Acclaim For

DEEP PACT

"DEEP PACT offers a powerful approach to leadership at the intersection of purpose, happiness, and performance. I recommend it to leaders at all levels."

—LISA EARLE MCLEOD,
best-selling author of
Selling with Noble Purpose and
Leading with Noble Purpose

"As we stand at the crossroads of a new era, this book serves as a rallying cry for leaders everywhere. It challenges us to rethink our approach to leadership, to break free from outdated models, and to create workplaces where people can realize their potential and find happiness in their work."

—ALYSON WATSON,
CEO and Chair, Board of Directors,
Woodard & Curran, *from the Foreword*

"An insightful guide to whole-person leadership, Saquib presents eight thought-provoking, transformative principles for leaders to embrace as they navigate the complexity of leading individuals and teams to their highest potential. Combining his own experiences, modern business theories, and timeless philosophical quotes, this book offers a roadmap for personal and professional excellence. Embracing these principles drives sustainable business success. A great read for anyone aiming to lead with purpose and achieve remarkable results."

—DAVID SWEENEY
President and CEO, RS&H

"The book is rich with insights from other learnings, and Saquib seamlessly blends them together with wonderful stories to provide a powerful leadership manual around his eight DEEP PACT principles. At a time when leadership needs to drive more than just shareholder returns, this book provides a provocative challenge for leaders. This 'manual' will help those leaders to find their voice and live out their leadership calling for sustained success and lifelong happiness."

—DOUG MCKEOWN
Former CEO and Chair, Board of Directors,
Woodard & Curran

"The California water community would benefit from practicing DEEP PACT leadership, founded on time-tested principles and cutting-edge research. Author Saquib Najmus brings to life a whole-person leadership approach and mindset by citing real-world examples from diverse disciplines and sectors. He makes the DEEP PACT journey attainable by describing practical steps for removing personal and interpersonal barriers and for releasing our potential. Integrating people, process, and technology is the power and secret sauce of DEEP PACT leadership, which is about leading—and living—collaboratively with character, compassion, humility, and commitment for happiness, success, and well-being at work, personally, and in the community."

—KAMYAR GUIVETCHI
Former division chief
California Department of Water Resources

"I worked with Saquib for many years and was continuously impressed with his management and leadership skills. Because of his successful leadership approach, individuals jockeyed to be on his teams and clients constantly sought his commitment to their projects. In DEEP PACT, Saquib has chronicled his approach to leadership allowing others to gain from his insights and approach to leading teams of individuals to success at the project, entity, and personal levels. I highly recommend DEEP PACT for anyone looking to improve their management and leadership skills."

—LYNDEL MELTON
Founder
RMC Water and Environment

"From my experience working with Saquib for over a decade, I knew he had wisdom to share for those (like me) engaged in the world of consulting and management. I was delighted to learn he put pen to paper to write DEEP PACT, which translates this wisdom into guidance and actionable advice for those embarking on, or already holding, positions of leadership. There is no time like the present to unlearn old bad habits and start learning new, better ones brought to life in DEEP PACT!"

—MATT TONKIN
President
S. S. Papadopulos & Associates

"DEEP PACT by Dr. Saquib Najmus is a powerful and thought-provoking read that blends science, compassion, and personal insight. It's both an intellectual and emotional journey—one that challenges you to see the world through a more compassionate lens.

In an era where leadership is being reshaped by AI and technological disruption, DEEP PACT provides a much-needed human-centered approach. Saquib's insights on purpose-driven whole-person leadership are a roadmap for leaders seeking meaning, impact, and happiness in both work and life. I highly recommend it."

—MOHAMMED ENAYETUR RAHMAN
President and CEO, Ulkasemi Inc.

"As Saquib's business partner, I had the privilege of witnessing these principles not only practiced daily but also personified by him long before they were written into DEEP PACT. Working alongside him, I closely experienced them in action—among my favorites are how he *"ensures excellence more than others think imaginable," "acts with more integrity than others think prudent,"* and *"trusts more than others think logical."* I saw the impact of these principles on our people, clients, and the company. As Chief Operating Officer of WRIME, Inc., I witnessed firsthand how embedding DEEP PACT principles into our organizational culture translated into measurable results—stronger collaboration, higher revenue, and sustainable growth. Most leadership books focus on performance, inspiration, or behavior, but DEEP PACT uniquely weaves beliefs, purpose, happiness, and performance into one powerful roadmap. This isn't theory; it's leadership proven in practice. For executives seeking lasting change rather than temporary fixes, this book is essential."

—ALI TAGHAVI
Cofounder and COO, WRIME, Inc.

"I've read countless leadership books over the years, but DEEP PACT rises above them all. It distills the most powerful leadership ideas into a single volume, offering clear, step-by-step methods for achieving both personal and interpersonal mastery. By blending psychology, philosophy, and a rare happiness-centered paradigm, it transforms timeless insights into daily, actionable habits. With its concise lessons, engaging personal stories, and effective daily practices, this is a book you'll return to again and again. DEEP PACT is an indispensable toolkit for leaders at every stage of their journey. For anyone aspiring to become a truly transformational leader, there is simply no substitute."

—ABDUL QUYYUM KHAN
Manager, Water Accounting
California Department of Water Resources

Elevate Your Leadership with *Purpose,*
Meaning, and *Happiness* in the Age of AI

DEEP PACT

8 Timeless Principles of
Whole-Person Leadership

SAQUIB NAJMUS, PhD, PE, PMP

INNOVATION AND INTEGRATION, INC.

For permission requests, write to the publisher at:
Innovation and Integration, Inc.
Email: manager.iandi@gmail.com

ISBNs:
Hardcover: ISBN-13: 978-0-9858-2325-2
Paperback: ISBN-13: 978-0-9858-2326-9
eBook (EPUB): ISBN-13: 978-0-9858-2327-6
eBook (Kindle): ISBN-13: 978-0-9858-2328-3

Cover and interior design by Caerus Kourt
Printed in the United States of America
First edition: September, 2025

This book is a work of nonfiction. While every effort has been made to ensure the accuracy and completeness of the content, the author and publisher assume no responsibility
for errors, omissions, or any consequences arising from the use of this material.

To my parents, Oheedun Noor and Ali Rawshana—
with gratitude for the roots you planted,
and the values you instilled.

And

To my beloved wife, Lubna,
and our daughters, Samhita and Samara—
with love for the light you bring to my days,
and the joy you place in my heart.

DEEP PACT
A Leadership Roadmap, Not Just a Book

This isn't just a book—it's the most comprehensive and deeply researched whole-person leadership manual available today. Rooted in happiness, purpose, and meaning, it operationalizes theory through a step-by-step process—turning research into impact and reflection into leadership.

Most Change Efforts Fail Because They:

⬦ Focus only on performance, not the person.
⬦ Offer inspiration but no structure.
⬦ Address behaviors, not beliefs.
⬦ Ignore emotional, interpersonal, and cultural blind spots.

DEEP PACT is different. It develops the whole person, pairs inspiration with a practical operating system, and dispels mistaken beliefs—reshaping mindsets and driving behaviors that build a happy, high-performing workplace. That's how change sticks.

Three-Part Manual For Lasting Leadership Change

PART ONE:
Problem and Solution
(Chapters 1 - 6)

✓ Understand why change doesn't stick.
✓ Discover what drives those you lead.
✓ Learn how to lead a multi-generational workforce in an AI-augmented world.

PART TWO:
Personal Mastery
(Chapters 7 - 10)

✓ Cultivate self-examination and excellence.
✓ Understand the belief-behavior connection.
✓ Learn how self-sabotage, not strategy, derails leaders.

PART THREE:
Interpersonal Mastery
(Chapters 11 - 15)

✓ Cultivate humility, trust, and influence.
✓ Lead with compassion and care without compromising performance.
✓ Turn feedback, care, and integrity into strategic advantages.

Built for Busy Leaders–and Deep Thinkers

⬦ **Practical leadership:** Over 200 actionable ideas, examples, and solutions.
⬦ **Daily practices:** Apply what you learn, every day.
⬦ **Personal stories:** Grounded in real-life leadership journeys.
⬦ **AI Playbook:** Navigate the future without losing your humanity.
⬦ **Bite-sized lessons:** 93% of book sections are less than 5 pages.

This is not a book you read once. It's a leadership **operating system.** You'll return to it again and again as your leadership deepens, your

We know what we are,

but know not what we may be.

—William Shakespeare, *Hamlet*

Contents

PART ONE—PROBLEM AND SOLUTION

PART TWO—PERSONAL MASTERY

PART THREE—INTERPERSONAL MASTERY

Fast Track for Busy Readers

I n a world overflowing with information and pressure to deliver results quickly, this book offers something different: **a path to lasting effectiveness and fulfillment** rather than superficial quick fixes. You may notice that the first part of the book focuses on exploring problems, challenges, context, and deeper questions before presenting solutions. **This is intentional.** To build real leadership capacity, you must first understand the landscape in which you lead.

To help you navigate the book in a way that fits your pace and priorities, here are four practical ways to get started without missing the deeper message.

1. **Start with what resonates.** Scan the table of contents and find the principle or section that speaks to your current leadership challenges or aspirations. You don't have to read sequentially.

2. **Read the introductory material.** Before diving into tactics, spend a little time with the introductory chapters to understand the "why" behind this approach. This will help you anchor the solutions in a powerful philosophical framework and overcome the resistance to change within yourself.

3. **Resist the lure of shortcuts.** Lasting change requires context and reflection. Skimming straight to solutions risks missing the underlying philosophy and mindset shifts that make new habits stick.

4. **Reflect and act.** Leadership is not just about knowledge but about action. Take time to reflect: *How does this principle change the way I lead? What immediate actions can I take?* The true power of these insights lies in their real-world application.

What This Book Can Do for You

No man was ever wise by chance.

—Seneca, *Letters to Lucilius*

Transform your mindset about leadership—so you can unlock your full potential, regardless of position or title.

Enrich yourself with the latest and greatest leadership insights—a **one-stop shop** for up-to-date knowledge as of August 2025—from the best leadership books and research at Harvard, Oxford, Stanford, MIT, Wharton, and Berkeley, so you can thrive in a world with rapidly changing expectations and priorities.

Adopt a purpose-driven, happiness-focused, and meaning-seeking leadership style—so you can find joy and fulfillment in both your professional and personal lives.

Cast off outdated leadership habits and break free from self-sabotaging tendencies—so you can inspire, empower, and create lasting impact.

Harness the power of DEEP PACT—so you can meet the demands of modern leadership and overcome daily barriers to success.

Elevate those around you with inspiration and support—true fulfillment comes from serving a cause greater than yourself.

Rekindle the joy of leadership in all peers—cultivating a shared spirit of energy and purpose.

Foreword

In an era where the rapid advancement of technology and artificial intelligence is reshaping every facet of our lives, the essence of leadership is undergoing a profound transformation. The traditional model of "command and control" is giving way to a more holistic, people-centered approach that places happiness, purpose, and ethics at its core. It is within this context that *DEEP PACT: Eight Timeless Principles of Whole-Person Leadership* emerges as a beacon of wisdom and guidance.

This book is not just a manual for leadership; it is a call to action for leaders to embrace a new paradigm—one that integrates the principles of whole-person leadership encapsulated in the DEEP PACT framework. The eight principles of leadership—decide, act, and lead; examine your beliefs and actions; ensure excellence; protect yourself from self-sabotage; practice more humility; act with more integrity; care more for people; and trust more—offer a comprehensive roadmap for navigating the complexities of modern leadership.

Through vivid storytelling and insights drawn from history, philosophy, psychology, and cutting-edge research, Saquib masterfully illustrates how leaders can cultivate a work environment grounded in empathy, care, trust, integrity, and joy. The book addresses the urgent challenges of our time, from burnout and disengagement to the post-pandemic complexities and the rise of remote management.

It provides practical strategies for overcoming these obstacles while fostering a culture of resilience and innovation.

Perhaps most importantly, these principles and their effectiveness in shaping culture are not merely theoretical. Having worked with Saquib for more than a decade, I have had the benefit of witnessing firsthand the meaningful impact of this approach in cultivating a culture of engagement, dynamism, and—yes—happiness. By distilling the core of his own leadership philosophy into a thoroughly researched and elegantly simple process, Saquib has shared with all of us the unique recipe that he himself has perfected for fostering resilience and innovative spirit in his teams.

As we stand at the crossroads of a new era, this book serves as a rallying cry for leaders everywhere. It challenges us to rethink our approach to leadership, to break free from outdated models, and to create workplaces where people can realize their potential and find happiness in their work. This book is a testament to the power of visionary leadership and a guide to transforming our organizations and ourselves.

I encourage you to embark on this transformative journey with an open mind and a willing heart, and to let this book inspire you to lead with purpose, elevate others, and both find and foster happiness in the age of AI.

—*Alyson Watson*
Board chair and CEO
Woodard & Curran, Inc.

Acknowledgments

Writing DEEP PACT: *Eight Timeless Principles of Whole-Person Leadership* has been a profound journey of discovery, reflection, and collaboration.

I extend my heartfelt gratitude to Alyson Watson, board chair and CEO of Woodard & Curran, for graciously writing the foreword. Her thoughtful words beautifully capture the essence of DEEP PACT. Her generosity in taking the time to read the entire manuscript, along with her encouragement and belief in my work, has been an enduring source of inspiration.

I am profoundly grateful to my dear friend Dr. Abdul Quyyum Khan, whose early review of the manuscript and years of thought-provoking conversations on leadership have deeply shaped my thinking and this work. My heartfelt gratitude to my business partner, Dr. Ali Taghavi, with whom I built WRIME, Inc. Ali's brilliance, unwavering support, thoughtful encouragement, and spirit of collaboration created an environment where the ideas in this book were able to flourish and be tested with rigor and confidence.

My sincere thanks to David Sweeney, president and CEO of RS&H; Kamyar Guivetchi, former division chief at the California Department of Water Resources; Doug McKeown, former chairman and CEO of Woodard & Curran; Lyndel Melton, founder of RMC Water and Environment; Dr. Matt Tonkin, president of S. S. Papadopulos & Associates; and Joe Barbagallo, president of consulting at Woodard & Curran, for their insightful feedback as reviewers. Their invaluable contributions enriched the manuscript and sharpened its ideas.

To my incredibly brilliant teammates at WRIME Inc., with whom we built an outstanding business together, thank you for your openness and trust in allowing me to test these principles during their early development. Your willingness to engage with and apply these ideas in real-world scenarios provided invaluable insights, refining the concepts that form the core of DEEP PACT. Our collaboration, discussions, and shared pursuit of excellence greatly expanded my perspective and strengthened my belief in whole-person leadership.

To my esteemed colleagues at CH2M Hill, RMC Water & Environment, and Woodard & Curran, thank you for the opportunities to explore and apply these principles in a project setting. Your engagement and feedback were vital in validating the real-world impact of DEEP PACT. To my clients, thank you for entrusting me with transformative projects. Your confidence fueled my commitment to DEEP PACT and enriched each of its principles.

I am grateful to the countless volunteers who contributed to the success of our nonprofit organization, Anandamela Inc., over the past two decades. They provided me with a space to apply DEEP PACT in a nonprofit setting, making the experience deeply meaningful. I want to offer special thanks to those who have worked alongside me on Anandamela for more than 10 years: Sheikh Abid Hossain, Mohammad Haider (Badal), Tasmin Eusuff (Lopa), Md. Haque (Manjur), Sirajul Chowdhury (Milon), Nasreen Kabir, Nilufer Begum (Nila), Abdul Khan (Quyyum), Shashwati Roy, Wahidul Islam, Zaffar Eusuff (Shaheen), and Zahangir Kabir—your enduring partnership and dedication have been invaluable in shaping my perspective on leadership.

Special thanks to Dr. Nazmul Hasan for the opportunity to serve as keynote speaker at a global leadership seminar organized by Bangladeshi Engineers and Computer Science Professionals in British Columbia during the pandemic—a moment when DEEP PACT truly crystallized. I am also grateful to Mohammed Enayetur Rahman, CEO of Ulkasemi, for inviting me to present DEEP PACT at a global all-hands meeting of his company. I extend my gratitude and thanks to Professor Dr. Mohammed Rashidul Kabir for the invitation to speak at Daffodil International University, and to Professor Dr. Abu Siddique for facilitating sessions at the Bangladesh University of Engineering and Technology, my alma mater. Each of these experiences enriched and refined my ideas. To the students and professionals who asked challenging questions, your curiosity and insights were instrumental in shaping this book. My thanks also to Professor Dr. Saif Islam of the University of California, Davis, whose thoughtful questions during an informal conversation prompted valuable additions to the book.

To my elder daughter, Samhita, I extend my heartfelt gratitude for her invaluable intellectual contributions from the earliest stages of this manuscript. Her insights on the perspectives of women, Millennials, and Gen Z, along with her comprehensive review of the entire book, have been instrumental in shaping its message and content. To my younger daughter, Samara, my deepest thanks for her love, support, and belief in this journey.

To my parents, Oheedun Noor and Ali Rawshana, thank you for instilling in me the values that form the foundation of *DEEP PACT* and for inspiring my lifelong pursuit of knowledge. Your unconditional love, wisdom, and encouragement have been my guiding light throughout this journey. To my brothers and sisters—the late Misbahun Noor (Molik), Mohius Sunnah, Rabeya Hussain, Khaleda Haque, Enayet Karim Saqui, Belayet Hussain Sohel, and Sadaquat Hussain Junayed—thank you for being my pillars of strength, my confidants, and my source of joy. Your steadfast belief in me, constant encouragement, and unwavering support have played a crucial role in shaping this work. I am deeply grateful for the bond we share and the inspiration you provide.

I am grateful to Glenn McMahan for his expert developmental editing and to Bob Land for his meticulous copyediting. My thanks to

Caerus Kourt for the cover design and formatting, and to Adam Fox for his brilliant graphics work and collaborative spirit in developing visuals for my client presentations—many of which now enrich this book.

Finally, with deepest love and gratitude, I thank my wife, Lubna, whose unwavering support, patience, and understanding have been the bedrock of this journey. Her encouragement during long hours of writing, her belief in me, and her steadfast presence through every challenge and milestone of my life have been invaluable. Over the past two decades, we have shared countless dinner-table conversations about what it truly means to lead with integrity, purpose, and empathy—especially in the context of our collaborative work in nonprofit leadership. Her insights and thought-provoking questions have challenged me in ways no one else could, deepening my perspective and refining my ideas in ways that may never be fully visible, yet are woven into every page of this work—an enduring gift of wisdom, patience, and love. Without her love and support, this work would not have been possible.

As I reflect on this journey, I feel profoundly privileged and deeply fortunate to have had the support of so many extraordinary individuals. Completing *DEEP PACT* has been a labor of love, made possible by their generosity of time, wisdom, and encouragement. This book is my way of giving back—to leadership, to those who shaped me, and to a life that has brought me so much joy and fulfillment. I hope readers find in these pages the inspiration to lead with purpose, cultivate meaningful connections, and ultimately, discover their own path to joy and happiness.

—*Saquib Najmus*
El Dorado Hills, California
September, 2025

DEEP PACT

8 Timeless Principles of Whole-Person Leadership

Part One

Problem and Solution

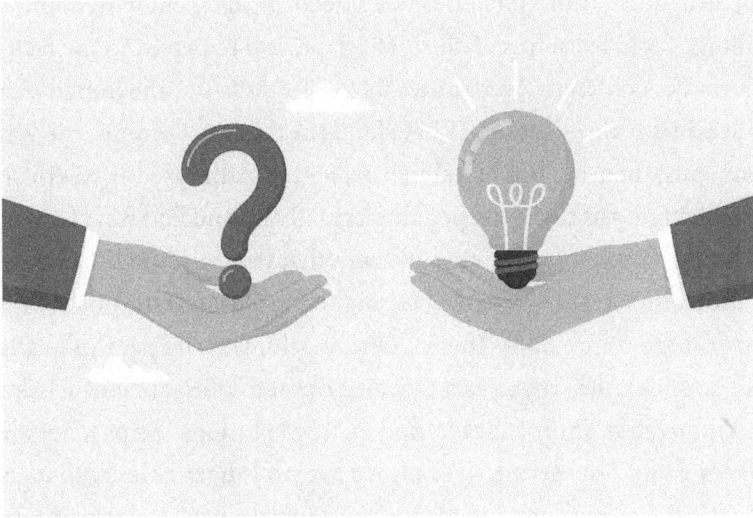

Identify your problems, but give your power and energy to solutions.
—Tony Robbins, author of *Awaken the Giant Within*

In Part One, we uncover the "why" and "what" behind this book, examining the urgent challenges confronting today's leaders and the transformative solutions that can overcome them. We'll explore the underlying causes of leadership failures, the shifting demands shaping the future, and a fresh, whole-person approach designed to empower leaders to rise above obstacles, foster resilience, and create lasting impact.

Life presents us with an endless array of problems, yet hidden within each challenge lies a solution waiting to be uncovered. As the Tao Te

Ching suggests, "The wise man is one who knows what he does not know," reminding us that while problems may appear insurmountable, wisdom comes from recognizing gaps in our understanding and having the courage to seek answers. This journey toward solutions is not an avoidance of difficulties but a deep engagement with them—a willingness to learn from failure, to adapt, and to persist in the face of adversity. As Marcus Aurelius wrote in *Meditations*, "The impediment to action advances action. What stands in the way becomes the way." Problems, then, are not merely obstacles but pathways to growth and insight, urging us to dig deeper, think creatively, and find ways forward.

In our search for solutions, we learn that true wisdom lies not only in problem-solving but in developing the mindset to see possibilities beyond the immediate. The modern world, with its pace of change and complexities, requires a mindset open to both ancient wisdom and innovative approaches to find lasting solutions. As psychologist Viktor Frankl observed, "When we are no longer able to change a situation, we are challenged to change ourselves." Solutions often require a transformation within—a shift in perception or approach that reveals the hidden answers in seemingly impossible situations. Let us begin our journey, opening the path to uncover the hidden possibilities within us all.

1 Introduction: Why This Book, Why Now

For those who have an open mind for new ideas, who seek to create long-standing success and who believe that your success requires the aid of others, I offer you a challenge. From now on, start with Why.
— Simon Sinek, author of *Start with Why*

In the late 1800s, an ambitious young engineer named Frederick Winslow Taylor stood in a bustling steel factory in Philadelphia, quietly observing the chaotic flow of workers. To the untrained eye, the factory seemed to hum with energy and purpose. But Taylor, with his stopwatch and notebook, saw something different—inefficiency, disorder, and what he considered a monumental waste of human potential. He believed he could transform this chaos into order, bringing an industrial symphony where every worker played a perfectly timed note.

Measuring every second, managing every move: the birth of scientific management.

What followed was the birth of Taylorism, or *scientific management*, a revolutionary approach that sought to maximize productivity by breaking every task down into its smallest components. Workers were instructed to perform repetitive tasks in the most efficient way possible, with every movement meticulously calculated to reduce wasted time. At first, it seemed brilliant. Factories became faster, and profits soared. Taylor was hailed as a genius who could squeeze every ounce of productivity from the industrial machine.

From this scientific management model emerged the *command-and-control* leadership approach, which remains deeply embedded in many organizations even today. Leaders were taught to view workers as resources to be managed and controlled. Efficiency was the supreme goal, and productivity ruled above all else, even at the cost of human fulfillment.

But beneath the surface of this so-called progress, something darker was brewing. The workers, who had once taken pride in their craft, were reduced to mere components of a larger machine, their individuality stripped away. With each tick of Taylor's stopwatch, the soul of work withered. Workers became numbers, their worth measured only by how efficiently they could perform mind-numbing tasks. The repetitive grind not only exhausted their bodies but also crushed their spirits.

1.1 The Dawn of Collaborative Leadership

As scientific management spread around the globe in the early 1900s, a wind of change was stirring in Boston. While factories continued to operate under the rigid structure of Taylor's scientific management, a new voice was beginning to emerge—one that would challenge the very foundation of how work and leadership were understood. Mary Parker Follett, a social worker deeply embedded in the community, was observing a different truth. Her work with neighborhood centers and social groups allowed her to see firsthand the frustrations and desires of ordinary people.

The turning point came during a tense meeting at a Boston community center, where workers and managers had been brought together to resolve conflicts. The air was thick with frustration. Workers complained about being treated like machines, while managers insisted that they were only following the best productivity models. Follett, who was moderating, did something unexpected—she didn't offer a solution. Instead, she asked both parties to work together, to share their concerns and find common ground. For Follett, the goal wasn't domination by one party over another; it was about integration—finding a win-win solution that allowed both sides to thrive.

This simple but profound idea became the cornerstone of her philosophy: *shared vision in management.* Instead of the rigid, top-down command structure of Taylor's scientific management, Follett advocated for a cooperative approach where employees had a say in how things were run. She argued that true power came not from *"power over"* but from *"power with,"* from listening to different voices and integrating their perspectives.

Follett's ideas were radical for the time. The industrial world wasn't ready for someone to say that workers should have a say in management. Yet she persisted. Follett's groundbreaking work culminated in her 1924 book, *Creative Experience,* where she articulated her vision of management as a collective endeavor. She believed that management wasn't about control but about empowering people, fostering creativity, and building shared responsibility.

Mary Parker Follett died in 1933. She was remarkably progressive for her era, embracing ideas for which society was not yet ready. Peter Drucker, one of the most renowned management thinkers of the 20th century, later called her the "prophet of management." He recognized that she had anticipated many of the ideas that would dominate management theory decades later—like teamwork, decentralized decision-making, and participatory leadership. While Taylor had focused on optimizing tasks, Follett was more interested in optimizing relationships and leadership. She foresaw a future where leaders wouldn't dictate from above but would work alongside their teams to co-create solutions.

Leadership is not defined by the exercise of power but by the capacity to increase the sense of power among those led.

—Mary Parker Follett

1.2 The Passing Glimmer of Collaborative Leadership

Follett's ideas, though powerful, were but a passing glimmer—a fleeting spark—in the rapidly expanding world of 20th-century business. As industries boomed, the initial promise of collaborative leadership began to fade, overshadowed by a relentless drive for profitability and control. The vision of shared empowerment and mutual respect between managers and workers soon found itself stifled by the rising tide of Taylorism, now evolving from a simple tool of improving efficiency into the backbone of an increasingly financialized view of management. In this new business landscape, employees ceased to be seen as contributors to a shared vision; instead, they became cogs within an intricate machine, valued solely for their ability to meet financial targets. All too quickly, Follett's vision of shared management was drowned out by the rise of **management by numbers—profits, targets, and metrics**.

In the heat of the postwar economic boom, companies adopted financial management techniques that emphasized maximizing shareholder value above all else. Command and control, derived from Taylor's rigid structures, became the dominant leadership model. Efficiency, now measured in quarterly profits and ever-growing margins, took precedence. Leaders began to gauge success by financial outcomes, not by the well-being of their people. Employees were overworked, driven to meet constantly shifting targets in an environment where profit trumped people. The workplace became a battleground of increasing demands, longer hours, and diminishing meaning.

1.3 The Rise of Progressive Leadership Models

Despite the dominance of management by numbers, Follett's voice rose from time to time. Over the years, various management theories would emerge echoing her ideas, offering hope for more inclusive, human-centered workplaces. Yet Follett's pioneering vision soon became overshadowed by subsequent management theories that, while borrowing selectively from her principles, repackaged them in more managerial, performance-driven frameworks. These newer models gained popularity due to their institutional appeal, ease of implementation, and alignment with existing hierarchical structures. Each promised to reshape organizational dynamics to create more inclusive and people-centered workplaces, yet ultimately failed to dislodge the entrenched command-and-control model.

This failure stemmed not from a lack of insight or intention but from a deeper tension: while these theories advanced more progressive principles, their implementation often coexisted with—or was constrained by—the enduring structures of top-down control. For instance, *situational leadership* by Hersey and Blanchard proposed that leadership should adapt based on the maturity and readiness of the team members, but ultimately kept the power to assess and direct squarely in the hands of the leader. *Transformational leadership*, championed by James Mac-Gregor Burns, focused on inspiring and motivating employees toward a shared vision, yet it often positioned the leader as the charismatic visionary rather than fostering mutual influence. *Servant leadership*, by Robert K. Greenleaf, emphasized that true leadership begins with serving others, but in many organizations, it was interpreted more as a personal ethic than a structural shift in power dynamics. *Transactional leadership*, introduced by Max Weber and expanded by Bernard Bass, maintained a rewards-based system, ensuring compliance through a series of carrots and sticks, reinforcing hierarchical control mechanisms.

Authentic leadership, advanced by Bill George, emphasized self-aware-ness, transparency, and values-based decision-making as essential to building trust and credibility, but placed the burden of transformation largely on the individual leader, not the system. *Coaching leadership*, introduced by Sir John Whitmore and popularized by Daniel Goleman, emphasized the leader's role in unlocking individual potential through guidance, feedback, and development, while still assuming a central figure with authority to direct growth. Lastly, *agile leadership*, born out of software development and formalized in the *Agile Manifesto* in 2001 by 17 software developers, called for flexibility and iterative learning, with leaders facilitating collaboration across functional teams, though it was often layered onto traditional reporting hierarchies that remained largely intact. Taken together, these examples illustrate how even well-intentioned models—though progressive in theory—were often implemented within existing systems that prioritized centralized authority and short-term productivity metrics, thereby limiting the emergence of the participatory leadership that Follett envisioned.

1.4 The Persistence of Command and Control

Thus, despite the proliferation of progressive leadership models, command and control solidified itself as the default, with top-down decision-making dominating organizations worldwide, primarily due to its emphasis on immediate results and efficiency. As industries became more diverse and complex, the idea that workers could have a say in management was often dismissed as impractical or inefficient. The workplace became an ever-accelerating treadmill, where the demand for more output, greater profits, and higher targets replaced the earlier vision of shared purpose.

Even today, the command-and-control approach prevails in many organizations. While some companies believe they have evolved beyond rigid hierarchies, data tell a different story. The 2016 HOW Report, drawing on input from over 16,000 employees in 17 countries, categorized organizations into three distinct governance archetypes. The first, "Blind Obedience" (30%), represents power-based, task-driven cultures rooted in authoritarian command and control. The second, "Informed Acquiescence" (62%), describes rules-based, process-driven, hierarchical structures aligned with traditional 20th-century management practices. The third and least common, "Self-Governance" (8%), characterizes purpose-driven organizations guided by shared values and moral authority.

At first glance, it may appear that only 30% of organizations still rely on command-and-control methods. However, in *Trust and Inspire*, Stephen M. R. Covey offers a more nuanced perspective. He differentiates between authoritarian command and control, which is rigid and fear-based, and enlightened command and control, which, while still structured, emphasizes transactional fairness and mutual respect. Covey equates Blind Obedience with authoritarian command and control and Informed Acquiescence with enlightened command and control—suggesting that, at the time of the study, up to 92% of organizations operated under some form of command and control, whether overt or disguised in more modern practices. Covey's own surveys of thousands of leaders reveal that *"the vast majority of people still say that the primary leadership style in their organization would best be described as command and control."* Command and control is no longer overtly authoritarian; instead, it manifests subtly through rigid hierarchies, performance metrics, and transactional management practices—often in disguised forms within business units, unnoticed by senior leaders. This reflects a persistent gap between leadership aspirations and organizational realities. Encouragingly, the command-and-control model is receding—slowly but surely across the board, and even more rapidly in technology companies and professional services firms.

While the prevalence of command-and-control leadership may no longer be as high as the 92% suggested by Covey in his 2022 book, its lingering presence—whether overt or subtly embedded within other progressive leadership models—continues to shape many corporate cultures. The persistence of this model—despite its inability to foster creativity and employee engagement—highlights how deeply rooted the culture of authority, hierarchy, and rigid control remains within organizational structures, often at the expense of innovation and worker well-being.

1.5 The Cracks in Prevailing Leadership Models

It wasn't until the pandemic that the massive cracks in prevailing leadership models began to show with startling clarity. The rapid shift to remote work left employees feeling disconnected, exhausted, and increasingly questioning the value and purpose of their work. *The Great Resignation* was a stark manifestation of this discontent, with millions choosing to walk away from jobs that no longer offered them meaning or fulfillment. The rigid structures of command-and-control leadership, built solely on financial targets and relentless pursuit of profits, proved unsustainable in a world where individuals yearned for *connection, purpose, meaning, and fulfillment.* After surveying over 10,000 business and HR leaders across 150 countries, Deloitte's 2023 *Global Human Capital Trends Report* emphasized that organizations must move beyond the outdated belief that leadership is about control. Instead, organizations are part of dynamic ecosystems where workers actively shape both organizational and societal outcomes. In such environments, leadership must evolve into something far more human and participatory. Deloitte further asserted, "A new brand of leadership will be required—one that focuses on where you show up and how you show up, and the mindset you adopt to drive work forward." Harvard's 2024 Global Leadership Development Study, *Time to Transform,* underscores a pivotal shift in leadership expectations. Drawing insights from over 1,100 leadership and development professionals, the study reveals that leaders must evolve beyond the competencies that once defined their success. As one senior executive put it, "The number one thing our business leaders need to do differently is to recognize that the things that have gotten them to the place they are—that they're very good at—will not get us to the next level." No single prevailing leadership style—regardless of context—can effectively address the diverse and complex challenges leaders face today. Today's leaders must develop a state-of-the-art skill set—blending emotional intelligence, digital fluency, empathy, strategic thinking, and adaptive decision-making—to effectively guide transformation in increasingly complex, dynamic, and uncertain environments.

These findings point to an undeniable truth: traditional, hierarchical leadership had failed to adapt to a new reality where human-centric values such as purpose, meaning, and happiness matter more than ever. Leadership has long been hailed as a noble pursuit, a path that embodies purpose, influence, and the potential to make positive change. But what is the true purpose of leadership if it fails to foster happiness and fulfillment? Leadership, at its core, should not just be about steering teams to achieve organizational goals or driving teams to peak productivity. While these outcomes are critical for businesses—and financial success serves as the fuel to achieve broader aspirations—they are not the entirety of what leadership should embody.

> *But what is the true purpose of leadership if it fails to foster happiness and fulfillment? Leadership, at its core, should not just be about steering teams to achieve organizational goals or driving teams to peak productivity.*

True leadership goes beyond metrics. It should inspire, energize, and elevate the collective human experience by helping others reach their potential, maximizing positive impact for the communities and society we serve, and fostering a cycle of fulfillment and well-being for both leaders and their teams.

If, instead, the process of leading leaves leaders and their teams feeling drained, unfulfilled, or trapped in a perpetual cycle of stress, one must ask: What is the true value of such leadership? Unfortunately, leadership today often falls short of delivering on what it is meant to achieve. This is no longer just theorization or opinion. New global research from Gallup provides compelling evidence of what followers around the world genuinely want from their leaders.

1.6 What Followers Want from Leaders

Gallup's groundbreaking *Global Leadership Report: What Followers Want*, launched at the 2025 World Governments Summit, offers an unprecedented global view of what people truly seek from their leaders. Based on surveys of more than 30,000 adults across 52 countries, this is the first study of its kind to examine followers' needs on such a massive global scale—covering 76% of the world's adult population and more than 86% of global GDP. The results reveal four universal needs that followers consistently expect from leaders—in every region, culture, and demographic: **hope, trust, compassion**, and **stability**.

Among these, hope emerged as the most dominant need. Followers look to leaders to help them believe in a better future, to cast vision, and to provide a sense of direction amid uncertainty. Trust follows as a critical foundation—leaders must be reliable and honest, acting in the best interests of those they serve. Compassion speaks to the emotional connection between leaders and followers; it reflects the desire to feel cared for, understood, and treated as more than just a role or function. Stability, though often undervalued, is essential for reducing anxiety. Leaders who are calm and consistent and who provide clarity offer the security that people need to focus and thrive.

Gallup also found a powerful link between these needs and well-being: when leaders deliver on hope and trust, the rate of thriving increases, while suffering decreases significantly. As the report concludes, "When leadership is done well, life improves for everyone."

This finding offers a profound reminder that leadership is not simply about competence—it is about connection, purpose, and humanity. Followers are not asking for perfect leaders; they are asking for leaders who can inspire hope, earn trust, show compassion, and create stability—especially in today's uncertain and fast-changing world. Clearly, the call for more human-centered leadership can no longer be ignored.

1.7 The Time for Change Is Now

The entrenched reliance on command and control over the years has overshadowed Follett's remarkable vision of collaboration and integration, which emphasized aligning leadership with the human elements of work—the very universal human needs affirmed anew by Gallup's global report. The time has come to revisit these ideas in a modern context, especially as the challenges of the post-pandemic world and AI-driven workplaces demand a more human-centered approach. As AI automates routine tasks, the qualities that Follett championed—creativity, collaboration, and emotional intelligence—are becoming increasingly important and necessary. The rise of AI reinforces the idea that the old model of managing workers like machines is obsolete.

The time for shared vision management has arrived, where leaders must listen to their people, empower them, and create workplaces that inspire purpose, meaning, and happiness. This shift is not merely a challenge to overcome but an opportunity to reimagine leadership in a way that embraces the values Follett promoted a century ago, balancing productivity with genuine human connection. The future of effective leadership lies in creating workplaces that value people as much as profits, inspiring not just productivity but also joy and shared purpose.

Start before you're ready. Don't prepare, begin.
—Mel Robbins, author of *The 5 Second Rule*

1.8 Immunity to Change Chains Us to the Past

We shackle ourselves to comfort, mistaking it for safety.

Do you know why we are so resistant to change or why we love the status quo so much? Our brains are wired to favor familiarity and routine because they require less cognitive effort and reduce the anxiety associated with uncertainty. This resistance to change is evident in how we handle New Year's resolutions. Statistics published in *U.S. News & World Report* show that about 80% of New Year's resolutions fail by February, with only 8% of people actually achieving their goals. This high failure rate highlights just how difficult it is to make and sustain meaningful behavioral change. Harvard psychologists Robert Kegan and Lisa Lahey explored the psychological mechanisms that prevent individuals from making necessary changes, even when they express a genuine desire to do so, and coined the concept of "immunity to change." This phenomenon is likened to a biological immune system that protects the body from perceived threats. In the context of personal growth and transformational change, these threats often come in the form of new ideas, unfamiliar situations, or changes that challenge deeply held assumptions and competing commitments, triggering resistance. Kegan and Lahey's work reveals that true transformation requires identifying and challenging these hidden commitments, allowing individuals to reframe their mindset and unlock their potential.

This idea finds resonance in ancient philosophy. In Plato's Allegory of the Cave, individuals are chained inside a cave, perceiving only shadows on the wall as reality. One day, a prisoner is freed from the cave and discovers the outside world, realizing that the shadows he once believed to be reality were mere illusions. However, when he returns to share this truth, those who remain in the cave resist and reject him. They are unwilling to accept a reality beyond their comfort zone. Instead of welcoming the freed prisoner as a source of new knowledge, they see him as misguided—or even dangerous.

This same resistance to change confronts enlightened leaders who challenge long-standing beliefs and drive transformation within their organizations. Many people are prisoners of old ideas and deeply ingrained convictions, making them reluctant to embrace new perspectives even when they lead to progress. Leaders who champion innovation, cultural shifts, or new strategies often face skepticism, rejection, or outright opposition—not because their ideas lack merit, but because change disrupts the familiarity of the status quo.

For leaders, understanding and addressing this immunity to change is crucial for driving effective transformation. Just as the freed prisoner must find ways to guide others toward the light, a visionary leader must recognize the psychological and emotional barriers that prevent people from accepting new realities. By fostering trust, communicating the benefits of change, and creating an environment where people feel safe stepping beyond the familiar, leaders can help their teams move out of the cave of outdated thinking and into a future of growth and possibility. In times of reinvention, the most impactful leaders won't simply be those who know the most; they'll be the ones who constantly challenge their own assumptions and ask not just, "What should we do next?" but also, "What must we leave behind?"

Stepping out of the cave is just the beginning. True transformation happens when leaders and teams not only leave behind old limitations but also dare to think beyond them, breaking free from rigid mindsets and embracing the limitless possibilities of thinking outside the box.

We laugh at people who still use Windows 95, yet we still cling to opinions that we formed in 1995.

—Adam Grant, author of *Think Again*

1.9 Think Outside the Box: Learn, Unlearn, Relearn, and Act

The memory is nearly four decades old, yet it remains as vivid as if it happened yesterday. I was a newly married foreign graduate student at UC Davis, and my wife and I were on our first trip to Disneyland—a place where dreams and imagination take flight. Excitement filled the air as we waited in line to enter Captain EO, a 3D sci-fi spectacle starring Michael Jackson, promising a futuristic adventure.

To keep the people in the long line entertained, a screen in the waiting area scrolled through texts and images. Then a quote flashed before my eyes on the screen:

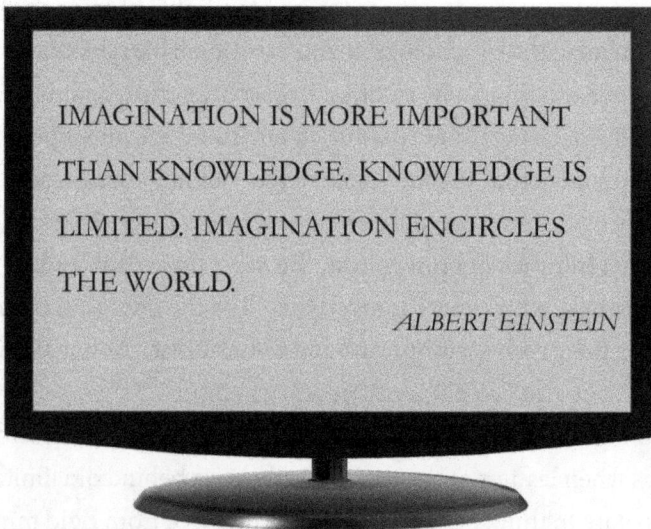

IMAGINATION IS MORE IMPORTANT THAN KNOWLEDGE. KNOWLEDGE IS LIMITED. IMAGINATION ENCIRCLES THE WORLD.

ALBERT EINSTEIN

Disneyland queue: before the ride thrills, imagination soars.

The words struck me with an intensity I hadn't expected. They resonated deeply, planting a seed in my mind that would grow into a guiding principle for my entire life. In that moment, I realized something profound: knowledge tells us what is; imagination envisions what could be. This single idea changed my perspective forever. Whether in business, nonprofit leadership, or strategic brainstorming sessions, I found myself quoting it time and again—whenever I needed to inspire others to break free from conventional thinking. I came to understand that the greatest breakthroughs often happen when we dare to think beyond the confines of what we know.

This realization reminded me of the *nine-dot puzzle,* a famous challenge where one must connect nine dots with four straight lines without lifting the pen. Most people instinctively confine their solutions within an imaginary box around the dots, failing to see that the only way to solve it is to go beyond the perceived boundaries.

This puzzle is a powerful metaphor for the need to reimagine leadership today—to break free from conventional models, challenge outdated assumptions, and embrace new ways of thinking that drive change rooted in purpose, meaning, and fulfillment. Thinking outside the box isn't just a phrase—it's

Connect all nine dots in four straight lines without lifting the pen. The solution is provided in Chapter 15.

a mindset, a discipline, and a commitment to continuous reinvention. It is not about rejecting traditional wisdom but about elevating it. It is about seeing opportunities where others see obstacles. It is about asking, "What if?" when others say, "This is how it's always been done." The future does not belong to those who cling to what they know but to those who dare to think differently, lead courageously, and imagine endlessly.

But thinking outside the box isn't only about imagination—it also demands courage to let go. To lead effectively today, leaders must not only acquire new knowledge but also unlearn obsolete habits, assumptions, and practices. As Vibhas Ratanjee, a global practice leader at Gallup, notes in a 2025 article in *Forbes*, "The challenge for leaders isn't just learning more. It's learning what to let go of." He asserted that innovation and relevance aren't achieved merely by knowing more—they come from "actively discarding what no longer serves."

This insight echoes futurist Alvin Toffler's timeless observation: "The illiterate of the 21st century will not be those who cannot read and write, but those who cannot learn, unlearn, and relearn." The essence of unlearning isn't forgetting—it's seeing again, reframing outdated mental models to align with new realities. Organizational resilience depends on it. The 2018 study by Kluge and Gronau, "Intentional Forgetting in Organizations," reinforces this point. Their research reveals that innovation doesn't arise solely from acquiring new competencies—it depends equally on the deliberate abandonment of practices, routines, and mental models that no longer serve current needs. Performance reviews designed for the in-office era—now applied to hybrid teams, succession plans that reward seniority over adaptability, and meetings that preserve rituals long past their usefulness are just a few examples of inherited systems misaligned with today's realities. These inefficiencies are not trivial—they are institutional barriers to relevance and agility.

This calls for deeper introspection. Leaders must regularly ask not just "What should we do next?" but also "What should we stop doing?" "Which beliefs, policies, or practices have quietly expired?" and "Where are we preserving rituals that belong to another time?" The answers may be uncomfortable, but they are essential to progress. In this light, unlearning becomes as critical as learning itself—both personally and organizationally.

Yet learning, unlearning, and relearning are meaningful only when followed by action. As Pablo Picasso once said, "Action is the foundational key to all success." Knowledge without action is like a map never used—full of promise but leading nowhere. Insights without implementation are merely potential. Wisdom without application is simply decoration. True growth begins only when we act.

A book can offer insights and perspectives that challenge conventional thinking and inspire you to let go of what no longer serves. It can even provide actionable steps. But only you can bring those insights to life—through daily choices, intentional reflection, and the courage to lead in new, wiser ways.

And that brings us to the next story—the story of the conception of a book inspired by out-of-the-box thinking and focused on learning, unlearning, relearning, and action.

1.10 Why I Wrote This Book

Today, a search for leadership books on Amazon yields over 60,000 results. So, why add another? Because the world has changed—profoundly. The leadership models we've leaned on—transactional, transformational, command-and-control, even servant leadership—have reached their limits. The old playbook—rooted in control, hierarchies, and profit over people—no longer works. Workplace happiness is in decline, leaders are challenged, employees are stressed, teams are disengaged. According to Gallup, declining employee engagement in 2024 resulted in an estimated $438 billion in lost productivity worldwide. People are no longer content with a paycheck alone; they crave meaning, fulfillment, and a sense of purpose. According to the 2025 HOW report titled *The State of Moral Leadership in Business*, an overwhelming 95% of employees want leaders who embody moral values: trust, fairness, and integrity. Employees want psychological safety—a workplace environment where they can speak openly, take risks, and be their authentic selves without fear of judgment or punishment.

These realities make it clear: more than ever, there is a pressing need to reimagine leadership—by unlearning outdated mindsets and relearning how to lead with purpose, humility, and happiness. True unlearning begins when we show the courage to confront flawed thinking, recognize our own biases, and engage openly with those who see the world differently. This is not only a time for change but also a time to rethink what leadership can—and should—be. **That's why I wrote this book: to reframe leadership through the lens of human happiness, centered on purpose, meaning, trust, excellence, and psychological safety.**

The Great Resignation, burnout, and widespread disengagement are not isolated trends; they signal a fundamental shift in how we view work today. Statistics paint a stark picture: Deloitte reports that 61% of employees are burned out, while a Gallup survey shows that only 23% are engaged. According to Gallup's 2024 *State of the Global Workplace* report, "Managers account for 70% of the variance in team employee engagement," indicating that leaders play an outsized role in organizational success. These are not just numbers—they are calls for change. **I wrote this book to help leaders overcome these stark realities** by becoming leaders who not only manage tasks and deliver results, but also inspire and elevate people.

I wrote this book because I believe in the untapped potential of people. Within each of us is a capacity for greatness waiting to be realized. Yet I have seen firsthand how countless self-limiting beliefs, misconceptions, and leadership myths have smothered the inner fire of individuals—brilliant minds held back and capable leaders settling for less than their potential. I wrote this book to help bust these myths and misconceptions so you can reignite your inner fire and achieve your full potential. I believe that unlocking human potential is the key to successfully navigating today's leadership challenges. Einstein said it best: "The significant problems we face cannot be solved at the same level of thinking we were at when we created them." It's time to rethink leadership entirely, and that is why this book exists.

I wrote this book to challenge you to think outside the box and disrupt the status quo. The future demands a new model of leadership—one that prioritizes people, happiness, and meaning while addressing the real challenges of a post-pandemic, AI-driven world, with a workforce made up of more than 54% Millennials and Gen Z. Research indicates that Gen Z places a high value on finding purpose and fulfillment in their professional lives. A survey by the Top Employers Institute revealed that 62% of Gen Z respondents are willing to accept lower salaries in exchange for better work-life integration. Unlike the outdated notion of work-life balance—which implies a rigid separation between work and personal life—work-life integration acknowledges that professional and personal responsibilities coexist and should complement rather than compete with each other. Additionally, 83% believe employers should support psychological health, and 82% value schedule flexibility. These preferences underscore Gen Z's commitment to mental health and a balanced lifestyle, marking a shift from previous generations' workplace priorities, which were dominated by financial security, stability, promotions, and job titles. This book offers an approach rooted in happiness, recognizing these shifting priorities. It blends timeless leadership principles with cutting-edge research to create a practical framework that aligns with modern expectations of purpose, well-being, and fulfillment at work. It provides the tools to overcome the psychological barriers—the *immunity to change*—that so often hold us back.

I wrote this book to help struggling leaders and managers overcome their challenges. These people are often labeled as "ineffective leaders," blamed for their teams' failures, and sacrificed at the altar of reorganization when the real issue isn't incompetence, but rather a lack of proper leadership preparation. Gartner's survey of over

1,400 HR leaders across more than 60 countries and major industries identified leader and manager development as the top priority for 2025; 75% of HR leaders report that managers are overwhelmed with the expanding scope of their responsibilities, and 70% believe that current leaders and managers are not adequately equipped to effectively develop midlevel leaders. The truth is that many leaders are not ineffective; they are simply **inadequately equipped**—thrust into high-stakes roles without the necessary training, mentorship, or tools to navigate the complexities of modern leadership. According to the Center for Creative Leadership, nearly six out of 10 first-time managers step into leadership roles without any formal training or preparation, highlighting a significant gap in organizational development practices. Yet we expect those new managers to meet performance targets, drive engagement, and manage teams effectively, while rarely equipping them with the skills to do so. This is especially concerning, given that many individuals pursue leadership positions primarily as a means to secure a promotion or advance their careers, rather than out of a deep understanding of or readiness for the responsibilities that leadership entails. Furthermore, conventional leadership training has failed them, as evidenced by data showing persistent leadership struggles across industries. Studies indicate that over 60% of new managers fail within their first 24 months, and that only 30% of employees feel their leaders effectively inspire and engage them. Additionally, according to a survey by the Society for Human Resource Management (SHRM), 84% of US workers report that poorly trained managers create a lot of unnecessary work and stress. Despite billions spent annually on leadership development programs, many of these efforts fail because they focus on abstract theories rather than equipping leaders with practical, actionable strategies required for success. A Harvard Business School professor rightly observed, "Corporations are victims of great training robbery." Instead of punishing leaders and managers for struggling, we must give them the right framework, principles, and strategies to grow into their full potential. DEEP PACT is that framework. It provides a structured yet adaptable approach to leadership that ensures leaders are not just promoted—but truly prepared.

I wrote this book to remind you that while we often hear inspiring stories of disruption by famous business leaders and innovators and may believe such opportunities are beyond our reach, the truth is different. Your imaginative power, when applied effectively, can bring about dramatic change in the way everyday tasks and processes are done. We are trapped by many mistaken beliefs about management and leadership, which this book seeks to dispel. You don't need to be a CEO or a renowned visionary to create meaningful disruption; what it takes is confidence in yourself and the drive to think differently—and *that* is leadership. Leadership, as defined in this book, is not only about the courage to innovate but also about pursuing a purpose bigger than yourself. That's why **I wrote this book with people of all levels and roles in mind**—to help them overcome their immunity to change and become the leaders that the modern world needs. If you're a CEO or senior leader, reading this book could be a game-changer both for your organization and your employees. And if you have someone on your team who is intellectually brilliant but struggles with decisiveness, self-examination, or empathy, consider gifting them a copy of this book. Sometimes, the right insights at the right time can help unlock a person's potential, transforming them into the leader your organization truly needs. If you're in middle management, just starting your career, running your own small business, or volunteering in a community or nonprofit organization, don't let your current role define your potential. This book will help you break free from limiting beliefs, overcome obstacles, and lead with confidence—no matter where you are on your journey.

I wrote this book because I have lived by these principles and found them to be powerful, practical solutions to today's challenges. I feel compelled to share my observations and humble personal stories so that others can harness these insights to enrich their lives and leadership. But this book is not just about my experiences. It is grounded in rigorous research and actionable strategies tested in the trenches of leadership.

Above all, **I wrote this book because I believe that leadership should bring happiness—not just to those who are led, but to those who lead**. According to Gallup, only 52% of workers in the United States and Canada were thriving in life evaluation in 2024—a measure of how workers feel about their lives overall, including everything outside the workplace. Globally, the situation is even worse: only 33% of workers worldwide are thriving in life evaluation. But it does not have to be this way. Creating a happier workplace is both possible and worth pursuing. Research has repeatedly shown that workplace happiness increases employee engagement, which in turn drives higher productivity and profitability. Clearly, fostering workplace happiness is not just possible—it is essential for human flourishing and organizational success. This is a new era, and it demands a new kind of leader. This book is your guide to becoming that leader.

More than just a book, this is a blueprint for leading in a way that brings greater purpose, deeper meaning, and lasting happiness into the lives of others—and your own. It reflects the legacy of a lifetime—carved through decades of hard-earned lessons, lived experience, and an unshakable belief in the human potential to achieve greatness. Informed by years of study, research, reflection, and practice, it offers a vision of leadership that is not only effective but also deeply human and profoundly transformative.

> *Whoever is happy will make others happy too. He who has courage and faith will never perish in misery!*
>
> —Anne Frank, *Diary of a Young Girl:*
> *Entry Dated March 7, 1944*

2 What's New and Why It Matters to Your Growth

Every particle of the world is a mirror,
In each atom lies the blazing light
of a thousand suns.
Cleave the heart of a raindrop,
a hundred pure oceans will flow forth.
Look closely at a grain of sand,
The seed of a thousand beings can be seen.

—Mahmud Shabistari,
14th-century Sufi poet

True to the motivations outlined in "Why I Wrote This Book" in the previous chapter, this book challenges the conventional view of leadership as merely a measure of productivity and results—often achieved through varying degrees of command and control. Abandoning this outdated model, this book expands the leadership conversation to a new paradigm—one that drives personal growth and organizational success by anchoring leadership in purpose, meaning, and happiness. In an era where leaders must navigate unprecedented complexities, this book presents a new holistic approach, embodied in five key differentiators, that reimagines leadership for the modern world and enables you to grow not by doing more but by leading with greater clarity, confidence, and impact.

2.1 Five Key Differentiators of This Book

Great execution is the ultimate differentiator.

—Margaret Molloy,
Global chief marketing officer, Siegel+Gale

First, **the book's focus on happiness is groundbreaking** in leadership literature. Unlike traditional leadership models that prioritize efficiency, this book looks beyond the surface of standard metrics like success, power, and prestige to consider the deeper, more personal impacts of our roles as leaders. It posits that when leaders prioritize their own well-being and that of their team members, they foster a more engaged, motivated, and productive workforce. This approach aligns with recent studies highlighting the strong correlation between employee happiness and overall organizational success.

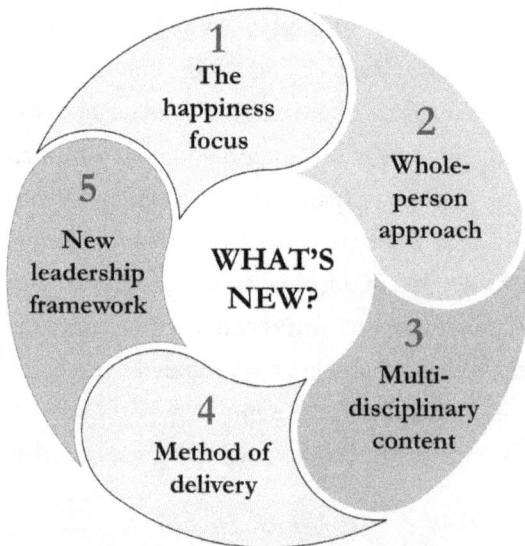

Five key differentiators that make this leadership journey unforgettable.

A Gallup study found that highly engaged employees contribute to a 21% increase in profitability. Similarly, a *Harvard Business Review* article titled "The Happiness Dividend" reported that happy employees are 31% more productive, 37% higher in sales, and three times more creative. Research from Oxford's Saïd Business School revealed that workers are approximately 20% more productive in weeks when they report being happy compared to weeks when they are unhappy. According to the Canada Human Resources Centre, unhappy workers cost the North American business economy well over $350 billion annually in lost productivity. By emphasizing happiness, this book addresses a gap in leadership literature, presenting it as central to successful leadership.

Second, the **whole-person approach in the book is new**, as it doesn't offer you a bag of tricks but instead seeks to transform your mindset and ultimately your character, from which greatness and happiness emanate. This approach represents a significant departure from traditional competency-based leadership training, which tends to focus solely on modifying attitudes and behaviors, often neglecting the deeper layers of the *belief-value-attitude-behavior* spectrum —layers that shape who we are and how we lead, decide, and connect with others. By examining and integrating beliefs and values into the leadership development process, the whole-person approach provides ample opportunities for self-reflection, mindset shifts, meaning-making, and overcoming psychological barriers to change. The whole-person approach recognizes, respects, and actively supports the full spectrum of an individual's humanity—including their intellectual, emotional, social, physical, and moral dimensions. It recognizes that leadership is not just about tactical skills or job performance—it is about developing the entire human being. It seeks to cultivate environments where people can thrive not merely as workers but as whole human beings, grounded in purpose and meaning.

Research highlighted in the *Harvard Business Review* and *MIT Sloan Management Review* shows that making work more meaningful is one of the most powerful—yet often underutilized—ways to boost productivity, happiness, engagement, and performance. In a survey of 12,000 employees, 50% said that they did not find a sense of meaning or significance in their work. However, those who did reported 1.7 times higher job satisfaction, were 1.4 times more engaged in their roles, and were more than three times as likely to stay with their current employer. These findings underscore the profound impact of meaningful work on both employee experience and organizational success. Moreover, meaning-making at work is closely linked to improved mental health and well-being.

The whole-person approach to leadership is also closely connected to employee experience—a critical driver of organizational success. Unlike employee well-being, which focuses on health and work-life balance, employee experience refers to the beliefs, interactions, and benefits that make an employee feel valued and connected to an organization. Leaders play an outsize role in shaping this experience, directly influencing how people perceive their workplace. MIT research shows that companies in the top quartile for employee experience achieve remarkable outcomes: they generate twice the innovation, double the customer satisfaction, and 25% higher profits compared to those in the bottom quartile. Yet, despite its clear importance, only 9% of surveyed leaders felt truly prepared to address employee experience—elevating it as a major strategic priority for leadership development.

In addition, this whole-person approach—enriched by personal and interpersonal mastery—empowers you to build and nurture the 12 data-driven habits that set top leaders apart, as demonstrated in a 15-year study of 30,000 top leaders conducted by the founder and CEO of an executive search firm.

Third, the **multidisciplinary content** of this book is both innovative and groundbreaking, as it seamlessly blends philosophy, psychology, literature, and social science with AI and cutting-edge research from prestigious journals. Notably, this book integrates the most recent studies and insights available as of April 2025, ensuring that readers benefit from the latest developments in leadership science. This wealth of contemporary research allows for a holistic understanding of effective leadership in today's increasingly complex and technology-driven world. For example, new findings published in 2024 by the Stanford Graduate School of Business highlight the growing importance of emotional intelligence in AI-integrated workplaces, revealing that leaders who balance technical and human-centered skills see a 27% increase in team engagement. Similarly, recent insights from MIT's Sloan School emphasize the critical role of ethical AI practices in leadership, noting that organizations with transparency-focused leaders experience up to 40% greater employee trust and satisfaction. Insights from the latest issues of the *Harvard Business Review* are also spread extensively throughout the book, illustrating the relevance of adaptability, trust, and diversity in modern leadership. For instance, Harvard Business Publishing's 2024 study on global leadership trends found that companies with leaders who embrace interdisciplinary thinking and inclusive decision-making are 30% more likely to sustain a competitive advantage. These insights underscore the value of fostering diverse perspectives and a generalist skill set in navigating the rapid changes and uncertainties of the modern business environment, as highlighted in *Range: Why Generalists Triumph in a Specialized World* by David Epstein. By blending the latest insights and studies on leadership with multidisciplinary content from ancient and modern sources, this book equips you not only with timeless leadership principles and their psycho-philosophical foundations but also with cutting-edge, evidence-based practices that address the needs and realities of today's world.

Fourth, the **method of delivery is new**, as it does not merely present ideas to you but also attempts to involve you in collaborative thinking by exploring together the **why, what, and how** of each principle of great and happy leadership presented in this book. Leadership thinker Simon Sinek famously said, "People don't buy what you do; they buy why you do it." By starting with "why," leaders can inspire and engage their teams, ensuring that their actions (the "what") and strategies (the "how") are aligned with a deeper, more meaningful mission.

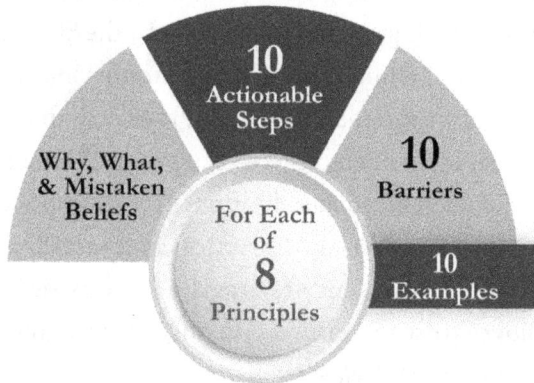

Delivering transformation: a step-by-step method to examine beliefs, remove barriers, and lead with purpose.

You'll find quick tips, happiness enablers, actionable steps for implementation, strategies to overcome barriers, examples, and daily practices—all illustrating how to effectively integrate each principle into your daily life. Another distinguishing feature of this book is its bite-size approach—big ideas and lessons are delivered in sections of just a few pages. Additionally, I include **personal stories** that demonstrate how these principles have shaped my life, proving that they are not just lofty ideas. This collaborative exploration and incremental implementation align with David A. Kolb's *experiential learning theory*, which posits that learning is most effective when individuals can experience, reflect, conceptualize, and experiment.

Finally, the proposed leadership framework (**DEEP PACT**) is new not only in its integrative formulation of eight timeless principles but also in its mnemonic, designed to help you easily recall these principles while evoking the emotion of a **personal pact, a deep one, with yourself**, tapping into your inner power to overcome the immunity to change.

At first glance, the concept of DEEP PACT might appear to be a mere feel-good, idealistic notion. However, by offering concrete strategies on how to navigate the complexities of modern work environments, this book demonstrates that it is not just idealism, but a unique and practical framework grounded in actionable principles essential for today's transformed workplace. Grounded in real-world evidence, contemporary research, and timeless truths, DEEP PACT provides a resilient and adaptable foundation for leaders to navigate today's challenges, from digital transformation to evolving workforce expectations.

By introducing these new elements, the book emphasizes that while the core principles of leadership remain timeless, their application must evolve to meet modern contexts and demands. This book invites you on a transformative journey into an innovative leadership paradigm, challenging you to rethink leadership at every step and offering insights from ancient wisdom, real-world examples, and cutting-edge research.

In addition, this text recognizes that while AI presents remarkable opportunities for efficiency and innovation, its use must be balanced with a deep commitment to human-centric values such as empathy, creativity, care, and ethics. This book will show you how, by incorporating the eight principles of DEEP PACT in our daily routine, we can ensure that technology serves to enhance, rather than diminish, our humanity in the workplace. This is not merely a book about acquiring a certain set of leadership skills to achieve success in your work life; it is about transforming your mindset and your character to foster happiness and success into every aspect of your life—work, personal, and community.

This is not merely a book about acquiring a certain set of leadership skills to achieve success in your work life; it is about transforming your mindset and your character to foster happiness and success into every aspect of your life—work, personal, and community.

Eight Principles Of

DEEP PACT

DECIDE, ACT, and LEAD
without waiting for approval.

EXAMINE YOUR BELIEFS and ACTIONS
more than others think wise.

ENSURE EXCELLENCE
more than others think imaginable.

PROTECT YOURSELF from SELF-SABOTAGE
more than others think necessary.

PERSONAL MASTERY

PRACTICE MORE HUMILITY
than others think possible.

ACT with MORE INTEGRITY
than others think prudent.

CARE MORE for PEOPLE
than others think reasonable.

TRUST MORE
than others think logical.

INTERPERSONAL MASTERY

2.2 What Problems Does DEEP PACT Solve?

Before we can answer the question, we must understand the primary problems and challenges of current leadership models and the imperatives for a change. Below, we discuss six critical challenges that highlight the urgency for a new approach to leadership.

1. Dismal Performance Data on Leadership

Leadership models today show significant shortcomings. Gallup's *State of the American Manager* report found that 50% of employees have left a job to get away from their manager at some point in their career. The Workplace Bullying Institute reports that 61% of bullies are bosses.

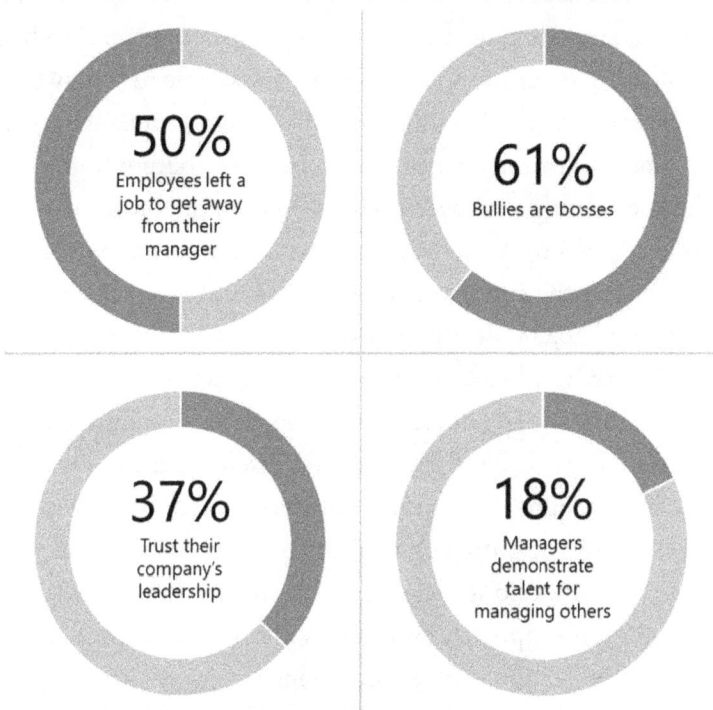

50%
Employees left a job to get away from their manager

61%
Bullies are bosses

37%
Trust their company's leadership

18%
Managers demonstrate talent for managing others

Leadership today: dismal performance data

Trust in leadership is also low, with only 37% of employees trusting their company's leadership, according to the Edelman Trust Barometer. A 2016 Gallup poll found that only 18% of managers demonstrate a high level of talent for managing others, meaning a staggering 82% fall short in their leadership roles, which contributes to two-thirds of employees being disengaged at work.

The Engagement Institute—a collaboration of the Conference Board, Sirota-Mercer, Deloitte, ROI, the Culture Works, and Consulting LLP—released a study of 1,500 respondents showing that disengaged employees cost companies between $450 billion and $550 billion a year.

2. The Health Imperative

The detrimental effects of modern-day failure of leadership extend far beyond organizational inefficiencies; they critically impact the health and well-being of employees and leaders alike due to long working hours, job insecurity, and insufficient work-life integration. These conditions create an environment ripe for chronic stress, burnout, and mental health issues among employees. A study by Stanford professors Jeffrey Pfeffer and Stefanos A. Zenios, along with their former student Joel Goh, highlights the grave consequences of such stressors, attributing them to over 120,000 deaths annually in the United States and up to $190 billion in healthcare costs. Leaders themselves are not immune from this situation. The demands of leadership, compounded by the responsibility of managing stressed and disengaged employees, can lead to significant health issues for leaders related to chronic stress, decision fatigue, and the constant pressure to deliver results. This situation creates a vicious cycle where stressed leaders are less capable of providing the supportive and effective leadership needed to create and maintain a healthy work environment.

3. The Generational Imperative

Millennials (born 1981 to 1996) and Gen Z (born 1997 to 2012), now representing over 50% of the global workforce, prioritize more than just a paycheck; they see work as an extension of their values and as a platform for positive change. These generations are driving the rising demand for moral leadership, where long-term societal impact takes precedence over short-term gains. For Millennials and Gen Z, alignment with an organization's purpose is essential, as 86% of Gen Z and 89% of Millennials report that a sense of purpose is crucial for job satisfaction and well-being, according to a 2024 Deloitte study. Moreover, these cohorts value a balanced, supportive work environment, with approximately 77% of Gen Z emphasizing the importance of work-life integration and flexible work arrangements, according to a 2022 McKinsey report. Studies conducted by Purdue Global report that career growth and skill development are equally vital, with 67% of Gen Z seeking roles that offer advancement opportunities, demonstrating the significance of continuous learning and growth. Additionally, a staggering 80% of Gen Z employees expect their employers to provide equitable support and development opportunities, reinforcing the growing demand for workplaces that prioritize fairness, inclusivity, and equal access to growth for all. Mental health and well-being support are also fundamental, with 68% of Gen Z stating that mental health benefits are crucial for workplace satisfaction.

Together, these values underscore a powerful shift in workplace expectations. Millennials and Gen Z are looking to leaders and organizations not only for a career path but for a sense of purpose, alignment with social responsibility, and a commitment to holistic well-being. Employers who actively meet these priorities are better positioned to attract and retain top talent from these purpose-driven generations.

This generational shift is also mirrored in the broader workforce. According to a study by the Global Strategy Group, a growing majority of Americans recognize the influence corporations wield beyond the marketplace. In fact, nearly nine in 10 believe that businesses have the capacity to drive meaningful social change, and over three-quarters agree that companies have a responsibility to actively engage with the pressing issues facing society today. These data reflect growing disapproval of purely profit-driven leadership models, signaling a fundamental shift in what employees, consumers, and stakeholders value in organizations.

Despite this, the current business landscape, dominated by outdated leadership models, often rewards leaders who deliver immediate financial results, regardless of the long-term consequences. This focus on short-term performance metrics has led to a culture where unethical behaviors are tolerated as long as targets are met. A stark example is Wells Fargo, where management ignored unethical practices in pursuit of financial goals, ultimately damaging trust and public confidence.

The widening gap between executive compensation and worker pay further illustrates how short-term profit motives overshadow ethical considerations. A 2024 report by the Economic Policy Institute revealed that from 1978 to 2023, CEO compensation skyrocketed by 1085%, while a typical worker's pay grew by just 24%. By 2023, the CEO-to-worker pay ratio reached 290:1, a stark contrast to 21:1 in 1965. According to a March 13, 2025, report posted on the Harvard Law School Forum on Corporate Governance website, data from the top 500 highest-revenue US companies shows that the CEO-to-worker pay ratio surged even higher, reaching 306:1 in 2024. Further illustrating this disparity, in 2022, CEOs earned nearly 10 times more than the top 0.1% of US wage earners.

Additionally, an August 2024 report from the Institute for Policy Studies exposed how the 100 largest low-wage employers in the United

States prioritized stock buybacks over worker pay. From 2019 to 2023, these corporations spent $522 billion on buybacks—enriching executives while neglecting wage growth. Retail giants like Lowe's and Home Depot led the way, spending $42.6 billion and $37.2 billion, respectively. Had those funds been redirected, Lowe's could have granted each of its 285,000 employees an annual $29,865 bonus for five years, while Home Depot could have given its 463,100 employees a $16,071 bonus annually for five years.

These findings underscore the widening gap between corporate leadership and the workforce, raising pressing questions about income distribution and corporate responsibility, a major concern for Gen Z and Millennials who prioritize corporate responsibility and fairness in the workplace. This growing disparity not only contributes to financial stress and insecurity among the workforce but also erodes trust in leadership.

4. The Great Resignation

The Great Resignation has emerged as a significant workforce phenomenon, with millions of employees voluntarily leaving their jobs in search of better opportunities, work-life integration, and meaningful work. According to the US Bureau of Labor Statistics, a record 4.3 million Americans quit their jobs in August 2021 alone, reflecting widespread dissatisfaction and shifting priorities. This trend underscores a critical shift in employee expectations and highlights the urgent need for a new approach to leadership that addresses these evolving demands.

The pandemic has acted as a catalyst for this mass exodus, prompting employees to reevaluate their career paths and seek roles that align more closely with their personal values and goals. A survey by Microsoft revealed that 41% of the global workforce considered leaving their employer in 2021, driven by factors such as burnout, lack of flexibility, and inadequate support from management. These findings point to a pressing need for leaders to adapt and create environments that prioritize employee well-being, offer flexibility, and promote a sense of purpose.

5. The AI Challenge

Artificial intelligence is profoundly transforming the business landscape, driving efficiency and innovation. AI technologies, from machine learning to natural language processing, are revolutionizing how companies operate, analyze data, and interact with customers. According to a report by McKinsey & Company, AI adoption has the potential to add $13 trillion to the global economy by 2030, underscoring its significant impact on business operations. However, this transformation also necessitates a new paradigm of leadership to navigate the complexities and ethical considerations that come with AI integration. AI systems, if not carefully managed, can perpetuate biases inherent in historical data and lead to unintended consequences. Overreliance on data-driven decision-making risks ushering in a new era of digital Taylorism — stripping the human element from workplace interactions, reducing employees to mere data points, and diminishing their sense of value and contribution. It can inadvertently compromise psychological safety and employee morale. This tension between technological advancement and human impact makes it imperative for leaders to address not only strategic goals but also emotional realities in the workplace.

In particular, AI integration often evokes fear and resistance among employees, primarily due to concerns about job displacement. Leaders play a crucial role in addressing these fears and motivating the workforce. By demonstrating empathy and showing that they care about their employees' futures, leaders can alleviate fears and build a culture of trust and collaboration. Leaders must reassure employees that **AI is a tool to enhance their roles, not replace them**. As AI continues to reshape industries and organizational structures in a post-pandemic world, more and more emphasis is placed on trust, transparency, empathy, humility, and care in the workplace.

6. *The Harvard Gap*

A 2023 article titled "What Makes Leadership Development Programs Succeed" in the *Harvard Business Review*, authored by professors Ayse Yemiscigil, Dana Born, and Horace Ling, highlighted that despite global organizations spending more than $60 billion annually on leadership development programs, the returns on these investments are dubious. The article noted that just 10% of this spending yields tangible results, with a dismal 90% going to waste. The authors identified three key gaps in leadership training: *a lack of a whole-person approach, insufficient opportunities for self-reflection and meaning-making, and a failure to recognize and address psychological barriers to growth.* In this book, these three gaps are collectively referred to as the Harvard Gap.

This alarming data on performance, healthcare costs, and burnout—combined with gaps in leadership training—underscore the urgent need for a paradigm shift in leadership practices. Leaders must prioritize the well-being of their employees, recognizing that a healthy work environment is not just beneficial but essential for business success. By addressing these workplace stressors, leaders can foster an environment of stability and well-being, ultimately reducing the devastating toll on both human lives and economic resources.

2.3 How DEEP PACT Addresses These Challenges.

This book aims to address the above-mentioned key problems and challenges of today's leadership by articulating a reimagined leadership framework—DEEP PACT—fully unpacked in Chapter 5. It meets the demands of a post-pandemic world by fostering ethical, dynamic, excellence-driven, compassionate, caring, and inclusive leadership.

DEEP PACT: The master key to today's leadership crisis.

DEEP PACT solves the dismal performance issue by providing psychological safety and meaningful work, fostering trust, transparency, and engagement across teams. By integrating employee well-being, both physical and mental, as a leadership priority, DEEP PACT helps create healthier work environments, reducing burnout, stress, and the associated health costs that come from toxic leadership models. DEEP PACT fosters purpose-driven ethical leadership that resonates with Millennials and Gen Z, aligning organizational goals with social responsibility, which appeals to the values-driven expectations of the modern workforce. DEEP PACT ensures ethical AI integration by promoting transparency, trust, and emotional intelligence in leadership, which counters the fear of job displacement and safeguards the human element in AI-driven workplaces. By offering a leadership model that focuses on empathy, care, and flexibility, DEEP PACT helps create a work environment where employees feel valued and supported, addressing the causes behind mass resignations and improving retention. Finally, DEEP PACT closes the Harvard Gap in leadership development, which sets this book apart from all other leadership literature in the following manner:

- ◈ **Happy leadership, not just leadership:** This book focuses on "happy leadership" by advocating a *whole-person approach*. It encourages you to make a solemn pact (DEEP PACT) with yourself, sparking a fundamental change of heart and mindset.
- ◈ **Belief-Value-Attitude-Behavior framework:** Unlike competence-based frameworks that assume that skill acquisition leads to better leadership, this book posits that meaningful behavioral changes occur when leadership training includes opportunities for *self-reflection*, shaping your beliefs and values in the process.
- ◈ **Philosophical underpinnings:** Every chapter of this book begins with the philosophical foundations of our beliefs and values associated with various leadership topics, offering data and information to facilitate *meaning-making*, a critical gap in our leadership training programs.
- ◈ **Implementation actions:** This book offers not only ground-breaking ideas but also practical steps for implementation, complete with examples to help you overcome both *psychological and operational barriers* to "happy leadership" in real-world scenarios.

Gallup identified four universal needs that followers consistently seek from their leaders—hope, trust, compassion, and stability—as documented in its 2025 *Global Leadership Report: What Followers Want,* based on surveys of more than 30,000 adults across 52 countries. Building on these insights, the DEEP PACT whole-person leadership model offers a clear and actionable path for cultivating these very qualities:

◈ **Hope** is inspired when leaders decide, act, and lead with vision and courage (Principle 1).

◈ **Trust** is earned through consistent humility, integrity, and the willingness to trust others in every interaction (Principles 5, 6, and 8).

◈ **Compassion** grows when leaders examine their own beliefs and actions and demonstrate genuine care for people beyond transactional roles (Principles 2 and 7).

◈ **Stability** is reinforced when leaders ensure excellence and protect against self-sabotage, fostering resilience and sustainable growth (Principles 3 and 4).

In short, practicing DEEP PACT equips leaders to meet the very needs followers most desire—building cultures of trust, purpose, and shared hope. As leadership expectations rise in an age of uncertainty, the future belongs to those who can lead, not just with expertise, but with humanity.

> *Progress is impossible without change; and those who cannot change their minds cannot change anything.*
> —George Bernard Shaw

2.4 Doubt This Book's Value? Think Again

In a world overflowing with empty promises, it's understandable why skeptics might initially view DEEP PACT leadership as just another feel-good, idealistic concept. They might dismiss ethical leadership as a lofty and impractical idea in a highly competitive world. They may question DEEP PACT's relevance in addressing the pressing challenges that keep leaders awake at night—such as future economic uncertainty, digital transformation, talent acquisition and retention, project delivery, quality assurance, customer expectations, and the relentless pace of innovation. Beyond these concerns, leaders also grapple with day-to-day workplace issues such as employee burnout, low engagement, high turnover, poor performance, and resistance to change—all of which stem from inadequate leadership, a lack of care for employees' well-being, unmanaged workloads, poor communication, low trust, and insufficient recognition.

However, upon closer examination, one will find that the DEEP PACT principles provide not only a strong foundation for developing the mindset and habits needed to tackle these challenges with resilience and confidence but also offer specific, actionable steps. These principles shape not just how you think but how you operate, make decisions, and lead through complexity. By fostering trust, practicing humility, leading with integrity, ensuring excellence, and empowering teams, leaders can transform challenges into opportunities for growth, collaboration, and sustainable success.

What sets DEEP PACT apart is that every argument for its principles is substantiated by research demonstrating a direct positive impact on an organization's financial performance. Studies consistently show that high-trust cultures and caring leadership drive greater profitability, ethical leadership reduces risk, and purpose-driven organizations outperform their competitors in long-term financial returns. This means that DEEP PACT is not just about ethics, feel-good leadership, or moral ideals—it is a proven framework that enhances business outcomes. Whether it's improving employee well-being, strengthening communication, or driving innovation, DEEP PACT serves as a guiding compass for ethical and whole-person leadership, equipping leaders to thrive in the modern professional landscape while ensuring sustainable financial success.

Many of us, conditioned by an immunity to change, tend to approach new ideas with doubt, trapping ourselves in cycles of skepticism and dismissiveness. Yet data tell a different story, revealing that bold actions and innovative thinking often lead to extraordinary achievements, defying common doubts and limitations. According to a report by the Corporate Executive Board (CEB, now Gartner), companies with strong ethical cultures outperform their peers by up to 10% in long-term financial returns, proving that ethical leadership is not just a lofty concept but a pathway to tangible results. History tells us that every major societal and leadership transformation—from civil rights movements to revolutionary technologies—began as an idealistic vision that challenged the status quo. It's an undeniable fact that a touch of idealism, fueled by a passion for elevating oneself and others, has always been at the heart of transformative, lasting change.

Even after setting aside skepticism about the merit of the book, some of you might still think, *This book isn't for me. I'm not a leader, and I don't see myself becoming one anytime soon.* This transition from skepticism to self-exempting bias is not uncommon, as it offers the comfort of *cognitive ease.* Renowned psychologist and Nobel Laureate Daniel Kahneman explained this concept in his book *Thinking, Fast and Slow* as a mental state where information that aligns with existing beliefs is easier to process, whereas information that contradicts those beliefs is met with cognitive strain. The question then becomes, do you want to fall prey to these limiting beliefs and dismiss your role in this world, or do you want to explore the possibilities within yourself?

Leadership isn't confined to formal titles; it is woven into the fabric of daily life. It emerges in countless situations: a parent guiding a child, an employee stepping up during a critical project, a friend offering unwavering support in difficult times, or a community member organizing local events. Each of these acts, no matter how small, carries weight and impacts others. Therefore, to say that this or any other leadership book is not relevant is simply to seek refuge in the comfort zone of self-exemption. The truth is, embracing these new ideas is relevant to all of us. New ideas challenge us to step out of that comfort zone and recognize the leader within ourselves.

In his bestseller *Think Again: The Power of Knowing What You Don't Know*, Adam Grant warns against the dangers of the "overconfidence cycle," where leaders become trapped in the illusion of certainty, believing they are right simply because their past successes have reinforced their confidence. This mindset discourages critical thinking, blinds leaders to new information, and stifles innovation. Instead of clinging to outdated assumptions, great leaders recognize that what worked yesterday may not work tomorrow.

The time has come for a major rethink in the leadership arena—one that embraces intellectual humility and the ability to unlearn outdated leadership theories and practices. Just as we update our software to stay relevant, we must continuously update our thinking, recognizing that holding onto outdated beliefs hinders growth and adaptability, while true confidence is best paired with curiosity rather than stubbornness. The leaders who will thrive are those who question their assumptions, integrate human-centered approaches with technological advancements, and foster a culture of innovation and continuous rethinking at every level.

In every role we play, we are either doing a poor job, an adequate job, or an exceptional one. But there is always room to improve, to strive for better. This book is for you—to show you how to lead better, how to bring more happiness into your life and the lives of those around you. After all, everything we do affects others in some form. As British primatologist Jane Goodall once said, "We have a choice to use the gift of our life to make the world a better place or not to bother." Choose to make a difference; choose to lead with intention and compassion.

Don't underestimate your potential either. You have more power than you realize. Each of us holds the potential to influence the world around us in profound ways. The Sufi poet Mahmud Shabistari's verse quoted at the beginning of this chapter powerfully illustrates the boundless potential and profound beauty inherent in even the smallest elements of our world. It reveals that within each particle, each atom, lies an immense, blazing light—symbolizing the extraordinary power within each of us. By recognizing and embracing this inner brilliance, we can unlock vast oceans of creativity, strength, and potential, transforming our lives and the world around us.

This book is designed to unleash your leadership potential by equipping you with the tools to harness your strengths, inspire change within yourself, and positively impact others. By following the principles of DEEP PACT, you can transform not just how you lead but how you live. **The ultimate goal of the book is to open up possibilities not only in your career but also within yourself.**

We have greatness inside each of us, though sometimes it is just as dormant as the wildflowers in Death Valley. The seed is always there—it just needs the right conditions to flourish.
—Stephen Covey

Imagine the ripple effect of your actions. By changing yourself, you start to change the people around you—and gradually the world begins to shift. You don't need a title to lead; leadership is about influence, inspiration, and action. Be a catalyst for change, no matter where you are in your journey. Embrace the possibility that you can be the spark that ignites transformation in your workplace, family, community, and beyond. Remember, the ocean is made up of countless drops, each contributing to its vastness and power. So take the first step: read this book. It is meant for you.

2.5 But What about My Performance Targets?

A final source of hesitation often arises from managers focused on meeting their annual performance targets, who might worry that DEEP PACT is just another set of feel-good principles for which they don't have time. However, this book dispels that notion by providing 10 practical, actionable steps for each principle to define and implement key performance indicators necessary for achieving tangible business outcomes. It challenges the mistaken belief that managing by metrics and efficiency is at odds with leading through care and empathy. In reality, these approaches are complementary aspects of effective leadership.

Research supports this integration. A 2023 *Harvard Business Review* article, "Leading with Compassion Has Research-Backed Benefits," argues that leaders who demonstrate compassion can significantly enhance employee engagement, reduce burnout, and improve overall organizational performance. A short-term, numbers-driven approach may yield immediate gains but often leads to burnout, disengagement, and high turnover—ultimately weakening an organization's long-term performance. When leaders prioritize short-term metrics over sustainable strategies, they risk creating a high-pressure environment where employees feel undervalued and expendable. This shortsighted approach can erode morale, stifle innovation, and create a toxic workplace culture that hinders long-term success.

DEEP PACT principles do not dismiss or undervalue metrics; instead, they harmonize them with empathy to foster trust and commitment. When employees feel valued and supported, their motivation and productivity naturally increase, leading to sustainable and consistent achievement of performance targets. This balanced approach shows that performance and human connection are not competing priorities but essential, synergistic elements of successful leadership, driving both exceptional results and a thriving workplace culture. But striking this balance is not always straightforward. It requires embracing the inherent paradoxes of leadership—the perennial tension between profit and purpose, short-term performance and long-term sustainability, and the relentless drive for excellence and employee well-being.

2.6 The Leadership Paradox: Embracing the Journey, Not Perfection

The paradox of leadership is that no single leader can equally embody every ideal—bold vision and deep empathy, relentless drive and genuine humility, or strategic foresight and unwavering trust in others. Each leader naturally excels in some areas while struggling in others, making leadership not a pursuit of perfection but a continuous journey of growth and self-awareness. A brilliant visionary may inspire the world with groundbreaking ideas yet struggle to connect deeply with the people bringing that vision to life. An empathetic and people-centric leader may build trust and belonging but hesitate when faced with tough, high-stakes decisions. The reality is that leadership is not about mastering all aspects at once but about embracing the journey, step by step, habit by habit, principle by principle.

I experienced this firsthand when I read *The 7 Habits of Highly Effective People* by Stephen R. Covey, a book that had an immense influence on me in the early days of my career. While I admired all seven habits, I couldn't internalize them equally. The one that became ingrained in my character was Habit 2: "Begin with the End in Mind." Every project I led began with a clear vision, and this approach significantly shaped my decision-making. Two other habits also guided my leadership journey: "Seek First to Understand, Then to Be Understood" and "Sharpen the Saw." While I practiced these three regularly, I was unable to pay equal attention to the rest of the seven habits all the time, although they inspired me. I was so inspired that I bought large, framed copies of each individual habit and hung them throughout our office as a daily reminder for my team and me.

Similarly, we do not expect you to internalize all eight principles of DEEP PACT equally. Leadership is not about rigid adherence to every ideal but about discovering the principles that matter most to you and applying them in ways that create real impact. The key is to start the journey of becoming the leader you are meant to be. Grow at your own pace. Leadership is not about being perfect—it's about being willing to evolve.

Begin the journey today.

2.7 One Step at a Time

The history of the cosmos
is the history of the struggle of becoming.

—D. H. Lawrence

Start small. Focus on one principle at a time for a month before moving to the next. Hang a page with the eight principles of DEEP PACT in a visible place at your desk. Look at the list of principles daily and contemplate how each one applies to your current work situation. Leadership growth is not about sudden, dramatic transformations but about consistent, intentional improvement. Suppose you incorporate only one of the eight principles into your life. That itself is a huge step toward great leadership and will lead to further success as you may choose to incorporate more principles into your leadership style over time. We recognize that there will be failures and setbacks from one day to the next, but what truly matters is maintaining a mindset committed to these principles. This persistent mindset will naturally guide your actions, and as you begin to see the benefits of implementing even a single principle, you will be motivated to adopt more. Each small success builds momentum, encouraging gradual improvement and reinforcing the value of these principles in fostering personal and organizational growth. This gradual approach allows you to deeply understand and embody each principle before moving on to the next, ensuring that the principles become a natural part of your leadership style and daily life. As Lao Tzu wisely said, "Nature does not hurry, yet everything is accomplished." Begin with the principle that resonates most with your immediate challenges.

The elevator to success is out of order. You'll have to use the stairs, one step at a time. —Joe Girard, American salesman

In each chapter, you will be introduced to the philosophical underpinnings of these principles as well as compelling and inspiring stories of leaders from diverse fields who have embodied these principles, transforming their visions into reality against all odds. Each chapter also includes 10 practical steps and solutions to 10 barriers that serve as tangible tools for real-life application. Spend a month actively working on incorporating the chosen principle into your behavior, reflecting on your progress, and observing the changes in yourself and your environment.

As you incorporate each principle, observe how it is changing you and your interactions with others. You might notice improvements in your stress levels, relationships, and overall job satisfaction. You might see improvements in your social and family interactions because of changed perspectives and mindset. These changes may be subtle at first, but over time, these small shifts can lead to significant personal and professional transformation. You may consider sharing the principles of DEEP PACT with your friends and colleagues, inviting them to explore the benefits and integrate the ideas into their own lives. When surrounded by individuals who are also committed to these principles, you are more likely to stay motivated and accountable. According to research published in the *Journal of Experimental Social Psychology*, individuals who share goals with others are more likely to stay motivated and achieve them due to mutual accountability.

Begin your journey into a new kind of leadership by implementing just one of the many actionable steps outlined in this book and you'll witness a profound change in yourself. Overcome even one of the many barriers identified here, and you'll realize the immense power you have, to transform your leadership and your life.

You were born with wings, why prefer to crawl through life?

—Rumi

2.8 Your Immense Creative Potential

David Kelley, the legendary designer and Stanford professor, asserts that "All people are naturally creative." He believes that many people lose their creative confidence as they grow older due to societal pressures and fear of judgment. As you embark on this journey of DEEP PACT, reclaim your creative spirit, knowing that you have the innate ability to innovate and inspire. It will guide you in prioritizing and applying these principles to fit your unique situational needs, style, and temperament. Your creativity will enable you to see possibilities others might overlook and lead with originality and vision.

Studies have shown that fostering creativity within leadership not only enhances problem-solving skills but also drives organizational innovation and success. Teresa Amabile, a Harvard Business School professor, emphasizes that creativity in leadership results in a more engaged and motivated workforce, as employees feel empowered to contribute unique ideas and solutions. Additionally, research by the World Economic Forum highlights creativity as one of the top skills needed for the future workforce, underscoring its critical role in navigating complex and rapidly changing environments. By embracing your creative potential, you not only strengthen your leadership capabilities but also cultivate an environment where innovation and inspiration thrive, positioning yourself and your team for sustained success.

The ideas presented here can ignite your leadership potential, but it is your commitment and creativity that will fuel the engine and propel you forward. Let your creativity shine, transforming challenges into opportunities, and making your leadership journey truly remarkable.

New horizons are not found by staying in the harbor.

—Unknown

2.9 Greatness, Character, and Resilience

Although this book offers a comprehensive framework and practical tools to unleash our inherent greatness, it must be noted that greatness in leadership cannot be achieved merely by learning and mastering new tools, whether from this book or any other books or training programs. As NVIDIA CEO Jensen Huang stated in a 2024 interview at Stanford University, "Greatness is not intelligence. Greatness comes from character, and character isn't formed out of smart people; it is formed out of people who suffered." This profound insight underscores that true greatness is rooted in character, forged through resilience and adversity, rather than just intelligence or skills. Huang's emphasis on character aligns with Aristotle's philosophy that virtues such as courage, temperance, and justice are cultivated through habitual actions, forming the foundation of true greatness. Character is not just about innate qualities but about the consistent practice of virtuous behavior, which builds resilience and strength over time.

Character, as Huang suggests, is forged in the crucible of adversity. It is through facing and overcoming challenges that individuals develop qualities like perseverance, empathy, and integrity. These traits are essential for leaders who must navigate the complexities and uncertainties of the modern world. Huang's own journey from a challenging childhood to leading NVIDIA, a powerhouse in the tech industry, underscores the importance of character. His experiences taught him resilience and the ability to persist through hardship, which he credits as key components of his success.

Character is not only about facing difficulties but also about how one responds to them. As the ancient Greek philosopher Heraclitus famously said, *"Character is destiny."* This highlights the idea that our character shapes our path and our ultimate impact on the world. Leaders with strong character are better equipped to build resilient organizations that can withstand and thrive amid change and uncertainty. Steve Jobs faced numerous failures and setbacks, including being ousted from Apple, the company he cofounded. However, his resilience and ability to learn from these experiences allowed him to return and lead Apple to unprecedented success. Similarly, Oprah Winfrey's early life was marked by significant challenges, including poverty and abuse. Her resilience helped her navigate these obstacles and become a leading media mogul and philanthropist. A study by the *Harvard Business Review* found that resilient leaders are better equipped to handle the pressures and uncertainties of today's fast-paced, ever-changing business environment.

The daily practice of DEEP PACT is ultimately a character-building tool. Character is a critical factor for success, and it teaches resilience. Stephen Covey, in *The 7 Habits of Highly Effective People*, emphasizes the importance of a character ethic over a personality ethic. Covey argues that qualities such as integrity, humility, and courage form the bedrock of true leadership. He asserts that sustainable success comes from building a strong moral foundation, which involves practicing virtues consistently. This aligns with findings from the 2016 HOW Report, which revealed that when managers prioritize shaping character and fostering freedom across an organization, not only do 96% of employees rate them as effective leaders (compared to just 52% otherwise), but they are also more than three times as likely to drive high performance. This underscores the profound impact of character-driven leadership, reinforcing that ethical foundations are not just moral imperatives but also key drivers of organizational success.

In the context of AI and the evolving business landscape, the importance of character becomes even more pronounced. The rapid advancements in technology and the increasing reliance on data-driven decision-making can sometimes overshadow the human element in leadership. However, it is precisely in this high-tech environment that character-driven leadership can provide balance. Leaders who demonstrate empathy, transparency, and ethical judgment can ensure that technological progress does not come at the expense of human values and well-being.

DEEP PACT can significantly aid in building the character necessary for happy and great leadership through daily practice of its principles. This daily practice not only fosters personal growth but also equips leaders to handle adversities with grace and determination.

Great leaders see greatness in others.
—Jon Gordon, author of *The Energy Bus*

2.10 Why DEEP PACT? Let Your Heart Decide

This leadership book is designed to be a beacon of inspiration and a roadmap to change, empowering you with the tools and knowledge to achieve great and happy leadership that effectively balances the needs of the business and its employees in a post-pandemic world. Through captivating narratives of philosophy, allegorical tales, and rich historical and hypothetical examples, this book illuminates our belief systems and inspires us to dismantle misconceptions and unlearn detrimental habits. Its profound wisdom transcends the workplace, enriching our personal lives and community interactions. This book offers a transformative journey, guiding readers to unlock their potential, embrace continuous improvement, and lead with passion and purpose. By the end of this enlightening journey, you will be equipped not only with the insights and strategies but also with actionable steps needed to create a lasting, positive change in your life and in the lives of those around you.

Great leadership is a joyful pursuit that brings immense personal happiness and job satisfaction. Opportunities for great leadership abound in your personal life, community, and workplace. It is not merely a position but a role you can assume without needing anyone's permission. Transforming your leadership potential into "happy leadership" ultimately requires a personal commitment, a pact with yourself.

Are you ready to ignite the leadership potential within you by embracing DEEP PACT? Harvard professor Theodore Levitt once said, "The future belongs to those who see possibilities before they become obvious and who effectively marshal resources and energies for their attainment or avoidance. Nor is anything great ever accomplished without high spirits." Do you aspire to be one of those high-spirited individuals? If so, I invite you to embark with me on this joyful journey of the mind and heart. Together, we will explore new horizons, unlock hidden potentials, and create meaningful connections that inspire growth and change.

A vision is not just a picture of what could be; it is an appeal to our better selves, a call to become something more.
—Rosabeth Moss Kanter,
professor, Harvard Business School

Let's walk along this path of discovery and enlightenment, making every step a celebration of knowledge and passion. Let's walk together with open minds and hearts, embracing every opportunity to learn and grow. Let's walk hand in hand with curiosity, exploring the depths of our potential and the heights of our aspirations. Let's walk with determination, breaking down barriers and overcoming obstacles that stand in our way. Let's walk with joy, finding inspiration in every moment and motivation in every achievement. Let's walk this journey with a shared vision, creating a brighter, more empowered future for ourselves and those around us through happy and great leadership.

In the spirit of creative self-discovery and personal transformation, let the words of 13th-century Sufi poet Fariduddin Attar inspire us to embrace the whole-person ethical leadership:

This ocean can be yours; why should you stop
Beguiled by dreams of evanescent dew?
The secrets of the sun are yours, but you
Content yourself with motes trapped in its beams.
Turn to what truly lives, reject what seems—
Which matters more, the body or the soul?
Be whole: desire and journey to the Whole.

3 Why Happiness Matters

Happiness is the meaning and the purpose of life, the whole aim and end of human existence.

—Aristotle

We are all happiness-seeking individuals, driven by the desire to find fulfillment and joy in various aspects of our lives. Aristotle's words quoted above illuminate the fundamental role that happiness plays in our existence. More than a fleeting emotion or momentary pleasure, happiness represents a state of being that we instinctively strive toward—an ultimate goal that underlies nearly every human endeavor.

Modern psychology affirms this ancient truth. Research in the field of positive psychology, particularly the work of Martin Seligman, has shown that happiness—or more precisely, *well-being*—is not just a byproduct of success or favorable circumstances. It is a composite of positive emotion, engagement, relationships, meaning, and accomplishment—the five pillars of Seligman's PERMA model. This framework reinforces the idea that we are wired to pursue purpose, mastery, and connection, echoing Aristotle's notion of *eudaimonia,* a deep sense of flourishing that transcends simple pleasure.

Contemporary voices continue to reinforce that Aristotle was right. Oprah Winfrey—one of the most influential storytellers and interviewers of the modern era—has observed this same hunger for happiness. She wrote in *Build the Life You Want*, "In my twenty-five years of doing the show, if there was one thing almost everyone in every audience had in common, it was the desire to be happy. As I've said before, after every show I'd chat with the audience, and I always asked what they most wanted in life. To be happy, they'd say. Just to be happy. Just happiness."

This longing for happiness is universal. It transcends culture, age, profession, and background. Whether we seek happiness through love, achievement, service, spirituality, or self-expression, the common thread is our shared human quest for a life that feels good and means something. Philosopher Bertrand Russell, in his seminal work *The Conquest of Happiness*, observed that many of the obstacles to happiness are internal—rooted in anxiety, self-absorption, and excessive competition. He wrote, "The secret of happiness is this: let your interests be as wide as possible, and let your reactions to the things and persons that interest you be as far as possible friendly rather than hostile." For Russell, happiness grows when we shift our focus outward—toward curiosity, community, and contribution—rather than inward toward self-centered striving. He emphasized that cultivating zest for life, engaging in meaningful work, and developing affectionate relationships are foundational to sustained joy.

In this light, happiness is not a luxury or an afterthought. It is a compass. It guides our choices, shapes our relationships, and defines our vision of a life well lived. Recognizing this truth—honoring it as both an ancient wisdom and a modern imperative—can fundamentally reshape how we lead ourselves and others. Our work life, personal life, and social life are intricately interconnected, each influencing our overall sense of happiness. The quality of our work environment, the depth of our personal relationships, and the richness of our social interactions all play crucial roles in shaping our emotional well-being and happiness.

3.1 Happiness and Leadership

Happiness at work doesn't just improve the bottom line—it transforms the workplace.
   —Michelle Gielan, author of *Broadcasting Happiness*

The impact of happiness becomes especially profound when viewed through the lens of leadership, where a leader's emotional well-being directly influences team morale, culture, and performance. Happy leaders not only experience greater personal fulfillment, but they also create the emotional conditions for thriving, resilient teams. Recognizing this truth, Harvard Business School introduced a now highly popular course, Leadership and Happiness, taught by best-selling author and professor Arthur Brooks. The course description states, "Leadership & Happiness is meant for anyone aspiring to be a leader— whether in business, or even as head of a family." The class has become so popular that it fills all 180 seats, with another 400 students on the waitlist—and even some attending via a secret Zoom link. In a 2023 interview with *Harvard Business Review* editor-in-chief Adi Ignatius, Brooks remarked, "If I had my way, every business school and every high school would have this class."

The importance of happiness in leadership is further reinforced by Shawn Achor and Michelle Gielan in their 2020 *Harvard Business Review* article "What Leading with Optimism Looks Like." Achor and Gielan argue that optimism is not naïve cheerfulness, but a learned habit that drives better outcomes in organizations. Their research shows that when leaders adopt optimistic behaviors—such as expressing gratitude, showing empathy, and encouraging positive communication—they help foster greater creativity, productivity, and resilience across their teams. True leadership means reflecting on how your work serves others—and helping employees see how their contributions make a difference. When people connect their efforts to service, they gain happiness, engagement, and purpose that ultimately fuel lasting success.

The significance of happiness as a core leadership competency is gaining recognition in academic circles. Cornell University offers a course, Maximizing Happiness as a Leader: Lessons from Ancient Rome, which explores strategies for leaders to achieve personal happiness and effectively manage workplace challenges. Similarly, the University of California, Berkeley, offers a professional certificate series called The Science of Happiness at Work, designed to teach the principles of fostering happiness within organizational settings. The MIT Sloan School of Management teaches a class, Pursuing Happiness and a Meaningful Life, and Stanford Graduate School of Business offers the online class Create a Happy and Meaningful Life. These classes reflect a broader trend among leading academic institutions to integrate the study of happiness into leadership education, emphasizing its critical role in effective management and organizational success.

> *"200 different studies show success won't make you happy. But science says happiness can make you more successful. Success typically doesn't result in happiness. But research shows happiness is a driver of success."*
> *– Jeff Haden, Inc., Aug. 21, 2025*

Together, the insights from Brooks, Achor, and Gielan—along with the growing attention devoted to happiness and leadership in academic programs—make a compelling case: happiness is not a distraction from leadership; it is a foundation for it. By nurturing enjoyment, satisfaction, and purpose, and by modeling optimism and emotional intelligence, leaders not only can elevate their own lives but also empower those they lead to flourish.

However, despite this recognition and the growing number of academic initiatives, happiness has yet to become mainstream in leadership training and corporate discourse. Many organizations still dismiss happiness as a mere "feeling" and a personal matter, rather than a measurable driver of organizational performance. This mindset persists despite substantial evidence highlighting the critical role of employee well-being and happiness in achieving business success.

3.2 The Ripple Effect of Leadership

You want to be the pebble in the pond that creates the ripple for change.
—Tim Cook, chief executive officer, Apple

Have you ever wondered why there are so many bad managers in our workplace spreading unhappiness across the board?

Imagine an employee who spends the day under the weight of relentless criticism and a lack of support from a manager. The stress doesn't simply disappear when the workday ends; it lingers, affecting energy levels and emotional well-being. This employee may come home feeling drained and emotionally distant, struggling to engage meaningfully with their loved ones. Over time, this chronic stress can shape the overall mood and atmosphere of their home, straining personal relationships.

Now, contrast this with an employee who, despite working just as hard, is supported, recognized, and encouraged by their manager. The sense of accomplishment fuels their energy, allowing them to return home with a more positive mindset. This positivity infuses warmth and enthusiasm into interactions at home, fostering connection rather than tension.

While each person is ultimately responsible for managing their emotions, research has shown that workplace experiences significantly influence mental well-being. The workplace is not the sole factor shaping home life, but when a significant portion of the day is spent in an environment that is either uplifting or toxic, it inevitably impacts one's emotional reserves. Professor Arthur Brooks, the instructor of Harvard's Leadership and Happiness class, once asserted, "If you're unhappy at work, you're probably unhappy in life." Therefore, when organizations prioritize positive leadership and employee well-being, they don't just enhance productivity—they create a ripple effect that extends beyond the workplace.

Shawn Achor's research in *The Happiness Advantage* provides compelling scientific evidence that happiness is not merely a byproduct of success but a critical driver of it—particularly in leadership. His research employs a blend of positive psychology experiments, cross-sectional studies, and workplace interventions to explore the link between happiness, performance, and leadership effectiveness. Grounded in empirical psychology and neuroscience, much of his work was conducted at Harvard University and later expanded to corporate environments, reinforcing its practical relevance.

Achor's central argument is that our brains function significantly better when we are in a positive state, leading to higher levels of intelligence, creativity, and resilience. His research shows that when leaders cultivate happiness, they enhance not only their own performance but also the performance of those they lead, which reinforces the idea that happiness is not incidental but foundational to effective leadership. Achor's studies reveal that a positive mindset boosts problem-solving abilities and innovation while reducing stress, allowing leaders to make better decisions and foster an environment of trust and engagement. In this way, happiness is not a passive emotional state but an active leadership tool that enhances productivity, motivation, and long-term success.

Furthermore, Achor's research highlights the ripple effect of happiness, reinforcing the idea that leadership influences extend far beyond individual leaders themselves. Happy leaders create more engaged, motivated teams, reducing turnover rates and increasing overall performance. Conversely, negative leadership can spread stress and disengagement throughout an organization, leading to decreased morale and productivity. By prioritizing happiness, leaders cultivate an environment where individuals thrive, reinforcing this book's assertion that joy and fulfillment are not luxuries but essential components of sustainable and impactful leadership.

In Charles Dickens's *A Christmas Carol*, Ebenezer Scrooge is a miserly boss whose stinginess and lack of compassion spread significant unhappiness to his employee, Bob Cratchit, and Cratchit's struggling family, including his sickly son, Tiny Tim. Scrooge's refusal to pay better wages and his indifferent attitude toward Bob's hardship create a bleak and joyless environment for the Cratchits. However, after being visited by the ghosts of Christmas Past, Present, and Yet to Come, Scrooge undergoes a profound transformation. He becomes generous and caring, improving the Cratchit family's circumstances by increasing Bob's salary and providing them with much-needed support, which helps ensure Tiny Tim gets the care he needs, ultimately saving his life. This change in Scrooge's character brings newfound happiness and stability to the Cratchit family. These stories underscore how leaders wield immense power to spread happiness or unhappiness far beyond the workplace.

If you are not happy in your role as a leader, it is essential to ask why and address the underlying issues. Happiness in leadership is not a luxury; it is a necessity that enhances your effectiveness, inspires those around you, and ensures that your leadership journey is both meaningful and sustainable.

True leadership begins with personal fulfillment and authenticity because happiness in leadership is not a superficial or selfish pursuit; it fuels genuine passion, creativity, and resilience. If you are not happy, it often signifies a misalignment between your values, your actions, and your environment. An unhappy leader may inadvertently create a toxic environment, leading to decreased morale, increased turnover, and lower productivity. An unhappy leader is more likely to be a "diminisher," defined in Liz Wiseman's book *Multipliers* as someone who unintentionally stifles the creativity and potential of their team by micromanaging and hoarding decision-making power. Conversely, a leader who finds joy and satisfaction in their role sets a powerful example, creating a ripple effect of positivity and engagement through-out the team. A happy leader is more likely to be a "multiplier," meaning they amplify their team's intelligence and capabilities by empowering and inspiring them to reach their full potential. In essence, happy leaders cultivate happy teams, which in turn drives better results and creates a healthier organizational culture. Harvard Business School professor Clayton Christensen once wrote, "Doing deals doesn't yield the deep rewards that come from building up people."

Happiness is also crucial for the long-term sustainability of your leadership. Burnout is real and pervasive in today's fast-paced world. Without a sense of happiness and fulfillment, the likelihood of burnout increases, threatening not only your well-being but also the stability and effectiveness of your leadership. By prioritizing happiness, you are investing in your capacity to lead sustainably and to continue making meaningful contributions over the long term. A January 2024 article in the *International Journal of Happiness and Development* titled "Happy Leadership, Now More Than Ever" emphasizes the essential role of happiness in organizational performance. The authors assert, "Management must remember that happy employees are a wave of creativity and innovation in the ocean of corporate cultures." This compelling metaphor highlights how employee happiness is not merely a soft benefit, but a dynamic force that drives innovation, engagement, and long-term success.

Finally, the purpose of leadership should be intrinsically linked to a vision that is larger than oneself, encompassing both personal and collective well-being and happiness. When leadership is driven by a genuine sense of purpose, it aligns more closely with ethical practices, compassionate actions, and visionary thinking. It transforms leadership from a mere role or responsibility into a powerful force for good, capable of creating lasting and positive impacts on individuals, organizations, and communities.

If you are not happy in your role as a leader, it is essential to ask why and address the underlying issues. Happiness in leadership is not a luxury; it is a necessity that enhances your effectiveness, inspires those around you, and ensures that your leadership journey is both meaningful and sustainable. The true purpose of leadership is to lead with joy, passion, and authenticity, creating a legacy of positive impact and fulfilled potential.

We reimagine leadership with happiness at its core, introducing a new paradigm that goes beyond traditional workplace boundaries to shape not just careers but also personal and social lives. By embracing the principles outlined here, you can cultivate a holistic approach to leadership that fosters happiness not only in professional settings but also in your personal relationships and social interactions. This paradigm posits that true leadership is about inspiring and empowering yourself as well as others to navigate life's challenges with resilience, empathy, and purpose.

3.3 Happiness Can't Be Universal or Constant

The modern world is a juggling act, and sometimes it can seem like an all-out circus.
> —Amy Blankson, author of *The Future of Happiness*

Although we place happiness front and center of leadership, we recognize that **happiness cannot be achieved universally across all aspects of life all the time.** For many individuals, mental health challenges, chronic illnesses, and unchangeable family situations can significantly impact their ability to experience happiness. According to the 2023 Fact Sheet on Depressive Disorder from the World Health Organization, about 3.8% (approximately 300 million) of the world's population suffer from depression, which can severely limit their capacity for joy and fulfillment. According to a 2023 Gallup poll, 29% (approximately 98 million) of Americans report having been diagnosed with depression in their lifetime, while 17.8% (approximately 48 million) report currently having depression.

Life is inherently filled with ups and downs, and true leaders understand that resilience is built through navigating these fluctuations. As a result, expecting to be happy or successful every day is unrealistic. Embracing the idea that setbacks and failures are integral parts of the journey helps in developing a resilient nature, which allows leaders to persevere through challenges, ultimately leading to deeper fulfillment and more sustainable success.

Ancient wisdom, such as the Stoic philosophy of Epictetus, teaches us that while we cannot control external events, we can control our responses to them. This mindset can help us navigate the vicissitudes of life, finding moments of contentment even amid adversity. Happiness should not be considered an all-or-nothing proposition. Life's circumstances will inevitably lead us to experience a spectrum of emotions, from joy to sorrow. Accepting this reality allows us to appreciate the fleeting moments of happiness without being overwhelmed by the pursuit of constant joy. The Greek philosopher Aristotle believed that true happiness comes from living a life of virtue and fulfilling our potential, rather than from external circumstances. Happiness can also be found through the quality of our relationships and our actions toward others. Modern research supports the idea that strong social connections and altruistic behavior are significant contributors to personal well-being. A study by Harvard Medical School found that people with strong social relationships are 50% more likely to live longer, healthier lives.

Leadership plays a critical role in either mitigating or exacerbating workplace depression. Poor leadership practices, such as lack of communication, insufficient support, unrealistic demands, or a hostile work environment, can lead to heightened stress levels among employees, significantly contributing to workplace depression. Published research highlights that employees with unsupportive supervisors are more likely to experience symptoms of depression and anxiety. Conversely, effective leadership that emphasizes empathy, clear communication, and support can create a positive work environment, reducing stress and improving overall mental health. By demonstrating genuine concern for the well-being of their team members, leaders can build trust and create a safe space where individuals feel valued and understood, which will improve the inner peace of the team members. Implementing practices such as regular mindfulness sessions, encouraging work-life integration, and offering resources for mental health support can also significantly contribute to an employee's sense of inner calm.

The DEEP PACT principles promote a transformative leadership style that can mitigate these negative outcomes. By encouraging open communication, demonstrating genuine care, and creating supportive partnerships, leaders can build a positive work environment where employees feel valued and understood.

3.4 Happiness or Success Cannot Be Pursued

Psychiatrist Viktor Frankl, in his seminal book *Man's Search for Meaning*, argues that happiness is not something that can be pursued directly but is a byproduct of living a meaningful life; he stated, "Happiness cannot be pursued; it must ensue." Frankl's philosophy emphasizes that happiness comes from finding purpose and meaning in life. He suggests that people find meaning through three primary avenues: work (doing something significant), love (caring for another person), and courage during difficult times. Frankl posits that success, much like happiness, emerges when individuals immerse themselves in meaningful and purposeful activities. He writes, "Success, like happiness, cannot be pursued; it must ensue, and it only does so as the unintended side-effect of one's personal dedication to a cause greater than oneself." This insight encourages a shift in focus from self-centered pursuits to actions that contribute to the well-being of others and the world.

Frankl's view on success is supported by research in positive psychology and motivational theory, which indicates that people who pursue intrinsic goals (personal growth, relationships, community involvement) rather than extrinsic goals (money, fame, image) tend to experience greater happiness and success. Self-determination theory (SDT), postulated by psychologists Edward Deci and Richard Ryan, posits that intrinsic motivation, which arises from internal satisfaction and personal interest, is a more powerful driver of human behavior than extrinsic motivation, which relies on external rewards or pressures. This is because intrinsic motivation encourages a sense of freedom and flexibility, which is essential for creative processes. The practice of the eight principles presented in this book can elevate you to new heights of meaningful engagement and intrinsic motivation, which are essential for true happiness and success through effective leadership.

3.5 The Goodness Connection

"Goodness," according to Michel de Montaigne, "is the demonstration of empathy and compassion toward others in everyday life." Goodness can generate happiness, as acts of kindness and compassion lead to a sense of fulfillment and joy for both the giver and the receiver. Unlike happiness, goodness can be pursued. Studies in positive psychology have shown that engaging in altruistic behaviors enhances overall well-being, reinforcing the intrinsic link between being good and feeling happy. All human beings are inherently good, but the complexities and challenges of world affairs often obscure this fundamental goodness inside us. Ancient philosophers and spiritual leaders have long recognized and articulated the intrinsic goodness within each person. Confucius, ancient Chinese philosopher and author of *Analects*, taught that humans have a natural inclination toward virtue and righteousness, emphasizing the importance of nurturing one's inner moral compass. Similarly, Mencius, another ancient Chinese philosopher and

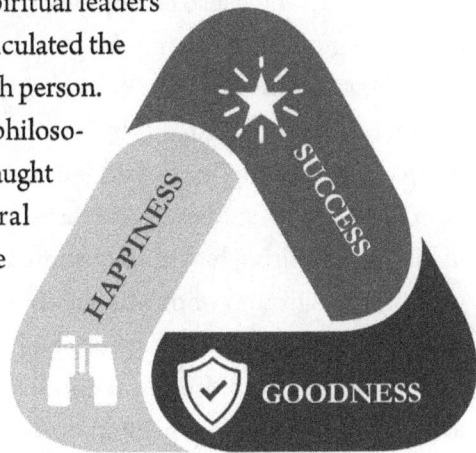

Three outcomes of DEEP PACT

author of the *Book of Mencius*, believed that human nature is inherently good and that individuals possess an innate sense of right and wrong. Greek philosopher Socrates argued that humans are naturally inclined toward the good, believing that knowledge and virtue are interconnected. According to Plato's *Meno*, Socrates posited that "no one does wrong willingly," asserting that people do wrong only out of ignorance and that "to know the good is to do the good." These philosophical teachings align with the idea that goodness is a core aspect of our humanity, driving us to seek out virtuous actions and compassionate behavior.

Psychological studies also support this philosophical notion, suggesting that acts of kindness and altruism are innate human behaviors. Research in positive psychology, elucidated by Sonja Lyubomirsky in her book *The How of Happiness*, has shown that helping others and engaging in prosocial behavior can enhance personal well-being and happiness. In *Thrive*, Arianna Huffington redefines success beyond wealth and power, emphasizing well-being, wisdom, wonder, and giving as essential pillars for a fulfilling life. She advocates for prioritizing self-care, mindfulness, and purpose to achieve true happiness and sustainable success. These ideas deeply resonate with the principles of DEEP PACT, which also champions a holistic approach to leadership by focusing on purpose, meaning, and whole-person development. Like *Thrive*, DEEP PACT underscores that happiness and well-being are not just personal pursuits but critical components of effective and impactful leadership in a world increasingly shaped by AI and rapid change. Moreover, studies by Martin Seligman and colleagues, captured in his book *Flourish*, have demonstrated that practicing kindness and expressing gratitude contribute significantly to overall life satisfaction and mental health. These findings highlight that our inherent goodness is not only a philosophical notion but also a practical pathway to achieving a fulfilling and meaningful life.

> *Human greatness does not lie in wealth or power, but in character and goodness.*
>
> —Anne Frank

External pressures such as conflict, injustice, and personal hardships, however, can overshadow this innate virtue, making it difficult to consistently act with compassion and integrity. It is critical to nurture the goodness within each of us, fostering a more harmonious and empathetic society despite the challenges we face. The eight principles of DEEP PACT are fundamentally oriented toward unleashing and nurturing the inherent goodness within each of us, ultimately transforming us into better individuals. These principles are designed not only to enhance our effectiveness in leadership roles but also to cultivate the goodness of our character. Whether we find ourselves in formal leadership positions or not, embodying these principles will lead us to become good, kind, and empathetic individuals. Such cultivated goodness brings us immense pleasure and happiness, derived from being kind and supportive to others.

Each principle of DEEP PACT serves as a step toward becoming a better person, enhancing our capacity for genuine connections and meaningful relationships. In the words of Roman emperor and philosopher Marcus Aurelius, "Waste no more time arguing about what a good man should be. Be one." As mentioned before, goodness, unlike happiness, can be pursued. DEEP PACT provides us with the roadmap to pursue goodness, ensuring that our legacy is defined by the goodness and happiness we impart in the world.

3.6 The Relationships Connection

The good life is built with good relationships.
—Robert Waldinger, Harvard professor

Happiness is not merely a personal aspiration—it is a strategic asset and a vital ingredient in effective leadership. Research shows that happy leaders are more likely to inspire, motivate, and foster collaboration, directly impacting their organization's performance and culture. Yet one of the most common—and underestimated—ways leaders sabotage their own happiness is by neglecting to nurture deep, meaningful relationships with friends, family, and their broader community. Many fall into the trap of emotional isolation, mistaking it for strength, independence, or laser focus. Others believe they are simply too busy—drowning in long hours and unrelenting responsibilities—to make time for connection. But this perceived lack of time can become a self-imposed barrier to well-being. Remaining aloof or disconnected is a subtle yet powerful form of self-sabotage. It erodes emotional resilience, weakens organizational culture, and undermines a leader's ability to cultivate trust and cohesion. When leaders pull away from meaningful engagement outside of work, they cut themselves off from one of the most proven sources of lasting happiness and vitality: human connection.

The importance of strong relationships is backed by decades of scientific research. In 2016, psychiatrist Robert Waldinger, director of the Harvard Study of Adult Development, delivered a TED Talk that has become one of the most viewed in history, with over 27 million views. Sharing insights from the longest-running study on human happiness—spanning more than 75 years and thousands of participants—Waldinger dispelled the myth that fame and wealth lead to fulfillment. Instead, the study revealed three critical findings: (1) people who are more socially connected to family, friends, and community are not only happier, but physically healthier and longer-lived; (2) warm, supportive relationships protect both emotional and physical health, while conflict and disconnection are deeply harmful; and (3) strong relationships support sharper cognitive function in later life, whereas isolation accelerates decline. Waldinger's message is simple yet deeply profound: "The good life is built with good relationships." That insight is echoed in the influential 2002 study "Very Happy People" by psychologists Ed Diener and Martin Seligman, which found that "very happy people have rich and satisfying social relationships and spend little time alone relative to average people. In contrast, unhappy people have social relationships that are significantly worse than average."

But effective leadership isn't about socializing more—it's about connecting intentionally. Building a few authentic, lasting relationships is far more powerful than maintaining dozens of shallow ones. Leaders must learn to balance connection with focus by setting healthy boundaries, protecting time for deep work, and carving out intentional space for meaningful interactions. This could mean regular conversations with trusted peers, informal check-ins with team members, or simply showing up for others as a genuine human being. When approached with purpose, social engagement becomes not a drain on energy but a multiplier of it. It builds culture, sharpens perspective, and elevates leadership impact.

Happiness is not a fringe benefit of great leadership—it is its foundation. The path to that happiness is paved by the quality of our relationships—the emotional bonds we form, the trust we build, and the kindness we extend to others. If we master every leadership theory and tool but neglect the humanity within us, we fall short of becoming truly fulfilled and effective leaders.

3.7 Leadership as a Choice

The heaviest penalty for declining to rule is to be ruled by someone inferior to yourself.

—Plato

Life often thrusts leadership upon us without warning, compelling us to rise, adapt, and discover strengths we never knew we possessed. In these moments, we are called not only to lead others but also to guide ourselves through uncertainty, growth, and transformation. While circumstances may dictate when leadership is needed, the choice to embrace that role is always ours. Even in the face of unexpected challenges, we retain the power to decide how we respond—whether we rise above adversity or allow it to hinder us. True leadership lies in recognizing that, although life may impose responsibilities upon us, it is ultimately our decision to act with courage, purpose, and unity.

Take the story of Harriet Tubman, who, born into slavery, became a beacon of hope for hundreds through her role in the Underground Railroad. Despite immense danger, Tubman repeatedly risked her life to lead over 300 people to freedom. Her leadership was not a choice, but a necessity driven by unwavering courage and a commitment to justice.

During the COVID-19 pandemic, we saw everyday heroes step into leadership roles. For instance, Kim Davis, a nurse, left her job in Arkansas to travel across Arizona, California, and Florida, helping hospitals manage the surge in COVID-19 patients. Her story, as documented in the *Harvard Gazette*, exemplifies the adaptability and determination needed during tough times.

Another example is the nurses at Massachusetts General Hospital who stepped into leadership roles during the pandemic, ensuring that patient care continued despite overwhelming challenges. They adapted quickly, setting up virtual family visits for patients, highlighting how leadership isn't just about grand gestures but often about small, meaningful actions that make a difference.

In August 2024, Nobel Laureate Muhammad Yunus was unexpectedly thrust into the national leadership of Bangladesh following a people's revolution that ousted an autocratic government. The revolution had no singular leader, no preordained successor—only a collective yearning for justice, equity, and a fresh start. Yunus had no direct connection to the revolution, aside from being a victim of harassment by the regime. Known globally for his pioneering work in microfinance and social business, Yunus had never sought political power. Yet, as the existing government collapsed and the autocrat fled, a broad coalition of activists and civil society leaders turned to him as a figure of trust and stability. Practically overnight, he found himself leading a nation in crisis.

His leadership reflected his lifelong philosophy—empowering people from the ground up. Just as he had revolutionized finance for the poor with Grameen Bank, Yunus now faced the enormous challenge of rebuilding a fractured country. His leadership was not about authority but about restoring faith in democracy and economic justice. Now the world watches as the man who once handed out small loans to the forgotten leads a nation toward an unprecedented experiment in social and economic transformation.

These real-life events demonstrate that leadership often arises not from a pursuit of power, but from the urgency of circumstance. Whether through personal conviction, moral duty, or circumstantial demands, individuals can find themselves in leadership roles that reveal their true capabilities and inspire others. This theme resonates across time and culture, reminding us that leadership is as much about choosing to rise to the occasion as it is about seeking the role. It isn't limited to the workplace or political arenas; it's a choice we make in every aspect of life—within families, friendships, and communities.

Choosing Leadership, Choosing Joy

The pursuit of leadership can bring immense happiness and joy to individuals by providing a sense of purpose, connection, and personal growth. Leading others toward a shared vision, overcoming challenges together, and witnessing the positive impact of one's guidance can be deeply rewarding. Leadership, when approached with a genuine commitment to making a difference, taps into the intrinsic human desires for contribution, connection, and accomplishment, thereby creating a lasting sense of fulfillment and joy.

Nelson Mandela's leadership during and after his imprisonment in South Africa demonstrates the profound connection between leadership and personal fulfillment. Mandela once said, "What counts in life is not the mere fact that we have lived. It is what difference we have made to the lives of others that will determine the significance of the life we lead." His commitment to ending apartheid and his subsequent efforts in promoting reconciliation and unity brought him immense personal satisfaction.

Individuals who embrace leadership roles often experience a heightened sense of purpose. According to a study by Steger and colleagues published in the *Journal of Positive Psychology*, having a clear purpose in life is associated with higher levels of happiness and life satisfaction. By leading initiatives, supporting loved ones, or volunteering in community projects, individuals not only contribute positively to their surroundings but also experience personal growth and self-improvement. This active engagement and the resulting sense of accomplishment and meaningful contribution are powerful drivers of happiness. As Abraham Maslow's hierarchy of needs suggests, self-actualization—the realization of one's full potential—is a key component of human happiness.

On the other hand, bad or poor leadership can have far-reaching negative consequences, causing unhappiness, demotivation, and failure within organizations and societies. Toxic leadership environments lead to high stress, burnout, and a lack of motivation among employees. This often results in high turnover rates, as unhappy employees leave in search of better workplaces.

The Enron scandal is a prominent example of corporate leadership that has gone awry, leading to widespread unhappiness and financial ruin for employees and investors. Enron's top executives, including Kenneth Lay and Jeffrey Skilling, engaged in fraudulent accounting practices to hide the company's financial losses and inflate stock prices. Their leadership was marked by greed, deception, and a lack of transparency. When the scandal broke, it led to the company's bankruptcy, massive job losses, and the destruction of employee retirement funds. Unethical leadership created a culture of mistrust and despair, demonstrating how poor leadership can have catastrophic consequences.

Uber, under the leadership of its cofounder and former CEO Travis Kalanick, faced severe backlash due to a toxic corporate culture. Reports of sexual harassment, gender discrimination, and unethical business practices plagued the company. Kalanick's aggressive and combative leadership style contributed to a hostile work environment, leading to widespread unhappiness among employees. The toxic culture not only harmed employee morale but also damaged the company's reputation. The leadership crisis at Uber highlights how a lack of ethical leadership and respect for employees can lead to internal turmoil and public scandal.

The synergy between leadership, personal happiness, and job satisfaction creates a virtuous cycle. Effective leadership leads to happy and satisfied employees, which in turn enhances organizational performance and success. This success further reinforces the positive environment, creating a feedback loop that benefits everyone involved.

> *Employees who believe that management is concerned about them as a whole person—not just as an employee—are more productive, more satisfied, more fulfilled. Satisfied employees mean satisfied customers, which leads to profitability.*
>
> —Anne M. Mulcahy,
> chief executive officer and chair, Xerox Corporation

An example of a positive culture can be drawn from the leadership approach at Woodard & Curran, a privately owned top-100 engineering design firm based in Portland, Maine. The foundation of Woodard & Curran's positive workplace culture is deeply rooted in its original mission, established by its founders nearly 50 years ago. In 2007, Doug McKeown succeeded cofounder Al Curran as the company's second CEO and continued to nurture this culture, leading to remarkable growth—nearly tripling revenue and doubling the workforce over the next decade. With this growth came the need to reinforce the company's mission with a clearly defined set of core values. McKeown recognized that while employees could articulate the company's mission, there was no formalized framework of values to guide behaviors and decision-making. Rather than imposing these values from the top down, he launched a company-wide engagement process in 2018, ensuring that employees themselves identified the fundamental values that truly represented the organization. Through open discussions, employee interviews, and leadership dialogues, Woodard & Curran employees collectively defined five core values that reflected the deeply ingrained behaviors shaping their workplace. By fostering this participatory approach, McKeown ensured that these values were not just words on paper but principles that employees genuinely embraced and owned. These values became a guiding force, rolled out just before the economic downturn triggered by the COVID-19 pandemic in 2020. They provided a strong cultural foundation as the company navigated through turbulent times.

This values-driven foundation played a crucial role when Alyson Watson took over as CEO at the end of 2020, just as the company was emerging from the worst of the pandemic. With the established values in place, Watson prioritized implementing them in a way that directly supported employee well-being and professional growth. This commitment was formalized in the company's value playbook, where "Put People First" became the number-one guiding principle, with the tagline "Well-being of our people is our top priority." Under her leadership, the company reinforced its dedication to work-life integration, mental health support, and transparent communication, ensuring that employees felt valued and supported in the evolving work environment.

The leadership transition from McKeown to Watson exemplifies the seamless evolution of a people-first culture at Woodard & Curran— moving from establishing core values to embedding them into daily operations—driven by the company's unwavering commitment to its core values and mission. The collaborative groundwork that began in 2018 ensured that employees already identified with these values, making it easier for Watson to build upon them and drive initiatives that enhanced job satisfaction, engagement, and business success manifested by continued growth during and since the pandemic. By embracing transparent communication, employee empowerment, and a strong emphasis on well-being, Woodard & Curran has sustained a workplace culture that not only drives performance but also fosters happiness and long-term success. This case illustrates how people-centric leadership, when implemented with authenticity and employee engagement, creates an environment where employees thrive—and organizations flourish.

3.8 Is Workplace Happiness a Pipe Dream or a Choice?

According to the best research available (which we will read in this class), to be a successful leader, you need to understand happiness and manage to it—yours and others'. Unfortunately, most leaders have to learn this fact by hard experience. Furthermore, they are never exposed to the expanding science of happiness, which contains a wealth of information on how to be happier as a leader and make others happier as well.

—Leadership and Happiness course overview,
Harvard University

Amid this theorization of leadership as a choice and workplace happiness, one may wonder, *Well, this doesn't apply in real life,* or *That's not what my experience has shown.* Many professionals feel trapped under ineffective, toxic, or uninspiring leaders, making the idea of great leadership seem idealistic rather than practical. For many, the concept of workplace happiness itself can feel like a pipe dream—something unattainable in the face of rigid hierarchies, office politics, and demanding managers. The long hours, unappreciated efforts, and constant stress can make it seem as though work is simply meant to be endured, not enjoyed. **I once felt the same way.**

My first job after completing my PhD in engineering was under a brilliant yet deeply flawed manager—a man whose intellect was undeniable but whose leadership style was demoralizing. He demanded long hours, expecting employees to sacrifice work-life balance without recognition or appreciation. He criticized far more than he encouraged, focusing on mistakes rather than progress. His meetings often felt like interrogations, where fear of reprimand stifled creativity and morale. Employees worked tirelessly, yet the atmosphere remained tense, driven by the anxiety of his relentless scrutiny.

At first, I thought the only way to survive was to endure, keeping my head down and avoiding attention. But over time, I realized that I had a choice—I could either become resentful and disengaged or take control of the one thing I could influence: how I treated others. I chose the latter. I started offering encouragement to colleagues, acknowledging their efforts where our manager would not. I sought fulfillment in my work rather than in external validation, and I began leading in small but meaningful ways—by mentoring junior employees, fostering collaboration, and creating a sense of camaraderie that counteracted the negativity from the top.

I volunteered my time to review the work products of junior employees before meetings with our manager, ensuring they were of high quality and well-prepared. This proactive effort not only improved our overall output but also helped shield the junior employees from harsh criticism, reducing stress and fostering a more supportive and confident team environment.

This experience fundamentally reshaped my view of leadership—it is not about position or power but about how we choose to influence those around us. Leadership, I realized, isn't just about those in charge; it's about the everyday choices we make to support, uplift, and inspire. Robin Sharma, in *The Leader Who Had No Title*, writes, "Leadership is not about a title or a designation. It's about impact, influence, and inspiration." No matter the external challenges, we all have the power to shape our professional lives.

Over time, I came to believe deeply that employees, regardless of their position, have the ability to influence workplace culture, create pockets of positivity, and inspire those around them. When faced with bad leadership, it can be tempting to surrender to frustration and disengagement. However, as Stephen R. Covey wrote in *The 7 Habits of Highly Effective People*, "Between stimulus and response, there is a space. In that space is our power to choose our response. In our response lies our growth and our freedom." Employees can choose to reclaim their power by fostering their own happiness, leading with integrity, and slowly influencing change.

The first step to happiness at work is focusing on what can be controlled—mindset and personal actions. A bad leader may set a toxic tone, but employees can create their own microclimate of positivity. Simple acts such as expressing gratitude, recognizing a colleague's effort, or celebrating small wins can counterbalance negativity. For example, an employee struggling under a micromanaging supervisor might focus on cultivating strong relationships with peers and taking pride in meaningful work rather than dwelling on frustration. As Marcus Aurelius, the Stoic philosopher, wisely said, "You have power over your mind—not outside events. Realize this, and you will find strength." By consciously directing attention to purpose and progress, employees reclaim control over their work experience, allowing them to find meaning and motivation even in challenging circumstances—until they can change their situation.

Another powerful way to foster happiness is by uplifting those below and around you. Employees with subordinates should lead by example, practicing the type of leadership they wish to see. This means that even if a leader at the top fails to inspire, employees can still create an engaging and motivating environment within their own teams. Consider a project manager dealing with an unappreciative executive; instead of mirroring that negativity, they can ensure their own team feels recognized and supported. By making others feel valued, employees contribute to a culture of trust and fulfillment, regardless of poor leadership above them.

By making intentional choices—supporting others, fostering teamwork, and focusing on what we can control—we take back our power.

3.9 Is Happiness Attainable in Hour-Based Professional Consulting?

Beware the barrenness of a busy life.

—Socrates

Can happiness truly be prioritized in a professional culture where the clock reigns supreme—where a consultant's value is tethered to utilization rates, billable hours, and constant availability? For many, the answer seems to be no. The traditional model of hour-based consulting operates on a mechanistic premise: input (hours billed) equals output (value delivered). In such environments, the most celebrated consultants are often those who consistently "go above and beyond"—burning the midnight oil, responding to clients on weekends, and living in service of utilization metrics. But this model of success, as widely accepted as it is, has a cost. Most of us either do not know or choose to ignore the fact that chronic overwork slowly chips away at our health, relationships, and overall happiness.

> *Over time, overwork not only dulls our cognitive edge but also amplifies the risk of serious health consequences. A 2021 World Health Organization study linked working more than 55 hours a week to a 35% higher risk of stroke and a 17% higher risk of dying from heart disease.*

This cost is not just anecdotal—it's measurable. A 2021 Deloitte workplace well-being study found that 77% of professionals experience burnout. And burnout doesn't just harm individuals; it undermines long-term performance. The *Harvard Business Review* article, "The Research is Clear: Long Hours Backfire for People and for Companies," echoes this concern: "The story of overwork is literally a story of diminishing returns: keep overworking, and you'll progressively work more stupidly on tasks that are increasingly meaningless." Over time, overwork not only dulls our cognitive edge but also amplifies the risk of serious health consequences. A 2021 World Health Organization study linked working more than 55 hours a week to a 35% higher risk of stroke and a 17% higher risk of dying from heart disease.

Even more compelling are findings that challenge the myth that more hours mean more results. In her study of consultants, Boston University professor Erin Reid discovered that managers could not distinguish between employees who actually worked 80 hours a week and those who merely appeared to. While honesty about working less was penalized, Reid found no evidence that employees who overworked achieved more.

Henry Ford discovered this truth more than a century ago. In the early 1900s, standard working hours ranged from 9 to 10 hours per day, six days a week, often totaling around 55 to 60 hours weekly. Facing pressure from labor activism to reduce working hours, along with significant employee retention issues, Henry Ford made a groundbreaking announcement in January 1914: he standardized the workday at Ford Motor Company to eight hours and more than doubled worker pay from $2.34 a day to $5 a day. This move made national headlines, attracted thousands of workers to Detroit, and sent shockwaves throughout the automobile industry. In 1926, Ford again captured attention by announcing a five-day workweek. Contrary to widespread skepticism, he discovered productivity actually increased, while costly errors and workplace accidents declined. It was not until 1938 that the US government officially recognized the 40-hour, five-day workweek through the Fair Labor Standards Act.

Nearly a century after Henry Ford's courageous decision, Harvard Business School professors Leslie Perlow and Jessica Porter conducted a study on knowledge workers. Their research demonstrated that when consulting teams were required to take predictable time off—nights and weekends—their productivity also improved significantly, reaffirming the timeless value of balanced work hours.

So, why do we still glorify overwork? Part of it stems from what psychologists call "internalized capitalism"—the deep-seated belief that our worth is directly tied to our productivity. In elite industries like professional consulting, this mindset becomes self-reinforcing: busyness becomes a badge of honor, and exhaustion a proxy for excellence. But this mindset is neither sustainable nor necessary for success. Sustainable high performance is less about clocked hours and more about energy management, autonomy, purpose alignment, and psychological safety.

If happiness is reframed not as fleeting pleasure but as engagement, meaning, and values alignment—as outlined in leadership models like DEEP PACT—then even in a time-focused professional consulting environment, well-being is attainable. It begins with cultural redesign: leaders must challenge the myth of overwork as virtue, recognize contributions beyond billables, and embed flexibility, empathy, and psychological safety into daily operations. Employees who feel valued, autonomous, and connected to a purpose report higher engagement and resilience: key drivers of both happiness and performance.

Real-world examples confirm this. When my partner and I launched our engineering consulting firm, we came from national firms that glorified overwork. We made a simple but radical commitment: our team would not routinely work more than 40 hours per week or be expected to sacrifice weekends. While occasional crises demanded extra hours, our baseline was clear—chronic overwork would not be the norm or be glorified. Our firm thrived for years with high retention, strong performance, and a reputation for quality. This experience reinforced my belief that success doesn't require excessive hours—when you plan your work effectively, you can work smart, stay within a 40-hour week, and still deliver outstanding results. Culture, it turns out, is a performance multiplier.

What I found to be the root causes of overwork in consulting were not heroism or necessity, but systemic dysfunctions: poor planning by project managers, accepting unrealistic timelines from clients, underbudgeting, a lack of courage to renegotiate schedules, waiting until the last minute to inform the client about problems, and the deep-seated belief that overwork is the only path to project success or career progress. On one occasion, a client asked me to develop a proof of concept for an innovative decision support system—on a timeline I knew was unrealistic. The pressure was intense, but I calmly told them what was actually possible: a six-week schedule with an appropriate budget and a well-defined scope. I told them, "I don't want to serve you half-cooked eggs." The client respected my honesty, and the project turned into a success, ultimately winning an award from the federal government. That moment reminded me that clarity and courage can outperform accommodation.

Another often-overlooked strategy to overcome overwork is seeking collaboration from peers—a practice known as *sideways delegation*. As leaders progress, their ability to work through peers—not just direct reports—becomes critical. A May 2025 *Harvard Business Review* article by Melody Wilding, "How to Delegate to Someone Who Doesn't Report to You," offers valuable guidance on how leaders can delegate sideways in order to share workload, foster ownership, and prevent burnout. Wilding stresses the importance of being selective and strategic when asking peers to take on work. She suggests framing requests as mutually beneficial partnerships. Instead of issuing directives, leaders should provide context, acknowledge their peers' strengths, and highlight shared value. Language matters: phrases like, "This could help both of us," or, "Would it make sense for your team to own this going forward?" turn a handoff into a collaborative opportunity. Once leaders are aligned, Wilding advises them to "contract" for accountability by co-creating timelines, checkpoints, and shared documents—making ownership clear without micromanaging. Follow-up should be tactful and respectful, signaling support rather than oversight. With trust, clarity, and diplomacy, sideways delegation becomes not only possible but a vital skill for modern leaders seeking to transform cultures overwhelmed by overwork.

My long experience in professional consulting has taught me to take the following proactive steps to stop the harmful practice of chronic overwork:

1. **Start with honest project scoping and budgeting.** Define success realistically and push back when expectations defy logic.
2. **Embed planning discipline.** Clearly establish the end product at the very beginning of the project and use project management methods and tools to avoid hidden overload.
3. **Model courageous and honest conversations.** Show that it's professional, not insubordinate, to renegotiate deadlines or budgets.
4. **Redefine career advancement.** Tie growth to outcomes and leadership behavior, not hours logged.
5. **Reward rest and effectiveness.** Normalize breaks, deep work, and true disconnection as productivity drivers.
6. **Communicate with clients in a timely manner.** Do not conceal problems until the last minute.
7. **Know that "hope" is not a good strategy.** Do not hope for 100% efficiency from everyone at all times, believe that more hours can solve all problems, or assume that adding more people to a late project will speed it up.

As leaders, we hold the levers to redesign the systems that glorify overwork. This isn't to say we should never work long hours—sometimes it is necessary in professional consulting, especially when an unanticipated crisis arises. And in today's knowledge-based workplace, there are moments when extended periods of focused effort—what psychologist Mihaly Csikszentmihalyi describes as "flow"—can be deeply engaging and even energizing. Immersing oneself in complex problem-solving or creative work can feel rewarding and purposeful. However, making such intense mental exertion a regular expectation isn't sustainable nor is it good for your health or happiness. Over time, chronic overwork erodes well-being and diminishes performance, ultimately undermining the very productivity it aims to boost. True leadership recognizes the difference between short-term sprints and chronic overextension—and has the courage to design work cultures that protect energy, support recovery, and promote lasting excellence.

As leaders, we should work toward normalizing rest as a productivity tool; we should reward outcomes over optics; and we should model behaviors that prioritize well-being and excellence. The real question, then, is not, "Can consultants be happy?" but, "Do we have the courage to stop glorifying overwork?" In a profession built on solving others' most complex problems, perhaps our greatest innovation is to solve this one for ourselves.

The challenge and the mission are to find real solutions to real problems on actual schedules with available resources.

—Frederick Brooks Jr.,
author of *The Mythical Man-Month*

3.10 Mistaken Belief: Leaders Don't Have Time for Joy

Happiness is what fuels success, not the other way around. When we are positive, our brains become more engaged, creative, motivated, energetic, resilient, and productive.

—Grace Ueng,
founder and CEO of Savvy Growth

Many accomplished professionals today appear to be living ideal lives—filled with achievement, purpose, and meaning. Their calendars are packed, their résumés reflect a distinguished record of success, and their teams rely on them. And yet beneath this outward success lies a quiet truth: a surprising number of them feel unfulfilled. An article titled "How the Busiest People Find Joy," published recently in the July–August 2025 issue of the *Harvard Business Review*, revealed that most of the 1,500 Harvard Business School alumni surveyed for a study felt high levels of accomplishment and meaning—but struggled to experience happiness in the moment.

Why is joy so elusive for so many high achievers? One major reason is our distorted relationship with time—specifically, how we perceive it and use it. We've been conditioned by the time management industry to believe that "time is money," fueling a culture that measures a good day by how much we get done. Productivity has become the yardstick of worth. But this efficiency mindset, while useful in moderation, has created a treadmill effect: the more we optimize, the faster we must run. In Western cultures especially, time is valued almost exclusively in terms of work output. As a result, many leaders believe they're simply too busy for joy. But this belief isn't just mistaken—it's strategically dangerous.

Joy is not an indulgence; it is a critical leadership asset. Positive emotions such as joy have been shown to expand cognitive capacity, enhance creative problem-solving, and strengthen relational connections. Barbara Fredrickson's "broaden-and-build" theory confirms that joy builds psychological resources and resilience over time. Leaders who cultivate joy report greater energy, creativity, and engagement—and these benefits extend to their teams. Research published in *The Leadership Quarterly* shows that leaders' emotional states are contagious: joyful leaders elevate morale, performance, and trust across their organizations.

Reclaiming joy, however, requires more than occasional smiles or short breaks. A recent research paper titled "Time Well Spent: A

New Way to Value Time Could Change Your Life," published in the summer 2025 issue of the *MIT Sloan Management Review*, introduced a revolutionary concept: **the subjective value of time.** The authors proposed that it be measured by the presence of three core elements in our lives—joy, achievement, and meaningfulness (JAM). Joy is the emotional spark of happiness that lifts our spirits. It's more than just feeling good—it's strongly tied to better mental and physical health, greater life satisfaction, and even a longer life. Achievement speaks to our drive to grow, to earn recognition, and to reach our goals. It reinforces our sense of competence and builds confidence in who we are. Meaningfulness, meanwhile, connects our daily actions to the deeper values and purposes that guide us. Unlike traditional time management approaches that focus on maximizing output, this concept emphasizes how time feels to the person experiencing it. It asks whether our hours are energizing or depleting, meaningful or mindless—and challenges us to evaluate the quality, not just the quantity, of how we spend our days.

Based on data from more than 3,000 professionals, the researchers found that each of the three elements in the JAM framework is essential for well-being. The authors asserted, "Everyone needs all three core elements to be fulfilled in their lives, but to varying degrees." To maintain high life satisfaction, individuals need to consistently experience a baseline amount of each—referred to as the "JAM minimum." People who met their JAM minimums experienced significantly higher life satisfaction. Alarmingly, only 30 percent of respondents did. Even those who prioritized purpose and achievement fell short when they neglected joy. The JAM model provides a diagnostic tool for assessing how time is being spent and whether it aligns with what individuals find fulfilling—shifting the focus from task completion to time quality. This insight reframes how we define a "productive day." Instead of asking *What did I get done?*, we must begin asking *How did my experiences enrich my life?*

For leaders, the JAM model is both a wake-up call and a roadmap. You may be delivering results and leading with vision—but if joy is missing, your effectiveness and influence are at risk. The JAM frame-work encourages reflection not on how efficiently time is used, but on how meaningfully it is experienced. Time spent on high-joy activities—such as catching up with family, pursuing hobbies with others, volunteering with others, attending social gatherings, or engaging in side projects with a team—correlates with higher satisfaction and sustainable performance. Conversely, time absorbed by low-joy activities—like watching TV alone, doing chores solo, or scrolling social media in isolation—tends to drain energy and diminish well-being. Research has shown that even the same activity—such as watching TV or movies—yields greater joy when done with family or others than when done alone. The presence of social connection elevates emotional value, reinforcing the importance of intentional time choices in both leadership and life. Researchers found that simply reallocating 1.5 hours per day from low-value to high-value experiences increased life satisfaction by 30 percent—and improved how people felt about their work hours as well.

Understanding this model also sheds new light on a deeper issue: it's not always the amount of time we have, but how we use the time available to us that matters most.

The HBR article, "How the Busiest People Find Joy," reported on a study of 1,500 Harvard Business School alumni with full-time careers and families, revealing that they spent an average of 50 hours per week on work and an additional 12 hours on nonwork responsibilities. After accounting for sleep, meals, hygiene, and commuting, they were left with about 26 discretionary hours per week—a little over three hours a day. And yet, what stood out was not the number of hours but how people spent them. Those who consciously invested this time in meaningful, joyful activities reported significantly higher happiness and satisfaction. Some participants managed to extract joy from limited leisure time far more effectively than others—proving that intentionality, not availability, is the true differentiator.

So what can leaders do to reclaim joy—and lead more fully as whole human beings? The *Harvard Business Review* article outlines five actionable practices, all of which align directly with the DEEP PACT philosophy of whole-person leadership.

First, engage with others. Time spent in social connection—even doing ordinary tasks—amplifies joy and contributes directly to leadership capacity. Leaders who intentionally prioritize connection create a human foundation that supports ethical, empathetic, and resilient leadership.

Second, avoid passive leisure. A meta-analysis by Kuykendall, Tay, and Ng found that active leisure (e.g., hobbies, volunteering, sports) contributes significantly more to happiness and psychological well-being than passive leisure (e.g., watching TV, browsing social media). When people engage in active pursuits—even alone—they report greater joy, energy, and motivation.

Third, follow your passion—not what others deem worthwhile. Research has consistently shown that intrinsic motivation—the desire to engage in activities for their own sake—is a strong predictor of well-being, vitality, and happiness in life.

Fourth, diversify your activities. Research published in the *Journal of Consumer Research* confirms that variety in leisure activities prevents hedonic adaptation and boosts overall happiness. Engaging in a mix of activities keeps experiences fresh, reduces emotional stagnation, and helps leaders maintain vitality over time.

Fifth, protect your time. Studies by Sabine Sonnentag have shown that psychological detachment from work during nonwork hours improves well-being and even enhances future job engagement and performance. Leaders must be intentional about creating boundaries that allow for genuine rest, joy, and recovery—key components of sustainable leadership.

The takeaway is clear—joy is not a byproduct of effective leadership. It is a precondition. Leaders must reject the myth that joy is optional and embrace it as a practice that fuels sustainable excellence and ethical influence. These principles reinforce the DEEP PACT values of emotional intelligence, purpose alignment, and care for self and others. They also echo MIT Sloan's call to redefine success through the lens of how we experience time, not just how we spend it.

Ultimately, leadership is not merely about doing more—it's about becoming more. Leaders who embrace joy and happiness as part of their identity create a sustainable rhythm that balances drive with restoration. They build not just high-performing teams but flourishing human ecosystems. DEEP PACT calls us to reject the false choice between happiness and high performance. The truth is, happiness enhances performance. Joy doesn't dilute excellence—it deepens it. And in a world desperate for ethical, resilient, and human-centered leaders, joy may be the most undervalued and transformative leadership strategy of our time. It is time to let go of the mistaken belief that leaders don't have time for joy.

3.11 The Choice Is Ultimately Yours

Choice, not chance, determines your destiny.

—Aristotle

The choices we make don't just influence our lives—they define them. Nowhere is this more critical than in the sphere of leadership today, where every decision holds the power to either entrench existing problems or unlock innovative solutions. The stakes are high, and the impact of our choices is undeniable. Will we choose to lead in ways that transform, or will we fall back into patterns that only maintain the status quo? The future of leadership hinges on this very question. To illustrate the importance of this choice, let me share a story that highlights the profound impact our decisions can have on our lives.

In a remote village nestled at the foot of a towering mountain in India, there lived an old monk known far and wide for his extraordinary wisdom and magical power. He had an uncanny ability to predict what people held in their hands without seeing it. This monk had lived atop the mountain for decades, devoting his life to meditation and spiritual growth, which, according to the villagers, had endowed him with extraordinary insight and perception.

Intrigued by the monk's reputation and somewhat skeptical, three teenagers from the village decided to put the monk to the test. They believed that they could outsmart him and prove to the villagers that the monk was not as infallible as he seemed. One day, they devised a plan to catch a small bird and visit the monk. They intended to hold the bird in their hands and ask the monk to predict what they were holding. If the monk guessed it correctly, they would then ask him whether the bird was alive or dead. Their plan was to either crush the bird or release it based on the monk's response, thus proving him wrong.

Confident and mischievous, the three teenagers climbed the mountain and found the monk sitting peacefully in meditation. They approached him and said, "Old monk, we have heard of your great wisdom and ability to predict things unseen. Can you tell us what we are holding in our hands?"

"The choice is yours."

The monk opened his eyes, looked at them with a gentle smile, and replied, "You are holding a bird."

The teenagers were astonished that the monk had guessed correctly. Determined to prove their point, they proceeded with their second question. "Tell us then, wise monk, is the bird in our hands alive or dead?"

The monk looked at them with deep compassion and wisdom in his eyes. After a moment of silence, he said softly, "The choice is yours."

The teenagers were taken aback by his response. They realized the profound truth in the monk's words: the fate of the bird was indeed in their hands. The monk had subtly imparted a lesson about responsibility and the power of choice. They stood there, reflecting on the implications of their actions. Instead of following through with their plan, they gently opened their hands and let the bird fly free into the sky.

This story of the monk of the mountain and the three teenagers highlights the critical lesson that while others may offer guidance, wisdom, or predictions, ultimately, the choices and consequences rest in our own hands. The monk's ability to foresee what was in their hands was not the true test; the real challenge lay in understanding the power and responsibility that come with choice. This story isn't just about the monk's wisdom or the teenagers' challenge; it's about the power of choice. Whether you choose to read this book and implement its insights or take another route, remember that your leadership journey and ultimate destiny are in your hands, waiting to be molded by the choices you dare to make.

May your choices reflect your hopes, not your fears.

—Nelson Mandela

4 Leadership Failure Is Not an Option

Let's work the problem, people. Failure is not an option.

—Gene Kranz

The year was 1970, and Apollo 13 was on its way to the moon. On April 13, at exactly 10:07 p.m. Eastern Time, a bone-chilling bang echoed through the spacecraft when Command Module Pilot Jack Swigert was in the middle of conducting routine instrument checks. The command module jolted, throwing the crew against their harnesses. Swigert's eyes widened, and he reached for his headset, his voice crackling with barely contained tension. "Houston, we've had a problem."

The words cut through the static and echoed in Mission Control in Houston, Texas, where engineers sat frozen, eyes locked on the flashing monitors. Spacecraft's

From crisis to courage: the mindset that shaped a mission.

oxygen tank No. 2 blew up, causing the No. 1 tank to also fail. Gene Kranz, the stoic flight director, stood in the center of the room, absorbing the enormity of the situation. Alarms blared, monitors beeped, but silence wrapped around the room like a vise as oxygen levels dropped, power reserves dwindled, and water supply plummeted. Over 200,000 miles away in the vast emptiness of space, three astronauts—Jim Lovell, Fred Haise, and Jack Swigert—were stranded, drifting in a crippled spacecraft. In that instant, the Apollo 13 mission was no longer a journey to the moon. It was a battle to survive.

Kranz clenched his fists, feeling the weight of lives balanced on his every decision. The engineers looked at him, waiting. He felt a heartbeat of fear but pushed it down. They had no contingency for this—a spacecraft gutted by an explosion in deep space. Yet the men in that room were the only hope for the men in that freezing capsule, their breaths visible in the dimming light. All eyes in the Mission Control room were fixed on Kranz, every person holding their breath in tense anticipation. Kranz raised his voice, steady and hard as steel. "Let's work the problem, people. Failure is not an option."

These words slammed into the room like a lifeline. Kranz had made a promise—a vow that failure was not on the table. With renewed focus, the engineers and scientists tore into their calculations, running tests, scrambling for anything that might work. Onboard, the three astronauts followed each update, their fate hanging on every syllable that crackled over the radio. Hour after hour, through day and night, Mission Control pushed the boundaries of ingenuity, improvising solution after solution. Engineers from the Earth guided the astronauts to build a makeshift carbon dioxide filter out of nothing but duct tape and plastic bags. For every problem, they created a solution, dragging the spacecraft inch by inch closer to home.

Four endless days later, on April 17 at 1:07 p.m. Eastern Time, Apollo 13 appeared on the edge of Earth's atmosphere. In Mission Control, the room was silent, breaths held as they tracked the descent. When the command module burst through the clouds, parachutes billowing, a roar erupted. Kranz felt a deep, exhausted relief. They had done it. They had brought the three stranded astronauts home.

That single, powerful phrase, "Failure is not an option," spoken in a moment of near hopelessness, would forever define the spirit of Apollo 13. It had carried them through, transforming the mission into a testament to courage, ingenuity, and the indomitable drive to refuse failure.

The lesson from Apollo 13 is clear. As we navigate today's leadership challenges, we can't afford the cost of failed leadership. It's time for today's leaders to adopt the resolve and innovation that saved a space mission—because failure is still not an option. But first, we need to understand the costs, the problems, and the needs of leadership in the modern world.

4.1 Costs of Failed Leadership Are Too High

Failure is simply the opportunity to begin again, this time more intelligently.

—Henry Ford

The cost of failed leadership is far greater than just missed business targets; it is a ticking time bomb for both human well-being and organizational sustainability, with widespread repercussions that extend into our communities and society. Workplace stress has emerged as one of the most critical health hazards of our time, and a growing body of research strongly suggests that poor leadership is a significant and modifiable contributor. A 2023 study by the American Psychological Association (APA) found that 57% of workers experience negative impacts due to work-related stress. The toll of workplace stress on human lives is staggering. According to a study by Stanford professors, workplace stress is responsible for over 120,000 deaths annually in the United States alone, and it drives up healthcare costs by as much as $190 billion each year.

120,000
deaths annually
in the U.S. due to
workplace stress

$550 billion
of lost productivity
per year due to
disengaged workers

4.3 million
Americans quit
their jobs in 2021 during
the Great Resignation

$190 billion
in annual
healthcare costs
related to job stress

57%
of employees cite experiencing
negative impacts due to work-
related stress

Costs of failed leadership in the United States

Stress-induced mortality is now comparable to major causes of
death like heart disease, accidents, and even diabetes. As Stanford
study points out, workplace stress surpasses diseases like Alzheimer's
and influenza in terms of deadliness. A joint global study by the World
Health Organization (WHO) and the International Labour Organization (ILO) revealed that in 2016, approximately 488 million people
worldwide were exposed to long working hours (defined as 55 or more
hours per week). In the same year, WHO and ILO estimated that
398,000 people died from stroke and 347,000 from heart disease as a
direct result of working such extended hours. Between 2000 and 2016,
deaths from heart disease linked to long working hours increased by
42%, while stroke-related deaths rose by 19%. The WHO/ILO study
concluded that working 55 or more hours per week is associated with a
35% higher risk of stroke and a 17% higher risk of death from ischemic
heart disease, compared to working a standard 35- to 40-hour week.
This is a reflection not just of poor health outcomes but of a colossal
leadership failure that permits toxic environments to persist. When
leaders prioritize profit and productivity over employee well-being, they

not only contribute to stress-related illnesses but also erode morale, loyalty, and overall organizational performance.

These grim statistics also carry with them a significant social cost. Poor leadership creates disengaged, overworked employees who are not just less productive at work—they are unfulfilled in life. This lack of purpose and well-being does not remain confined to the office; it reverberates through personal relationships, family life, and community engagement. When leadership fails, it's not just the individual who suffers. Family and social networks are impacted as well.

Leadership is not just about business outcomes—it's about human outcomes.

Beyond the immediate human toll, the economic implications of poor leadership are equally severe. Financially, poor leadership is costing businesses billions of dollars annually. Gallup data show that disengaged employees cost US corporations up to $550 billion in lost productivity each year. High turnover, lower innovation, and reduced efficiency are just some of the cascading effects of ineffective leadership. But this doesn't just hurt businesses—it weakens local economies. A disengaged workforce spends less money, participates less in community activities, and is less likely to contribute to the civic and social fabric of their communities.

The Great Resignation, where millions left their jobs in search of meaning and better work environments, is perhaps the clearest indicator of the leadership crisis we face. In August 2021 alone, 4.3 million Americans voluntarily left their jobs, a reflection of the widespread dissatisfaction with current leadership approaches. Workers today aren't just looking for a paycheck—they want purpose, flexibility, and a sense of belonging. A Microsoft survey revealed that 41% of the global workforce considered leaving their employer in 2021, driven by factors like burnout, lack of flexibility, and inadequate support from management. This mass exodus has profound implications for society. As people leave toxic environments, they take with them valuable skills and experience, creating labor shortages that ripple across industries and communities, slowing economic recovery and innovation.

The societal costs of poor leadership cannot be overstated. According to the WHO, stress—much of it stemming from workplace conditions—is a leading cause of mental health disorders, which now affect over one billion people globally. Untreated mental health disorders, many of which are linked to workplace stress, cost the global economy nearly $1 trillion annually, according to a 2024 fact sheet published by the organization. The strain on healthcare systems, the erosion of trust in leadership, and the growing disconnect between work and personal fulfillment all point to one undeniable truth: leadership is not just about business outcomes—it's about human outcomes.

4.2 Leadership: The Lever for Change

Every wall is a door.

—Ralph Waldo Emerson

Leadership is the single most significant lever we have to change the trajectory of this crisis. Leaders today hold the power to either perpetuate harmful work environments or transform them into spaces that foster well-being, innovation, and sustainable growth. The ripple effects of poor leadership are not confined to the workplace; they permeate our personal lives, communities, and society as a whole. Failure is not an option, because the stakes—in terms of dollars and human lives—are simply too high.

Leadership, much like life, is about perspective. The obstacles we encounter—whether in our careers, personal growth, or organizational challenges—often appear as impenetrable walls. But what if we saw them differently? What if, instead of barriers, we viewed them as doorways to new opportunities, innovation, and transformation?

This quote, "Every wall is a door," resonated with me so deeply that when I bought my house in El Dorado Hills, California, I decided to quite literally make it part of my home. The doorbell to my house was positioned on a wall perpendicular to the front door—an unusual placement that often left guests searching for it. To turn this quirky feature into a meaningful experience, I hired a painter to inscribe, "Every Wall Is a Door," next to the doorbell.

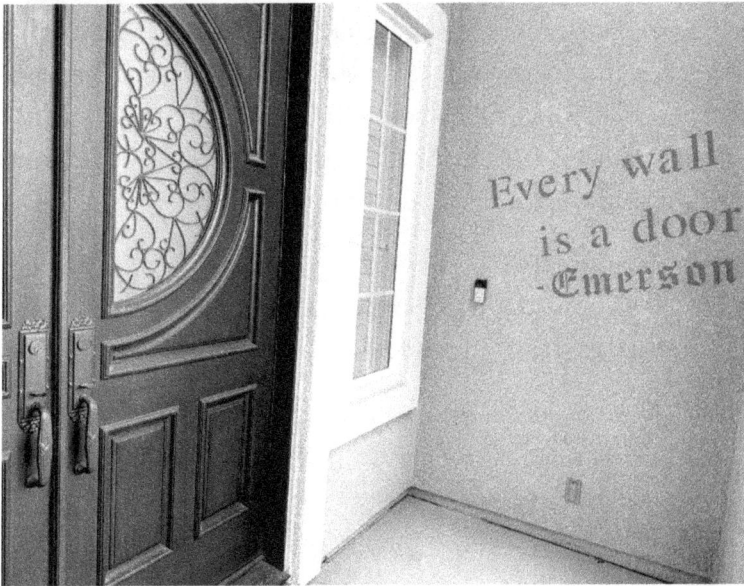

Each time you ring the bell, remember: the world belongs to those who see doors where others see walls.

Over time, I noticed how guests reacted. Many would pause, read the inscription, and ask me about it. It became a conversation starter—a reflection of how we perceive obstacles in life. But what truly fascinated me was what happened beyond my immediate circle. One day, while reviewing footage from my front-door camera, I saw an Amazon delivery driver stop, take out his phone, and photograph the inscription. It clearly resonated with him. Then, it happened again. And again. Different delivery workers, people passing by—they were capturing this simple yet profound message, likely taking it with them beyond my doorstep.

This experience reaffirmed my belief that leadership is about shaping perspectives. The world is evolving at an unprecedented pace, and traditional leadership paradigms—once thought to be absolute—are proving inadequate for the challenges of today. If we continue to see outdated leadership models as fixed walls rather than adaptable door-ways, we risk stagnation. The DEEP PACT framework presented in this book offers a way to challenge these barriers, reimagine leadership, and open doors where others see walls.

So, the question remains: Will you stand before the wall and stop, or will you see the door within it and step forward?

4.3 Limitations of Dominant Leadership Models

Intelligence is traditionally viewed as the ability to think and learn. Yet in a turbulent world, there's another set of cognitive skills that might matter more: the ability to rethink and unlearn.

—Adam Grant, author of *Think Again*

In today's rapidly evolving world, leadership models that once seemed effective are increasingly being recognized as less suited and inadequate for addressing contemporary challenges. To build a future-ready lead-ership framework, it is essential to critically examine the limitations of these established paradigms and explore new approaches that align with the demands of the modern world.

1. Command-and-Control Model of Leadership

Despite significant advancements in leadership theory and the proliferation of literature advocating for more progressive, inspirational, and inclusive leadership styles, the command-and-control model, characterized by hierarchical decision-making and rigid control, remains surprisingly prevalent in many organizations today.

The persistence of command-and-control leadership is not merely a matter of habit or individual choice—it has systemic roots. Research shows that while most leaders acknowledge command-and-control as outdated, many still revert to it out of fear: fear of looking bad, missing targets, losing control, or falling behind in competitive environments. These fears are not unfounded—they're often reinforced by organizational cultures that reward performance over people, control over trust, and appearance over authenticity. In this light, command-and-control is not just a leadership problem—it's a structural one. Real change requires more than evolved leaders; it demands organizations that are willing to rethink what they value, measure, and reward. Letting go of control doesn't start with individuals alone. It begins with cultures that make trust safe and transformation possible.

One of the clearest indicators of the prevalence of command-and-control leadership can be found in a 2020 survey by McKinsey & Company, which found that only 30% of organizations reported having a decentralized decision-making structure, which implies that a majority (70%) still rely on centralized, top-down management approaches. These data underscore the persistence of the command-and-control model, particularly in large, traditional organizations resistant to change. According to Gallup's 2024 *State of the Global Workplace* report, only 23% of employees worldwide are engaged at work. This low level of engagement is often linked to management styles that do not empower employees or involve them in decision-making processes. Disengaged employees are less motivated, less productive, and more likely to leave their jobs, creating a cycle of low morale and high turnover that can cripple an organization's performance. It is estimated that this disengagement costs the global economy $8.9 trillion in lost productivity annually.

The financial repercussions of poor leadership, often fueled by a hierarchical management structure, extend beyond lost productivity. The Work Institute's *2025 Retention Report* provides comprehensive insights into employee turnover and retention strategies. According to the report, analysis of over 14,000 exit interviews in 2024 revealed that 76% of employee departures could be prevented by better management practices. This finding is consistent with trends from the last five years (2019–2023), during which more than 123,000 exit interviews were conducted, showing that preventable turnover ranged from 71% to 80%. According to the report, the cost of replacing an employee averages 33% of their annual salary, adding significant expenses related to recruitment, training, and lost productivity during the transition period. For a mid-level employee earning $50,000 per year, this equates to a replacement cost of $16,500.

An article published in the *Harvard Business Review* in 2016 revealed that a global survey spanning eight major industrial nations, including the United States, found that trust in the workplace was alarmingly low, with only 49% of full-time employees reporting "a great deal of trust" in their bosses and colleagues. According to a 2018 *Forbes* article, a *Harvard Business Review* survey found that 58% of employees would trust a stranger more than their own manager, suggesting a significant disconnect between employees and management. This distrust is often rooted in rigid hierarchical structures where decisions are made at the top and communicated down the chain of command without input from lower levels. Additionally, a 2019 study by SHRM found that 58% of employees who quit their jobs cited their managers as the primary reason for their departure, underscoring the direct link between leadership quality and employee retention. According to a comprehensive study by Zenger Folkman, which analyzed 360-degree feedback data from over 20,000 leaders, poor leadership significantly correlates with lower organizational performance. The study revealed that the bottom 10% of leaders, based on their effectiveness ratings, contributed to organizations that were in the bottom 10% in terms of profitability. Conversely, the top 10% of leaders were associated with organizations in the top 10% for profitability.

2. Profit-Centric Leadership Model

The profit-centric leadership model, which prioritizes shareholder value and short-term financial gains over other considerations, has also come under intense criticism. Lynn Stout—formerly a professor at Cornell University—in her book *The Shareholder Value Myth* provides a compelling critique of profit-centric leadership, arguing that it harms corporations, investors, employees, and society. She challenges the prevailing notion that corporations exist solely to maximize shareholder value, asserting that this belief is neither legally mandated nor beneficial for long-term corporate success. The profit-centric approach often overlooks critical aspects such as employee well-being, corporate social responsibility, and long-term sustainability. The profit-only model neglects employee well-being, leading to burnout and decreased productivity. A 2020 survey by the Chartered Institute of Personnel and Development (CIPD) found that stress-related absences in the workplace have increased by 37% over the past decade. Companies that invest in employee well-being, however, see substantial benefits. Google's extensive wellness programs, for example, have contributed to high levels of employee satisfaction and retention, which in turn have supported the company's continuous innovation and profitability.

Poor leadership stemming from a profit-centric model also stifles innovation and competitiveness. A Deloitte study found that companies with ineffective leadership are 2.5 times less likely to be innovative compared to those with strong, supportive leadership. Furthermore, the American Psychological Association (APA) reports that stress-related absenteeism, often exacerbated by poor leadership, costs US businesses an estimated $300 billion annually. These statistics highlight how inadequate leadership can lead to a toxic workplace culture, increased stress, and decreased ability to adapt to market changes, ultimately hindering an organization's long-term success and growth.

3. Servant Leadership Model

The servant leadership model, introduced by Robert K. Greenleaf in the 1970s, advocates for leaders to prioritize the needs of their followers, supporting and empowering them to reach their full potential. This approach emphasizes values such as empathy, humility, and steward-ship, positioning the leader as a caretaker whose primary role is to serve others. Research has shown that servant leadership positively correlates with job satisfaction and retention, making it an appealing leadership model for various organizations. Several prominent US businesses, including Southwest Airlines, Starbucks, and Marriott International, are recognized for embracing servant leadership principles.

However, in many organizations, servant leadership has been inter-preted primarily as a personal ethic—encouraging leaders to be kinder, more empathetic, and supportive—rather than as a structural shift in how power, decision-making, and voice are distributed throughout the organization. As a result, while leaders may have adopted a more benevolent tone, the underlying hierarchies and top-down authority often remained unchanged. This limited the model's ability to drive deeper transformation in organizational culture, especially when systemic inequities or imbalances of power went unaddressed.

The profit-driven nature of for-profit organizations often creates tension between servant leadership principles and shareholder expectations, leading to inconsistent implementation. In contrast, the adoption of servant leadership is higher in the nonprofit sector, where it aligns more naturally with mission-driven objectives. Nonprofits prioritize social impact and community service, making servant leadership a logical fit for their organizational culture. A 2021 study highlighted that servant leadership positively influences volunteer retention and organizational citizenship behavior. However, some research suggests potential challenges, such as followers becoming overly reliant on servant leaders, which may constrain empowerment and organizational commitment.

In the post-pandemic world, the effectiveness of the servant leadership model has increasingly been called into question although its core ideas remain highly relevant—particularly in light of the evolving workplace expectations of Millennials and Gen Z, who increasingly seek meaningful employment, inclusive leadership, psychological safety, and a sense of purpose and belonging in their professional lives. However, the sudden shift to remote work and the rapid acceleration of digital transformation have introduced challenges that this traditional model may struggle to address. With the blurring of personal and professional boundaries in remote work settings, employees are seeking leaders who can provide structure, set clear expectations, and maintain accountability. While servant leadership's emphasis on empowerment and autonomy can be beneficial, it may not offer the level of guidance and clarity that employees now need.

Furthermore, the current business environment demands leaders who can navigate complex and uncertain situations with clear vision and strong direction. While servant leadership traditionally emphasizes humility and self-effacement, today's challenges require leaders who can inspire confidence and unite teams around a shared goal. The need for visionary leadership, which often contrasts with the self-effacing nature of servant leadership, has become more critical as organizations face unprecedented challenges and the necessity to innovate to remain competitive.

In a rapidly changing world, where agility and speed are paramount, servant leadership's focus on consensus-building and follower needs can sometimes slow decision-making processes, potentially hindering an organization's ability to respond quickly to disruptions. As businesses increasingly seek leaders who can balance empathy with efficiency and innovation, the servant leadership model, while still valuable, will need to evolve to meet effectively the demands of the new era.

4. Noble Purpose Leadership

Lisa Earle McLeod introduced the concept of *noble purpose selling* in her 2012 book, *Selling with Noble Purpose: How to Drive Revenue and Do Work That Makes You Proud,* where she demonstrated that sales performance and employee engagement improve dramatically when driven by a meaningful mission rather than just quotas. This idea laid the groundwork for her expanded framework of *noble purpose leadership,* which she developed further in her 2016 book, *Leading with Noble Purpose: How to Create a Tribe of True Believers.* In this follow-up, McLeod shifts the focus from individual sales to organizational culture, making the case that leaders who embed a noble purpose throughout their teams inspire greater trust, performance, and long-term success. This model shares foundational values with the servant leadership model, but differs in focus, framing, and execution.

In a 2023 *Harvard Business Review* article, "How to Be a Purpose-Driven Leader without Burning Out," Lisa Earle McLeod and Elizabeth Lotardo examined the suitability of servant leadership in the face of today's rampant burnout, less hierarchical workplaces, and the increasingly demanding schedules of leaders. While acknowledging the compassionate intent behind the servant leadership model, the authors observed that it often places unsustainable emotional and operational burdens on already overextended managers. When a leader's primary focus becomes serving others at all costs, the temptation to please everyone can turn into a never-ending and unproductive pursuit. Difficult conversations, tight deadlines, and honest feedback are inherently uncomfortable—regardless of how empathetic the leader may be. When leaders frame decisions solely around being helpful or accommodating, they risk burnout and may inadvertently foster entitlement, where employees begin to expect that the leader's role is to shield them from all discomfort. This emotional weight can erode clarity, weaken accountability, and ultimately impair a leader's ability to make tough but necessary decisions.

McLeod and Lotardo advocated for a shift toward noble-purpose leadership—a model grounded in a broader organizational mission to make a positive difference in the world and fulfill people's intrinsic need for meaning in their work. Rather than focusing solely on serving internal teams (as in servant leadership) or maximizing shareholder returns (as in traditional profit-centric models), noble-purpose leadership centers on an organization's external impact, especially on its customers. Noble-purpose leadership aligns teams around a shared cause greater than themselves, enabling leaders to channel their energy strategically rather than reactively. This model emphasizes contribution over compliance, purpose and meaning-making over people-pleasing, and long-term impact over immediate approval. McLeod and Lotardo argue that "servant leadership was a crucial stepping-stone to a more humane world of work, but 'noble-purpose leadership' is better suited for today's chaotic environment." When leaders and employees are united by a noble purpose, they demonstrate greater resilience, motivation, and clarity in decision-making—because they are driven not by ego or obligation, but by the pursuit of making a difference. In essence, noble-purpose leadership builds on the core principles of servant leadership while adding a more intentional focus on impact and shared purpose.

Noble purpose leadership is a powerful and compelling model that brings meaning and direction to organizations by aligning work with a higher mission. However, despite its strengths, this approach to leadership also presents a unique set of challenges that leaders must navigate to ensure lasting impact and engagement. For example, if the stated noble purpose is not consistently reinforced and clearly connected to the organization's daily operations, it can quickly lose relevance or be misunderstood. This disconnect—or mission drift—between declared intentions and everyday actions may lead to confusion, erode stakeholder trust, and ultimately result in employee disengagement, as the stated purpose may be perceived as merely a feel-good HR initiative.

An *MIT Sloan Management Review* article, "A Noble Purpose Alone Won't Transform Your Company," warned of the risks of relying solely on the aspirational aspects of a company's mission to attract and retain talent. Based on two decades of research involving more than 300 companies and numerous executive interviews, the study found that while having a noble purpose is a powerful performance driver, the level and quality of interpersonal collaboration have the greatest impact on employee engagement and overall workplace experience. The authors emphasized that although a noble purpose is important, it must be supported by deliberate efforts to cultivate interpersonal relationships and collaboration in order to truly transform an organization.

To sustain relevance and impact in an ever-changing world, leadership must continue to evolve—building on the foundations of service and purpose while developing new capacities that meet today's emerging challenges.

4.4 Emergence of Whole-Person Leadership

The strengths of servant and noble-purpose leadership are clear—but so are their limits. Both models have significantly contributed to humanizing the workplace and anchoring leadership in service, meaning, and mission. Servant leadership taught us the power of humility and trust. Noble purpose leadership reminded us that performance is elevated when people know that their work matters. These models remain highly relevant and continue to shape ethical and effective leadership. However, as the complexity of the workplace grows—with multigenerational teams, blurred work-life boundaries, and a relentless pace of change—there is a growing need to expand the leadership conversation and equip leaders with new capacities.

Whole-person leadership has emerged in response to this need. It is a model that recognizes that effective leadership cannot be separated from the leader's full humanity. Rather than viewing leaders as compartmentalized professionals, it sees them as integrated beings whose work is shaped by their inner life, personal commitments, and broader social context.

At its core, whole-person leadership integrates four essential domains of a leader's life: work, friends and family, community, and self. It acknowledges that each of these dimensions profoundly influences how a leader thinks, acts, and relates. Rather than encouraging leaders to "balance" these areas in isolation, whole-person leadership promotes alignment and mutual reinforcement. A leader who is grounded in self-awareness and purpose (self), nurtures meaningful personal relationships (friends and family), contributes to collective well-being (community), and drives business performance (work) leads with authenticity, vitality, and happiness.

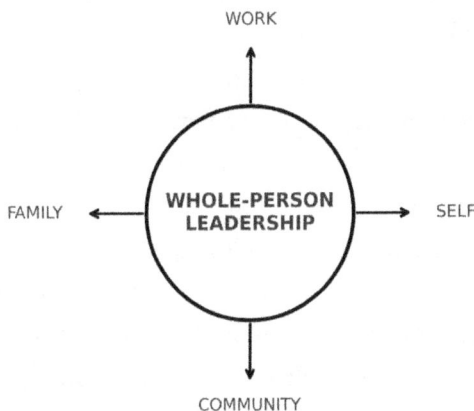

WORK

FAMILY ← **WHOLE-PERSON LEADERSHIP** → SELF

COMMUNITY

Leadership that aligns who you are with what you do.

The emergence of this leadership model reflects a growing understanding that fragmentation—between personal values and professional roles, or between individual well-being and organizational performance—is unsustainable. Today's leaders face a world of accelerating complexity and constant disruption. To thrive, they must lead not just with competence, but with wholeness. This means drawing strength from all dimensions of their lives and showing up fully and humanly in every sphere of their leadership.

Although whole-person leadership is gaining momentum in the 21st century, its roots run deep. Ancient traditions across cultures have long emphasized the unity of mind, body, spirit, and moral action. In Confucian thought, cultivating one's character (*xiūshēn*) was the basis for public responsibility. In the *Bhagavad Gita*, leadership arose from inner clarity, disciplined action, and selfless service. In classical Greek philosophy, the pursuit of the good life (*eudaimonia*) required harmony of reason, emotion, and virtue. Indigenous wisdom traditions similarly affirm that a leader must be in right relationship with self, others, community, and nature. These perspectives remind us that leadership has always been a human act—not just a strategic one.

In more recent history, the whole-person idea gained traction through humanistic psychology, authentic leadership, and frameworks like Stewart Friedman's "Total Leadership," which emphasized integration across life domains. As executive coaches, psychologists, and leadership scholars observed the burnout and fragmentation plaguing modern organizations, they began to advocate for more holistic models of development. Whole-person leadership emerged as both a personal and organizational imperative.

DEEP PACT, as proposed in this book, builds on these ancient and modern insights to offer a practical, research-informed framework for cultivating happiness-centered whole-person leadership. This approach doesn't replace noble purpose leadership—it builds upon it. It challenges leaders not only to inspire with a meaningful purpose but also to deliver on that purpose with precision, accountability, and emotional maturity. Personal mastery is not about serving others directly, but about advancing and consistently delivering on a noble purpose through decisiveness, focus, self-examination, and the pursuit of excellence—qualities that are critical for business growth and success in a competitive environment. Without personal mastery, noble purpose risks becoming an aspirational slogan rather than a lived reality. Interpersonal mastery, on the other hand, focuses on the ability to serve and connect with others, fostering trust, empathy, care, humility, and collaboration—qualities that lie at the heart of servant leadership and resonate strongly with the evolving workplace aspirations of Millennials and Gen Z. Employees today are not just looking for leaders who are visionary; they are looking for leaders who are human.

A whole-person leadership approach unites the head and the heart, aligning strategy with compassion, and purpose with practice. It is not just an evolution in leadership thinking—it is a step forward in leadership being. Unlike traditional models that emphasize either service to others (as in servant leadership) or driving performance through purpose (as in noble-purpose leadership), whole-person leadership integrates the leader's internal landscape—self-awareness, emotional resilience, and disciplined focus—with their external impact on people and systems. It recognizes that sustainable leadership requires not just inspiration but integration: the ability to lead with authenticity, navigate complexity, and foster meaningful relationships while delivering real results. Where other models often focus on what leaders do for others, whole-person leadership also asks who the leader is—and how that identity shapes their decisions, presence, and legacy.

Whole-person leadership refuses to treat leaders as disembodied skillsets or productivity machines. It views the leader as a full human being—not a divided personality where only their leadership competencies are evaluated or valued. It affirms that a leader's personal well-being, happiness, and sense of purpose and meaning are not peripheral—they are foundational. Leaders must be whole to lead well. Accordingly, success is measured not only by business outcomes but also by the leader's ability to flourish, sustain energy, uplift others, and model a balanced, fulfilling life. In this way, whole-person leadership reconnects modern organizational life with timeless wisdom—placing the well-being of the individual and the health of the collective at the center of leadership practice. This is the leadership model for a world that demands not only high performance but also deeply human presence.

4.5 Failure of Leadership Training Programs

Corporations are victims of the great training robbery. American companies spend enormous sums on training and education, but they are not getting a good return on their investment.

—Harvard Business Review

The problem with today's leadership doesn't lie solely with prevailing leadership models. Another critical issue is at play: leadership training programs themselves are falling short. In 2016, a *Harvard Business Review* article titled "Why Leadership Training Fails—And What to Do about It" made a bold claim: "**Corporations are victims of the great training robbery.**" The article highlighted a troubling reality—companies around the world invest billions in employee education and training, yet they see little return on investment. The authors, Harvard professors who conducted extensive research on this issue, reached a striking conclusion: learning alone does not lead to better organizational performance. Employees may acquire new knowledge and skills through training, but they often revert to their old ways once they return to their workplace. This cycle renders most training efforts ineffective.

The fundamental flaw, according to the authors, lies in a deeply ingrained but misguided assumption—that problems in organizational behavior and performance stem from individual deficiencies.

Companies believe that improving employees' knowledge, skills, and attitudes will automatically enhance overall effectiveness. However, the real issue often lies elsewhere. Rather than addressing systemic flaws—such as poorly designed structures, ineffective management practices, or a lack of support for new behaviors—organizations focus on training individuals in isolation. Without meaningful changes in the work environment, even the best-trained employees struggle to apply their newfound skills.

Seven years later, in 2023, another *Harvard Business Review* article, "What Makes Leadership Development Programs Succeed," reported that global organizations spend more than $60 billion annually on leadership development programs, yet only 10% of this spending yields tangible results, with a staggering 90% going to waste. The primary reason for this failure lies in the poor design based on a traditional competency framework for leadership development, which promotes a one-size-fits-all approach and assumes that by mastering a predefined set of skills and attributes, anyone can become an effective leader.

Leadership is not a thing. It is not merely a set of competencies to be acquired but a holistic, adaptive process that involves deep human connections and continuous learning.

These leadership training programs follow a structured curriculum, typically delivered through classroom-based, logical approaches focused on individual learning. Participants are removed from their regular work environments to engage with expert instructors, analyze case studies, receive personalized feedback, and absorb the latest leadership theories. A super-efficient one-week program dumps 40 hours of information on participants, assuming that this intensive content delivery will create confident, competent leaders. This competence-based training, focused merely on exposure to selected topics and rushed attempts at acquiring a set of skills through group exercises, operates under the mistaken belief that checking the box and printing a certificate are enough to ensure effective leadership. According to the authors of the 2023 *HBR* article, such training fails to equip leaders with the flexibility and innovative thinking necessary to respond to the unpredictable challenges of today's fast-paced business world. These programs often culminate in participants earning credentials that enhance their résumés. This is usually the extent of their impact, except in cases where individuals are particularly self-driven and apply the knowledge proactively.

Consider the case of General Electric (GE), which famously invested heavily in its leadership development programs. Despite its rigorous competency frameworks, GE faced significant challenges in maintaining its leadership edge in the rapidly changing business environment of the 21st century. The rigid adherence to competencies did not equip its leaders with the agility needed to adapt to new market dynamics.

Leadership is not a thing. It is not merely a set of competencies to be acquired but a holistic, adaptive process that involves deep human connections and continuous learning. In contrast, management is about acquiring and applying a set of competencies and skills to ensure organizational efficiency and effectiveness.

4.6 Failure to Address the Priorities of Millennials and Gen Z

If you don't understand the needs and aspirations of the younger generation, you risk being left behind.

—Simon Sinek

According to an August 2024 report by the US Department of Labor, Millennials and Gen Z made up 54% of the workforce in the second quarter of 2024. Globally, that figure is slightly higher at 59%, according to the World Economic Forum. This percentage is expected to continue rising as more members of Gen Z enter the workforce. As a result, their unique priorities and expectations have become critical to organizational success. However, many leaders continue to operate under outdated leadership models that do not align with the values and needs of these younger generations. This disconnect between traditional leadership approaches and employee expectations is a significant barrier to fostering a motivated and productive workforce. To bridge this gap, it is crucial to understand the priorities of Millennials and Gen Z, as this knowledge is essential for developing a new leadership model that effectively meets their needs. The following are the top 10 priorities shaping the values and aspirations of Millennials and Gen Z:

1. **Sense of purpose:** Desire for meaningful work that aligns with their values and contributes to a greater good.
2. **Work-life integration:** Emphasis on flexible schedules and the ability to blend professional and personal responsibilities in a way that supports overall well-being and productivity. Unlike traditional work-life balance, which emphasizes a strict separation between work and personal life, work-life integration enables individuals to navigate both seamlessly, providing greater flexibility and alignment with their unique needs and lifestyles.
3. **Career growth opportunities:** Importance of professional development, skill enhancement, and clear pathways for advancement.
4. **Mental health support:** Access to mental health resources and a workplace culture that prioritizes employee well-being.
5. **Whole self to work:** Preference for organizations that foster an inclusive and psychologically safe culture, where employees feel valued not just for their skills but also for

their identities, beliefs, and perspectives, and can express themselves freely without fear of judgment or punishment.

6. **Technology integration:** Comfort with and expectation for the latest technology that facilitates productivity, communication, and collaboration.

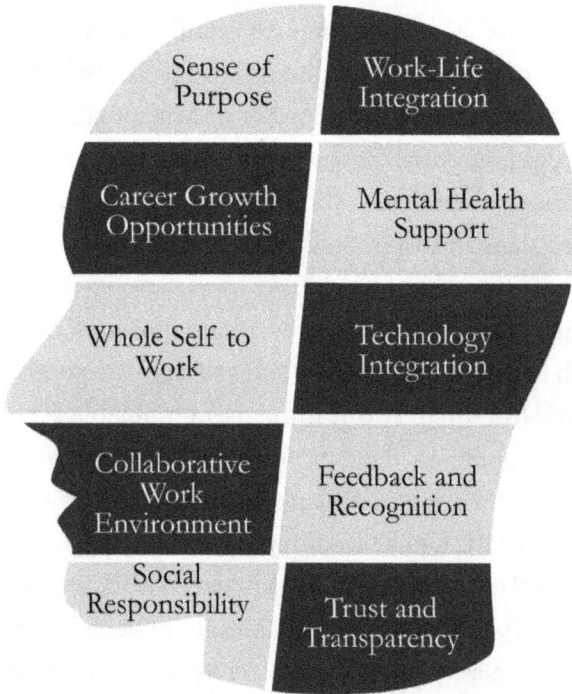

Top 10 Priorities of Millennials and Gen Z

7. **Collaborative work environment:** Preference for teamwork and open communication over hierarchical structures.

8. **Feedback and recognition:** Desire for regular feedback and acknowledgment of their contributions and efforts.

9. **Trust and transparency:** Importance of transparent leadership and open communication about company decisions and policies.

10. **Social Responsibility**: Preference for employers that take active roles in addressing social issues and demonstrate corporate social responsibility.

4.7 Leadership Needs of the Post-Pandemic World

Life is never made unbearable by circumstances, but only by lack of meaning and purpose.
> —Viktor Frankl, author of *Man's Search for Meaning*

The COVID-19 pandemic has triggered unprecedented changes in how we live, work, and lead. People are no longer content with merely earning a salary; they now seek roles that allow them to prioritize their personal and family needs, contribute to the greater good of society, and find deeper fulfillment. This shift aligns closely with Viktor Frankl's ideas in *Man's Search for Meaning*, where he emphasizes that true happiness comes from finding purpose and making meaningful contributions. As remote work blurred the boundaries between professional and personal life, people began to reassess their priorities, seeking jobs that align with their values and aspirations. Remote work has expanded their choices, providing more opportunities to find roles that resonate with their sense of meaning-seeking and purposeful living.

Consequently, the leadership landscape is experiencing a profound transformation. Professor George Kohlrieser, an organizational psychologist and author of the award-winning book *Hostage at the Table*, notes, "The pressures of remote work, increasing organizational complexity, and a new generation of digitally savvy workers valuing more than just a paycheck have changed the requirements of leadership." Leadership thinker Stephen M. R. Covey, in his insightful book *Trust and Inspire*, identified five pivotal forces behind this transformation: (1) the change in the global landscape and our interconnectedness, (2) the change in the nature of work through new technologies and approaches, (3) the change in workplace structures from traditional physical spaces to include remote and hybrid models, (4) the change in workforce composition with a diverse, multigenerational cohort seeking purpose and flexibility, and (5) the change in the nature of choice with the rise of virtual work, allowing for greater career choice and decision-making power. Covey argues that these transformative forces are not just incremental changes but are reshaping the very essence of how we lead, work, and interact.

The pandemic has accelerated several trends that were already beginning to reshape leadership. Remote work, digital transformation, and an increased focus on employee well-being have all taken center stage. According to a 2020 survey by McKinsey & Company, organizations significantly accelerated their implementation of digital tools and technologies during the pandemic. This rapid shift has demanded that leaders be more technologically savvy and adaptable.

Moreover, the pandemic has underscored the importance of empathy and emotional intelligence in leadership. Catalyst's report, "The Power of Empathy in Times of Crisis and Beyond," emphasizes that empathy from senior leaders significantly enhances employee outcomes, including innovation, engagement, and retention. Notably, 76% of employees with highly empathic senior leaders report being engaged at work, compared to only 32% with less empathic leaders. Furthermore, empathic leadership is linked to increased employee retention, as employees with empathic senior leaders are more likely to remain with their organizations. The values that underpin leadership have also shifted dramatically. The pandemic has brought to the forefront issues such as mental health, work-life integration, and social responsibility.

In the post-pandemic world, people are also looking for leaders who are transparent, resilient, and inclusive. Transparency has become a critical attribute, as employees and stakeholders seek honest and clear communication about the challenges and uncertainties facing their organizations. A 2021 survey by Edelman revealed that trust in government, business, and media declined significantly during the pandemic, emphasizing the need for transparent leadership to rebuild and maintain trust.

Resilience is another key quality that has gained prominence. The ability to navigate crises, adapt to rapid changes, and maintain stability in turbulent times is now seen as essential. Inclusivity has also become a paramount concern. Employees and consumers are increasingly demanding that leaders prioritize diversity, foster inclusive cultures, and implement policies that ensure equitable treatment and opportunities within their organizations. A report by McKinsey found that companies with diverse leadership teams were 25% more likely to have above-average profitability. Such data underscore the business case for diversity and the growing expectation for leaders to champion inclusive practices. Despite recent political resistance and shifting narratives, diversity, equity, and inclusion are not just moral imperatives—they are strategic necessities that drive innovation, resilience, and long-term organizational success.

In addition, the pandemic and the advent of artificial intelligence have accentuated more than ever the need for character in leaders, highlighting that integrity and moral fortitude are crucial in guiding teams through changing times. Character in leadership not only builds resilience but also ensures that advancements like AI enhance rather than undermine the human element in the workplace.

In summary, the pandemic has exposed the limitations of traditional leadership theories that prioritize command-and-control styles and hierarchical structures. These outdated models are increasingly seen as inadequate in addressing the complexities and uncertainties of the modern world. The hierarchical approach, which emphasizes top-down decision-making, has proven to be too rigid and slow in responding to the rapid changes that COVID brought. In contrast, more agile and decentralized leadership models have shown greater effectiveness. For instance, companies that empowered their frontline employees to make decisions quickly were better able to adapt to changing circumstances and meet customer needs during the crisis.

The companies that survive longest are the ones that work out what they uniquely can give to the world, not just growth or money but their excellence, their respect for others, or their ability to make people happy. Some call those things a soul.

—Charles Handy

Moreover, traditional leadership theories often fail to account for the importance of emotional intelligence and empathy. Leaders who lack these qualities are ill-equipped to support their teams through psychological and emotional challenges. The growing recognition of the importance of mental health and well-being in the workplace necessitates a compassionate, human-centered approach to leadership.

Finally, traditional leadership paradigms no longer adequately address the growing importance of social responsibility and ethical leadership. The pandemic underscored the deep interconnection between businesses and society, leading to rising expectations for leaders to act with integrity and accountability. This shift is evident in the increasing commitment of companies worldwide to sustainable and responsible business practices. According to a 2021 report by the Global Sustainable Investment Alliance, global sustainable investment now exceeds $35 trillion, highlighting the growing emphasis on ethical leadership and corporate accountability.

The post-pandemic world demands a new paradigm of leadership that is adaptable, empathetic, inclusive, and transparent.

4.8 Leadership Needs in an AI-Augmented World

I definitely fall into the camp of thinking of AI as augmenting human capability and capacity.

—Satya Nadella

Artificial intelligence is revolutionizing the workplace, creating both opportunities and challenges for modern leadership. As AI integrates into business processes, it demands a shift in leadership paradigms to manage effectively the complex interplay between technology and human elements. Traditional leadership approaches, which often emphasize control and hierarchy, are proving increasingly inadequate in addressing the dynamic and unpredictable nature of an AI-driven world. Leaders must now embody a blend of technical acumen and emotional intelligence to navigate this new landscape.

The rise of AI has heightened the demand for greater empathy, transparency, and adaptability in leadership. A 2025 blog post from Harvard Business Publishing, titled "AI-First Leadership: Embracing the Future of Work," emphasized the need for leaders to rethink the collaboration between humans and AI to fully leverage AI's potential and align technological advancements with strategic objectives. It highlighted the importance of organizations investing in a structured development process for leaders, focusing on foundational AI knowledge, fostering an AI-first mindset, enhancing AI-related skills, and leading with confidence in an AI-driven environment. Wharton professor Ethan Mollick, in his book *Co-Intelligence: Living and Working with AI*, delves into the transformative potential of AI in business and education, promoting a synergistic relationship between humans and this increasingly ubiquitous technology. He advocates for viewing AI as a collaborator—serving as a coworker, co-teacher, and coach—rather than merely a tool, emphasizing that such a partnership can significantly enhance human capabilities. Mollick also underscores the importance of continuous experimentation with AI to understand its strengths and limitations, encouraging leaders to foster a culture of adaptability and learning to effectively integrate AI into their organizations. As AI continues to evolve, leaders must move beyond passive adoption and actively shape its role within their organizations, ensuring that technology serves to augment, rather than diminish, human potential. To successfully navigate this evolving landscape of AI adoption, today's leaders must shift from a command-and-control hierarchical model to a whole-person ethical leadership approach—one that harnesses AI's full potential while preserving trust and organizational integrity.

4.9 Closing Reflections

A journey of a thousand miles begins with a single step.

—Lao Tzu

The necessity for a new leadership paradigm arises not only from failures of today's dominant leadership models and training programs but also from the changing needs and increasingly high stakes of the future. Leadership failure is no longer an option in a world where ineffective models contribute to widespread burnout, disengagement, and organizational instability. The financial and human tolls of poor leadership make it clear that failure in leadership is a burden that organizations and society can no longer afford.

Stress-induced workplace conditions driven by unfit leadership are directly linked to the erosion of mental health, family well-being, and community involvement. The interconnectedness of leadership with personal fulfillment, economic success, and societal health means that leaders now bear far greater responsibility; failure in leadership not only weakens businesses but disrupts the very fabric of society. Leaders of the future must be able to navigate these unprecedented challenges with empathy, transparency, and integrity to ensure that well-being and productivity go hand in hand.

This realization sets the stage for the introduction of a transformative leadership framework, DEEP PACT, described in detail in the next chapter. This new leadership model aims to equip leaders with the tools they need to embrace empathy, resilience, and ethical responsibility while fostering innovation and organizational growth. DEEP PACT is designed to inspire a leadership revolution, ensuring that the failures of the past are not repeated and that leaders are empowered to guide their teams and themselves to new heights of success and fulfillment.

5 DEEP PACT: A Whole-Person Approach

Shoot for the moon. Even if you miss, you'll land among the stars.
—Norman Vincent Peale

How do you tackle the vast problems and needs of today's leadership described in the previous chapters? By thinking beyond what is obvious, by embracing a new way of thinking that transcends the limitations of the present and imagines possibilities that reshape the future. Shoot for the moon, they say; because, even if you miss, you'll land among the stars. This is the mindset behind "cathedral thinking," where the seeds of grand ideas are planted not for immediate harvest but for future generations. Let me share a story that perfectly exemplifies the essence of cathedral thinking.

In a bustling medieval town, the townsfolk were enthralled by a grand project that would take decades to complete—a magnificent cathedral destined to be a beacon of faith and beauty for generations. This cathedral, with its towering spires and intricate carvings, symbolized the collective dreams and aspirations of the entire community.

Among the myriad workers contributing to this monumental task were three bricklayers, each with a distinct perspective on their labor. One day, a traveler passing through the town approached the three men, curious about their work.

The first bricklayer, his face etched with fatigue, muttered, "I am laying bricks." His tone was flat, and his eyes betrayed a sense of drudgery. To him, each brick was just another in an endless series of monotonous tasks, devoid of meaning or purpose.

"I am laying bricks" vs. "I am building a cathedral."

The second bricklayer, slightly more engaged, responded, "I am building a wall." He saw beyond the individual bricks to the structure they formed. However, his vision was still limited to the immediate task, and he failed to grasp the grandeur of the final creation.

Then the traveler approached the third bricklayer, who was humming a tune as he worked, his eyes gleaming with enthusiasm. "What are you doing?" the traveler asked.

With a broad smile and a hint of pride, the third bricklayer replied, "I am building a cathedral—a place where people will find solace and inspiration for centuries to come." He understood that his work was part of a grand vision, one that transcended the present moment and would stand the test of time.

This third bricklayer had embraced a concept that we now understand as *cathedral thinking*—the ability to see beyond the immediate tasks and envision the lasting impact of one's efforts.

Much like the third bricklayer's foresight into future magnificence, this book goes beyond merely teaching the tricks and tools of leadership; it stretches its arms toward constructing a transformative leadership framework that will not only create lasting positive change but also leave a legacy as enduring and inspiring as the grandest cathedrals.

5.1 DEEP PACT: Leadership Reimagined

What is now proved was once only imagined.

—William Blake

The rapid pace of technological advancement, changing societal expectations, and growing emphasis on employee well-being demand a new approach to leadership. More than ever, employees seek purpose in their work that goes beyond financial compensation. They want to feel that their efforts contribute to something meaningful and align with their values and passions. As a result, leaders must embed a sense of purpose within their organizations to drive engagement and foster fulfillment.

Lisa McLeod, in her influential book *Leading with Noble Purpose*, argues that when leaders focus on a higher mission beyond profits—such as making a positive impact on customers, employees, and society—they inspire greater engagement, increase job satisfaction, drive better performance, and achieve more sustainable success. A groundbreaking global study, the first of its kind, from Oxford's Saïd Business School highlights the critical role of purpose-driven leadership in business success. Surveying 450 C-suite executives, the research found that 71% of leaders in high-performing firms report that purpose actively guides their decision-making, while only 7% of leaders in underperforming companies do the same. These findings underscore that a clear and authentic corporate purpose is not just an abstract ideal—it is a fundamental driver of long-term success and competitive advantage.

We are in the midst of the Fourth Industrial Revolution, a period defined by rapid advancements in technologies like artificial intelligence, robotics, the Internet of Things (IoT), genetic engineering, and quantum computing. These innovations are reshaping industries and society at an unprecedented pace. In response to these transformative changes, the *Davos Manifesto 2020* emphasizes the need for companies to serve all stakeholders—customers, employees, communities— emphasizing that businesses should pursue not just profit but also a noble purpose, focusing on long-term societal well-being alongside economic success. This manifesto sets forth the universal purpose of a company, championing shared and lasting value for society, as stated in the excerpt below:

> *The purpose of a company is to engage all its stakeholders in shared and sustained value creation. In creating such value, a company serves not only its shareholders, but all its stakeholders—employees, customers, suppliers, local communities and society at large.*
>
> *A company is more than an economic unit generating wealth. It fulfils human and societal aspirations as part of the broader social system. Performance must be measured not only on the return to shareholders, but also on how it achieves its environmental, social and good governance objectives.*
>
> —*The Davos Manifesto 2020:*
> *Universal Purpose of a Company in the*
> *Fourth Industrial Revolution*

Leadership, noble purpose, social responsibility, and meaningful work may seem like abstract concepts, but they are deeply intertwined and essential for creating a positive impact in the world. In an age flooded with information, true leadership can be distilled into a powerful and actionable definition: **Leadership is doing things differently for a purpose larger than yourself.** This perspective moves beyond personal ambition or mere efficiency, focusing instead on the greater good—driving change and serving a higher cause that benefits others and society as a whole.

Leadership is doing things differently for a purpose larger than yourself.

This definition of leadership embodies two key attributes: innovation (doing things differently) and a noble purpose (larger than yourself). True leadership involves stepping outside conventional methods and practices to do things differently to inspire and create meaningful change. Leaders challenge the status quo, see opportunities where others see obstacles, and are not afraid to take risks to achieve something greater. This aspect of leadership requires creativity, vision, and the courage to forge new paths.

The second critical attribute of leadership, as defined here, is focusing on something larger than yourself. True leadership is not about personal glory or individual success; it is about working toward a greater good—a noble purpose. This could be the betterment of a community, the success of an organization, or the advancement of a cause. Leaders inspire and mobilize others by demonstrating a commitment to a purpose that transcends their own interests. They understand that their actions have a ripple effect, impacting not just their immediate surroundings but also broader society. This selfless dedication to a larger mission not only amplifies their impact but also fosters a sense of fulfillment and happiness that goes beyond personal achievements. As we embrace this mindset, we realize that our true strength lies in our ability to uplift and empower those around us, creating a lasting and positive legacy that endures through collective success and well-being.

However, a definition or a new theory of leadership alone will not suffice. The initial excitement that accompanies the introduction of a new definition or theory often fades, leaving organizations to revert to their old ways. This has happened with leadership concepts like servant and noble purpose leadership, which gained initial traction but were often implemented superficially, failing to drive the deep, systemic change that organizations need. It is time to challenge the status quo of leadership. What is needed is not just a new approach or theory but a profound shift in mindset and behavior—a personal commitment and a change of heart, a happiness-seeking, meaning-making, purpose-driven, whole-person approach that recognizes that leadership is not just about tactical skills or job performance—it is about developing the whole human being. When leaders grow as whole people, they foster cultures of trust, psychological safety, purpose, and sustained impact. As Simon Sinek writes in *The Infinite Game*, we must replace the status quo with a "reality that is vastly more conducive to our deep-seated human need to feel safe, to contribute to something bigger than ourselves and to provide for ourselves and our families."

Within this context, we not only articulate a new definition of leadership, encompassing innovation and noble purpose, but also introduce the DEEP PACT—a reimagined framework that meets the demands of a post-pandemic world by fostering ethical, dynamic, excellence-driven, compassionate, and inclusive leadership.

The DEEP PACT, a mnemonic representing eight principles, consists of specific insights, strategies, and actions designed to help leaders navigate the challenges and demands of future leadership. These principles—introduced below and elaborated on in subsequent chapters—not only challenge conventional wisdom but also align with the evolved expectations of society, inspiring a higher standard of leadership that is transformative and enduring. The DEEP PACT fills three key gaps in leadership training identified in the 2023 *Harvard Business Review* article titled "What Makes Leadership Development Programs Succeed": (1) a lack of a whole-person approach, (2) insufficient opportunities for self-reflection and meaning-making, and (3) a failure to recognize and address psychological barriers to growth. While these principles are undeniably aspirational, they are firmly rooted in a whole-person approach that seeks to influence belief systems, which in turn shape values, attitudes, and actions.

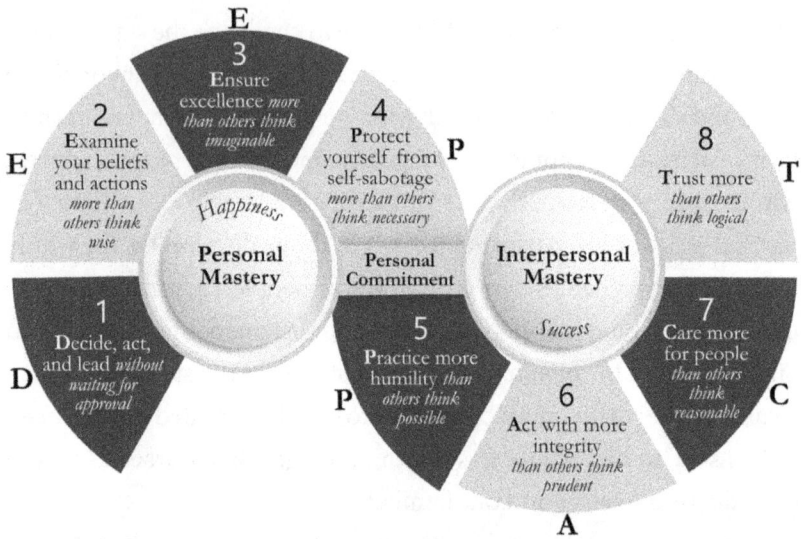

DEEP PACT: linking personal and interpersonal
mastery through the power of commitment.

Personal Mastery

The first four principles of DEEP PACT are about achieving **personal mastery** or self-mastery, which is the art of gaining control over one's thoughts, emotions, and behaviors to achieve personal and professional goals. This foundational aspect of personal development allows individuals to harness their inner strengths and mitigate weaknesses that create barriers to success. Often, we are our own worst enemies, as immunity to change, lack of initiative, ego, a fixed mindset, and limiting beliefs can sabotage our efforts to unleash our inherent greatness. According to Peter Senge, author of *The Fifth Discipline*, personal mastery involves continually clarifying and deepening our personal vision, focusing our energies, and seeing reality objectively. Leadership missionary Robin Sharma, in his books *The Leader Who Had No Title* and *The 5 AM Club*, emphasizes personal mastery as the foundation of exceptional leadership. He argues that before a leader can effectively lead others, they must first lead themselves. It is not a one-time achievement but an ongoing pursuit of becoming the best version of oneself. By becoming more aware of our thoughts and feelings, we can better manage them, leading to more consistent and intentional actions aligned with our goals. This journey of personal mastery requires a commitment to personal growth and a willingness to confront and overcome internal obstacles.

Interpersonal Mastery

The last four principles of DEEP PACT are about achieving **interpersonal mastery**. While personal mastery focuses on controlling and regulating one's internal world, interpersonal mastery involves effectively managing and influencing the external environment, including people, situations, and systems. Interpersonal mastery is essential for building strong relationships, fostering collaboration, and leading others effectively. Successful leaders who possess interpersonal mastery are adept at communication, conflict resolution, and team-building. They create environments where trust and mutual respect thrive, enabling their teams to perform at their best. John C. Maxwell, in his book *The 21 Irrefutable Laws of Leadership*, emphasizes the importance of influence and the ability to inspire and motivate others as critical components of effective leadership. Leaders who excel in interpersonal mastery can navigate complex social dynamics, foster a sense of belonging, and drive collective success.

The integration of personal mastery and interpersonal mastery completes the cycle of total leadership, creating a foundation for happiness and success personally and professionally. As leaders achieve personal mastery, they become more self-aware, resilient, self-reliant, and capable of navigating the complexities of their own emotions and behaviors. When leaders excel in interpersonal mastery, they inspire and motivate their teams, cultivate strong relationships, and drive collective success.

Such leaders embody a holistic approach to leadership that integrates personal growth with relational excellence, ultimately leading to greater fulfillment, effectiveness, and happiness in their leadership roles.

Personal Commitment

DEEP PACT's four principles of personal mastery and four principles of interpersonal mastery are bound together by a powerful force: personal commitment—a pact with oneself. This commitment is more than a promise; it is a deep, intrinsic dedication to self-improvement and leadership excellence. By making this pact, a leader acknowledges the importance of mastering the internal and external dimensions of their leadership journey. DEEP PACT addresses critical gaps in leadership development by aligning inner purpose with outward impact. While aspirational, its principles are firmly grounded in the belief that lasting leadership begins from within. Each principle is supported by actionable tools and real-world examples, offering a practical roadmap for leaders to inspire, decide, and deliver.

Making a pact with yourself is the most profound aspect of this new leadership paradigm, where you are your own checkpoint. You may falter, but dedication to these principles will guide you back to your true self, fostering personal happiness and aligning your motivations with a higher purpose—an essential element of our leadership definition. What else could be more practical?

All truth passes through three stages. First, it is ridiculed. Second, it is violently opposed. Third, it is accepted as being self-evident.
—Arthur Schopenhauer

Eight Principles Of
DEEP PACT

Descriptions and Happiness Advantages

Principle 1—Decide, act, and lead without waiting for approval.

Leadership is not a title bestowed but a role embraced. This principle embodies the essence of proactive leadership. Waiting for permission or approval implies a need for external validation, which can stifle initiative and innovation. True leaders recognize opportunities to make a difference and seize them without hesitation. This proactive approach to maximize one's potential not only fosters positive change but also brings profound happiness and satisfaction.

Consider the example of Malala Yousafzai, who, despite facing grave dangers, championed the cause of girls' education in Pakistan. Malala did not wait for societal approval to lead; she recognized a critical need and acted on it, becoming a global symbol of courage and advocacy. Her story illustrates that leadership, at its core, is about responding to challenges with determination and a sense of duty, regardless of whether one has been granted explicit authority.

☼ **The Happiness Advantage:** This principle is a powerful catalyst for happiness because it empowers individuals to take control of their own destiny and pursue their passions without waiting for external validation. When you seize opportunities to lead or chase your dreams without seeking permission or approval, you align your actions with your true desires and values, creating a deep sense of purpose and happiness. When you refuse to wait for permission, you take responsibility for your impact on the world, infusing your journey with purpose and meaning as you pursue goals that resonate with your deepest aspirations.

Principle 2—Examine your beliefs and actions more than others think wise.

Self-reflection is a cornerstone of effective leadership. By *examining their beliefs more than others think wise*, leaders cultivate a deeper understanding of their motivations, biases, and values. This introspection fosters a mindset of continuous learning and adaptability, enabling leaders to navigate complex situations with greater clarity and insight.

This principle encourages leaders to question their assumptions, seek diverse perspectives, and remain open to new ideas. Such rigorous self-examination prevents stagnation and promotes intellectual growth, equipping leaders to make informed and ethical decisions. In an ever-changing world, the ability to adapt and evolve is paramount —and that begins with a willingness to scrutinize and refine one's own beliefs. Correcting mistaken beliefs helps avoid unnecessary pitfalls and paves the way to greater happiness and fulfillment.

Nelson Mandela's life story is a powerful testament to the importance of examining and challenging deeply entrenched beliefs. During his fight against apartheid in South Africa, Mandela scrutinized not only the oppressive regime but also the tactics of his own movement. After spending 27 years in prison, he emerged with a commitment to reconciliation and unity, rejecting the notion of retributive justice that many expected. By advocating for forgiveness and collaboration, Mandela dismantled the apartheid system and laid the groundwork for a democratic South Africa, showing that examining and evolving one's beliefs can lead to profound societal transformation.

☼ **The Happiness Advantage:** This principle fosters happiness by encouraging a deep alignment between your inner values and outward behaviors. When you engage in a deep level of self-reflection, you gain clarity about what truly matters to you, enabling you to make decisions that are more authentic and fulfilling. When your actions consistently reflect your true beliefs, you create a life that is genuinely your own, filled with purpose and meaning, rooted in self-awareness.

Principle 3—Ensure excellence more than others think imaginable.

Excellence is not an occasional act but a consistent pursuit. Leaders who *ensure excellence more than others think imaginable* set a high standard for themselves and their teams. This commitment to surpassing expectations drives innovation, fosters a culture of continuous improvement, and inspires others to elevate their performance.

Steve Jobs exemplified this principle with his relentless pursuit of perfection at Apple. Jobs's insistence on excellence resulted in groundbreaking products that revolutionized industries and set new benchmarks for quality and innovation. His leadership demonstrated that when leaders demand and model excellence, they can achieve extraordinary results. Striving for excellence requires discipline, vision, and an unwavering commitment to high standards, all of which are essential for long-term success.

☼ **The Happiness Advantage:** The principle is a powerful driver of happiness because it allows you to fully realize your potential and take pride in your accomplishments. The joy derived from knowing you've given your very best, and exceeded expectations, creates a lasting sense of achievement and happiness in your personal and professional life. When you voluntarily hold yourself to the highest standards, you not only contribute value to the world but also craft a life story filled with purpose, meaning, and enduring impact.

Principle 4—Protect yourself from self-sabotage more than others think necessary.

Self-sabotage is a pervasive threat to effective leadership. By *protecting themselves from self-sabotage more than others think necessary*, leaders safeguard their potential and ensure sustained success. This principle involves recognizing and mitigating behaviors that undermine one's effectiveness, such as procrastination, perfectionism, and negative self-talk.

Howard Schultz, the former CEO of Starbucks, faced significant internal and external challenges as he built the company. Early in his journey, Schultz struggled with self-doubt and fear that his vision for Starbucks—to create a coffeehouse experience centered around community rather than just selling coffee—might not resonate with people. This fear, coupled with the pressure to deliver perfection, often led him to second-guess himself and question whether he was making the right choices. However, Schultz learned to protect himself from the self-sabotaging effects of perfectionism and doubt by embracing a growth mindset and leaning into his vision, even when others doubted his unconventional approach. Schultz once reflected, "I always saw Starbucks as a different kind of company . . . that could nurture the human spirit, one person, one cup, and one neighborhood at a time." By staying committed to this purpose and silencing the internal voice of doubt, Schultz transformed Starbucks into a global brand.

Leaders must develop the resilience to persevere through challenges and the self-awareness to avoid behaviors that impede progress. By fostering a growth mindset and cultivating positive habits, leaders can maintain their trajectory toward success.

☼ **The Happiness Advantage:** This principle brings happiness because it helps you recognize and overcome the internal obstacles that can hinder your success and fulfillment. When you actively guard against self-sabotaging behaviors, you avoid unnecessary stress and disappointment and create the conditions for a happier, more fulfilled life. When you protect yourself from self-sabotage, you safeguard the integrity of your life's purpose, ensuring that your journey is guided by clarity, intention, and a deep sense of meaning.

Principle 5—Practice more humility than others think possible.

Humility is a defining trait of great leaders. *Practicing more humility than others think possible* fosters authentic connections, facilitates collaboration, and creates a culture of respect and openness. Humility enables leaders to acknowledge their limitations, seek feedback, and value the contributions of others, thereby enhancing team dynamics and performance.

Mahatma Gandhi's leadership in India's struggle for independence was characterized by profound humility. Gandhi's approach to leadership, based on nonviolence and servant leadership, galvanized millions and brought about significant social change. His humility allowed him to connect deeply with people and inspire collective action. In today's context, leaders who practice humility can build trust, encourage open communication, and foster an inclusive environment where everyone feels valued.

☼ **The Happiness Advantage:** The happiness that comes from practicing humility is rooted in the fulfillment of knowing that you are contributing to the well-being of others and creating an environment where everyone feels valued and respected. When you embrace humility, you reduce ego-driven stress and conflict, allowing you to create a life rich in relationships, collaboration, and collective achievement. When you practice humility, you infuse your actions with profound meaning as you shift the focus from self-centered ambition to something larger than yourself.

Principle 6—Act with more integrity than others think prudent.

Integrity is the bedrock of trust and credibility. *Acting with more integrity than others think prudent* involves adhering to ethical principles even when it is inconvenient or unpopular. Leaders who prioritize integrity earn the respect and loyalty of their followers, creating a foundation of trust that is essential for effective leadership.

In 1982, Johnson & Johnson CEO James Burke faced a crisis when cyanide-laced Tylenol capsules resulted in several deaths. Despite the significant financial cost and potential damage to the brand, Burke made the bold decision to recall all Tylenol products from store shelves, prioritizing consumer safety over profits. This action was guided by the company's credo, which emphasized responsibility to customers first. Burke's integrity-driven response not only mitigated a public health crisis but also restored public trust and set a new standard for corporate responsibility.

☼ **The Happiness Advantage:** This principle brings deep and lasting happiness because it ensures that your actions are always aligned with your core values, creating a life of authenticity and self-respect. When you consistently choose integrity, you achieve peace of mind by eliminating the inner turmoil and regret that often accompany ethical compromises. When you uphold integrity, you infuse your life with meaning, knowing that your contributions are not only successful but also morally significant, leaving a lasting impact that goes beyond mere accomplishments.

Principle 7—Care more for people than others think reasonable.

Empathy and compassion are critical components of effective leadership. *Caring for people more than others think reasonable* emphasizes the importance of prioritizing the well-being of team members. Leaders who genuinely care for their people create supportive environments that enhance morale, engagement, and productivity.

Jacinda Ardern, the prime minister of New Zealand, exemplifies this principle through her empathetic leadership style. Her compassionate responses to crises, such as the Christchurch Mosque shootings and the COVID-19 pandemic, have been widely praised. Ardern's focus on the well-being of her citizens has strengthened social cohesion and trust in her leadership. By prioritizing the needs of their people, leaders can foster loyalty and create a positive organizational culture.

☼ **The Happiness Advantage:** This principle brings happiness because it strengthens the bond of connection, creating a supportive and fulfilling environment. When you genuinely care for others, you cultivate meaningful relationships by elevating your interactions from transactional to transformational. When you extend care and compassion beyond what is expected, you create a profound positive impact on the lives of those around you, fostering an environment of all-around happiness.

Principle 8—Trust more than others think logical.

Trust is the cornerstone of effective leadership. *Trusting more than others think logical* involves placing confidence in others, delegating responsibilities, and fostering a culture of autonomy and accountability. While it may seem risky, extending trust beyond your comfort zone empowers individuals, encourages innovation, and strengthens team cohesion.

Warren Buffett's leadership at Berkshire Hathaway is a testament to the power of trust. Buffett's decentralized approach to management, where he entrusts the leaders of subsidiary companies with significant autonomy, has been instrumental in the conglomerate's success. His willingness to trust his managers has fostered a culture of responsibility and innovation. Leaders who extend trust to their teams create an environment where individuals feel empowered to take initiative and contribute their best efforts.

☼ **The Happiness Advantage:** This principle fosters happiness by creating an environment of openness, collaboration, and mutual respect. When you choose to trust others beyond what is typically expected, you build deeper, more meaningful relationships, which are a key source of joy and fulfillment. When you trust others, you signal to others that you believe in their abilities and intentions, which often inspires them to live up to that trust and brings happiness to them.

5.2 Why Is the Word "Others" So Prominent in Each Principle?

Others can have a surprising and profound effect on almost every aspect of our behavior. They shape how we dress, what we buy, how we vote, and even how we name our children.

—Jonah Berger

The prominence of the word "others" in the principles of DEEP PACT is a deliberate choice, highlighting the pervasive influence that others have on practically every element of our lives. In his book *Invisible Influence: The Hidden Forces That Shape Behavior*, Jonah Berger, a marketing professor at the Wharton School of the University of Pennsylvania, discusses how our behavior is continuously shaped by those around us, often without our conscious awareness. Arthur Schopenhauer once said, "We forfeit three-fourths of ourselves in order to be like other people." From the clothes we wear to the food we eat, and from our judgments to our choices, the impact of others is profound and inescapable. Recognizing this influence is crucial because it allows us to understand and navigate the subtle forces that can either propel us forward or stifle our growth.

Moreover, the concept of "others" extends beyond external influences to include our internal dialogues—our "other self" or ego. This internal influence can be just as dangerous, if not more so, as the external pressures we face. Our ego often whispers doubts, fears, and negative thoughts, shaping our actions and decisions in ways that may hinder our progress and well-being. By acknowledging this internal other, we become more aware of the dual influences shaping our lives and can take steps to mitigate their negative impacts. Berger's insights into how we strive to be optimally distinct—not too different, not too similar—underscore the delicate balance we must maintain in managing these influences to achieve personal and professional growth.

In DEEP PACT, the emphasis on others serves as a reminder of the constant interplay between external and internal influences. It encourages us to be mindful of how we are shaped by those around us and by our inner thoughts. By understanding the power of these influences, we can better harness the positive aspects and guard against the negative ones. This awareness empowers us to lead more intentional, authentic lives, grounded in self-awareness and resilience against the pervasive effects of others.

5.3 How Does DEEP PACT Help Build Powerful Leadership Habits?

Sow a thought, reap an action; sow an action, reap a habit; sow a habit, reap a character; sow a character, reap a destiny.

—Stephen Covey

The primary benefit of DEEP PACT lies in its holistic approach to personal and professional development. The daily practice of DEEP PACT principles can significantly aid in building and nurturing the leadership habits necessary for happy and great leadership, as shown in Table 1 below. The latest leadership literature also reiterates the importance of cultivating desirable habits to enhance leadership effectiveness and form the character of a leader. DEEP PACT will make you a better person, empowering you to lead with integrity, resilience, and compassion. By embracing these principles, you'll find yourself not only more capable in your professional roles but also more grounded, self-aware, and fulfilled in every aspect of life. This approach encourages growth from within, aligning your actions with your highest values and igniting the greatness that lies within all of us.

> *DEEP PACT will make you a better person, empowering you to lead with integrity, resilience, and compassion.*

Table 1: How DEEP PACT Helps Build Powerful Leadership Habits

Principle 1. Decide, act, and lead without waiting for approval helps build and nurture the following habits:

Decisiveness	Leaders become more confident in making quick, informed decisions, reducing delays and enhancing agility.
Ownership	Taking initiative encourages a sense of responsibility for outcomes, promoting accountability and commitment.
Risk-taking	Embracing calculated risks becomes a habit, leading to greater resilience and adaptability in the face of challenges.

Principle 2. Examine your beliefs and actions more than others think wise helps build and nurture the following habits:

Self-reflection	Leaders develop the habit of regularly assessing their beliefs, motivations, and actions, fostering personal growth and awareness.
Critical thinking	This practice encourages leaders to analyze situations deeply, consider multiple perspectives, and make informed decisions.
Continuous learning	Leaders cultivate a mindset of lifelong learning, seeking feedback and new information to refine their beliefs and practices.

Principle 3. Ensure excellence more than others think imaginable helps build and nurture the following habits:

High standards	Leaders set and maintain elevated expectations for themselves and their teams, fostering a culture of excellence.
Continuous improvement	A commitment to lifelong learning encourages leaders to seek feedback, invest in personal development, and embrace innovation.
Proactive mindset	Anticipating potential issues and addressing them before they escalate allows leaders to maintain a focus on excellence.

Principle 4. Protect yourself from self-sabotage more than others think necessary helps build and nurture the following habits:

Self-awareness	Leaders develop a keen understanding of their strengths, weaknesses, triggers, and patterns that lead to self-sabotage, enabling more effective decision-making.
Boundary-setting	Leaders learn to establish healthy boundaries, protecting their time and energy from external distractions and demands.
Emotional regulation	Leaders learn techniques to manage their emotions effectively, reducing impulsive reactions that could lead to self-sabotage.

Principle 5. Practice more humility than others think possible helps build and nurture the following habits:

Active listening	Humble leaders prioritize listening to their team members, valuing their insights and fostering a culture of open communication.
Embracing feedback	Leaders who practice humility actively seek and welcome feedback, viewing it as a tool for growth rather than criticism.
Valuing others' contributions	Leaders acting from a position of humility recognize and celebrate the achievements of team members, fostering a sense of appreciation and motivation.

Principle 6. Act with more integrity than others think prudent helps build and nurture the following habits:

Transparency	Acting with integrity encourages openness in communication, fostering trust among team members and stakeholders.
Ethical decision-making	A commitment to integrity leads to a habit of considering the ethical implications of decisions, prioritizing long-term impact over short-term gains.
Trust-building	Consistently acting with integrity helps leaders build strong, trusting relationships with their teams, enhancing collaboration and loyalty.

Principle 7. Care more for people than others think reasonable helps build and nurture the following habits:

Empathy	Leaders develop a deep understanding of their team members' feelings and perspectives, fostering stronger relationships and trust.
Personal connections	Taking the time to know team members personally helps build rapport, making individuals feel valued beyond their professional roles.
Work-life integration advocacy	They prioritize and promote a healthy work-life integration, demonstrating genuine concern for their team's well-being.

Principle 8. Trust more than others think logical helps build and nurture the following habits:

Empowerment	Leaders learn to delegate responsibility, giving team members the autonomy to make decisions and take ownership of their work.
Open communication	By trusting their teams, leaders create an environment where open dialogue is encouraged, fostering transparency and collaboration.
Resilience	By encouraging a trusting environment, leaders create a supportive culture that helps teams bounce back together from setbacks.

5.4 How Does DEEP PACT Shape Your Character?

Character cannot be developed in ease and quiet. Only through experience of trial and suffering can the soul be strengthened, ambition inspired, and success achieved.

—Helen Keller

William Vanderbloemen, founder and CEO of an executive search firm, identified 12 key habits—or more accurately, character traits—that distinguish exceptional leaders. Vanderbloemen's conclusion is based on 15 years of extensive research involving more than 30,000 top leaders and proprietary data. In his 2023 book, *Be the Unicorn; 12 Data-Driven Habits That Separate the Best Leaders from the Rest*, Vanderbloemen documented 12 character traits that separate the best leaders from the rest. Those are: (1) The Fast, (2) The Authentic, (3) The Agile, (4) The Solver, (5) The Anticipator, (6) The Prepared, (7) The Self-Aware, (8) The Curious, (9) The Connected, (10) The Likable, (11) The Productive, and (12) The Purpose-Driven. The figure below depicts the connection between the eight DEEP PACT principles and the 12 key habits, which ultimately shapes a leader's character.

Complementing the insights from *Be the Unicorn*, other contemporary leadership literature also highlights the significance of good habits in forming the character of a leader. For instance, in *Atomic Habits*, James Clear emphasizes the power of small, incremental changes in behavior that can lead to significant improvements over time. Clear's research indicates that habits are the compound interest of self-improvement, underscoring how minor adjustments in daily routines can accumulate to produce substantial outcomes. Similarly, BJ Fogg's *Tiny Habits* explores the psychology behind habit formation, suggesting that starting with small, manageable changes can lead to the development of sustainable habits. Both books provide valuable frameworks for leaders looking to embed desirable habits into their daily practices.

Leadership journal articles further reinforce the critical role of habits in shaping character and effective leadership. Research published in the *Harvard Business Review* and the *Journal of Applied Psychology* consistently shows that leaders who demonstrate high levels of emotional intelligence, adaptability, and integrity tend to achieve better organizational outcomes. These habits not only enhance a leader's ability to navigate complex challenges but also build trust and credibility with their teams. As Vanderbloemen's study illustrates, the most effective leaders are those who continuously cultivate and refine their habits, leading to sustained personal and organizational growth.

3. Ensure
excellence

4. Solver &
6. Prepared

*excellence-driven,
meticulous,
diligent*

2. Examine
your beliefs
and actions

5. Anticipator
& 8. Curious

*introspective,
contemplative,
analytical*

7. Self-Aware
&
11.Productive

*emotionally
intelligent, growth
mindset, prudent*

4. Protect
yourself from
self-sabotage

1. Fast &
3. Agile

*confident, brave,
determined,
resilient*

1. Decide,
act, and
lead

Character

10. Likable

*unpretentious,
respectful, down-
to-earth, self-
effacing*

5. Practice
more
humility

12. Purpose
Driven

*inspiring,
dependable,
collaborative,
transparent*

8. Trust
more

9. Connected

*caring,
compassionate,
understanding,
sensitive*

2. Authentic

*honest, principled,
ethical, sincere,
fair*

6. Act
with more
integrity

7. Care more
for people

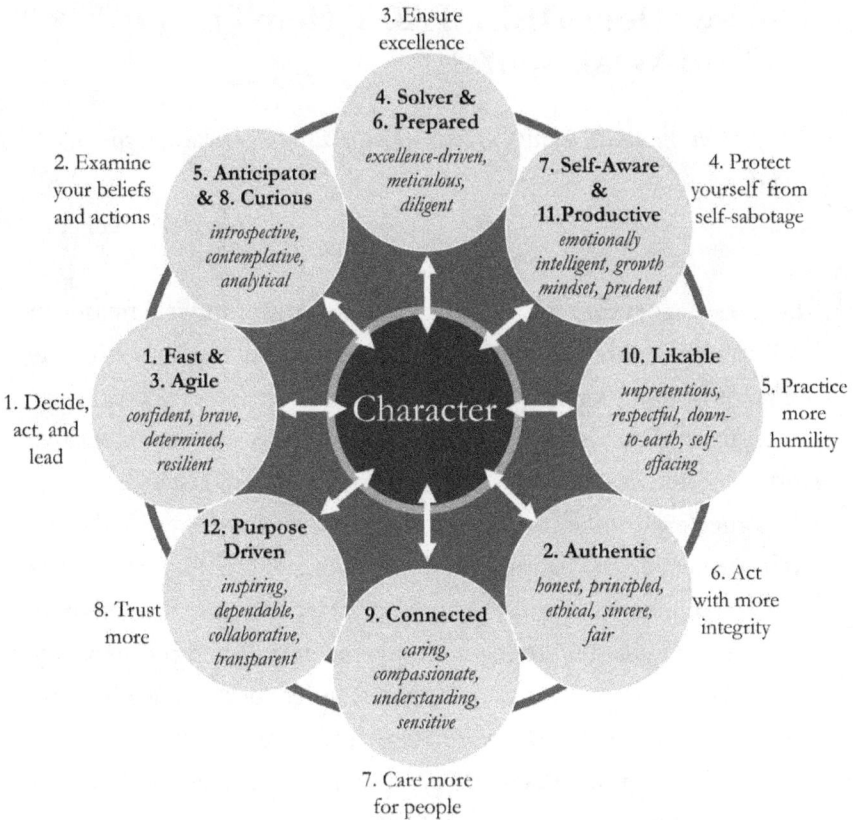

*DEEP PACT in motion: eight principles, twelve traits,
one unshakable foundation—character.*

*(Each bold number within the circles represents a key character trait of great
leaders, while the outer ring links these traits to the eight DEEP PACT principles)*

Ultimately, DEEP PACT is not just a leadership framework; it is
a comprehensive approach to character development that ensures
lasting impact and success in all areas of life. This transformative leadership style enables us to leave a lasting legacy, much like the grandest
cathedrals, built not just for the present but for future generations to
benefit from and admire.

5.5 How Does DEEP PACT Help Fix Your Weak Spots?

Although the world is full of suffering, it is also full of the overcoming of it.

—Helen Keller

The latest leadership literature highlights common weaknesses in leaders, often rooted in outdated practices that don't align with the demands of today's workplace. Addressing these issues is crucial for leaders to navigate the complexities of the modern world, foster positive work environments, and drive sustainable success. For instance, leaders who struggle with adaptability may find it challenging to respond effectively to unexpected changes, hindering their team's ability to innovate and stay competitive. Similarly, micromanagement can stifle creativity and autonomy, leading to lower employee morale and productivity, while a lack of empathy can create a disconnect between leaders and their teams, resulting in decreased trust and engagement.

DEEP PACT principles offer a comprehensive framework to address these flaws, as presented in Table 2 below.

Table 2: How DEEP PACT Helps Fix Your Weak Spots

Principle 1. Decide, act, and lead without waiting for approval helps overcome the following weak spots of leaders:	
Fear of taking risk	Encourages leaders to take initiative and make bold decisions without waiting for approval, fostering a culture of innovation and rapid integration of technology into business operations.
Indecisiveness	Promotes decisive action and self-reliance, reducing delays and increasing confidence in decision-making processes.

Dependency on authority	Empowers mid-level managers and leaders to act independently and confidently, reducing overreliance on higher-ups and fostering a sense of autonomy.
Inability to inspire	Empowers leaders to inspire others through decisive and independent actions.

Principle 2. Examine your beliefs and actions more than others think wise helps overcome the following weak spots of leaders:

Lack of self-awareness	Promotes continuous self-reflection and assessment, helping leaders understand their strengths, weaknesses, and areas for improvement.
Lack of adaptability	Encourages leaders to regularly evaluate and adapt their beliefs and actions, making them more open to change and new ideas.
Bias and prejudice	Fosters critical self-examination, helping leaders identify and overcome personal biases and prejudices.
Ignoring feedback	Encourages leaders to seek and integrate feedback into their actions and beliefs.

Principle 3. Ensure excellence more than others think imaginable helps overcome the following weak spots of leaders:

Complacency	Drives leaders to strive for high standards and continuous improvement, preventing stagnation and fostering a culture of excellence.
Inattention to detail	Promotes thoroughness and precision, ensuring that all aspects of work meet high standards of excellence.
Failure to foster innovation	Drives leaders to continuously pursue excellence and foster a culture of innovation.
Poor communication skills	Promotes high standards in communication and clarity in leadership.

Principle 4. Protect yourself from self-sabotage more than others think necessary helps overcome the following weak spots of leaders:

Fixed mindset	Helps leaders recognize and challenge negative thought patterns and self-serving behaviors, fostering a positive mindset and boosting self-confidence.
Inadequate delegation	Promotes trust in others and effective delegation to prevent burnout and inefficiency.
Overemphasis on short-term results	Encourages long-term thinking and resilience against short-term pressures.

Principle 5. Practice more humility than others think possible helps overcome the following weak spots of leaders:

Ego/arrogance	Fosters a culture of humility, allowing leaders to remain grounded, open to feedback, and respectful toward others' perspectives.
Poor listening skills	Promotes active listening and valuing others' perspectives, enhancing communication and collaboration.
Overconfidence	Encourages humility and self-awareness, helping leaders balance confidence with a realistic understanding of their limitations.
Inadequate digital literacy	Encourages continuous learning and adopting new digital tools and technologies.

Principle 6. Act with more integrity than others think prudent helps overcome the following weak spots of leaders:

Ethical lapses	Instills a strong ethical framework, guiding leaders to make principled decisions even in challenging situations.
Manipulative behavior	Encourages honesty and ethical behavior, fostering trust and respect within the team.
Lack of accountability	Promotes integrity and accountability in leadership roles.

Principle 7. Care more for people than others think reasonable helps overcome the following weak spots of leaders:

Lack of empathy	Encourages leaders to prioritize the well-being and needs of their team, fostering a supportive and compassionate work environment.
Disregard for work-life integration	Promotes a caring attitude toward employees' personal lives, helping to create a balanced, integrated, and supportive work environment.
Lack of inclusivity	Encourages caring and inclusive behavior toward all team members.
Ignoring mental health	Promotes caring for the mental health and well-being of the team.

Principle 8. Trust more than others think logical helps overcome the following weak spots of leaders:

Micro-management	Promotes trust in employees' abilities and autonomy, reducing the need for excessive control and fostering a sense of ownership and empowerment.
Lack of delegation	Encourages leaders to delegate effectively, trusting their team to take on responsibilities and make decisions.
Inability to develop others	Reduces the tendency to overcontrol by fostering trust and empowering team members to take initiative.

5.6 How DEEP PACT Can Protect You from Common Mistakes

Uneasy lies the head that wears a crown.

—William Shakespeare

Leaders fail. Startups fail even faster. Companies collapse, sometimes overnight. The landscape of leadership and business is riddled with failure, and the numbers are staggering. A 2023 *Forbes* article, citing research from the Corporate Executive Board (CEB), now part of Gartner Inc., reports that 60% of new leaders fail within their first 24 months. Even seasoned executives are not immune; 40% of externally hired executives fail within 18 months.

At the heart of many of these failures lies a critical factor: the role of the manager. Managers are not just operational enablers—they are culture-setters, motivators, and the connective tissue between leadership vision and team execution. When a transitioning leader struggles, their direct reports perform 15% worse, on average, than those reporting to high-performing managers. The struggling leader's team members are also 20% more likely to leave or become disengaged, according to Gartner research. As the saying goes, *"People don't leave bad companies—they leave bad managers."* These numbers highlight a harsh truth: success is never guaranteed, and a leader's failure ripples far beyond themselves, affecting a company's employees, culture, and overall performance.

Leadership is a privilege, but it comes with immense responsibility and pressure. Shakespeare's words—"Uneasy lies the head that wears a crown"—remind us that leadership is not just about holding power but about the weight of expectations, scrutiny of decisions, and the ever-present risk of failure. Many leaders rise to success through talent, vision, and hard work, but staying at the top requires more than skill—it demands vigilance, adaptability, and self-awareness. The true test of leadership is not reaching the summit but ensuring you don't stumble on the way down.

But why do once-successful leaders suddenly fail? The *MIT Sloan Management Review* article "Why Good Leaders Fail?" identifies derailment as a process, not a single event. Leaders often fail not because of incompetence but due to subtle shifts in behavior, an inability to adapt, or misalignment with their organization's evolving needs. The article highlights some of the biggest causes of leadership failure, including unchecked ego, resistance to feedback, and a lack of self-awareness. Many leaders, once celebrated for their success, fall victim to hubris, stagnation, or poor decision-making—often because they stop learning, stop listening, and stop evolving. Leadership is not a one-time achievement but a continuous journey of growth, adaptation, and self-examination. Those who fail to recognize this reality eventually find themselves replaced, outpaced, or irrelevant. The difference between those who thrive and those who fall is not just talent or vision. It is the ability to remain humble, adaptable, and relentlessly committed to learning.

To safeguard against failure, leaders must understand the most common leadership mistakes and recognize early warning signs. Awareness is the first step toward prevention—without it, even the most promising leaders risk falling into patterns that undermine credibility, trust, and effectiveness. Leadership is not just about decisiveness and strength but also about humility and resilience—the ability to course-correct before a misstep turns into a fall. By staying vigilant, intentional, and open to growth, leaders can avoid the fate of those who falter despite their initial success and sustain their impact for the long term.

This is where DEEP PACT offers a unique advantage. While many leadership models focus on growth and achievement, DEEP PACT also emphasizes protection from failure. It is not just about developing the right leadership qualities but also about fortifying yourself against the most common pitfalls that derail leaders.

The table below outlines the top 10 mistakes a leader makes and how each DEEP PACT principle serves as a safeguard, helping leaders stay resilient, adaptable, and successful in an ever-evolving world.

Table 3—Top 10 Mistakes Leaders Make and How
DEEP PACT Protects You from These Mistakes

Leadership Mistake	DEEP PACT Principle That Helps	How It Helps
1. Failing to develop future leaders	*Decide, act, and lead without waiting for approval.*	Taking decisive action to mentor and develop others ensures the continuity of strong leadership.
2. Neglecting effective communication	*Examine your beliefs and actions more than others think wise.*	Self-reflection helps leaders recognize communication gaps and adjust their approach.
3. Micromanaging employees	*Trust more than others think logical.*	Trusting employees fosters autonomy, reducing the need for micromanagement.
4. Avoiding difficult conversations	*Care more for people than others think reasonable.*	Caring for people involves having honest conversations that help them grow rather than avoiding issues.
5. Ignoring employee development	*Ensure excellence more than others think imaginable.*	Focusing on excellence means investing in employees' growth and long-term success.
6. Inconsistent and unethical behavior	*Act with more integrity than others think prudent.*	Consistency and integrity in leadership build trust and reliability among employees.
7. Resisting change	*Practice more humility than others think possible.*	Being open to change requires examining beliefs and embracing new ideas.
8. Lack of recognition and appreciation	*Care more for people than others think reasonable.*	Caring for employees includes recognizing their contributions and making them feel valued.

Leadership Mistake	DEEP PACT Principle That Helps	How It Helps
9. Overemphasis on short-term results	*Ensure excellence more than others think imaginable.*	A focus on excellence ensures a balance between immediate results and sustainable success.
10. Failing to address toxic leadership	*Protect yourself from self-sabotage more than others think necessary.*	Protecting against self-sabotage helps leaders recognize and eliminate toxic behaviors in them-selves and their teams.

5.7 A Special Note to Nonprofit Leaders

Volunteers do not necessarily have the time; they just have the heart.
—Elizabeth Andrew, US spiritual teacher

Leading a nonprofit or community organization of volunteers requires a unique approach—one that goes beyond traditional business practices and embraces the deeper motivations that inspire volunteerism. Volunteers are driven by a shared purpose and personal commitment rather than financial incentives. From my experience working with multiple community organizations and founding and leading one as a CEO, I have learned invaluable life lessons that shape effective volunteer leadership.

DEEP PACT Principle 5—*Practice more humility than others think possible*—should primarily guide all interactions with volunteers. This means recognizing that while you may hold a leadership role, fostering a spirit of equality and mutual respect is crucial. Volunteers need to feel valued, heard, and empowered. Humility in leadership opens the door for collaborative engagement and deepens trust, creating an environment where everyone feels included and motivated.

Furthermore, Principle 8—*Trust more than others think logical*—should be a dominating principle when working with volunteers. Trusting in others' capabilities and valuing their ideas over letting your ego take control are vital for maintaining harmony. Your role as a leader should focus on actively listening to and integrating others' suggestions to create a sense of collective ownership. This approach will keep the volunteer team intact and encourage a culture of shared leadership. Remember to always follow Principle 2—*Examine your beliefs and actions more than others think wise*—by examining your beliefs and actions to identify and remove biases or blind spots. This is especially important in the language you use, as subtle cues can greatly influence how people perceive their value within the team.

It is also essential to collaboratively define what excellence looks like in the context of our collective volunteer work, so that activities remain joyful and sustainable rather than stressful. Without a positive and fulfilling environment, volunteers may gradually withdraw.

Acknowledging the contributions of others regularly and putting the spotlight on their efforts will reinforce a positive dynamic. Nonprofit leaders should remember the wise words of US president Harry Truman: "It is amazing what you can accomplish if you do not care who gets the credit." This statement emphasizes the power of selfless teamwork and humility, suggesting that when individuals prioritize the greater good over personal recognition, they can achieve far more collectively than if they were focused on claiming credit for their contributions.

Finally, ensure that the highest standards of integrity are adhered to, especially when handling funds collected through public fundraising events. Treat the funds of the nonprofit with as much care as you would your own, ensuring transparency and accountability. This practice reinforces trust and credibility, which are indispensable to a successful volunteer organization.

5.8 Closing Reflections

The difference between what we are doing and what we are capable of doing would solve most of the world's problems.

—Mahatma Gandhi

In a world that is seeking new forms of leadership, DEEP PACT offers a transformative approach that is both visionary and practical. It challenges you to think beyond traditional boundaries and embrace a holistic and inclusive approach to leadership. By making a personal pact, you are not only committing yourself to your own growth and success but also to creating a positive impact on your organization and community. A pact to change is just the beginning; true transformation requires discipline and consistent effort. Leaders must approach these principles like a muscle that strengthens through daily practice and dedication.

Benjamin Franklin, one of America's most revered Founding Fathers, embarked on an extraordinary journey of self-improvement in his youth, driven by a fervent desire to build impeccable character. As a young boy, Franklin was keenly aware of his imperfections and sought a systematic approach to self-betterment. With meticulous care, he devised a plan centered around 13 virtues, each representing a pillar of moral excellence. Armed with a small book, Franklin created a chart to track his progress, dedicating each week to a specific virtue while maintaining vigilance over the others. Every night, he would reflect on his actions, marking his successes and shortcomings with a dot for each infraction, turning the process into an intense personal discipline of moral accountability.

Franklin faced the relentless challenge of adhering to his virtues amid the temptations and chaos of everyday life. Each week presented a new test, from the struggle to remain temperate at social gatherings to the effort to maintain silence and avoid frivolous chatter. The young Franklin's determination was unwavering, yet the journey was fraught with setbacks. His evenings of reflection often revealed a startling number of infractions, but instead of deterring him, these failures fueled his resolve. With the wisdom of a seasoned strategist, Franklin analyzed his shortcomings and adjusted his approach, determined to master his own nature. Over time, this rigorous practice of self-examination and disciplined effort forged a character of remarkable integrity and wisdom, setting the stage for his future as a leading statesman and thinker.

Franklin's childhood story is a testament to the fact that daily remembrance and practice are essential for internalizing and effectively applying any set of principles, such as the eight DEEP PACT principles. To truly unlock our leadership potential and achieve personal happiness and job satisfaction, we must first train our minds to believe in the value of these principles. Let us not forget that training is akin to sweeping the floor; cleaning it once does not ensure it will stay clean forever. Just as everyday dust and debris accumulate, so do the challenges and obstacles in our professional and personal lives. Training requires consistent attention and effort, much like maintaining a clean floor.

Each day brings fresh learning opportunities and areas for improvement, akin to the daily dust that needs sweeping away. By dedicating ourselves to continuous training and conscious practice, we sharpen and enhance our skills, ensuring that we remain effective and ready to face any challenge. This relentless commitment to practice keeps our minds and abilities in peak condition, enabling us to achieve our full potential. Just as a clean floor creates a welcoming environment, regular practice of these principles ingrains them in our behavior, allowing us to respond intuitively and effectively to various situations.

Ingraining these principles through daily practice not only reinforces our understanding but also equips us to handle the challenges that come our way each day. Consistent dedication to training and development ensures that we stay prepared, adaptable, and resilient, ready to lead with confidence and wisdom. Embrace the ongoing journey of growth and improvement, knowing that each step brings you closer to mastering the art of leadership and living a fulfilled life.

Practice like you've never won. Perform like you've never lost.

—Unknown

5.9 Daily Practice of Whole-Person Leadership

1. **Choose wisely.** Choose wisely, for your decisions shape the path of your life and profoundly impact those around you.

2. **Renew DEEP PACT.** Reflect on the DEEP PACT principles and choose one to apply today. Observe how it profoundly enhances your interactions and relationships.

3. **Stay focused.** Stay focused on your own path; do not be swayed by the limiting thoughts and doubts of others.

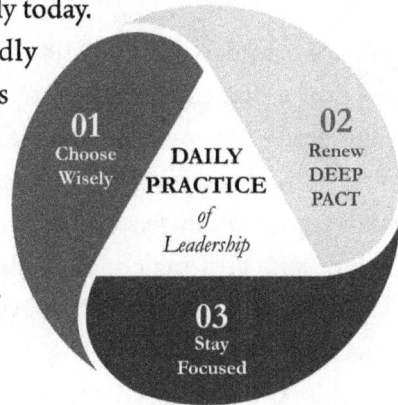

6 The AI Playbook of DEEP PACT

I think of AI as the most profound technology humanity is working on. More profound than fire, electricity, or anything that we have done in the past.

—Sundar Pichai,
chief executive officer, Google and Alphabet

Once considered a futuristic concept, artificial intelligence (AI) has now emerged as a transformative force, equipping leaders with unprecedented tools to enhance decision-making, drive innovation, and boost organizational success. In today's rapidly evolving business landscape, no leadership book is complete without a chapter on AI, despite growing concerns about its ethical and responsible use. Additionally, the rapid pace of AI advancement presents a significant challenge: what is cutting-edge today can become outdated in no time.

This AI playbook chapter is written acknowledging both of these challenges. It is designed to empower leaders with the knowledge, insight, and foresight needed to navigate AI's evolving landscape while upholding the values that define the DEEP PACT framework. As AI becomes deeply embedded in leadership and decision-making, the DEEP PACT principles take on an even greater significance.

Ethical leadership, a core tenet of DEEP PACT, is supported through AI's ability to monitor compliance, ensuring transparency and accountability. AI systems can detect ethical breaches, ensuring that practices like hiring or financial management align with the highest ethical standards. This reinforces a culture of integrity, crucial for modern leadership. Personalized learning programs, tailored through AI, foster continuous improvement and development, contributing to a culture of excellence, another core tenet of DEEP PACT. Caring leadership, rooted in Principle 7 of DEEP PACT, can be enhanced through AI by using sentiment analysis and employee well-being and feedback tools. Leaders can address concerns in real time, demonstrating empathy and creating an environment where employees feel supported.

The relationship between AI and the DEEP PACT framework is synergistic, with each mutually amplifying the other. AI enhances dynamic, ethical, excellence-driven, compassionate, and inclusive leadership, while DEEP PACT ensures that AI is leveraged responsibly and ethically to create a future-ready, high-performing, happy workforce.

Whether you are a CEO, mid-level manager, or aspiring leader—or simply seeking to improve your personal productivity—you have the power to integrate AI into your daily workflows, setting the pace for those around you. By elevating yourself and empowering those around you with ethical and responsible AI-driven strategies, you cultivate a leadership approach that fosters fulfillment and success—in work and in life.

6.1 The Ancient Origins of AI

Hephaestus, the famous crippled smith, had fashioned twenty tripods upon wheels, and these could move of themselves into the assembly of the gods and back again, marvels to look upon.

—Homer, *The Iliad*

The concept of artificial intelligence or AI-like entities has roots that stretch back to the earliest mythologies, reflecting humanity's enduring fascination with creating intelligent, autonomous beings. Around 1500 BCE, in Hindu mythology, the epic *Mahabharata* describes divine weapons like the *Brahmastra*, which functioned with precision and intelligence, targeting enemies based on preset conditions—much like an early vision of smart weapons. Similarly, in Greek mythology (circa 700 BCE, as documented in Hesiod's *Theogony*), the god Hephaestus created self-operating machines, including Talos, a giant bronze automaton programmed to defend Crete by patrolling its shores. Hephaestus also fashioned mechanical golden handmaidens capable of independent movement and intelligence, foreshadowing later concepts of humanoid robots and AI-driven assistants.

By the third century BCE, stories of artificial life were expanding into broader mythologies. The Pygmalion myth, first recorded in Ovid's *Metamorphoses* (8 CE, Roman mythology), tells of a sculptor whose statue, Galatea, is brought to life by divine intervention—reminiscent of modern AI's quest to create lifelike machines. Meanwhile, Chinese legends from the fourth century BCE, particularly in the writings of Liezi of Yan Shi, an engineer who allegedly built an automaton so lifelike it could sing and dance, astounding the Zhou king.

These myths, spanning thousands of years, reveal that the idea of AI is not a modern invention but a timeless aspiration, deeply embedded in the human imagination. The myths remind us that the pursuit of creating intelligent machines is as old as civilization itself, reflecting our innate desire to push the boundaries of what is possible.

6.2 AI Today: A Spectrum of Intelligence

Artificial intelligence, deep learning, machine learning—whatever you're doing, if you don't understand it, learn it. Because otherwise, you're going to be a dinosaur within three years.

—Marc Cuban

Today, AI is no myth. It spans a spectrum of technologies, each building on the last to create increasingly sophisticated systems. At its core, AI mimics human intelligence, enabling machines to reason, learn, and solve problems. This spectrum ranges from simple rule-based systems to advanced concepts like Generative AI, Large Language Models, and the futuristic vision of Artificial General Intelligence, as summarized below.

1. **Rule-based AI:** Operates on predefined rules (e.g., a thermostat adjusting temperature). Effective for narrow tasks but lacks adaptability.

2. **Machine learning (ML):** Learns from data to make predictions or decisions (e.g., Netflix recommendations). Improves over time with more data.

3. **Deep learning (DL).** Uses deep neural networks (DNNs) to model complex patterns in unstructured data like images, audio, and text (e.g., facial recognition, self-driving cars). DL now powers the most advanced vision and speech systems, from autonomous vehicles to real-time translation apps.

4. **Generative AI.** Creates new content, such as images, music, or text (e.g., DALL-E for images, ChatGPT and DeepSeek for text). Tools like Midjourney for visual art and Suno for music generation are transforming creative industries.

5. **Large language models (LLMs).** A subset of generative AI, LLMs like GPT-4, Claude 3 (Anthropic), and Gemini 1.5 (Google DeepMind) master human language, enabling tasks like translation, summarization, and creative writing. These models now support advanced reasoning, multi-modal input (text + image + audio), and real-time interaction.

6. **Artificial general intelligence (AGI).** A theoretical system with humanlike intelligence, capable of reasoning and learning across any domain. Represents the future frontier of AI. While no system today fully meets the criteria for AGI, top labs—including OpenAI, DeepMind, and Anthropic—are actively exploring its boundaries.

7. **Beyond AGI.** The concept of **superintelligence**—AI surpassing human intelligence—raises ethical questions about control, safety, and humanity's role in an AI-dominated world. Global discussions are underway regarding AI governance, risk mitigation, and ensuring beneficial outcomes for all.

6.3 Tread Carefully: Navigating AI's Promise and Peril

O, it is excellent
To have a giant's strength; but it is tyrannous
To use it like a giant.

—William Shakespeare

While the promise of AI is immense, its implementation must be approached with caution and responsibility. AI is meant to augment human intelligence, not replace it. However, as organizations rush to integrate AI, failing to address psychological barriers and ethical concerns can lead to unintended resistance and negative consequences. A 2025 *Harvard Business Review* article by Professor Julian De Freitas revealed that many resist AI due to perceptions that it is "too opaque, emotionless, rigid, and independent, and that interacting with humans is far more preferable." If these concerns are not properly addressed, efforts to increase AI adoption may backfire, deepening skepticism rather than fostering trust. Transparency, explainability, and human-centered design must be at the core of any AI adoption strategy.

Popular culture has long fueled a man-versus-machine narrative, portraying AI as a threat to humanity rather than a tool for progress. From HAL 9000 in *2001: A Space Odyssey* to Skynet in *The Terminator*, films have depicted AI as an entity that inevitably turns against its creators. Most recently, the 2023 film *The Creator* echoed this fear with its ominous warning: "We should never have let AI out of the box."

These stories resonate with growing real-world concerns, as leading scientists and tech pioneers have issued urgent warnings about AI's risks, urging against unchecked development. Yet, despite the cautionary tales and calls for restraint, AI is already out of the box, permanently reshaping our world in ways we must now learn to navigate responsibly. AI is neither a shortcut to success nor an automatic disruptor; its impact depends on how it is integrated and governed. Leaders must ensure that AI enhances human creativity, decision-making, and well-being, rather than merely driving efficiency at the expense of trust and ethical responsibility. The road to AI-driven transformation is not just about progress—it is about progress done right.

6.4 Facts, Fears, Trust, and Transparency

The superior man is modest in his speech but exceeds in his actions.
—Confucius

AI's current and potential impact on the workforce is often met with anxiety and uncertainty, particularly regarding job displacement. While these concerns are valid, historical trends show that while technological advancements do eliminate jobs, they also create new ones. Studies indicate that approximately 60% of the jobs available in 2018 did not exist in 1940, underscoring the constantly evolving job market. Similarly, as AI reshapes industries today, it is not merely eliminating positions—it is transforming roles, generating new career paths, and shifting the nature of work itself. Looking ahead, the World Economic Forum's *Future of Jobs Report 2025* predicts that while AI and automation may displace 9 million jobs by 2030, they will simultaneously create 11 million new roles—roles designed to leverage human creativity, problem-solving, and collaboration alongside AI systems.

To ease concerns and build trust, leaders must go beyond simply implementing AI. They must communicate and clarify with empathy and care the data and plans behind AI-driven change. The DEEP PACT Principle 7—*Care more for people than others think reasonable*—calls for a dedicated effort to ensure that AI-driven changes prioritize employee well-being, inclusion, and long-term career growth; Principle 6—*Act with more integrity than others think prudent*—calls for transparency, fairness, and ethical decision-making to build trust and accountability in AI implementation.

Unchecked AI systems can introduce bias, privacy concerns, and unintended consequences that may undermine trust among employees and customers. Leaders must ensure that AI operates transparently, fairly, and in alignment with the organization's ethical principles and values. This includes establishing AI ethics committees, conducting bias audits, and educating teams on responsible AI use. Employees need to understand the impact AI will have on their roles and how they can upskill to remain competitive. By providing transparency, education, and reskilling opportunities, organizations can empower their workforce, ensuring that AI is perceived not as a threat but as a catalyst for growth and opportunity.

6.5 AI—The Competitive Edge

AI is not just a tool or a fad. It is a game-changer that enhances decision-making, accelerates efficiency, and unlocks unprecedented growth. In 2017, JPMorgan Chase introduced COIN (Contract Intelligence), an AI-driven system that automated commercial loan reviews, saving 360,000 hours of manual labor annually. This allowed legal teams to shift their focus to high-value strategic work, demonstrating that AI's true power is not merely automation but workforce optimization.

DeepMind's AlphaFold2, a revolutionary AI-driven protein structure predictor, has transformed drug discovery by enabling researchers to synthesize a potential treatment for hepatocellular carcinoma—the most common type of liver cancer—in just 30 days, a process that would typically take up to 10 years. This breakthrough not only showcases AI's ability to accelerate medical advancements but also paves the way for a future where life-saving treatments can be developed in weeks rather than decades.

At Jindal Steel & Power, AI-driven market analysis led to a market capitalization surge from $750 million to over $12 billion in just four years. In the entertainment industry, Netflix employs AI-powered recommendation systems, with 80% of viewed content discovered through its algorithms. This has not only enhanced user engagement but also saved the company over $1 billion annually by boosting customer retention and reducing churn. AI is not a trend. It is the key to staying competitive in an increasingly digital world.

6.6 AI in Action: Efficiency, Job Satisfaction, Growth

AI is revolutionizing not only business processes but the workforce itself. Companies like Chipotle Mexican Grill have leveraged AI to streamline hiring, using the AI-powered assistant Ava Cado to increase job application completion rates to over 85% and reduce hiring time from 12 days to just four days. AI is also playing a crucial role in reducing bias in recruitment. A study by LinkedIn Talent Solutions found that 68% of recruiters believe AI helps eliminate unconscious bias, resulting in more diverse and inclusive workplaces.

Beyond hiring, AI is enhancing employee experience and satisfaction. A Salesforce survey found that 89% of employees felt automation made their jobs more fulfilling, while 91% reported improved work-life balance due to AI-driven efficiency. This underscores a critical insight: AI is not just about business growth. It is about empowering people to work smarter and with greater purpose.

The future of leadership is no longer about keeping up with AI; it is about leading with it.

For companies that hesitate, the risk of falling behind is real. Deloitte reports that organizations integrating AI in knowledge-based work have already seen cost reductions of up to 20% in areas such as document processing, customer service, and data analysis. A McKinsey study estimates that AI could automate up to 25% of knowledge worker tasks, leading to a 20 to 30% increase in productivity in fields like finance, marketing, and IT. The acceleration is clear: a 2024 Accenture report found that companies with fully AI-integrated operations achieved 2.5 times higher revenue growth compared to their peers.

6.7 The Changed Workplace

AI will not replace managers, but managers who use AI will replace those who don't.
—Erik Brynjolfsson, AI researcher, Stanford University

As Generation Z and Millennials become increasingly dominant in the workforce, leaders must align with their values. These generations prioritize social responsibility, career development, and technology integration while expecting flexibility and well-being in the workplace. Companies that fail to meet these expectations risk losing top talent to AI-savvy competitors.

The rise of remote and hybrid work is further redefining leadership. According to a Gartner survey, 64% of employees are more likely to choose a job with flexible work options over one without them. Companies like Automattic have fully embraced AI-powered collaboration tools, such as Slack AI and Notion, to maintain seamless global communication among employees spread across 90 countries. Leaders must transition from traditional decision-makers to facilitators of AI-driven insights, making faster, smarter, and more strategic choices.

The future of leadership is no longer about keeping up with AI; it is about leading with it. Those who embrace AI not just to survive but to innovate will emerge as the visionaries of tomorrow. The question is no longer if AI should be integrated, but how quickly leaders can leverage it to shape the future.

6.8 A Growing Leadership Crisis

Leadership today demands strategic thinking, yet many leaders struggle to find the time for it. A *Harvard Business Review* study, based on a survey of 10,000 senior leaders conducted by the Management Research Group, found that 97% of executives identified strategic thinking as the most critical leadership behavior for their organization's future success. Despite recognizing its importance, many leaders have little time to engage in high-level, forward-thinking decision-making, as their days are often consumed by operational tasks: endless meetings, emails, distractions, and urgent demands.

Research shows that executives' time is often consumed by administrative and operational tasks, leaving limited room for strategic planning and innovation. Many executives report that they struggle to dedicate adequate time to long-term strategic thinking, with most admitting they are often caught in daily firefighting.

The result? A leadership crisis where reactive decision-making replaces strategic foresight. This relentless busyness doesn't just impact work—it spills over into personal life, compromising what matters most: quality time with family, health, and overall happiness. Leaders need a way to reclaim their time—a solution that allows them to focus on what truly matters. AI, when used as a thought partner, provides that solution.

6.9 Make AI Your Thought Partner

If you see AI as just another Google or a tool for writing better emails, you're selling yourself short. It can be a strategic Thought Partner, ready 24/7 to help you make faster, smarter decisions.

—Geoff Woods

In *The AI-Driven Leader*, Geoff Woods argues that leaders must shift their mindset when it comes to AI and embrace AI as a strategic thought partner to free up valuable time. A strategic thought partner is more than just an assistant—it is a trusted advisor that challenges your thinking, expands your perspective, and enhances decision-making. Traditionally, executives and leaders have relied on mentors, coaches, or advisory teams for strategic insight. Now AI can serve a similar role, offering data-driven recommendations, predictive insights, and real-time analysis to help leaders make smarter, more informed decisions quickly. But to fully embrace AI as a thought partner, leaders must shift their mindset from viewing AI as just a productivity tool to recognizing it as a collaborator that enhances strategic thinking.

Instead of asking, *How do I solve this problem?* a more effective question is, *How can AI help me solve this problem?* This small yet fundamental shift in perspective changes how leaders engage with AI. Rather than relying solely on human effort for every decision, drafting reports, or manually analyzing data, AI can accelerate processes, uncover deeper insights, and enhance strategic thinking. Woods suggests an **interactive approach** where leaders use AI to interview it one question at a time when facing complex decisions. This method helps leaders identify blind spots they might otherwise overlook. Additionally, AI can process large volumes of data to detect patterns and trends—work that would typically take hours, if not days, to complete manually.

To make AI an effective thought partner, start by asking AI the right questions—not just seeking quick answers, but using AI to challenge your assumptions and explore different viewpoints. Use AI to assist you in self-reflection, identifying gaps in logic, suggesting alternatives, and analyzing historical patterns to refine decision-making. However, AI alone is not enough. The most successful leaders will adopt a hybrid approach, combining AI-driven insights with human intuition, experience, and ethical judgment to ensure balanced, people-centered decisions. Research shows that AI-generated document drafts can complete 50 to 60% of the work toward a finished product, saving leaders a substantial amount of their time.

For nonprofit leaders and community organizers, this is a game-changer, as they often struggle with limited resources and time constraints. AI can streamline messaging, vision-setting, and strategic planning, allowing them to focus on mission-driven impact. The leaders who thrive in the AI era will be those who continuously ask, *How might AI help me do this better?* and refine their approach to extract maximum value from AI. AI is not just a tool—it is a strategic ally, a thought partner that enables leaders to operate with greater clarity, efficiency, and impact. Those who embrace AI as a leadership multiplier will not only stay ahead of the curve but also inspire innovation, drive smarter decision-making, and shape the future of leadership.

6.10 From Thought Partnership to Co-Intelligence

Wharton professor Ethan Mollick, in his 2024 book *Co-Intelligence: Living and Working with AI*, takes us beyond the concept of a strategic thought partner, presenting a vision of AI as an active collaborator that enhances human creativity, decision-making, and problem-solving through a dynamic and synergistic relationship. He outlines four essential principles for knowledge workers:

- ◈ *"Always invite AI to the table,"* encouraging the integration of AI in all projects.
- ◈ *"Be the human in the loop,"* stressing the importance of human oversight to prevent AI errors.
- ◈ *"Treat AI like a person,"* viewing it as an intelligent yet inexperienced intern needing guidance.
- ◈ *"Assume this is the worst AI you will use,"* preparing for future advancements.

These principles provide a clear and actionable framework for integrating AI into the workplace without compromising human judgment, ethics, or innovation. Those who embrace this collaborative intelligence approach will not only stay ahead of technological shifts but also redefine the future of work—one where AI and human ingenuity thrive side by side.

6.11 Co-Intelligence and the Magic of Smart Prompts

The role of a leader is not to have all the answers, but to ask the right questions—AI helps us ask better ones.
                    —Satya Nadella, chief executive officer, Microsoft

The effectiveness of co-intelligence—the collaboration between humans and AI—depends heavily on the quality of the prompts you provide to tools like ChatGPT or DeepSeek, because the precision of your input directly shapes the relevance and depth of AI-generated responses. A smart prompt is one that is clear, specific, and context-rich, guiding the AI to generate more insightful, relevant, and actionable responses. In his book *The AI-Driven Leader,* Geoff Woods emphasizes that the key to unlocking AI's potential lies in how you frame your questions. He advises that rather than simply requesting information, leaders should use AI to challenge their thinking, communicate back and forth, explore alternative perspectives, and uncover blind spots. Smart prompts encourage AI to think critically, structure responses effectively, and provide richer insights, transforming it from a basic tool into a strategic advisor.

To experience this firsthand, try testing some of the examples below. Enter both a weak prompt and a smart prompt into an AI tool and compare the responses. You'll quickly see how a well-crafted question (smart prompt) leads to more precise, actionable, and insightful answers, in contrast to a weak prompt, which is likely to produce a vague, generic, and overly voluminous response that may lack depth or feel overwhelming. Mastering smart prompts is like learning a new language—one that, when used correctly, can turn AI into an invaluable leadership asset.

Weak Prompt: Tell me about leadership.
Smart Prompt: What are the top five leadership strategies used by CEOs of Fortune 500 companies, and how can a mid-level manager apply them effectively?

Weak Prompt: How do I think strategically?
Smart Prompt 1: I'm a mid-level manager in a retail company facing increased competition from e-commerce platforms. What are three strategic initiatives I can propose to leadership to help our brick-and-mortar stores stay competitive, and how can I present these ideas effectively?
Smart Prompt 2: I'm a knowledge worker in a fast-paced consulting firm, often juggling multiple projects and client demands. What are three proven strategic thinking techniques I can use to

anticipate industry trends, provide higher-value insights to clients, and position myself as a thought leader within my organization?

Weak Prompt: How do I communicate better?
Smart Prompt: I need to deliver a difficult message to my team about upcoming layoffs due to budget cuts. How can I communicate this transparently while maintaining trust and morale? Provide a sample script and key talking points.

Weak Prompt: To remain competitive in my work, I need to launch a new product. What advice can you give me?
Smart Prompt: I am brainstorming ideas for a new product. I would like you to act as a board member with expertise in product positioning to help me come up with a product concept that will be successful in the market. Interview me and ask me one question at a time based on my responses to help me clarify the need of my customers, the gaps that exist in the market today, and how this product will give us a competitive edge. Once you have all the information a board member may require to approve a plan, generate some potential product ideas.

Weak Prompt: How do I show empathy as a leader?
Smart Prompt: One of my team members is struggling with burnout after working long hours on a high-pressure project. How can I show empathy while also ensuring the project stays on track?

Weak Prompt: How do I become an effective leader?
Smart Prompt: As a new leader in a tech startup, how can I balance fostering innovation with maintaining accountability among my team? Provide three actionable strategies.

Weak Prompt: How can I improve my decision-making?
Smart Prompt: Give me a structured framework for improving decision-making, including practical examples of how top executives use data and intuition to make better choices.

Weak Prompt: How can I be more transparent?
Smart Prompt: My team has expressed concerns about a lack of communication regarding recent organizational changes. How can I improve transparency while maintaining confidentiality about sensitive information? Provide a step-by-step approach.

Weak Prompt: I run a small e-commerce business selling eco-friendly products. How can I grow my business?
Smart Prompt: I run a small e-commerce business selling eco-friendly products. My target audience is Millennials. What are three actionable strategies to increase online sales by 20% in the next six months, and how can I measure their success?

Weak Prompt: Write a blog post for small business owners, explaining how AI can streamline customer service.
Smart Prompt: Write a 500-word blog post aimed at small business owners, explaining how AI can streamline customer service. Use a conversational tone, include three real-world examples, and end with a call-to-action encouraging readers to explore AI tools for their own businesses.

Weak Prompt: How do I help my team embrace change?
Smart Prompt: What are the key psychological barriers to organizational change, and how can I, as a leader, proactively address them to drive a smooth transition?

Weak Prompt: What is the future of AI?
Smart Prompt: Provide three evidence-based predictions about AI's impact on leadership in the next decade, referencing recent studies and expert opinions.

The difference is clear: Smart prompts provide context, specify the type of response desired, and push AI toward producing more valuable insights. By framing AI interactions strategically, leaders can use it for scenario planning, brainstorming, and high-level decision-making.

6.12 MELDS—An Innovative Approach for AI Implementation

To successfully implement AI and harness its potential, leaders should explore various frameworks that guide its integration into organizations. One such approach is MELDS—mindset, experimentation, leadership, data, and skills—introduced in *Human + Machine* by Paul R. Daugherty and H. James Wilson. This framework is built on the premise that AI is not merely a tool but a transformative force that demands a shift in how organizations think, operate, and innovate. While MELDS provides one perspective on AI adoption, leaders must critically assess its principles alongside other strategies to determine what best aligns with their organizational needs and ethical considerations.

The first and most critical pillar of MELDS is *mindset*. Leaders must move beyond viewing AI as a mere automation tool and instead embrace it as a co-intelligence partner that enhances human capabilities. This shift requires fostering a culture of curiosity, adaptability, and collaboration, where AI is not a replacement for workers, but a tool to elevate their potential. The next pillar, experimentation, involves structured experimentation, starting with small pilots, with the intent to learn because organizations cannot afford to wait for a perfect AI solution. Companies that experiment boldly gain a competitive edge, while those that hesitate risk being left behind. *Leadership*, the third pillar, requires that CEOs make a commitment from the very beginning to the responsible use of AI in their organization with due consideration to the ethical, moral, and legal dimensions of AI technologies. CEOs also should avoid delegating the responsibility solely to CIOs because the stakes are too high. The fourth pillar of MELDS is *data*, the lifeblood of AI. Without clean, reliable, and well-structured data, even the most advanced AI models will fail. Organizations must invest in data integrity, governance, and accessibility to maximize AI's impact. *Skills*, which determine whether AI will drive growth or stagnation, is the fifth and final pillar. AI-driven workplaces require continuous learning, upskilling, and adaptability, where employees are equipped to collaborate with AI rather than fear it. The MELDS framework is more than just a strategy—it is a call to action. Organizations that embrace it will not only implement AI successfully but also redefine leadership, drive innovation, and shape the future of work with intelligence, agility, and purpose.

The MELDS framework and the DEEP PACT principles of whole-person leadership share a common foundation, both championing the integration of AI with human-centered leadership. At the heart of MELDS is the idea that AI should augment human capabilities, not replace them—a philosophy that aligns seamlessly with DEEP PACT's emphasis on purpose, meaning, care, empathy, and continuous growth. Together, MELDS and DEEP PACT provide a holistic approach to AI-driven leadership, ensuring that AI adoption is about not just efficiency but also elevating human potential, strengthening integrity, and driving purpose-driven success.

6.13 Five Focus Areas of Effective AI-Augmented Leadership

Artificial intelligence is not a substitute for human intelligence; it is a tool to amplify human creativity and ingenuity.

—Fei-Fei Li, codirector,
Stanford Institute for Human-Centered AI

The literature on AI and its applications is booming, offering theoretical insights and practical strategies for leveraging this transformative technology. However, rather than diving into exhaustive details, this section provides key ideas and general guidelines, along with examples, to help you develop a structured framework for AI implementation in your workplace.

AI adoption is not solely the responsibility of CEOs. Leaders at all levels of an organization play a crucial role in driving and overseeing AI initiatives. By leveraging sound leadership practices—such as strategic communication, cross-functional collaboration, and a focus on impact—they can influence key decision-makers, including the CIO or CEO, to ensure AI is implemented strategically and responsibly.

To succeed in the AI era, leaders must pay attention to five core focus areas that integrate AI into decision-making, leadership strategies, and workforce development. These are not just isolated actions but fundamental leadership priorities that collectively enable organizations to harness AI's potential while maintaining a human-centric approach. These focus areas, along with action statements, are as follows:

1. **AI-augmented decision-making.** Leverage AI for data-driven, predictive insights to enhance strategic choices.
2. **Agile and adaptive leadership.** Cultivate flexibility and resilience to navigate an AI-driven world.

3. **Ethical AI governance.** Ensure responsible AI adoption by addressing biases and maintaining transparency.
4. **Empathy and human-centric leadership.** Balance AI integration with emotional intelligence and human connection.
5. **Continuous learning and AI literacy.** Equip yourself and your teams with AI fluency to stay future-ready.

Each of these actions is essential for thriving in an AI-driven world as elaborated further below. The AI tools mentioned in this book are provided as examples only and are not recommendations or endorsements. These tools may not be suitable for all organizations, industries, or circumstances. AI technology evolves at an extraordinarily rapid pace, with existing tools being continuously upgraded, replaced, or outperformed by newer innovations. A truly AI-savvy leader should actively explore emerging tools, stay informed about the latest advancements, and engage their colleagues and teams in researching and evaluating AI solutions to determine their appropriateness for specific business needs. Leaders should exercise due diligence and consider factors such as security, scalability, ethical implications, and compatibility before adopting any AI technology.

Focus Area 1: AI-Augmented Decision-Making

AI enables leaders to shift from intuition-based decision-making to data-driven precision, offering real-time analytics, predictive modeling, and automation that allow them to anticipate challenges and seize opportunities before they arise.

Actionable Strategies for Leaders

⟡ *Integrate AI tools into decision-making* (e.g., IBM Watson for AI-powered business insights, ChatGPT for language-based analytics, Microsoft Copilot for productivity augmentation).

❖ *Adopt a hybrid approach,* balancing AI-driven insights with human intuition.

❖ *Develop AI literacy* to interpret AI-generated reports accurately (e.g., Google Cloud AutoML for understanding machine learning predictions).

❖ *Leverage AI analytics tools* (e.g., Power BI, Tableau, or Google Analytics for data visualization, business analytics, and trend analysis).

❖ *Collaborate with AI experts* to understand how AI-generated insights apply to your team.

❖ *Implement AI-driven efficiency improvements* such as automated scheduling, workflow optimization, and trend analysis (e.g., Monday.com for workflow automation, Notion AI for smart task organization).

Focus Area 2: Agile and Adaptive Leadership

The traditional hierarchical leadership model is fading as AI-driven workplaces demand agility, adaptability, and innovation.

Actionable Strategies for Leaders

❖ *Encourage experimentation.* AI thrives on iteration and learning (e.g., Google's AI Test Kitchen for AI experimentation).

❖ *Decentralize decision-making.* Empower teams to act autonomously with AI support (e.g., Microsoft Viva for AI-enhanced team autonomy).

❖ *Adopt flexible work models.* Use AI collaboration tools (e.g., Trello for task management, Zoom AI for meeting summaries and assistance, Otter.ai for real-time transcription and automated summaries, Asana for workflow automation and project management).

❖ *Facilitate cross-functional collaboration* with AI and digital transformation teams (e.g., Miro for AI-powered brainstorming and whiteboarding).

❖ *Automate repetitive tasks* to free up time for strategic initiatives (e.g., UiPath for robotic process automation, Zapier for AI-driven workflow integration).

❖ *Stay open to AI-driven processes and encourage a culture of innovation.*

Focus Area 3: Ethical AI Governance

With AI's immense power comes ethical responsibility. Leaders must ensure that AI is transparent, equitable, and free from bias to maintain trust and credibility.

Actionable Strategies for Leaders

❖ *Establish AI ethics committees* (e.g., Google's AI Ethics Board for corporate AI governance).

❖ *Implement transparency policies* (e.g., IBM OpenScale for AI fairness monitoring and explainability).

❖ *Educate employees on responsible AI use and bias detection* (e.g., OpenAI's AI Ethics Curriculum for responsible AI education).

❖ *Advocate for AI transparency.* Ask vendors about AI decision-making processes (e.g., explainable AI tools in AWS and Google Cloud).

◈ *Proactively conduct AI audits* to ensure fairness and compliance (e.g., AI Fairness 360 by IBM for bias detection in AI models).

◈ *Stay informed on AI ethics* by following regulatory updates and corporate responsibility guidelines (e.g., EU AI Act and AI policy frameworks by the World Economic Forum).

Focus Area 4: Empathy and Human-Centric Leadership

While AI excels in automation and analysis, it lacks human qualities such as empathy, creativity, and moral judgment—traits that will define exceptional leadership in the AI era.

Actionable Strategies for Leaders

◈ *Prioritize human connection* even in AI-driven environments.

◈ *Use AI-powered coaching tools* to enhance leadership development (e.g., BetterUp for AI-driven executive coaching).

◈ *Align AI adoption with purpose-driven leadership.* Ensure that AI enhances well-being (e.g., Replika AI for AI-driven mental well-being support).

◈ *Enhance communication using AI-driven feedback tools* (e.g., Humu for AI-powered behavioral coaching).

◈ *Ensure that AI complements (not replaces) human interactions* in hiring and team development (e.g., HireVue for AI-assisted recruitment while maintaining human oversight).

◈ *Develop active listening skills* to foster meaningful workplace relationships.

Focus Area 5: Continuous Learning and AI Literacy

As AI evolves, continuous learning and upskilling are essential for leaders and their teams to remain competitive.

Actionable Strategies for Leaders

- *Stay ahead of AI trends* by following AI thought leaders and industry updates (e.g., *MIT Technology Review*'s AI section, OpenAI Blog, DeepMind Research Papers).
- *Invest in team upskilling.* Encourage AI training programs for future readiness (e.g., Coursera's AI for Everyone by Andrew Ng, Udacity AI Nanodegree).
- *Foster an AI-curious mindset.* Promote a workplace culture that embraces AI-driven learning (e.g., LinkedIn Learning AI courses for professional development).
- *Take AI and digital transformation courses* to strengthen AI literacy (e.g., Harvard Online's AI in Business Strategy, Stanford AI for Leaders).
- *Engage in AI-focused leadership workshops* to stay ahead of emerging trends (e.g., World Economic Forum's AI Leadership Forum, Singularity University AI Summits).
- *Encourage AI upskilling initiatives within teams* to ensure long-term adaptability (e.g., Microsoft Learn AI Fundamentals, Google AI Training for businesses).

6.14 Navigating AI Risks: Dos and Don'ts

A knife cuts because it has a blade, but a wise man uses it to carve his path rather than wound himself.

—Ancient Chinese proverb

As AI becomes increasingly integrated into decision-making, leadership, and everyday business operations, it is critical to strike a balance between harnessing its benefits and mitigating its risks. While AI can enhance productivity, streamline workflows, and drive innovation, overreliance on it or misuse can lead to misinformation, bias, security vulnerabilities, and even ethical dilemmas. AI adoption, by leaders and employees alike, must always be approached with caution and responsibility.

Just as one would not remove guardrails from a dangerous road, leaders must not deploy AI recklessly, assuming it is infallible. AI is rapidly evolving, and its limitations are not always fully understood—making human expertise and judgment indispensable, especially when AI is used for creative, analytical, or decision-making work. This necessity aligns with DEEP PACT Principle 2—Examine Your Beliefs and Actions, urging leaders to critically assess their assumptions about AI's accuracy and risks, as summarized below.

1. AI Hallucinates

AI can hallucinate, meaning it can generate entirely false information while presenting it as fact. This is particularly concerning when AI provides survey statistics, research findings, or citations. Always verify AI's responses—ask it to confirm its own accuracy, provide sources, or explain its reasoning. If uncertainty remains, go directly to the original source and cross-check the information.

AI is not infallible. In 2018, an Uber self-driving car failed to recognize a pedestrian crossing the street, resulting in a fatal accident. On November 15, 2022, Meta, the parent company of Facebook, launched Galactica, an AI model intended to assist scientific research by summarizing academic papers. It was taken offline after just three days due to generating incorrect and biased content, which highlighted concerns about AI reliability in providing accurate scientific information.

Furthermore, AI's knowledge is time-bound—it is only up to date up to a certain period. Always ask AI about the recency of its knowledge, and verify any information beyond its training cut-off date. AI can also misinterpret information if analysis extends beyond its capabilities, further reinforcing the need for human oversight.

2. AI Has Limitations

A 2023 Boston Consulting Group (BCG) study, conducted in collaboration with Harvard Business School, serves as a prime example of AI's power and limitations. In this study, 758 consultants from BCG were assigned 18 different business-related tasks, ranging from creative and analytical problem-solving to strategic decision-making. When consultants used AI for tasks within its capabilities, they completed 12.2% more work, performed 25.1% faster, and produced over 40% higher-quality results. However, when assigned tasks that extended beyond AI's current technological frontier—such as highly complex reasoning or novel strategic insights—consultants relying on AI were 19 percentage points less likely to produce the correct solution. This contrast underscores a crucial lesson: AI should be used as a productivity enhancer, not as an absolute authority. Leaders must develop the discernment to know when to trust AI and when to rely on independent judgment.

3. Bias in AI: Questioning Assumptions

Bias in AI systems is no longer a theoretical concern—it's a documented reality with serious consequences. A US Department of Commerce study conducted by the National Institute of Standards and Technology (NIST) found that facial recognition software is significantly more likely to misidentify people of color than white individuals, raising alarm over its use in law enforcement where such errors could result in wrongful arrests. This concern is not hypothetical. Robert Williams, a Black man in Detroit, was wrongfully arrested in 2020 due to a faulty facial recognition match. Similarly, researchers at Georgia Tech discovered that self-driving cars using AI were less accurate at detecting pedestrians with darker skin tones, a potentially life-threatening flaw in autonomous navigation systems. In the financial sector, a University of

California, Berkeley study revealed that mortgage algorithms charged Black and Latino borrowers higher interest rates than white borrowers with similar financial profiles—costing these communities up to $500 million annually in extra interest. These examples reflect what the root of AI bias: flawed training data and systemic inequalities embedded into algorithmic design.

A commonly held belief is that AI can eliminate bias in recruitment, but this assumption should be critically examined. AI's ability to reduce bias depends entirely on how it is designed and trained. A University of Washington study found that some AI résumé screening tools favored white-associated names 85% of the time, reinforcing racial bias rather than mitigating it. However, other AI-driven hiring platforms have successfully reduced bias by anonymizing certain details, such as names, genders, and photos, ensuring that hiring decisions focus instead on skills and qualifications. Leaders must not blindly accept AI's promises but rather evaluate the specific ways in which AI is used to determine whether bias is actually being reduced or merely shifting in another form.

4. AI's Environmental and Ethical Cost

Beyond accuracy and bias, AI presents another often-overlooked risk: its environmental impact. The energy consumption of AI models is exponentially higher than traditional search engines. A single Google search consumes about 0.3 watt-hours of energy, whereas an AI-powered query on ChatGPT can consume 10 to 100 times more energy, depending on its complexity. Large-scale AI training requires massive computing power, contributing significantly to carbon emissions. Before using AI for trivial tasks, leaders should consider: Is this necessary? Could a simpler method suffice? AI should be used judiciously, with its environmental cost in mind.

5. *Confidentiality and Security Risks*

AI also poses serious risks to confidentiality and data privacy. Leaders must not share sensitive company information with AI tools, as AI platforms can store, process, or even inadvertently expose proprietary data. Similarly, customer privacy must be safeguarded. Organizations handling financial, healthcare, or personal data must ensure that AI does not compromise compliance with applicable regulations and data protection standards.

6.15 Closing Reflections

As we head down this road, it's time to discard outdated notions of humans versus machines and instead embrace an exciting new world of human and machine.

—Paul Daugherty and James Wilson,
authors, *Human + Machine*

Leaders must not outsource their thinking to AI. While AI can be an exceptional tool for brainstorming, data synthesis, and strategy formation, the final judgment must always remain human. AI is a thought partner, not a replacement for leadership. Leaders should use AI to enhance their decision-making, not to delegate responsibility to an algorithm. Critical thinking, ethical judgment, and leadership vision cannot—and should not—be automated.

By understanding these risks and applying principled, responsible leadership, organizations can harness AI's benefits while mitigating its downsides, ensuring that AI remains a tool for empowerment rather than a source of harm.

The future of leadership is not about resisting AI but about mastering its potential while upholding human-centered values. The question is no longer whether AI will change the landscape but whether leaders will harness its power with wisdom, adaptability, and ethical integrity—or be left behind.

Winston Churchill once said, "To each, there comes in their lifetime a special moment. . . . What a tragedy if that moment finds them unprepared." This is that moment for leaders. The rapid acceleration of AI presents an unprecedented opportunity to drive progress, enhance productivity, and create new possibilities. However, seizing this potential requires more than enthusiasm—it demands strategic leadership, ethical foresight, and a commitment to developing the skills necessary for success.

Despite AI's promise, significant challenges remain. Many executives cite a lack of skilled talent as a primary barrier to AI adoption, while others express concerns about ethics, trust, and bias in AI systems. These issues raise critical questions about fairness, accountability, and the societal impact of AI-driven decision-making. These concerns are not only . They are leadership challenges that require deliberate action.

To navigate this era of transformation, organizations must prioritize upskilling. According to LinkedIn's *Workplace Learning Report*, "Four in five people want to learn more about how to use AI in their profession." A Microsoft *Work Trend Index* report revealed that, as of March 2023, US job postings on LinkedIn mentioning GPT had already increased by 79% year over year. At the same time, 82% of leaders believe employees will need new skills to work effectively with AI. The message is clear: without investment in learning, individuals and organizations both risk becoming obsolete.

The data speak clearly: companies that effectively integrate AI into their workflows will gain a decisive advantage, while those that resist will struggle to remain competitive. But AI is not just a tool; it is a force multiplier for vision, agility, and impact. The future belongs to leaders who do not merely adapt but who actively shape the integration of AI with purpose and ethical responsibility.

The time for action is now. Will you lead the change, or will you be led by it?

Part Two

Personal Mastery

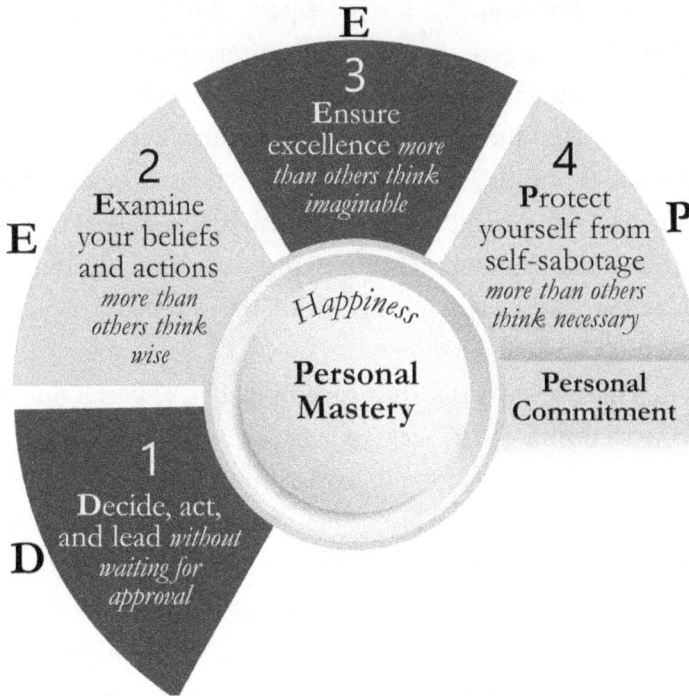

Most powerful is he who has himself in his own power.

—Seneca

n **Part Two**, we examine why **personal mastery** is essential for successfully navigating today's leadership challenges. We also explore how personal mastery can be achieved through inner practices that prepare leaders to meet future needs, inspire others authentically, pursue excellence, and transform obstacles into opportunities for growth.

Personal mastery is the foundation of the change we must pursue to meet the demands of future leadership. True leadership begins within, with a disciplined understanding of oneself, and as Lao Tzu says, "He who conquers others is strong; he who conquers himself is mighty." This self-conquest is not merely an act of discipline but an invitation to align our actions, values, and purpose—a prerequisite for leading others with clarity and authenticity. As we cultivate personal mastery, we develop the resilience and adaptability necessary to face the unknown, for "until you make the unconscious conscious, it will direct your life, and you will call it fate," as Carl Jung observed. Leaders of tomorrow must illuminate their inner landscapes, understanding the motivations and patterns that guide their decisions, if they hope to inspire transformation in others.

Personal mastery is not about reaching a state of perfection but embracing a continuous process of learning and growth. In an era defined by rapid shifts and complexities, future leaders must view personal mastery as a journey of alignment between vision and action. Only through understanding and cultivating one's inner strengths and weaknesses can a leader inspire others to bring forth their best selves. As Peter Senge suggests in *The Fifth Discipline*, "Personal mastery is the discipline of continually clarifying and deepening our personal vision, of focusing our energies, of developing patience, and of seeing reality objectively."

7 Principle 1: Decide, Act, and Lead without Waiting for Approval

Whatever you can do, or dream you can do, begin it. Boldness has genius, power, and magic in it.

—Goethe

In a faraway land, where mysteries shrouded every corner, there stood a grand and imposing gate. This was no ordinary gate; it was the Gate of the Law. Guarding this gate was a stern, formidable doorkeeper whose presence alone could make one hesitate.

One day, a man from the countryside arrived, his heart filled with a burning desire to gain entry into the Law. He approached the gate with cautious anticipation, and as he drew closer, the doorkeeper's piercing gaze met his. The countryside man felt a chill run down his spine but mustered the courage to speak.

"I seek entry into the Law," he declared, his voice trembling slightly. The doorkeeper, with an almost imperceptible smirk, replied, "It is possible, but not now."

The countryside man was taken aback. "Why not now?" he asked, desperation creeping into his voice. The doorkeeper's eyes twinkled with a mysterious light as he said, "If you truly desire entry, you must wait. But be warned, it might be a very long wait."

Do not wait for approval.

The man, undeterred by the ambiguity, decided to wait. He found a small stool and sat by the gate, hoping that his patience would eventually grant him passage.

Days turned into weeks, and weeks into months. The countryside man remained steadfast, never leaving his post. He observed the doorkeeper carefully, trying to find any sign or hint that might indicate when he would be allowed to enter. The doorkeeper, however, remained impassive, occasionally exchanging a few words but mostly silent, watching over the gate with unwavering vigilance.

Seasons changed, and the countryside man aged. His hair turned gray, and his face grew lined with the passage of time— yet his resolve did not wane. He continued to sit by the gate, now frail but still filled with the hope that one day he would be allowed to enter the Law.

As he neared the end of his life, the man, now bent and weak, summoned the last of his strength to ask one final question. With a voice quivering from age and anticipation, he said, "I have waited all my life. Why has no one else come to seek entry through this gate?"

The Gatekeeper leaned closer, and for the first time, his eyes softened with a hint of compassion. "This gate was made just for you," he revealed. "Only you could pass through it, and now it will be closed forever, because you kept asking for permission to enter."

With that, the Gatekeeper stepped aside, and the countryside man, filled with a bittersweet realization, saw the gate in a new light. It had always been his journey, his struggle, and his understanding that mattered. The gate had been made just for him, but he waited for someone's permission to enter the gate.

7.1 The Illusion of Permission

Do not ask for permission to dance in the rain; just let your soul move with the storm.

—Rumi

This poignant parable, depicting an enigmatic encounter between a countryside man and a gatekeeper, is derived from the esteemed German author Franz Kafka's "Before the Law," originally part of his novel *The Trial*. It stands as a timeless narrative, exploring the dichotomy between asking for permission or approval and taking action. Day after day, the man implores the gatekeeper for entry, offering gifts and displaying unwavering determination. Yet the man's fixation on obtaining permission becomes a paralyzing force, trapping him in a state of perpetual waiting and dependence, ultimately leading to his failure in gaining entry to the Law.

The parable raises questions about the nature of authority and the power dynamics inherent in systems of control. It challenges individuals to question the legitimacy of external barriers and consider the potential consequences of defying conventional norms. True leadership emerges from the willingness to challenge existing paradigms, defy conventional wisdom, and chart new courses of action.

In the business world, those who take the initiative often find themselves at the forefront of innovation and success. When Steve Jobs and Steve Wozniak started Apple, they did not wait for established tech companies to validate their vision. They saw an opportunity to revolutionize personal computing and took bold steps to bring their vision to life. Their initiative not only created a world-leading company but also transformed an entire industry.

> *It is in the act of taking action that we truly set ourselves free from the confines of the status quo and embark on a journey of discovery, growth, and empowerment.*

Similarly, when Sheryl Sandberg joined Facebook, she did not wait for permission to make significant changes. She identified areas where the company could grow and improve and took decisive action to implement those changes. Her leadership helped transform Facebook into one of the most influential companies in the world, demonstrating the power of taking initiative.

Don't wait for opportunity. Create it.
—George Bernard Shaw

In a world filled with complexity and rapid change, the call for effective leadership has never been more pressing. Too often, though, potential leaders hesitate, waiting for permission or validation from others before stepping into their roles. This hesitation stems from a deeply ingrained belief that leadership is a position conferred by titles or authority figures.

However, true leadership is about action, initiative, and the courage to make a difference regardless of one's official status. Much like Kafka's enduring parable, the gate to leadership is uniquely tailored for each of us. It is in the act of taking action that we truly set ourselves free from the confines of the status quo and embark on a journey of discovery, growth, and empowerment.

7.2 The Essence of Leadership

Twenty years from now you will be more disappointed by the things that you didn't do than by the ones you did do. So, throw off the bowlines. Sail away from the safe harbor. Catch the trade winds in your sails. Explore. Dream. Discover.

—Mark Twain

Leadership is not confined to boardrooms or high offices; it exists wherever there are people willing to make a positive impact. Each of us has the potential to lead, to influence, and inspire. The essence of leadership lies in recognizing opportunities to contribute and taking decisive action to address them without waiting for anyone's approval. It is about seeing a need, envisioning a solution, and rallying others to join you in creating change. Leadership is about stepping up when it matters most, without waiting for someone to give you the green light.

Many potential leaders are held back by the fear of overstepping boundaries, of being seen as presumptuous or arrogant. This fear is rooted in the societal norms that often equate leadership with formal titles and hierarchical positions. However, history and experience teach us that waiting for permission can lead to missed opportunities and unfulfilled potential.

Empower yourself with the knowledge that leadership is not about having all the answers but about being willing to find solutions. It is about fostering collaboration, encouraging dialogue, and mobilizing others to work toward a common goal. When you take the initiative, you inspire others to do the same, creating a ripple effect of positive change.

7.3 Who Am I to Lead?

If you hear a voice within you say, "You cannot paint," then by all means paint, and that voice will be silenced.

—Vincent Van Gogh

Self-doubt is a common barrier to leadership. The internal dialogue of *Who am I to lead?* can be paralyzing, yet every great leader has faced moments of doubt and uncertainty. What sets them apart is their decision to act despite their fears. They understand that leadership is a journey of growth and learning, not a destination of perfection.

Rosa Parks's refusal to give up her seat to a white passenger on a Montgomery bus in 1955 sparked the Montgomery Bus Boycott, a pivotal event in the civil rights movement. Her act of defiance was not orchestrated by any organization or by any leadership role. It was a personal decision driven by her conviction that the racial segregation laws were unjust; her action gave voice to oppressed Blacks.

Malala Yousafzai's journey to becoming a global advocate for girls' education began without seeking permission or waiting for an invitation to lead. Growing up in the Swat Valley of Pakistan, Malala witnessed the Taliban's oppressive regime, which banned girls from attending school. At just 11 years old, she began blogging for the BBC under a pseudonym, fearlessly detailing her experiences and advocating for the right to education. Her courageous voice drew international attention, but it also made her a target. In 2012, she survived a brutal assassination attempt by the Taliban, which only strengthened her resolve. Her relentless pursuit of education for all girls, despite the dangers she faced, exemplifies her natural leadership and unwavering commitment to justice. Malala did not wait for permission; she stepped forward with courage and conviction, inspiring millions around the world to join her cause.

Reflect on the story of Amelia Earhart, the pioneering aviator who broke numerous flying records. Earhart's achievements were not the result of waiting for approval but of pursuing her passion with determination and resilience. She faced numerous challenges and societal expectations that questioned her abilities as a female pilot. However, her boldness to lead in an uncharted field paved the way for future generations of women in aviation and beyond.

Imagine a workplace where innovation and collaboration thrive because employees feel empowered to propose new ideas and take charge of projects. Picture a community where residents come together to address local issues because they feel a shared responsibility for their environment. This is the transformative power of leadership that does not wait for permission.

Your journey as a leader begins now, with the choices you make and the actions you take. Embrace this call to leadership and transform the world around you.

7.4 Choose to Act. Don't Wait for Permission

When we are no longer able to change a situation, we are challenged to change ourselves.

—Viktor Frankl

Success favors those who take initiative, stepping forward with confidence instead of waiting for approval. When you choose to act without waiting for permission, you empower yourself to create opportunities and drive meaningful change.

Remember the story of the monk and the boys in chapter 3 of this book. Instead of feeling like the boys who hold choices in their hands in the story, some of you might actually feel like the helpless bird caught in the grasp of your manager. The reality of your work environment might be filled with challenges that make the principle *Decide, act, and lead without waiting for approval* seem untrue or even unattainable. It's completely understandable to feel trapped and powerless under such conditions. The pressures and constraints of a difficult workplace can make it hard to see any way out, leaving you feeling like you have no control over your situation. Or you might be facing a community situation where people are quarreling with each other in an unhealthy manner over some simple issues because of big egos. You may feel helpless amid this discord and conflict, and it is affecting your personal happiness because relationships are at risk.

However, even with the most stringent constraints, there are choices to be made or created that can transform your workplace experience. For instance, in a toxic environment where a manager is overly critical, maintaining your professionalism and positivity can set a different tone and gradually influence the team's morale. When unrealistic deadlines are imposed, negotiating priorities or seeking collaborative support can help manage the workload more effectively. If your role feels stagnant and uninspiring, proactively seeking new projects, training, or additional responsibilities can reignite your passion and facilitate growth. In situations where team communication is poor, initiating regular check-ins or proposing the use of collaborative tools can enhance clarity and teamwork. Even if your job doesn't wholly align with your personal values, making incremental changes in your approach or finding ways to incorporate your values into your daily tasks can provide deeper fulfillment. Even in conflict-ridden community situations, there is always a glimmer of hope. By embracing patience, empathy, and the power of leading by example, you can gradually mend relationships and cultivate a more harmonious community.

For personal happiness and fulfillment, it is crucial to take action, even in the smallest of ways. Remaining passive is not a viable option if you want to improve your situation. While it might seem that you have little power, the cumulative effect of small, deliberate actions can lead to significant improvements in your work experience. The power to shape your environment and job satisfaction lies within you, and by focusing on what you can influence, you can create a more positive and fulfilling professional life. Remember, even in the most challenging environments, your choices and actions can pave the way for meaningful change. You owe it to yourself to strive for happiness and satisfaction, even when the path seems difficult.

7.5 Lead Yourself through Workplace Struggles: Happiness Will Ensue

Some things are within our power, while others are not.

—Epictetus

Over the years in my mentorship of young professionals, I have heard countless stories of frustration—micromanagers breathing down their necks, managers withholding crucial information, unrealistic expectations, endless last-minute emergencies, and a lack of recognition. Their instinct was often to complain, feeling like victims of poor leadership and broken systems. But I always advised them: rather than dwelling on what they can't control, they should focus on what they can. By taking proactive steps, they could transform their work environment, regain a sense of control, and ultimately find fulfillment in their careers. Workplace challenges don't have to be a source of constant stress. When handled with a strategic mindset, they can lead to personal growth, professional success, and a greater sense of happiness.

When circumstances allowed, I also spoke with their managers, providing constructive feedback. In many cases, those managers appreciated the insight, as they were often unaware of how their approach or attitude was affecting their employees. At the same time, I encouraged employees to self-reflect—to examine their own actions and behaviors to see if they were unintentionally contributing to their struggles. Growth and improvement, after all, come from both external change and internal self-awareness.

However, this does not mean you can always lead yourself successfully through a workplace struggle. Some environments are simply too toxic to fix, and in those cases, the best way to lead yourself is to walk away. I had to make that choice once myself, after recognizing that staying in an unhealthy environment was stifling my growth rather than advancing it. Leaving a toxic leadership culture is not failure; it is an act of self-leadership, choosing to prioritize your well-being and professional integrity.

Below, I describe a few real-world scenarios from my personal mentorship experience, using fictitious names, job roles, and settings to protect the identities of the professionals involved.

> *People will do something—including changing their behavior—only if it can be demonstrated that doing so is in their own best interests as defined by their own values.*
>
> —Marshall Goldsmith

Scenario 1: The Micromanager Trap: Setting Expectations Early

One young engineer, Aisha, was constantly frustrated by her micromanager. He would review her work excessively, redo parts of it, and never seemed to trust her judgment. She felt suffocated. Instead of continuing the cycle of frustration, I suggested she proactively schedule brief, structured check-ins with her manager before he could swoop in unannounced. She started sending him concise progress updates, identifying potential concerns early, and preemptively addressing them. Over time, her manager saw that she was capable and began to trust her judgment.

By thinking outside the box, she turned her micromanager into a mentor rather than a roadblock. With more autonomy and trust, Aisha not only became more productive but also found greater satisfaction in her work.

Scenario 2: The Information Hoarder: Asking for What You Need

Then there was John, a junior analyst who often found himself working on projects without all the necessary details. His manager rarely provided clear direction or set expectations, leaving him to piece together information like a detective. Instead of waiting for information to trickle down, I advised John to take the lead in structuring his assignments. Before starting any new task, he would identify the expected outcome and send a structured list of questions to clarify and confirm the scope, deliverables, schedule, and key stakeholders. He also started summarizing conversations via email to ensure alignment.

His initiative forced his manager to communicate better, and soon John was seen as a problem-solver rather than just a follower. With fewer roadblocks and clearer direction, John was able to focus on meaningful work, reducing stress and increasing his sense of accomplishment.

Scenario 3: The Late-Night Workload Dump: Setting Boundaries Professionally

Maria, a marketing associate, was constantly blindsided by her manager with urgent requests late at night. She was exhausted and on the verge of quitting. I encouraged her, instead of complaining, to take control of her schedule. She started sending a Monday morning check-in email, outlining key priorities for the week and requesting alignment upfront on urgent tasks. She also set clear, polite boundaries, responding to late-night requests with, "I'll prioritize this first thing in the morning. If it's an emergency, let's discuss a process for identifying true urgencies ahead of time."

By creating a proactive approach, Maria not only regained control of her personal time but also helped her manager improve planning.

As a result, her workload became more predictable, and she enjoyed a healthier work-life balance, leading to greater job satisfaction.

Scenario 4: The Underestimated Effort: Managing Expectations Early

Then there was Jake, a software developer whose manager frequently underestimated the time required for tasks. Deadlines were always impossible, and he was left scrambling. Instead of suffering in silence, I advised him to start every new project with a detailed effort estimation matrix. He would break tasks into components, estimate time for each, and present it to his manager before work began.

This forced his manager to acknowledge the real workload and adjust timelines accordingly. Rather than waiting for a crisis, Jake set the narrative early. With realistic deadlines in place, he no longer felt overwhelmed, and his workdays became more manageable and rewarding.

Scenario 5: The Lack of Recognition: Showcasing Your Own Value

Jeff, a mid-career engineer, worked tirelessly, solving complex issues and mentoring his team, yet promotions always went to others. He assumed his hard work would speak for itself, but leadership never took notice. Instead of staying invisible, I advised Jeff to track his achievements and send structured monthly updates highlighting key contributions—efficiency improvements, problem-solving successes, and mentorship efforts. He also began speaking up in meetings and volunteering for high-visibility projects.

Within six months, leadership recognized his impact, and he finally earned the promotion he had long deserved. Rather than waiting for recognition, he took control of his own narrative. With his efforts finally acknowledged, Jeff felt valued and motivated, proving that advocating for oneself can lead to both professional growth and personal happiness.

Scenario 6: The Poorly Managed Project: Becoming the Leader You Wish You Had

Finally, there was Stefanie, who worked in a company where projects were chaotic, with shifting deadlines and unclear objectives. I told her that if the leadership isn't managing well, then step up and fill the gap. She began taking the initiative to create clear project timelines, identify risks early, and set informal check-ins with team members to ensure alignment.

Before long, her manager relied on her for structure, and she became the de facto project lead—eventually leading to a promotion. She turned dysfunction into an opportunity to shine. As she took control of the chaos, she found joy in her ability to lead, gaining confidence and a deep sense of fulfillment in her work.

Scenario 7: Breaking the Chains: Leading Yourself through Challenges

Each of these professionals could have continued feeling stuck, weighed down by poor management, or left their jobs without any guarantee that the next workplace would be better. Instead, by thinking outside the box, anticipating problems, and taking proactive steps, they broke the chains of frustration and turned obstacles into stepping-stones for growth.

More importantly, they didn't just survive their workplace challenges—they thrived. By taking ownership of their circumstances, they created environments where they felt valued, empowered, and ultimately happier. True happiness at work doesn't come from the absence of challenges but from the ability to navigate them with confidence and purpose.

7.6 Dream. Don't Wait for Permission

The future belongs to those who believe in the beauty of their dreams.
                                        —Eleanor Roosevelt

At the core of every great leader lies a dream. This dream is not a mere fantasy, but a powerful vision of what could be—a beacon that guides their actions and inspires others to follow. Leaders are made of dreams, and it is this visionary quality that distinguishes them from mere managers or caretakers of the status quo. They do not wait for anyone's permission to pursue their dreams. By embracing and nurturing their dreams, leaders ignite the potential within themselves and those around them, driving progress and creating a better future.

A leader's dream is a catalyst for change—the spark that ignites innovation, motivates action, and propels societies forward. Without dreams, there is no vision, and without vision, there can be no meaningful progress. Leaders who dare to dream set the stage for transformative change by envisioning a future that others may not yet see. They are driven by a sense of purpose and a belief in possibilities beyond the present reality.

> *Leaders who dare to dream set the stage for transformative change by envisioning a future that others may not yet see.*

One of the most inspiring stories of a big dream that started without asking for permission is that of Muhammad Yunus and the creation of Grameen Bank. While teaching economics at Middle Tennessee State University in the early 1970s, Yunus grew increasingly frustrated with the traditional economic theories that failed to address the real-life struggles of the impoverished. Upon returning to his native Bangladesh in 1972, he saw firsthand the devastating effects of poverty during the famine of 1974 and was determined to find a practical solution. Yunus began by lending small amounts of money from his own pocket to poor women in local villages, allowing them to start small businesses and achieve financial independence. This initiative grew into Grameen Bank, which challenged conventional banking practices and provided microloans to millions of impoverished individuals without requiring collateral. Yunus's innovative approach to microfinance demonstrated the profound impact of empowering the poor with financial resources, sparking a global movement, and earning him the Nobel Peace Prize in 2006. His story is a testament to the power of big dreams and the courage to pursue them, regardless of the traditional boundaries and expectations.

Today, Grameen America, inspired by the ideas of Muhammad Yunus, serves low-income entrepreneurs in the United States by providing microloans, financial training, and support to help them build small businesses and lift themselves out of poverty. Operating in over 20 cities across the United States, Grameen America has impacted more than 100,000 individuals, while the Grameen Bank model operates in over 40 countries worldwide, demonstrating its global reach and effectiveness in addressing poverty.

7.7 Cast a Bold Vision. Don't Wait for Permission

When you are inspired by some great purpose, some extraordinary project, all your thoughts break their bonds: Your mind transcends limitations, your consciousness expands in every direction, and you find yourself in a new, great and wonderful world. Dormant forces, faculties and talents become alive, and you discover yourself to be a greater person by far than you ever dreamed yourself to be.

—The Yoga Sutras of Patanjali

To dream beyond limits without permission or validation from others is to cast a vision that defies conventional wisdom and transcends the ordinary. Visionary leaders possess the unique ability to see beyond the present and imagine a future that others might deem unattainable. This vision is not confined to the top echelons of leadership; it permeates every level of an organization. It's a common misconception that only CEOs or top executives should have a vision. In reality, anyone can and should cultivate their own vision for their future or for specific projects without asking for anyone's permission. When everyone on a team feels empowered to be creative and innovative without seeking constant approval, it fosters a dynamic environment where ideas can flourish. As Gary Pisano illustrates in *Creative Construction: The DNA of Sustained Innovation*, successful innovation in large organizations hinges on a shared vision that guides efforts across all departments and levels. This collective vision aligns individual aspirations with organizational goals, fostering a sense of purpose and direction. By encouraging a culture where creativity is not just allowed but expected, organizations can harness the full potential of their teams, driving continuous innovation and growth.

When leaders at all levels embrace visionary thinking, it transforms the entire organizational culture. Moreover, having a vision empowers individuals to navigate the complexities and uncertainties of the modern workplace. It provides a roadmap for achieving personal and professional goals, fostering resilience and adaptability in the face of challenges. By encouraging a culture where everyone is motivated to think big and pursue their dreams, organizations can unlock the full potential of their workforce, driving innovation and growth.

Martin Luther King Jr. is a quintessential example of casting a bold vision. His dream of racial equality and justice, articulated in his famous "I Have a Dream" speech, was a vision that many considered unrealistic, given the deeply entrenched racial prejudices of the time. Despite widespread skepticism and fierce opposition, King remained steadfast in his vision, galvanizing a movement that brought about significant civil rights advancements. His dream continues to inspire generations, demonstrating the enduring power of a bold vision.

Luis von Ahn, a computer scientist and entrepreneur, came up with the idea of Duolingo after co-creating CAPTCHA and reCAPT-CHA, tools designed to help digitize books. When von Ahn launched Duolingo in 2012, the concept of offering free, high-quality language education seemed improbable in a market dominated by expensive software. Skeptics doubted a free app could be sustainable or impactful. However, von Ahn and his team worked tirelessly, experimenting with monetization models that aligned with their mission of making education accessible. Today, Duolingo is the world's most popular language-learning platform, democratizing education for millions around the globe.

Bangladeshi Nobel Laureate Muhammad Yunus's dream of a world with zero poverty, zero unemployment, and zero net carbon emissions—what he calls the "**world of three zeros**"—once seemed radical in a system driven by profit and inequality. Yet his unwavering belief in the power of social business has transformed this vision into a global movement, gaining traction in universities, boardrooms, and political circles worldwide. Yunus argues that the current capitalist system, built on self-interest, is fundamentally flawed—leading to growing inequality, widespread unemployment, and environmental devastation. He envisions a new economic model that harnesses altruism as a creative force, proving that businesses can thrive while prioritizing human well-being over wealth accumulation.

What began as a bold idea is now a global reality, embraced by thousands of individuals and organizations working toward a more inclusive and sustainable economy. Social businesses are driving real change—from solar energy initiatives lighting up millions of homes in Bangladesh to programs transforming unemployed youth into entrepreneurs through equity investments. In the United States, funding initiatives are empowering women-led businesses, while in France, enterprises are tackling rural poverty by providing mobility, housing, and infrastructure. A global support network is now helping young entrepreneurs launch startups centered on sustainability and social impact.

Universities such as Harvard, Oxford, and HEC Paris have integrated social business into their curricula, training future leaders to build enterprises with purpose. The United Nations and the World Economic Forum have recognized Yunus's work, and world leaders—including former US president Barack Obama, French president Emmanuel Macron, and German chancellor Angela Merkel—have praised his vision as a viable path to addressing global challenges. His concept of the three zeros is no longer just a theory—it is reshaping policies, influencing economies, and redefining the future of capitalism itself. Yunus has proven that when bold ideas are backed by action, belief, and systemic change, business can truly be a force for good, where economic success and social progress go hand in hand.

7.8 Beware of Excessively Realistic People

Don't be trapped by dogma—which is living with the results of other people's thinking. Don't let the noise of others' opinions drown out your own inner voice.

—Steve Jobs

Beware of those who question your bold vision under the guise of being realistic—those who advise you to seek permission before action. Individuals who are excessively realistic or cautious can be profoundly detrimental to your aspirations and ambitions. They often focus relentlessly on potential obstacles and limitations, effectively stifling creativity and innovation. When every idea is met with a barrage of practical concerns and worst-case scenarios, it becomes nearly impossible to explore bold, unconventional solutions.

This constant negativity not only dampens your enthusiasm but also restricts your ability to envision and pursue extraordinary achievements. In an ever-changing world where adaptability and forward-thinking are essential, being anchored by overly realistic perspectives can prevent you from seizing new opportunities and realizing your full potential. Had Orville and Wilbur Wright listened to those who deemed human flight impossible, they would never have pursued their groundbreaking experiments, leading to the invention of the airplane.

The Wright brothers' story has always resonated with me—not just as history, but as something deeply personal. It echoes an early experience that quietly shaped how I deal with people who dismiss bold ideas as unrealistic. I was in sixth or seventh grade when I came across a quote by Napoleon: "Impossible is a word only found in the dictionary of fools." In my youthful literalism, I took the quote at face value and boldly struck out the word "impossible" from the shared household dictionary. As a regular user of that dictionary, I didn't want to be a fool. My elder brother, a more frequent and serious user of the volume, was not amused. He scolded me for defacing what he considered a sacred academic tool, and it was then that I realized Napoleon had spoken metaphorically, not literally. Still, the quote left a lasting impression on me. Even decades later, it continues to inspire me to tackle what others might call impossible—and often, to prove them wrong.

This mindset isn't just personal—it matters in teams and organizations too. Surrounded by people who constantly say, "That won't work," even the most promising efforts can wither before they begin. Their unyielding focus on practicality often creates a negative atmosphere that stifles motivation and enthusiasm.

The dangers of excessive realism are also vividly portrayed in movies like *Dead Poets Society*. The character of Mr. Keating, played by Robin Williams, inspires his students to "seize the day" and pursue their passions despite societal pressures to conform. The film contrasts Keating's inspirational leadership with the rigid realism of the school's administration, which ultimately stifles the students' creativity and spirit. This poignant story underscores how an overly realistic mindset can crush dreams and limit potential.

High-reaching goals and ambitious endeavors require an environment filled with optimism and a willingness to embrace calculated risks. By distancing yourself from those who are too realistic, you can cultivate a more positive, dynamic atmosphere that encourages growth, innovation, and resilience. This shift not only enhances personal and professional fulfillment but also sets the stage for transformative success, driven by a mindset unafraid to dream big and tackle challenges head-on.

7.9 "You Got a Dream, You Gotta Protect It"

All men dream, but not equally. Those who dream by night in the dusty recesses of their minds, wake in the day to find that it was vanity: but the dreamers of the day are dangerous men, for they may act on their dreams with open eyes, to make them possible.

—T. E. Lawrence

Dreaming beyond what society deems realistic is often frowned upon, yet it's the foundation of many extraordinary accomplishments. As we embark on this voyage of discovery, let us draw inspiration from the silver screen, where timeless tales of resilience and fortitude serve as beacons of hope. Witness the indomitable spirit of a single father, played by Will Smith, in the 2006 film *Pursuit of Happyness*, based on the true story of Chris Gardner, a struggling salesman who faces homelessness, financial hardship, and personal setbacks while striving to build a better life for himself and his son, Christopher. Yet Gardner's dedication to his dream of securing a better life for himself and his son never wavered.

This story underscores the importance of maintaining faith in one's aspirations, regardless of external opinions. In a pivotal moment between a father and son, the child excitedly shares his dream of becoming a professional basketball player, his eyes filled with hope. The father, burdened by the weight of his own disappointments and struggles, responds pragmatically, telling his son that he should set more realistic goals because dreams like that are often out of reach. The boy's face falls, his enthusiasm dampened by the words of someone he trusts most.

As they stand together on a basketball court, the father notices his son's disappointment and quickly realizes his mistake. He softens, looking at his son with a newfound determination, and says, "Don't ever let somebody tell you—you can't do something. Not even me. You got a dream, you gotta protect it." The boy listens intently, absorbing the gravity of the lesson—that people often project their own limitations onto others, but true success comes from believing in oneself. The father continues, "People can't do something themselves, they want to tell you—you can't do it. If you want something, go get it. Period." The message echoes throughout the story, emphasizing the significance of forging one's own path despite external doubts. This sentiment is also echoed by Steve Jobs, who once said, "Your time is limited, so don't waste it living someone else's life."

In essence, Chris's message to his son in the film *Pursuit of Happyness* extends beyond mere encouragement—it's a reminder of the importance of resilience, determination, and unwavering faith in the face of adversity. It's a testament to the power of dreams to sustain us through life's darkest moments and propel us toward a brighter future. As the story unfolds, Chris's steadfast commitment to his dream ultimately leads to triumph, proving that with perseverance, resilience, and unrelenting determination, anything is possible. And in imparting this invaluable lesson to his son, Chris not only protects his own dream but instills in Christopher a powerful belief in the limitless potential of dreams and the resilience of the human spirit.

7.10 Overcoming Obstacles and Doubt

Our doubts are traitors
And make us lose the good we oft might win
By fearing to attempt.

—William Shakespeare

Dreaming beyond limits invariably attracts obstacles and doubt, both from internal and external sources. The biggest obstacle to dreaming big is often our own mindset, which convinces us that we are not supposed to dream, but merely to work within predefined boundaries. This mindset also ingrains the belief that we need the approval or permission of our superiors before daring to pursue bold visions, effectively limiting our potential. Those who can break away from this mindset begin their journey of becoming visionary leaders, fully aware that this path is often fraught with challenges that test their resolve and resilience.

Thomas Edison, one of history's greatest inventors, exemplified the spirit of overcoming obstacles and doubt. Edison's dream of creating a practical and affordable electric lightbulb faced countless failures. He famously conducted over 1,000 experiments before achieving success. Critics doubted his ability to deliver on such a grand vision, but Edison's persistence and innovative spirit ultimately led to a breakthrough that illuminated the world. His story underscores the importance of resilience and perseverance in the face of adversity.

Fred Smith's idea for FedEx, a global overnight delivery service, was initially met with skepticism. While studying at Yale University, he submitted the concept in an economics class paper and reportedly received a C, as the professor deemed it impractical. After founding FedEx in 1971, Smith faced significant financial challenges. In 1973, with the company nearly out of funds, he famously took the last $5,000 to Las Vegas and won $27,000 playing blackjack—just enough to keep the planes fueled and operations running for a few more days. That gamble gave him the time he needed to secure additional funding. "The $27,000 wasn't decisive, but it was an omen that things would get better," Smith says. And indeed they did. Returning to his quest for funds, he raised another $11 million. Today, FedEx stands as a multibillion-dollar global enterprise, built on Smith's vision, risk-taking, and determination.

To overcome obstacles and doubt, visionary leaders follow a set of best practices. First, they recognize fear and self-doubt as signals—not stop signs—and take action despite them. Second, they set bold but achievable goals, breaking them into smaller steps that create early wins and build momentum. Third, they surround themselves with believers—mentors, peers, and teams—who challenge and support them in equal measure. Fourth, they reframe failure not as defeat but as data, learning from setbacks rather than being paralyzed by them. Finally, they practice self-reflection and resilience, reminding themselves regularly of their deeper purpose and why they started. These habits do not eliminate obstacles, but they empower leaders to face them with clarity, confidence, and courage.

7.11 The Leap of Faith: A Personal Story

Faith is taking the first step even when you don't see the whole staircase.
— Martin Luther King Jr.

It was 1998. I was working for a large international company, steadily climbing the leadership ladder. From the outside, it looked like I was living the dream. But inside, I felt a growing restlessness and a deep desire to create something of my own, something that truly aligned with my passions. At the peak of my corporate career, I made a decision that surprised many around me. Without asking for permission or seeking validation, I decided to step away from the comfort of my job and embark on an uncertain journey to start my own company. I formed a partnership with a college friend who shared my vision.

I vividly remember the day we designed our first business card for the new venture. On the back, I proposed to inscribe a quote from the Greek philosopher Aristotle that had always resonated with me: *"We are what we repeatedly do. Excellence, then, is not an act, but a habit."* This quote became a quiet mantra, reminding me of the high standards I aspired to uphold—not just for myself, but for the team we hoped to build. I was far from perfect and knew that success would be a collective effort, one that depended on inspiring and empowering those around me.

The early years were filled with challenges, many of which tested our resolve and humility. Despite the obstacles, our company managed to rise to prominence in California, becoming a leader in our field. This wasn't solely due to strategic wins or my efforts alone; it was the shared commitment to excellence that our team embodied. I learned that success is not about the individual achievements of one leader but about creating an environment where everyone feels driven to pursue excellence as a collective mission.

Reflecting on my journey, I realized that the lessons I learned could apply to anyone striving to lead in any capacity. Leadership isn't about being the smartest person in the room or having all the answers; it's about fostering a culture that values persistence, learning, and collective growth. Dreams aren't always things we find; they are often born from our passions and nurtured by the people who support us. These passions are not random; they are your calling and can guide you toward fulfilling work.

For those struggling to find their dream or purpose, I often suggest starting with small steps. One exercise that helped me—and that I share with others—is to write, "I want to . . . ," and fill in the blank 30 times on a piece of paper. It's a way to dig deep and unearth your true aspirations. My leap of faith wasn't just about starting a company; it was about answering a calling and doing so with the support and shared belief of those around me. In taking that step, I found not only professional success but also personal fulfillment, a journey that anyone can embark on by embracing their passions and striving for excellence, not alone, but together.

QUICK TIP

Write, "I want to . . . ," 30 times. Start filling it in and a personal vision will emerge.

7.12 Inspiring Innovation and Change

If your actions inspire others to dream more, learn more, do more and become more, you are a leader.

—John Quincy Adams

Visionary leaders are catalysts for innovation and change. Their dreams often challenge the status quo and pave the way for transformative advancements that benefit society. They do not ask for permission or validation from others; they do not wait for approval.

Nelson Mandela's dream of a democratic and free South Africa, where all citizens enjoyed equal rights, seemed impossible under the oppressive apartheid regime. Mandela's unwavering commitment to his vision, even during 27 years of imprisonment, inspired a nation and the world. His leadership and sacrifice were instrumental in dismantling apartheid and establishing a new era of democracy in South Africa. Mandela's story is a testament to how visionary leadership can inspire monumental change.

Bill Hewlett and Dave Packard cofounded Hewlett-Packard (HP) and revolutionized the electronics and computing industry. Their visionary leadership not only advanced technology but also set new standards for corporate culture with "The HP Way"—a philosophy that emphasized innovation, employee empowerment, and ethical business practices. Their leadership style reshaped the corporate world, proving that a successful business could prioritize both technological advancement and employee well-being.

Dr. Rajendra Singh, known as the Waterman of India, took on the challenge of reviving dry river systems in the arid region of Rajasthan, India. When he started his work in the 1980s, many experts doubted his traditional methods of water management, such as building small dams and check dams using ancient techniques. Singh persisted, involving local communities and teaching them sustainable water conservation practices. His work eventually revived five major rivers and replenished the water table, transforming barren lands into fertile areas and inspiring other regions to implement similar practices for water management and sustainability. He was awarded the Ramon Magsaysay Award for Community Leadership in 2001 and the Stockholm Water Prize in 2015.

Elif Bilgin, a Turkish teenager, was passionate about reducing environmental waste and finding sustainable solutions. At age 16, she developed a method for creating bioplastics from banana peels, despite being told it was an impractical idea. Bilgin faced multiple failed attempts before perfecting her process. Her breakthrough won her global recognition, including the Science in Action Award at the Google Science Fair. Bilgin's story is a testament to the potential of young innovators to inspire change through perseverance and a commitment to sustainability.

Innovation is the heart of economic progress and business growth. However, a common misconception is that innovation is solely the domain of nimble startups. Gary Pisano, in his book *Creative Construction: The DNA of Sustained Innovation*, demonstrated how both small and large organizations can foster innovation with the right strategies, systems, and culture because innovation is a systematic process rather than a stroke of genius. Pisano emphasizes the importance of a well-defined innovation strategy. This involves aligning innovation efforts with the organization's overall strategic goals, prioritizing initiatives that leverage the firm's unique strengths, and ensuring that innovation is not an isolated activity but integrated into the core business operations.

An effective innovation system comprises the right talent, processes, structures, and behaviors. Pisano highlights that large companies often fail to innovate due to structural inertia and fragmented processes. To counter this condition, he suggests building a cohesive system that encourages collaboration, risk-taking, and continuous learning. This system should facilitate the seamless flow of ideas across different parts of the organization, much like how Apple's integrated approach enabled it to outpace competitors like Sony in developing portable electronic devices.

Cultural alignment is another critical aspect Pisano stresses. This includes fostering an environment where employees feel safe to experiment and fail, where diverse perspectives are valued, and where leadership actively promotes and rewards innovative thinking. Ed Catmull's book *Creativity, Inc.: Overcoming the Unseen Forces That Stand in the Way of True Inspiration* similarly advocates for creating a safe environment for creativity within large organizations. In the book, Catmull shares insights from his experience at Pixar, detailing strategies for nurturing an open culture where candid feedback is encouraged and failures are seen as opportunities for learning and growth. He emphasizes that true creative excellence requires a commitment to supporting and trusting teams to explore bold ideas.

Your legacy is every life you have touched.

—Maya Angelou

7.13 The Transformative Power of Dreams

There is nothing like a dream to create the future.

—Victor Hugo

Dreams have the power to transform not only organizations and societies but also leaders themselves. The pursuit of a dream requires leaders to grow, adapt, and evolve. It challenges them to develop new skills, embrace creativity, and take bold risks. This personal transformation is a testament to the profound impact that a visionary dream can have on an individual's leadership journey.

One of the most inspiring examples of this transformation is Oprah Winfrey's remarkable rise from a challenging childhood to becoming a global media icon and advocate for education, health, and social justice exemplifies how dreams can shape a leader's identity and legacy. Born in 1954 in Kosciusko, Mississippi, to a single teenage mother, Winfrey faced significant hardships, including poverty and abuse. Despite these challenges, she pursued her passion for media, starting her career in radio and local television before launching *The Oprah Winfrey Show* in 1986. The show became the highest-rated talk show in television history, running for 25 years and reaching millions worldwide. Beyond her media success, Winfrey has been a powerful advocate for various causes. In 2007, she opened the Oprah Winfrey Leadership Academy for Girls in South Africa, providing education and leadership opportunities to disadvantaged girls. Her philanthropic efforts also include significant contributions to health initiatives and disaster relief. Winfrey's story is a shining example of how dreams can drive personal and societal transformation.

> *Reach high, for stars lie hidden in your soul. Dream deep, for every dream precedes the goal.*
>
> —Rabindranath Tagore,
> first Asian Nobel Laureate

To become leaders made of dreams, individuals must nurture their visions with intention and commitment without seeking approval from others. This involves setting clear goals, continually refining their vision, and persistently pursuing their aspirations despite challenges. It also requires a willingness to inspire and empower others, fostering a culture of shared purpose and collective effort.

As we reflect on the stories of Martin Luther King Jr., Thomas Edison, Nelson Mandela, Oprah Winfrey, and others, we are reminded of the transformative power of dreaming beyond limits. Their journeys teach us that visionary leadership is not confined to extraordinary individuals but is a mindset that anyone can adopt.

Leaders should create environments that encourage dreaming and innovation. By fostering a culture that values creativity and encourages the exploration of new ideas, leaders can unlock the potential within their teams and organizations. This environment not only supports the realization of individual dreams but also drives the collective success of the group.

7.14 Concrete Examples of Visionary Leaders

Here's to the crazy ones, the misfits, the rebels, the troublemakers, the round pegs in the square holes . . . the ones who see things differently—they're not fond of rules. . . . You can quote them, disagree with them, glorify or vilify them, but the only thing you can't do is ignore them because they change things. . . . They push the human race forward, and while some may see them as the crazy ones, we see genius, because the ones who are crazy enough to think that they can change the world, are the ones who do.

—Steve Jobs

To understand how the principle *Decide, act, and lead without waiting for approval* can bring extraordinary success, let's look at some examples of visionary leaders who dreamed beyond what was considered realistic.

Born Sarah Breedlove, Madam C. J. Walker was America's first female self-made millionaire. Rising from poverty, she created a line of beauty and hair products for Black women that revolutionized the beauty industry in the early 20th century. Her keen business acumen, innovative marketing, and commitment to empowering other women made her a trailblazer. Walker's legacy includes not just her successful business but also her philanthropy and activism supporting social causes and the African American community. She believed deeply in giving back to the community that supported her rise and used her wealth and influence to make a difference in the lives of others. Walker was a major financial contributor to numerous organizations, including the National Association for the Advancement of Colored People (NAACP), to which she donated large sums to support their antilynching campaigns and civil rights initiatives.

Sheryl Sandberg's rise to becoming one of the most powerful women in tech was fueled by her relentless vision and pioneering spirit. As the former COO of Meta (formerly Facebook), Sheryl Sandberg played a pivotal role in transforming the company into a global powerhouse. Her vision for expanding the company's advertising model and fostering a culture of empowerment was instrumental in Meta's growth. Sandberg's influential book, *Lean In*, sparked a global conversation on gender equality in the workplace and ignited a worldwide movement, challenging women to break free from societal constraints and step confidently into leadership roles. Through both her work and her advocacy, Sandberg's vision was clear: a world where technology and empowerment walk hand in hand, paving the way for transformative change in both business and society.

Whitney Wolfe Herd founded Bumble with a disruptive vision to create an online dating platform where women make the first move, challenging traditional norms in dating. Her innovative approach empowered women in the digital dating space and quickly propelled Bumble to become one of the most popular dating apps worldwide. Wolfe Herd's resilience and ambition also made her the youngest female

CEO to take a company public, cementing her status as a trailblazer for women in tech and business.

Angela Ahrendts is a visionary leader who shattered expectations and redefined what it means to lead in the luxury and tech industries. At Burberry, she didn't just revamp a legacy brand—she catapulted it into the future with a bold vision that merged digital innovation with timeless luxury. Under her leadership, Burberry became synonymous with cutting-edge digital experiences and unwavering brand consistency, setting a new standard for what a luxury fashion house could be in the modern world.

7.15 When Dreams Become Fantasies

It is not because things are difficult that we do not dare; it is because we do not dare that things are difficult.

—Seneca

While the principle *Decide, act, and lead without waiting for approval* is empowering, it must be balanced with a sense of practicality. Dreaming big without a practical action plan risks transforming these ambitious visions into mere fantasies. The distinction between transformative dreams and mere fantasies hinges on the implementation of a robust action plan. Dreams become actionable when they are grounded in reality through strategic planning, resource allocation, and continuous evaluation. WeWork's ambitious vision to revolutionize office space with shared work environments initially captivated investors. However, the lack of a sustainable business model and financial discipline turned this dream into a fantasy, leading to significant financial losses and a failed IPO.

Another example is the downfall of Theranos, a company that promised to revolutionize blood testing with minimal samples. Founder Elizabeth Holmes's vision was undoubtedly groundbreaking, but the absence of transparent, reliable technology and the disregard for scientific validation transformed this vision into a dangerous fantasy. The company's inability to deliver on its promises led to its collapse, illustrating the importance of pairing visionary ideas with practical, evidence-based execution.

7.16 Ten Actionable Steps for Applying Principle 1

As you start to walk out on the way, the way appears.

—Rumi

Application of the principle *Decide, act, and lead without waiting for approval* to lead requires taking initiative and making decisive moves, even in the face of uncertainty or lack of formal authority. This approach necessitates a blend of bold vision and pragmatic execution. A set of 10 actionable steps, with examples, is provided below to help you embrace the principle, empowering you to take bold initiatives and pursue your grandest ambitions with confidence. You are not required to follow all 10 steps to apply the principle, nor are you required to follow them in any specific order. Pick one, two, or three steps that best suit your needs or circumstances and work on those. Every single step will bring you closer to internalizing the principle, and that is the main point. You can refer back to these steps when you are consciously attempting to follow this principle in your work life, personal life, or community life. Each action you take strengthens your capacity to lead boldly, without waiting for permission.

> *You are not required to follow all 10 steps to apply the principle, nor are you required to follow them in any specific order. Pick one, two, or three steps that best suit your needs or circumstances and work on those.*

QUICK TIP

Action: Encourage your team to experiment with AI tools for process automation and decision-making without waiting for top-down directives. Implement AI-driven project management tools like Asana or Trello with AI plugins to streamline workflows autonomously.

Example: Allowing employees to integrate AI chatbots for customer service enhancements independently.

Caveat: Ensure that a clear policy and framework are in place to manage and monitor the use of AI tools to avoid potential misuse or security risks.

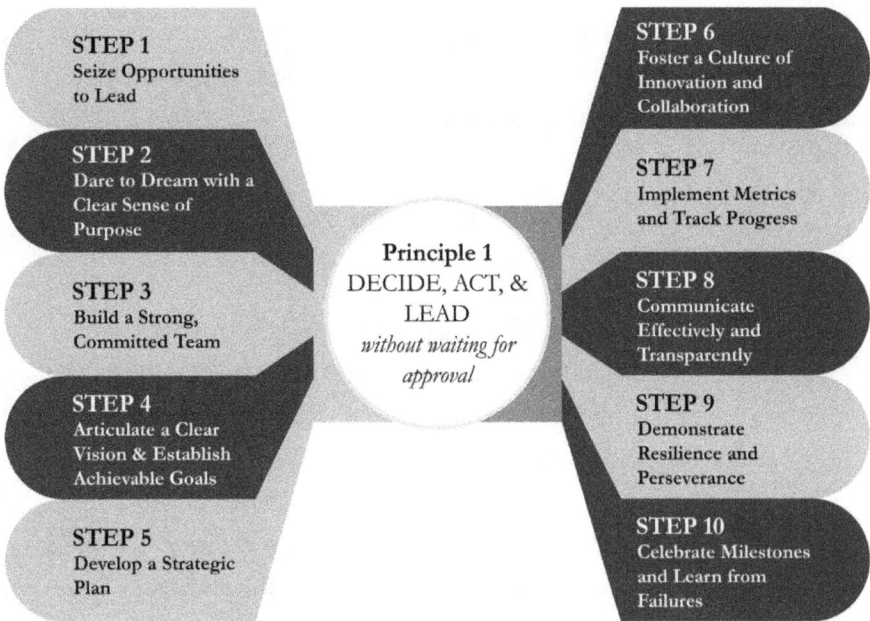

STEP 1
Seize Opportunities to Lead

STEP 2
Dare to Dream with a Clear Sense of Purpose

STEP 3
Build a Strong, Committed Team

STEP 4
Articulate a Clear Vision & Establish Achievable Goals

STEP 5
Develop a Strategic Plan

Principle 1
DECIDE, ACT, & LEAD
without waiting for approval

STEP 6
Foster a Culture of Innovation and Collaboration

STEP 7
Implement Metrics and Track Progress

STEP 8
Communicate Effectively and Transparently

STEP 9
Demonstrate Resilience and Perseverance

STEP 10
Celebrate Milestones and Learn from Failures

Turning intention into momentum: ten actionable steps for applying Principle 1

💡 *Principle 1, Step 1: Seize Opportunities to Lead*

Action: Identify opportunities to take charge and step up, even if you haven't been formally designated as a leader. Leadership isn't always about having a formal title—it's about recognizing moments where you can step up and make a difference. Whether in your personal life, community, or workplace, identifying these moments allows you to influence and inspire others, proving that leadership is an action, not just a role.

Example: You can start a nonprofit organization with the goal of eliminating homelessness in your city. Joan of Arc took the initiative to lead the French army despite having no formal military training, believing she was guided by divine voices. Rosa Parks refused to give up her seat on a segregated bus, sparking a movement that changed civil rights history. Greta Thunberg, at 15, started skipping school on Fridays to protest climate change, sparking a global youth-led movement called Fridays for Future. During the Apollo 13 crisis, flight director Gene Kranz took decisive control, demonstrating leadership that ultimately led to the safe return of the astronauts.

💡 *Principle 1, Step 2: Dare to Dream with a Clear Sense of Purpose*

Action: Allow yourself to dream big, setting ambitious goals that challenge the status quo and push the boundaries of what's possible. Great leaders are fueled by big dreams and bold visions. They see beyond the current limitations and imagine a future filled with possibilities.

Example: *charity: water*, founded by Scott Harrison, envisioned a world where everyone has access to clean drinking water. This ambitious dream has driven innovative fundraising strategies and partnerships, bringing clean water to over 11 million people in 29 countries. Walt Disney famously dreamed of creating a theme park unlike any other, where families could enjoy magical experiences together. Despite numerous obstacles, including financial setbacks and skepticism from peers, Disney turned his dream into reality with Disneyland, a legacy that endures today.

💡 *Principle 1, Step 3: Build a Strong, Committed Team*

Action: Gather a team of talented, dedicated individuals who share your vision and are willing to work toward it. Delegate tasks and empower your team members to take ownership of their roles and decisions. Ultimately, the team is what makes the difference between success and failure. A cohesive team working toward a shared goal can overcome challenges, adapt to changes, and achieve results that are greater than the sum of individual efforts.

Example: Jeff Bezos built Amazon by hiring smart, passionate people who were excited about innovation and customer service. Reed Hastings assembled a team at Netflix that embraced the shift from DVD rentals to streaming, driving the company's success. Abraham Lincoln's "team of rivals" was a strategic assembly of his political adversaries into his cabinet, fostering a diverse range of perspectives that ultimately strengthened his leadership and the Union during the Civil War. For your nonprofit organization, talk to people in your social circle and ask them to join you to help you refine your vision and mission.

💡 *Principle 1, Step 4: Articulate a Clear Vision and Establish Achievable Goals*

Action: Clearly articulate what you want to achieve and why it matters. A clear vision is the foundation of any big dream. It provides direction and purpose, guiding the actions and decisions of everyone involved.

While the overall vision may be grand, breaking it down into smaller, manageable goals can make it more attainable. Your vision should be specific, inspiring, and aligned with your core values. Create a vivid mental image of what success looks like. Ensure that your goals are SMART (specific, measurable, achievable, relevant, and time-bound). This makes it easier to track progress and adjust your plan as needed. Identify key milestones that represent significant steps toward your vision. Celebrate these milestones to maintain momentum and motivation.

Example: Amazon's goal to become "Earth's most customer-centric company" drives continuous innovation in customer service, delivery, and product offerings, keeping the company ahead of its competitors. A nonprofit organization aiming to eliminate homelessness in a city could define its vision as "A city where every person has a safe and stable place to call home." A milestone goal for the nonprofit organization could be securing funding for the first 100 housing units. TOMS Shoes was founded with the audacious goal of providing a pair of shoes to a child in need for every pair sold. This bold vision has not only driven the company's success but also inspired a global movement of socially responsible businesses. Tesla's vision of transitioning the world to sustainable energy is broken down into SMART goals, such as producing 500,000 electric vehicles per year by 2020, with key milestones like launching the Model 3 to achieve broader market adoption. In 2022, Tesla delivered 1,313,851 electric vehicles and produced 1,369,611 units. The Bill & Melinda Gates Foundation's goal to eradicate malaria is structured with specific milestones, such as reducing malaria deaths by 50% within a decade, using SMART targets to measure progress and adjust strategies accordingly.

💡 *Principle 1, Step 5: Develop a Strategic Plan*

Action: Develop a strategic plan that outlines the steps required to achieve your goals and realize your vision. Conduct a SWOT analysis to assess your strengths, weaknesses, opportunities, and threats. This helps you understand your current position and identify potential challenges and opportunities. Determine the resources needed to achieve your goals, including time, money, and talent. Ensure that these resources are allocated efficiently.

Example: The nonprofit organization might develop a strategic plan that includes fundraising strategies, partnerships with local businesses, and volunteer recruitment. Starbucks' strategic plan to expand globally included specific steps such as market research, local partnerships, and store design adaptations, leading to successful growth and strong international presence. Kodak's failure to develop a strategic plan for transitioning from film to digital photography led to its downfall, as it missed the opportunity to adapt to market changes and new technology.

💡 *Principle 1, Step 6: Foster a Culture of Innovation and Collaboration*

Action: Create an environment where team members feel comfortable sharing new ideas and experimenting with different approaches. Innovation and collaboration are critical for achieving ambitious goals. Foster a culture of teamwork and collaboration. Encourage cross-functional teams to work together toward common goals.

Example: Google's policy of allowing employees to spend 20% of their time on projects of their own choosing has led to innovative products like Gmail and Google Maps. This practice encourages risk-taking and creativity within the company. At Pixar, Ed Catmull empowers teams to take risks and innovate, leading to a string of successful animated films. In the nonprofit sector, organizations like Habitat for Humanity engage volunteers, community members, and local partners in collaborative brainstorming sessions to develop innovative solutions for affordable housing—ranging from sustainable building designs to wraparound support services for families in need. The Bill & Melinda Gates Foundation takes on high-risk, high-reward projects to tackle global health and education issues. By funding innovative solutions and approaches, they have made significant strides in reducing diseases like malaria and improving educational outcomes.

💡 Principle 1, Step 7: Implement Metrics and Track Progress

Action: Select metrics that are directly related to your goals and vision. These key performance indicators (KPIs) should provide clear insights into your progress and enable you to assess the effectiveness of your strategies. Continuously monitor your progress and make adjustments as needed. Regular reviews help you stay agile and responsive to changing circumstances. Align and realign resources with vision and strategic plan. Ensure that budgetary allocations reflect the strategic priorities of the organization. Invest in areas that drive the vision forward and support key initiatives.

Example: The nonprofit organization could track metrics such as the number of housing units secured, funds raised, and the number of individuals transitioned from homelessness to stable housing. Amazon's use of detailed metrics to track customer satisfaction, shipping times, and inventory levels has enabled it to continually optimize its operations, leading to unmatched efficiency and customer loyalty.

The World Wildlife Fund (WWF) tracks KPIs like the number of protected areas and species population trends, helping them measure the impact of their conservation efforts and adjust strategies for greater effectiveness. Kodak's failure to allocate resources toward digital photography, despite early awareness of its potential, led to its decline. The company's continued investment in traditional film technology, rather than embracing digital advancements, prevented it from capitalizing on market shifts. BlackBerry's lack of effective metrics to track changing consumer preferences and technology trends led to a significant loss of market share to competitors like Apple and Samsung.

💡 *Principle 1, Step 8: Communicate Effectively and Transparently*

Action: Regularly communicate your vision and progress to your team, supporters, and stakeholders. This helps maintain alignment and enthusiasm. Keep everyone informed about milestones, achievements, and any changes to the plan. Transparency builds trust and fosters a sense of shared purpose.

Example: A nonprofit organization could use newsletters, social media, and community meetings to keep stakeholders informed and engaged. When Microsoft CEO Satya Nadella effectively communicated the company's shift toward cloud computing and artificial intelligence, it aligned the entire organization and led to significant growth and innovation. Winston Churchill's speeches during World War II conveyed strength and resolve, rallying the British people. Ray Dalio's principles at Bridgewater Associates emphasize radical transparency, fostering a culture of openness and trust. Johnson & Johnson's handling of the Tylenol crisis involved transparent communication, which helped rebuild consumer trust. On the contrary, during the Boeing 737 Max crisis, poor communication with regulators, airlines, and the public severely damaged the company's reputation and trust, leading to massive financial losses and prolonged grounding of the aircraft.

💡 Principle 1, Step 9: Demonstrate Resilience and Perseverance

Action: View challenges as opportunities for growth and learning. Use setbacks as a chance to refine your strategies and improve your approach. Maintain your determination and persistence, even when progress is slow. Celebrate small victories to keep morale high and stay motivated.

Example: A nonprofit organization might face setbacks such as funding shortfalls or regulatory hurdles. By staying resilient and persistent, they can find alternative solutions and continue working toward their vision. After facing near bankruptcy in the early 2000s, Apple's resilience and perseverance in innovating new products like the iPod, iPhone, and iPad led to a remarkable turnaround and solidified its position as a tech industry leader.

The Kony 2012 campaign was a viral social media campaign launched by the nonprofit organization Invisible Children in March 2012. The campaign aimed to raise awareness about Joseph Kony, the leader of the Lord's Resistance Army (LRA), a militant group responsible for widespread atrocities in Central Africa, including the abduction of children to be used as soldiers and sex slaves. The video sought to make Joseph Kony globally infamous to prompt international action to arrest him and dismantle the LRA. While the Kony 2012 campaign was groundbreaking in its use of social media to mobilize global action and raise awareness, it also faced significant criticism and challenges. Critics argued that the campaign oversimplified a complex issue and portrayed a "white savior" narrative. Concerns were also raised about the allocation of funds by Invisible Children, with critics pointing out that only a portion of the donations was spent on direct aid in Africa. The campaign lacked the resilience and perseverance to sustain its initial momentum and address criticism, leading to a rapid loss of public interest and support for its cause.

Principle 1, Step 10: Celebrate Milestones and Learn from Failures

Action: Acknowledge and celebrate significant milestones to maintain enthusiasm and morale. Recognizing progress reinforces the value of hard work and dedication. View failures as learning opportunities. Analyzing what went wrong and why can provide valuable insights for future strategies and improvements.

Example: A company can hold quarterly meetings to celebrate major accomplishments, such as reaching sales targets or completing important projects. These events can include awards, public recognition, and team-building activities to boost morale and keep the team motivated. Nonprofit Habitat for Humanity showcases each completed home and community project, reinforcing the impact of their work and motivating volunteers and donors. Apple unveils milestones with high-profile product launches and events that build excitement and engage both employees and customers. These occasions reinforce Apple's innovative culture and keep the brand strong and dynamic. 3M's Post-it Notes, now a ubiquitous office product, originated from a failed attempt to create a super-strong adhesive. The company's culture of learning from failure allowed this accidental invention to become a massive success.

7.17 Ten Barriers to Applying Principle 1

Your task is not to seek for love, but merely to seek and find all the barriers within yourself that you have built against it.

—Rumi

The principle *Decide, act, and lead without waiting for approval* encourages individuals to take initiative and pursue their visions without waiting for approval. However, various barriers, including internal insecurities, organizational constraints, and societal norms, can impede this proactive mindset. Here we explore these barriers and provide solutions for overcoming them. The essential role of a leader is to recognize these barriers and proactively dismantle them to pave the way for innovation and progress. It is the leader's responsibility to be vigilant and committed to identifying obstacles and implementing strategies to eliminate them, thereby fostering an environment where creativity and leadership can thrive without restrictions.

⚠ *Principle 1, Barrier 1: Fear of Failure*

Barrier: Fear of failure is a significant internal obstacle that can prevent individuals from taking bold steps without seeking approval. This fear often stems from potential negative consequences such as loss of reputation, financial risk, or personal disappointment.

Solution: Cultivate a growth mindset by encouraging leaders to embrace challenges and view failures as learning opportunities. Promote a culture that celebrates learning from mistakes and continuous improvement, as Carol Dweck discusses in *Mindset: The New Psychology of Success*.

Principle 1
DECIDE, ACT, & LEAD
without waiting for approval

Barrier 1
Fear of Failure

Barrier 6
Gender and Diversity
Issues

Barrier 2
Lack of Confidence

Barrier 7
Resource Constraints

Barrier 3
Rigid Hierarchies

Barrier 8
Fear of Repercussions

Barrier 4
Lack of Support
Systems

Barrier 9
Inadequate Training
and Development

Barrier 5
Cultural Norms

Barrier 10
Resistance to Change

What holds us back: ten hidden barriers to applying Principle 1

⚠ *Principle 1, Barrier 2: Lack of Confidence*

Barrier: A lack of self-confidence and self-efficacy can inhibit individuals from stepping into leadership roles or pursuing ambitious dreams independently.

Solution: Build self-confidence through small successes and positive reinforcement. Encourage individuals to experience mastery through achievable tasks, as theorized by Albert Bandura in *Self-Efficacy: The*

Exercise of Control. Support this effort by providing opportunities for skill development and celebrating incremental achievements.

⚠ Principle 1, Barrier 3: Rigid Hierarchies

Barrier: Rigid hierarchical structures can stifle initiative and innovation. Employees may feel constrained by bureaucratic processes and the need for explicit permission from higher-ups to lead or implement new ideas.

Solution: Create flexible and empowering organizational structures. Implement flatter hierarchies and promote cross-functional teams to enhance flexibility and innovation. Emphasize transformational leadership, as described by James MacGregor Burns in his book *Leadership*, to empower individuals at all levels.

⚠ Principle 1, Barrier 4: Lack of Support Systems

Barrier: Without adequate mentorship, resources, and support from colleagues and superiors, individuals may find it challenging to take initiative or pursue their ideas.

Solution: Foster supportive leadership and a collaborative culture. Implement mentorship programs and ensure access to resources to encourage employees to pursue their ideas. As James Kouzes and Barry Posner suggest in *The Leadership Challenge: How to Make Extraordinary Things Happen in Organizations*, prioritize building an environment where employees feel equipped and encouraged to lead.

⚠ Principle 1, Barrier 5: Cultural Norms

Barrier: Societal expectations and cultural norms can influence individuals' willingness to act independently and take risks. In some cultures, there is a strong emphasis on collective harmony and respecting authority, which can discourage individuals from standing out or challenging the status quo.

Solution: Promote cultural awareness and flexibility by understanding and navigating cultural differences using Geert Hofstede's *Culture's Consequences: Comparing Values, Behaviors, Institutions and Organizations across Nations.* Encourage leaders to value diverse perspectives and foster an environment where questioning the status quo is welcomed.

⚠ *Principle 1, Barrier 6: Gender and Diversity Issues*

Barrier: Women and minority groups often face additional barriers due to systemic biases and stereotypes that cast doubt on their talents, capabilities, and creative potential.

Solution: Address biases and promote diversity and inclusion by implementing training programs and antidiscrimination policies. Support the advancement of underrepresented groups, as recommended by Alice Eagly and Linda Carli in *Through the Labyrinth: The Truth about How Women Become Leaders.* Ensure that leadership opportunities are inclusive and accessible.

⚠ *Principle 1, Barrier 7: Resource Constraints*

Barrier: Limited access to resources such as funding, technology, or personnel can inhibit individuals from taking initiative without seeking permission.

Solution: Ensure equitable access to resources by establishing clear allocation processes and providing training on leveraging resources effectively. Empower employees with the tools and support needed to act independently and encourage innovation and initiative.

⚠ *Principle 1, Barrier 8: Fear of Repercussions*

Barrier: Concerns about potential negative repercussions—such as job loss, demotion, or workplace retaliation—can deter individuals from acting independently.

Solution: Create a safe environment by establishing policies that protect employees who take calculated risks. Foster psychological safety and encourage open dialogue, ensuring that employees know constructive risk-taking is valued and rewarded.

⚠ *Principle 1, Barrier 9: Inadequate Training and Development*

Barrier: Lack of proper training and development opportunities can leave individuals feeling unprepared to take on leadership roles or pursue their dreams.

Solution: Provide comprehensive training programs and continuous development opportunities. Bridge the skill gap through mentorship, coaching, and leadership workshops, equipping employees with the skills and confidence needed to lead.

⚠ *Principle 1, Barrier 10: Resistance to Change*

Barrier: Organizational resistance to change can stifle innovation and discourage individuals from taking initiative without approval.

Solution: Cultivate a change-friendly culture by communicating the benefits of change and involving employees in the process. Create urgency and build support, as John P. Kotter recommends in his book *Leading Change*. Recognize and reward innovative efforts to foster an environment that embraces new ideas.

7.18 Ten Examples of Applying Principle 1

1. Jane proposes a new project idea during an open forum strategic planning session, seizing the opportunity to present it directly to senior management without first consulting her immediate supervisor.
2. Mark takes the initiative to lead a team meeting when the scheduled leader is absent.
3. Lisa implements a new software tool to improve team efficiency without waiting for formal approval.
4. Tom starts a company-wide recycling program after noticing excessive waste.
5. Olivia takes the initiative to mentor new and junior employees, creating an informal training program to help them develop their skills.
6. During a critical project deadline, an employee implements a new efficient process without seeking prior approval, significantly improving workflow.
7. A team member takes the initiative to contact a potential client directly, securing a new business opportunity.
8. A store manager reconfigures the product display to enhance customer experience without waiting for corporate directives.
9. A sibling takes the initiative to organize a family get-together, resulting in a delightful reunion.
10. A community member starts a neighborhood clean-up initiative without waiting for the local council's approval.

7.19 Closing Reflections

Now this is not the end. It is not even the beginning of the end. But it is, perhaps, the end of the beginning.

—Winston Churchill

By following these guidelines on how to implement the principle *Decide, act, and lead without waiting for approval,* leaders can inspire their organizations to achieve extraordinary outcomes and drive meaningful change in the nonprofit and for-profit sectors.

By recognizing and addressing the barriers mentioned above, individuals and organizations can more effectively embrace the principle of not asking for permission to lead or dream. This proactive approach fosters innovation, creativity, and dynamic leadership, ultimately resulting in greater personal and organizational success. Effective leaders must be vigilant and committed to identifying and dismantling these obstacles, paving the way for a more empowered and visionary workforce.

True leaders are those who do not ask for permission or wait for approval to lead. True leaders are those who dare to dream big. Their unparalleled initiative and visionary quality set them apart and drive them to make a difference. Dreams serve as catalysts for change, sources of resilience, and inspirations for collective action. They transform not only the world but also the leaders themselves. By embracing and nurturing their dreams, leaders can create a future that is brighter and more promising than the present. The power of a dream lies in its ability to inspire, motivate, and unite. As we look to the leaders of tomorrow, let us remember that their greatest strength lies not in their titles or positions, but in the dreams that drive them forward. Embrace your dreams, and you too can become a leader who changes the world.

7.20 Daily Practice

1. **Seize initiative.** Identify opportunities where you can take initiative and step up.

2. **Protect your dream.** Take daily actions in the pursuit of your dreams, undeterred by those who say it is unrealistic.

3. **Empower your team.** Give your team members responsibility and authority, enabling them to think big without seeking approval at every step.

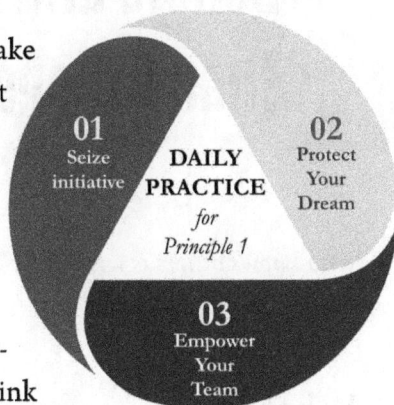

01 Seize initiative

DAILY PRACTICE *for Principle 1*

02 Protect Your Dream

03 Empower Your Team

8 Principle 2: Examine Your Beliefs and Actions More Than Others Think Wise

He who knows others is wise; he who knows himself is enlightened.

—Lao Tzu

8.1 What If . . .

What if the very beliefs that shape your life, the very convictions you hold dear, are the same forces that obscure your vision and shackle you from attaining true understanding and knowledge? What if the truths you cling to are the very chains that prevent you from unleashing the inherent greatness in you to become a happy and successful leader?

8.2 Socrates and the Unexamined Life

The unexamined life is not worth living.

—Socrates

It is often said that we rely on deeply held convictions that prevent us from breaking free and seeing the world as it truly is. This is the paradox that Socrates sought to unravel in ancient Athens through his legendary method of inquiry. By relentlessly questioning everything, Socrates revealed that true wisdom starts with acknowledging our own ignorance and biases. Known as the *Socratic method*, his approach challenged accepted norms and encouraged deep self-reflection, helping to overcome the blind spots created by our beliefs. For Socrates, this journey of introspection was the key to a meaningful life, as he famously declared, *"The unexamined life is not worth living."* This statement emerged during his trial, as chronicled by his disciple Plato in *The Apology*. Socrates was sentenced to death for allegedly corrupting the youth and impiety. Rather than fleeing or pleading for his life, Socrates used his defense to emphasize the importance of self-examination and moral integrity. He argued that living without introspection, without questioning one's beliefs, values, and actions, leads to a life devoid of purpose and true understanding.

Socrates's timeless wisdom "The unexamined life is not worth living" left such a profound impact on me that I had it inscribed on the back wall of my house. It became a daily checkpoint as I stepped into my backyard—a quiet yet firm nudge to pause, reflect, and renew my commitment to self-examination, ensuring that I never drifted too far from a life of awareness, purpose, and growth. What intrigued me most was how every visitor, without fail, was drawn to it. Friends, colleagues, and even first-time guests would pause, reading it aloud as if absorbing its depth for the first time. Many would ask about its meaning, sparking deep conversations, while others simply stood beside it, posing for a picture as if to capture a piece of its wisdom for themselves. Over time, that inscribed wall became more than just an architectural detail. It became a symbol of thoughtfulness, curiosity, and the pursuit of a life well-examined.

Effective leadership mirrors Socratic philosophy in that it necessitates continuous self-examination. Self-examination is crucial for personal and professional growth, as it allows us to confront and understand our deepest wounds and challenges. Leaders who fail to reflect on their beliefs and actions risk making decisions that are misaligned with their core values and organizational goals. By adopting a Socratic approach, leaders can ensure that their actions are thoughtful, deliberate, and ethical.

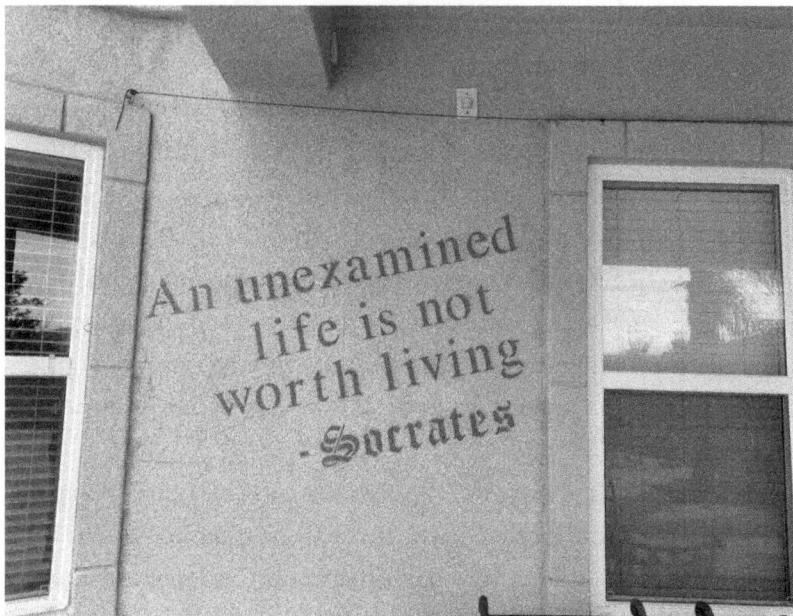

My everyday encounter with Socrates

8.3 Why Self-Examination?

Knowing yourself is the beginning of all wisdom.

—Aristotle

Leaders should examine their beliefs and actions more than others think wise because self-awareness and critical self-reflection are essential for authentic and effective leadership. By reflecting on our experiences and learning from them, we can uncover inner strengths and insights that lead to a more fulfilling and authentic life. Leaders who consistently scrutinize their beliefs and actions are better equipped to align their decisions with their core values and the organization's mission, fostering trust and credibility among their followers. This deep level of introspection enables leaders to identify and correct any biases or assumptions that may impede their judgment, promoting a culture of integrity and transparency. According to the article "What Makes a Leader?" published in the *Harvard Business Review*, self-aware leaders are more effective because they understand their strengths and weaknesses, enabling them to make better decisions and connect more deeply with their team. However, organizational psychologist and *New York Times* best-selling author Tasha Eurich found that self-awareness is a rare quality. In a five-year research study, she and her team discovered that while most individuals perceive themselves as self-aware, only 10 to 15% actually meet the criteria. This gap between perception and reality underscores the challenges leaders face in accurately understanding their own strengths, weaknesses, and impact on others.

Leadership is not just about having the right answers; it is about continuously questioning assumptions, refining perspectives, and updating strategies in response to new information. Adam Grant, in *Think Again: The Power of Knowing What You Don't Know*, highlights the dangers of cognitive rigidity and the importance of intellectual humility. Leaders who fail to challenge their own thinking fall into what he calls the "overconfidence cycle," where success in the past breeds complacency and a false sense of certainty. The most effective leaders embrace a "scientist mindset"—constantly testing their ideas, seeking evidence, and remaining open to new perspectives. By fostering a culture of rethinking, leaders can ensure that both they and their organizations remain adaptive and resilient in an ever-changing world.

One of the greatest barriers to rethinking is the natural tendency to defend our beliefs rather than question them. According to Adam Grant, leaders often fall into the trap of operating in preacher, prosecutor, or politician mode—either preaching their ideas, attacking opposing views, or seeking approval rather than truth. The alternative, as Grant suggests, is to think like a scientist: embrace doubt, test assumptions, and adjust conclusions when faced with new evidence. Rethinking does not mean a lack of conviction; rather, it is a commitment to continuous learning and growth. When leaders detach their ego from their ideas, they become more capable of making informed decisions, navigating uncertainty, and fostering an organizational culture that values critical thinking and adaptability.

The principle *Examine your beliefs and actions more than others think wise* is deeply connected to the concept of whole-person leadership, an approach that emphasizes integrating into one's leadership style all aspects of a person's life—mental, emotional, physical, and spiritual. Whole-person leadership recognizes that effective leadership stems not just from professional competencies but from the alignment of one's beliefs, values, attitudes, and actions across all areas of life. By rigorously examining one's beliefs and actions, a leader can ensure that their leadership approach is authentic and grounded in a deeper understanding of themselves and their impact on others. This self-awareness fosters a leadership style that is not only effective but also deeply meaningful, as it resonates with the leader's core values and personal identity.

Moreover, a leader's willingness to critically examine her beliefs and actions sets a powerful example for the entire organization, encouraging a culture of continuous improvement and learning. By modeling introspection and accountability, leaders inspire their team members to also reflect on their behaviors and strive for personal growth. This practice not only enhances individual performance but also drives organizational success by fostering a resilient and adaptive workforce. As noted by Kouzes and Posner in their book *The Leadership Challenge*, the best leaders are those who continuously challenge themselves and seek feedback to improve, demonstrating a commitment to personal and professional development. Therefore, leaders who engage in rigorous self-examination are better positioned to lead with authenticity, inspire their teams, and navigate effectively the complexities of modern organizational life.

Leaders who embrace Socratic self-examination cultivate a culture of continuous improvement and ethical integrity. They encourage their teams to question assumptions, seek out diverse perspectives, and align their actions with shared values. This approach not only enhances decision-making but also builds trust and loyalty within the organization.

Abraham Lincoln's leadership during the American Civil War provides a compelling case of a leader examining and evolving his beliefs and actions. Initially, Lincoln's primary goal was to preserve the Union, and he was hesitant about addressing the issue of slavery directly. However, as the war progressed, Lincoln began to see the moral and strategic necessity of ending slavery. Lincoln's initial reluctance to tackle slavery head-on reflected a belief in prioritizing the Union's survival. However, the prolonged conflict and the moral imperative pushed him to reevaluate his stance. The issuance of the Emancipation Proclamation in 1863 marked a significant shift in Lincoln's actions, aligning them more closely with a moral opposition to slavery. This decision, though fraught with political and social risks, demonstrated Lincoln's capacity to reconcile his evolving beliefs with his leadership actions.

Examining one's beliefs and aligning them with actions is a profound challenge for leaders. Figures like Abraham Lincoln show how evolving beliefs can lead to significant shifts in leadership actions, often requiring immense courage and integrity. These examples underscore that true leadership involves continuous self-reflection and the courage to act in accordance with one's deepest values, despite external pressures and personal risks.

8.4 Lessons from History

Back of every mistaken venture and defeat is the laughter of wisdom, if you listen.

—Carl Sandburg

The failure to critically examine one's deeply held beliefs has all too often led to catastrophic outcomes, as tragically demonstrated by the disasters of the *Titanic* and the *Challenger*.

Despite warnings about the dangers of icebergs and the need for caution in navigating the North Atlantic, the builders and operators of the *Titanic* failed to adequately examine their beliefs and actions regarding the ship's safety and emergency preparedness. The *Titanic* was deemed "unsinkable" by its designers and operators, leading to complacency and a lack of thorough safety protocols. As a result, when the *Titanic* struck an iceberg on its maiden voyage in 1912, the consequences were catastrophic, with the loss of over 1,500 lives.

In 1986, the Space Shuttle *Challenger* exploded shortly after liftoff, resulting in the deaths of all seven crew members on board. An investigation into the disaster revealed that NASA engineers had raised concerns about the safety of the shuttle's O-rings in cold weather conditions, but their warnings were dismissed by senior management. Despite ample evidence suggesting potential risks, NASA failed to adequately examine its beliefs and actions regarding the safety of the shuttle.

8.5 Self-Examination, Happiness, and Meaning-Making

I am the hunter of the invisible game. I am not ready to give up the chase yet.

—Fariduddin Attar, 13th-century Sufi poet

Self-examination can significantly contribute to happiness and meaning-making in a leader's life. When leaders engage in deep self-examination, they are more likely to uncover the underlying beliefs and values that drive their actions, enabling them to make more intentional choices that align with their true selves. This alignment between beliefs and actions is a key factor in achieving *eudaimonia*, or human flourishing, as described by Aristotle. Aristotle argued that true happiness comes from living in accordance with one's virtues, which requires continuous self-reflection and moral integrity. By examining their beliefs and actions, leaders can ensure that their work is not just about achieving external success but about fulfilling their own sense of purpose and contributing to the greater good.

In a practical sense, adopting this principle can also lead to more meaningful relationships and a greater sense of fulfillment. Leaders who take the time to understand their own motivations are better equipped to empathize with others and create environments where everyone feels valued and understood. This not only enhances the well-being of those they lead but also fosters a culture of mutual respect and collaboration. As a result, leaders and their teams can both experience greater satisfaction and a deeper sense of meaning in their work. Ultimately, the principle of *examining one's beliefs and actions more than others think wise* is not just about becoming a better leader—it is about becoming a more authentic, fulfilled, and happy person.

8.6 Embracing Vulnerability

The wound is the place where the Light enters you.

—Rumi

Through self-examination, we uncover our true vulnerabilities, and it is by embracing these vulnerabilities as they are that we can transform them into strengths. When we confront our weaknesses and fears, we open the door to deeper understanding, greater resilience, and more meaningful connections with others. This process not only empowers us but also enriches our relationships, both personally and professionally. Leaders who are willing to confront their imperfections and learn from their mistakes can foster a culture of openness and continuous improvement. Rumi's message "The wound is the place where the Light enters you" emphasizes that our pain and struggles can be powerful catalysts for enlightenment and transformation.

Abraham Lincoln's presidency was marked by his willingness to embrace vulnerability and learn from his experiences. During the Civil War, Lincoln faced immense pressure and criticism. Instead of becoming defensive, he actively sought advice from his cabinet and was open to changing his strategies. This humility and willingness to learn were pivotal in his leadership, ultimately preserving the Union and ending slavery. Lincoln's ability to embrace vulnerability and grow from it set a powerful example for future leaders.

When Angela Ahrendts moved to Apple as senior vice president of retail, she transformed the Apple Store from a simple retail outlet into a vibrant, immersive space that embodied the brand's elite status. She infused the stores with elements of community and engagement, turning them into "town squares" where innovation met experience. Ahrendts's vision made Apple Stores destinations—not just places to buy products but spaces where customers felt inspired and connected. Her legacy is one of relentless pursuit of excellence and a fearless commitment to reshaping how the world interacts with iconic brands.

8.7 Invaluable Lessons from Self-Examination: A Personal Story

The fault, dear Brutus, is not in our stars,
But in ourselves, that we are underlings.
—William Shakespeare

Early in my career, I approached projects with a very structured mindset. I prided myself on my detailed and methodical work, and my track record reinforced this confidence. In the words of Adam Grant, author of *Think Again*, I was entrapped in an overconfidence cycle fueled by my past successes. Then came a complex project that proved to be a humbling experience—one that changed how I viewed my approach to project execution.

I had worked tirelessly to complete a comprehensive project report, investing countless hours to ensure that it met the highest technical standards. To my dismay, when I presented the final report to the client, I realized that their expectations for content, approach, length, and focus were completely different from mine. While they didn't question the technical merit of my work, the presentation and focus were not aligned with what they had envisioned.

It was a devastating blow to my ego, which had been fueled by my past achievements. I felt embarrassed, and my confidence took a hit. Thankfully, my supervisor was supportive and helped me step back and examine the assumptions I had made about the client's expectations. He pointed out that I had approached the report from my perspective of rationality without fully considering how the client defined success for the project, which included irrational political elements common in a public water supply project. It was a difficult but valuable lesson. I learned that assuming my structured and familiar approach was inherently correct could lead to misunderstandings and disappointment.

From that experience, I adopted new practices that have stayed with me throughout my career. Now, at the start of every project, I make it a standard practice to conduct a vision-setting meeting with the client to align our expectations and understand their perspective. I also make it a priority to get early approval on an annotated outline for any report, ensuring that we are on the same page before I dive into the detailed work. Frequent check-ins with clients about the project's quality and progress have become another essential part of my workflow. These adjustments not only improve the final product but also strengthen trust and collaboration with clients.

Another pivotal experience came from my work in a community organization. We were planning a large public event, and there were differing opinions on the focus and format. I had my own ideas about what would work best, based on past events and my understanding of community needs. However, there were opposing viewpoints from other committee members, each equally passionate about their own approach. Tensions began to rise as we debated the format, and what started as constructive discussions quickly turned into conflict.

I found myself frustrated and defensive, but I heeded the advice of a close friend and took a moment to step back and examine my own beliefs and actions. I realized that I was so focused on what I thought was the most rational approach that I hadn't taken the time to truly listen and understand why others felt so strongly about their ideas. My assumption that my perspective was the most practical had blinded me to the merits of the alternative viewpoints.

With humility, I reached out to a few members of the committee and asked them to share more about their reasoning and priorities. I listened without judgment, trying to understand their concerns and what they hoped to achieve. What I discovered was that our goals were not so different; it was our approach that varied. By acknowledging this point and validating their ideas, we were able to come up with a plan that incorporated elements from all sides, resulting in a more inclusive and successful event.

These experiences taught me that examining my beliefs and assumptions, especially when I thought I was being rational, was essential for growth and effective collaboration. They showed me that being open to feedback, seeking alignment early, and actively listening to others' perspectives can turn potential conflicts into opportunities for shared success.

8.8 Confronting Bias and Blind Spots

Prejudice is a burden that confuses the past, threatens the future, and
renders the present inaccessible.

—Maya Angelou

Self-examination allows us to confront our personal biases and blind
spots. As leaders, we must continuously examine our assumptions and
seek diverse perspectives to make inclusive and equitable decisions.

Plato's Allegory of the Cave, presented in *The Republic*, is a profound
philosophical narrative that explores the nature of human perception,
knowledge, and enlightenment. Through a vivid and thought-provoking
metaphor, Plato illustrates how biases and blind spots can trap individuals in ignorance and illusion, mistaking shadows for reality, and
how true understanding requires a difficult but transformative journey
toward intellectual and spiritual awakening.

In Plato's Allegory of the Cave, we are asked to imagine a group of
prisoners who have been chained inside a dark cave since birth. These
prisoners are bound in such a way that they can only face the cave wall
in front of them. Behind them, there is a large fire, and between the
fire and the prisoners is a raised walkway where people and objects
occasionally pass by. However, the prisoners cannot see these people
or objects directly; they can only see the shadows cast on the wall by
the fire's light. To the prisoners, these shadows constitute the entirety of
their reality. They have never seen the actual objects or people casting
the shadows and have no concept of a world beyond the cave. The
shadows are the only things they know, and they believe them to be
the most real things in the world.

One day, one of the prisoners is freed and exposed to the world
outside the cave. At first, he is blinded by the intense light of the sun and
overwhelmed by the unfamiliar sights. As his eyes adjust to the light, he

begins to see the world in its true form—full of color, depth, and life. He realizes that the shadows on the cave wall were mere illusions, and that a much richer and more complex reality exists outside. Eager to share this revelation, the freed prisoner returns to the cave to enlighten his fellow captives. However, upon reentering the dark cave, he is no longer accustomed to the darkness and struggles to see the shadows as clearly as before. When he tells the other prisoners about the world outside and the true nature of the shadows, they ridicule and reject him. They are so deeply entrenched in their belief that the shadows are the only reality that they refuse to accept the possibility of anything beyond what they see.

This story shows how biases and limited perspectives can trap individuals in a false reality, and how challenging it can be to break free from these constraints and embrace a deeper understanding of the world. The story underscores the importance of self-examination, critical thinking, and the courage to seek and accept the truth, even when it is uncomfortable or difficult to comprehend.

Eleanor Roosevelt's evolution as a leader exemplifies the importance of confronting biases. Initially, her perspectives were shaped by her privileged background. However, through her extensive travels and interactions with marginalized communities, she recognized her blind spots and became a fierce advocate for civil rights and social justice. Roosevelt's ability to confront her biases and expand her worldview enabled her to champion causes that had a lasting impact on society.

Tim Ryan, US chair of PwC, realized that the company, like many others, had inherent blind spots when it came to racial and social justice issues. Following high-profile events around racial inequality in the United States, Ryan committed to addressing these biases head-on. He launched the CEO Action for Diversity & Inclusion, a coalition that brought together over 2,000 CEOs from various industries who pledged to promote open conversations, tackle unconscious bias, and implement strategies that foster an inclusive workplace. This move encouraged corporate leaders to confront their own blind spots and led to more transparent, equitable policies across participating companies.

Alyson Watson, CEO of Woodard & Curran, was determined to transform her company's commitment to inclusivity and fairness from words into meaningful action. In a bold move, she authorized a comprehensive 27-hour mandatory training program on equity for over 70 of the company's managers. The training was a significant investment in time and resources, but it was necessary to challenge ingrained biases and promote understanding among the leadership team. This initiative was designed not only to educate but to create a safe space for difficult conversations, self-reflection, and the development of actionable insights to incorporate into daily operations.

8.9 Question Workplace "Truths"

The truth is rarely pure and never simple.

—Oscar Wilde

In the workplace, we often find ourselves guided by established "truths"—beliefs about how things work and what drives success. These ideas can feel so ingrained that we rarely pause to question them. However, as Marcus Buckingham and Ashley Goodall argue in *Nine Lies About Work: A Freethinking Leader's Guide to the Real World*, many of these widely held beliefs don't hold up under scrutiny. They challenge us to look beyond what we've accepted as common knowledge and to examine these "truths" critically. The principle *Examine your beliefs and actions more than others think wise* is essential here: by accepting these norms without question, we may blind ourselves to more effective ways of fostering performance, engagement, and satisfaction within our teams.

One example Buckingham and Goodall explore is the idea that "people leave their managers." This statement or so-called truth is often taken at face value and used to attribute employee turnover directly to managerial shortcomings. While poor management can indeed contribute to dissatisfaction, the authors suggest that this assumption may prevent us from looking at deeper, systemic issues. Instead of focusing solely on the manager as the root cause, the authors encourage us to consider the broader work environment. People might leave because they lack meaningful work, a sense of purpose, or connection within their teams—not simply because of a single individual. Furthermore, a poor manager may be a direct product of upper management's leadership approach, organizational culture, or decision-making processes. Without questioning this "truth" that "people leave their managers," organizations risk overlooking crucial factors, addressing only surface-level symptoms rather than the true causes of employee turnover.

Another workplace "truth" often accepted without examination is that feedback is essential for growth. Many organizations emphasize the importance of providing frequent feedback to drive improvement, assuming it always leads to positive outcomes. Yet *Nine Lies About Work* points out that feedback can sometimes be counterproductive, especially if it's overly critical or doesn't align with the employee's strengths. Instead of using feedback as a tool for critique, the authors propose that people benefit more from support and recognition for their strengths, which can boost motivation and engagement. This shift challenges traditional feedback models and encourages us to question the impact of our methods on individual performance and development.

By questioning so-called workplace truths, *Nine Lies About Work* invites us to think critically about our beliefs and practices. When we fail to examine the assumptions that drive our actions, we may inadvertently hinder our own growth and that of our teams. Adopting a mindset that questions accepted norms allows us to uncover what truly drives performance, engagement, and satisfaction. In doing so, we create an environment that values individual strengths and fosters genuine connection, ultimately leading to a healthier and more productive workplace.

8.10 Leaving a Lasting Legacy

We can easily forgive a child who is afraid of the dark; the real tragedy of life is when men are afraid of the light.

—Unknown

Leaders who engage in deep self-reflection and continuous self-improvement leave a lasting legacy. Their commitment to examining and refining their beliefs and actions inspires future generations and creates enduring positive change.

Anne Mulcahy, former CEO of Xerox, exemplified the power of self-reflection in effective leadership. By thoroughly examining the company's difficulties and her own leadership strategies, she led a remarkable recovery, guiding Xerox from the brink of bankruptcy to financial stability. Her magic was to focus on collaborative efforts and adapt the business model to meet market demand.

As the first woman to lead IBM, Ginni Rometty spearheaded the company's pivot to cloud computing, artificial intelligence, and cybersecurity. Her vision reshaped IBM's future, focusing on innovative technologies such as the development of Watson, the AI platform. Rometty's leadership emphasized the importance of reinvention and adaptability in the tech industry, leaving a legacy of transformation and forward-thinking strategy.

As the first female CEO of a major global automaker, Mary Barra has redefined General Motors' future by pushing for sustainability and innovation. Her bold commitment to transitioning GM to an all-electric vehicle lineup by 2035 has positioned the company as a leader in the shift toward eco-friendly transportation. Under her leadership, GM has invested heavily in electric and autonomous technology, showcasing her forward-thinking approach to steering the company through an evolving industry.

8.11 Holistic Approach to Self-Examination

Look well into thyself; there is a source of strength which will always spring up if thou wilt always look.

—Marcus Aurelius

Many modern companies have adopted practices such as regular reflection sessions and feedback loops, where leaders and employees alike are encouraged to discuss their past actions and the rationale behind their decisions. The intent is to create an environment of self-reflection and self-examination, reminiscent of the Socratic dialogues that sought to uncover deeper truths.

However, a large majority of these reflection sessions fail to bring any meaningful and lasting change in organizational practices because they often are focused solely on actions, neglecting the underlying beliefs and values that drive those actions. Actions are the outward manifestations of deeper cognitive and emotional processes. Without examining the foundational beliefs and values, we fail to understand the true motivations behind our behaviors and cannot address the root causes of any issues. For example, a manager who only assesses their actions in managing a team may notice poor team performance but might miss the deeper issue of a belief in autocratic leadership styles over collaborative ones.

This incomplete self-examination prevents meaningful change and growth. According to psychological theories such as the *theory of planned behavior*, postulated by University of Massachusetts psychology professor Icek Ajzen, attitudes and behaviors are deeply influenced by underlying beliefs and values. Furthermore, studies in organizational behavior have shown that effective self-reflection includes examining one's values and beliefs to align actions with long-term goals and ethical standards. Thus, a holistic approach to self-examination that includes a deep understanding of the *belief-value-attitude-behavior* spectrum is essential for genuine personal and professional development.

8.12 Examine Your Belief-Value-Attitude-Behavior Spectrum

Belief creates the actual fact.

—William James

The interplay between beliefs, values, attitudes, and behaviors is a foundational concept in psychology and behavioral science. This spectrum, shown in the figure below, illustrates how deeply held beliefs shape our values, how these values inform our attitudes, and how our attitudes ultimately drive our behaviors. It provides critical insights into human behavior. Successful self-examination requires a deep understanding of this intricate relationship and how our internal beliefs influence our outward actions, allowing us to make more informed choices and align our behaviors with our true values.

Beliefs form the bedrock of our values, which in turn shape our attitudes and drive our behaviors. By examining this spectrum, we can better predict and influence behaviors in various contexts, from personal habits to organizational practices and societal norms. This understanding is not only academically enriching but also practically valuable for leaders, educators, and policymakers aiming to foster positive change through effective training programs.

By unpacking this spectrum with concrete examples, we can better understand the mechanisms that underlie decision-making and action, which in turn will enable us to influence others and bring about changes in our organizations.

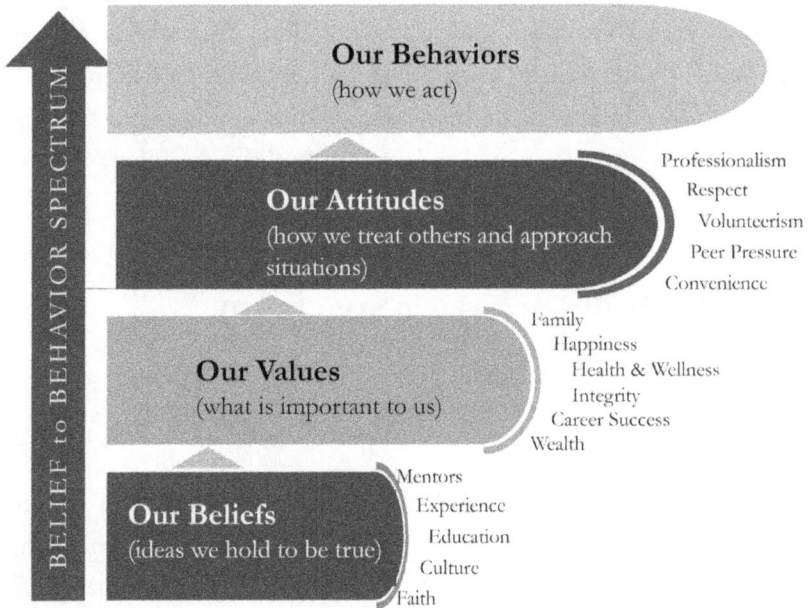

From Belief to Behavior: The hidden architecture of who we are.

Beliefs as the Foundation

Beliefs are convictions and ideas that we hold to be true. We often seek in our own way sound reasons or evidence for these potential beliefs. As shown in the figure, these are cognitive judgments that can be formed through personal experiences, faith, mentors, cultural norms, education, social influences, and the information available to us.

Beliefs are foundational because they shape our understanding of the world and our place within it. Consider the belief in the importance of environmental conservation. This belief might stem from scientific understanding, personal experiences with nature, or cultural emphasis on sustainability.

Values Emerging from Beliefs

Values are deeply held principles that guide our judgments about what is important in life. In a 1992 paper published in *Advances in Experimental Social Psychology*, Schwartz concluded that values are "desirable, trans-situational goals, varying in importance, which serve as guiding principles in people's lives."

Values emerge from our beliefs and represent what we consider to be right, beneficial, and important, such as happiness, family, wealth, health, and so on. They often become the standards by which we order our lives and prioritize our choices.

For example, from the belief in environmental conservation may arise the value of sustainability. This value influences how we prioritize actions and decisions regarding resource use, waste management, and lifestyle choices.

Attitudes Shaped by Values

Attitudes are mental dispositions or feelings toward particular objects, people, or events. In their book *Belief, Attitude, Intention, and Behavior: An Introduction to Theory and Research*, Fishbein and Ajzen defined attitudes as "learned predispositions to respond in a consistently favorable or unfavorable manner with respect to a given object."

Attitudes are shaped by our values and reflect how we respond emotionally and cognitively to various stimuli. A person who values sustainability will likely have a positive attitude toward recycling programs, renewable energy sources, and policies aimed at reducing pollution. Their attitude toward these initiatives will be one of support and advocacy. However, factors that may not have been internalized as beliefs and values can still influence a person's attitudes at the point of decision-making. Typical influences include the desire to please, political correctness, convenience, peer pressure, and psychological stressors.

Behaviors Driven by Attitudes

Behaviors are the outward expressions of our attitudes. Ajzen's theory of planned behavior suggests that attitudes significantly influence the intention to perform behaviors, which in turn predicts actual behavior.

Behaviors are the actions we take in response to our attitudes, which are informed by our values and underpinned by our beliefs. An individual with a positive attitude toward environmental conservation will engage in behaviors such as recycling, reducing energy consumption, and supporting green policies. This behavior is a direct manifestation of their belief in the importance of protecting the environment and their value of sustainability.

Here are some examples of the *belief-value-attitude-behavior* spectrum from various fields.

Example 1. Health and Wellness

Belief: Regular physical exercise is crucial for maintaining good health.
Value: Health and wellness.
Attitude: Positive outlook toward exercise and fitness activities.
Behavior: Regularly attending the gym, participating in sports, or engaging in daily walks. A study by Biddle and Mutrie highlights that "attitudes toward physical activity, influenced by the value placed on health, significantly predict engagement in exercise behaviors."

Example 2. Workplace Integrity

Belief: Honesty is the best policy for long-term success.
Value: Integrity and transparency.
Attitude: Favorable disposition toward ethical behavior and honesty in professional settings.

Behavior: Reporting accurate information, avoiding deceitful practices, and encouraging a culture of openness. Treviño, Weaver, and Reynolds state that "organizational values of integrity directly impact employee attitudes toward ethical behavior, which in turn, shape their actions and decision-making processes."

Social Justice

Belief: All individuals deserve equal rights and opportunities.
Value: Equality and justice.
Attitude: Supportive stance toward policies and actions that promote social equity.
Behavior: Participating in or supporting advocacy groups, voting for inclusive policies, and actively promoting diversity. According to a study by Sagiv and Schwartz, published in the *Journal of Personality and Social Psychology*, "Values of equality and social justice influence positive attitudes toward diversity, which are manifested in behaviors that support equitable and inclusive practices."

Example 3. Environmental Sustainability

Belief: Protecting the environment is essential for future generations.
Value: Sustainability and conservation.
Attitude: Positive disposition toward eco-friendly practices and reducing environmental impact.
Behavior: Implementing recycling programs, reducing plastic use, and supporting green initiatives. A study by Kollmuss and Agyeman published in *Environmental Education Research* found that "values related to environmental concern significantly influence attitudes toward sustainable behaviors, leading individuals to adopt more eco-friendly practices."

Example 4. Educational Achievement

Belief: Education is a key factor in personal and professional development.
Value: Knowledge and lifelong learning.
Attitude: Positive outlook toward education and continuous learning.
Behavior: Attending classes, seeking additional learning opportunities, and engaging in intellectual discussions. According to Eccles and Wigfield, "The value placed on education can shape students' attitudes toward learning, which in turn affects their academic behaviors and performance."

Example 5. Community Service

Belief: Helping others is a fundamental duty of being a good citizen.
Value: Altruism and community support.
Attitude: Positive view toward volunteerism and community engagement.
Behavior: Regularly volunteering, participating in community events, and donating to charitable causes. A study by Penner and colleagues published in *Annual Review of Psychology* suggests that "values related to altruism influence attitudes toward helping behaviors, which significantly predict the frequency and type of volunteer activities individuals engage in."

Belief-Driven Actions: Real-Life and Fictional Examples

In 1968, at just 20 years old, Kareem Abdul-Jabbar (then Lew Alcindor) was already a prominent basketball star at UCLA and a top prospect for Team USA in the Mexico City Olympics. Yet he made a bold and risky decision—to boycott the Olympics in protest of racial injustice in America. His belief in justice and equality was deeply shaped by the civil rights movement and the systemic racism Black Americans faced daily.

Rather than basking in the glory of international competition, he saw sports as a potential distraction from the urgent fight for social change.

Guided by his values of integrity, solidarity, and moral courage, Abdul-Jabbar chose principle over prestige. While many saw Olympic participation as a patriotic duty, his attitude was clear: silence in the face of injustice was complicity. Despite immense pressure and potential career risks, he took action, sacrificing a once-in-a-lifetime opportunity and enduring public criticism to stand for his convictions. His decision became a defining moment in sports activism, proving that true leadership—at any age—is about aligning beliefs, values, attitudes, and actions in pursuit of meaningful change.

In Harper Lee's novel *To Kill a Mockingbird*, Atticus Finch serves as a powerful fictional example of a leader grappling with his beliefs and actions. Atticus, a white lawyer in the racially segregated South, chooses to defend Tom Robinson, an African American man falsely accused of raping a white woman. Atticus firmly believes in justice and equality, values that are severely tested in the prejudiced society he lives in. Despite facing social ostracism and threats, Atticus's defense of Robinson is a direct action that aligns with his deep-seated beliefs in fairness and moral integrity. His leadership is marked by the courage to uphold his principles in the face of overwhelming opposition.

8.13 The Problem of a Two-Legged Stool of Leadership

Strong leadership stands on people, not just processes and tools.

Despite the importance and relevance of the *belief-value-attitude-be-havior* spectrum model, most leadership books and training programs even today continue to focus predominantly on attitudes and behavior modification. This prevailing approach is rooted in competency-based leadership thinking, which suggests that by simply learning specific skills or behaviors—"Do this, do that, learn this, learn that"—one can become an effective leader. This reductionist view neglects the deeper, more foundational elements of belief and value systems that truly drive sustainable leadership. Consequently, this approach to training our leaders and managers contributes to the troubling statistic that only 18% of managers possess a high level of talent in managing others, as highlighted by the 2016 Gallup Poll.

Training programs and leadership books constitute a massive indus-try, continuously churning out new content and methodologies aimed at improving leadership skills. However, this relentless focus on skills and behaviors overlooks the critical aspect of internal alignment and self-awareness. The result is a revolving door of leadership development initiatives that fail to produce lasting change. Leaders trained in this manner may exhibit temporary improvements but often revert to old habits under pressure because the underlying beliefs and values that drive their actions remain unexamined and unchanged. This explains why the vast majority of leadership development efforts fall short of their goals, leaving organizations with a deficit of truly effective leaders.

Effective leadership can be likened to a three-legged stool, with the legs of *process, tools, and people.* Focusing training efforts solely on processes and tools to modify behavior creates an unstable, two-legged stool, leading to inconsistency and instability in leadership practices. Leaders become unpredictable, changing their approaches from one day to the next without a solid foundation of aligned beliefs and values to guide their actions. Truly effective leadership training must integrate all three legs—addressing not just what leaders do (*process*) and how they do it (*tools*), but also why they do it (*people*). By cultivating self-awareness and aligning personal beliefs and values with organizational goals, leaders can achieve greater stability and effectiveness, ultimately leading to more sustainable success for their teams and organizations.

Because leadership training has historically focused on behavior modification rather than examining the underlying belief systems, we often fail to see the expected improvements in business performance. Below, we explore some illusions and mistaken beliefs that have hindered true progress.

8.14 Examine Your Illusions about Rationality in Project Management

Man stands face-to-face with the irrational.

—Albert Camus

As part of our applying the principle *Examine your beliefs and actions more than others think wise,* let us examine a common belief in rationality, especially in the context of project management. Project managers are universally trained on the five key aspects of project management— scope, schedule, budget, deliverables, and project team—all of which drive product quality. The common thinking is that these are all quantifiable, measurable, and rational elements that can be controlled and optimized through rigorous methodologies. Project management tools and techniques—such as the *PMBOK Guide* from the Project Management Institute, Agile development, and Scrum methods—are designed to increase efficiency and ensure project success by controlling these five aspects of a project.

However, the reality of project success often tells a different story. The 2020 CHAOS study of IT projects in the United States revealed that only 31% of projects are deemed successful—less than a third. Additionally, about 19% of projects fail outright, and a staggering 50% are over budget, delivered late, and with reduced scope. These statistics highlight a significant gap between the theoretical rationality of project management practices and the actual outcomes achieved in practice.

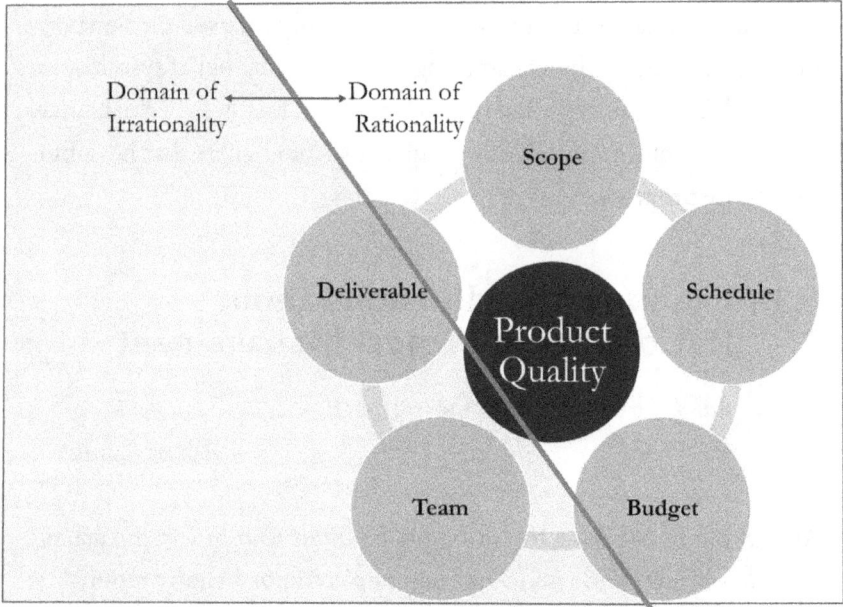

Rational plans meet irrational realities: the project management paradox.

One of the primary reasons for these poor results is the mistaken belief that everything in project management lies within the rational domain. This mindset guides our approach, focusing on quantifiable and measurable elements while neglecting the irrational aspects influenced by human emotions and perceptions. Project teams and perceptions of the deliverables are not just mechanical components; they are deeply affected by the psychological and emotional states of the individuals involved, which are difficult to control through rational methods alone because they belong to the irrational domain of project management.

Dan Ariely, in his books on behavioral economics such as *Predictably Irrational* and *The Upside of Irrationality*, explores the concept of irrational behavior and how it affects decision-making processes.

Ariely's research demonstrates that humans are not always rational actors and that their decisions are often influenced by emotions, biases, and cognitive shortcuts. This insight is crucial for project management, where the human element plays a significant role in the success or failure of projects.

For instance, consider the impact of team dynamics and morale on project performance. A project team that is demotivated or experiencing interpersonal conflicts is likely to perform poorly, regardless of how well-defined the scope, schedule, and budget are. Similarly, stakeholder perceptions and expectations can influence the perceived success of a project. If stakeholders feel that their needs and concerns are not being addressed, they may deem a project unsuccessful even if it meets its technical specifications.

Moreover, the complexity and uncertainty inherent in many projects further complicates the rational approach. Projects often face unforeseen challenges and changes, requiring flexibility and adaptability rather than rigid adherence to predefined plans. The failure to anticipate and manage these uncertainties can lead to project delays, cost overruns, and scope creep, undermining the rational foundations of project management.

The solution lies in embracing a more holistic approach to project management that recognizes the interplay between rational and irrational elements. This involves developing emotional intelligence and soft skills among project managers, fostering a positive and collaborative team culture, and being attuned to the needs and concerns of all stakeholders. Additionally, incorporating agile methodologies can help manage uncertainty and complexity by promoting iterative development and continuous feedback.

In conclusion, the illusion of rationality in project management is a significant barrier to achieving better project outcomes. By acknowledging and addressing the irrational elements influenced by human emotions and perceptions, project managers can develop more effective strategies and approaches. This shift in mindset, supported by insights from behavioral economics, can lead to more successful projects that meet their objectives and deliver value to stakeholders.

We can expand this idea of the importance of emotion from a project to business transformations—or major changes in business organizations—that require employee buy-in and cooperation for success. Collaborative research from Oxford's Saïd Business School with Ernst & Young indicates that business transformations prioritizing workforce emotions are 2.6 times more likely to succeed. Leaders who provide emotional support during transformations can reduce workforce strain by 136%.

8.15 Mistaken Belief about Leader's Responsibility

Seldom, very seldom, does complete truth belong to any human disclosure; seldom can it happen that something is not a little disguised, or a little mistaken.

—Jane Austen

There is a prevalent mistaken belief in many organizations that leaders are responsible for the job or the product. This misconception can lead to a narrow focus on deliverables and outputs, rather than on the people who are ultimately responsible for creating those deliverables and achieving those outputs. The truth is: leaders are not directly responsible for the job; they are responsible for the people who are responsible for the job. This distinction is crucial for fostering a productive and supportive work environment where employees feel valued and empowered.

By shifting the focus from the job to the people doing the job, leaders can create a more engaged and motivated workforce. This approach acknowledges that while processes and tools are important, the true drivers of success are the people who use them. When leaders prioritize their team's well-being and development, they not only enhance individual performance but also foster a culture of trust and collaboration. This, in turn, leads to better overall outcomes for the organization. As Simon Sinek aptly puts it, "Leadership is not about being in charge. It is about taking care of those in your charge."

Understanding that people are both rational and irrational is fundamental to effective leadership. Human behavior is complex, and employees may sometimes act in ways that seem illogical or counterproductive. These actions can stem from a variety of factors, including emotional responses, personal biases, and external stressors. Leaders who recognize this complexity are better equipped to address the root causes of irrational behavior and guide their teams toward more consistent and rational actions, rather than focusing only on the measurable metrics of organizational performance.

A leader's ability to navigate the irrational aspects of human behavior hinges on their emotional intelligence, which involves the ability to understand and manage one's own emotions, as well as the emotions of others. For example, a project manager who focuses solely on deadlines and deliverables may miss underlying team issues such as low morale or interpersonal conflicts. In contrast, a leader who prioritizes their team's well-being and development can address these issues proactively, ensuring that the team remains motivated and cohesive. This approach not only enhances the overall performance of the team but also leads to more sustainable success. By shifting the focus from the job to the people responsible for the job, leaders can create a more dynamic and effective organization that is capable of navigating both rational and irrational challenges.

8.16 A Costly Management Myth

Myths, which are believed in, tend to become true.

—George Orwell

A widely circulated misquote attributed to Dr. Edward Deming, the renowned management guru, states, "You can't manage what you can't measure." However, according to the Deming Institute, Dr. Deming actually said, "It is wrong to suppose that if you can't measure it, you can't manage it—a costly myth." This misquote has led to a popular but fundamentally flawed belief among many managers and leaders who are trained to prioritize metrics as the primary tool for running their businesses.

The prevalence of this misquote can be attributed to the managerial inclination toward quantifiable metrics. Many leaders focus heavily on metrics such as revenue, profit, productivity, and billability to gauge the health of their companies. While these metrics are undoubtedly crucial, overemphasizing them can have detrimental effects. It can dishearten top performers who feel their contributions are reduced to mere numbers, and it can disable weaker performers who may struggle to meet these rigid numerical targets.

Dr. Deming identified "Running a company on visible figures alone" as one of the seven deadly diseases of management. He believed that an exclusive focus on quantifiable metrics overlooks the qualitative aspects of management that are equally important. Factors such as employee engagement, morale, creativity, and the overall work environment cannot always be measured but are critical to an organization's long-term success and health. When employees feel they are seen only as numbers, their engagement and morale suffer, leading to a decline in overall performance.

The myth perpetuated by the misquote undermines the essence of Deming's teachings. He advocated for a holistic approach to management, where metrics are used as one of many tools to understand and improve a company's operations. Effective management requires looking beyond the numbers to understand the underlying processes, motivations, and human elements that drive those numbers. By doing so, managers can foster a more engaged, motivated, and productive workforce, ultimately leading to sustainable success.

While metrics are important, they should not overshadow the qualitative aspects that are vital to managing a successful organization. Embracing Deming's true teachings encourages a balanced approach, integrating measurable and immeasurable elements to create a more holistic and effective management strategy.

8.17 Limiting Belief of "It Does Not Apply to Us"

Make not your thoughts your prisons.

—William Shakespeare

Many leaders and managers often dismiss new ideas with the limiting belief that "It does not apply to us." This mindset stifles innovation and undermines potential growth opportunities. For instance, managers of consulting firms might argue that Google's 20% rule, which allows employees to spend 20% of their time on projects they are passionate about, cannot be applied to their business model because their profits are directly tied to the billability of each employee. They believe setting high billability targets is essential to remain profitable, unlike tech companies. However, this limiting belief overlooks the possibility of creatively adapting the idea to fit their context.

For example, a consulting company might consider dedicating 5% (equivalent to two hours per week) of indirect time to professional development or research and idea generation. Alternatively, it could allow a select group of employees, perhaps the most creative and passionate ones, to have 10% of their time dedicated to innovation. This adaptation of Google's 20% rule can foster a culture of innovation without significantly impacting overall billability. By encouraging employees to explore new ideas and solutions, consulting firms could discover new services or efficiency improvements that ultimately benefit the company. This practice can be seen as an investment in long-term innovation rather than an immediate cost.

Deloitte Consulting provides a compelling example with its Greenhouses initiative, which offers creative spaces designed to foster innovative problem-solving and collaboration, where consultants can brainstorm and prototype new solutions for clients.

Another common example of a limiting belief is the outright rejection of remote work before the pandemic, when many companies believed that remote work was not feasible for their operations. However, when forced to adapt, numerous organizations found that remote work not only maintained productivity but also offered employees greater flexibility and satisfaction. Companies like Twitter and Microsoft have since embraced remote work as a permanent option, recognizing the long-term benefits it brings.

Breaking free from the limiting belief that innovative ideas do not apply to certain contexts can unlock significant potential for growth and employee satisfaction. This shift not only enhances productivity and profitability but also cultivates a more engaged and motivated workforce. Embracing new ideas and approaches, even in small, manageable ways, can lead to substantial long-term benefits for any organization.

8.18 Examine Your Mindsets and Beliefs

The mind is everything. What you think you become.

—Buddha

Beliefs are the fundamental assumptions and convictions we hold about ourselves, others, and the world. They serve as the foundation upon which our mindsets are built. Mindsets, in turn, are the lenses through which we view and interpret our experiences. The relationship between beliefs and mindsets is profound, as our beliefs shape our attitudes, behaviors, and ultimately our success in various aspects of life. Understanding and examining this relationship is crucial for personal development and growth.

Carol Dweck, a renowned psychologist, introduced the concepts of fixed and growth mindsets in her seminal work *Mindset: The New Psychology of Success*. According to Dweck, individuals with a fixed mindset believe that their abilities and intelligence are static traits that cannot be changed. This belief leads them to avoid challenges, give up easily, and see effort as fruitless. They tend to view failure as a reflection of their inherent limitations and seek validation of their intelligence through success.

Conversely, individuals with a growth mindset believe that their abilities and intelligence can be developed through effort, learning, and perseverance. This belief fosters a love for challenges, resilience in the face of setbacks, and a recognition that effort is essential for growth. Those with a growth mindset view failure as an opportunity to learn and improve, and they seek feedback as a valuable tool for development.

Our beliefs, whether they align with a fixed or growth mindset, significantly influence our behavior and outcomes. For example, employees with a growth mindset are more likely to seek out learning opportunities, take on new challenges, and contribute to a culture of innovation and collaboration. An employee with a fixed mindset may believe, *I'm not good at public speaking, so I'll avoid presenting at meetings,* and consequently they miss opportunities for growth and visibility within the company. In contrast, an employee with a growth mindset thinks, *Public speaking isn't my strength yet, but I'll take on more presentation opportunities to improve my skills,* actively seeking feedback and practicing persistently to enhance their abilities.

The role of our beliefs in shaping our mindsets extends beyond individual success to impact relationships and organizational dynamics. Leaders with a growth mindset are more likely to foster an environment that encourages learning, collaboration, and resilience. According to Carol Dweck, they view their team's potential as something that can be developed, leading to higher levels of engagement and performance. On the other hand, leaders with a fixed mindset may inadvertently stifle growth by failing to provide opportunities for development and by focusing solely on outcomes rather than the learning process.

Examining and reshaping our beliefs is essential for cultivating a growth mindset. This process involves self-reflection and critical analysis of our thought patterns and reactions to challenges. It requires us to question the origins of our beliefs, observe how they affect our behavior, and consider alternative perspectives. By actively seeking feedback, embracing new experiences, and remaining open to change, we can shift from a fixed mindset that limits to a growth mindset that empowers.

In summary, our beliefs play a pivotal role in shaping our mindsets, which in turn influence our behavior, relationships, and overall success. By understanding the relationship between beliefs and mindsets, and by actively working to cultivate a growth mindset, we can unlock our potential for personal and professional development. The work of scholars like Carol Dweck has provided valuable insights into this process, offering a framework for fostering resilience, innovation, and continuous improvement in various aspects of life.

8.19 Examine Your Actions: Paradox of Emotion and Rationality

The intuitive mind is a sacred gift and the rational mind is a faithful servant. We have created a society that honors the servant and has forgotten the gift.

—Albert Einstein

Leaders often grapple with the paradox of balancing emotion and rationality. Traditional fixed mindsets suggest that excessive emotion undermines rationality, asserting that a rational leader must suppress emotions to make sound decisions. Conversely, a growth mindset embraces the idea that emotions are integral to rational decision-making. Research supports this view, showing that emotions influence our rational brain for good reasons, highlighting the complex interplay between these forces.

To resolve this paradox, we can draw wisdom from the 13th-century Sufi poet Rumi, who said, *"Water in the boat is the ruin of the boat, but water under the boat is its support."* This metaphor illustrates that emotions, like water, are essential for leadership. However, unchecked emotions can lead to poor decisions and instability. Therefore, the goal is not to eliminate emotions from our lives but to manage them effectively, fostering emotional intelligence.

Be a boatman; don't let the waters of emotion sink your lifeboat—let them become the current that carries you forward with wisdom and strength.

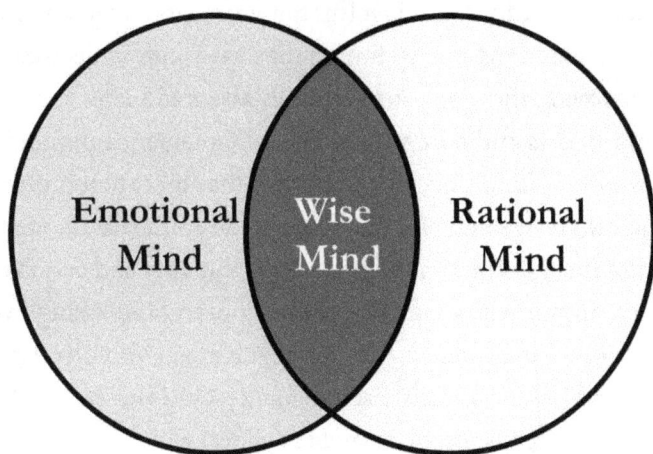

Where emotion meets logic, wisdom emerges.

A leader must strive for a "wise mind," integrating both rationality and emotional intelligence. As illustrated in the figure, the wise mind sits at the intersection of the emotional mind and the rational mind—a balanced mental state where logic and feeling coexist in harmony. The emotional mind alone may react impulsively, while the rational mind may overlook human nuance. But the wise mind brings clarity through balance, allowing leaders to make decisions that are both thoughtful and compassionate. Wise leaders don't suppress emotions or ignore reason. They skillfully steer between emotions and reason to stay afloat, even in turbulent times. Be a boatman; don't let the water of emotion sink your lifeboat, but let it carry you forward with wisdom and strength.

8.20 Examine Your Emotional Intelligence

When dealing with people, remember you are not dealing with creatures of logic, but with creatures of emotion.

—Dale Carnegie

Emotional intelligence (EI) is deeply connected to the principle of examining your actions, as it involves the awareness and understanding of your own emotions and the impact they have on your decision-making and behavior, allowing you to critically assess and align your actions with your beliefs and core values. Daniel Goleman, a pioneer in EI research, notes, " Emotional intelligence is the ability to monitor one's own and others' feelings and emotions, to discriminate among them, and to use this information to guide one's thinking and actions." It is a critical component of effective leadership, encompassing five key elements: (1) self-awareness. (2) self-regulation, (3) motivation, (4) empathy, and (5) social skills. Each element plays a vital role in shaping a leader's ability to inspire, manage, and connect with their team. Daniel Goleman, who popularized the concept of EI, asserts that these traits are integral to successful leadership. Let's explore each of these five elements to understand why they are essential for leaders and what actions one can take to acquire emotional intelligence.

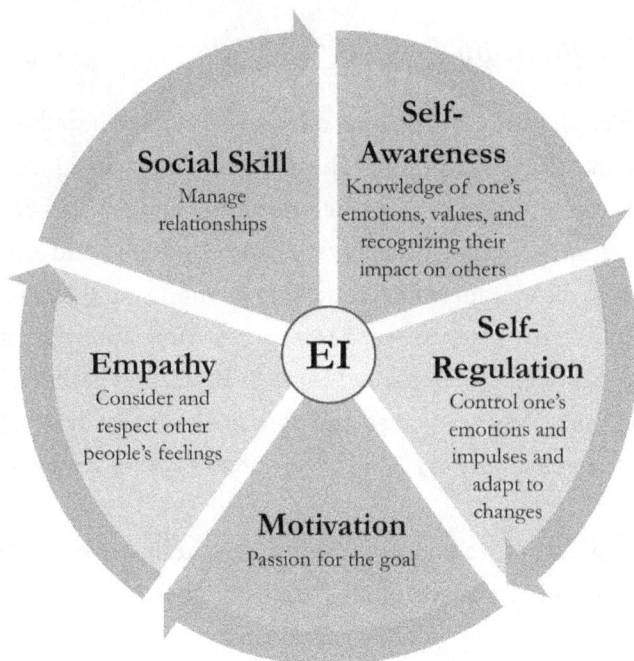

The five pillars of emotional intelligence:
mastering the self to lead with others.

1. Self-Awareness

Self-awareness is the ability to recognize and understand one's own emotions, strengths, weaknesses, and values. It involves being conscious of how emotions affect behavior and decision-making. A self-aware leader is reflective and knows how their emotions affect their interactions with others. Self-awareness allows leaders to understand their emotional triggers and how their mood affects their team. As Aristotle noted, "Knowing yourself is the beginning of all wisdom." Leaders who are self-aware can better manage their reactions, fostering a stable and reliable environment that builds trust and respect within their team.

Action: Regularly reflect on your emotions and seek feedback; practice mindfulness and journaling to increase self-awareness.

2. Self-Regulation

Self-regulation involves managing one's emotions and impulses, maintaining control, and adapting to changing circumstances. It requires a leader to stay composed, think before acting, and express emotions appropriately. Self-regulation prevents hasty decisions and emotional outbursts that can undermine leadership credibility and team morale. It helps leaders navigate stress and remain calm under pressure, demonstrating resilience and dependability. As Founding Father Thomas Jefferson said, "Nothing gives one person so much advantage over another as to remain always cool and unruffled under all circumstances."

Action: Pause before you speak or react, practice stress-reduction techniques, and stay adaptable to change.

3. Motivation

Motivation in the context of EI is about having an inner drive to achieve goals for reasons beyond external rewards. It involves a passion for work, optimism, and a strong commitment to personal and organizational objectives. Motivated leaders inspire and energize their teams, fostering a culture of excellence and persistence. They set high standards and are proactive in pursuing goals, even in the face of setbacks. US president John Quincy Adams captured this essence: "If your actions inspire others to dream more, learn more, do more, and become more, you are a leader." Motivated leaders can ignite the same passion and drive in their teams, resulting in higher performance and achievement.

Action: Set personal goals, maintain a can-do positive attitude, and focus on what inspires and drives you.

4. Empathy

Empathy is the ability to understand and share the feelings of others. It involves active listening, recognizing emotions in others, and responding compassionately. Empathy allows leaders to connect with their team on a deeper level, fostering trust and loyalty. It helps in understanding team members' perspectives, addressing their concerns, and resolving conflicts amicably. Carl Rogers emphasized the importance of empathy: "Empathy is a special way of coming to know another and ourselves." Empathetic leaders create an inclusive and supportive work environment, enhancing collaboration and morale.

Action: Actively listen to others, put yourself in their shoes, and respond with compassion and understanding. Learn from emotionally intelligent individuals by observing how they handle various situations.

5. Social Skills

Social skills encompass a broad range of competencies, including effective communication, conflict resolution, and the ability to build and maintain relationships. It involves being adept at managing social interactions and influencing others positively. Strong social skills are essential for leaders to navigate the complexities of organizational dynamics. Leaders who excel in social skills can build networks, foster teamwork, and lead change effectively. They are persuasive and can rally support for their vision and initiatives. As Dale Carnegie famously said, "You can make more friends in two months by becoming interested in other people than you can in two years by trying to get other people interested in you." Leaders with strong social skills can cultivate a cooperative and motivated workforce, driving collective success.

Action: Communicate clearly and assertively but politely, nurture strong relationships, and resolve conflicts amicably.

These five elements of emotional intelligence are indispensable traits for effective leadership. By cultivating these traits, leaders can create a positive, productive, and resilient organizational culture, driving sustained success.

8.21 Emotional Intelligence Is No Soft Skill

Emotional intelligence is the sine qua non of leadership. Without it, a person can have the best training in the world, an incisive, analytical mind, and an endless supply of smart ideas, but he still won't make a great leader.

—Daniel Goleman

Despite extensive research and numerous best-selling books, many managers still dismiss emotional intelligence as a touchy-feely, soft skill. While the importance of traits like empathy and self-awareness is acknowledged, intelligence and technical capability are often viewed as the primary drivers of professional success. This attitude stems from the belief that EI is solely about being nice rather than recognizing its importance in managing behavior, navigating social complexities, and making decisions. A common belief is that rationality and objectivity are the keys to success, leading to the dismissal of emotions as irrational or irrelevant in professional settings.

Furthermore, some cultures or industries place strong emphasis on technical skills and cognitive intelligence (measured by IQ) over emotional intelligence and interpersonal skills. This bias can lead to undervaluing EI. Many educational and professional systems prioritize hard skills and technical knowledge over emotional skills like EI, leading to a lack of awareness and training in EI.

In addition, EI often involves long-term development and subtle benefits, whereas people and organizations may favor immediate, tangible results and quick fixes.

Despite these perceptions, research has shown that emotional intelligence is critical for effective leadership, teamwork, and overall success. Emphasizing EI can lead to better decision-making, stronger relationships, and improved organizational outcomes.

A 2011 CareerBuilder survey involving more than 2,600 hiring managers in the United States revealed that 71% of employers value EI over IQ. This preference highlights the increasing recognition of EI as crucial for professional success. According to this survey, 75% of employers stated they are more likely to promote employees with high EI over those with high IQ. Additionally, 59% of employers stated they would not hire someone with a high IQ but low EI. This finding illustrates the critical importance of emotional intelligence in fostering a collaborative and effective work environment, emphasizing that technical skills alone are insufficient for professional success.

EI's critical role in professional success is underscored with compelling evidence in the blog article "Emotional Intelligence Is No Soft Skill" by the Harvard University Division of Continuing Education. Research from the *Harvard Business Review* reveals that EI accounts for nearly 90% of what distinguishes top performers from their peers when IQ and technical skills are similar. Furthermore, Sanofi, a global pharmaceutical company, saw a 12% increase in performance after emphasizing EI in their sales force, while Motorola, a leader in telecommunications, noted improved productivity in over 90% of staff following EI training. These statistics highlight that EI is a fundamental component of effective leadership and organizational success, not just a peripheral skill.

8.22 Psychological Safety and Emotional Intelligence

Psychological safety gives people the confidence to express their thoughts and admit mistakes, knowing that they won't be shot down.
                    —Amy Edmondson, Harvard Business School

Psychological safety—the belief that one can speak up without risk of punishment or humiliation—is a critical driver of team performance and innovation. Emotional intelligence (EI) plays a central role in creating this environment. Leaders with high EI are self-aware and empathetic, fostering trust and open communication within their teams. They manage emotions constructively, resolve conflicts productively, and encourage diverse viewpoints. By recognizing and addressing the emotional needs of their teams, they cultivate a climate in which people contribute fully and take the risks necessary for growth and success.

Google's landmark Project Aristotle, which analyzed more than 250 team variables, found that psychological safety was the single most important factor in high-performing teams—outranking dependability, structure, clarity, meaning, and impact of work. Teams with high psychological safety are more collaborative, innovative, and effective. Yet McKinsey research reveals that only 26 percent of leaders consistently create this kind of environment, despite its proven benefits.

Part of the challenge lies in widespread misunderstandings about what psychological safety truly means. In their June 2025 *Harvard Business Review* article, "What People Get Wrong About Psychological Safety," Amy C. Edmondson and Michaela J. Kerrissey identify six common misconceptions that can undermine well-intentioned efforts. First, psychological safety is not about being nice or avoiding discomfort—it is about permission for candor, where constructive truth-telling matters more than keeping things pleasant. Second, it does not mean always getting your way—your ideas should be heard, but decisions must serve the team's shared goals. Third, it is not synonymous with job security—layoffs may still occur, but people should feel free to voice concerns without fear of retaliation. Fourth, it is not at odds with high performance—true excellence requires both rigorous standards and open dialogue. Fifth, it cannot be legislated into existence—trust and openness are built interaction by interaction through leaders' messaging, modeling, and mentoring. And sixth, it is not solely a top-down mandate—anyone, at any level, can strengthen safety by inviting input and responding constructively.

When leaders dispel these myths, keep the focus on meaningful goals, elevate the quality of team conversations, and embed regular reflection into their teams' rhythms, psychological safety shifts from a vague ideal to a lived reality. As Edmondson and Kerrissey observe, "Ironically, talking less about psychological safety and more about the goal and the context and why everyone's input matters is the first step in building psychological safety." In such environments, people are energized to share ideas, surface hard truths, and collaborate with purpose—driving the innovation, adaptability, and sustained performance that organizations need to thrive in uncertainty.

8.23 Examine Your Language Actions

The limits of my language mean the limits of my world.
—Ludwig Wittgenstein

The language we use has a powerful connection to the principle of examining your beliefs and actions, as the words and phrases we choose not only reflect our underlying beliefs but also shape our perceptions and behaviors, making it essential to critically assess and align our language with our true values and intentions. In leadership, the power of language is paramount, as it shapes vision, inspires action, mitigates conflicts, and builds trust among team members. Effective communication can motivate and guide individuals toward a common goal, making language a critical tool for successful leadership. Cofounder of Intel Corporation Andy Grove famously said, "Communication is not what is being said but what is being heard," highlighting the critical importance of ensuring that our messages are clearly understood by others and emphasizing that effective communication relies not just on expression but also on perception and interpretation.

In *The Fearless Organization*, Amy Edmondson emphasizes that leaders play a vital role in creating psychological safety by using language that fosters trust and openness. When leaders approach conversations with curiosity rather than judgment, it encourages employees to express their ideas, take risks, and collaborate more effectively. For example, asking someone, "Can you walk me through your thought process?" rather than, "Why did you do it that way?" can invite dialogue rather than defensiveness. This kind of thoughtful communication helps dismantle hierarchical barriers, promotes inclusivity, and contributes to a culture where innovation and high performance can thrive. Edmondson's work highlights how small shifts in leadership behavior and language can lead to profound changes in how teams function and grow.

The importance of language in leadership is also underscored by Marshall Goldsmith in his book *What Got You Here Won't Get You There*. Goldsmith points out that successful leaders must be mindful of how their words impact their teams. Subtle shifts in communication can lead to significant improvements in how leaders are perceived and how effectively they can inspire and guide their teams. For example, instead of saying, "You need to improve your performance," a leader might say, "I believe you have the potential to excel even more. Let's discuss how we can support your growth." Effective communication helps build a shared vision, align efforts, and foster a sense of collective purpose, all of which are essential for driving organizational success.

Seven Transformative Languages of Leadership Communication

Harvard psychologists Robert Kegan and Lisa Lahey emphasize that the way leaders speak profoundly influences individual behavior and organizational change. They argue that the way we communicate can significantly influence our ability to bring about change by making us aware of how our "immunity to change" works against our personal growth. In their book *How the Way We Talk Can Change the Way We Work*, the authors introduce seven powerful shifts in language that restrict a leader's language patterns to ones that foster growth. The examples provided below are not verbatim quotes from their book but illustrative examples drawn from real-life situations I have encountered and navigated during my years of leadership in both for-profit and non-profit organizations, reflecting the practical application of the principles discussed in *How the Way We Talk Can Change the Way We Work.*

For example, instead of saying, "I can't meet deadlines because we never have enough resources" (*language of complaint*), project managers and leaders can shift to, "I am committed to finding ways to meet our deadlines with the resources we have and exploring new ways to optimize our processes" (*language of commitment*). This change from the language of complaint to the language of commitment in phrasing not only reframes the issue positively but also demonstrates a proactive attitude. Similarly, moving from the *language of blame* to the *language of personal responsibility* can have profound effects on team dynamics. Consider a team member who blames a colleague for a failed presentation, saying, "The presentation failed because John didn't do his part." In contrast, shifting to personal responsibility might sound like, "I take responsibility for my role in the presentation and will work on better coordination with John to ensure success next time." This shift encourages accountability and collaborative problem-solving, fostering a more supportive and effective team environment.

Kegan and Lahey also emphasize the importance of recognizing competing commitments when setting goals. An employee might resolve to work fewer overtime hours but find himself consistently staying late. Instead of saying, "This year, I will work fewer overtime hours" (*language of New Year's resolution*), he could acknowledge his competing commitments by saying, "I am committed to working fewer overtime hours, but I recognize I have a competing commitment to ensure all tasks are completed, which I need to address" (*language of competing commitments*). This acknowledgment helps in identifying underlying assumptions and creating realistic, achievable goals. Moreover, moving away from the *language of strongly held beliefs* to the *language of assumptions* we hold is crucial for personal growth. Instead of saying, "If I delegate this task, it will be done poorly," say, "I need to explore my belief that delegating tasks will lead to poor results and find ways to delegate effectively."

In addition to the four internal language shifts for personal growth just mentioned, Kegan and Lahey introduce us to three more language shifts that are crucial for social and organizational growth. Replacing the *language of prizes and praising* with the *language of ongoing regard* shifts the focus from occasional recognition of an employee to consistent appreciation. A supervisor might typically acknowledge efforts only during annual reviews. Instead of saying, "You did an excellent job this month," say, "I value the effort you put into your work every day and the positive impact it has on our team." Transitioning from the *language of rules and policies* to the *language of public agreements* can also transform organizational behavior. An organization enforcing strict meeting punctuality might say, "Everyone must be in meetings by 9 a.m. according to policy." Changing this to, "We all agree that starting meetings on time at 9 a.m. helps us be more productive and respectful of everyone's schedule," promotes shared responsibility and commitment. Finally, the shift from the *language of constructive criticism* to the *language of deconstructive criticism* is vital for maintaining morale and fostering improvement. Instead of a leader saying, "You need to improve your communication skills," they might say, "Let's explore together how you can enhance your communication skills and what support you might need." This approach encourages a collaborative and supportive environment, essential for continuous improvement and growth.

By adopting these transformative languages, leaders can create environments that support growth, innovation, and mutual respect, ultimately driving personal and organizational success.

8.24 Pay Attention to the Power of Magic Words

Subtle shifts in language can make a huge difference.

—Jonah Berger

Wharton Business School professor Jonah Berger, in his highly instructive book *Magic Words*, explores the profound impact that specific types of words can have on our ability to persuade, connect, and influence others. Magic words are not just about linguistic manipulation; rather, they reflect and promote emotional intelligence. The examples provided below are not direct quotes from *Magic Words* but are crafted based on my own experiences and insights, demonstrating the real-world applicability of Jonah Berger's concepts, as well as the DEEP PACT principles of humility and care.

One powerful real-life example is substituting, "I can't help you," with, "Let's see how we can solve this." This change transforms a negative, dismissive statement into a positive, collaborative invitation. A leader who says, "Let's see how we can solve this," shows care and empathy and willingness to engage, which can make employees feel supported and valued, leading to higher morale and stronger team dynamics.

Another example is replacing, "It's too late," with, "There's still time to. . . ." This shift conveys optimism and possibility, which can inspire hope and motivation in others. When a project appears to be behind schedule, saying, "There's still time to make a difference," encourages the team to continue striving rather than abandoning the effort. This type of language fosters a growth mindset, where challenges are seen as opportunities rather than insurmountable obstacles.

Using "I believe" instead of "I think" can significantly impact how one's statements are received. "I believe this strategy will work" sounds more confident and assured than, "I think this strategy will work." This confidence can be contagious, making others more likely to support and engage with the idea. Leaders who express belief in their plans and teams can inspire greater commitment and effort from their colleagues.

Professor Berger asserts that inclusive language—such as changing "You must" to "I suggest"—can also enhance emotional intelligence in communication. Saying, "I suggest we explore this option," rather than, "You must explore this option," respects the listener's autonomy and encourages a collaborative approach. This shift can make others feel more valued and respected, promoting a more positive and cooperative working environment.

Another subtle yet powerful change is substituting "You're wrong" with "Let's look at it differently." This reframing avoids direct confrontation and instead promotes open-mindedness and a willingness to explore alternative perspectives. It helps maintain a respectful dialogue, even in disagreement, which is crucial for maintaining healthy professional relationships.

Transforming "I hope" into "I am confident" can also significantly enhance how messages are received. "I am confident we can achieve this" projects certainty and assurance, which can motivate and reassure others. This change conveys a strong belief in the possibility of success, which can be very encouraging, especially in challenging situations.

Changing "I can't make it" to "I'll be there as soon as I can" communicates commitment and reliability, even if there are delays. This phrasing helps build trust and shows that you are dependable. It acknowledges the challenge while also showing a clear intention to fulfill your obligations as soon as possible.

Replacing "I don't know" with "Let me find out for you" can also enhance communication. "I don't know" leaves the issue unresolved, whereas, "Let me find out for you," shows a willingness to assist and provides assurance that the matter will be addressed.

Instead of saying, "I'm busy," you can say, "I'm currently focused on another task." This subtle shift conveys the same message but in a way that highlights your engagement and productivity rather than simply stating a limitation.

When providing feedback, using "Consider" instead of "You need to" can be more constructive. For example, saying, "Consider approaching the task this way," is less authoritative and more suggestive, which can make the recipient more open to the feedback and willing to make changes.

When discussing potential actions, "could" instead of "should" can foster more creative thinking. Asking, "What could we do to solve this?" encourages brainstorming and exploring various possibilities, while "What should we do?" can limit thinking to conventional solutions. This simple change can lead to more innovative and effective outcomes.

In a situation where a project goal is not met, changing "It's not my fault" to "Let's find a solution" can improve conflict resolution. The former statement deflects responsibility, while the latter focuses on resolving the issue collaboratively. This fosters a more positive and solution-oriented dialogue.

Finally, using "Let's" instead of "You should" can be a powerful way to include others and promote teamwork. For instance, saying, "Let's brainstorm some solutions," rather than, "You should brainstorm some solutions," involves others in the process and shows that you value their input. This inclusive language fosters a sense of belonging and shared responsibility, which can strengthen team cohesion and collaboration.

The magic words above are just a few examples of numerous instances that Professor Berger mentions in his book. By incorporating these and other emotionally intelligent magic words into our daily interactions, we can significantly improve our communication. These changes not only enhance how we are perceived but also foster more positive, collaborative, and productive interactions. Jonah Berger's insights in *Magic Words* provide a powerful toolkit for anyone looking to increase their influence and effectiveness through the strategic use of language. These examples demonstrate that by tweaking our language, we can create a more emotionally intelligent and supportive environment, ultimately leading to better outcomes in personal and professional contexts.

8.25 Examine Your Body Language

Only 7% of meaning is in the words spoken. Thirty-eight percent is in tone of voice, and 55% is in body language.
—Albert Mehrabian, professor of psychology, UCLA

Leadership is not only about what we say—it's equally about what we signal. Studies suggest that over 50% of our communication is conveyed nonverbally, with body language playing a critical role in how others perceive our presence, confidence, and trustworthiness. As a leader or manager, your posture, gestures, and facial expressions are constantly communicating—often louder than your words. These signals can either reinforce your credibility or subtly undermine it.

In professional settings, body language shapes how your team interprets your mood, intent, and authority. Avoiding eye contact may signal discomfort or lack of confidence, while a weak handshake can erode others' perception of your leadership strength. Even seemingly minor habits—like fidgeting, slouching, or crossing your arms—can make you appear disengaged, disinterested, or unapproachable. These unconscious cues can hinder your ability to influence, inspire, and connect with others. The table below highlights common body language habits, what they may unintentionally communicate to others, and practical adjustments leaders can make to convey greater confidence, presence, and respect.

The good news is that effective body language can be learned and practiced. Sitting upright, maintaining steady eye contact, and moving naturally during presentations all project assurance and openness. Simple improvements—such as smiling when greeting someone, keeping your arms relaxed, or showing attentiveness when others speak—help you build rapport and foster a positive leadership presence.

Ultimately, watching your body language is about intentional leadership. The most successful leaders are those who align their verbal and nonverbal messages—communicating trust, competence, and authenticity not just through what they say but in how they show up.

Body Language, What It Says about You, and What to Do Instead

Body Language	What It Says about You	What to Do Instead
Avoiding eye contact	You appear nervous, unprepared, or lacking confidence; possibly hiding something.	Maintain natural eye contact with speakers and listeners.
Slouching or slumping in your chair	You seem careless, disengaged, or unprofessional.	Sit upright to show attention and authority.

Body Language	What It Says about You	What to Do Instead
Fidgeting or playing with objects	You come across as impatient or unsure.	Keep still and stay composed.
Standing still during a presentation	You may seem stiff, boring, or disconnected.	Move purposefully to engage the audience.
Hands in pockets	You might be perceived as nervous or disinterested.	Keep hands visible and gesture naturally.
Weak handshake	You may lack confidence or conviction.	Offer a firm, warm handshake.
Blank or frowning facial expression	You appear uninterested or unapproachable.	Smile genuinely and maintain an engaged expression.
Overused or phony gestures	You seem rehearsed or insincere.	Use gestures naturally and sparingly.
Crossed arms	You appear defensive or closed off.	Let arms rest at your sides in a relaxed position.
Tapping feet or fingers	You may seem anxious or inattentive.	Remain still and focused.
Yawning or gulping water	You look bored or disengaged.	Avoid these habits during conversations or meetings.
Doing something else while someone speaks	You signal disrespect or lack of interest.	Give full attention to the speaker.

8.26 Examine Your Drive for Efficiency: Don't Sacrifice Effectiveness

Efficiency is doing things right; effectiveness is doing the right things.
—Peter Drucker

In the realm of leadership, the relentless pursuit of efficiency—maximizing outputs with minimal inputs—is often celebrated. However, this focus can overshadow the equally vital goal of effectiveness, which emphasizes achieving meaningful and strategic outcomes. Stephen R. Covey, in his book *The 8th Habit: From Effectiveness to Greatness*, introduces the concept of finding one's "voice"—a unique personal significance—and inspiring others to find theirs, suggesting that true leadership transcends mere task completion and delves into purpose-driven action. Leaders must constantly ask themselves, *Am I optimizing for short-term efficiency at the cost of long-term effectiveness?* Efficiency that comes at the expense of morale, creativity, or strategic vision becomes counterproductive.

An understanding of the distinction between efficiency and effectiveness is crucial for successful leadership. Efficiency focuses on processes and the optimization of tasks, often within the purview of management. Effectiveness, on the other hand, is concerned with setting the right goals and achieving them, aligning closely with leadership. An *MIT Sloan Management Review* article on efficiency, effectiveness, and balance emphasizes that "to be successful, companies must strike the right balance between driving for efficiency and achieving effectiveness while also supporting employees to balance work and life in meaningful ways." Striking this balance requires leaders to ensure that speed and cost-cutting measures do not undermine innovation, employee engagement, or strategic priorities. A key watchpoint is when processes become so rigid in the name of efficiency that they stifle adaptability.

Leaders should foster a culture of continuous improvement rather than rigid optimization, ensuring that efficiency serves the broader mission rather than dictating it.

What to Watch for and How to Strike the Balance

To help leaders put these principles into practice, here are key areas to watch—and strategies to maintain a healthy balance between efficiency and effectiveness in everyday decision-making.

- ◈ **Watch for overautomation.** Automating processes can improve efficiency, but excessive reliance on automation can diminish effectiveness by eliminating critical human judgment. Ensure that automation complements, rather than replaces, strategic thinking.
- ◈ **Avoid a short-term mindset.** Cost-cutting and time-saving measures may offer immediate gains but can erode long-term growth and innovation. Be cautious of decisions that sacrifice sustainability for the sake of short-term efficiency.
- ◈ **Prioritize outcomes over metrics.** Metrics such as speed and cost reduction are important, but they should not over-shadow meaningful outcomes like customer satisfaction, employee well-being, and innovation.
- ◈ **Foster an adaptive mindset.** Instead of enforcing rigid efficiency models, cultivate a culture of learning, feedback, and flexibility that allows teams to pivot when necessary.

Consider the case of a company that, in its drive for increased efficiency, decides to reduce office space and encourage remote work. While this move cuts costs, it may inadvertently hinder team cohesion and innovation if not managed effectively. An effective leader would recognize this potential pitfall and implement strategies to maintain collaboration and morale, such as regular virtual team-building activities or periodic in-person meetings. This approach ensures that the organization remains efficient in its operations and effective in achieving its strategic goals. Similarly, in product development, an overly rigid, efficiency-driven process may force teams to rush to market with an inferior product. Leaders must help strike a balance by allowing time for quality control, creative iteration, and customer feedback.

8.27 Ten Actionable Steps for Applying Principle 2

Follow effective action with quiet reflection. From the quiet reflection will come even more effective action.

—Peter Drucker

Now that we have explored the many facets of self-examination—from Socrates' timeless warning about the unexamined life to confronting our biases and blind spots, from questioning workplace "truths" and inherited myths to understanding the paradoxes of emotion and rationality, and from embracing vulnerability to scrutinizing our belief-value-attitude-behavior spectrum—it is time to translate this knowledge into deliberate action. For knowledge, without courageous application, is little more than an illusion of progress.

Applying the principle *Examine your beliefs and actions more than others think wise* in a project management and leadership setting demands more than passive reflection. It requires boldness to question, humility to learn, and discipline to change course when necessary. The following steps and guidelines are designed to help you put this principle into practice, turning insight into impact and self-awareness into tangible results. You do not need to follow every suggestion at once; instead, choose those most relevant to your current journey. Each step you take builds your capacity to lead with greater wisdom, clarity, and purpose—laying the foundation for extraordinary leadership that is both ethical and effective.

💡 *Principle 2, Step 1: Conduct Introspection*

Action: Contemplate regularly to gain a deep understanding of your beliefs and how they influence your actions. In an era of constant change and uncertainty, introspection and self-awareness are not just luxuries—they are essential tools for navigating complexity and leading with integrity.

Identify core beliefs: Write down your core beliefs about leadership, teamwork, and project management. Reflect on how these beliefs were formed and how they influence your decision-making.

Daily reflection: Set aside time each day to reflect on your actions and decisions. Ask yourself questions like, *Why did I make that decision?* and *How did my beliefs influence my actions today?*

Example: A project manager might believe that strict adherence to deadlines is paramount. Reflect on how this belief influences their interactions with the team and decisions about resource allocation. A manager at a tech startup found that his belief in micromanagement was stifling innovation. Through daily reflection, he realized the need to trust his team's expertise and delegate more effectively. Imagine a CEO faced with an ethical dilemma: should the company prioritize short-term profits at the expense of environmental sustainability, or take a principled stand for corporate social responsibility? Rather than making a snap decision based on external pressures or conventional wisdom, the CEO engages in deep introspection, examining their values, beliefs, and long-term vision for the company. Through careful reflection, the CEO gains clarity and conviction, ultimately choosing to align the company's actions with its core values and principles. At Intel, former CEO Andy Grove practiced regular introspection to stay grounded and make informed decisions during the company's transformative years.

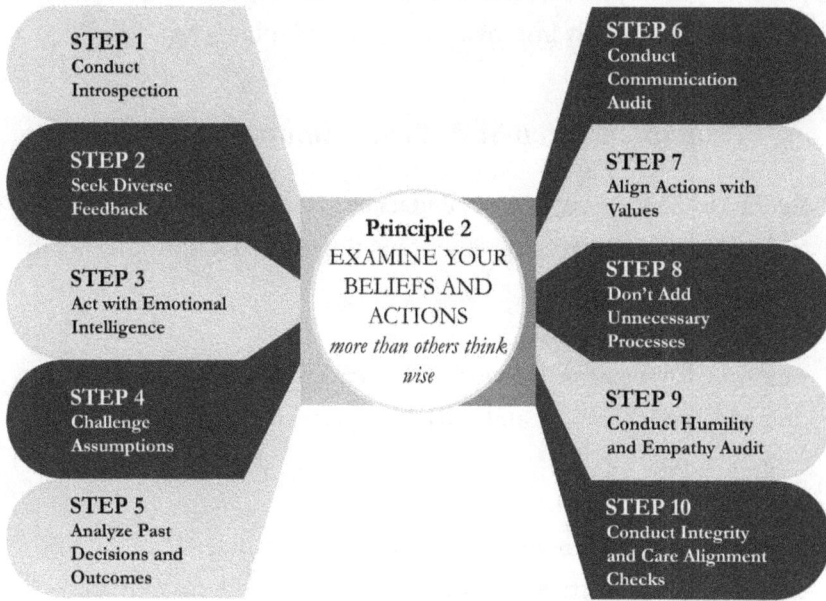

Self-examination in action: ten bold steps for applying Principle 2.

💡 Principle 2, Step 2: Seek Diverse Feedback

Action: Obtain diverse perspectives to challenge and refine your beliefs and actions.

360-degree feedback: Implement a 360-degree feedback process where peers, subordinates, and supervisors provide feedback on your leadership style and decision-making.

Open dialogue: Create opportunities for open dialogue with your team. Encourage them to share their thoughts on your leadership and project management approach.

Example: A project manager might discover through feedback that their belief in strict hierarchy is causing communication breakdowns. At Google, project managers use "retrospectives" after each project phase to gather candid feedback from team members. This process helps in continuously improving management practices.

💡 *Principle 2, Step 3: Act with Emotional Intelligence*

Action: Enhance your ability to understand and manage your emotions and those of others to improve interactions and decision-making in the workplace.

Emotional awareness: Develop a keen sense of your emotions and how they affect your thoughts and behaviors. Regularly reflect on your emotional responses to different situations to build greater self-awareness.

Empathetic engagement: Actively listen to and understand the emotions of others. Practice empathy by considering others' perspectives and responding with compassion and support.

Use magic words: Use emotionally intelligent communication techniques and appropriate magic words to resolve conflicts, provide constructive feedback, and foster a positive team environment. Ensure that your communication is clear, respectful, and considerate of others' feelings.

Example: If a team member appears disengaged or frustrated, use emotional awareness to recognize your initial reaction, empathetic engagement to understand their perspective, and effective communication to address the issue constructively. During the COVID-19 pandemic, Qantas CEO Alan Joyce demonstrated high emotional intelligence. By communicating transparently and empathetically about necessary staff cuts, Joyce maintained trust and engagement among employees and customers. This approach balanced difficult business decisions with stakeholder relationships, helping the company manage the crisis effectively.

💡 *Principle 2, Step 4: Challenge Assumptions*

Action: Identify and question underlying assumptions that influence your beliefs and actions.

Assumption inventory: List out the assumptions underlying your key beliefs and actions. Challenge each assumption by seeking evidence that supports or refutes it.

Scenario analysis: Use scenario analysis to envision different outcomes based on changing key assumptions. This helps in understanding the potential impact of different beliefs on project outcomes.

Example: If you assume that remote work reduces productivity, test this assumption by comparing team performance metrics before and after implementing remote work policies. IBM conducted a scenario analysis before transitioning to a hybrid work model, challenging the assumption that in-office presence was necessary for collaboration. The analysis showed that hybrid work could maintain, if not enhance, productivity.

💡 *Principle 2, Step 5: Analyze Past Decisions and Outcomes*

Action: Reflect on previous decisions and their results to identify patterns and areas for improvement.

Retrospective analysis: Conduct a retrospective analysis (previously called postmortem analysis) after the completion of major projects or initiatives. This involves reviewing what went well, what didn't, and what could be done differently in the future. Encourage team members to participate and provide their insights, but do not forget to celebrate successes at the same time.

Data-driven reviews: Use data and metrics to evaluate the outcomes of your decisions. Look at key performance indicators, timelines, and budget adherence to understand the impact of your choices and identify areas for improvement.

Example: A marketing manager might discover through a postmortem analysis that their decision to launch a campaign during a holiday period resulted in lower engagement than expected. They could then use this insight to better plan future campaigns. At Amazon, teams use Correction of Error (COE) reports to analyze failures and learn from them. This process not only helps in identifying what went wrong but also in establishing preventive measures for future projects. After the failure of Google Glass —a wearable augmented reality device that projected information onto a small optical display—Google analyzed what went wrong to improve future innovation strategies. Toyota's implementation of the Five Whys technique in their production process helps identify the root causes of issues and improve decision-making.

💡 *Principle 2, Step 6: Conduct Communication Audit*

Action: Enhance your ability to understand and improve communication within your team and organization by regularly evaluating your communication.

Clarity and consistency: Assess the clarity and consistency of messages across different channels. Ensure that important information is communicated clearly and consistently, without conflicting messages. Standardize communication templates and guidelines to maintain a consistent tone and style.

Regular reviews: Schedule regular reviews of your communication strategies. During these reviews, analyze key metrics such as response times, engagement levels, and feedback scores. Adjust your strategies based on these insights to continually improve communication effectiveness.

Example: At Google, regular "pulse surveys" are conducted to gather employees' feedback on communication effectiveness. These surveys help the company continuously refine its communication practices to enhance clarity and engagement. A tech company noticed that team members often missed important project updates. The company instituted a biweekly communication review meeting where they analyzed engagement metrics from their internal communication platforms. This practice helped them identify the best times to send updates and the most effective formats for them, leading to higher engagement and fewer missed updates.

💡 *Principle 2, Step 7: Align Actions with Values*

Action: Ensure that your actions consistently reflect your core values.

Values clarification: Clearly define your core values and communicate them to your team. Ensure that these values are reflected in your project goals and daily operations.

Consistency check: Regularly review your actions to ensure they are aligned with your stated values. Adjust your behavior if there are discrepancies.

Example: If innovation is a core value, encourage risk-taking and create a safe environment for experimentation. Patagonia aligns its actions with its core value of environmental sustainability by implementing eco-friendly business practices and encouraging employees to engage in environmental activism. When I formed my company, I set "excellence" as the core value, ensuring that every decision, process, and interaction was guided by an uncompromising commitment to quality and high performance. This singular focus on excellence became the driving force behind our culture; our employees rallied around the concept, setting high standards for themselves and each other. As a result, we built a reputation for delivering superior results, and our firm rose to become the top company in California in our industry. This experience reinforced my belief that a clearly defined and consistently reinforced core value can unify teams, drive performance, and establish lasting organizational success.

💡 *Principle 2, Step 8: Don't Add Unnecessary Processes*

This step, drawn from the *Harvard Business Review* article "Rid Your Organization of Obstacles That Infuriate Everyone," emphasizes the importance of simplifying processes and removing unnecessary complexities rather than layering on additional steps, rules, or initiatives.

Action: Foster a culture that prioritizes removing inefficiencies and unnecessary complexities over introducing new layers of processes or policies.

Identify barriers to productivity: Start by examining processes, policies, and routines that frustrate employees, slow down workflows, or hinder innovation. Look for areas where steps are redundant, approvals are excessive, or outdated rules persist without purpose.

Employee-driven input: Empower employees, especially those on the front lines, to voice their frustrations about obstacles they encounter and suggest areas for simplification.

Lean decision-making: Streamline decision-making by reducing approval chains and eliminating unnecessary bureaucracy, which can lead to faster action and improved morale.

Make subtraction a habit: Build a culture that continuously questions, "What can we stop doing?" Instead of automatically introducing new initiatives or procedures, regularly evaluate which existing practices have outlived their usefulness and could be retired.

Example: At Procter & Gamble, A. G. Lafley, the former CEO, implemented the principle of subtraction by reducing complex decision-making processes and cutting down unnecessary layers of management. This simplification allowed teams to focus on innovation and customer-centricity, leading to more agile and effective operations. Similarly, Toyota's lean manufacturing approach exemplifies this philosophy by continuously identifying and eliminating waste in their processes to maintain efficiency and quality.

💡 *Principle 2, Step 9: Conduct Humility and Empathy Audit*

Action: Regularly assess how well you are practicing humility and empathy in your interactions and decision-making processes.

Humility audit. Reflect on recent decisions and interactions to identify instances where humility was demonstrated or where arrogance may have taken precedence. Ask yourself questions like, *Did I listen more than I spoke?* and *Did I acknowledge the contributions of others?*

Empathy audit. Evaluate your ability to understand and share the feelings of your team members. Consider questions like, *Did I take the time to understand the perspectives of others?* and *Did I respond with compassion and support?*

Example: A leader at a nonprofit organization might review how they handled a team conflict, assessing whether they allowed all voices to be heard and showed understanding and respect for different viewpoints.

💡 Principle 2, Step 10: Conduct Integrity and Care Alignment Checks

Action: Regularly evaluate how well your actions align with your core values of integrity and care.

Integrity check: Review recent decisions and behaviors to ensure they reflect your commitment to honesty and ethical principles. Ask yourself, *Did I make decisions that were honest and fair?* and *Did I uphold the company's ethical standards?*

Care alignment check: Assess how your actions demonstrate care and concern for your team and stakeholders. Consider questions like, *Did I prioritize the well-being of my team?* and *Did I show genuine concern for the impact of my decisions on others?*

Example: A supervisor might review how they implemented a bonus program, ensuring that decisions were fair and equitable. A project manager facing formidable budget and schedule constraints on a project may consider accepting the discomfort of renegotiating the budget and schedule with the client rather than putting pressure on the employees.

QUICK TIP

Action: Use AI-driven analytics to evaluate your leadership decisions and their impacts. Implement AI-based feedback systems to collect and analyze team sentiments and productivity.

Example: Utilizing AI sentiment analysis tools to understand team morale and adjust leadership strategies accordingly.

Caveat: Be mindful of data privacy and consent issues when collecting and analyzing employee feedback to maintain trust and comply with regulations.

8.28 Ten Barriers to Applying Principle 2

The impediment to action advances action. What stands in the way becomes the way.

—Marcus Aurelius

The principle *Examine your beliefs and actions more than others think wise* encourages deep introspection and continuous self-improvement. However, several barriers can hinder individuals from engaging in this level of self-examination. Understanding such barriers can help individuals overcome them and embrace a more reflective and intentional approach to their beliefs and actions.

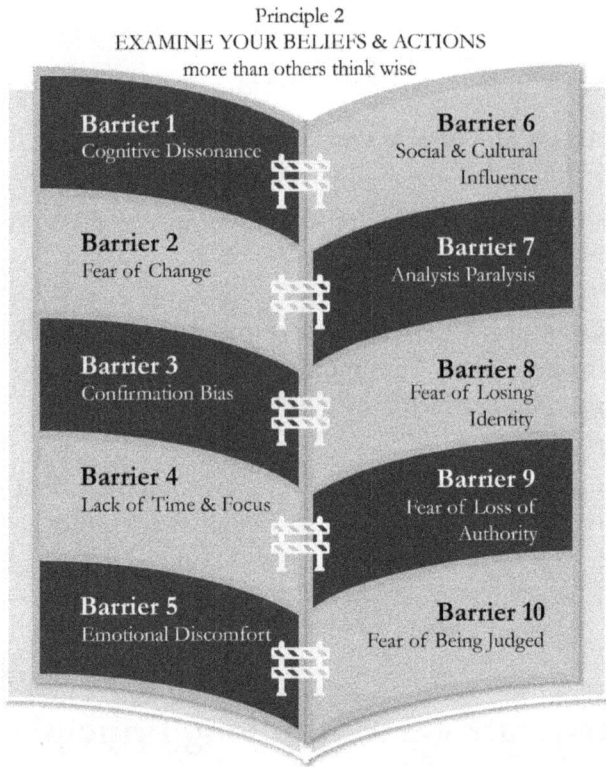

Principle 2
EXAMINE YOUR BELIEFS & ACTIONS
more than others think wise

Barrier 1
Cognitive Dissonance

Barrier 2
Fear of Change

Barrier 3
Confirmation Bias

Barrier 4
Lack of Time & Focus

Barrier 5
Emotional Discomfort

Barrier 6
Social & Cultural
Influence

Barrier 7
Analysis Paralysis

Barrier 8
Fear of Losing
Identity

Barrier 9
Fear of Loss of
Authority

Barrier 10
Fear of Being Judged

The psychology of resistance: ten barriers to applying Principle 2

⚠ *Principle 2, Barrier 1: Cognitive Dissonance*

Barrier: Cognitive dissonance occurs when a conflict is present between one's beliefs and actions or between different beliefs. This discomfort can lead to resistance to examining beliefs and actions too closely, as it may force individuals to confront inconsistencies and make difficult changes.

Solution: Cultivate a mindset that welcomes discomfort as a necessary part of growth. Understand that recognizing and resolving cognitive dissonance can lead to a more coherent and fulfilling life. Engage in regular reflection and seek feedback from trusted sources to identify and address inconsistencies.

⚠ *Principle 2, Barrier 2: Fear of Change*

Barrier: Deep self-examination often reveals areas where change is needed, which can be daunting. People may fear the uncertainty and effort associated with changing long-held beliefs and habits.

Solution: Embrace change as an opportunity for growth rather than a threat. Focus on the potential positive outcomes of change and take small, manageable steps toward making necessary adjustments. Support from friends, family, or a coach can also provide encouragement and accountability.

⚠ *Principle 2, Barrier 3: Confirmation Bias*

Barrier: Confirmation bias is the tendency to seek out information that confirms existing beliefs and ignore information that contradicts them. This bias can hinder objective self-examination and reinforce flawed beliefs and actions.

Solution: Actively seek out diverse perspectives and challenge your own assumptions. Engage in discussions with people who hold different views and be open to new information. Practicing critical thinking and skepticism can help counteract confirmation bias.

⚠ *Principle 2, Barrier 4: Lack of Time and Focus*

Barrier: In today's fast-paced world, finding time and mental space for deep self-reflection can be challenging. The demands of daily life often leave little room for introspection.

Solution: Prioritize self-reflection by setting aside dedicated time for it, such as through journaling, meditation, or quiet contemplation. Integrate reflective practices into your daily routine, even if only for a few minutes each day. Consider regular retreats or breaks to create space for deeper introspection.

⚠ *Principle 2, Barrier 5: Emotional Discomfort*

Barrier: Examining beliefs and actions deeply can bring up uncomfortable emotions, such as guilt, shame, or regret. This emotional discomfort can deter individuals from engaging in thorough self-examination.

Solution: Develop emotional resilience by practicing self-compassion and understanding that all humans have flaws and make mistakes. View self-examination as a compassionate act aimed at personal growth rather than a punitive one. Seek support from therapists or counselors if needed to process difficult emotions.

⚠ *Principle 2, Barrier 6: Social and Cultural Influence*

Barrier: Social and cultural norms can exert pressure to conform to certain beliefs and behaviors. Challenging these norms through deep self-examination can lead to social friction and feelings of isolation.

Solution: Build a supportive network of individuals who value introspection and personal growth. Communicate your journey and findings with empathy and understanding to foster constructive dialogue. Recognize that true growth often requires the courage to stand apart from societal expectations.

⚠ *Principle 2, Barrier 7: Analysis Paralysis*

Barrier: The prospect of continuously examining every belief and action can be overwhelming, leading to analysis paralysis where individuals feel stuck and unable to make decisions or take action.

Solution: Focus on one area of self-examination at a time to avoid feeling overwhelmed. Set specific, achievable goals for self-reflection and action. Celebrate progress and incremental improvements rather than striving for perfection.

⚠ *Principle 2, Barrier 8: Fear of Losing Identity*

Barrier: Deep self-examination can challenge core aspects of one's identity. The fear of losing or changing fundamental parts of oneself can be a significant barrier to introspection.

Solution: Recognize that identity is not static, and that growth and change are natural parts of life. Approach self-examination with curiosity and openness, understanding that evolving your beliefs and actions can lead to a more authentic and fulfilling sense of self.

⚠ *Principle 2, Barrier 9: Fear of Loss of Authority*

Barrier: Fear of loss of authority arises when leaders worry that demonstrating emotional intelligence—such as empathy and openness—will undermine their authority and control. This fear can result in leaders avoiding emotionally intelligent behaviors, leading to a lack of trust and poor team dynamics.

Solution: Cultivate a mindset that values emotional intelligence as a strength rather than a threat to authority. Understand that demonstrating empathy, active listening, and emotional regulation can actually enhance your authority by building trust and respect within your team. Engage in regular self-reflection to identify any insecurities about authority and seek feedback from trusted colleagues and mentors to gain perspective. Embrace the discomfort of vulnerability as an essential part of authentic leadership and recognize that empowering others and fostering a supportive environment can lead to greater overall team success and stronger leadership.

⚠ *Principle 2, Barrier 10: Fear of Being Judged*

Barrier: Fear of being judged by others for one's beliefs and actions can discourage individuals from engaging in deep self-examination. This fear can stem from a desire to conform to social expectations or avoid criticism.

Solution: Develop resilience to external opinions by focusing on personal values and intrinsic goals. Practice self-acceptance and understand that constructive criticism can be valuable for personal growth. Engaging in supportive communities and seeking feedback from trusted sources can provide a safe space for honest self-reflection and help mitigate the fear of judgment.

8.29 Ten Examples of Applying Principle 2

1. Rachel reevaluates the company's hiring practices, which favor graduates from elite universities, and advocates for a more inclusive approach.
2. Daniel questions the long-held belief that only senior staff can lead projects, opening opportunities for junior members.

3. A community leader reexamines their stance on local development projects, prioritizing environmental sustainability.
4. Jason challenges his department's traditional methods by introducing a flexible work policy despite initial resistance.
5. Janyce seeks to understand her implicit biases by attending a diversity and inclusion workshop.
6. John critically evaluates his leadership style after noticing a drop in team morale.
7. A volunteer in a nonprofit reviews the impact of their efforts and seeks ways to address deeper systemic issues.
8. A manager reevaluates their decision-making process and bias after receiving feedback, leading to more inclusive team meetings.
9. Mike questions his approach to handling a difficult client and seeks feedback from colleagues to improve.
10. Olivia reassesses her belief that working late equals productivity and starts setting healthier boundaries.

8.30 Closing Reflections

We ought to entertain our opinions with some measure of doubt. I shouldn't wish people dogmatically to believe any philosophy, not even mine.

—Bertrand Russell

By following the guidelines and the solutions to these barriers, leaders can inspire their organizations to achieve extraordinary outcomes by promoting profound personal growth and self-awareness.

By engaging in self-assessment and reflection, examining beliefs, seeking diverse feedback, acting with emotional intelligence, challenging assumptions, aligning actions with values, and fostering a culture of continuous improvement, leaders develop a deeper understanding of themselves and their impact on their teams. This holistic approach not only enhances personal effectiveness but also drives better project outcomes and organizational success. However, the journey to personal growth and self-awareness is rarely smooth and is often filled with challenges and obstacles. Barriers such as cognitive dissonance, fear of change, confirmation bias, lack of time, emotional discomfort, social influences, fear of losing identity, and fear of loss of authority can hinder deep introspection. By recognizing and addressing these barriers, individuals can cultivate a more reflective and intentional approach to their lives, ultimately leading to greater fulfillment and authenticity.

8.31 Daily Practice

1. **Challenge yourself:** Ask yourself why you believe the decision you are about to take is the right choice and reexamine your assumptions.

2. **Seek and value feedback:** Discuss your actions and decisions with a trusted peer or mentor and ask for constructive feedback.

3. **Stay curious:** Learn something new every day—read five to 10 pages of a book that challenges the status quo and observe others—not to judge, but to learn.

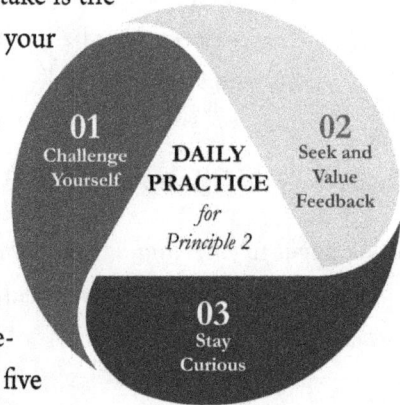

01 Challenge Yourself

DAILY PRACTICE *for* Principle 2

02 Seek and Value Feedback

03 Stay Curious

9 Principle 3: Ensure Excellence More Than Others Think Imaginable

If it falls your lot to be a street sweeper, sweep streets like Michelangelo painted pictures, sweep streets like Beethoven composed music, sweep streets like Leontyne Price sings before the Metropolitan Opera. Sweep streets like Shakespeare wrote poetry. Sweep streets so well that all the host of heaven and earth will have to pause and say, "Here lived a great street sweeper who swept his job well."

—Martin Luther King Jr.,
sermon delivered in Atlanta, 1967

9.1 Aristotle and the Pursuit of Excellence

Aristotle, one of history's greatest philosophers, profoundly shaped our understanding of ethics, logic, science, and politics, leaving a legacy that continues to influence modern thought and intellectual discourse. His philosophy on excellence is particularly influential, encapsulated in his famous statement "We are what we repeatedly do. Excellence, then, is not an act, but a habit." This insight emphasizes that true excellence is cultivated through consistent and deliberate practice. Aristotle believed that virtues, which are habitual actions aligned with moral and ethical standards, are central to achieving excellence. By ingraining virtuous behaviors into our daily lives, individuals develop a character predisposed to excellence in all pursuits. This process of habitual excellence underscores the importance of daily actions and decisions in shaping one's destiny. As mentioned earlier, when we founded WRIME Inc., an engineering consulting firm, in California, we placed Aristotle's quote on the back of our company's business card. It had an amazing effect on all of us, and soon our company garnered the reputation of being the best in California in our core business area.

Moreover, Aristotle viewed excellence as the result of intentional and intelligent effort rather than mere chance. He asserted, "Excellence is never an accident. It is always the result of high intention, sincere effort, and intelligent execution; it represents the wise choice of many alternatives—choice, not chance, determines your destiny." This perspective highlights the critical role of purposeful action in the pursuit of excellence. Aristotle's philosophy encourages individuals to take responsibility for their choices and to recognize that excellence stems from continuous improvement and the wise application of effort and intelligence. This notion empowers individuals to actively shape their paths to success through thoughtful and consistent actions.

Furthermore, Aristotle's concept of excellence extends beyond individual achievement to societal well-being. He posited that the highest good for humanity is achieved when individuals and societies strive for excellence in all their endeavors. This holistic view integrates personal virtues with communal responsibilities, suggesting that the pursuit of excellence contributes to the greater good. By fostering a culture of excellence, societies can enhance overall well-being and progress. Aristotle's teachings, therefore, advocate for a balanced approach where personal growth and societal development are intertwined, promoting a virtuous cycle of continuous improvement and collective success.

9.2 Why Excellence?

Happiness is the full use of one's talents along lines of excellence.
—John F. Kennedy

Excellence plays a crucial role in bringing personal happiness and job satisfaction, as it aligns with personal fulfillment, growth, and a sense of accomplishment. When individuals strive for and achieve excellence, they experience a profound sense of satisfaction and well-being. This connection between excellence and happiness is supported by various psychological theories and real-world examples, demonstrating that excellence is about not only external achievements but also internal contentment.

Achieving excellence provides a powerful sense of accomplishment. When individuals set high standards for themselves and reach those goals, they experience a deep sense of pride and satisfaction. This sense of purpose and contribution is further echoed by leadership guru Simon Sinek, who notes, "Happy employees ensure happy customers. And happy customers ensure happy shareholders—in that order." This underscores the idea that excellence benefits not only the individual but also positively impacts the organization and its stakeholders.

According to psychologist Albert Bandura's theory of self-efficacy, described in *Self-Efficacy: The Exercise of Control*, individuals who believe in their capabilities are more likely to take on challenging tasks and succeed, which in turn boosts their overall happiness. This sense of achievement reinforces their belief in their abilities, creating a positive feedback loop that enhances their overall well-being.

Excellence often aligns with personal values and a sense of purpose, which are critical components of happiness. When people pursue excellence in areas that matter to them, they feel that their efforts are meaningful and significant, which leads to a state of "flow"—a term coined by psychologist Mihaly Csikszentmihalyi. He argued, in *Flow: The Psychology of Optimal Experience*, that individuals are happiest when they are fully immersed in activities that challenge them and align with their skills and values. Individuals experience joy, creativity, and total involvement when they achieve excellence in such activities.

Excellence also enhances relationships and community engagement. When individuals pursue excellence, they often inspire those around them, fostering a culture of mutual respect and admiration. This can strengthen personal and professional relationships, leading to greater social support and a sense of belonging.

In summary, excellence is a powerful driver of happiness because it fosters a sense of accomplishment, aligns with personal values, and enhances social connections. By striving for excellence, individuals can experience profound personal fulfillment and contribute positively to their communities. The pursuit of excellence is, therefore, not just a pathway to success but also a vital component of a happy and meaningful life.

9.3 The Essence of Excellence

Excellence is not a skill. It's an attitude.

—Ralph Marston

Excellence is not merely a goal; it is a continuous pursuit that transcends ordinary expectations. It is the relentless drive to achieve and maintain the highest standards in every aspect of life: personal endeavors, professional pursuits, or community contributions. The principle *Ensure excellence more than others think imaginable* serves as a call to push beyond conventional limits and strive for extraordinary achievements. In this chapter, we explore the essence of excellence through historical examples and fictional stories, illustrating how setting high standards, embracing continuous improvement, fostering a culture of excellence, overcoming adversity, and leaving a lasting legacy can transform individuals and societies.

Excellence is the unwavering commitment to surpass ordinary standards and achieve greatness in every endeavor. It is not merely a goal but a way of life, a relentless pursuit of the highest quality and performance. Excellence embodies the spirit of continuous improvement, where every challenge is seen as an opportunity to grow and every setback as a stepping-stone to greater achievements. It is about setting lofty goals and dedicating oneself to the discipline, hard work, and perseverance required to attain them. Excellence is a reflection of one's dedication to personal and professional mastery—a testament to the belief that the pursuit of the extraordinary is not only possible but essential.

At its core, excellence is an attitude that transforms the mundane into the magnificent. It is the belief that greatness is achieved not through isolated acts but through consistent, intentional actions. This mindset fuels passion, inspires innovation, and cultivates resilience. Excellence is the driving force behind iconic achievements and remarkable transformations, motivating individuals to push beyond their limits and organizations to redefine what is possible. It is a beacon that lights the path to success, guiding us to realize our fullest potential and leave an indelible mark on the world. Embracing excellence means committing to a journey of relentless pursuit, where the joy of accomplishment is matched only by the satisfaction of knowing one has given their absolute best.

9.4 First Thing First: Building a Team for Excellence

Great things in business are never done by one person. They're done by a team of people.

—Steve Jobs

In the modern world of both for-profit and nonprofit organizations, the importance of building a strong team cannot be overstated. A cohesive, high-functioning team is an absolute necessity for achieving excellence, driving innovation, and fostering resilience in the face of challenges. Research studies indicate that employees who feel a strong connection to their teams are less likely to leave their companies and more engaged in their work. These findings send a clear message: team dynamics are at the heart of job satisfaction, productivity, and retention. In a post-pandemic, AI-driven world where adaptability and collaboration are paramount, building an exceptional team is the foundation upon which true excellence is built.

One of the most striking insights into team importance comes from *Nine Lies About Work* by Marcus Buckingham and Ashley Goodall. The book challenges conventional beliefs, revealing that people do not necessarily care about the organization they work for; instead, they care deeply about the team they work with—because human connections are central to motivation and performance. When employees feel that they are part of a supportive, aligned, and high-functioning team, they are more willing to contribute their best efforts. This aligns with Deloitte's 2020 Global Human Capital Trends report, which found that 79% of organizations identified fostering a sense of belonging in the workforce as important to their success, and 93% agreed that a sense of belonging drives organizational performance—highlighting that belonging is not just a cultural aspiration but a critical business priority.

In 2012, Google launched Project Aristotle, a comprehensive internal research initiative to determine what makes teams successful. Named for the philosopher who said, "The whole is greater than the sum of its parts," the project analyzed over 180 teams at Google over a span of two years. These were not experimental groups; they were real-world working teams. Google conducted over 200 interviews and assessed more than 250 team attributes, including personality types, skill sets, team structure, and communication styles. The goal was to identify patterns that correlated with high team performance.

Project Aristotle researchers discovered that several commonly assumed factors believed to impact team performance and effectiveness actually had little influence. These included frequently cited attributes such as:

- Collocation of teammates (sitting together in the same office)
- Consensus-driven decision making
- Extroversion of team members
- Individual performance of team members
- Seniority

Instead they found, to their surprise, that the following five elements actually drive effective teamwork:

- **Psychological safety.** Team members feel comfortable taking risks and voicing ideas without fear of judgment or embarrassment.
- **Dependability.** Everyone can rely on each other to deliver high-quality work on time.
- **Structure and clarity.** Team members have clearly defined roles, responsibilities, and goals.
- **Meaning.** Team members see the value and purpose in their work.
- **Impact.** Team members believe their work matters and contribute to a greater mission.

When these essential elements come together, the results are transformative, and the business world offers numerous inspiring examples. Companies like Google, Netflix, and Spotify have thrived by focusing on building teams that are empowered, transparent, and unified in purpose. Their emphasis on fostering psychological safety, trust, clear communication, and shared goals has propelled them to industry-leading success.

To build and sustain high-performing teams, leaders must prioritize creating an environment of trust, openness, and collective purpose. An African proverb states, "If you want to go fast, go alone. If you want to go far, go together." This saying encapsulates the essence of teamwork—the understanding that collective effort, not individual brilliance, is the cornerstone of enduring success. In today's complex and fast-paced world, particularly with the rise of remote teams, no project of significance can thrive without a cohesive, motivated, and diverse group. Building and nurturing such a team requires leaders to put aside their egos, embrace humility, and foster an environment where every voice is valued. Even a simple act like allowing team members to voice their opinions first in a meeting before the leader speaks can create an atmosphere of psychological safety and encourage more open and honest discussions and lay the foundation for excellence.

However, forming a high-performing team still comes with challenges. Patrick Lencioni's seminal work *The Five Dysfunctions of a Team* identifies five key pitfalls that can derail even the most talented groups: (1) absence of trust, (2) fear of conflict, (3) lack of commitment, (4) avoidance of accountability, and (5) inattention to results. To overcome these dysfunctions, leaders must actively cultivate trust through transparency, encourage healthy conflict to surface diverse perspectives, secure commitment through a shared purpose, ensure accountability with clearly defined roles and responsibilities, and maintain a relentless focus on high standards of excellence. Additionally, leaders should discourage pursuing individual status and personal recognition, which can erode the focus on collective success. True leadership is about sharing accolades and fostering a culture where success is celebrated as a team.

Beyond overcoming dysfunctions, effective team-building requires laying the groundwork for meaningful communication. Research from the MIT Human Dynamics Laboratory found that communication patterns are the most significant predictor of a team's success—more important than intelligence, personality, or skill. Their study identified three key dynamics in high-performing teams: energy (frequent interactions), engagement (balanced participation), and exploration (seeking insights beyond the team). Leaders who encourage these behaviors create environments where ideas flow freely, creativity flourishes, and solutions emerge organically. Moreover, in an era where remote work and AI-driven collaboration tools are transforming workplace dynamics, effective communication is more critical than ever. AI-powered tools that monitor and balance participation in virtual meetings can help mitigate power imbalances, ensuring that every team member has a voice and an opportunity to contribute.

Best Practices for Team Building

To put these ideas into practice, you can start with a few simple but powerful actions. Establish clear team norms that encourage open dialogue and create psychological safety—for example, invite others to speak first during meetings and reinforce that every idea has value. Assign well-defined roles and responsibilities to eliminate ambiguity and promote accountability. Schedule regular check-ins to build trust and ensure everyone feels heard and supported. Use feedback tools and shared dashboards to promote transparency and dependability. Most importantly, help your team connect their daily work to a larger purpose so that meaning and impact are lived experiences, not abstract ideals.

Equally important is knowing what to avoid. Resist the urge to micromanage, dominate conversations, or prioritize individual recognition over team wins—these behaviors erode trust and psychological safety. Avoid confusing consensus with clarity; not every decision needs agreement, but every team member deserves to understand the direction. Do not rely on charisma, seniority, or individual brilliance alone—the strongest teams thrive on mutual respect, balanced participation, and shared ownership.

By consistently practicing these behaviors and avoiding these common traps, you can build a team culture where collaboration flourishes, problems are solved together, and excellence becomes a habit, not an exception.

9.5 Setting High Standards

Where tireless striving stretches its arms toward perfection.
—Rabindranath Tagore

Setting high standards is the cornerstone of excellence. Visionary leaders and innovators have always set ambitious goals that challenge the status quo and inspire others to aim higher.

Michelangelo, the renowned Renaissance artist, exemplified the pursuit of excellence through his commitment to setting high standards. His masterpiece, the Sistine Chapel ceiling, is a testament to his meticulous attention to detail and unwavering dedication to perfection. Michelangelo's ability to envision and execute such a monumental work of art, despite the physical and creative challenges, set a new standard for artistic excellence that continues to inspire generations of artists.

In the 2016 Indian movie *Dangal*, based on a true story, the pursuit of excellence is vividly portrayed through the story of Mahavir Singh Phogat and his daughters Geeta and Babita. Mahavir, a former wrestler, dreams of winning a gold medal for India but is unable to achieve this himself. Determined to realize his dream through his daughters, he rigorously trains them in the sport of wrestling, despite societal pressures and gender stereotypes. Mahavir instills in them the values of high standards, discipline, hard work, and perseverance, pushing them to their limits. The rigorous training and relentless pursuit of excellence lead Geeta to become India's first female wrestler to win a gold medal at the 2010 Commonwealth Games. The film beautifully captures the essence of striving for greatness against all odds, highlighting that excellence is achieved through unwavering dedication and an unyielding spirit.

The 1976 American film *Rocky* is a quintessential story of the underdog's pursuit of excellence. The film follows Rocky Balboa, a small-time boxer who gets an unexpected opportunity to fight the heavyweight champion Apollo Creed. Despite being considered a long shot, Rocky trains rigorously, pushing his physical and mental limits. The match goes the full 15 rounds, and Creed wins by split decision. Rocky's journey is marked by relentless determination and an unyielding spirit to "go the distance." Rocky's commitment to excellence, even when faced with insurmountable odds, serves as an inspiring reminder that greatness is achieved through grit, hard work, and the courage to keep moving forward, no matter the challenges.

9.6 Embracing Continuous Improvement

Continuous improvement is better than delayed perfection.

—Mark Twain

Excellence is not a static achievement but a dynamic process of continuous improvement. Embracing a mindset of perpetual growth and learning is essential for maintaining high standards and achieving sustained success.

Jeffrey K. Liker's work in organizational behavior, particularly his study of the Toyota Production System (TPS), reinforces this idea. Liker's research demonstrates that cultures built on continuous improvement (kaizen), respect for people, and high performance standards consistently achieve superior quality, greater efficiency, and long-term success. Developed by Taiichi Ohno and Eiji Toyoda, TPS embodies these principles, having revolutionized manufacturing through its relentless focus on eliminating waste, enhancing quality, and empowering employees at all levels to drive innovation. This commitment to incremental improvement has enabled Toyota to become one of the world's leading automobile manufacturers, celebrated for its reliability and operational excellence.

Stephen Covey's principle of "Sharpen the Saw" from his book *7 Habits of Highly Effective People* underscores the importance of continually honing our skills and abilities. Covey argues that excellence and effectiveness require us to engage in regular self-renewal across physical, mental, emotional, and spiritual dimensions. Individuals must prioritize continuous personal growth to stay resilient and adaptable in a changing world. "Sharpen the Saw" reminds us that, to sustain high performance and embrace new challenges, we must invest in ourselves through learning and self-care, ensuring that we are always ready to face what lies ahead. A good leader is one who actively seeks out new knowledge, embracing ideas that challenge conventional thinking and exploring concepts that can drive improvement.

9.7 Pursuit of Continuous Improvement: A Personal Story

Perfection is not attainable, but if we chase perfection, we can catch excellence.

—Vince Lombardi, American football coach

From day one at WRIME Inc., our newly founded engineering consulting firm, I understood we had to challenge conventional thinking to stand out in a competitive industry. The prevailing belief in the consulting world was that billable hours were everything; research and development were seen as luxuries that cut into profit margins. I hoped that investing in innovation and continuous improvement would pay off, though I knew it was far from guaranteed. We decided to allocate time for research and development (R&D) in our core business areas, even though it meant sacrificing some billable hours, critical at the start of a new company. It was a gamble, and we had moments of doubt, but the approach resonated with my belief in setting high standards and striving to push beyond the status quo.

We didn't stop at technical development; we placed significant emphasis on training for our employees in project management, writing skills, and career growth. I encouraged the team to read broadly and learn from various fields, and we built an in-house library stocked not only with technical manuals but also with books on leadership, communication, and management. Every new hire received a pocket version of *7 Habits of Highly Effective People*, a small gesture that symbolized our shared commitment to growth and the pursuit of excellence. We also offered lunch with the CEO to employees who took the initiative to read *The Elements of Style*, a classic on writing, hoping to help them refine their communication skills.

This investment in our people and commitment to continuous improvement started to pay off in ways that sometimes surprised even me and my partner. We began winning new projects and standing out in competitive bidding processes, occasionally surpassing firms that were 100 times our size. Our proposals stood out not just for their technical accuracy but for the thought leadership and vision we brought to the table. We earned a reputation as a company that didn't just meet standards but set them. This journey reminded me that excellence is not a one-time achievement but a habit, as Aristotle so wisely observed.

Over time, I came to realize that fostering continuous improvement wasn't only about achieving business success; it was about nurturing a culture where everyone felt empowered to grow and contribute. Just as Stephen Covey's "Sharpen the Saw" principle suggests, investing in self-renewal and development helped keep our team resilient and adaptable. Encouraging the team to pursue personal and professional growth became a cornerstone of our company's philosophy, reflecting the idea that true leadership and excellence come from constant learning and a commitment to improvement.

For those aspiring to lead, I humbly offer this advice: embrace a mindset that values continuous growth and challenge the limits of conventional thinking. By investing in your people, even at the cost of short-term gains, you build a foundation of excellence that fuels long-term success and demonstrates leadership that prioritizes not just business outcomes but the growth and fulfillment of the entire team.

9.8 Fostering a Culture of Excellence

The thing I have learned at IBM is that culture is everything.
— Louis V. Gerstner Jr.,
former chief executive officer, IBM

Creating an environment that nurtures and promotes excellence is crucial for achieving extraordinary results. Leaders play a pivotal role in fostering a culture where high standards, innovation, and collaboration are valued and encouraged.

Steve Jobs, cofounder of Apple Inc., was instrumental in instituting and maintaining a culture of excellence that propelled the company to the forefront of the tech industry. Jobs's uncompromising commitment to quality and innovation set the tone for Apple's culture. He inspired his team to think differently, push boundaries, and strive for perfection in every product. This culture of excellence resulted in iconic products such as the iPhone, iPad, and MacBook, which revolutionized technology and design. Jobs's leadership at Apple exemplified how fostering a culture of excellence can lead to groundbreaking achievements.

Striving for excellence is closely linked to happiness and meaning-making because it involves a continuous pursuit of personal and professional growth, which contributes to a deeper sense of fulfillment.

Adopting an attitude of excellence can transform not only individual performance but also organizational culture. Brian Tracy, author of *Eat That Frog*, notes, "Excellence is not a destination; it is a continuous journey that never ends." This journey requires a collective commitment to high standards and the willingness to embrace change and innovation. Research in leadership and management underscores the importance of leaders who inspire and model this attitude of excellence, creating an environment where employees feel motivated to strive for their best. Organizations that cultivate this attitude among their teams tend to see higher levels of employee engagement, job satisfaction, and overall performance, leading to sustained competitive advantage.

Striving for excellence is closely linked to happiness and meaning-making because it involves a continuous pursuit of personal and professional growth, which contributes to a deeper sense of fulfillment. A study at the University of Chicago found that individuals who engage in activities requiring high levels of skill and concentration, often associated with the pursuit of excellence, experience greater levels of happiness and life satisfaction. This pursuit helps individuals align their actions with their core values, leading to a more meaningful and purpose-driven life. Additionally, Gallup's research indicates that employees who feel they are working toward excellence are 3.6 times more likely to be engaged at work, which is a significant predictor of overall well-being.

9.9 Inspiring vs. Motivating: What Drives Excellence?

A good leader inspires people to have confidence in the leader. A great leader inspires people to have confidence in themselves.

—Eleanor Roosevelt

The concepts of inspiration and motivation, though often used inter-changeably, have distinct differences that profoundly impact the pursuit of excellence. In his book *Trust and Inspire*, Stephen M. R. Covey argues that while motivation can drive people to achieve short-term goals through external rewards or punishments, inspiration taps into an individual's intrinsic values and desires, fostering long-lasting com-mitment, creativity, and excellence. Motivation tends to be temporary and situational, often requiring constant reinforcement. In contrast, inspiration resonates deeply within individuals, catalyzing sustained passion and initiative from within.

Motivation is frequently linked to the idea of pushing individuals toward a goal— often through incentives such as bonuses, promotions, or recognition—but not necessarily toward *exceeding* that goal. Daniel H. Pink, in his book *Drive: The Surprising Truth about What Motivates Us*, discusses how traditional motivational techniques, like rewards and punishments, are not as effective in the long run, particularly for complex, creative tasks. Instead, Pink argues for the importance of intrinsic motivators such as autonomy, mastery, and purpose. These intrinsic motivators align closely with the concept of inspiration, where individuals feel a sense of ownership and meaning in their work, which ignites a passion for excellence. Inspiration pulls individuals toward a vision that resonates with their core values and aspirations. As Simon Sinek outlines in *Start with Why*, inspirational leaders communicate a compelling vision that connects deeply with their followers' beliefs and values. This connection fosters a sense of purpose and belonging, encouraging people to invest their best efforts not because they have to, but because they want to. Inspirational leaders ignite a passion within their followers that transcends mere compliance, driving them to innovate and excel. An understanding of the distinction between inspiration and motivation is crucial for leaders who aim to foster a resilient and high-performing team.

9.10 Inspire, Infuriate Not

Our chief want is someone who will inspire us to be what we know we could be.

—Ralph Waldo Emerson

Leadership is a double-edged sword; it can either elevate and inspire or frustrate and alienate. In *Inspire: The Universal Path for Leading Yourself and Others*, Adam Galinsky presents a compelling argument that all individuals exist on a spectrum between inspiration and infuriation, and the way we lead—whether in our personal or professional lives—determines where we fall on this continuum. Leaders in particular wield an amplified influence; their words and actions resonate deeply, shaping the emotional and psychological landscapes of those they lead. While some leaders naturally inspire through their vision, authenticity, and ability to uplift others, others alienate and frustrate by failing to communicate effectively, disregarding the needs of their teams, or lacking self-awareness. Galinsky argues that inspiration is not an inherent trait but a skill that can be cultivated through conscious effort, making leadership a matter of deliberate practice rather than innate ability.

To navigate this spectrum successfully, Galinsky introduces three distinct archetypes of inspiring leaders: visionaries, exemplars, and mentors. *Visionaries* articulate a compelling, optimistic future, giving people a sense of purpose and direction. *Exemplars* lead with integrity, remaining consistent in their words and actions, and demonstrating courage in the face of challenges. *Mentors* focus on uplifting and empowering others, recognizing potential and guiding individuals toward growth. The most effective leaders often embody aspects of all three archetypes, seamlessly integrating vision, authenticity, and encouragement. By identifying where they currently stand and actively working to strengthen these leadership traits, individuals can move closer to the inspirational end of the spectrum.

Inspiration, however, is not just about understanding the leadership theory behind it—it's about putting that theory into action. Galinsky provides actionable strategies for enhancing one's leadership presence and impact. He emphasizes the importance of self-awareness, urging leaders to assess how their actions affect others and adjust accordingly. Small yet meaningful practices—such as expressing gratitude, clearly defining the purpose of meetings, and offering timely recognition—can create a positive ripple effect. Leaders who consciously amplify their influence for good can transform their teams and organizations, fostering a culture of trust, motivation, and high performance. By recognizing that leadership is an evolving practice rather than a static position, anyone can shift their impact from being merely transactional to truly transformational.

9.11 Engage an "Invisible Manager" to Inspire

Culture eats strategy for breakfast.

—Peter Drucker

In *The Core Value Equation*, Darius Mirshahzadeh introduces the concept of core values as an "invisible manager"—a guiding force that shapes decision-making, behaviors, and company culture. When core values are authentically embedded within an organization, they become more than just words on a wall; they serve as a constant source of inspiration, driving employees to act with purpose, take ownership, and exceed expectations. He introduces the formula "Core values = Words = Conversations Decisions = Actions = Results," highlighting that core values serve as a foundational decision-making engine within a company. Here, the equal signs illustrate how values cascade through the organization—first expressed in words, then shaping conversations, guiding decisions, driving actions, and ultimately producing results. This idea of an invisible manager aligns closely with DEEP PACT, where leadership is not about rigid oversight but about creating an environment where values naturally inspire action. When leaders clearly define and reinforce core values, they instill a shared sense of mission that empowers employees to navigate challenges and opportunities with confidence and passion. This improves efficiency, strengthens teamwork, and enhances the overall workplace culture. It also builds trust and consistency, as employees and leaders alike understand that their actions are rooted in shared principles. Ultimately, an organization with a well-integrated invisible manager experiences higher engagement, stronger retention, and a deeper sense of purpose, as individuals feel empowered to contribute meaningfully without constant direction.

Mirshahzadeh stresses the importance of designing core values to be memorable and actionable, stating, "The difference between the almost right word and the right word is a large matter. It's the difference between the lightning bug and the lightning." This underscores the need for precision in articulating values to ensure they resonate throughout the organization.

9.12 Mastering Conflict Resolution

Be kind, for everyone you meet is fighting a hard battle.

—Socrates

Conflict is a natural and inevitable part of life—and business. Whether it's a clash of ideas, priorities, personalities, or values, unresolved conflict can quietly erode trust, disrupt collaboration, and stall the pursuit of excellence. In high-performing organizations, the absence of open dialogue around conflict often leads to underperformance, lower employee satisfaction, diminished engagement, higher turnover, and missed opportunities for innovation. Unresolved conflict also contributes significantly to workplace unhappiness.

Harvard Business Review contributor Amy Gallo points out in her 2024 article "How to Master Conflict Resolution," that there's no such thing as a conflict-free office. She asserts, "If you're involved in conflicts at work, it's not that there's something wrong with you, or the other person." It can also be said that there is no such thing as a conflict-free family or nonprofit organization. Conflict is not a sign of dysfunction— it is a natural consequence of ambitious people working together to pursue excellence. In fact, the presence of conflict often indicates that people care deeply about their work, the mission, and the outcomes. Leaders must recognize that how conflict is handled often matters more than whether it arises in the first place. What distinguishes excellent leaders and teams is not the absence of conflict, but their ability to navigate it skillfully, constructively, and urgently.

Reinforcing this urgency, Peter T. Coleman's article "The Conflict-Intelligent Leader," published in the July–August 2025 issue of the *Harvard Business Review*, underscores the strategic cost of unresolved conflict. He cites that 76% of employees have witnessed incivility in the workplace, with nearly half encountering it weekly and 13% experiencing it daily—costing businesses over $2 billion a day in productivity losses and absenteeism. Coleman argues that leaders must develop "conflict intelligence," a learnable leadership competency anchored in four core capabilities: self-regulation, situational adaptivity, systemic awareness, and social-emotional skills. Leaders with high conflict intelligence don't just resolve issues—they build resilient, inclusive cultures where innovation and trust thrive. These leaders model calm, intentional responses and promote feedback even in times of tension.

To begin mastering conflict resolution, leaders must first recognize the critical difference between task-related conflict and relationship conflict. Task conflict arises from differing ideas, viewpoints, or problem-solving strategies. When managed constructively, this kind of friction can be healthy; it challenges groupthink, sharpens thinking, and often leads to better decisions and innovation. Leaders should not only tolerate task conflict—they should welcome it as a source of creative tension. In contrast, relationship conflict stems from personal friction, perceived disrespect, or clashing egos. It erodes trust, undermines collaboration, and breeds resentment. Left unaddressed, it spreads silently and corrodes team morale.

Gallo's article outlines a practical four-step process for conflict resolution: (1) assess the situation, (2) prepare for the conversation, (3) conduct it skillfully, and (4) reflect and follow up. This structure helps leaders and teams navigate emotionally charged situations with clarity and purpose. Assessment requires understanding the nature of the conflict and deciding whether to address it immediately or to allow emotions to cool first. Preparation includes identifying what's really at stake and anticipating the other person's perspective. The conduct of the conversation should embody openness and mutual respect, aiming to resolve the issue rather than to prove who is right. Finally, reflection and follow-up allow leaders to reinforce trust, capture lessons learned, restore relationships, and ensure forward progress.

But mastering conflict resolution goes beyond following a stepwise process—it also requires affirming the dignity of every person involved. In a 2024 *MIT Sloan Management Review* article titled "To Navigate Conflict, Prioritize Dignity," Merrick Hoben defines dignity as our inherent sense of value, self-worth, and desire to contribute meaningfully. He outlines four practices for honoring dignity in conflict: (1) deepen acknowledgment by recognizing others' concerns, (2) strengthen agency by ensuring they feel heard, (3) build reciprocity through mutual respect, and (4) ensure clarity of path through agreed next steps. These practices are not add-ons. They are the core of enduring, trust-filled relationships in dynamic workplaces.

By integrating the structural clarity of Gallo's four steps with the human depth of Hoben's dignity practices, leaders can transform conflict into a catalyst for excellence. This approach doesn't just resolve disagreements—it builds resilience, strengthens relationships, and cultivates a culture where excellence is not derailed by tension but reinforced through it. It teaches leaders to balance outcomes with emotional intelligence, creating space for both resolution and human connection.

Coleman emphasizes that conflict intelligence is not a personality trait—it's a teachable and necessary leadership skill. And it is more relevant than ever in today's volatile climate of polarization, disengagement, and workplace incivility. As he concludes, "The question for leaders isn't whether to build conflict intelligence—it's how quickly they can begin."

Of course, conflict resolution paths are rarely linear. The key is to shift from "me versus you" to "us versus the problem." This mindset fosters collaboration and unlocks shared creativity and learning. In conflicts with peers, a shared commitment to the relationship can often ease resolution. Begin by affirming what you value about the other person's contributions, then clearly express your concerns.

In conflicts with superiors, it's essential to prepare well, focus on shared objectives, and frame feedback as a mutual interest in better outcomes. Avoid public confrontation and seek a safe space for discussion instead. In a 2023 article titled "The Delicate Dynamics of Challenging a Superior" in the *MIT Sloan Management Review*, author Benjamin Laker emphasizes the importance of "I" statements. Instead of saying "You ignored my work," say, "I felt that my work didn't receive the attention I had hoped for." Shifting from accusatory language ("You never listen") to ownership language ("I feel unheard in meetings") can de-escalate tension and keep the conversation productive. These small changes in word choices can mean the difference between defensiveness and dialogue. Timing also is critical—avoid initiating tough conversations in high-stress moments. Instead, choose a time when both parties can focus without distraction or embarrassment. And most importantly, stay open. The goal is not to "win" the conversation but to reach understanding and build mutual respect. Above all, view conflict not as a threat but as an opportunity to grow, realign, and ultimately, lead with greater clarity, courage, and compassion. Excellence does not come from avoiding discomfort—it comes from working through it with integrity.

Ultimately, the ability to resolve conflict constructively is not a soft skill—it's a strategic leadership imperative. Conflict avoidance as a leadership style is not just ineffective, it's dangerous. As Amy Jen Su, author of *The Leader You Want to Be*, warns, efforts to be "nice" often come with significant hidden costs. Leaders who sidestep difficult conversations create relationships that are neither authentic nor constructive. This avoidance can erode their own health and self-esteem, signal weakness or victimhood, and ultimately compromise organizational outcomes. When leaders avoid conflict, they risk empowering the loudest voices in the room, losing diversity of thought, and sacrificing the innovation and clarity that come from open debate. Avoiding conflict may seem like a path to harmony, but in reality, it undermines team cohesion, decision quality, and long-term success. Strong leaders don't fear conflict. They learn to face it and resolve it.

Best Practices for Conflict Resolution

To put these ideas into practice, follow this outline of best practices for resolving conflict—highlighting both what to do and what to avoid to foster trust, clarity, and progress.

You should:

- ◈ **Address conflict early.** Delay only if emotions need to cool—otherwise, silence breeds assumptions.
- ◈ **Clarify the type of conflict.** Welcome task-related tension; defuse relationship-driven friction quickly.
- ◈ **Prepare, don't improvise.** Know what's at stake, anticipate reactions, and lead with empathy.

- ❖ **Use "I" statements.** They express ownership and reduce defensiveness.
- ❖ **Create safety.** Choose the right time and setting for honest, respectful dialogue.
- ❖ **Affirm dignity.** Make others feel seen, heard, and valued—even when disagreeing.

You should not:
- ❖ **Avoid the issue** to keep the peace. Avoidance erodes trust and compounds tension.
- ❖ **Attack or blame.** "You never listen" shuts doors. "I feel unheard" opens them.
- ❖ **Try to win.** Seek resolution, not victory. Conflict isn't a contest—it's a conversation.
- ❖ **Go public with private issues.** Hard conversations belong in safe, discreet settings.
- ❖ **Dismiss emotion.** People remember how you made them feel more than what you said.

Conflict handled well can build trust, clarity, and cohesion. Conflict avoided can destroy them. Choose wisely. When leaders create space for candid dialogue, grounded in empathy and purpose, conflict becomes a source of clarity, alignment, and forward momentum. Excellence, after all, is not the absence of tension—but the presence of courage, clarity, and connection in how we work through it.

9.13 Overcoming Adversity

Being challenged in life is inevitable, being defeated is optional.
—Roger Crawford

The pursuit of excellence often involves overcoming significant challenges and setbacks. Resilience, the ability to adapt and persevere in the face of adversity, is a critical trait for achieving and maintaining excellence.

Helen Keller's life story is a remarkable testament to resilience and the pursuit of excellence. Despite losing her sight and hearing at a young age, Keller overcame immense obstacles to become a renowned author, activist, and lecturer. With the help of her teacher, Anne Sullivan, Keller learned to communicate and excel academically. She graduated from Radcliffe College with honors and dedicated her life to advocating for people with disabilities. Keller's indomitable spirit and relentless pursuit of excellence continue to inspire individuals worldwide.

California resident Roger Crawford is a unique and accomplished individual, recognized as a Hall of Fame athlete and speaker. *Sports Illustrated* acknowledged Roger as "One of the most accomplished, physically challenged athletes in history," and he was given the ITA Achievement Award, presented by the International Tennis Hall of Fame, in recognition of his athletic success.

Crawford's story is a powerful testament to the relentless pursuit of excellence despite overwhelming adversity. Born with ectrodactylism, a rare condition that left him with only one finger on his right hand and a thumb and a finger on his left hand, and with his legs severely impaired, Roger faced challenges that would seem insurmountable to many. Doctors told his parents that he would never walk or be able to care for himself. However, Roger and his parents refused to accept this prognosis.

From an early age, Roger refused to let his physical limitations define him. Encouraged by his parents to pursue his passions and live a life without limits, he developed an unyielding resolve to achieve his dreams. He fell in love with sports, particularly tennis, a game that demands precision, agility, and strength—qualities that most would think impossible for someone with Roger's physical condition.

However, Roger's pursuit of excellence was relentless. He practiced tirelessly, often facing setbacks and frustrations that tested his will-power. Yet he grew stronger and more determined with every obstacle he faced. Roger believed that excellence wasn't about being the best in the world but about being the best version of himself. His hard work and perseverance paid off when he not only competed but also succeeded in collegiate tennis, becoming the first athlete with four impaired limbs to compete in a Division I sport.

Roger's story doesn't end with his personal achievements. He turned his experiences into a mission to inspire and motivate others. As a renowned motivational speaker, he shares his journey of overcoming adversity and striving for excellence, touching countless lives with his message of hope, resilience, and determination. Roger Crawford's life exemplifies that true excellence is not defined by the absence of challenges but by the courage and tenacity to overcome them. His relentless pursuit of excellence, despite all odds, is a beacon of inspiration, reminding all of us that our limitations do not define us. Our determination does.

9.14 Collaborative Intelligence and Excellence

Collaborative intelligence leverages the diverse perspectives within an organization, leading to more informed decisions and greater buy-in from all stakeholders.
—California Management Review

The myth that excellence is solely a result of individual heroics is increasingly being debunked in today's business world, where collaboration and collective effort are recognized as the true drivers of extraordinary achievements. Collaborative intelligence, which leverages the diverse insights and knowledge of teams, is now seen as essential for achieving high levels of excellence. A compelling example is the case of a European consumer goods company that engaged over 8,000 employees in digital deliberations focused on identifying opportunities for process improvements, cost efficiencies, and innovation across the organization. This large-scale collaboration, as reported in the *California Management Review,* resulted in increased operational efficiency and significant cost savings, highlighting the effectiveness of collaborative intelligence in driving organizational success. This example underscores the potential of collaborative intelligence to not only streamline operations but also to enhance the overall performance of the organization. Further reinforcing this idea, the "Competing in the Age of Digital Convergence" article from the *California Management Review* emphasizes that successful digital convergence requires not just technological innovation but also strategic combinations of existing knowledge and collaborative efforts across different sectors.

The rise of digital tools and platforms in the 2020s has significantly facilitated the implementation of collaborative intelligence. These tools enable seamless communication and collaboration across various departments and geographic locations, breaking down traditional silos and fostering a more integrated approach to problem-solving. Recent real-world examples of collaborative intelligence further illustrate its impact. Companies like Google and Microsoft have implemented collaborative platforms that allow employees to contribute ideas and solutions to complex problems, leading to breakthroughs in product development and innovation. Google's use of internal forums and idea-sharing platforms, such as Google Moderator, enables employees to suggest and vote on new ideas, fostering a culture of continuous improvement and innovation. Similarly, Microsoft's use of Teams has revolutionized the way its global workforce collaborates, resulting in more cohesive and effective project management. These examples highlight the critical role of collaborative intelligence in driving organizational success and adaptability in an ever-evolving business landscape.

By embracing this approach, leaders can unlock the full potential of their teams, ensuring sustained growth.

Collaborative intelligence aligns with contemporary leadership theories that emphasize inclusivity, transparency, and the democratization of decision-making processes.

9.15 Attracting and Retaining Talent for Excellence

Hire character. Train skill.

—Peter Schutz, former president and chief executive officer, Porsche

Talent matters, but so does character—and perhaps more so than anything else. Greatness comes from character, not from intelligence alone. A candidate might have the perfect set of skills necessary for the job, but if they lack the right values and character, they will not fit into the organization. Attitude is not something you can easily teach. If someone needs to be constantly reminded to act or behave in a certain way to achieve the desired outcome, it does little to benefit the company. As Jim Collins wrote in *Good to Great*, organizations thrive when they "get the right people on the bus, the wrong people off the bus, and the right people in the right seats," prioritizing character and potential over credentials—a concept he calls "First Who, Then What."

In today's world, where skills become outdated quickly and technology disrupts entire industries, hiring for potential ensures that you have individuals who can adapt to new challenges and innovations. To thrive, you need to identify those with the right attitude and the highest potential, bring them onto your team, and help them grow. In a *Harvard Business Review* video titled "Hire for Potential, Not Just Experience," Claudio Fernández-Aráoz, a top global expert on talent and leadership, asserts that "the art of great 'who' decisions" marks the difference between success and failure. He urges leaders and managers to assess current and prospective employees on five key indicators: the right motivation, curiosity, insight, engagement, and determination.

Hiring highly talented people is just the beginning; retaining them is a critical challenge for organizations committed to excellence. It requires more than just offering attractive salaries and perks; it demands a deep understanding of what truly motivates employees to join, stay, or leave. Research shows that employees often quit due to unmet needs for growth, autonomy, and alignment with organizational values. By addressing these core drivers, organizations can position themselves as employers of choice, fostering loyalty and engagement among their workforce. At the heart of this effort lies the principle of ensuring excellence: when organizations prioritize employee well-being, psychological safety, and professional growth, they create a culture where individuals and teams consistently strive to deliver their best.

To retain top performers, companies must prioritize career development opportunities. Employees crave the ability to grow and advance within their roles, and organizations that invest in mentorship, upskilling, and clear pathways for promotion demonstrate a commitment to their team's success. Moreover, empowering employees through greater autonomy is equally critical. Providing flexibility in how and where work gets done not only boosts satisfaction but also fosters innovation by encouraging employees to take ownership of their responsibilities.

Finally, a strong organizational identity rooted in shared values can be a powerful retention tool. When employees feel connected to their company's mission and culture, their work gains deeper meaning. Leading organizations like Google and Spotify have demonstrated the effectiveness of this approach, offering environments where employees feel valued, supported, and aligned with the organization's purpose.

It is not enough just to pay attention to what motivates, attracts, and retains top talent—it is equally important to avoid behaviors and practices that drive people away. Organizations should not rely solely on salaries and perks, as compensation alone does not build long-term loyalty; purpose and growth matter more. Ignoring feedback is also detrimental, as dismissing employee concerns erodes trust and engagement. Micromanagement stifles innovation and damages morale, while tolerating toxic behavior undermines culture and pushes away high performers. Finally, leaders should never assume loyalty is automatic; it must be earned through consistent respect, recognition, and meaningful opportunities for growth.

By integrating these strategies and insights, organizations can build a workforce that is not only talented but also loyal, inspired, and invested in long-term success.

9.16 Designing Leadership Training for Sustained Excellence

This is the new war for talent—not wooing employees away from competitors, but unleashing the enthusiasm that is already there within employees, but dormant.

—Daniel M. Cable,
London Business School

Winning the war for talent is just the beginning. The true differentiator is not just hiring great people—it's keeping them engaged and unlocking their leadership potential. Without strong leadership at every level, organizational excellence cannot be ensured. Therefore, effective leadership training is not optional; it is a strategic imperative. Organizations must deliberately design leadership training that drives sustained excellence and meaningful behavioral change—not simply to bestow a certificate from a prestigious program. Yet, as discussed earlier, leadership development programs continue to disappoint, often delivering a minimal return on investment. According to *Harvard Business Review*, most corporate leadership programs are part of a "great training robbery," with companies spending billions yet seeing little change in actual leadership behavior. Reports estimate that over 90% of leadership development investments fail to produce measurable results.

The problem isn't a lack of effort, but a flawed approach. Many organizations still select leadership programs based on superficial factors such as the charisma of facilitators, aesthetic presentation, or institutional brand prestige. Designing leadership training for sustained excellence means ensuring that your programs are appropriately scaled, targeted, and aligned with your organization's real needs and challenges—avoiding both generic solutions and overengineered approaches that waste resources. Some companies invest in top-tier business school programs that cost upward of $150,000 per executive yet fail to ask critical questions: *Does the program reflect our strategic needs and priorities? Will our leaders be able to practice and apply these skills at work? Is there a mechanism to reinforce and measure progress?* As highlighted in McKinsey & Company's 2023 article "Why Leadership Development Programs Fail," most organizations lack clarity on what great leadership looks like, and they often don't link development efforts to measurable business outcomes. In *MIT Sloan Management Review*'s "Leadership Development Is Failing Us. Here's How to Fix It," published in December 2023, authors Leroy, Anisman-Razin, and Detert echo this concern, noting that many programs lack coherence between vision, method, and impact.

This is where the DEEP PACT's model of whole-person leadership offers a breakthrough. Rather than treating leadership as a checklist of competencies, DEEP PACT emphasizes mindset transformation, character development, and human connection as the foundation of effective leadership. Whole-person leadership—one that integrates purpose, integrity, humility, care, and trust—helps organizations right-size their development programs by anchoring them in what truly drives influence and impact: who the leader is, not just what the leader knows. When training is built around the whole person, not just job performance, it unleashes enthusiasm within the trainees and fosters resilience, ethical clarity, and strategic courage—capabilities that today's environments demand.

Best Practices for Designing Leadership Training

To build an effective leadership pipeline, you must rethink how leadership training is selected, delivered, and measured. Successful programs do three things exceptionally well:

- ◈ **Clarify the program's vision and desired outcomes.** Define the specific leadership attributes and behaviors that matter most in your context. Avoid vague ambitions and anchor your efforts in what your organization truly needs.
- ◈ **Use evidence-based, contextual methods.** Move beyond lectures and theoretical case studies. Embed learning into real-time business challenges. Leverage peer feedback, coaching, and reflective practices. As the McKinsey article emphasizes, leaders grow best through personalized learning journeys, grounded in self-awareness and business relevance.
- ◈ **Measure and reinforce impact.** Leadership growth is not a one-time event—it's a behavioral transformation. Create structures for follow-up, feedback, and ongoing application. Track how leadership behaviors are changing and how that change impacts team performance, culture, and business outcomes.

Equally important is avoiding the four critical mistakes identified in the *MIT Sloan* article: Don't design one-size-fits-all solutions, don't isolate training from real work, don't underestimate the cultural shifts required, and don't forget to measure results over time. Deloitte reinforces this by advocating for leadership as an ongoing developmental process, not a box to be checked once. Leadership must be embedded into the culture, supported by systems and peers, and linked to strategic execution.

DEEP PACT helps bridge the gap between leadership theory and personal transformation. It redefines training success not by how much content is delivered but by how deeply beliefs are examined, actions aligned, and character strengthened. By centering leadership on the whole person, organizations move beyond temporary performance gains and cultivate enduring leaders equipped to thrive amid uncertainty.

The bottom line? Don't settle for programs that simply look good or check a skill or competency box. Don't design leadership training around the volume of information delivered or the number of competencies covered. Instead, design it to spark mindset shifts, build meaningful capabilities, and drive lasting behavioral change. Choose leadership development that unleashes enthusiasm and creativity within your employees. As a leader, you're responsible for ensuring that your investment in people drives real returns—for your teams, your culture, and your mission. Select wisely. Build intentionally. Measure relentlessly. Because when you get leadership right, you don't just shape better leaders—you shape better organizations, stronger communities, and a future worth leading.

9.17 READ, or Be Left Behind!

Not all readers are leaders, but all leaders are readers.

—Harry Truman

Reading is not just a habit—it is a strategic advantage. The world is evolving at an unprecedented pace, and leaders who fail to stay informed risk becoming outdated, ineffective, and disconnected. Whether the text is the latest research in management, insights from thought leaders, or emerging social and economic trends, reading equips leaders with the knowledge necessary to adapt, innovate, and make informed decisions. Those who do not read miss out on critical ideas, industry disruptions, and shifting employee, customer, and investor expectations, leaving them ill-prepared for the future.

Whenever I faced a challenge, my instinct was not to sit and struggle alone but to turn to books and the latest research. Reading has always given me access to perspectives I might never have discovered on my own, helping me jump-start my creative process instead of spending years trying to piece together insights through trial and error. That said, books don't have all the answers. They won't solve your problems for you, but they will expand your thinking, challenge your assumptions, and introduce you to ideas you may not have considered. They provide guidance and perspective, but it is up to you to apply that knowledge, connect it to real-world experiences, and turn insights into action. The true power of reading is not in memorizing information but in developing the wisdom to use it effectively.

In a rapidly changing world, leaders cannot afford to be confined to one rigid way of thinking. The only way to stay ahead is to continuously read and learn, ensuring you are aware of the latest advances in business thinking and technology. Today, being ahead of new developments in leadership, AI, automation, and digital transformation is no longer optional—it is the key differentiator between those who thrive and those who are left behind. Leadership is about seeing what others don't, making decisions with clarity, and staying ahead of change. The best leaders understand that learning never stops, and reading provides access to diverse perspectives, timeless wisdom, and cutting-edge strategies. It strengthens critical thinking, enhances communication, and fosters a deep understanding of the human, technological, and global factors shaping business and society.

This commitment to continuous learning aligns directly with the DEEP PACT principle *Ensure excellence more than others think imaginable.* True excellence is not achieved by standing still—it is fueled by curiosity, knowledge, and the relentless pursuit of growth. Leaders who prioritize reading are not satisfied with "good enough"—they seek insights that push boundaries, challenge assumptions, and elevate their impact beyond what others believe is possible.

Books and business magazines do not hand you ready-made solutions, but they give you the tools to think better, adapt faster, and lead with greater confidence. In today's world, you either stay current or you get left behind.

The choice is simple: READ, or be left behind!

9.18 Leaving a Lasting Legacy

Carve your name on hearts, not tombstones. A legacy is etched into the minds of others and the stories they share about you.

—Shannon Alder,
inspirational author and therapist

The pursuit of excellence leaves a lasting legacy that continues to influence and inspire future generations. Leaders who embody this commitment create a ripple effect that extends beyond their immediate sphere of influence; it transcends personal ambition and touches the lives of others in meaningful ways.

One of the most profound impacts of striving for unimaginable excellence is the cultural shift it can create within an organization or community. When leaders and individuals commit to this level of excellence, they inspire people around them to also elevate their own standards and aspirations. Historical examples like Toyota's implementation of the kaizen philosophy, which emphasizes continuous improvement and employee involvement, demonstrate how a commitment to excellence can transform organizational culture.

Leonardo da Vinci's legacy as a polymath and visionary remains unparalleled. His relentless pursuit of excellence across various fields—including art, science, and engineering—left an indelible mark on history. Da Vinci's masterpieces, such as the *Mona Lisa* and *The Last Supper*, as well as his scientific discoveries and inventions, continue to inspire and educate. His dedication to excellence serves as a timeless example of how one individual's commitment can leave a profound and lasting impact on the world.

Indra Nooyi, former CEO of PepsiCo, embodies a pursuit of excellence that goes beyond imagination. During her tenure, Nooyi not only transformed the company's product line to emphasize healthier options but also integrated sustainability and social responsibility into the corporate strategy. Her vision for Performance with Purpose redefined what it meant to be a global leader by showing that a commitment to excellence can balance profitability with positive social impact. Nooyi's unwavering dedication to high standards inspired those around her to push boundaries and rethink what a corporation could achieve. Her legacy is evident in the way PepsiCo continues to innovate and uphold values that prioritize both business success and community well-being. This pursuit of excellence generated financial success and set a new standard for responsible and visionary leadership that future generations strive to emulate.

Moreover, the legacy of excellence extends beyond tangible achievements and encompasses the values and principles instilled in others. For instance, the impact of Steve Jobs at Apple goes beyond groundbreaking products; it includes a culture of creativity and perfectionism that continues to drive the company. As Jobs famously said, "Be a yardstick of quality. Some people aren't used to an environment where excellence is expected." This quote encapsulates the idea that excellence, when pursued relentlessly, becomes a benchmark that others aspire to reach. *Ensuring excellence more than others think imaginable* leaves a lasting legacy not only through the success it generates but also through the inspiration and aspiration it seeds in future generations.

QUICK TIP

Action: Deploy AI quality-assurance tools to maintain high standards in deliverables. Use machine-learning algorithms to predict and mitigate risks in projects.

Example: Implementing AI-driven quality control in manufacturing processes to reduce defects and ensure product excellence.

Caveat: Continuously validate and update AI models to ensure accuracy and relevance and prevent overreliance on potentially outdated or biased algorithms.

9.19 Ten Actionable Steps for Applying Principle 3

Excellence is a continuous process and not an accident.

—A. P. J. Abdul Kalam,
former president, India

In exploring the many dimensions of excellence—from Aristotle's timeless lessons on the pursuit of virtue to building high-performing teams, fostering cultures of continuous improvement, mastering conflict resolution, and leaving a legacy that endures—we have uncovered both the ideals and the challenges that define true excellence. But knowledge alone is never enough to achieve excellence, for it is a disciplined practice, built step by step through commitment, courage, and consistency.

Applying the principle *Ensure excellence more than others think imaginable* requires an integrated approach that weaves together vision, strategy, and culture. The following guide offers practical steps with examples to help you bring these principles to life. You need not tackle every idea at once; begin with those that resonate most deeply with your current challenges and aspirations. Every step you take strengthens your foundation to build something greater, inspire others, and bring you closer to unimaginable excellence.

Good is the enemy of great.

—Jim Collins

STEP 1
Define and Communicate a Clear Vision of Excellence

STEP 2
Foster a Culture of Continuous Improvement

STEP 3
Set High Standards and Hold Everyone Accountable

STEP 4
Invest in Talent and Development

STEP 5
Encourage Innovation and Risk-Taking

Principle 3
ENSURE EXCELLENCE
more than others think imaginable

STEP 6
Leverage Technology and Data

STEP 7
Measure and Celebrate Success

STEP 8
Develop Resilience

STEP 9
Communicate Clearly and Frequently about Quality

STEP 10
Build a Collaborative Environment

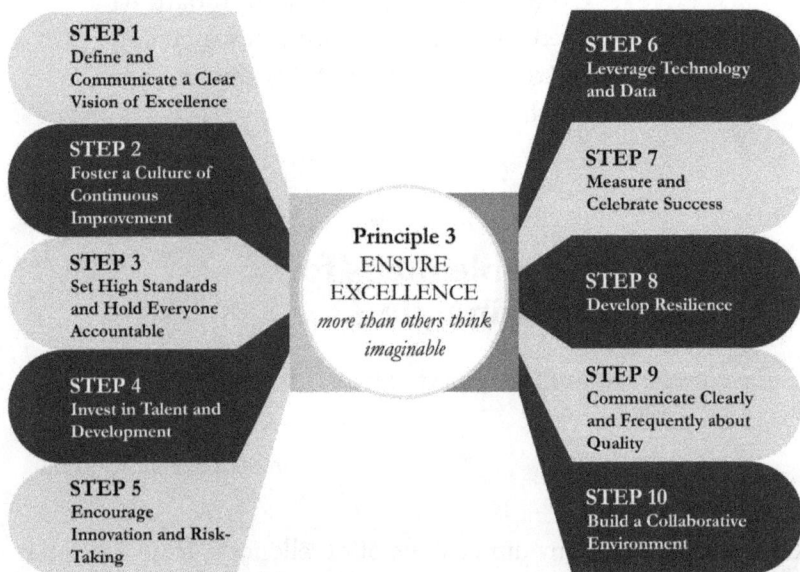

The pursuit of excellence: ten actionable steps for applying Principle 3

💡 *Principle 3, Step 1: Define and Communicate a Clear Vision of Excellence*

Action: Articulate a compelling vision that sets a high standard of excellence and communicates it clearly across the organization.

Example: Walt Disney envisioned Disneyland as "the happiest place on Earth," a standard that drove the company's commitment to an exceptional customer experience. Disney's clear vision has become a benchmark for excellence in the entertainment industry. Apple Inc. under Steve Jobs exemplified the pursuit of excellence. Jobs's vision for innovative and user-friendly products led to the creation of ground-breaking devices like the iPhone and iPad. This vision was clearly communicated and relentlessly pursued, setting Apple apart as a leader in technology and design.

💡 *Principle 3, Step 2: Foster a Culture of Continuous Improvement*

Action: Promote the concept of a learning organization, where continuous learning and improvement are embedded in the culture that supports career growth opportunities, a top priority for Millennials and Gen Z. Encourage team members to take ownership of their professional development and provide resources for continuous learning. Conduct regular workshops and training sessions focused on self-awareness, emotional intelligence, and adaptive leadership.

Example: At Zappos, regular training sessions on company culture and values help ensure that employees' actions are aligned with the company's mission of delivering exceptional customer service. Gary Ridge, the CEO of WD-40, has championed a culture of servant leadership by focusing on creating a learning environment for his employees. He believes in making sure that employees are growing and thriving professionally and personally, and his leadership style has contributed to the company's high employee satisfaction and retention rates. Toyota's implementation of the kaizen philosophy emphasizes continuous improvement and employee involvement. This approach has been critical in Toyota's rise to become one of the world's leading automobile manufacturers. Toyota's production system, which includes practices like just-in-time (JIT) and *Jidoka* (automation with a human touch), has resulted in significant efficiency gains and product quality improvements. The company's culture of continuous improvement has been a cornerstone of its long-term success.

💡 *Principle 3, Step 3: Set High Standards and Hold Everyone Accountable*

Action: Establish high standards for performance and hold everyone in the organization accountable for meeting them. Do not settle for good enough under strenuous circumstances. Make excellence a habit.

> *Do not settle for good enough under strenuous circumstances. Make excellence a habit.*

Example: Steve Jobs's insistence on perfection in design and functionality at Apple set a high bar for innovation and quality. Jeff Bezos at Amazon did the same for customer service and operational efficiency. Amazon's "customer obsession" philosophy has driven the company's relentless pursuit of excellence in all aspects of its operations. The focus on fast and reliable delivery, exemplified by the introduction of Amazon Prime, has redefined customer expectations and set new standards for the e-commerce industry. The company's commitment to high standards and accountability has been a key factor in its growth and success. The Ritz-Carlton's motto, "We are Ladies and Gentlemen serving Ladies and Gentlemen," sets a high standard for service excellence, ensuring exceptional customer experiences.

Principle 3, Step 4: Invest in Talent and Development

Action: Attract, retain, and develop top talent to ensure that the organization has the skills and capabilities needed to achieve excellence. Millennials and Gen Z care a lot about professional growth opportunities and recognition.

Example: Google's strategy of hiring the best talent and providing them with a supportive and stimulating work environment has been crucial to its innovation and success. Google's investment in employee development programs—such as Google University and the promotion of a collaborative culture—has fostered an environment where excellence and innovation thrive. This focus on talent has enabled Google to maintain its leadership position in the tech industry. Microsoft's investment in training programs for its employees to enhance their skills in cloud computing and AI has been critical to the company's transformation under Satya Nadella.

Principle 3, Step 5: Encourage Innovation and Risk-Taking

Action: Create an environment that encourages innovation and tolerates calculated risks and failures.

Example: 3M's culture of innovation encourages employees to spend 15% of their time on projects of their choosing, fostering creativity and breakthrough innovations. The development of the Post-it Note is a prime example of how this culture of experimentation and risk-taking can lead to revolutionary products. The company's willingness to invest in and support innovative ideas has driven its long-term success.

Principle 3, Step 6: Leverage Technology and Data

Action: Utilize the latest technologies and data analytics to drive efficiency and excellence in operations.

Example: FedEx's use of advanced tracking systems to ensure timely delivery and customer satisfaction demonstrates the impact of technology on achieving high standards of excellence. FedEx's investment in real-time tracking technology has revolutionized the logistics industry, providing customers with unparalleled visibility into their shipments and ensuring timely deliveries. This technological edge has been a critical factor in FedEx's reputation for reliability and excellence.

Principle 3, Step 7: Measure and Celebrate Success

Action: Implement robust metrics to measure performance and celebrate achievements to motivate and inspire continued excellence.

Example: General Electric (GE) under Jack Welch implemented rigorous performance measurement systems and celebrated successes to maintain high standards and motivate employees. GE's and Welch's use of Six Sigma for quality control and process improvement significantly enhanced operational efficiency and product quality. The company's practice of recognizing and celebrating employee achievements helped sustain a high-performance culture.

💡 *Principle 3, Step 8: Develop Resilience*

Action: Strengthen your ability to cope with challenges and bounce back from setbacks to continue to pursue excellence.

- ◈ **Resilience training.** Engage in resilience training programs that teach coping strategies, stress management techniques, and adaptive thinking, all of which help with achieving excellence.
- ◈ **Mindfulness practices.** Incorporate mindfulness practices such as meditation and yoga into your routine to build mental fortitude and clarity.

Example: After experiencing a major project failure, a tech company CEO implemented resilience training for the entire team. This included stress management workshops and mindfulness sessions, which significantly improved the team's ability to handle future challenges and maintain productivity under pressure. During the 2008 global financial crisis, the resilience of leaders like Howard Schultz of Starbucks helped the company navigate through tough times without losing sight of its core values and mission.

💡 *Principle 3, Step 9: Communicate Clearly and Frequently about Quality*

Action: Enhance your ability to understand and improve communication within your team and organization by regularly evaluating your communication strategies and practices regarding product quality requirements and expectations.

- ◇ **Communication inventory.** Create an inventory of all communication channels and methods currently in use within your organization. Evaluate the effectiveness of each channel by gathering feedback from your team.
- ◇ **Feedback mechanism.** Implement a system for regular feedback on communication effectiveness. Encourage team members to share their experiences and suggestions for improvement.

Example: A marketing firm conducted a comprehensive communication audit after realizing that product quality requirements were frequently misunderstood. They discovered that their reliance on lengthy email chains was causing confusion. By switching to a project management tool with real-time updates and direct messaging, they streamlined communication, significantly reducing misunderstandings.

💡 Principle 3, Step 10: Build a Collaborative Environment

Action: Foster a collaborative environment where team members are encouraged to work together and share ideas openly.

- ◇ **Collaboration tools.** Utilize collaboration tools and platforms that facilitate teamwork and idea sharing.
- ◇ **Team-building activities.** Regularly organize team-building activities to strengthen relationships and improve teamwork.

Example: Pixar's open office design encourages spontaneous collaboration and idea sharing among employees, leading to creative breakthroughs and innovative projects. This collaborative environment has been instrumental in Pixar's success in creating critically acclaimed and commercially successful films. Similarly, Salesforce emphasizes collaboration through its use of the Chatter platform, which allows employees to connect and collaborate in real time, fostering a culture of teamwork and innovation.

9.20 Ten Barriers to Applying Principle 3

Excellence is not being the best; it is doing your best.

—Unknown

Striving for excellence beyond what others think imaginable is an admirable goal, but it comes with significant challenges. Understanding these barriers can help individuals and organizations develop strategies to overcome them and achieve exceptional standards of excellence.

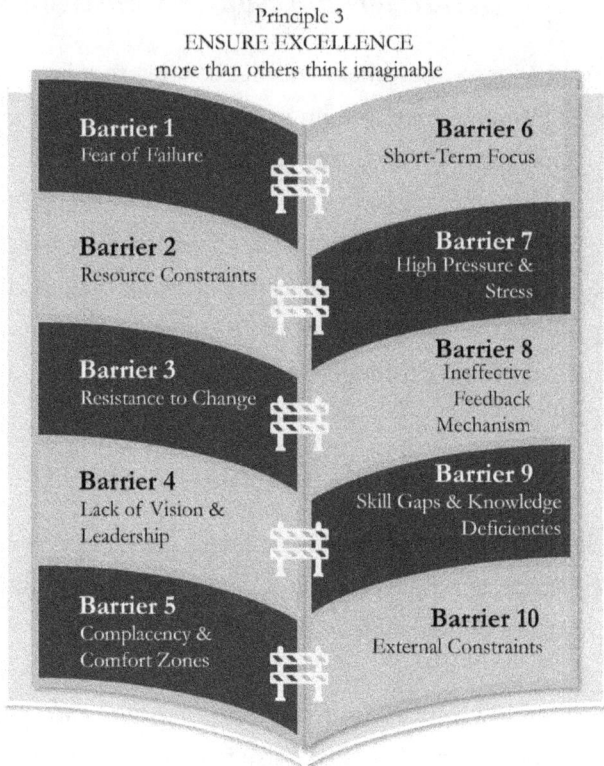

Principle 3
ENSURE EXCELLENCE
more than others think imaginable

Barrier 1
Fear of Failure

Barrier 2
Resource Constraints

Barrier 3
Resistance to Change

Barrier 4
Lack of Vision &
Leadership

Barrier 5
Complacency &
Comfort Zones

Barrier 6
Short-Term Focus

Barrier 7
High Pressure &
Stress

Barrier 8
Ineffective
Feedback
Mechanism

Barrier 9
Skill Gaps & Knowledge
Deficiencies

Barrier 10
External Constraints

What gets in the way: ten barriers to applying Principle 3

⚠ *Principle 3, Barrier 1: Fear of Failure*

Barrier: The pursuit of excellence often involves taking risks and pushing boundaries, which can lead to a heightened fear of failure. This fear can paralyze individuals and organizations, preventing them from striving for the highest standards.

Solution: Cultivate a growth mindset that views failure as a learning opportunity rather than a setback. Encourage a culture that supports calculated risk-taking and innovation. Celebrate efforts and progress, not just outcomes.

⚠ *Principle 3, Barrier 2: Resource Constraints*

Barrier: Achieving extraordinary excellence often requires significant investment of time, money, and human resources. Limited resources can make it challenging to reach and sustain high levels of performance.

Solution: Prioritize and allocate resources strategically, focusing on areas where excellence will have the most significant impact. Seek additional funding, partnerships, or collaborations to support ambitious projects. Optimize resource usage through efficient processes and technologies.

⚠ *Principle 3, Barrier 3: Resistance to Change*

Barrier: Striving for unimaginable excellence often requires changing established practices, which can encounter resistance from individuals and organizations comfortable with the status quo.

Solution: Foster a culture of continuous improvement and openness to change. Communicate the benefits of striving for excellence and involve stakeholders in the change process. Provide training and support to ease transitions and reduce resistance.

⚠ *Principle 3, Barrier 4: Lack of Vision and Leadership*

Barrier: Without a clear vision and strong leadership, it is difficult to inspire and guide individuals and teams toward extraordinary excellence. A lack of direction can result in mediocrity and complacency.

Solution: Develop a compelling vision for excellence and communicate it clearly and consistently. Leaders should model excellence and inspire others through their actions and commitment. Encourage visionary thinking and strategic planning at all levels of the organization.

⚠ *Principle 3, Barrier 5: Complacency and Comfort Zones*

Barrier: Success can lead to complacency, where individuals and organizations become satisfied with good enough and stop pushing for higher standards. Comfort zones can limit innovation and progress.

Solution: Set challenging but achievable goals that push the boundaries of current performance. Regularly assess and raise performance standards. Encourage a mindset of relentless improvement and avoid settling for mediocrity.

⚠ *Principle 3, Barrier 6: Short-Term Focus*

Barrier: A focus on short-term results and immediate gains can undermine efforts to achieve long-term excellence. Pressure for quick wins can lead to shortcuts and compromise on quality.

Solution: Balance short-term objectives with long-term goals. Develop and implement strategic plans that prioritize sustainable excellence over quick fixes. Communicate the importance of long-term vision and invest in initiatives that build lasting value.

⚠ *Principle 3, Barrier 7: High Pressure and Stress*

Barrier: The relentless pursuit of excellence can lead to high levels of pressure and stress, which can negatively impact mental and physical well-being, leading to burnout and reduced performance.

Solution: Promote a healthy work-life integration and provide support for flexibility, stress management, and mental health. Create a supportive work environment that values well-being as much as performance. Encourage regular breaks and downtime to recharge.

⚠ *Principle 3, Barrier 8: Ineffective Feedback Mechanisms*

Barrier: Without effective feedback mechanisms, individuals and organizations may struggle to identify areas for improvement and track progress toward excellence. Lack of constructive feedback can hinder growth.

Solution: Establish robust feedback systems that provide regular, constructive, and actionable feedback. Encourage a culture of open communication where feedback is seen as a tool for improvement rather than criticism. Use performance metrics and benchmarks to guide progress.

⚠ *Principle 3, Barrier 9: Skill Gaps and Knowledge Deficiencies*

Barrier: Achieving excellence often requires a high level of expertise and knowledge. Skill gaps and lack of access to the latest information can limit the ability to perform at an exceptional level.

Solution: Invest in continuous learning and professional development. Provide training, mentoring, and access to resources that enhance skills and knowledge. Encourage knowledge sharing and collaboration within the organization.

⚠️ *Principle 3, Barrier 10: External Constraints*

Barrier: External factors such as market conditions, regulatory requirements, and competitive pressures can pose significant challenges to achieving excellence. These constraints can limit flexibility and innovation.

Solution: Stay informed about external trends and developments that impact the pursuit of excellence. Develop strategies to navigate and mitigate external constraints. Foster adaptability and resilience to respond effectively to changing conditions.

9.21 Ten Examples of Applying Principle 3

1. Lucy benchmarks her department's performance against industry leaders and sets higher standards.
2. Ben insists on thoroughly testing a new product feature before release, despite tight deadlines.
3. Maria develops a comprehensive training program to ensure that her team can handle complex tasks with confidence.
4. Sophie continuously updates the team's training materials to ensure they are at the cutting edge of industry standards.
5. Daniel sets clear expectations for high-quality work from his team and provides regular feedback and support to help them achieve it.
6. Chloe sets up a peer review system for all major deliverables, ensuring multiple perspectives and feedback loops.

7. Noah demands a higher standard of data accuracy, implementing double-checking procedures that slow down the workflow but increase reliability.

8. A project manager sets higher quality standards for a product launch, resulting in exceptional client satisfaction.

9. A community organizer plans a local event with meticulous attention to detail, ensuring that everything runs smoothly.

10. A parent goes above and beyond to create a memorable birthday party for their child, paying attention to every detail.

9.22 Closing Reflections

Do not wait for leaders; do it alone, person to person.

—Mother Teresa

The principle *Ensure excellence more than others think imaginable* challenges individuals to push beyond conventional limits and strive for extraordinary achievements. Through historical examples and fictional stories, we see how setting high standards, embracing continuous improvement, fostering a culture of excellence, overcoming adversity, and leaving a lasting legacy define the pursuit of excellence.

From Michelangelo's artistic mastery to Steve Jobs's innovative leadership, from Helen Keller's resilience to Leonardo da Vinci's enduring impact, these stories highlight the transformative power of excellence. They teach us that excellence is not a destination but a continuous journey of growth, learning, and unwavering commitment to the highest standards.

Believing in the principle *Ensure excellence more than others think imaginable* is a commendable first step, but implementing it requires strategic and sustained effort. By applying the step-by-step guidelines presented here, organizations can surpass conventional expectations and achieve unparalleled levels of success. These actions drive innovation, fuel growth, and secure long-term success by embedding excellence into the very fabric of the organization's culture. The commitment to this principle not only transforms individual performance but also propels the entire organization toward a future defined by resilience and excellence.

Ensuring excellence at all levels of an organization requires overcoming numerous barriers, including fear of failure, resource constraints, resistance to change, lack of vision and leadership, complacency, short-term focus, high pressure, ineffective feedback mechanisms, skill gaps, and external constraints. By addressing these challenges with strategic planning, strong leadership, continuous improvement, and a supportive culture, individuals and organizations can achieve extraordinary levels of excellence.

In an era marked by rapid change and unprecedented challenges, the need for excellence is more critical than ever.

9.23 Daily Practice

1. **Set high standards:** Set and communicate high standards for everything you do and strive to go beyond mere requirements.

2. **Sharpen your saw:** Dedicate time each day to continuous learning, self-care, and personal growth, ensuring that you maintain peak performance and well-being.

3. **Seek feedback:** Ask a peer or mentor about the quality of your work for the purpose of continuous improvement.

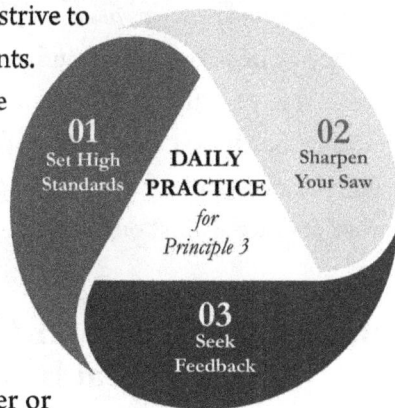

01 Set High Standards — DAILY PRACTICE *for Principle 3* — 02 Sharpen Your Saw — 03 Seek Feedback

10 Principle 4: Protect Yourself from Self-Sabotage More Than Others Think Necessary

For a man to conquer himself is the first and noblest of all victories.

—Plato

10.1 What If . . .

What if the greatest obstacle to your success isn't external—but you? By the end of this chapter, you might come to the unsettling realization that you've been sabotaging your own progress all along. This self-defeating behavior isn't a new struggle; it's rooted in an ancient Greek concept known as **akrasia**. *Akrasia* describes the perplexing state of acting against your better judgment due to a lack of self-control. It mirrors today's battle with self-sabotage—where internal conflicts and irrational behavior cause us to undermine our own goals and potential. By understanding *akrasia*, we gain valuable insights into why we sometimes act against our best interests, even when we know better.

10.2 Akrasia and Self-Sabotage: Philosophical Insights

Self-will in the man who does not reckon wisely is by itself the weakest of all things.

—Aeschylus

Aristotle offered a detailed examination of *akrasia* in his *Nicomachean Ethics*. He explores how overpowering desires can undermine rational decisions, leading to behavior that contradicts one's values or intentions. Aristotle distinguishes between akrasia arising from impulsiveness (*propeteia*) and that driven by weakness (*astheneia*), reflecting a complex interplay between reason and emotion. He notes that "the incontinent man knows that what he does is bad, but he does it because of his passion." These reflections can be seen as an early philosophical framework for understanding self-sabotage: when people recognize the right course of action yet fail to pursue it due to internal conflict or lack of self-mastery.

Stoic philosopher Epictetus later emphasized rational control and inner freedom, arguing that peace comes not from changing external events but from mastering one's reactions to them. He famously said, "Men are disturbed not by things, but by the views they take of them," encapsulating the Stoic belief that internal attitudes, not external circumstances, are the true sources of distress.

Modern psychology mirrors these ancient insights, defining self-sabotage as behaviors that interfere with long-term goals. These behaviors often arise from inner conflicts, much like the akratic actions described by Aristotle and the irrational disturbances noted by Epictetus. According to Dr. Judy Ho, a clinical and forensic neuropsychologist and the author of *Stop Self-Sabotage: Six Steps to Unlock Your True Motivation, Harness Your Willpower, and Get out of Your Own Way*, self-sabotage involves "acting in ways that are counterproductive to one's own success" and is driven by underlying cognitive and emotional processes.

These timeless concepts underscore the necessity of self-awareness and discipline to overcome self-sabotage, paving the way for personal and professional success, because self-sabotage can prevent leaders from fully leveraging their strengths and achieving their strategic goals.

Leaders with a fixed mindset or those who struggle with their ego may shy away from taking necessary risks or making bold decisions, fearing failure or criticism. This hesitation can stagnate growth and innovation within the organization.

10.3 The Enemy Within

For him who has conquered the mind, the mind is the best of friends; but for one who has failed to do so, his mind will remain the greatest enemy.
—Bhagavad Gita

In the pursuit of personal and professional success, one of the greatest obstacles individuals face is not external adversity but the enemy within—self-sabotage. This insidious force can undermine achievements, derail goals, and diminish leadership potential.

Self-sabotage manifests in various forms, often subtly undermining a leader's efforts to succeed. Among the various factors that contribute to self-sabotage, five stand out:

1. Ego
2. Fixed mindset
3. Distrust
4. Profit/loss obsession
5. Power blindness

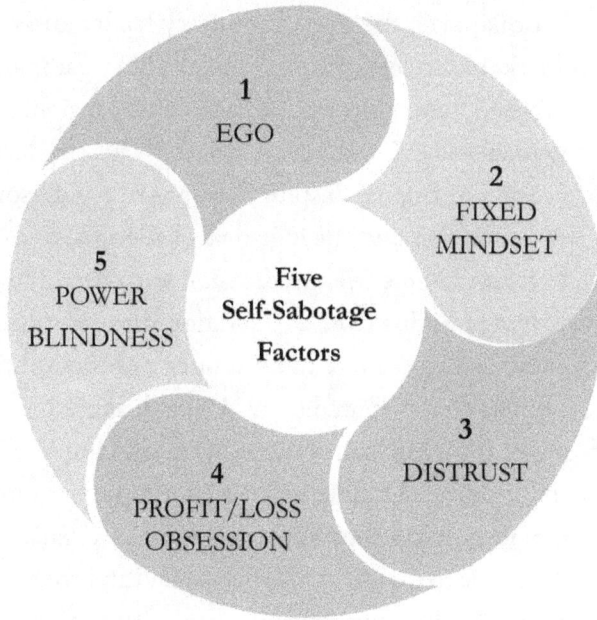

What derails leaders: the inner enemies of progress

By addressing and minimizing these detrimental factors, leaders can unlock their full potential and lead more effectively.

10.4 Self-Sabotage Factor 1: Ego

Ego, characterized by selfishness and self-orientation, is the greatest enemy of effective leadership. Inflated by power and success, ego is the insidious whisper in one's ear that tells people they are inherently better than others. This inflated sense of self-importance leads leaders to operate out of self-interest—constantly seeking praise, ignoring feedback, and taking all the credit. When leaders prioritize their own egos over the collective good, they sabotage their potential and harm their organizations. History is replete with examples where ego-driven decisions led to downfall.

Napoleon Bonaparte, the French military leader and emperor, achieved remarkable success through his military campaigns and conquests. However, his ambition and desire for expansion ultimately led to his downfall. In 1812, Napoleon, driven by his ego, launched a disastrous invasion of Russia, despite warnings from advisors about the harsh Russian winter and the logistical challenges of such a vast campaign. The campaign ended in disaster, with Napoleon's army suffering massive losses due to cold, starvation, and guerrilla warfare. Napoleon's overreach and failure to heed warnings about the risks of his actions ultimately contributed to his downfall and exile.

The sinking of the *Titanic* in 1912 is another example of an ego-driven leadership failure. Despite receiving multiple warnings about the presence of icebergs in the North Atlantic, the *Titanic's* captain, Edward Smith, chose to maintain the ship's speed and continue on its course, believing that the ship was unsinkable. This overconfidence and failure to heed warnings led to the tragic collision with an iceberg and the sinking of the *Titanic*, resulting in the loss of over 1,500 lives, including his own.

When leaders prioritize their own interests over those of their team or organization, they erode trust and collaboration. This is vividly illustrated in the fall of Enron, where executive egos led to unethical practices and the company's ultimate downfall in the early 2000s. Despite presenting itself as a model of corporate innovation and success, Enron engaged in widespread accounting fraud and financial manipulation to artificially inflate its stock price. Senior executives, including CEO Jeffrey Skilling and CFO Andrew Fastow, misled investors, regulators, and employees about the company's financial health, leading to massive losses for shareholders and employees alike.

As Ryan Holiday points out in *Ego Is the Enemy,* this self-serving behavior undermines leadership potential, as it alienates team members and stifles collaboration. Effective leadership, in contrast, requires humility, the ability to listen, and the willingness to share credit. By recognizing and controlling their ego, leaders can foster a more inclusive and dynamic environment, ultimately leading to greater success for their organizations.

Ego is the root cause of all relationship problems.

Research underscores the detrimental impact of ego on leadership. Studies show that leaders with high levels of narcissism and hubris often make poor decisions due to overconfidence and lack of empathy. For instance, a study published in the *Journal of Applied Psychology* by Resick and colleagues found that narcissistic leaders are prone to decisions that prioritize their interests over the organization's welfare. Individuals with narcissistic personality traits often exhibit an inflated sense of self-importance, exaggerate their accomplishments, fixate on fantasies of power and success, and display excessive self-admiration, along with a defensive hostility toward criticism and a strong resistance to compromise. These behaviors can adversely affect organizational effectiveness by undermining collaboration, trust, and sound decision-making.

Controlling one's ego is challenging because success and adulation often reinforce it. Leaders in high positions frequently receive praise and deference, which can inflate their sense of self-importance. This phenomenon, often referred to as "CEO disease," leads to isolation from honest feedback and critical perspectives. Historical figures like Adolf Hitler exemplify this danger. Hitler's unchecked ego and delusions of grandeur drove him to make increasingly irrational decisions, culminating in the catastrophic consequences of World War II.

> ### QUICK TIP
>
> Keep your ego in check. Everything else will fall in place.

Leadership Is Not about You; It Is about the Team

Leadership is not a platform for personal success or accolades. It is a responsibility to drive the collective forward. Frances Frei and Anne Morriss, in *Unleashed: The Unapologetic Leader's Guide to Empowering Everyone around You*, assert that the essence of leadership lies in creating an environment where others can thrive. A leader's role is not to bask in the glow of individual achievements but to channel their influence into enabling their team's success. This shift in perspective, from self-centered authority to fostering collaboration and shared purpose, is what separates mediocre leadership from transformative leadership. Leaders who prioritize their team's success cultivate resilience, innovation, and lasting results that endure beyond their own tenure.

The concept of "teamship," first articulated by Sir Clive Woodward, coach of England's Rugby World Cup–winning team in 2003, captures the idea that leadership is a shared responsibility, not a singular privilege. Woodward focused on building a culture of discipline, commitment, and collective accountability among players, demonstrating that leadership thrives when responsibilities and successes are shared. Similarly, Lisa Earle McLeod, in *Leading with Noble Purpose*, underscores that great leaders inspire their teams by connecting daily efforts to a larger mission. By fostering a sense of purpose, leaders transform work into a meaningful pursuit, turning hierarchical leadership into a partnership founded on shared goals. When leaders illuminate the significance of their team's contributions, they inspire peak performance and foster a culture of commitment, collaboration, and mutual accountability.

Leadership that prioritizes the team fosters trust, adaptability, and sustainability. Frei and Morriss emphasize that leaders who focus on building systems and processes to empower their teams create organizations that outlast any individual leader. Peter Hawkins, in *Leadership Team Coaching: Developing Collective Transformational Leadership*, echoes this sentiment by advocating for systemic coaching to develop leadership teams that collaborate across functions. Likewise, the article "Collectivistic Leadership Approaches: Putting the 'We' in Leadership Science and Practice," published in *Industrial and Organizational Psychology*, highlights how effective leadership is rooted in collective effort rather than individual power. By embracing principles of teamship, leaders shift from command-and-control figures to stewards of shared success. In this way, leadership becomes less about the individual and more about empowering the collective to thrive together. A simple but powerful practice is to **remove the word "I" from your emails. Instead, use "we."** For example, rather than saying, "I completed the report," a leader might say, "We've completed the report," or "Our team finalized the document." This intentional use of inclusive language reinforces unity, recognizes shared contributions, and cultivates a culture of collaboration and mutual respect.

QUICK TIP

Remove the word "I" from your emails; use "we" instead.

Modern leadership theories emphasize the importance of humility and emotional intelligence in combating the detrimental effects of ego. Jim Collins, in his book *Good to Great*, identifies Level 5 Leaders as those who combine humility with fierce resolve. These leaders are more likely to build enduringly successful organizations because they prioritize the organization's success over personal recognition. They listen to others, acknowledge their limitations, and foster a culture of collaboration and mutual respect.

Ultimately, controlling the ego requires conscious effort and self-discipline. Leaders must seek out and value honest feedback, surround themselves with diverse perspectives, and remain committed to personal growth and self-awareness. As Ryan Holiday eloquently states, "Ego is the enemy of what you want and of what you have: Of mastering a craft. Of real creative insight. Of working well with others. Of building loyalty and support. Of longevity. Of repeating and retaining your success. It repulses advantages and opportunities. It is a magnet for enemies and errors." By recognizing and mitigating the influence of ego, leaders can avoid self-sabotage and lead their organizations to sustainable success.

10.5 Self-Sabotage Factor 2: Fixed Mindset

A fixed mindset, characterized by the belief that abilities and intelligence are static and unchangeable, can be a significant barrier to effective leadership, leading to self-sabotage. Because of this belief, people will avoid challenges, give up easily, and view effort as fruitless if they do not immediately succeed. They may also feel threatened by the success of others and perceive feedback or criticism as a direct attack on their inherent abilities rather than as opportunities for growth and improvement. Historical examples abound to illustrate how this mindset has undermined leadership potential. Take the case of King George III of Britain during the American Revolution. King George's rigid mindset and inability to adapt to changing circumstances contributed to the loss of the American colonies. His refusal to consider the evolving aspirations and grievances of the colonists, along with his insistence on maintaining traditional policies, ultimately caused a devastating defeat for the British Empire.

In the corporate world, the story of Blockbuster serves as a cautionary tale of how a fixed mindset can sabotage leadership. Blockbuster's leaders failed to recognize and adapt to the rapidly changing landscape of digital streaming. Despite having opportunities to innovate and even acquire Netflix, Blockbuster's executives clung to their established business model, believing their market dominance was unassailable. This rigid adherence to the status quo and refusal to embrace new technologies led to the company's decline and eventual bankruptcy, while Netflix soared to industry dominance, first in rentals, then in streaming and production.

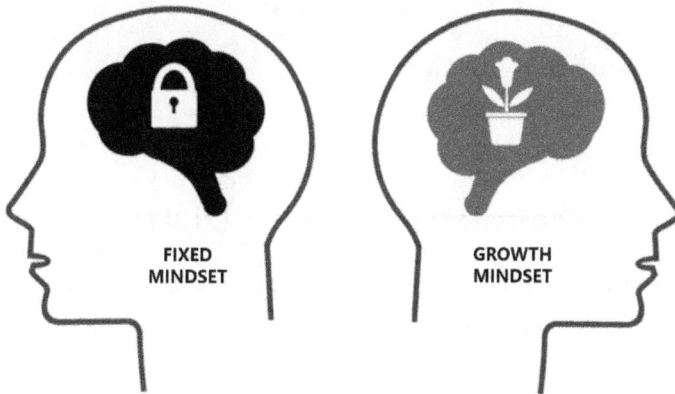

Two minds, two worlds: one locked in rigidity,
the other blooming in possibility

On the other hand, leaders with a growth mindset, who believe in the potential for development and learning, often drive innovation and success. This belief fosters a love for learning and resilience in the face

of challenges, viewing effort as a path to mastery and failures as opportunities to improve. People with a growth mindset embrace challenges,
persist despite setbacks, and find inspiration in the success of others,
leading to continuous personal and professional growth. Microsoft's
turnaround under Satya Nadella is a prime example. Nadella's emphasis on fostering a growth mindset within the company transformed
Microsoft's culture. By encouraging continuous learning and adaptability, Nadella revitalized Microsoft, leading to significant advancements in cloud computing and artificial intelligence, and propelling
the company to new heights. This shift in mindset from fixed to growth
illustrates how adaptability and a willingness to embrace change are
crucial for sustaining leadership success in a rapidly evolving business
environment.

QUICK TIP

Nurture a growth mindset.

10.6 Self-Sabotage Factor 3: Distrust

Distrust is one of the most corrosive forces in leadership—and when
it originates from the leader themselves, it becomes a potent form of
self-sabotage. Leaders who operate from suspicion, control, or fear
of vulnerability often build walls instead of bridges, stifling the very
relationships and insight they need to thrive. Without trust, leadership
becomes increasingly isolated, reactive, and fragile.

A striking historical example is the downfall of Julius Caesar. Though
Caesar's assassination on the Ides of March is often seen as a betrayal
by others, a deeper look reveals how his own inability to trust and
engage with the Roman Senate fueled his demise. Caesar centralized

power and ignored growing dissent among the senators, choosing dominance over dialogue. His failure to foster mutual trust or address their concerns created a breeding ground for conspiracy. In the end, Caesar was blindsided not only by his assassins—but by his own leadership blind spots. His distrust of shared governance sabotaged the long-term stability of his leadership, plunging Rome into years of civil unrest.

In the corporate world, the collapse of Enron offers another cautionary tale. CEO Jeffrey Skilling and chair Kenneth Lay cultivated a secretive, high-pressure environment built on mistrust. Information was hoarded, whistleblowers were silenced, and internal dissent was suppressed. The leaders themselves operated from a place of deep suspicion—of regulators, of the media, even of their own employees. This deep-seated distrust created a culture where fraud thrived, and ethical concerns went unaddressed until it was too late. The result was one of the most devastating corporate scandals in history, proving how distrust at the leadership level can poison not just culture but accountability itself.

Distrust can also be fatal to innovation. Nokia, once a global leader in mobile technology, faltered not because of a lack of resources or talent, but because its leadership became increasingly insular and dismissive of external ideas. Their resistance to collaboration and skepticism of emerging technologies—especially the rise of smartphones—kept them from adapting. While competitors like Apple and Samsung embraced openness, Nokia clung to internal legacy thinking. This reluctance to trust outside innovation caused Nokia to miss the smartphone revolution altogether, leading to a steep decline from which it has never fully recovered.

In contrast, trust can be a leader's greatest strategic advantage. Consider Howard Schultz, former CEO of Starbucks, who returned to the company during a time of decline. Rather than tighten control, Schultz listened—to baristas, store managers, and customers. He trusted his team to speak the truth, and he acted on their input. This trust-based approach helped turn the company around, revitalizing both morale and performance. Schultz's story shows that when leaders extend trust, they build cultures where people feel safe, heard, and motivated to contribute.

Leadership thrives on trust. It opens the door to honest feedback, shared accountability, innovation, and loyalty. When leaders let distrust take hold—whether toward others, new ideas, or change itself—they unknowingly set themselves up for failure. Building trust isn't a soft skill; it's a strategic imperative that anchors lasting influence and organizational success.

10.7 Self-Sabotage Factor 4: Profit/Loss Obsession

Obsession with profit and loss can lead leaders to make short-sighted decisions that ultimately sabotage their long-term success. One historical example is the fall of the East India Company. Initially a trading company, the East India Company became obsessed with maximizing profits, often at the expense of ethical considerations and sustainable practices. This relentless focus on profit led to exploitative practices, such as harsh taxation and oppressive control over local populations in India. These actions sparked widespread resentment and rebellion, ultimately culminating in the Indian Rebellion of 1857. The company's profit-driven policies not only led to its downfall but also significantly damaged British colonial interests, demonstrating how prioritizing short-term financial gains over ethical governance can lead to catastrophic consequences.

In the corporate world, the story of Lehman Brothers epitomizes the dangers of profit obsession. In the years leading up to the 2008 financial crisis, Lehman Brothers engaged in increasingly risky financial practices to maintain and boost profits. The firm heavily invested in subprime mortgages and used complex financial instruments to hide its true financial condition. This focus on short-term profit maximization led to the accumulation of significant risk. When the housing market collapsed, Lehman Brothers found itself unable to cover its losses, leading to its bankruptcy. This event triggered a global financial crisis, illustrating how a singular focus on profit without regard for risk management can result in monumental failure that extends beyond the company itself.

QUICK TIP

Don't sacrifice people for profit—personal or monetary.

Another example is the case of Sears, once a retail giant. Under the leadership of Eddie Lampert, Sears became fixated on cutting costs and improving short-term financial performance. Lampert implemented severe cost-cutting measures, including reducing staff, closing stores, and minimizing maintenance and reinvestment. While these strategies temporarily improved financial metrics, they eroded employee morale, customer satisfaction, and overall brand strength. The lack of investment in the core business led to a decline in the quality of service and products, ultimately causing a sharp decline in sales and market share. Sears' focus on short-term profits at the expense of long-term sustainability resulted in its downfall, highlighting the dangers of prioritizing immediate financial gains over a holistic, long-term strategy.

A powerful literary example of this self-sabotage factor can be found in Arthur Miller's play *Death of a Salesman*, which explores the corrosive effects of pursuing profit at the expense of personal integrity and human dignity. The protagonist, Willy Loman, sacrifices his values and relationships in pursuit of material success, only to realize too late the emptiness of his achievements and the tragic consequences of his actions. Through Willy's story, Miller highlights the importance of prioritizing human connection, authenticity, and moral integrity over the pursuit of profit and external validation.

These examples underscore the critical importance of balanced leadership. Leaders who focus solely on profit and loss risk neglecting other essential aspects of sustainable success, such as ethical practices, risk management, and long-term strategic planning. By balancing financial objectives with broader considerations, leaders can avoid the pitfalls of profit obsession and steer their organizations toward enduring success.

10.8 Self-Sabotage Factor 5: Power Blindness

Blind spots, the unseen gaps in our knowledge or awareness, become particularly perilous when combined with power blindness, a phenomenon where individuals in positions of authority lose sight of their limitations and the perspectives of others. British philosopher and mathematician Bertrand Russell famously noted, "Power corrupts, and absolute power corrupts absolutely." This timeless insight remains highly relevant in today's leadership landscape, where the acquisition of power often brings about significant challenges and potential pitfalls that could lead to self-sabotage. As leaders ascend in power, they may become increasingly insulated from candid feedback and diverse viewpoints, fostering an environment where their decisions are less informed and more prone to error. This power-induced myopia can result in overconfidence and misguided actions, ultimately stifling innovation and alienating team members. The famed investor and entrepreneur Ray Dalio, in his book *Principles*, asserted, "The two biggest barriers to good decision-making are your ego and your blind spots." The context of the quote emphasizes the need for leaders to be aware of their limitations and seek diverse perspectives to make well-rounded decisions.

Dacher Keltner, in *The Power Paradox: How We Gain and Lose Influence*, argues that power is not about dominance, control, or coercion but about the ability to make a positive difference in the lives of others. Power is earned through emotionally intelligent behaviors such as empathy, kindness, and collaboration. However, the paradox lies in how power can corrupt individuals, leading them to lose the very qualities that helped them gain it. Keltner warns of *power blindness*, where leaders tend to focus more on what they need and want and less on the challenges and inconveniences that others face. Leaders may misinterpret the struggles of less powerful individuals as incompetence rather than the effect of systemic barriers, further alienating their followers and creating a feedback loop where disengaged employees withdraw their trust and support. Power, Keltner emphasizes, is relational and sustained only through humility, gratitude, and ethical responsibility. It is not a license for self-interest but a mandate to serve. Leaders who nurture relationships and stay grounded in these values retain influence, inspire others, and avoid the self-sabotage of power blindness.

To counteract the effects of power blindness, leaders need to cultivate self-awareness, seek regular feedback, and actively engage with their teams, ensuring that diverse voices and critical insights are heard and valued. Recognizing and addressing blind spots is essential for effective, ethical, and inclusive leadership.

Five Power Traps That Contribute to Power Blindness

As leaders rise in influence, they must recognize and carefully navigate certain power traps that can sabotage their effectiveness and integrity. The June 2024 *Harvard Business Review* article "5 Traps to Avoid as You Gain Power as a Leader" elaborates on these challenges, offering critical insights into how leaders can avoid these pitfalls and wield power responsibly and ethically. Notably, the *HBR* article describes these traps in general terms without providing specific real-world examples. The examples below are drawn from external case studies to illustrate these concepts in practice.

The first trap, according to the authors of the *HBR* article mentioned above, is the ***savior trap***. As leaders gain power, they often develop an inflated sense of self-belief, leading them to "giving advice, having all the answers, being overly helpful, . . . and trying to solve everyone's problems." This overengagement can disable a team, stifle innovation, and alienate team members who feel their contributions are ignored and undervalued. To avoid this trap, leaders should cultivate humility, regularly solicit feedback, ask more questions to engage, and remain open to new ideas. This approach not only fosters a collaborative environment but also ensures that decisions are well-informed and balanced.

To illustrate this trap, consider the case of John Sculley, the CEO of Apple Inc. in the late 1980s. Hired from PepsiCo for his marketing genius, Sculley initially led Apple to great success with innovative marketing campaigns. However, as Apple's market share started to decline due to increased competition, Sculley felt compelled to take on the role of the savior. He began micromanaging every aspect of the company's operations, believing that his direct involvement was crucial for turning the tide. Sculley overrode the decisions of his experienced executives, centralizing control and stifling the creative freedom that had been the hallmark of Apple's success.

Sculley's micromanagement led to internal conflicts and an oppressive work environment, driving away key talent, including the company's cofounder Steve Jobs. The lack of delegation and empowerment caused innovation to stall, and Apple's product line became cluttered and unfocused. The company's financial performance continued to suffer, and Sculley was eventually forced out in 1993. This period highlighted the dangers of the savior trap, showing how a leader's overreach can hinder a company's ability to innovate and respond to market changes. Not until Steve Jobs returned in 1997, emphasizing collaborative leadership and streamlined decision-making, did Apple regain its innovative edge and market dominance.

The second trap is the *complacency trap*. With power, leaders may become less curious about knowing the truth about market shifts because they think they know everything. In the early 2000s, Kodak, once a giant in the photography industry, fell into the complacency trap. Leadership, increasingly insulated from their team and market realities, relied on a close-knit circle of advisors and continued to see silence as agreement, assuming it represented consensus. Despite inventing the first digital camera in 1975, Kodak's executives feared it would cannibalize their film business and dismissed the digital revolution. As digital photography emerged, Kodak's leaders ignored the shift, believing their dominance in film would persist. They continued investing heavily in film-based products while competitors like Sony and Canon captured the burgeoning digital market. This disconnect led to misguided strategies, ignoring the clear trend toward digital technology. To combat such complacency, leaders should engage with employees at all levels, asking questions like, "Am I missing something? What might I have overlooked? What have you tried?" Unfortunately for Kodak, their failure to stay grounded and informed about the evolving market, coupled with an unwillingness to pivot from film to digital, ultimately led to their decline and bankruptcy in 2012.

The third trap of power is the *avoidance trap*. Power can sometimes erode a sense of responsibility, causing a leader to avoid unpleasant tasks, such as having a hard conversation with a manager or stepping in firmly when ethical lapses occur at work or someone has blatantly trampled organizational values. Avoidance may give an immediate feeling of comfort when shrugging off a conflict or difficult conversations, but the leader's lack of actions weakens their credibility and authenticity; employees lose trust in the leader who picks and chooses tasks based on their comfort zone, not based on their obligations as a leader to be fair and consistent. To combat this trap, you should pay attention to the obligations in your role as a leader and consider the benefits and costs of your inaction. Tackling tough situations head-on makes you a stronger leader.

A classic but tragic example of the avoidance trap is the story of Boeing's quality failure during Dennis Muilenburg's tenure as CEO. PBS's documentary *Boeing's Fatal Flaw* detailed how Boeing's leadership ignored critical safety issues with the 737 MAX, leading to tragic crashes in October 2018 and March 2019 that caused the loss of 346 lives. PBS revealed that despite multiple warnings from engineers and safety experts about the flaws in the Maneuvering Characteristics Augmentation System (MCAS), Boeing's top executives avoided engaging in the necessary but difficult discussions about addressing these safety concerns. This avoidance was driven by a focus on meeting production deadlines and financial targets rather than prioritizing passengers' safety and well-being. By sidestepping unpleasant interventions and critical conversations, Boeing's leaders avoided fulfilling their obligations, ultimately resulting in catastrophic consequences. The documentary highlighted how this failure to act responsibly and transparently not only led to the tragic crashes but also severely damaged Boeing's reputation and financial standing. It underscored the crucial need for leaders to face tough issues head-on, prioritize ethical standards, and maintain open lines of communication to prevent such devastating outcomes. Dennis Muilenburg was eventually ousted in December 2019, and David Calhoun took over as CEO with a mandate to restore trust and overhaul the company's safety practices.

The fourth trap is the *friend trap*, one of the most difficult of the five mentioned here. It consists of compromising the power of position or authority to play favorites with a former peer. The newly promoted leader might have difficulty in holding former peers accountable or sharing confidential information that is privy only to his or her position. To combat this, rejuvenate your confidence in the new role by making a list of skills and capabilities that got you promoted and reemphasize the roles, responsibilities, and decision-making framework for your team in a clear and explicit manner. According to the authors of the article, "These intentional discussions remove doubt and confusion about how you will use your new positional power."

In October 2012, Marissa Mayer, then CEO of Yahoo, hired Henrique de Castro from Google, where they had previously worked together. This hiring decision quickly became contentious as de Castro struggled to adapt to Yahoo's unique challenges. Despite multiple internal warnings about his lack of fit and difficult personality, Mayer proceeded with the hire, possibly influenced by their past professional relationship. Over the next 15 months, de Castro's tenure was marked by poor performance and clashes with other executives. Mayer's hesitation to address these issues directly, due to their previous connection, exemplified the friend trap.

Ultimately, Mayer had to make the difficult decision to fire de Castro in January 2014, acknowledging that their working relationship was not productive. This decision, although delayed, was necessary to address Yahoo's leadership and performance issues. The incident highlighted the importance of maintaining professional boundaries and the challenges leaders face in balancing personal relationships with their responsibilities. By confronting the issue head-on, Mayer demonstrated the need for decisive action to maintain organizational integrity and performance.

The fifth trap is the ***stress trap***. With power comes stress from the pressure to deliver results. A leader's unmanaged stress, however, could cause secondary stresses among their direct reports, who may hold back on sharing the bad news because of fear of the leader's uncertain or unpleasant reaction. Your team may bring the bad news to your attention when they can't keep it away from you any longer, which may be too late to address the problems. To avoid falling into the misery of this trap, leaders should practice mindfulness and learn to better manage their stresses.

In the early 2000s, Ford Motor Company, under CEO Jacques Nasser, faced significant challenges. Known for his aggressive management style, Nasser was under immense pressure to deliver results, leading to a high-stress environment. This stress permeated the organization, causing his direct reports to fear his reactions to bad news and often delaying the communication of critical issues. A prominent example was the Firestone tire recall crisis. Defective tires on Ford Explorers were linked to numerous accidents, but the severity of the problem was not promptly communicated to Nasser. By the time the issue reached him, it had escalated into a full-blown crisis, severely damaging Ford's reputation and finances. This delay highlighted the dangers of the stress trap, where unmanaged stress from leadership trickled down, creating a culture of fear and poor communication.

Nasser's inability to manage stress effectively and foster open communication contributed to his removal as CEO in 2001. This incident underscored the importance for leaders to manage their stress and cultivate an environment where employees feel safe to share critical information promptly.

Understanding and avoiding these five traps of power blindness is crucial for leaders who aspire to wield their power responsibly. By avoiding these power traps, leaders can harness their influence to drive meaningful and positive change, not only within their organizations but also in the wider community. The true measure of leadership lies in the ability to use power responsibly and for the greater good.

10.9 Self-Sabotage and the Leadership Effectiveness Formula

Pure mathematics is, in its way, the poetry of logical ideas.
—Albert Einstein

The presence of self-sabotage factors diminishes one's leadership potential, whereas emotional intelligence (EI), discussed in the previous chapter, acts as a multiplier. The interplay between emotional intelligence and self-sabotage factors in determining effective leadership can be expressed in a mathematical formula as follows:

$$LE = LP \times (EI)^2$$

where

LE (leadership effectiveness) is an indicator of the strength of a leader's overall effectiveness and impact;

LP (leadership potential) represents the capabilities and talents of a leader. A score of 5 is assigned to those who exhibit no self-sabotage factors, with 1 point deducted for each of the five self-sabotage factors that is present in a leader.

and

EI (emotional intelligence) represents the number of emotional intelligence attributes present in a leader. A score of 5 is assigned to those who exhibit all five EI attributes, with 1 point deducted for each of the five attributes that is absent in a leader.

A few example scenarios can arise, as described below:

Leadership Effectiveness is shown in the Table using the formula, $LE = LP*EI^2$		Leadership Potential (LP) *Full score of 5 decreases by 1 point for presence of each self-sabotage factor*					
Emotional Intelligence (EI) *Full score of 5 decreases by 1 point for absence of each EI attribute*	EI Score ↓	Full LP Score (0 Self-sabotage factors present)	1 factor present	2 factors present	3 factors present	4 factors present	5 factors present
		5	4	3	2	1	0
Full EI Score (All 5 EI Attributes Present)	5	125	100	75	50	25	0
Missing 1 EI Attribute	4	80	64	48	32	16	0
Missing 2 EI Attributes	3	45	36	27	18	9	0
Missing 3 EI Attributes	2	20	16	12	8	4	0
Missing 4 EI Attributes	1	5	4	3	2	1	0
Missing 5 EI Attributes	0	0	0	0	0	0	0

← LE Score

Scenario 1   Scenario 3   Scenario 4   Scenario 2

Two forces, one outcome: how EI and self-sabotage shape your leadership effectiveness score

Scenario 1—Maximum LP and EI: If an individual is free from all five self-sabotage factors, her LP score would be 5. If this individual demonstrates the presence of all five EI attributes, her EI score will also be 5. Hence, her leadership effectiveness score would be:

$$LE = 5 \times 5^2 = 125$$

In this scenario, the individual achieves a score of 125, reflecting maximum leadership effectiveness.

Scenario 2—Decreased Leadership Potential due to Self-Sabotage: Suppose the individual exhibits four of five self-sabotage factors, resulting in an LP score of 1, after deducting 4 points. If the individual demonstrates the presence of all five EI attributes, her leadership effectiveness score would be as follows:

$$LE = (5\text{-}4) \times 5^2 = 25$$

Despite possessing high emotional intelligence, the individual's leadership score plummets to 25, one-fifth of the maximum of 125, due to the prevalence of four self-sabotage factors.

Scenario 3—Absence of Emotional Intelligence: If the individual lacks EI entirely, her leadership effectiveness score would be reduced to 0, even if she does not exhibit any self-sabotage factor.

$$LE = 5 \times 0^2 = 0$$

In this scenario, the absence of emotional intelligence nullifies the individual's leadership effectiveness, resulting in a score of 0, regardless of their LP score.

Scenario 4—Decreased Leadership Potential and Decreased Emotional Intelligence: Suppose the individual exhibits two self-sabotage factors, resulting in a deduction of 2 points from the LP score. Assuming that the individual exhibits only 2 of the 5 EI components, the leadership effectiveness score would be as follows:

$$LE = (5\text{–}2) \times 2^2 = 12$$

These illustrative scenarios provide a clear, quantifiable framework that helps leaders identify where they can make the most significant improvements. By visualizing the interplay between these elements, leaders can develop targeted strategies to enhance their EI and reduce self-sabotage, thereby unlocking their full potential for leadership effectiveness.

Implementing this formula in leadership development programs can revolutionize how organizations approach training and development. By emphasizing the exponential impact of emotional intelligence and the need to address self-sabotage, organizations can cultivate more effective leaders. Leaders who understand and apply this formula will be better equipped to navigate complex challenges, inspire their teams, and drive sustainable success. This holistic approach ensures that leaders are aware not only of their potential but also actively working to enhance it through continuous learning and self-improvement.

QUICK TIP

Action: Consider using AI-driven personal productivity, emotion recognition, and feedback analyzer tools to assess the level of emotional intelligence and self-sabotage factors. Employ AI for mental health support and stress management.

Example: Leveraging AI tools like Affectiva, Culture Amp, Headspace, or Calm.

Caveat: Ensure that AI tools for mental health support are used as a supplement to, and not a replacement for, professional human intervention when necessary.

10.10 Overcoming Self-Sabotage: A Personal Story

It is not the strongest of the species that survive, nor the most intelligent, but the one most responsive to change.

—Charles Darwin

Early in my career, I was entrusted with managing a groundbreaking and complex project—a $4 million consulting contract with a federal agency, the largest I had ever overseen. This project was innovative, involving multiple subconsultants, including a Canadian software company with a unique product that played a pivotal role in our plan. I took great pride in leading this one-of-a-kind endeavor and had developed an elaborate project management plan complete with a detailed schedule, critical paths, and all the meticulous tools that project management courses teach. I was confident in my approach and determined to prove myself capable of delivering excellence.

However, this overconfidence soon turned into a source of trouble. Managing such an unprecedented project made it difficult to keep everyone aligned, and the biggest challenge came from the Canadian software company. Their platform—essential for building the decision support system for a major US river basin—turned out to be less developed than expected. The software was unable to handle some of the advanced features I envisioned and had promised to the client. The president of the software company tried to persuade me to redefine the problem, adjust the vision, and tailor our goals to fit the existing software capabilities. But I was adamant about maintaining the original vision. I thought compromising would mean failure, and I became unyielding, micromanaging every step of the process—including aspects like software data models and system design, areas where I lacked expertise.

Fueled by my ego, I began immersing myself in software and systems design books, convinced that I needed to know enough to challenge our subconsultant at every turn. My intention was to ensure excellence, but instead it created confusion and stalled progress. The friction escalated, and the president of the software company even complained to my manager. When my manager confronted me, I defended my approach fiercely, insisting that the subconsultant was trying to cut corners and push additional costs onto us.

At this juncture my manager helped me take a step back. He encouraged me to consider the perspectives and constraints of everyone involved—my own team, the subconsultants, and the client. He reminded me that leadership wasn't about having my way at all costs; it was about finding solutions that worked within our budget, schedule, and scope while maintaining our promise of excellence to our client. His words struck a chord, and I realized that I had let my ego take the reins, risking the success of the entire project.

Humbled, I sat down and began to look at the situation from all sides. I reached out to the president of the software company for a one-on-one meeting, setting aside the tension we had built. We talked openly and collaboratively, and together we found a middle ground. We agreed to make some modifications to their software design, while I made adjustments to my vision of the product. We jointly reached out to the client as a team and obtained buy-in from the client for minor adjustments in the product design. This approach preserved the integrity of the project and kept us within our constraints, while still delivering a quality product to the client. In the end, our project received recognition from the US federal government for excellence.

That experience was a turning point for me. I realized how close I had come to self-sabotage by letting my ego, fixed mindset, distrust, and power blindness take control. It taught me that true leadership isn't about rigidly sticking to an ideal; it's about being adaptable, listening, and finding collaborative paths forward, enriched by mutual trust. Since then, I have made it a habit to work with subconsultants as partners, respecting their expertise and seeking solutions that push the boundaries of possibility without breaking them. I learned that while striving for excellence is vital, humility and collaboration are the true foundations for avoiding self-sabotage and achieving sustainable success.

10.11 Don't Let Personality Labels Sabotage Your Leadership

It's hard to let go of the comfort that comes from thinking you've figured someone out.

—Peter Bregman,
chief executive officer, Bregman Partners

One of the most subtle forms of leadership self-sabotage is believing that personality defines potential. In many leadership coaching programs and training workshops, the first exercise often involves a personality assessment. Whether it's the Big Five, Myers-Briggs Type Indicator (MBTI), or the Enneagram, these tools provide valuable insights into who we are and how we lead. Each model approaches personality from a different angle. The Big Five describes personality as a set of five continuous traits—openness, conscientiousness, extraversion, agreeableness, and neuroticism—and is widely regarded as the most scientifically validated framework. The MBTI categorizes people into one of 16 personality types based on cognitive preferences, such as introversion versus extraversion, sensing versus intuition, thinking versus feeling, and judging versus perceiving. It aims to highlight how individuals perceive the world and make decisions. The Enneagram, by contrast, focuses on core motivations, emotional patterns, and under-lying fears, offering nine distinct personality "types" that emphasize inner drivers and patterns of behavior.

Other widely used tools include the DiSC Personality Profile, which assesses behavioral tendencies across four styles—dominance, influence, steadiness, and conscientiousness—to improve communication and teamwork; the Hogan Personality Inventory (HPI), which evaluates normal personality characteristics, potential career derailers, and core values to help organizations assess leadership potential, performance risks, and cultural fit; the Herrmann Brain Dominance Instrument (HBDI), which measures thinking preferences across analytical, practical, relational, and experimental styles to enhance collaboration and innovation; and CliftonStrengths (formerly StrengthsFinder), which helps individuals identify and leverage their top natural talents to drive engagement and performance.

All of these tests are based on self-assessments, which, by their nature, tend to reinforce an individual's existing self-perceptions. You report how you see yourself, and the results echo that view back to you—creating the illusion of accuracy. In reality, these assessments are simply reflecting the information you provided. Rather than revealing hidden traits, they often reinforce blind spots by confirming what you already believe about yourself. Yet these personality assessments can provide valuable insights for enhancing self-awareness, team building, and understanding how we interact with others.

However, without thoughtful use, they can easily reinforce limiting beliefs—especially the pervasive myth that personality is fixed and defines the limits of who someone can become as a leader. What many forget is that personality assessment results are based on how you have shown up in the past—not on your future aspirations or potential. Anchoring your leadership identity to results based on past behavioral patterns can unconsciously limit your vision for who you are capable of becoming.

While personality traits show relative stability over time, modern psychology, neuroscience, and leadership research clearly demonstrate that personality is malleable and adaptive. As Dr. Benjamin Hardy argues in *Personality Isn't Permanent*, traits shift in response to new environments, life experiences, intentional learning, and future self-vision. Hardy points out that our personality at any moment is shaped by our current role, relationships, and goals—not by an inherent, unchangeable type. He gives the example of entrepreneurs who started out shy and risk-averse but, through intentional learning and identity work, became confident, visionary leaders. Neuroplasticity—the brain's capacity to rewire itself—means that core behaviors, attitudes, and even aspects of temperament can evolve with purposeful effort. Leadership is a dynamic journey of becoming—not a static expression of a past-based personality type.

In an article titled "Employees Can't Be Summed Up by a Personality Test" in the *Harvard Business Review*, Peter Bregman, CEO of Bregman Partners, an executive coaching firm, makes a compelling case that personality tests can dangerously oversimplify people. Bregman argues that these assessments provide the illusion of understanding, reinforcing self-image and blind spots, while discouraging curiosity and deeper connection. Once we label someone, he writes, we stop seeing how they are growing and changing. True leadership requires seeing people as evolving, not as static types, and staying open to the surprise of who they are becoming.

The myth of fixed personality becomes especially dangerous in leadership because it encourages a fixed mindset. Leaders may begin to excuse limitations with phrases like, "I'm just not a visionary," or "I'm not good with people," simply because a test once suggested it. But such beliefs are self-sabotaging. Traits such as resilience, adaptability, courage, empathy, and strategic thinking are not hardwired—they are developed through deliberate practice and conscious identity shifts. Hardy emphasizes that one of the greatest predictors of future personality change is the clarity of one's future self vision: when leaders actively define who they want to become, their behaviors, habits, and even personality traits begin to shift toward that desired identity. In fact, many great leaders describe themselves as having evolved dramatically in how they show up—often in ways that contradict their early personality assessments. When Satya Nadella began his career at Microsoft, he was a highly technical, task-focused engineer—not known for emotional intelligence or people leadership. Over time, through deliberate self-work and leadership coaching, he transformed into a highly empathetic leader, championing growth mindset and cultural transformation at Microsoft.

Personality tests can become socially acceptable, demographically neutral ways of labeling people—offering convenient explanations for conflict or performance issues without addressing their root causes. For example, rather than confronting difficult dynamics—such as trust breakdowns or destructive competition for limited resources—teams may fall back on personality labels as justification: "She's just introverted," or "He's too extroverted." These explanations may feel tidy, but they are often misleading. When you view others through the static lens of personality labels, you risk misjudging your team members, underestimating their potential, or even passing them over for growth opportunities and promotion.

As you pursue whole-person leadership, beware of the subtle ways personality myths can sabotage not only your own leadership evolution but also the growth and potential of those you lead. To use personality tools effectively, treat them as starting points for meaningful dialogue and self-awareness—not as final verdicts. Don't let the results of your personality test limit how you see yourself. Encourage your team to explore who they want to become, not just who they've been. Use these tools to spark curiosity, deepen empathy, and support growth—not to explain away challenges or avoid real conversations.

Remember: personality is not a cage; it is a canvas.

10.12 Disconnect to Connect: Stop Sabotaging Your Presence

Presence is one of the most powerful yet underappreciated qualities of effective leadership—an essential force that builds trust, fosters deep connections, and drives meaningful impact. Yet in today's hypercon-nected world, leaders unknowingly sabotage their own presence every day, allowing digital distractions to fracture their attention—tethering them to devices and pulling them away from the very people and moments that matter most.

Presence is more than just physical availability—it is the ability to be fully engaged, mentally attuned, and emotionally connected in every interaction. Harvard Business School professor Amy Cuddy, author of *Presence*, defines *presence* as "the state of being attuned to and able to comfortably express our true thoughts, feelings, values, and potential." Similarly, another Harvard professor, Bill George, author of *True North*, describes presence as "offering oneself and one's spirit"—a quality that fosters trust, deepens relationships, and strengthens influence.

The paradox of technology is that while it was designed to connect us, it often keeps us from being truly present. When leaders allow digital distractions to dominate their time, they risk losing credibility, empathy, and the deeper understanding necessary to lead effectively. To counteract this, leaders must create intentional blocks of time to unplug. Disconnecting is not a luxury—it is a leadership necessity. Amy Blankson writes in *The Future of Happiness* that we need to find "a balanced calculus that works in the modern world for deciding how to integrate the steady stream of technology into our lives in a way that fuels our success and happiness, instead of serving as a stumbling block." By setting intentional, device-free moments to fully engage with employees, teams, and loved ones, leaders not only reclaim their own mental clarity but also cultivate an environment where deep connection, trust, and meaningful collaboration can thrive.

By embracing intentional disconnection, embodied in the phrase "Disconnect to Connect," leaders send a powerful message: that true connection is not built through notifications or emails but through genuine presence and mindful engagement. Small but deliberate actions—such as tech-free mornings, deep-work sessions, or simply putting devices away during conversations—serve as powerful reminders that true leadership is about being fully present in the moments that matter most. In a world where constant connectivity is the norm, the ability to step away and be fully present is not just a skill—it is a leadership superpower.

10.13 Self-Sabotage in Disguise: Say No to Distractions

Clarity about what matters provides clarity about what does not.
                                    —Cal Newport, author of *Deep Work*

In an age dominated by constant notifications, multitasking demands, and digital noise, distractions have become the silent saboteurs of leadership success. The 2024 research report *Lost Focus: The Cost of Distractions on Productivity in the Modern Workplace*, published by Insightful in collaboration with Pollfish, reveals the growing impact of workplace distractions on employee productivity. The study surveyed 1,200 participants across the United States, equally divided between 600 employees and 600 company leaders, providing a balanced perspective on the issue. An overwhelming 92% of employers expressed concern about focus loss among employees, with many estimating significant weekly productivity losses. Specifically, 36% of leaders reported that employees lose one to five hours per week due to distractions, while 34% cited losses of six to 10 hours per employee. Alarmingly, 15% of leaders estimated losses of 11 to 15 hours, and 9% reported 16 to 20 hours lost weekly, meaning that nearly a quarter of leaders believe that distractions consistently consume more than 25% of the workweek.

Leaders are often pulled in multiple directions, and without deliberate focus, they risk losing clarity of purpose. As the Roman philosopher

Seneca wisely wrote in *Letters from a Stoic*, "To be everywhere is to be nowhere." This ancient wisdom still resonates: When leaders scatter their attention across too many fronts, they dilute their effectiveness and vision. The creeping nature of distractions—often disguised as opportunities, urgent tasks, or harmless browsing—can slowly erode strategic thinking and decision-making capabilities.

Modern research supports this assertion. A study from the University of California, Irvine found that it takes an average of 23 minutes and 15 seconds to fully regain focus after an interruption. For leaders, this means a single distraction can derail not just a moment but an entire strategy session or decision-making process. Daniel Goleman, in his book *Focus: The Hidden Driver of Excellence*, emphasizes that attention is the foundation of empathy, clarity, and leadership itself. Without mastering our attention, we lose the very tools that make us effective leaders. Distractions, while often small and seemingly benign, compound over time and can quietly sabotage long-term leadership success.

To overcome the stealthy pull of distractions, leaders must take deliberate action to reclaim their focus. This begins with practicing time blocking—setting aside dedicated, interruption-free windows for deep, strategic work. Equally important is maintaining a "not-to-do list" that reminds leaders what to avoid, whether it's reactive email checking or unplanned meetings. Grouping shallow tasks like emails and admin work into focused batches helps preserve mental energy for what truly matters. By delegating small decisions and eliminating unnecessary meetings, leaders free themselves from low-value noise. Regularly reviewing one's week for distraction patterns and practicing mindfulness, even for just a few minutes a day, sharpens attention over time. Leaders who say no to distractions are not just protecting their calendars—they are preserving their clarity, integrity, and ability to lead others with purpose. In the end, saying no to distractions is saying yes to leadership that matters.

10.14 Prioritize Sleep: Don't Sabotage Your Health

Sleep-deprived employees cost US businesses an estimated $411 billion annually due to lost productivity and increased absenteeism.
                                        —RAND Corporation study

In the relentless pursuit of success, many leaders unknowingly sabotage their potential by neglecting one of the most critical pillars of well-being: sleep. Arianna Huffington, in her book *The Sleep Revolution*, argues that sleep deprivation has become a global epidemic, fueled by a culture that glorifies overwork and minimizes rest. This mindset, she asserts, undermines both our health and our capacity for effective decision-making. *National Geographic*'s August 2018 cover story, "The Science of Sleep," delves into the critical role sleep plays in human health and performance. The article examines how chronic sleep deprivation disrupts cognitive function, creativity, and emotional regulation—all essential traits for successful leadership. Studies show that individuals who sleep fewer than six hours per night are significantly more likely to experience impaired judgment, reduced empathy, and an inability to manage stress effectively, which can lead to poor leadership outcomes.

The science is clear: Sleep is foundational to peak performance. The National Sleep Foundation and the American Academy of Sleep Medicine both recommend that, for optimal health and functioning, adults ages 18 to 64 should get seven to nine hours of sleep per night. Sleep is not merely a passive state but an active process during which the brain consolidates memories, organizes information, and resets for the challenges ahead. Leaders who prioritize sleep are better equipped to make strategic decisions, foster collaboration, and inspire their teams. Conversely, sleep deprivation can lead to burnout, decreased productivity, and even long-term health issues such as cardiovascular disease and depression. A study published in *Nature* found that even one night of sleep deprivation can reduce brain efficiency by as much as 30%, underscoring its immediate and tangible impact on cognitive function. Leaders who undervalue sleep may find themselves in a cycle of diminishing returns, where working longer hours actually undermines their ability to perform a task well and to completion.

To lead with purpose and resilience, sleep must be reframed as a strategic advantage rather than a luxury. Whole-person leadership, as emphasized in DEEP PACT, recognizes that personal well-being, including adequate sleep, is inseparable from professional success. By creating routines that prioritize rest—such as setting boundaries on work hours, embracing mindfulness practices, and fostering a culture of well-being within organizations—leaders can model a sustainable path to success and happiness. As Arianna Huffington aptly states, "Sleep is a performance-enhancing tool." When leaders treat sleep as an essential investment in their potential, they cultivate their own success and also the well-being and productivity of those they lead.

10.15 Move, Don't Die

Exercise is the single best thing you can do for your brain in terms of mood, memory, and learning.

—John J. Ratey, M.D.,
Harvard Medical School

In leadership, self-neglect often masquerades as dedication. We work harder, push further, and sacrifice more—all in the name of service, excellence, and results. But beneath this noble pursuit lurks a dangerous delusion: that we are invincible. That our health can wait. That movement is optional. The truth? Movement is not optional. It's the bare minimum. Without it, leaders don't just burn out—they break down.

Many entrepreneurs wear overwork like a badge of honor. They pull eighty-hour weeks, convinced they are building a legacy. Meals are skipped, sleep is sacrificed, and the body's quiet warnings are ignored—until one day the warning is no longer quiet. What seems like ordinary fatigue escalates into a medical emergency. In hindsight, the signs are often obvious, yet the drive to push the business forward blinds leaders to the toll on their health. Beneath it lies a common belief: that self-care is indulgence and that slowing down means falling behind. It is a costly mistake—and they are not alone in making it.

In the high-stakes world of leadership, movement is often the first sacrifice and the last priority. The lack of regular physical activity becomes a hidden form of self-sabotage—an invisible drain on personal well-being, energy, and resilience. We spend hours in meetings, glued to screens, and chasing deadlines—unaware that neglecting our bodies undermines our ability to lead effectively. Research is unequivocal: regular physical activity is one of the most powerful, accessible, and underutilized tools for boosting both individual well-being and professional performance. Whole-person leadership is not just about driving business outcomes—it's about taking care of yourself and your employees, so that everyone can thrive.

The World Health Organization (WHO) affirms that exercise reduces depression risk and improves cognitive function, energy, and emotional regulation—traits essential for effective leadership. A 2018 study in *The Lancet Psychiatry* found that individuals engaging in moderate aerobic activity (30–45 minutes, three to five times per week) had 43 percent fewer days of poor mental health per month compared to those who didn't. Consistency is key.

Harvard Business Review (HBR) confirms this leadership–exercise connection in an article titled "To Improve Work Performance, Get Some Exercise." The researchers found that daily physical activity leads to measurable improvements in next-day task performance, creativity, and health by enhancing sleep quality, physical vigor, and cognitive focus.

Exercise doesn't just elevate mood—it sharpens the mind. A *Psychological Bulletin* meta-analysis reported that aerobic activity consistently improves executive function—decision-making, attention, and problem-solving—the very functions leaders rely on in moments of crisis. Moreover, exercise regulates stress: it lowers cortisol while boosting endorphins and brain-derived neurotrophic factor (BDNF), vital for learning and memory. *Harvard Health* notes that exercise acts like a "natural antidepressant," enhancing neuroplasticity and buffering against chronic stress. Yet despite these proven benefits, many workplaces continue to undervalue physical activity, overlooking its role in boosting concentration, decision-making, and emotional resilience.

MIT Sloan Management Review reinforces how well-designed work—including breaks and autonomy that often include movement—bolsters cognitive skill and ongoing learning. And it doesn't stop with individual benefit. An HBR-featured study on corporate wellness reveals that when leaders model healthy behaviors—like regular exercise—employees are significantly more likely to adopt them, resulting in higher morale, lower absenteeism, and increased productivity.

So why don't we move? In theory, the benefits are indisputable. Yet in practice, movement falls to the bottom of the list. Psychological barriers—time scarcity, guilt, and habit inertia—keep us sedentary. We cling to packed schedules and the illusion that one more meeting is more productive than a short walk. HBR highlights how leaders often override self-care in favor of immediate work demands—believing there's "no time" for exercise, even though just 15 to 30 minutes of activity can dramatically improve energy and focus.

To break this cycle, we must address both mindset and structure, as shown below:

⟡ **First**, reframe exercise as productivity time, not downtime. *MIT Sloan* research shows that deliberate breaks and movement enhance creativity and problem-solving.

⟡ **Next**, implement specific strategies from behavior-change research: use "if-then" plans (e.g., "If it's 3 p.m., then I'll walk for 15 minutes") as shown by psychologists Oettingen and Gollwitzer to dramatically increase follow-through.

⟡ **Incorporate** "Booster Breaks"—short, intentional pauses that reduce fatigue and elevate mood, as confirmed by workplace studies.

⟡ **And most critically**, model the behavior publicly: an HBR case study shows that leaders who visibly prioritize wellness see up to 60 percent higher employee engagement in health initiatives.

We move because it sustains us. We lead better because we move. We are not invincible—and that's the point. To protect the lives we lead and the people who count on us, we must protect the bodies that carry us.

So move—before your body forces you to stop.

Move, don't die.

10.16 Ten Actionable Steps for Applying Principle 4

Believe you can and you're halfway there.

—Theodore Roosevelt

In the preceding pages, we have examined the many forces that undermine our leadership from within—from the ancient notion of akrasia to the subtle traps of ego, fixed mindset, distrust, and power blindness. We have explored how obsession with profit and loss can distort decisions, how personality labels and constant distractions sabotage presence, and how even neglecting sleep can erode our effectiveness. These insights have illuminated the hidden enemy within us all.

But understanding alone is not enough. It is through deliberate practice and conscious effort that we break free from self-sabotage and cultivate the emotional intelligence needed to lead with integrity, resilience, and clarity. The following steps provide practical guidance to help you protect yourself from these pitfalls and build the foundation for truly effective leadership. You do not need to tackle every area at once—choose what resonates most and begin there. Each decision you make to improve brings you closer to becoming the leader your team, your organization, and the world need.

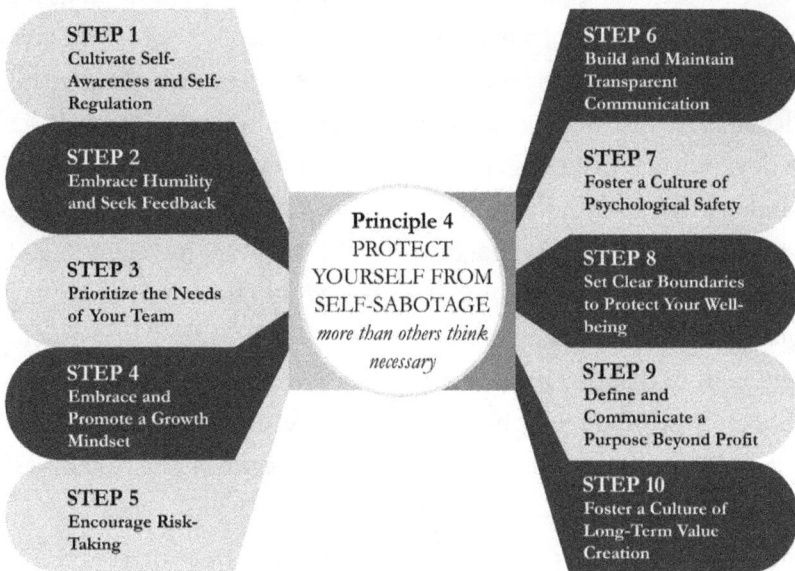

STEP 1
Cultivate Self-Awareness and Self-Regulation

STEP 2
Embrace Humility and Seek Feedback

STEP 3
Prioritize the Needs of Your Team

STEP 4
Embrace and Promote a Growth Mindset

STEP 5
Encourage Risk-Taking

Principle 4
PROTECT YOURSELF FROM SELF-SABOTAGE
more than others think necessary

STEP 6
Build and Maintain Transparent Communication

STEP 7
Foster a Culture of Psychological Safety

STEP 8
Set Clear Boundaries to Protect Your Well-being

STEP 9
Define and Communicate a Purpose Beyond Profit

STEP 10
Foster a Culture of Long-Term Value Creation

Safeguard your potential from silent saboteurs: ten actionable steps for applying Principle 4.

💡 *Principle 4, Step 1: Cultivate Self-Awareness and Self-Regulation*

Action: Regularly reflect on your thoughts, emotions, and behaviors to identify patterns of self-sabotage. Think before you act. Self-regulate yourself and set realistic goals.

Example: Benjamin Franklin's practice of daily reflection helped him identify and correct his own flaws. Ray Dalio, founder of Bridgewater Associates and author of *Principles*, uses a set of clearly defined principles—centered on radical transparency, open-mindedness, and thoughtful decision-making— along with personal reflections to maintain self-awareness and avoid self-sabotage. According to him, principles are fundamental truths that serve as the foundations for behavior that gets you what you want out of life. At Microsoft, Satya Nadella encourages leaders to engage in self-reflection to understand their impact on the organization and avoid detrimental behaviors. Indra Nooyi, former CEO of PepsiCo, practiced self-regulation by maintaining a rigorous routine and focusing on physical fitness and mental well-being. She regularly sought feedback from peers and mentors and encouraged transparent communication within her team. By staying grounded and prioritizing work-life balance, Nooyi avoided the burnout and poor decision-making that can result from overwork and stress. Google's use of OKRs (objectives and key results) helps set realistic, achievable goals that drive progress without overwhelming employees.

💡 *Principle 4, Step 2: Embrace Humility and Seek Feedback*

Action: Foster a mindset of humility and actively seek feedback from peers, subordinates, and mentors to keep your ego in check.

Example: Abraham Lincoln, known for his humble leadership, regularly sought advice and feedback from his cabinet members, even those who were his political rivals. This openness to feedback helped him navigate the complexities of leadership during the Civil War. At General Electric, former CEO Jack Welch implemented a culture of candid feedback and "boundaryless behavior," encouraging employees at all levels to share their ideas and feedback. This approach helped break down hierarchical barriers and fostered a culture of continuous improvement.

💡 *Principle 4, Step 3: Prioritize the Needs of Your Team*

Action: Adopt a servant leadership approach, focusing on the growth and well-being of your team members to protect yourself from acting on the basis of self-interest.

Example: In the movie *Remember the Titans,* Coach Herman Boone demonstrates servant leadership by putting the needs of his team above his own, fostering unity and resilience among the players. Howard Schultz, the former CEO of Starbucks, emphasized servant leadership by focusing on the needs of his employees, providing them with comprehensive health benefits and stock options. This approach helped create a loyal and motivated workforce, driving the company's success.

💡 *Principle 4, Step 4: Embrace and Promote a Growth Mindset*

Action: Cultivate a growth mindset by encouraging continuous learning, resilience, and the belief that abilities and intelligence can be developed through dedication and hard work.

Example: Thomas Edison's approach to invention exemplified a growth mindset. Despite numerous failures while inventing the lightbulb,

Edison famously said, "I have not failed. I've just found 10,000 ways that won't work." His persistence and willingness to learn from each attempt led to groundbreaking success. Satya Nadella's leadership at Microsoft is a contemporary example. Upon becoming CEO, Nadella shifted the company culture from a fixed mindset to a growth mindset by emphasizing learning and collaboration. He encouraged employees to adopt a learn-it-all rather than a know-it-all attitude, which revitalized Microsoft's innovation and market position.

💡 Principle 4, Step 5: Encourage Risk-Taking

Action: Foster an environment where taking calculated risks is encouraged, and failures are viewed as valuable learning opportunities rather than setbacks.

Example: In the movie *The Pursuit of Happyness*, Chris Gardner takes significant risks in his career despite numerous failures and rejections. His resilience and ability to learn from each setback ultimately lead to his success as a stockbroker. Google's Project Aristotle emphasizes the importance of psychological safety, where team members feel safe to take risks and make mistakes without fear of retribution. This approach has been fundamental in fostering innovation and high performance within teams at Google. Pixar Animation Studios, under the leadership of Ed Catmull, has consistently encouraged a culture of creative risk-taking. Catmull implemented the concept of "fail early, fail fast, fail cheap," allowing employees to experiment and learn quickly from their mistakes. This philosophy has contributed to Pixar's long string of successful and innovative films, as described by Catmull in his book *Creativity, Inc.: Overcoming the Unseen Forces That Stand in the Way of True Inspiration*.

💡 *Principle 4, Step 6: Build and Maintain Transparent Communication*

Action: Establish open and honest communication channels within the organization to build trust and reduce suspicion.

Example: During World War II, Winston Churchill's transparent and direct communication with the British public, including his "We Shall Fight on the Beaches" speech, fostered trust and resilience among the populace. At Radisson Hotels, former CEO Kurt Ritter implemented a culture of transparency and open communication. By regularly sharing both successes and challenges with employees, Ritter built a high level of trust within the organization, which was crucial for its turnaround and success.

💡 *Principle 4, Step 7: Foster a Culture of Psychological Safety*

Action: Create an environment where employees feel safe to express their ideas and concerns without fear of retribution.

Example: In the movie *Remember the Titans*, Coach Herman Boone builds a culture of trust by ensuring that all team members feel valued and heard, leading to a unified and successful team. Google's Project Aristotle found that psychological safety, where team members feel safe to take risks and be vulnerable in front of each other, was the most important factor in creating effective teams. This practice led to higher performance and innovation within the company. At Pixar, Ed Catmull emphasized the importance of creating a safe environment for creativity. By encouraging employees to take risks and openly share ideas without fear of criticism, Pixar fostered an innovative culture that produced numerous successful films.

💡 *Principle 4, Step 8: Set Clear Boundaries to Protect Your Well-Being*

Action: Establish and maintain boundaries to prevent burnout and protect your mental and physical health, ensuring long-term productivity and well-being. Sleep at least seven hours every night.

Example: Arianna Huffington, founder of the *Huffington Post*, emphasizes the importance of setting boundaries to avoid burnout. She recounts a pivotal moment in 2007 when she collapsed at her desk due to extreme exhaustion and woke up in a pool of blood with a broken cheekbone, an incident that served as a wake-up call. This experience ultimately inspired her to launch Thrive Global, a company dedicated to well-being, stress management, and workplace wellness. Similarly, at Basecamp, CEO Jason Fried advocates for a work environment that emphasizes work-life integration, ensuring that professional responsibilities align harmoniously with personal well-being. Basecamp maintains a strict 40-hour workweek, reduced to 32 hours during summer months. This approach encourages employees to prioritize essential tasks, fostering efficiency and focus during designated work periods. By limiting work hours, Basecamp promotes a culture where work responsibilities are balanced with personal life, reducing the risk of burnout.

💡 *Principle 4, Step 9: Define and Communicate a Purpose beyond Profit*

Action: Articulate a compelling vision that prioritizes purpose and values over mere financial metrics and communicates this clearly across the organization.

Example: Patagonia's founder, Yvon Chouinard, envisioned a company dedicated to environmental sustainability and ethical business practices. This commitment has driven Patagonia's business strategy, attracting customers and employees who share these values. Unilever, under the leadership of former CEO Paul Polman, redefined its mission to focus on sustainable living and long-term value creation. Polman's vision emphasized social and environmental impact alongside financial performance, leading to increased trust and loyalty from consumers and stakeholders.

💡 Principle 4, Step 10: Foster a Culture of Long-Term Value Creation

Action: Develop and promote strategies that emphasize long-term value creation over short-term financial gains, ensuring that all stakeholders—including employees, customers, and the community—benefit.

Example: In the movie *It's a Wonderful Life,* George Bailey focuses on the long-term well-being of his community through his family-run building and loan, rather than maximizing short-term profits, which ultimately strengthens the community and his business. Costco, under cofounder Jim Sinegal, is known for its commitment to employee well-being, offering higher wages and benefits compared to industry standards. This long-term investment in employees has led to high productivity, low turnover, and strong financial performance over time. The Toyota Production System, with its focus on continuous improvement and respect for people, emphasizes long-term efficiency and quality over short-term financial metrics. This approach, as documented by Jeffrey Liker in his book *The Toyota Way,* has helped Toyota maintain its position as a leader in the automotive industry while fostering innovation and employee engagement.

10.17 Ten Barriers to Applying Principle 4

*Your net worth to the world is usually determined by what remains
after your bad habits are subtracted from your good ones.*
                                        —Benjamin Franklin

Self-sabotage is a common but often overlooked issue that can impede
personal and professional growth. Protecting oneself from self-sabotage
requires heightened self-awareness and proactive strategies. However,
several barriers can make this challenging. Here are some of the main
obstacles and ways to address them.

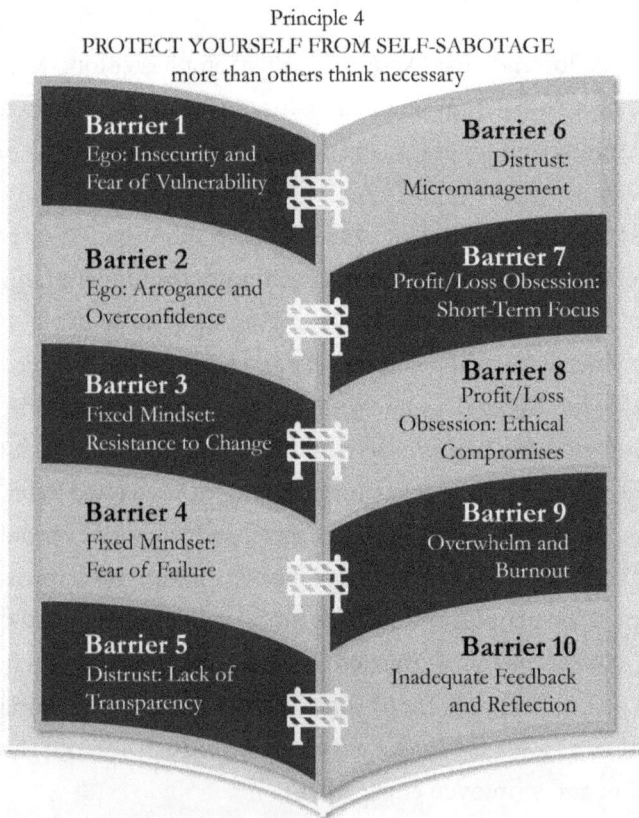

Principle 4
PROTECT YOURSELF FROM SELF-SABOTAGE
more than others think necessary

Barrier 1
Ego: Insecurity and
Fear of Vulnerability

Barrier 2
Ego: Arrogance and
Overconfidence

Barrier 3
Fixed Mindset:
Resistance to Change

Barrier 4
Fixed Mindset:
Fear of Failure

Barrier 5
Distrust: Lack of
Transparency

Barrier 6
Distrust:
Micromanagement

Barrier 7
Profit/Loss Obsession:
Short-Term Focus

Barrier 8
Profit/Loss
Obsession: Ethical
Compromises

Barrier 9
Overwhelm and
Burnout

Barrier 10
Inadequate Feedback
and Reflection

The inner blockage: ten insidious barriers to applying Principle 4

⚠ *Principle 4, Barrier 1: Ego—Insecurity and Fear of Vulnerability*

Barrier: Many individuals are not fully aware of their egotistic behaviors. These behaviors can be subtle and ingrained, making them difficult to recognize. Leaders with inflated egos may struggle to acknowledge their mistakes, refuse to listen to others, act defensively, and prioritize their own interests over the team's needs.

Solution: Cultivate humility and foster a growth mindset. Encourage self-awareness and emotional intelligence through regular self-reflection and feedback from peers and mentors. Implement practices that promote vulnerability and transparency, such as admitting mistakes and openly discussing challenges. Create an organizational culture that values collaboration, continuous learning, and the collective success of the team over individual accolades.

⚠ *Principle 4, Barrier 2: Ego—Arrogance and Overconfidence*

Barrier: Arrogance and overconfidence can lead to a disregard for others' opinions and a belief that one is always right.

Solution: Encourage humility by seeking diverse perspectives and valuing others' contributions. Implement regular feedback mechanisms and peer reviews to ensure that all voices are heard and respected.

⚠ *Principle 4, Barrier 3: Fixed Mindset—Resistance to Change*

Barrier: A fixed mindset leads to resistance to change and an inability to adapt to new circumstances or feedback.

Solution: Promote a growth mindset by emphasizing learning and development. Provide training and resources that encourage continuous improvement and adaptability. Celebrate failures as learning opportunities rather than setbacks.

⚠ *Principle 4, Barrier 4: Fixed Mindset—Fear of Failure*

Barrier: Fear of failure can prevent leaders from taking risks and exploring new opportunities.

Solution: Create a safe environment where risks are encouraged, and failures are viewed as valuable learning experiences. Highlight stories of innovation and success that came from taking calculated risks.

⚠ *Principle 4, Barrier 5: Distrust— Lack of Transparency*

Barrier: A lack of transparency can foster suspicion and distrust among team members.

Solution: Implement open communication channels and regularly share information with the team. Encourage leaders to be honest about challenges and decisions to build trust and credibility.

⚠ *Principle 4, Barrier 6: Distrust— Micromanagement*

Barrier: Micromanagement can signal a lack of trust in employees' abilities and judgment.

Solution: Delegate responsibilities and empower team members to take ownership of their work. Provide support and resources but avoid unnecessary oversight. Trust your team to deliver results.

⚠ *Principle 4, Barrier 7: Profit/Loss Obsession—Short-Term Focus*

Barrier: An obsession with short-term profits can lead to decisions that undermine long-term sustainability and success.

Solution: Develop and communicate a long-term vision that prioritizes sustainable growth and ethical practices. Align performance metrics and rewards with long-term goals rather than short-term financial gains.

⚠ *Principle 4, Barrier 8: Profit/Loss Obsession—Ethical Compromises*

Barrier: Prioritizing profit over ethics can damage a company's reputation and stakeholder trust.

Solution: Establish and enforce a strong code of ethics. Ensure that all business practices align with ethical standards and that leaders model ethical behavior.

⚠ *Principle 4, Barrier 9: Overwhelm and Burnout*

Barrier: Taking on too much at once can lead to overwhelm and burnout, which in turn can trigger self-sabotaging behaviors as a way to cope with stress.

Solution: Prioritize tasks and break them down into manageable steps. Learn to say no and delegate responsibilities when necessary. Make time for rest and relaxation to prevent burnout and maintain balance.

⚠ Principle 4, Barrier 10: Inadequate Feedback and Reflection

Barrier: Without regular feedback and reflection, leaders may continue self-sabotaging behaviors without realizing it.

Solution: Implement regular feedback loops and encourage reflective practices. Use tools such as 360-degree feedback, mentorship programs, and self-assessment exercises to continually improve self-awareness and leadership effectiveness.

Addressing these barriers involves fostering a culture of transparency, humility, continuous learning, ethical integrity, and long-term thinking. By systematically tackling these issues, leaders can mitigate self-sabotage and unlock their full potential for themselves and their organizations.

10.18 Ten Examples of Applying Principle 4

1. A manager steps back and lets competent senior developers take the lead on projects, fostering collaboration and trust.
2. A CEO encourages the team to see a recent product launch failure as a learning experience and explore innovative improvements for the next iteration.
3. A department head starts an open-door policy, inviting team members to share their concerns and ideas freely, knowing they won't be judged.

4. A director decides to invest in better working conditions and professional development programs, even if it means short-term financial sacrifices.
5. Olivia acknowledges her tendency to micromanage and actively works on delegating more tasks to her team.
6. Ethan takes a break from a high-stress project to focus on his mental health, despite fears of being perceived as weak.
7. Ben steps back from a project to reassess his strategy after a series of setbacks, seeking external advice.
8. A volunteer sets realistic goals to ensure they can consistently contribute without overwhelming themselves.
9. An individual sets clear boundaries to avoid overcommitting and maintains a healthy work-life integration.
10. A manager delegates tasks effectively to prevent burnout and ensure balanced workload distribution.

10.19 Closing Reflections

The greatest enemy will hide in the last place you would ever look.
—Julius Caesar

The journey of leadership is fraught with internal obstacles, often more challenging than any external barrier. Among these, ego stands out as a significant threat. It whispers deceitful affirmations that cloud judgment and foster arrogance. To protect oneself from this form of self-sabotage, leaders must practice humility and self-awareness. By continually reflecting on their actions and seeking honest feedback, leaders can keep their ego in check, ensuring it does not overshadow their mission. This humility not only builds stronger relationships but also cultivates a culture of trust and respect within the organization.

A fixed mindset can be equally destructive, stifling innovation and growth. Leaders must embrace a growth mindset, which sees challenges as opportunities and failures as learning experiences. By fostering an environment that encourages experimentation and values continuous improvement, leaders can break free from the constraints of a fixed mindset. This approach not only enhances personal development but also drives organizational success, as it empowers teams to innovate and adapt in an ever-changing landscape. Companies like Microsoft, under Satya Nadella's leadership, have demonstrated how shifting to a growth mindset can transform an organization and unlock its full potential.

Distrust and an excessive focus on profit and loss are other common pitfalls that can derail even the most capable leaders. Building trust requires transparency, integrity, and consistent actions that align with one's words. When leaders prioritize trust, they create a foundation for collaboration and loyalty, both of which are essential for long-term success. Additionally, while financial performance is crucial, an obsessive focus on profit and loss at the expense of values can lead to ethical compromises and short-term thinking. Leaders must balance financial goals with a commitment to their core values and broader mission, ensuring that their decisions promote sustainable growth and positive impact. By protecting themselves from these self-sabotaging factors, leaders can navigate their path with clarity and integrity, fostering a legacy of excellence and enduring success.

10.20 Daily Practice

1. **Check your ego:** Avoid doing things for personal gain or to seek praise, approval, or validation. Replace the word "I" in your emails; use "we" instead.

2. **Nurture a growth mindset:** Stay positive and consider failures as learning opportunities.

3. **Value people over money:** Do not sacrifice people, purpose, or quality for profit.

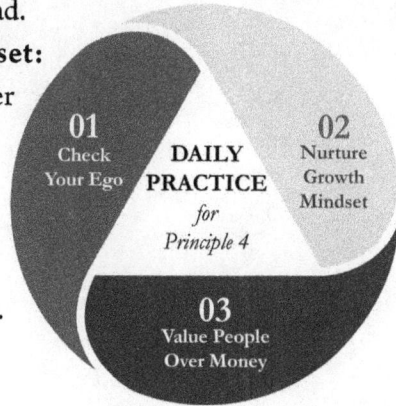

01 Check Your Ego

DAILY PRACTICE *for Principle 4*

02 Nurture Growth Mindset

03 Value People Over Money

Part Three

Interpersonal Mastery

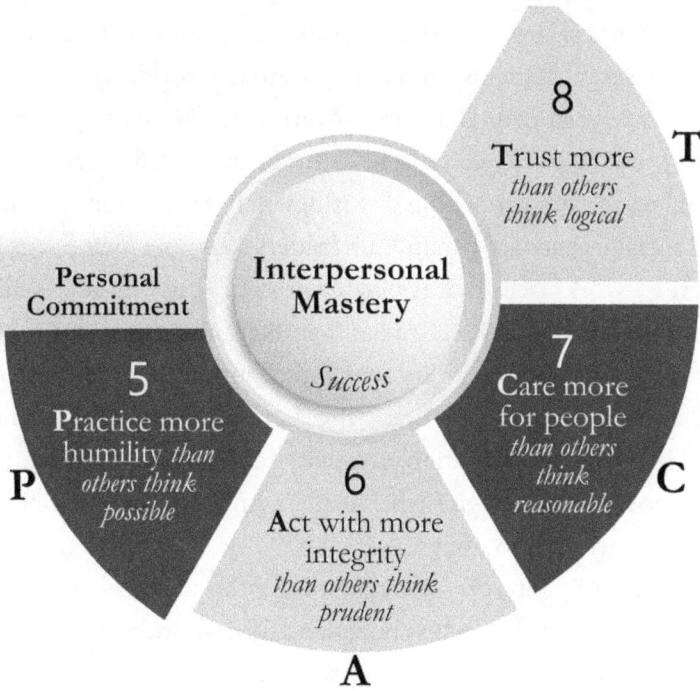

If you treat an individual as he is, he will remain how he is. But if you treat him as if he were what he ought to be and could be, he will become what he ought to be and could be.

—Goethe

n Part Three, we examine why **interpersonal mastery** is essential for successfully navigating today's leadership challenges, exploring how it can be achieved through intentional practices that prepare leaders to create workplaces rooted in purpose, care, trust, and integrity, and drive meaningful and lasting social impact.

Interpersonal mastery is the essential skill leaders need to truly inspire others, especially in a workplace where employees now seek more than a salary, they desire meaning, genuine care, and ethical guidance. As Confucius wrote, "To govern the world, first govern your state; to govern your state, first govern your family; to govern your family, first cultivate yourself; to cultivate yourself, first set your heart right." In today's professional world, where transparency, empathy, and social impact are paramount, leaders must "*set their hearts right*" to create workplaces that resonate with purpose. A leader skilled in interpersonal mastery recognizes that their influence is not rooted in authority but in their ability to connect authentically, listen deeply, and act with integrity. As Brené Brown reminds us, "Vulnerability is the birthplace of innovation, creativity, and change," a reminder that genuine leadership begins when leaders embrace openness and build trust through shared values.

In mastering interpersonal relationships, leaders become not only mentors but also allies who understand the importance of a collective vision. With societal expectations shifting, today's leaders must foster spaces where employees feel genuinely valued and are empowered to contribute to a larger purpose. This level of mastery allows leaders to act not as distant figures but as accessible guides, offering respect, recognition, and collaboration. "People will forget what you said, people will forget what you did, but people will never forget how you made them feel," said Maya Angelou, a truth that underscores the power of human connection.

11 Principle 5: Practice More Humility Than Others Think Possible

A great man is always willing to be little.

—Ralph Waldo Emerson

11.1 Close to the Ground

The word "humility" finds its origins in the Latin word *humilitas*, which derives from *humus*, meaning ground or earth. This etymology reflects the concept of being grounded or lowly, emphasizing a sense of modesty and a lack of arrogance. The notion of humility as being "close to the ground" is a powerful metaphor for understanding one's place in the larger scheme of things, recognizing one's limitations, and valuing the contributions of others.

One of the earliest and most profound stories illustrating humility comes from the Bible, specifically the Old Testament. Moses, who led the Israelites out of Egypt and received the 10 Commandments from God, is often cited as a paragon of humility. Despite his critical role, Moses is described in Numbers 12:3 as "very humble, more than all men who were on the face of the earth." Moses's humility is demonstrated through his reluctance to lead, his constant dialogue with God seeking guidance, and his willingness to put the needs of his people above his own desires. His humility allowed him to lead effectively, with empathy and patience, even through great adversity.

In Greek mythology, Prometheus is a figure who embodies humility in his actions and intentions. Although a Titan, Prometheus chose to side with humanity, bestowing upon people the gift of fire and knowledge of the arts. His actions were not motivated by a desire for power or recognition, but by a genuine concern for humanity's welfare. Prometheus's humility is further highlighted when he accepts his punishment from Zeus without regret, demonstrating his willingness to endure suffering for the benefit of others. This story underscores the idea that true humility involves self-sacrifice and a commitment to the greater good.

Nelson Mandela's life story is a testament to the power of humility. Imprisoned for 27 years for his fight against apartheid in South Africa, Mandela emerged without bitterness, ready to lead his country toward reconciliation and unity. Despite his immense influence and the adulation he received globally, Mandela remained grounded, often deflecting praise, and emphasizing the collective effort of his fellow activists and citizens. His ability to listen, forgive, and lead with humility was instrumental in South Africa's peaceful transition to democracy.

These stories, spanning various cultures and historical periods, illustrate the enduring value of humility. Whether through religion, myth, or history, the concept of humility as being close to the ground remains a powerful and timeless lesson in leadership and human behavior.

11.2 Why Humility?

A leader is best when people barely know he exists, when his work is done, his aim fulfilled, they will say: we did it ourselves.

—Lao Tzu

Humility is a profound virtue characterized by a modest view of one's own importance, an openness to learning, and a genuine appreciation for the contributions of others. It involves recognizing one's limitations and imperfections, which fosters an environment of continuous personal growth and mutual respect.

Humility is often misunderstood as self-deprecation or an underestimation of one's abilities and achievements. However, true humility is not about diminishing oneself but rather about having an accurate and balanced view of one's strengths and limitations. It involves recognizing and appreciating the value and contributions of others while maintaining confidence in one's abilities. As Rick Warren, author of *The Purpose Driven Life*, wrote, "Humility is not thinking less of yourself; it is thinking of yourself less." This means that humility allows individuals to focus outwardly on others, fostering collaboration and mutual respect, rather than inwardly on their own ego.

Humility is a crucial attribute in leadership because it promotes a culture of learning and growth. Leaders who exhibit humility are open to feedback and willing to admit their mistakes, which creates an environment where continuous improvement is possible.

Moreover, humility fosters authentic relationships and trust, essential components of any successful team or organization. When leaders and team members approach each other with humility, they create a space where everyone feels valued and heard. This leads to higher levels of engagement and productivity. In the business world, Satya Nadella, CEO of Microsoft, exemplifies this principle. Nadella's humble leadership style, which emphasizes empathy and inclusivity, has transformed Microsoft's corporate culture and driven its resurgence. His approach demonstrates that humility is not about downplaying one's role but about empowering others to reach their full potential. Humility, therefore, is a powerful and dynamic force that enhances both personal and organizational success.

11.3 Lessons in Humility: A Personal Story

Do you wish to rise? Begin by descending. You plan a tower that will pierce the clouds? Lay first the foundation of humility.
　　　　　　　　　　　　　　　　　　　　—St. Augustine

Organizing community events has always been one of my passions. Early on, I found myself drawn to the leadership role, confident in my ability to guide the planning and execution. I thought my past experience and knowledge would naturally position me as the best person to direct these events. However, over time, I realized that my approach, while well-intentioned, lacked an essential element: humility.

At one point, I was helping plan a large event for our community that would involve various activities and performers. As the CEO of the community nonprofit organization, my initial instinct was to take charge of the entire process, ensuring that everything met my vision. I had a lot of ideas about how to structure the event, from the themes to the scheduling of performers and activities. I believed I knew what would work best and felt compelled to guide every decision. However, as I began sharing my vision in planning meetings, I noticed that some members of the committee were quieter than usual, and others would nod without much enthusiasm. I realized that in my eagerness, I was unintentionally dominating the conversation and leaving little space for others to contribute.

One day, a colleague gently suggested that we open the floor to hear more from others. I felt a pang of defensiveness at first—after all, I thought my ideas were well-grounded. But I took a breath and decided to do something different. At the next meeting, instead of presenting my vision as a starting point, I invited others to share their ideas first. I practiced the art of listening, really listening, without formulating a response or critique in my head. To my surprise, people brought forward ideas that I hadn't considered. Some of these ideas were outside of my comfort zone, and at first I thought they might dilute the quality of the event. But then I reminded myself that practicing humility meant being open and recognizing that my idea didn't have to be the best one for the event to be successful; another idea could still work, and I needed to give everyone's suggestion a chance. The discussion format turned out to be more engaging than I expected, encouraging more participation and dialogue among attendees.

During the event, I consciously stepped back from the spotlight. Instead of speaking or moderating, I encouraged others to take the lead. I introduced speakers, facilitated transitions, and let others shine. There was a moment when someone publicly acknowledged the efforts of the organizing committee. I felt the urge to step forward and share a few words, but I resisted. I watched from the side as another committee member spoke on behalf of all of us. The pride on their face and the appreciation from the audience was worth more than any acknowledgment I could have given myself.

That experience taught me that true leadership isn't about being in the spotlight or ensuring that your ideas are always at the forefront. It's about creating a space where everyone feels valued, listened to, and empowered. By practicing humility—more than I ever thought possible—I discovered the power of collective ownership and collaboration. Not being the center of attention didn't diminish my role; it amplified my impact by fostering a community where everyone felt they belonged and could contribute. The lesson reshaped how I approach leadership, teaching me that stepping back often allows the most meaningful progress to move forward.

11.4 Humility Begins Where Judgmentalism Ends

It is the mark of an educated mind to be able to entertain a thought without accepting it.

—Aristotle

Leadership falters when we reach for labels before we reach for understanding. It's important to distinguish between being judgmental—rushing to conclusions, categorizing people, and reacting from ego—and exercising good judgment, which is a critical leadership skill rooted in discernment, reflection, and wisdom. While good judgment enables leaders to assess people and situations with clarity and wisdom, judgmentalism tends to shortcut that process through assumption and bias. It reacts rather than reflects. It labels rather than understands. True leadership begins when judgmentalism ends—and humility takes root.

In positions of power, it's all too easy to fall into the trap of sizing people up quickly, reducing them to personality types, assigning labels to behaviors, and deciding who fits or fails. But when we judge or categorize others based on surface behaviors or limited information, we risk closing the door on empathy, curiosity, and the very growth we are meant to inspire. As Ron Carucci writes in the *Harvard Business Review*, when a team labels someone as "difficult," it rarely considers that person's backstory, pressures, or unrealized potential. We begin to see people not as evolving humans but as problems to manage. The result? We stop listening, we stop learning—and we stop leading with heart.

This is especially critical because, as Carucci's case study shows, the anger and stress we carry often say more about our own unexamined expectations than the other person's behavior. Nonjudgmental leadership enhances psychological safety and collaborative trust. It cultivates space for risk-taking, vulnerability, and growth. When we approach people with humility and curiosity, we give them permission to show up more fully.

Judgmentalism not only hardens our hearts; it hinders learning and suppresses innovation. Judgmental leadership diminishes psychological safety—making employees less likely to speak up, share ideas, or admit mistakes. In contrast, nonjudgmental leaders foster a culture where people feel seen, heard, and valued. Nonjudgment doesn't mean accepting mediocrity—it means choosing discernment over assumption, and growth over ego. It is entirely possible to uphold accountability and standards while also leading with humility and understanding.

In her *Harvard Business Review* article "Don't Let Anchoring Bias Weigh Down Your Judgment," Helen Lee Bouygues offers an important caution: even seasoned leaders can be misled when they anchor their evaluations to biased or incomplete reference points. Anchoring bias leads us to fixate on early impressions, which can distort how we assess others. Humility, she argues, is essential to counteracting this bias. It invites leaders to pause, reflect, and ask better questions. There is a profound difference between being discerning and being judgmental. The former is thoughtful; the latter, reactive. Good leaders evaluate with wisdom, not ego. They uplift rather than diminish. They lead not with superiority but with deep respect for the complexity of human beings.

Ben Heady echoes this in his LinkedIn Pulse article, "Judgment Is the Enemy of Empathy." He explains that judgment activates defensive behaviors and blocks the neural pathways of empathy, whereas humility builds stronger, more productive teams. When leaders suspend judgment and practice empathy, they create space for connection and accountability to thrive side by side.

Ultimately, humility expands our capacity to lead. It softens our gaze so that we can see more clearly. It strengthens our teams by making them feel safe. And it transforms our leadership from being about control and correctness to being about connection and growth. Because, in the end, the most humane and powerful leaders are not the ones who judge most quickly—but the ones who understand most deeply.

11.5 Active Listening: The Heart of Humility

Most people do not listen with the intent to understand; they listen with the intent to reply.

—Stephen Covey

In the world of leadership, one of the most underrated yet powerful skills is active listening. Effective leaders know that true listening goes beyond hearing words; it involves understanding, empathy, and a sincere commitment to engaging with others. Active listening is the heart of humility—it's a conscious choice to set aside one's ego and focus on the speaker, showing that their thoughts and experiences are valued. Understanding others creates a foundation of trust and respect, which is essential for any leader looking to inspire and guide effectively.

However, barriers to active listening are pervasive in today's fast-paced environment. Leaders often fall into the trap of being preoccupied with formulating responses, multitasking, or making assumptions, which undermines their ability to listen fully. Recent research has highlighted that active listening is not just about nodding or maintaining eye contact; it involves expressing genuine interest by asking probing questions that deepen the conversation. These questions signal that the listener is truly engaged and seeking to understand the speaker's perspective. Leaders who practice active listening, including asking thoughtful questions, are more likely to inspire trust and build strong team rapport.

Amy Gallo, in her 2024 *Harvard Business Review* article "What Is Active Listening?" expands on this by emphasizing that active listening involves three main components: comprehension, retention, and response. Comprehension requires fully focusing on the speaker and absorbing what they say, while retention is about processing and remembering the information shared. The response phase involves demonstrating understanding, not just through body language, but also by summarizing what was heard and asking relevant, probing questions.

Gallo asserts that active listening requires effort, feedback, and interaction to show that the listener values and understands the speaker's message. Amy Gallo provides an excellent example of how asking questions that explore what might not have been said can help the other person feel truly heard and lead to valuable insights for both parties. The scenario she provided goes like this:

> An employee expresses, "I'm anxious about my presentation to senior management tomorrow."
> With the good intention of reassuring the employee, you might respond by saying, "You'll do just fine. No worries. Honestly, it took me years to present confidently without feeling nervous."

While this may be an attempt to relate and offer comfort, it inadvertently shifts the focus away from them and onto you, failing to acknowledge or explore their deeper concern. A more effective approach would be to respond with, "I remember feeling that way when I first started presenting. What specifically is making you feel uneasy?" Notice the difference? This response shows empathy, invites them to share more, and demonstrates that you are truly invested in their experience.

Traditional books on listening may suggest asking clarifying questions, which can be helpful at times. However, when overused or applied without sensitivity, they can have the opposite effect—creating frustration rather than fostering connection.

Consider this scenario: An employee shares, "I'm feeling uncertain about the direction of this project." A leader, aiming to show they are listening, responds with, "Did I hear you correctly? You're saying you're uncertain about the project?" or, "I understand you to mean that you're feeling unsure—is that right?"

While these responses might seem like active listening in action, excessive repetition of such phrases can come across as robotic, overly cautious, or even condescending and offensive. Instead of reinforcing trust, they may signal skepticism or a lack of attentiveness—as though the listener is more focused on getting the phrasing right than on truly engaging with the speaker's concerns.

A more natural and effective approach would be to acknowledge and expand on what was shared: "That makes sense. What specifically is causing you uncertainty?" or, "Tell me more about what's making you feel that way." These responses invite deeper discussion without making the speaker feel like their words are being scrutinized. Active listening should feel like a conversation, not an interrogation. Leaders who balance clarification with genuine curiosity and warmth create an environment where employees feel heard, valued, and safe to express their thoughts openly.

To develop active listening skills, leaders should focus on a few key strategies. Maintaining eye contact, using nonverbal cues like nodding, and paraphrasing what the speaker says are important, but engaging through questions elevates listening to the next level. Leaders should practice asking open-ended and clarifying questions, such as, "Can you tell me more about that?" or, "What do you think led to this situation?" This demonstrates genuine curiosity and helps build deeper under-standing. Practicing patience, eliminating distractions, and responding thoughtfully can further enhance this skill. By committing to these habits, leaders can transform their ability to connect, motivate, and lead with humility and impact, fostering a culture of trust and collaboration.

11.6 The Synergy of Leadership, Connection, and Humility

And we are all connected to each other
In a circle, in a hoop that never ends

. . .

For whether we are white or copper-skinned
We need to sing with all the voices of the mountain
We need to paint with all the colors of the wind.

Stephen Schwartz,
Pocahontas (Disney film)

In Disney's *Pocahontas*, the song "Colors of the Wind" beautifully encapsulates the profound message that "we are all connected to each other," which serves as a reminder of the interconnectedness of humanity and nature, transcending cultural and racial boundaries—"whether we are white or copper-skinned." The necessity of connecting to each other is highlighted by the idea that we all share the same fundamental human experiences, emotions, and aspirations. Connection lies at the heart of effective leadership, and humility is the key to unlocking it.

As a foundational trait, humility allows us to acknowledge that we are not the center of the universe but part of a larger, interconnected web of life. Humility involves recognizing the worth and contributions of others, regardless of their background or status. This perspective fosters empathy and openness, essential components of emotional intelligence. Just as Pocahontas sings about understanding the world through different perspectives and seeing the connections between all living things, humility enables leaders to appreciate diverse viewpoints and cultivate inclusive environments. According to Jim Collins in *Good to Great*, the most successful leaders exhibit a paradoxical blend of personal humility and professional will. They do not seek to dominate but to empower their teams, fostering a collaborative environment where everyone's voice is heard.

Connecting with others through humility is not just a moral imperative; it is a practical necessity for effective leadership. Leaders who approach their roles with humility are more likely to build trust and loyalty within their teams. They are seen as approachable and relatable, which encourages open communication and honest feedback. This has been exemplified by leaders such as Nelson Mandela, whose humility and empathy allowed him to bridge deeply entrenched divides and foster a sense of unity and purpose among South Africans.

The necessity of connecting to each other is highlighted by the idea that we all share the same fundamental human experiences, emotions, and aspirations. This connection is vital for building strong, resilient communities and organizations. When leaders understand and embrace the interconnectedness of their team members, they can foster a sense of belonging and purpose. This connection enhances engagement, motivation, and overall well-being by integrating emotional intelligence into leadership, when leaders learn, as stated in the *Pocahontas* song, to "sing with all the voices of the mountain" and "paint with all the colors of the wind."

Connection goes beyond simple communication, a concept that John Maxwell eloquently explores in his book *Everyone Communicates, Few Connect*. Maxwell argues that despite their ability to communicate effectively, many leaders struggle to connect because they focus more on delivering their message rather than understanding and relating to their audience. Maxwell's central theory posits that leaders often fall into the trap of talking to people instead of engaging with them, which can create a barrier to genuine connection. To bridge this gap, leaders must develop emotional intelligence and be willing to show vulnerability. By doing so, they create an atmosphere of trust and respect, making their communication efforts more impactful and meaningful.

As Patrick Lencioni points out in *The Five Dysfunctions of a Team*, a lack of trust stemming from an absence of vulnerability can lead to dysfunctional team dynamics. Brené Brown, the author of *Daring Greatly*, states, "Vulnerability is not winning or losing; it's having the courage to show up and be seen when we have no control over the outcome." This act of being open about one's imperfections and challenges requires a profound sense of humility, which, in this context, means recognizing that one does not have all the answers and being open to learning and growth.

Research from Oxford's Saïd Business School after the pandemic indicates that leaders who openly express self-doubt and vulnerability in a measured way foster greater trust among their teams. This approach contrasts with traditional command-and-control authoritative leadership styles, suggesting that acknowledging uncertainty can enhance decision-making and leader credibility. However, self-doubt must be balanced; excessive uncertainty can undermine confidence in leadership and destabilize an organization. Leaders who strategically embrace doubt while maintaining clarity and direction can create a culture of trust and adaptability without compromising organizational stability.

The interplay between leadership, connection, and humility creates a powerful synergy that enhances a leader's influence and effectiveness. Leaders who combine these qualities can navigate complex challenges with grace and resilience. For example, the leadership style of Jacinda Ardern, the prime minister of New Zealand, exemplifies the power of connection. Her empathetic and inclusive approach has not only garnered her widespread respect but has also united her country during times of crisis. Ardern's ability to connect with people on a human level, understanding their fears and hopes, has been pivotal in her leadership success.

11.7 Interplay between Competence and Humility

Raise your words, not voice. It is rain that grows flowers, not thunder.
—Rumi

Competence and humility are both indispensable qualities for effective leadership, each enhancing the other in significant ways. Competence ensures that a leader has the necessary skills, knowledge, and ability to guide their team toward achieving goals. It builds trust and confidence among team members, who rely on their leader's expertise to navigate challenges and seize opportunities.

However, competence without humility can indeed be perceived as arrogance. This perception arises when a leader's display of skills and knowledge is not tempered with an understanding and acknowledgment of their limitations or the contributions of others. As former General Electric CEO Jack Welch famously said, "Before you are a leader, success is all about growing yourself. When you become a leader, success is all about growing others." Arrogant leaders often struggle with receiving constructive feedback, which is essential for personal and organizational growth. Their unwillingness to admit mistakes or learn from others can stifle development and create a culture of fear and disengagement.

On the other hand, when humility stands alone without the reinforcement of competence, it can be misconstrued as a weakness. A leader who exhibits humility without demonstrating their skills and knowledge might be perceived as lacking authority or capability. This perception can undermine their credibility and effectiveness, leading to a lack of confidence from their team. Therefore, competence is crucial in making humility not just an admirable trait but a powerful and respected component of leadership.

Competence provides the foundation upon which humility stands strong and visible. Competence is what validates humility. When leaders are competent, their humility is seen as a sign of maturity and emotional intelligence, rather than a lack of confidence. When leaders showcase their skills and expertise, they establish themselves as capable and knowledgeable. This competence garners respect and trust from their team, creating a stable platform from which their humility can shine. For instance, Satya Nadella, CEO of Microsoft, exemplifies this balance. His technical expertise and innovative vision have driven Microsoft's resurgence, while his humble leadership style has fostered a collaborative and inclusive corporate culture. Nadella's humility is respected because it is backed by his clear competence and achievements. The combination of humility and competence creates a powerful synergy that enhances a leader's influence.

The interplay between competence and humility is what distinguishes truly great leaders from merely good ones. Competence ensures that a leader can effectively guide their team and make informed decisions, while humility ensures that they remain approachable, open to feedback, and empathetic. This blend makes leaders more relatable and trustworthy. For instance, Indra Nooyi, former CEO of PepsiCo, exemplified this balance by consistently demonstrating her strategic vision and business acumen while remaining approachable and empathetic. Her leadership style not only drove the company's success but also created a supportive and inclusive corporate culture. In essence, the fusion of competence and humility creates a leadership style that is both effective and deeply resonant, leading to sustained success and a positive organizational climate.

11.8 Warmth: The Conduit of Influence

Warmth is the conduit of influence: It facilitates trust and the communication and absorption of ideas.
                    —A. Cuddy, M. Kohut, and J. Neffinger

Warmth, born from humility, is a key element in building strong, positive relationships within a team. It is the embodiment of empathy, kindness, and genuine care for others. It is the ability to connect with team members on a personal level, making them feel valued and understood. Leaders who demonstrate warmth create an environment of trust and psychological safety, where individuals feel comfortable sharing their ideas and concerns without fear of judgment. Research from Harvard Business School highlights that leaders who project warmth are more effective at gaining trust and fostering cooperation than those who rely solely on demonstrating competence. This warmth is not a superficial trait but a genuine reflection of the leader's humility and commitment to their team.

Warmth is not merely a soft skill; it is a powerful driver of engagement and performance, enabling leaders to inspire and uplift their teams and influence them. John C. Maxwell, one of the foremost voices in leadership development, famously declared, "The true measure of leadership is influence—nothing more, nothing less." Yet it is warmth—expressed through empathy, authenticity, and connection—that often becomes the conduit through which that influence flows.

Warm leaders are approachable and relatable, which encourages open communication and authentic relationships. This connection enhances the leader's ability to guide and support their team, driving collective success. As Amy Cuddy of Harvard highlights, "People judge you really quickly, at first just on your facial features. They're first judging you on warmth." This initial perception sets the tone for all subsequent interactions, emphasizing that warmth is foundational to impactful leadership. This initial judgment determines whether others perceive us as trustworthy and approachable. For example, Howard Schultz, former CEO of Starbucks, emphasized creating a company culture grounded in warmth and care for employees. This approach not only fostered loyalty and dedication but also drove the company's success by ensuring that employees felt valued and engaged.

11.9 Interplay between Competence and Warmth

When we judge others—especially our leaders—we look first at two characteristics: how lovable they are (their warmth, communion, or trustworthiness) and how fearsome they are (their strength, agency, or competence).

—A. Cuddy, M. Kohut, and J. Neffinger

Many leaders and individuals often complain about not being respected, without realizing the critical shortfall in their display of warmth and competence. Before lamenting the lack of respect, one should introspectively evaluate their abilities in these areas. Are you approachable and empathetic? Do you consistently demonstrate expertise and reliability? By honestly assessing and addressing these aspects, you can identify what needs improvement to earn genuine admiration from others.

Amy Cuddy, along with Matthew Kohut and John Neffinger, explores the interplay between competence and warmth in their article "Connect, Then Lead" published in the *Harvard Business Review* in 2013. They presented a matrix that categorizes leaders based on high and low levels of competence and warmth. This matrix helps explain why people admire or resent certain leaders and how these traits influence leadership effectiveness.

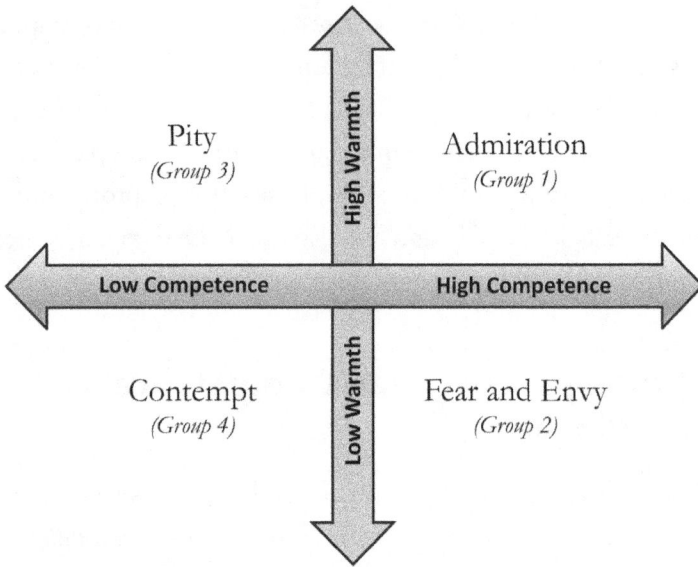

The lens of perception: how warmth and competence shape our judgments.

Group 1. High Competence, High Warmth

Characteristics: Leaders who exhibit both high competence and high warmth are often admired and trusted. They are perceived as capable and approachable, balancing their skills with genuine care for others. They receive admiration from those who they lead.

Example: Nelson Mandela epitomizes this quadrant. His profound competence in navigating the political landscape of apartheid South Africa, combined with his deep empathy and humility, made him a beloved leader. Mandela's ability to connect with people on a human level, while demonstrating exceptional leadership skills, earned him respect and admiration globally.

Group 2. High Competence, Low Warmth

Characteristics: Leaders with high competence but low warmth are often respected for their skills and abilities but can be resented or feared due to their perceived lack of empathy and approachability. This kind of leader garners fear and envy, not admiration.

Example: Steve Jobs is a notable example. While widely recognized for his visionary competence and innovation at Apple, Jobs was often seen as intimidating and demanding, which created a fear-based work environment. His high competence was undeniable, but his lower warmth sometimes led to strained relationships with colleagues and employees.

Group 3. Low Competence, High Warmth

Characteristics: Leaders who are warm but not particularly competent may be liked on a personal level but often struggle to gain respect and authority. People may enjoy their company but doubt their ability to lead effectively. This type of leader receives neither admiration nor envy, but pity.

Example: Michael Scott, the fictional boss from the TV show *The Office*, falls into this category. He is known for his personable and caring nature toward his employees, but his lack of competence often leads to ineffective management and poor decision-making. His warmth makes him likable, but his lack of competence diminishes his effectiveness as a leader.

Group 4. Low Competence, Low Warmth

Characteristics: Leaders who lack both competence and warmth are generally neither liked nor respected. They are seen as ineffective and unapproachable, often leading to low morale and disengagement among their team members. This type of leader receives contempt from their peers and subordinates.

Example: A less prominent example from history could be certain ineffective political figures who failed to connect with their constituents or demonstrate the necessary skills to govern effectively. These leaders often face widespread disapproval and lack the support needed to lead successfully.

QUICK TIP

Action: Integrate AI to facilitate transparent decision-making processes and acknowledge the contributions of all team members. Use AI to analyze performance data objectively, removing personal biases.

Example: Using AI-driven dashboards to share team performance metrics and credit contributions transparently.

Caveat: Be cautious of AI biases and ensure that diverse datasets are used to train AI systems to promote fairness and inclusivity.

11.10 Humility and Confidence Are Not Opposites

Believe in yourself! Have faith in your abilities! Without a humble but reasonable confidence in your own powers you cannot be successful or happy.

—Norman Vincent Peale

A persistent misconception holds that humility and confidence are mutually exclusive. In truth, humility is not about shrinking or playing small. It is not about avoiding attention or minimizing one's strengths. Rather, humility is about having a grounded sense of self—being aware of your value without arrogance, and being open to others' contributions without insecurity. Presenting ourselves with confidence does not betray humility; instead, it empowers us to engage with authenticity, courage, and connection.

In her now-iconic TED Talk, watched by more than 26 million people worldwide, Harvard professor Amy Cuddy shared a deceptively simple yet transformative insight: "Your body language may shape who you are." Drawing on years of research in social psychology, Cuddy demonstrated that how we hold our bodies influences not only how others perceive us but also how we perceive ourselves. Through powerful experiments, she showed that even just two minutes of expansive, open posture—what she calls "power posing"—can lower cortisol (the stress hormone), increase testosterone (the dominance hormone), and lead to greater feelings of confidence and presence in high-stakes situations such as interviews, negotiations, or public speaking.

Consider the "Wonder Woman" pose: standing tall with feet wide, hands on hips, chest lifted. Or imagine sitting with a relaxed posture, arms open, fingers lightly steepled—both of which convey self-assurance without aggression. In contrast, shrinking into ourselves—crossed arms, hunched shoulders, downcast eyes—signals powerlessness, not just to others, but to our own brain. Cuddy found that candidates who power-posed before a job interview were consistently rated more competent and confident—even though their qualifications were no different. It was their presence—not their résumé—that made the difference.

The impact of power posing has real-world application across a range of leadership contexts. A manager heading into a difficult performance review might take two minutes beforehand to stand tall in a private space, reset their nervous system, and center themselves. A young professional preparing to pitch an idea in a high-stakes meeting can use a subtle seated power pose—upright posture, relaxed arms, steady gaze—to project clarity and conviction. These micro-adjustments not only influence perception—they shape real outcomes. Entering a boardroom, addressing a team, or facing a difficult conversation, the question is not whether to be humble or confident—it's how to embody both. For leaders, this balance is essential.

These insights underscore a powerful truth: that humility and confidence are not in conflict—they are complementary forces—and that warmth and competence, two foundational qualities of trusted leadership, are communicated first not through words but through posture, gestures, and expression. When leaders align their physical presence with their inner purpose—when they stand tall not to dominate, but to connect—they inspire trust, clarity, and courage. True humility is grounded, not diminished.

11.11 Ten Actionable Steps for Applying Principle 5

There is nothing noble in being superior to your fellow man; true nobility is being superior to your former self.

—Ernest Hemingway

In the preceding pages of this chapter, we have explored humility from many angles—from letting go of judgmentalism to practicing active listening, from balancing competence with warmth to understanding how humility and confidence strengthen rather than oppose one another. We have seen how humility fosters connection, trust, and genuine influence, and how it transforms not just leadership but the culture of entire organizations.

Yet humility is not simply a perspective to be admired—it must be lived. It is a daily discipline, an attitude reflected in the smallest moments of listening, acknowledging others, and remaining open to learning and growth. The following section offers practical steps with examples to help you put humility into action. You need not adopt every idea at once; begin with those that resonate most, and build from there. Each choice to lead with humility deepens your impact and helps create environments of respect, collaboration, and trust, ultimately fostering both organizational success and personal fulfillment.

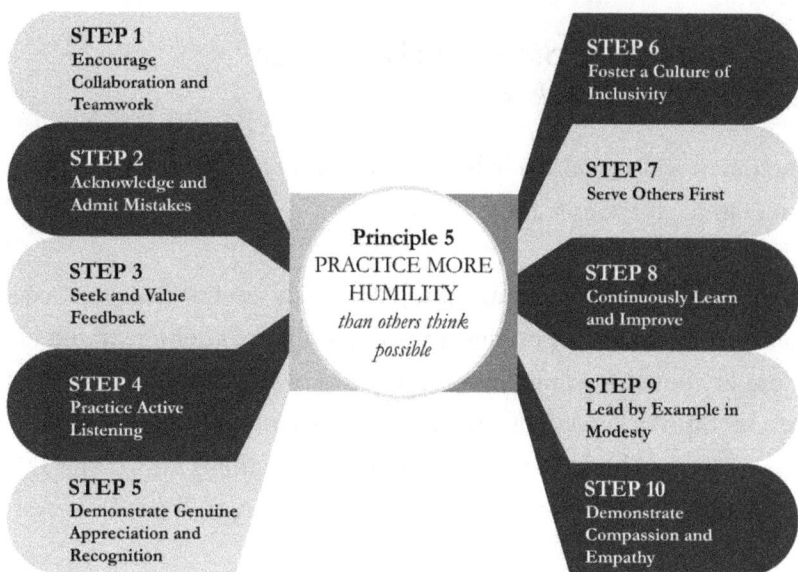

STEP 1
Encourage Collaboration and Teamwork

STEP 2
Acknowledge and Admit Mistakes

STEP 3
Seek and Value Feedback

STEP 4
Practice Active Listening

STEP 5
Demonstrate Genuine Appreciation and Recognition

Principle 5
PRACTICE MORE HUMILITY
than others think possible

STEP 6
Foster a Culture of Inclusivity

STEP 7
Serve Others First

STEP 8
Continuously Learn and Improve

STEP 9
Lead by Example in Modesty

STEP 10
Demonstrate Compassion and Empathy

The quiet strength of leadership: ten bold steps for applying Principle 5.

💡 *Principle 5, Step 1: Encourage Collaboration and Teamwork*

Action: Foster a collaborative environment where teamwork is prioritized over individual achievement. Remove the word "I" from your emails and speech; use "we" instead. At the end of each day, reflect on all the people who were part of making you successful that day. Regularly express gratitude to your team for their hard work and dedication.

Example: At NASA, the successful Apollo 11 mission was a result of extraordinary teamwork and collaboration among engineers, scientists, and astronauts. The mission's success demonstrated how diverse expertise, shared goals, and mutual support can lead to groundbreaking achievements. At IDEO, a global design company, teamwork and collaboration are central to the company's success, demonstrating the humility to recognize that great ideas often come from collective effort.

💡 *Principle 5, Step 2: Acknowledge and Admit Mistakes*

Action: Regularly acknowledge and admit your mistakes openly, setting an example for your team.

Example: When President John F. Kennedy admitted his mistakes publicly after the Bay of Pigs invasion, it not only demonstrated his humility but also gained him respect and restored confidence in his leadership. At Toyota, the principle of kaizen (continuous improvement) involves leaders admitting mistakes and learning from them. This culture of humility and transparency has been key to Toyota's success.

💡 *Principle 5, Step 3: Seek and Value Feedback*

Action: Actively seek feedback from all levels of your organization and act on it.

Example: Satya Nadella at Microsoft encourages a growth mindset by asking for feedback from his employees and making changes based on their input. The development of the IBM Watson AI involved constant feedback from employees at all levels, demonstrating a commitment to humility and collaborative improvement.

💡 *Principle 5, Step 4: Practice Active Listening*

Action: Make a conscious effort to actively listen and listen more than you speak in meetings and discussions.

Example: Abraham Lincoln was known for his "listening tours" where he would visit soldiers and civilians to hear their concerns, which informed his decisions during the Civil War. At Pixar, Ed Catmull's leadership style emphasizes listening to the creative ideas of his team members, fostering an environment where innovation thrives.

💡 *Principle 5, Step 5: Demonstrate Genuine Appreciation and Recognition*

Action: Regularly acknowledge and celebrate the contributions and achievements of your team members to foster a positive and supportive environment.

Example: Nelson Mandela's leadership was marked by his ability to recognize and uplift the efforts of those around him, creating a sense of unity and shared purpose during South Africa's transition from apart-heid. Doug Conant, former CEO of Campbell Soup Company, wrote over 30,000 handwritten notes to employees, recognizing their efforts and achievements. This personal touch significantly boosted employee morale and engagement. Tony Hsieh, the late CEO of Zappos, was known for his practice of writing thank-you notes to employees, which helped build a positive and humble company culture. Former PepsiCo CEO Indra Nooyi would write personal letters to the parents of her senior executives, acknowledging their contributions and expressing gratitude, which fostered loyalty and respect. Pixar Animation Studios has a tradition of celebrating the achievements of its employees. By publicly recognizing individual contributions to successful projects, Pixar fosters a strong sense of community and appreciation within the company.

💡 *Principle 5, Step 6: Foster a Culture of Inclusivity*

Action: Promote an inclusive environment where diverse perspectives are valued and considered.

Example: Jacinda Ardern, as the prime minister of New Zealand, emphasized inclusivity by creating one of the most diverse cabinets in the country's history. She involved representatives from different ethnic backgrounds and ensured that women held leadership positions, fostering a governmental culture where diverse voices shaped national policies. Google's diverse hiring practices and inclusive work culture have made it a leader in innovation, reflecting the humility to recognize and integrate different viewpoints. Under Satya Nadella's leadership, Microsoft has focused on fostering inclusivity through its commit-ment to accessibility. The company's inclusive design efforts, such as developing technology for people with disabilities, reflect a culture of recognizing diverse needs and ensuring that technology benefits everyone, demonstrating humility in leadership to acknowledge all users.

💡 *Principle 5, Step 7: Serve Others First*

Action: Adopt a servant leadership approach by prioritizing the needs of your team and organization over your own.

Example: Mahatma Gandhi's leadership in the Indian independence movement was characterized by his selfless service and putting the needs of the people first. Howard Schultz of Starbucks prioritized employee welfare with benefits and opportunities, ensuring a motivated and loyal workforce.

💡 *Principle 5, Step 8: Continuously Learn and Improve*

Action: Dedicate time to continuous learning and encourage your team to do the same.

Example: Leonardo da Vinci, despite his genius, was always in pursuit of new knowledge, demonstrating humility in his recognition that there was always more to learn. Amazon's Jeff Bezos attributes part of the company's success to its "Day 1" philosophy, which is about continuous learning and staying humble in the face of success. The Day 1 philosophy emphasizes maintaining a startup mindset focused on innovation, customer obsession, and long-term thinking to avoid complacency and ensure continuous growth and agility.

💡 *Principle 5, Step 9: Lead by Example in Modesty*

Action: Lead by example through modest behavior and actions.

Example: Pope Francis was known for his humble lifestyle and actions, such as choosing simpler living quarters and driving a modest car, setting an example for others. Warren Buffett, despite his immense wealth, lives a relatively modest lifestyle and is known for his humble demeanor, which garners respect and trust. Another example is Satya Nadella, CEO of Microsoft, who consistently credits his team for success and demonstrates modesty in his leadership style.

💡 *Principle 5, Step 10: Demonstrate Compassion and Empathy*

Action: Show genuine care and understanding for others' perspectives and feelings.

Example: During his time as CEO of Starbucks, Howard Schultz introduced several policies that demonstrated his commitment to employee well-being. Schultz ensured that all employees, including part-timers, received health benefits, showing empathy for their financial and health concerns. Chade-Meng Tan, a former Google engineer, helped develop the Search Inside Yourself program, which focused on mindfulness, compassion, and emotional intelligence in the workplace. His efforts to cultivate a culture of empathy and emotional well-being within Google helped employees manage stress and fostered a more compassionate work environment.

11.12 Ten Barriers to Applying Principle 5

Practicing humility is powerful and transformative, but it can be challenging, especially when striving to exceed societal expectations. Here are the main barriers to *practicing more humility than others think possible*, along with potential solutions to overcome these challenges.

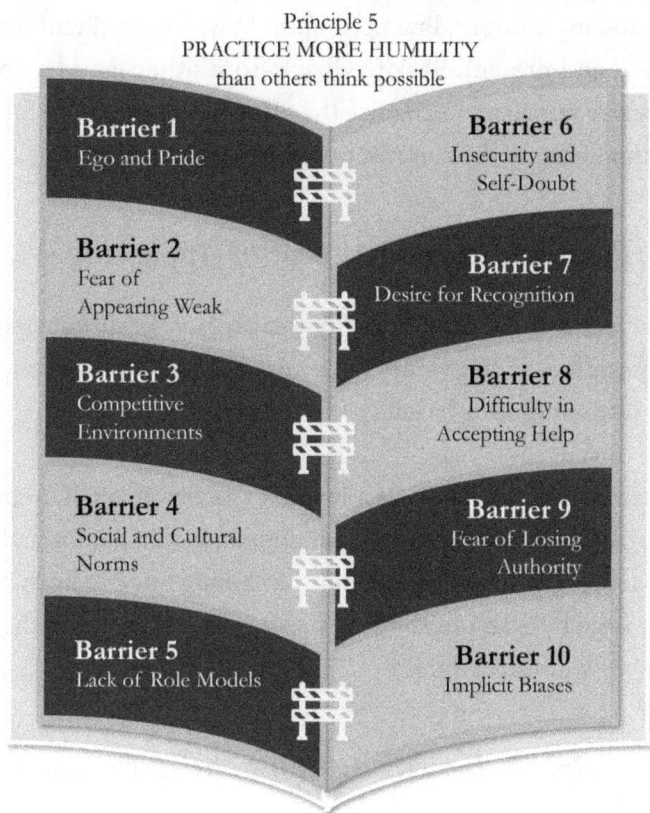

Principle 5
PRACTICE MORE HUMILITY
than others think possible

Barrier 1
Ego and Pride

Barrier 6
Insecurity and
Self-Doubt

Barrier 2
Fear of
Appearing Weak

Barrier 7
Desire for Recognition

Barrier 3
Competitive
Environments

Barrier 8
Difficulty in
Accepting Help

Barrier 4
Social and Cultural
Norms

Barrier 9
Fear of Losing
Authority

Barrier 5
Lack of Role Models

Barrier 10
Implicit Biases

Invisible Armor: Ten Hidden Barriers to Applying Principle 5

⚠️ *Principle 5, Barrier 1: Ego and Pride*

Barrier: Ego and pride can make it difficult to acknowledge mistakes, accept criticism, and appreciate others' contributions. These traits can hinder the practice of genuine humility.

Solution: Cultivate self-awareness by regularly reflecting on your actions and motivations. Practice mindfulness and meditation to stay grounded and present. Seek feedback from others and be open to constructive criticism. Recognize the value in learning from mistakes and acknowledging the contributions of others.

⚠️ *Principle 5, Barrier 2: Fear of Appearing Weak*

Barrier: In many cultures, humility can be mistakenly equated with weakness or lack of confidence. This misconception can prevent individuals from practicing humility.

Solution: Redefine humility as a strength that involves self-awareness, empathy, and respect for others. Demonstrate confident humility by acknowledging your strengths while remaining open to learning and growth. Lead by example, showing that humility enhances rather than diminishes your capabilities.

⚠️ *Principle 5, Barrier 3: Competitive Environments*

Barrier: Highly competitive environments can discourage humility, as individuals may feel pressured to assert their superiority to succeed or gain recognition.

Solution: Focus on collaboration rather than competition. Emphasize teamwork and collective success over individual achievements. Recognize and celebrate the strengths and contributions of your peers. Promote a culture that values mutual respect and support.

⚠ *Principle 5, Barrier 4: Social and Cultural Norms*

Barrier: Societal and cultural norms that prioritize individualism and self-promotion can make it challenging to practice humility. These norms often reward assertiveness and self-praise.

Solution: Challenge societal norms by embodying and advocating for humble behavior. Surround yourself with individuals who value humility and provide mutual support. Highlight the benefits of humility in fostering strong relationships, collaboration, and long-term success.

⚠ *Principle 5, Barrier 5: Lack of Role Models*

Barrier: The absence of humble role models can make it difficult to understand and practice humility in a workplace or community. Seeing others who embody humility can inspire and guide your own behavior.

Solution: Seek out and learn from individuals who exemplify humility, whether through personal relationships, biographies, or public figures. Study their behaviors and adopt practices that align with their approach to humility. Become a role model yourself by consistently demonstrating humility in your actions.

⚠️ *Principle 5, Barrier 6: Insecurity and Self-Doubt*

Barrier: Insecurity and self-doubt can lead individuals to overcompensate by seeking validation and recognition, which can hinder the practice of humility.

Solution: Build self-confidence through self-reflection and acknowledgment of your strengths and achievements. Practice self-compassion and understand that humility does not mean devaluing yourself. Focus on personal growth and self-improvement rather than external validation.

⚠️ *Principle 5, Barrier 7: Desire for Recognition*

Barrier: The desire for recognition and praise can conflict with the practice of humility. Seeking acknowledgment for accomplishments can lead to self-promotion rather than humble behavior.

Solution: Shift your focus from seeking external recognition to finding intrinsic satisfaction in your efforts and contributions. Recognize that true humility often garners genuine respect and admiration from others over time. Celebrate others' successes and contributions as much as your own.

⚠️ *Principle 5, Barrier 8: Difficulty in Accepting Help*

Barrier: Humility involves recognizing the need for and accepting help from others. Pride and a desire for independence can make it difficult to seek or accept assistance.

Solution: Understand that accepting help is a sign of strength and wisdom, not weakness. Practice gratitude for the support you receive and acknowledge the interdependence of human relationships. Offer help to others, fostering a reciprocal culture of humility and support.

⚠ *Principle 5, Barrier 9: Fear of Losing Authority*

Barrier: Leaders and individuals in positions of authority may fear that practicing humility will undermine their authority and respect from others.

Solution: Demonstrate that humility enhances leadership by building trust, respect, and strong relationships. Show that acknowledging your limitations and valuing others' input strengthens your authority rather than diminishing it. Balance humility with confident decision-making and clear communication.

⚠ *Principle 5, Barrier 10: Implicit Biases*

Barrier: Implicit biases and prejudices can affect how we perceive and practice humility, leading to unconscious behaviors that contradict humble intentions.

Solution: Engage in continuous self-examination and education to identify and address implicit biases. Practice empathy and actively listen to others' perspectives. Foster an inclusive environment that respects and values diverse experiences and contributions.

11.13 Ten Examples of Applying Principle 5

1. Victoria openly admits her mistakes during a team meeting and outlines her plan to correct them.
2. Jack publicly credits his team for the company's recent success.

3. Emma defers to a junior colleague's expertise on a technical issue, recognizing their superior knowledge.
4. Laura defers to another department's expertise on a critical project decision, despite her higher rank.
5. Luke regularly asks for feedback from his team, showing he values their opinions.
6. Jacob credits his team's collective efforts during a high-stakes presentation, rather than taking the spotlight himself.
7. Sarah volunteers for the least desirable tasks in the office, setting an example for her team.
8. A CEO openly acknowledges the contributions of their leadership team and employees, giving credit where it's due and fostering a positive, high-trust work environment.
9. A volunteer listens to the needs of the community rather than imposing their own ideas.
10. A partner acknowledges mistakes in a relationship and works to make amends.

11.14 Closing Reflections

One of the criticisms I've faced over the years is that I'm not aggressive enough or assertive enough, or maybe somehow, because I'm empathetic, it means I'm weak. I totally rebel against that. I refuse to believe that you cannot be both compassionate and strong.

—Jacinda Ardern

It's essential to remember that humility is not about diminishing our worth but about recognizing the value and contributions of others. Humility fosters an environment where collaboration, growth, and mutual respect can thrive. It allows us to acknowledge our limitations, learn from our mistakes, and remain open to new ideas and perspectives.

This mindset not only enriches our personal lives but also enhances our professional relationships and organizational culture. By practicing humility, we create a space where everyone feels valued and empowered to contribute their best.

In a world that often celebrates self-promotion and individual achievement, choosing humility can seem counterintuitive. However, true leadership and personal fulfillment stem from our ability to uplift others and work together toward common goals. As you reflect on the principles discussed in this chapter, consider how you can incorporate humility into your daily interactions and decision-making processes. Embrace the power of humility to build stronger connections, foster a culture of continuous improvement, and ultimately achieve greater success and satisfaction in all areas of your life. Let humility be the foundation upon which you build your leadership legacy.

11.15 Daily Practice

1. **Stay humble:** At the end of each day, take a moment to reflect deeply and express gratitude to those who have played a pivotal role in your success.

2. **Create psychological safety space:** Foster an environment where everyone feels safe to express their opinions, admit mistakes, and ask for help without fear.

3. **Acknowledge your mistakes:** Accept responsibility for your errors and learn from them instead of shifting blame to others.

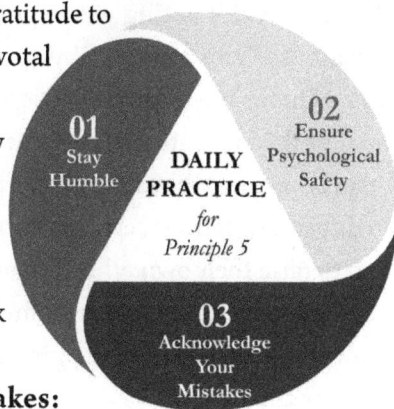

12 Principle 6: Act with More Integrity Than Others Think Prudent

Integrity is not something you show others. It is how you behave behind their back.

—Unknown

12.1 What If . . .

What if compromising your integrity for short-term gains leads to long-term consequences, eroding the trust others have in you? What if, by not acting with enough integrity, you find yourself in situations where your credibility is questioned and opportunities slip away? On the other hand, what if acting with uncompromising integrity became the foundation of every decision you make, leading to trust and respect beyond what others think possible? What if choosing integrity in difficult situations sets a powerful example, inspiring those around you to raise their own ethical standards?

Now, consider the scenarios in which you would like to see yourself. How would your goal of happiness and meaning-making be impacted by your choice?

12.2 Socrates and Gandhi: Paragons of Integrity

This above all: to thine own self be true,
And it must follow, as the night the day,
Thou canst not then be false to any man.

William Shakespeare

Integrity is a complex and multifaceted concept, often challenging to define because it encompasses a range of qualities that include honesty, consistency, and moral courage. It requires a deep alignment between one's values, actions, and words, making it a virtue that is not only about adherence to ethical principles but also about authenticity and steadfastness in the face of adversity. The lives of Socrates and Mahatma Gandhi provide profound illustrations of integrity.

Socrates's Unwavering Commitment to Principles

More than 2,400 years ago, in 399 BCE, Athens was a bustling city-state renowned for its intellectual, artistic, and political achievements, yet it was also a place of significant tension and strife, recovering from the Peloponnesian War and experiencing internal political upheaval. A short, snub-nosed man with protruding eyes, Socrates, later hailed as the greatest philosopher of all time, was accused of corrupting the youth and impiety.

The tension was palpable as he faced the jury, his fate hanging in the balance. The powerful elites, threatened by his relentless questioning and critique, sought to silence him forever. Yet Socrates, unwavering in his principles, defended his actions with a calm conviction. "*The unexamined life is not worth living,*" he declared, emphasizing the importance of seeking truth and integrity above all else.

The jury, unmoved by his eloquence, sentenced him to death by hemlock poisoning. In the days following the trial, Socrates's friends and followers were devastated. They devised a plan for his escape, believing that his life was too valuable to be lost. As night fell in his prison cell, his closest friend Crito whispered urgently, "Socrates, we have arranged everything. You can escape tonight. No one needs to know."

Socrates looked at Crito with a serene smile. "And what of the laws of Athens? If I escape, would I not be betraying everything I have taught? Would I not be undermining the very principles of justice I have lived by?" His voice was calm, yet resolute. Crito pleaded, "But you have been wronged, Socrates! The trial was unjust!"

Socrates responded with unwavering integrity, "Whether the trial was just or unjust, escaping would be wrong. I must accept the consequences of my actions, even if they lead to my death. My duty is to uphold the laws and principles, not to flee from them." His words hung heavily in the air, a testament to his steadfast commitment to integrity.

On the final day, as the hemlock was brought to him, Socrates faced death with remarkable composure. His friends wept, but Socrates reassured them, "Do not be afraid. I am not afraid. To die is either to pass into nothingness or to migrate to another place where I may continue to seek wisdom."

With dignity and calmness, Socrates drank the poison. As his strength waned, his commitment to truth and integrity remained unwavering. His final moments were a powerful demonstration of living and dying by one's principles.

The trial and death of Socrates offer a powerful story of integrity, demonstrating that true adherence to one's principles often requires the ultimate sacrifice. His refusal to escape, choosing instead to face death with dignity, continues to inspire and teach the value of living a life grounded in unwavering moral commitment.

The Steadfastness of Gandhi

In the heat of India's struggle for independence in the 1940s, tensions ran high among the leaders of the Indian National Congress. Amid the rising clamor for immediate and forceful action against British rule, Mahatma Gandhi stood resolute in his commitment to nonviolence. His closest associates, Jawaharlal Nehru and Muhammad Ali Jinnah, frequently pressed him to reconsider his stance, arguing that the British would never relinquish control without a more aggressive approach.

One evening, in a dimly lit room filled with anxious energy, Nehru approached Gandhi with a sense of urgency. "Bapu, the people are restless. They are ready to fight for their freedom. We cannot afford to wait any longer. Nonviolence has its limits."

Gandhi, calm and composed, responded, "Violence only begets more violence. Our struggle is not just for independence, but for the soul of our nation. We must not compromise our principles."

Jinnah, equally concerned, added, "The world is watching. We need to show strength. The British will only respond to force. Your methods may not achieve the swift results we need."

Gandhi looked at both men, his eyes filled with conviction. "True strength lies in our ability to endure and to uphold righteousness. Our path is not easy, but it is just. Violence will only corrupt our cause."

Despite the mounting pressure, his integrity remained unshaken. Historical incidents such as the violent crackdown during the Quit India Movement were used by his peers to argue their point, yet he remained steadfast. He reminded them of the Amritsar Massacre of 1919, where British troops killed hundreds of unarmed Indians. "Do you not see," he argued, "that violence will only lead to more such atrocities? We must rise above it."

The drama of these conversations and the weight of the decisions at hand filled the atmosphere with suspense. Would Gandhi bend to the collective pressure? Would he abandon his lifelong principle of nonviolence? But Gandhi's resolve was clear. His commitment to truth and nonviolence was absolute. He believed deeply that the ends did not justify the means, and that true independence could only be achieved through peaceful resistance.

In the end, Gandhi's steadfastness in his principles of nonviolence triumphed. His integrity became a beacon of hope and moral strength, not just for India, but for oppressed people worldwide. His refusal to succumb to pressure, his unwavering commitment to nonviolence, and his profound integrity ultimately led India to independence, leaving a legacy that continues to inspire generations.

Mahatma Gandhi's philosophy of nonviolence deeply influenced Martin Luther King Jr. and Nelson Mandela. King and Mandela admired Gandhi's unwavering commitment to peaceful resistance and his belief in the power of nonviolent protest to achieve social and political change. This admiration led King and Mandela to adopt similar principles in their struggles against injustice in the United States and South Africa, respectively. King wrote in his essay "My Pilgrimage to Nonviolence" that nonviolence is "the only morally and practically sound method open to oppressed people in their struggle for freedom." Similarly, Mandela's leadership in the African National Congress was marked by efforts to apply nonviolent methods, inspired by Gandhi's success in securing India's independence. Gandhi's legacy of dignity, integrity, and peaceful defiance provided a powerful framework for King and Mandela's fight for justice and equality.

12.3 The Essence of Integrity

Real integrity is doing the right thing, knowing that nobody's going to know whether you did it or not.

—Oprah Winfrey

Integrity is a complex and multifaceted concept, often difficult to define in mere words. The word "integrity" traces its roots to the Latin term *integritas*, meaning wholeness, completeness, and purity. Initially, it referred to the state of being whole or undivided. Over centuries, its meaning evolved to encompass moral and ethical steadfastness, emphasizing honesty and adherence to strong moral principles and values. To truly capture the essence of integrity, one must look beyond definitions and delve into stories of individuals who embodied this virtue. These stories—like those of Socrates and Gandhi, from ancient philosophers to modern leaders—provide a window into the profound impact that integrity has on personal character and ethical leadership.

In Harper Lee's *To Kill a Mockingbird*, a character profoundly remarks that Atticus Finch is "the same in his house as he is on the public streets." This statement highlights Atticus's unwavering commitment to his moral code, driven by personal integrity rather than public opinion. His steadfast consistency earns him the trust and respect of those around him. The expression "sound as a bell" illustrates this idea of consistency perfectly; a well-cast bell emits the same clear note regardless of when and where it is struck. Similarly, a person with integrity consistently exhibits the same moral behavior, regardless of the situation. Their core values and principles remain unshaken, guiding their actions even in the face of adversity, making them a reliable and trustworthy figure in any context. Integrity requires a deep alignment between one's values, actions, and words, making it a virtue that is not only about adherence to ethical principles but also about authenticity and steadfastness in the face of adversity. It fosters trust, respect, and authenticity, which are essential for effective leadership and sustainable success.

Warren Buffett, CEO of Berkshire Hathaway, who is set to retire at the end of 2025 after serving as CEO for nearly 50 years, is renowned for his integrity. During the 2008 financial crisis, Buffett maintained transparent communication with shareholders and made ethical decisions that prioritized long-term stability over short-term gains.

Similarly, Johnson & Johnson's handling of the Tylenol crisis showcased corporate integrity. In 1982, Johnson & Johnson faced a crisis when seven people died after ingesting cyanide-laced Tylenol capsules. Despite the potential for devastating financial and reputational consequences, Johnson & Johnson acted with integrity, prioritizing the safety and well-being of customers above all else. The company issued a nationwide recall of Tylenol products, implemented tamper-resistant packaging, and communicated openly and transparently with the public. By demonstrating integrity and putting people before profits, Johnson & Johnson regained the trust of customers while setting a new standard for crisis management and corporate responsibility.

The stories of Socrates, Gandhi, and contemporary leaders illustrate that integrity is not a static concept but one that evolves with societal needs. In today's context, integrity demands that leaders not only act ethically but also inspire others to uphold these values. As the world navigates the complexities of a post-pandemic landscape, integrity has become synonymous with resilience, trust, and the moral courage to lead with authenticity and purpose. From ancient Greece to modern-day governance, integrity remains a cornerstone of ethical leadership. It is a guiding principle that challenges us to align our actions with our deepest values, fostering a world where trust, justice, and moral clarity prevail.

12.4 Integrity: A Rare Commodity

Common sense is not so common.

—Voltaire

Integrity, while universally acknowledged as a cornerstone of ethical leadership, is often conspicuously absent in practice among modern corporate leaders. Despite inspiring historical examples of high integrity and its touted importance for business success, integrity is frequently overshadowed by the pursuit of short-term business gains, leading to widespread ethical breaches.

One glaring example of the lack of integrity in modern leadership is the Volkswagen emissions scandal. In 2015, it was revealed that Volkswagen had installed software in millions of cars worldwide to cheat emissions tests. This deceit, orchestrated at the highest levels of the company, resulted in significant environmental damage and loss of consumer trust. The scandal highlighted how the pursuit of profit and market dominance can lead to ethical breaches that ultimately harm the company's reputation and financial stability. Volkswagen's integrity was called into question, leading to billions in fines and a severe hit to its brand image.

The Wells Fargo scandal, which came to light in 2016, is another example of integrity being compromised. Employees, under pressure to meet unrealistic sales targets, created millions of unauthorized bank accounts without customers' knowledge. This fraudulent activity was encouraged by a corporate culture that prioritized profits over ethical behavior. The fallout included hefty fines, legal actions, and significant damage to Wells Fargo's reputation. This incident underscores the importance of fostering an ethical culture where integrity is not just a value on paper but a practiced principle.

Even in the tech industry, where innovation and progress are celebrated, issues of integrity can arise. For instance, the Cambridge Analytica scandal involving Facebook highlighted serious ethical breaches related to user data privacy. The unauthorized harvesting of personal data for political advertising exposed the vulnerabilities in Facebook's oversight and governance. This case illustrates how even the most successful and innovative companies must prioritize integrity to maintain trust and credibility in the eyes of the public and regulators.

These examples demonstrate that while integrity is highly valued, it is often compromised in the pursuit of short-term objectives. The consequences of such breaches are far-reaching, affecting not only the immediate stakeholders but also the broader societal trust in corporate institutions. Therefore, it is imperative for modern leaders to commit to integrity, ensuring that their actions align with their ethical values. Only by doing so can they foster sustainable success and restore faith in corporate leadership.

Many corporations claim to value integrity, yet their actions often tell a different story. The 2024 Edelman Trust Barometer reveals that trust in US corporate institutions has plummeted from 62% in 2014 to 53% in 2024. This decline in trust is indicative of a broader integrity gap within organizations. While a significant number of Fortune 500 companies include integrity in their value statements, studies show that these values are not always reflected in their operational practices. For instance, the 2024 *Global Business Ethics Survey* report by the Ethics & Compliance Initiative found that the percentage of employees who indicate that they are working in a strong-leaning ethical culture has reduced from 45% in 2020 to 40% in 2023 and the percentage who have reported observed misconduct has also decreased, from 71% in 2020 to 64% in 2023, often due to fear of retaliation. According to the 2025 HOW report *The State of Moral Leadership in Business*, only 13% of managers and 10% of CEOs are reported to consistently demonstrate key moral leadership behaviors, such as upholding ethical standards, seeking truth, and acting with courage.

This rarity of moral leadership and integrity in modern leadership, despite its proclaimed value, highlights a critical challenge for corporations today. Bridging the integrity gap requires more than just espousing values; it necessitates a concerted effort to embed these values into the organizational culture, ensuring that actions align with principles. By fostering a culture of transparency, accountability, and ethical behavior, companies can rebuild trust and create a more sustainable and morally sound business environment.

12.5 Why Integrity?

Integrity: without it nothing works.
 —Michael Jensen, professor, Harvard Business School

Integrity is a foundational principle that underpins all aspects of effective leadership and organizational success. Author and motivational speaker Charles Marshall is widely credited with articulating one of the most enduring definitions of integrity. In his 2001 book *Shattering the Glass Slipper*, he wrote, "Integrity is doing the right thing when you don't have to—when no one else is looking or will ever know—when there will be no congratulations or recognition for having done so." This quote powerfully captures the essence of personal ethics: the quiet, often unseen choices that reveal a person's true character. Unlike external measures of success, Marshall's view of integrity emphasizes internal consistency and moral courage, even in the absence of reward or recognition.

Harvard professor Michael Jensen, in his paper "Integrity: Without It Nothing Works," argues that integrity is essential for the proper functioning of individuals and organizations. He posits that integrity is about being whole and complete, which translates into actions that align consistently with one's values and commitments. Without integrity, trust erodes, and the very fabric of organizational relationships begins to unravel, leading to inefficiencies and failures.

The necessity of integrity in leadership cannot be overstated. Leaders who demonstrate integrity build trust, which is the cornerstone of any successful relationship, whether personal or professional. Trust, born out of integrity, ensures that employees feel secure and valued, fostering an environment where they can perform at their best.

Furthermore, integrity is critical for sustaining organizational performance. The research clearly demonstrates that moral leadership—especially at the CEO level—has a profound impact on organizational success. Organizations led by top-tier moral leaders consistently outperform others in several key areas, including customer satisfaction, resilience during economic challenges, and readiness for future business success.

For the past 19 years, Ethisphere—a global organization committed to "building a better world by advancing business integrity"—has tracked the performance of the World's Most Ethical Companies, consistently finding that these organizations outperform their industry peers, a phenomenon Ethisphere refers to as the "Ethics Premium." In 2025, 136 companies were honored for their steadfast commitment to integrity and ethical business practices. Between January 2020 and January 2025, these companies outperformed a comparable global index by 7.8%, further reinforcing the strong correlation between ethical leadership and sustained financial performance. These advantages are often driven by leaders who model integrity, trust, foresight, inclusive decision-making, and authentic connection.

Importantly, the impact of moral leadership is not limited only to the CEO. Its influence extends throughout the organization, particularly through managers at all levels, as documented in the 2025 HOW report. Teams led by high-integrity managers demonstrate significantly greater loyalty and reduced turnover. For instance, only 10% of employees under top-tier managers were seeking new jobs, compared to 31% under bottom-tier managers. The reason? Employees are more likely to stay committed to organizations where leaders and managers demonstrate ethical behavior and consistency between their words and actions. Moreover, the business benefits of integrity extend to financial performance as well. High-integrity leaders create environments where ethical practices are the norm, reducing the risks associated with unethical behavior and fostering long-term sustainable growth. In contrast, a lack of integrity can lead to catastrophic failures, as evidenced by the collapse of Enron, Lehman Brothers, and others, where unethical practices and dishonesty were rampant.

Jensen's argument also highlights that integrity is not just about avoiding wrongdoing but about actively doing the right thing, even when it is difficult. This proactive stance on integrity ensures that leaders make decisions that are not only legally compliant but also morally sound.

In the post-pandemic world, the importance of integrity has become even more pronounced. Organizations are navigating unprecedented challenges, and the need for trustworthy, transparent, and ethical leadership is critical. As businesses rebuild and adapt, those that prioritize integrity are more likely to earn the trust and loyalty of their stakeholders, ensuring resilience and long-term success. Thus, integrity is not merely a value to be aspired to but a fundamental necessity for any functioning and thriving organization.

12.6 No Alternative to Integrity: A Personal Story

Better is a poor man who walks in his integrity than a rich man who is crooked in his ways.
—Proverbs 28:6 (English Standard Version)

Thanks to my parents and teachers, integrity has always been a guiding principle for me—both in my professional life and in how I contribute to my community. I learned early on that integrity is not just about doing the right thing when it's easy or convenient; it's about doing the right thing even when it's difficult or goes unnoticed. It's about maintaining your standards with humility, even when others might think you're being overly cautious or impractical.

One of the most telling moments of integrity in my career came during a time when our firm was paid by physical checks. I was reviewing our annual bookkeeping records when I noticed that a government client had paid an invoice twice for an amount just shy of $2,000. It was a small amount in the grand scheme of our operations, and the client hadn't caught the error. I could have easily let it slide without anyone knowing, but it didn't sit right with me. Even though I knew that bringing it up would create more work for both sides and might seem excessive, I felt a responsibility to act. We reached out to the government office to notify them of the mistake. They were surprised and initially unsure how to handle a repayment from a private firm. It took some time, extra effort, and coordination, but we ultimately sorted out the process and returned the money. Looking back, I'm grateful for the guidance of my parents, who instilled these values in me. It was a moment that reinforced the importance of acting with integrity, even when it felt cumbersome.

During a fundraising event for a community cause, we had some donations coming in cash, which posed a challenge for transparent accounting. To ensure there could be no doubts about the handling of funds, we conducted all accounting and receipt tracking in a public setting, in front of a group of organizers. Every dollar received and spent was itemized, and we made the reports available to any community member who wanted to review them. It was more work and required extra attention to detail, but it left no doubt in anyone's mind that we were acting with complete integrity. This approach strengthened trust within the community and also inspired others in the group to adopt similar standards.

I also strive to bring integrity into everyday interactions at the office. One of my core beliefs is that everyone, regardless of race, religion, gender, or background, deserves to be treated with fairness and respect—which means being consistent in my actions and decisions, ensuring that everyone in the office receives the same consideration and opportunities. Whether it's resolving conflicts, evaluating performance, or making decisions that impact the team, I try to set an example by being fair and unbiased. By living as a role model of high integrity, I aim to create a work culture where everyone feels valued and trusts that they will be treated equitably.

Moments in my life outside of work also test my commitment to integrity—like when a cashier accidentally gives me too much change. Acting with integrity in such situations may seem like a small gesture, but consistently doing so reinforces the habit.

Ultimately, I have come to see that acting with integrity is not just about individual moments; it's a way of life. It builds a reputation not just for me but for everyone who shares in that commitment. It sets a standard for my team, my community, and myself—a standard that no amount of convenience, gain, or approval could ever replace.

12.7 Is Integrity Overvalued and Unachievable?

Somebody once said that in looking for people to hire, you look for three qualities: integrity, intelligence, and energy. And if they don't have the first, the other two will kill you.

—Warren Buffett

While integrity is widely hailed as a cornerstone of ethical leadership and organizational success, some argue that it is an overvalued and often unachievable trait in the harsh realities of the business world, where the primary goal is to generate profit. Critics suggest that the relentless pursuit of integrity can sometimes clash with the demands of achieving financial performance, leading to challenging dilemmas for business leaders.

One argument against the absolute necessity of integrity is the case of successful leaders who have operated in morally grey areas. For instance, Steve Jobs, cofounder of Apple, was known for his relentless drive for perfection and innovation. While undeniably successful, Jobs was often criticized for his harsh management style and sometimes questionable ethical practices, such as denying stock options to early employees and engaging in "poaching" agreements with other tech companies to prevent talent from leaving. Despite these issues, Jobs's leadership resulted in Apple becoming one of the most valuable companies in the world, raising questions about whether strict adherence to integrity is always necessary for business success.

Furthermore, in highly competitive industries, the pressure to meet quarterly earnings expectations can lead to compromises on integrity. Wells Fargo's scandal involving the creation of millions of fake accounts to meet sales targets is a glaring example. The bank's leadership prioritized short-term financial gains over ethical practices, resulting in significant fines and reputational damage. However, despite these issues, Wells Fargo remains a major player in the banking industry, suggesting that the pursuit of profit can sometimes overshadow the importance of integrity.

Additionally, the pharmaceutical industry often faces criticism for prioritizing profits over ethical considerations. Martin Shkreli, former CEO of Turing Pharmaceuticals, famously increased the price of a life-saving drug by 5000%, leading to widespread outrage. While Shkreli's actions were legal, they were widely deemed unethical. This case illustrates how the focus on maximizing shareholder value can sometimes lead to decisions that starkly contrast with broader societal values.

The concept of "creative accounting" also highlights the tension between integrity and business practices. Companies like Enron and WorldCom engaged in accounting practices that, while technically legal at times, were designed to mislead investors and inflate stock prices. These practices ultimately led to their downfall, but for years they enabled the companies to present a façade of financial health and profitability. This raises questions about whether integrity can coexist with the financial engineering often necessary to meet market expectations.

Finally, in the highly competitive global market, companies sometimes resort to outsourcing and labor practices that, while legal, raise ethical concerns. Major corporations, including Nike and Apple, have faced criticism for labor practices in their supply chains. These practices often involve low wages and poor working conditions, highlighting the conflict between maintaining high ethical standards and achieving cost efficiencies necessary for competitive advantage.

These counterexamples suggest that while integrity is an admirable and important trait, the realities of the business world can sometimes make it difficult to maintain. The drive for profit, market competition, and shareholder expectations often creates situations where compromises on integrity are made.

12.8 Balancing Integrity and Financial Goals

The purpose of a business is to create and keep a customer. . . . Not so long ago a lot of companies assumed something quite different about the purpose of a business. They said quite simply that the purpose is to make money. But that proved as vacuous as saying that the purpose of life is to eat.

—Theodore Levitt,
Harvard Business School

A leader must strike a balance between integrity and financial goals to ensure sustainable success and ethical governance. While financial performance is crucial for the survival and growth of a business, it should not come at the expense of ethical standards and integrity.

Leaders who prioritize short-term financial gains over ethical behavior risk damaging their reputation, losing stakeholder trust, and facing legal repercussions, as seen in the cases of Enron and Wells Fargo. By incorporating integrity into their decision-making processes, leaders can build a strong foundation of trust and loyalty, which ultimately contributes to long-term profitability and organizational resilience.

However, there are compelling arguments for maintaining unwavering integrity even when financial goals are at stake. Leaders in the financial sector, such as Paul Volcker, former Federal Reserve chairman, and Christine Lagarde, president of the European Central Bank, exemplify the power of steadfast principles— demonstrating that true leadership involves upholding ethical values even under intense market pressures. Integrity fosters a culture of transparency and accountability, attracting employees, customers, and partners who value ethical behavior. Thus, while the pressures of financial performance are undeniable, leaders must remain committed to their core values, ensuring that their actions align with ethical principles to achieve sustainable and responsible success.

Furthermore, Theodore Levitt's assertion "The true purpose of a business is to create and keep a customer, not to make you money," highlights a fundamental principle of customer-centric business philosophy. This statement emphasizes that businesses should focus on satisfying customer needs and building lasting relationships rather than solely pursuing profits. Integrity plays a crucial role in this customer-centric approach, fostering trust and loyalty.

12.9 Employees as Customers: The Case for Ethical Leadership

Customers will never love a company until the employees love it first.
—Simon Sinek

In a post-pandemic world characterized by a talent shortage and an intense "war for talent," the lines between employees and customers have blurred, compelling businesses to pay unprecedented attention to their employees' needs. Today, employees expect more than just a salary; they seek workplaces that value their well-being, purpose, and professional growth. Companies must recognize that their workforce is also their customer base, driving the necessity to create an environment that attracts, retains, and nurtures talent. As Richard Branson, founder of the Virgin Group, famously said, "Clients do not come first. Employees come first. If you take care of your employees, they will take care of the clients." This holistic approach is critical in fostering loyalty, enhancing performance, and securing a sustainable competitive edge in the evolving business landscape. Theodore Levitt's assertion can be enhanced to say, "The true purpose of a business is to create and keep a customer" *and to hire and retain an employee.*

The demand for ethical leadership and integrity has never been greater. This shift is driven by a renewed focus on the well-being of employees, societal impact, and sustainable business practices. Companies are no longer judged solely by their financial performance but also by their commitment to ethical standards and their role in contributing positively to society. According to a report by the International City/County Management Association (ICMA), the COVID-19 pandemic highlighted the importance of ethical decision-making in leadership, emphasizing the need for leaders who prioritize the common good over short-term gains.

Harvard Law School's analysis of business ethics in the tech industry underscores the tangible benefits of ethical behavior. Businesses that uphold ethical standards are more likely to attract and retain top talent, foster trust with customers and stakeholders, and achieve long-term success. Conversely, companies that compromise on ethics, such as those led by figures like Elon Musk, face significant challenges, including loss of trust, employee attrition, and financial instability.

In a February 2022 article published on the British Broadcasting Corporation (BBC) website cited research from Blue Beyond Consulting showing that employees increasingly expect companies to be a force for good in society, particularly in response to recent crises such as the pandemic, racial injustice, and political polarization. The research revealed that company values now significantly influence employment decisions, with only one in four knowledge workers willing to accept a job if their values do not align with those of the organization. Research studies also reveal that employees would leave their current job for an employer with an excellent ethical reputation, even during economic downturns. These revelations highlight the growing importance of integrity in the workplace and suggest that employees value ethical leadership over financial incentives alone. Moreover, companies with strong ethical foundations tend to perform better in the long run, as they build lasting relationships with their stakeholders based on trust and mutual respect.

However, a significant gap remains between the espoused values of integrity and their practical application in the corporate world. Many organizations claim to value integrity but fail to implement policies that genuinely uphold ethical standards. This discrepancy is often reflected in employee dissatisfaction and distrust toward management. For instance, the ICMA report notes that while many leaders profess a commitment to ethics, their actions during crises, such as layoffs and resource cuts, often betray a primary focus on financial outcomes over employee welfare.

In summary, the post-pandemic era has underscored the critical need for ethical leadership, which means practicing integrity more than others think logical. While financial performance remains important, the ability to lead with integrity and uphold ethical standards is increasingly seen as essential for sustainable success. Companies that bridge the gap between their stated values and actual practices are likely to thrive, attracting top talent and building stronger, more resilient organizations.

QUICK TIP

Action: Employ AI to ensure compliance with ethical standards and regulations. Use blockchain technology for transparency and traceability in transactions and decisions.

Example: Implementing AI tools to monitor and ensure compliance with industry regulations and company policies.

Caveat: Regularly audit AI systems to ensure they are functioning as intended and not perpetuating unethical practices or oversights.

12.10 Ten Actionable Steps for Applying Principle 6

Without being a person of integrity, you can forget about being a leader. And, being a person of integrity is a never-ending endeavor. Being a person of integrity is a mountain with no top—you have to learn to love the climb.

—Michael Jensen,
Harvard Business School

In the preceding pages of this chapter, we have examined integrity from many vantage points—from the timeless lessons of Socrates and Gandhi to the challenges of balancing ethical leadership with financial pressures, from questioning whether integrity is overvalued or unachievable to seeing it brought to life in personal stories of sacrifice and courage. We have seen that integrity is not merely a lofty ideal, but a rare and essential quality that anchors every meaningful relationship and every lasting success.

Integrity is not declared; it is demonstrated. It lives in the daily choices you make, in the culture you build, and in the values you uphold even when no one is watching. The following section offers practical steps with examples to help you transform your convictions into consistent actions. You do not need to adopt every practice immediately; start with those that resonate most, and build steadily from there. Each choice you make strengthens the foundation of trust and authenticity upon which extraordinary leadership—and enduring success—are built.

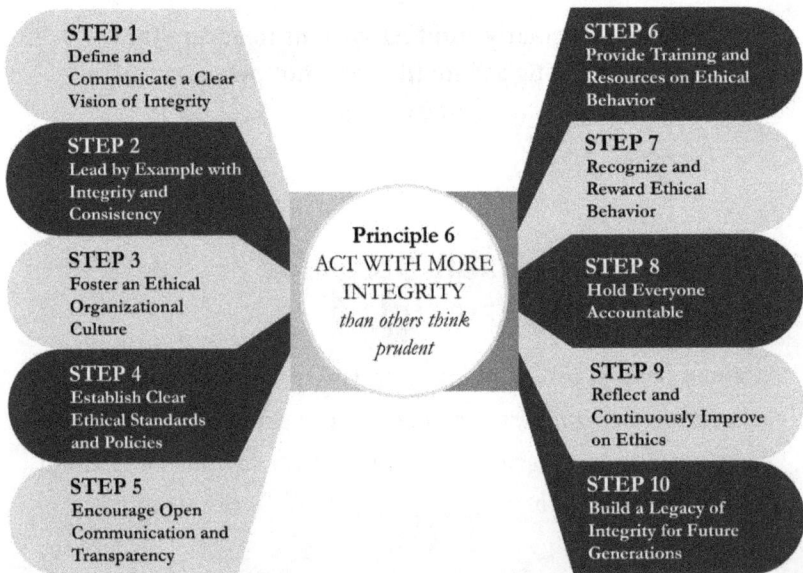

STEP 1
Define and Communicate a Clear Vision of Integrity

STEP 2
Lead by Example with Integrity and Consistency

STEP 3
Foster an Ethical Organizational Culture

STEP 4
Establish Clear Ethical Standards and Policies

STEP 5
Encourage Open Communication and Transparency

Principle 6
ACT WITH MORE INTEGRITY
than others think prudent

STEP 6
Provide Training and Resources on Ethical Behavior

STEP 7
Recognize and Reward Ethical Behavior

STEP 8
Hold Everyone Accountable

STEP 9
Reflect and Continuously Improve on Ethics

STEP 10
Build a Legacy of Integrity for Future Generations

The integrity imperative: ten actionable steps for applying Principle 6

💡 *Principle 6, Step 1: Define and Communicate a Clear Vision of Integrity*

Action: Articulate a compelling vision that prioritizes integrity and communicates it clearly across the organization.

Example: As the first US president, George Washington emphasized the importance of honesty and ethical behavior in governance, setting a precedent for future leaders. Patagonia, an outdoor clothing company, is known for its commitment to environmental sustainability and ethical business practices. Founder Yvon Chouinard's clear vision of integrity has shaped the company's culture and reputation.

💡 *Principle 6, Step 2: Lead by Example with Integrity and Consistency*

Action: Demonstrate integrity and consistency in actions and decisions to build credibility and trust within the organization.

Example: Mahatma Gandhi's leadership in the Indian independence movement was characterized by his integrity and consistency in adhering to the principles of nonviolence and truth. His actions inspired trust and loyalty among his followers. Warren Buffett, CEO of Berkshire Hathaway, is renowned for his integrity and transparent communication with shareholders. His consistent and ethical approach to business, documented by Alice Schroeder in her book *The Snowball: Warren Buffett and the Business of Life*, has earned him immense trust and respect in the corporate world. Similarly, Mary Barra, CEO of General Motors, led with integrity when she took swift responsibility for the company's ignition switch crisis, promoting a culture of accountability and transparency. Arvind Krishna, CEO of IBM, has consistently focused on maintaining IBM's long-standing commitment to trust and responsibility in the use of artificial intelligence and data. His leadership emphasizes transparent practices in AI ethics, ensuring the technology is used in a way that benefits society.

💡 Principle 6, Step 3: Foster an Ethical Organizational Culture

Action: Create an environment where ethical behavior is valued and encouraged.

Example: Roman emperor Marcus Aurelius led with Stoic principles, emphasizing the importance of virtue and moral integrity, which influenced his governance and military leadership. Google's "Don't be evil" motto reflects its commitment to ethical business practices and nurturing a positive work environment. The turnaround of Ford Motor Company under CEO Alan Mulally involved cultivating a culture of transparency, accountability, and ethical behavior, which helped revive the company's fortunes.

💡 Principle 6, Step 4: Establish Clear Ethical Standards and Policies

Action: Develop and enforce policies that promote integrity and ethical behavior.

Example: President Theodore Roosevelt's anticorruption efforts and establishment of ethical standards in public office set a benchmark for future administrations. Microsoft's implementation of strict anticorruption policies and ethical guidelines has helped maintain its reputation and operational integrity. The whistleblower policies at Enron, had they been enforced, could have potentially prevented the catastrophic downfall of the company due to unethical practices.

💡 *Principle 6, Step 5: Encourage Open Communication and Transparency*

Action: Promote a culture of openness where employees feel safe to speak up about ethical concerns.

Example: Abraham Lincoln's leadership during the Civil War involved open communication and transparency, earning him the trust and respect of the nation. Starbucks' commitment to transparent communication with both employees and customers has been integral to its brand and business success. The implementation of an open-door policy at IBM encouraged employees to share concerns and suggestions, encouraging a more ethical and collaborative workplace.

💡 *Principle 6, Step 6: Provide Training and Resources on Ethical Behavior*

Action: Offer regular training sessions and resources to educate employees about ethical standards and expectations.

Example: The teachings of Confucius emphasized the importance of ethical education and moral development, principles that guided many leaders in ancient China. Deloitte's comprehensive ethics training programs help employees understand and adhere to the company's ethical standards. The ethics training programs at Lockheed Martin are designed to promote a culture of integrity and accountability within the organization.

💡 *Principle 6, Step 7: Recognize and Reward Ethical Behavior*

Action: Acknowledge and reward employees who demonstrate exceptional integrity in their roles.

Example: Johnson & Johnson's Credo Awards recognize employees who go above and beyond in practicing the company's values, particularly the focus on health and ethical responsibility. This award celebrates employees who demonstrate integrity and ethical leadership in critical situations, reinforcing the company's long-standing reputation for ethical business practices. Zappos' rewards program for employees who exemplify the company's core values, including integrity, helps reinforce ethical behavior. The recognition programs at Salesforce celebrate employees who demonstrate ethical leadership and integrity, reinforcing the company's commitment to ethical business practices. Patagonia actively rewards employees who advocate for environmental and social justice causes, aligning with its mission of ethical responsibility. The company encourages employees to take time off to volunteer for environmental causes and even provides bail money for employees arrested in peaceful protests.

💡 *Principle 6, Step 8: Hold Everyone Accountable*

Action: Ensure that all employees, regardless of their position, are held accountable for their actions.

Example: The Athenian democracy had a practice of banishing individuals from the city by majority vote as a means to hold leaders accountable for their actions and decisions. Intel's policy of holding all employees, including executives, accountable for ethical breaches has helped maintain its reputation for integrity. The accountability measures at Volkswagen after its emissions scandal aimed to rebuild trust and ensure ethical compliance throughout the organization.

Principle 6, Step 9: Reflect and Continuously Improve on Ethics

Action: Regularly assess and improve the organization's ethical standards and practices.

Example: Benjamin Franklin's practice of daily reflection on his virtues and ethical behavior guided his leadership and personal development. Toyota's commitment to continuous improvement (kaizen) includes a focus on ethical business practices and integrity.

Principle 6, Step 10: Build a Legacy of Integrity for Future Generations

Action: Focus on creating long-term impact by embedding integrity into the organization's culture and systems to sustain ethical practices for future generations.

Example: Unilever, under Paul Polman's leadership, institutionalized sustainability and ethical practices into its operations, making them a core part of the company's identity. As chair of the Tata Group—one of India's largest and most respected multinational conglomerates—Ratan Tata prioritized ethical business practices and social responsibility, embedding these values into the company's DNA. The Tata Group's charitable trusts own over two-thirds of the company, ensuring that profits are reinvested into societal causes and maintaining a legacy of integrity that defines the organization. The founding principles of institutions like the Red Cross, rooted in humanitarian values, have created a legacy of integrity that continues to guide their mission across generations. Jacinda Ardern's empathetic and inclusive leadership, especially during crises like the Christchurch mosque shootings, emphasized compassion, transparency, and ethical governance. Her actions and policies set a benchmark for integrity-driven leadership that will influence future leaders of New Zealand.

By following these steps, leaders can effectively apply the principle *Act with integrity more than others think prudent* and nurture a culture of ethical behavior and trust within their organizations.

12.11 Ten Barriers to Applying Principle 6

Integrity is choosing courage over comfort; choosing what is right over what is fun, fast, or easy; and choosing to practice our values rather than simply professing them.

—Brené Brown

Acting with integrity is a powerful and transformative practice, but it can be challenging, especially when striving to exceed societal expectations. Here are the main barriers to *acting with integrity more than others think prudent*, along with potential solutions to overcome these challenges.

Principle 6
ACT WITH MORE INTEGRITY
than others think prudent

Barrier 1	Barrier 6
Ego and Pride	Cultural Differences
Barrier 2	Barrier 7
Fear of Consequences	Personal Gain
Barrier 3	Barrier 8
Peer Pressure	Lack of Accountability
Barrier 4	Barrier 9
Lack of Clear Ethical Guidelines	Overwhelm and Burnout
Barrier 5	Barrier 10
Misaligned Incentives	Rationalization

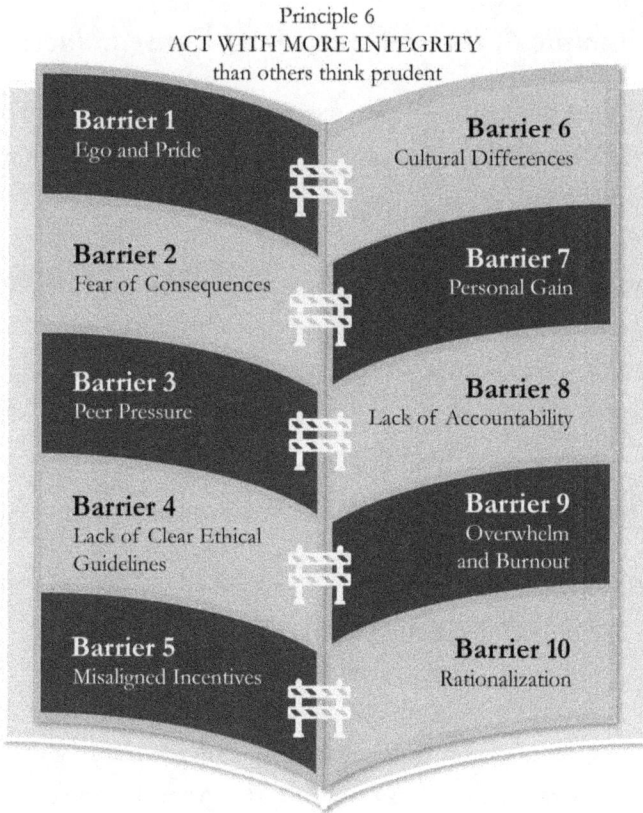

The silent erosion: ten barriers to applying Principle 6

⚠ Principle 6, Barrier 1: Ego and Pride

Barrier: A high ego and excessive pride can lead to arrogance and a refusal to acknowledge mistakes, undermining integrity.

Solution: Cultivate humility by seeking feedback and reflecting on personal shortcomings. Encourage a culture of openness and learning, where admitting mistakes is seen as a strength rather than a weakness.

⚠️ *Principle 6, Barrier 2: Fear of Consequences*

Barrier: Fear of negative repercussions can deter individuals from acting with integrity, leading to dishonest or unethical behavior to avoid punishment.

Solution: Create a supportive environment where transparency and honesty are valued and rewarded. Ensure that the organization has clear policies protecting those who report unethical behavior (whistleblower protections).

⚠️ *Principle 6, Barrier 3: Peer Pressure*

Barrier: Pressure to conform to the unethical practices of peers can compromise an individual's integrity.

Solution: Promote a strong ethical culture within the organization where integrity is valued and celebrated. Provide training on ethical decision-making and encourage individuals to speak up against unethical practices.

⚠️ *Principle 6, Barrier 4: Lack of Clear Ethical Guidelines*

Barrier: Ambiguity in ethical standards can lead to confusion and inconsistent behavior.

Solution: Establish and communicate clear ethical guidelines and standards. Regularly review and update these guidelines to ensure they remain relevant and effective.

⚠ *Principle 6, Barrier 5: Misaligned Incentives*

Barrier: Incentive structures that prioritize results over ethical behavior can lead to compromised integrity.

Solution: Align incentives with ethical behavior by incorporating integrity metrics into performance evaluations and reward systems. Recognize and reward individuals who demonstrate ethical behavior.

⚠ *Principle 6, Barrier 6: Cultural Differences*

Barrier: Diverse cultural backgrounds can result in varying interpretations of ethical behavior.

Solution: Foster an inclusive environment that respects cultural differences while establishing a common ethical framework. Provide cross-cultural training to enhance understanding and collaboration.

⚠ *Principle 6, Barrier 7: Personal Gain*

Barrier: The pursuit of personal gain can lead to conflicts of interest and unethical decisions.

Solution: Implement policies that identify and manage conflicts of interest. Encourage a culture of selflessness and service, emphasizing the importance of greater good over individual gain.

⚠ *Principle 6, Barrier 8: Lack of Accountability*

Barrier: Without accountability, individuals may feel they can act without consequence.

Solution: Establish robust accountability mechanisms, including regular audits and transparent reporting systems. Ensure that ethical breaches are addressed promptly and fairly.

⚠ *Principle 6, Barrier 9: Overwhelm and Burnout*

Barrier: Taking on too much at once can lead to overwhelm and burnout, which in turn can trigger self-sabotaging behaviors as a way to cope with stress.

Solution: Prioritize tasks and break them down into manageable steps. Learn to say no and delegate responsibilities when necessary. Make time for rest and relaxation to prevent burnout and maintain balance.

⚠ *Principle 6, Barrier 10: Rationalization*

Barrier: Justifying unethical behavior through rationalization can erode integrity over time.

Solution: Encourage critical self-reflection and ethical decision-making. Provide training on recognizing and combating rationalization. Develop and support an environment where ethical behavior is the norm and deviations are openly discussed and corrected.

By addressing these barriers and implementing the solutions, individuals and organizations can create a culture that supports and promotes integrity, leading to more ethical and effective leadership.

12.12 Ten Examples of Applying Principle 6

1. Mike stands up against unethical practices in his department, risking his job security.

2. Rachel reports a compliance issue to the board, despite potential backlash from her direct supervisor.
3. Kevin refuses to cut corners on a project, even when pressured by management to meet deadlines.
4. Liam insists on full transparency about a project's risks with stakeholders, even if it might jeopardize the approval.
5. Mia stands by her decision to report financial inaccuracies, despite pressure from colleagues to overlook them.
6. Emma refuses a lucrative contract from a client known for unethical practices, prioritizing the company's values.
7. John declines a job offer that involves compromising his principles, even though it offers significant financial rewards.
8. Julia ensures that all her dealings with clients are transparent and honest, even if it means losing a potential sale.
9. A local politician remains transparent about their funding sources, maintaining public trust.
10. A community member ensures fairness in distributing resources, even when pressured otherwise.

12.13 Closing Reflections

The truth is always the strongest argument.

—Sophocles

The imperative to *act with integrity more than others think prudent* underscores the profound necessity of unwavering ethical conduct in all aspects of life. Integrity is not merely a virtue but a foundational principle that shapes character, builds trust, and fosters authentic relationships. It transcends the immediate calculations of rationality, anchoring decisions in a moral compass that guides actions even when the path is challenging or obscure.

Acting with integrity also cultivates a sense of inner peace and fulfillment. When our actions align with our values, we experience a harmony that is personally gratifying and socially commendable. This internal alignment propels individuals toward greater personal and professional success, as their actions are driven by conviction rather than convenience.

Historical and contemporary examples abound, demonstrating that integrity is a critical differentiator between transient success and enduring greatness. Companies that have embedded integrity into their core values consistently outperform those that do not. This correlation between ethical behavior and financial performance underscores that integrity is not just a moral imperative but a strategic advantage.

In a world where short-term gains often tempt individuals to compromise their principles, maintaining integrity can appear difficult or impractical—but it remains essential for long-term trust and success. History and experience show that those who prioritize integrity over expediency often achieve lasting success and fulfillment. They build legacies that stand the test of time, rooted in the unwavering commitment to doing what is right rather than what is easy.

The challenges of maintaining integrity are real, but they are surmountable. By addressing barriers such as ego, peer pressure, and fear of consequences, and by promoting a culture of accountability and ethical behavior, leaders can overcome obstacles to acting with integrity. It requires continuous effort, self-reflection, and a commitment to ethical principles, but the rewards—trust, loyalty, and long-term success—are well worth the investment.

Let integrity be the beacon that guides our actions. Let us strive to exceed the rational expectations of others by adhering to a higher standard of ethical conduct. In doing so, we not only elevate ourselves but also inspire those around us to pursue a path of righteousness and honor. Integrity is not just a choice; it is the cornerstone of a life well-lived and a legacy worth leaving.

12.14 Daily Practice

1. **Be authentic:** Demonstrate the behaviors and values you want to see in your team.
2. **Be fair and consistent:** Apply rules and policies fairly, uniformly, and consistently to all people under all circumstances.
3. **Be ethical:** Prioritize ethical considerations in your decision-making.

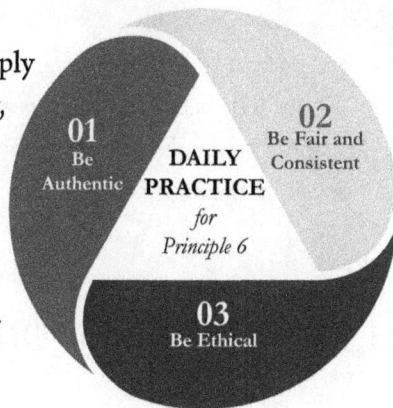

01
Be
Authentic

DAILY PRACTICE
for
Principle 6

02
Be Fair and
Consistent

03
Be Ethical

13 Principle 7: Care More for People Than Others Think Reasonable

The one who is free from selfish attachments, who has no desire for personal gain, who has no egoism, and is filled with the spirit of service, alone attains true peace.

—Bhagavad Gita

13.1 Why Care for Others?

Throughout human history, the evolution of caring for others has been shaped by the recognition of our shared humanity and the ethical frameworks developed by various cultures and religions. From the communal support systems of early humans to the moral teachings of ancient civilizations and religious traditions, the practice of caring for others has been fundamental to the development of social cohesion and moral progress. These historical lessons continue to influence modern ethical thought and underscore the enduring importance of compassion and care in human societies.

To lead with genuine care for others is to unlock a deeper sense of purpose and meaning in both life and work. This caring mindset could be an immense source of happiness and peace. Leaders who prioritize the well-being of others over their own interests are not only likable and warm, they also inspire those around them to find value in serving the greater good. Caring for others isn't just a leadership trait—it's a pathway to discovering the true essence of life. When we practice caring, we cultivate environments where people feel valued, respected, and motivated to contribute meaningfully. As Aristotle, one of the greatest thinkers of ancient Greece, profoundly noted, "The essence of life is to serve others and to do good." His philosophy of life has resonated through the ages, encapsulating the Greek ideal of *philoxenia*, which translates to the love of strangers, and *eunoia*, meaning goodwill. It serves as a timeless reminder that true leadership lies not in personal accolades but in the impact we have on others through acts of care and service.

Aristotle's teachings often emphasized the importance of living a virtuous life, a concept he explored deeply in his works such as *Nicomachean Ethics*. In this text, Aristotle argued that the highest good for humans is *eudaimonia*, often translated as happiness or flourishing, which is achieved through virtuous living. Virtue, according to Aristotle, is not just about personal excellence but also about contributing to the well-being of others.

Aristotle viewed *philoxenia* as an expression of the virtue of generosity, where showing hospitality and kindness to strangers was a demonstration of moral excellence. By treating others with respect and care, individuals cultivate a society rooted in mutual support and cooperation, essential for the well-being of the community. Regarding *eunoia*, Aristotle considered it a crucial aspect of friendship, which he categorized as one of the highest forms of virtue. He argued that genuine goodwill and a selfless attitude toward others are foundational for forming deep, meaningful relationships. This positive regard for others engenders trust and mutual respect, enabling individuals to live harmoniously and contribute to the greater good of society.

Aristotle believed that humans are social animals, inherently connected to one another. This connection means that our happiness is intertwined with the happiness of others. Serving others and doing good are not just moral obligations but essential elements of achieving personal fulfillment. By helping others, we enhance our own lives and contribute to a harmonious society. Aristotle's influence on subsequent philosophical thought helped to spread and entrench these values within global cultural and ethical frameworks.

Caring for others is not merely a noble trait, but a foundational principle of spiritual and moral life as expounded by all major world religions. More than 200 years before the birth of Aristotle, in the sixth century BCE, Siddhartha Gautama—later known as the Buddha—founded Buddhism, a spiritual tradition that places a strong emphasis on compassion and care for all living beings. Buddha taught that suffering is a fundamental part of human existence, and that caring for others through acts of compassion can alleviate this suffering. The concept of *karuna* (compassion) became central to Buddhist ethics, encouraging followers to extend care and empathy to all beings, transcending social and cultural boundaries. This ethic of care, rooted in ancient spiritual and philosophical traditions, resonates across the world's major religions, diverse cultures, and historical eras. Whether expressed through compassion, duty, justice, love, or mercy, they all converge on a shared truth: true leadership, purpose, and human flourishing arise when we serve and uplift those around us.

Fast-forward to modern times, and we find similar sentiments echoed by influential figures. German philosopher Immanuel Kant's moral philosophy emphasizes the categorical imperative, which includes the principle of treating others as ends in themselves, not just as means. He advised, "Act in such a way that you treat humanity, whether in your own person or in the person of another, always at the same time as an end, never merely as a means." According to Kant, we have a moral obligation to care for others because every individual has inherent worth and dignity. French philosopher Jean-Paul Sartre, a key figure in existentialism, argued that we create meaning through our choices and actions, particularly in our relations with others. He posited that caring for others is a way to create authentic relationships and find meaning in an otherwise indifferent universe.

Mother Teresa famously said, "Give your hands to serve, and your hearts to love." One remarkable story is of her rescuing children from a war zone in Beirut in 1982. Despite the ongoing conflict, she negotiated a temporary ceasefire, allowing her to evacuate 37 children from a devastated hospital. Her unwavering commitment to service and compassion left an indelible mark on the world. Mother Teresa's life exemplified the principle that true fulfillment comes from helping others.

US Supreme Court justice Ruth Bader Ginsburg's life exemplified the principle that leadership, grounded in care and empathy, can bring about true and lasting change. Ginsburg's approach to justice was not limited to the black-and-white of the law; it was infused with a deep, unwavering commitment to equity and compassion. In her early career, she fought for gender equality not just with intellect, but with a genuine desire to uplift those facing discrimination. She famously said, "Fight for the things that you care about, but do it in a way that will lead others to join you," capturing the essence of her empathetic leadership.

Her dissent in *Ledbetter v. Goodyear Tire & Rubber Co.* was more than a legal argument—it was a clarion call for justice for countless women experiencing pay discrimination. Ginsburg's carefully chosen words, filled with care for the real people affected, laid the foundation for legislative change, leading to the Lilly Ledbetter Fair Pay Act. Her care and empathy extended beyond her decisions; she believed in bringing people together, even those who disagreed with her. Her deep friendship with Justice Antonin Scalia was a testament to her belief in connection and respect across ideological divides. Ginsburg found happiness in her dedication to justice and in her role as a trailblazer for women's rights. Her legacy is not only in the cases she championed but in the generations she inspired—people who saw that leadership could be fierce and compassionate, rigorous and understanding. Like Mother Teresa's acts of service and compassion, Ginsburg's life showed that caring leadership is both powerful and transformative, leaving a lasting and profound impact on society.

Utilitarian Value of Caring for Others

Beyond philosophical, religious, and moral reasoning, caring for others has tangible benefits from leadership and utilitarian perspectives. Companies with caring leadership practices see a 21% increase in profitability and a 41% reduction in absenteeism, according to a study by Gallup published in 2017. Additionally, research studies found that leaders who prioritize the well-being of their employees spark higher levels of engagement, resulting in increased productivity. A leader who is caring, helpful, and thoughtful not only improves others' lives but also benefits personally from better health due to the biochemical changes that occur when practicing kindness. According to an article published by SSM Health, engaging in acts of kindness decreases blood pressure and lowers cortisol, a stress hormone linked to stress levels. Caring for others has been demonstrated to bring personal happiness and fulfillment, with a study published in the *Journal of Social Psychology* revealing that acts of kindness can boost life satisfaction. Additionally, research from the Greater Good Science Center at UC Berkeley indicates that "a strong correlation exists between the well-being, happiness, health, and longevity of people who are emotionally and behaviorally compassionate, so long as they are not overwhelmed by helping tasks."

13.2 Tolstoy "Unleashed"

> *Leadership is about empowering other people as a result of your presence—and making sure that impact continues into your absence.*
> —Frances Frei and Anne Morris, authors of *Unleashed*

In Russian novelist Leo Tolstoy's short story "Three Questions," a king seeks the answers to three crucial questions to ensure he always acts correctly: What is the right time to act? Who are the most important people? What is the most important thing to do? He consults a wise hermit, who initially offers no direct answers. The king helps the hermit with his work, and they are interrupted by a wounded man, whom they care for together. The next day, the man, who had intended to kill the king, expresses gratitude for saving his life and pledges loyalty. The hermit then reveals that the king's questions were answered through his actions: the most important time is now, the most important person is the one you are with, and the most important action is to do good for that person.

This timeless wisdom aligns seamlessly with the leadership principles articulated in *Unleashed: The Unapologetic Leader's Guide to Empowering Everyone Around You* by Frances Frei and Anne Morriss. The authors emphasize the power of leadership through trust, empathy, and the prioritization of people. Tolstoy's story and Frei and Morriss's book each highlight the importance of being present, valuing those around you, and acting with compassion and integrity

In *Unleashed*, Frei and Morris ask current and potential leaders to consider three powerful questions, much like the king of Tolstoy's story: "Are your teammates and colleagues better off when you're around? Are they more productive and more engaged? More willing to innovate and take smart bets?"

Frei argues in *Unleashed* that effective leadership is not about wielding power but about unleashing the potential of others. This requires leaders to be attuned to the needs of their people, much like the king in Tolstoy's story learns to value the present moment and the person in front of him. By focusing on building trust and fostering an environment where everyone can thrive, leaders create a culture of mutual respect and shared purpose.

Both works teach that leadership is grounded in everyday actions and decisions. The king's experience with the hermit and the wounded man illustrates that wisdom and effective leadership come from serving others and making the most of every moment. Frei's book provides a modern framework for this timeless principle, showing leaders how to cultivate trust, empathy, and purposeful action in their organizations.

In essence, Tolstoy's narrative and Frei's insights converge on a powerful message: true leadership is about being present, prioritizing people, and consistently doing good. By internalizing these principles, leaders can inspire and empower those around them, creating the conditions for the people around them to become more effective and fully realize their own potential.

13.3 Mindfulness and Caring Leadership

People don't care how much you know until they know how much you care.

—Theodore Roosevelt

Mindfulness is the practice of being fully present and engaged in the current moment, fostering awareness of one's thoughts, emotions, and surroundings. It aligns perfectly with the central theme of Tolstoy's story that revolves around the significance of living in the present and caring for those around us. Mindfulness is crucial for becoming a happy and great leader—because when leaders practice mindfulness, they cultivate a deeper awareness of the needs and feelings of those around them. This heightened awareness encourages a nonjudgmental, accepting attitude, which is fundamental to truly caring for others, rather than reacting impulsively or inattentively. By being fully present with others, leaders can better understand their team members' challenges, strengths, and aspirations. This understanding fosters a supportive environment where people feel valued and heard, which is fundamental to effective and compassionate leadership. A study published in *Psychological Science* by Condon and colleagues has shown that mindfulness practices can increase prosocial behaviors, such as helping and cooperation, thereby strengthening our ability to care for and connect with others on a deeper level. Another study published in *Mindfulness* by Boellinghaus and colleagues found that regular mindfulness practice is associated with greater compassion and empathy, which are critical components of caring relationships.

Mindfulness practice brings personal benefits to leaders by enhancing their capabilities across multiple aspects. It improves emotional regulation, enabling leaders to manage stress, remain calm under pressure, and respond thoughtfully rather than react impulsively. This emotional stability fosters better decision-making, as leaders can approach challenges with clarity and objectivity. Mindfulness also sharpens focus and concentration, allowing leaders to prioritize tasks effectively and maintain productivity amid distractions.

Ultimately, mindfulness empowers leaders to create a balanced, resilient, and supportive leadership style that drives both personal and organizational success. For leaders, this translates into a greater sense of fulfillment and happiness.

To practice mindfulness, focus on your breathing for a few minutes daily, paying close attention to each inhale and exhale. Additionally, engage in activities like meditation or mindful walking, where you stay fully present and aware of your thoughts, sensations, and surroundings without judgment.

13.4 Genuine Concern and Interest for Employees

To win in the marketplace you must first win in the workplace.
—Doug Conant, former chief executive officer,
Campbell Soup Company

In today's interconnected and often remote work environment, demonstrating genuine concern and interest in others is more important than ever. One effective way to show this concern is through active listening. Active listening goes beyond merely hearing words; it involves engaging with the speaker, asking thoughtful questions, and providing feedback that shows understanding and empathy. This type of listening promotes discovery and insight, allowing individuals to feel truly heard and valued. By practicing active listening, leaders can demonstrate warmth and can connect with their employees, fostering a culture of respect and collaboration.

Another critical aspect of showing genuine concern is attending to the personal needs of employees, especially when unexpected circumstances arise. Whether it's a family emergency, health issue, or any other personal challenge, providing support and flexibility demonstrates that you care about your employees as individuals, not just as workers. This can be done through flexible work arrangements, additional leave, or simply offering a listening ear and emotional support. When employees feel that their personal well-being is a priority, they are more likely to remain loyal, productive, and engaged in their work.

Moreover, when people believe that you care for them genuinely, they become more amenable to your influence. They are more likely to go above and beyond in their roles, showing higher levels of productivity and engagement. They are also more open to feedback and more willing to adapt to changes. This level of trust is not built overnight but through consistent actions that demonstrate genuine concern and interest in their well-being.

Sharing information and knowledge is another powerful way to show that you care. Transparency in communication and providing opportunities for learning and development can significantly impact how employees perceive their value within the organization. Leaders who take an active interest in their employees' growth by offering training, mentorship, and career development opportunities signal a deep investment in their future. This not only enhances the skills and capabilities of the workforce but also strengthens their commitment to the organization.

Lastly, taking a strong interest in the personal and professional growth of employees can have a transformative effect on organizational culture. By recognizing and nurturing individual talents and aspirations, leaders can create an environment where everyone feels valued and motivated to contribute their best. This approach leads to a more engaged and innovative workforce, driving the organization toward greater success. In conclusion, showing genuine concern for and interest in others is not just a moral imperative but a strategic one—essential for building trust, fostering engagement, and achieving long-term organizational success.

13.5 Stop Carewashing: Make Your Wellness Program Work

Sometimes, leaders aren't aware that what they're doing is ineffective. Sometimes, they're consciously ignoring it, potentially.

—Deloitte Insights

"Carewashing" is the organizational equivalent of a shiny car wash: it polishes the surface with feel-good wellness slogans and token gestures, while leaving the deeper issues—work overload, burnout, toxic culture, or poor leadership—untouched. Just as a clean exterior can't fix a broken engine, performative care without structural change does little to truly support employees.

Is your company's wellness program a case of carewashing? Examine your beliefs and actions in light of the reality on the ground—and what your employees think.

Wellness programs are everywhere these days, widely promoted as essential tools for boosting employee retention and reducing healthcare costs. Corporate wellness gained momentum in the 1990s and 2000s, fueled by a combination of economic pressures, cultural shifts toward preventive health, and mounting concerns over chronic illness from work stress. Influential studies—such as those cited in a 2010 *Harvard Business Review* article titled "What's the Hard Return on Employee Wellness Programs?"—claimed that such programs could deliver impressive returns. One study cited a $6 return for every dollar spent on wellness initiatives, while Johnson & Johnson estimated saving $250 million on healthcare costs between 2002 and 2008, with a return of $2.71 for every dollar invested. These figures helped cement the belief that wellness programs weren't just ethically sound. They made economic sense.

But if wellness is so widely embraced and financially supported, why is it failing to deliver in today's workplace, dominated by Millennials and Gen Z? In January 2024, the *New York Times* reported findings from a study by an Oxford researcher involving 46,333 workers across 236 organizations. The study concluded that the use of a wide range of digital wellness solutions—mindfulness seminars, massage classes, resilience workshops, coaching sessions, and sleep apps—made no meaningful difference between those who participated and those who did not. According to the 2024 *Harvard Business Review* article "Why Workplace Well-Being Programs Don't Achieve Better Outcomes," companies are pouring billions into employee wellness with little to show for it. Nearly 85% of large US employers now offer some form of well-being program, and global corporate spending on wellness is projected to surpass $94.6 billion by 2026. Despite this investment, burnout, disengagement, and mental health challenges among employees continue to rise. This troubling disconnect points to a deeper issue—not a lack of concern or good intention, but a lack of meaningful action.

The authors of the *HBR* article—Jazz Croft, Acacia Parks, and Ashley Whillans—argue that many organizations have fallen the carewashing trap: superficially promoting wellness without addressing the systemic causes of stress, exhaustion, and disengagement. The authors outline five key reasons why wellness programs frequently fall short:

1. **They ignore root causes**—Programs target individual behavior instead of fixing systemic stressors like workload and poor job design
2. **They feel hypocritical**—Promoting self-care feels hollow when workplace pressures remain unchanged.
3. **They suffer from low engagement**—Many employees don't participate due to stigma, lack of time, or unclear benefits.
4. **They don't delivery measurable outcomes**—Studies show minimal impact on well-being, often because healthier employees are the main users, and
5. **They lack leadership buy-in**—Without visible support and accountability, programs lose credibility and momentum.

At the heart of this failure is what the authors describe as the *I-frame* (individual-level interventions) versus the *S-frame* (systemic interventions) approach to wellness. The *I-frame* focuses on individual behaviors—offering mindfulness apps, sleep challenges, or stress management tips—assuming that personal improvement alone will lead to well-being. While these tools can be helpful, they often miss the mark by ignoring organizational realities. The *S-frame*, by contrast, targets the structural causes of stress: inflexible work hours, excessive workloads, poor management, and lack of autonomy. Without addressing these systemic issues, well-being efforts come across as tone-deaf, or, worse, manipulative. When leaders tell employees to "breathe deeply" while keeping them chronically overworked and unsupported, employees rightly see it as hypocrisy.

The failures of the wellness programs are often rooted in an overreliance on the *I-frame*. Leaders who are serious about employee well-being must shift their focus to the *S-frame*—acknowledging and changing the organizational structures that drive employee distress. That means aligning policies with what employees say they need, rethinking workloads, granting flexible schedules, creating psychologically safe teams, and training managers to lead with emotional intelligence. It also means embedding well-being into leadership KPIs and tying executive compensation to engagement and retention metrics. Leaders must go beyond symbolic gestures and demonstrate commitment through transparent action and accountability.

A caring organization is not one that simply encourages people to meditate—it's one that listens, reforms, and empowers. When wellness becomes a structural value rather than a superficial perk, it begins to truly work.

13.6 Caring Leadership and Inclusive Employee Engagement

We are more alike, my friends,
than we are unalike.

Maya Angelou

Fostering a culture of belonging, fairness, and opportunity has become a defining principle of modern leadership—particularly in an era when organizations recognize that fairness and inclusivity are not only moral imperatives but also strategic assets. True inclusive leadership extends beyond surface-level representation; it involves creating environments where diverse perspectives can flourish through constructive dialogue and equitable decision-making.

Andy Grove, Intel's former CEO, exemplified this philosophy through his principle of "constructive confrontation." He encouraged open, data-driven debates that allowed employees at all levels to challenge ideas, ensuring that decisions were scrutinized from multiple perspectives. Grove's approach fostered transparency and mutual respect, breaking down hierarchical barriers and ensuring that innovation emerged from collaborative problem-solving rather than top-down directives. This model highlights that true leadership isn't about avoiding disagreements but about creating an inclusive environment where differing viewpoints lead to better, well-informed decisions.

Importantly, by "inclusivity," we don't mean diversity, equity, and inclusion (DEI)—a framework often centered on identity-based representation, equity policies, and demographic targets. Rather, we advocate for creating a culture where everyone feels genuinely valued, heard, and empowered—regardless of background. As noted in the *Harvard Business Review* article "Achieve DEI Goals Without DEI Programs," published in the July–August 2025 issue, many well-intentioned DEI efforts falter when they rely solely on formal programs and compliance checklists instead of embedding inclusive practices in everyday work. The authors caution that overemphasizing formal DEI policies and dashboards can foster resentment and superficial compliance. When inclusion becomes a strategy instead of a shared value, employees may experience the workplace as fragmented or politicized. Instead, the authors recommend integrating inclusion into core talent systems—recruitment, onboarding, team support, and retention—so that fairness and engagement become organizational norms rather than checkbox exercises. Inclusivity, in this sense, is not about special treatment;

it's about ensuring equal opportunity, fair treatment, and a sense of belonging for all.

This kind of leadership calls for actively identifying and removing barriers—such as bias, unclear policies, or unequal access—that prevent people from fully contributing. Bias doesn't always come from ill intent—often, it hides behind comfort and routine. But when ignored, it quietly warps decisions about who gets hired, heard, supported, or promoted. Ask yourself: Whose voice carries weight? Who's allowed to stumble and recover? Whose struggles prompt empathy—and whose don't? The truth lies not in metrics, but in your answers.

The solution to the recent backlash against DEI, according to the HBR article, is to shift from programmatic DEI to human-centered inclusion. This means creating "everyday systems of care" where fairness and empathy are baked into hiring, team dynamics, recognition, and conflict resolution. Leaders must become culture shapers—not just policy enforcers—by setting the tone, modeling inclusive behavior, and making inclusion an organizational norm, not an exception. When fairness is embedded in workplace culture, it benefits everyone. It fosters trust, drives innovation, strengthens cohesion, and anchors inclusivity as a foundation of effective leadership and organizational excellence. The importance of such inclusivity is underscored by research indicating that diverse teams are more innovative and effective, because they bring a wider range of ideas and solutions to the table. For instance, McKinsey's research shows that companies within the top 25% for racial and ethnic diversity are 39% more likely to financially outperform the bottom 25% companies. The business case for gender diversity on executive teams has strengthened significantly over the past decade, with top-quartile companies now 39% more likely to financially outperform their bottom-quartile peers—up from 15% in 2015. Additionally, research by the Boston Consulting Group found that companies with more diverse management teams have 19% higher revenues due to innovation.

The advantages of constructive, inclusive leadership extend beyond financial performance. They shape company culture, attract top talent, reduce turnover, and enhance an organization's reputation. Companies seen as leaders in inclusivity are more likely to gain the trust and loyalty of employees and customers. For instance, a report by Glassdoor revealed that 76% of job seekers consider a diverse workforce an important factor when evaluating companies and job offers. By fostering an environment where everyone feels valued and empowered, leaders unlock the full potential of their workforce. By integrating principles of constructive dialogue, trust, and inclusivity, leaders drive sustainable innovation, employee satisfaction, and long-term organizational success. Great leadership creates a culture where diverse ideas are actively sought out, welcomed, and leveraged to fuel meaningful growth.

13.7 Leaders and Followers: A Symbiosis of Care

Leadership is not about being in charge. It is about taking care of those in your charge.

—Simon Sinek

There exists a powerful symbiosis between leaders and followers, a delicate balance where each relies on the other for success. If leaders and followers do not genuinely care for the success of each other, both are destined to falter. A leader without committed followers is a voice in the wilderness, and followers without a leader's guidance are a ship without a compass. This mutual care and investment are not just beneficial—they are imperative. When leaders and followers engage in this reciprocal relationship, they create a resilient, unstoppable force capable of surmounting any challenge and reaching new heights of collective achievement.

Followers are not merely the backbone of a leader's success—they are the lifeblood, the driving force that transforms vision into reality. They offer essential support, carry out critical actions, and provide invaluable feedback that propels an organization toward achieving its goals. Buckingham and Goodall, in their book *Nine Lies About Work*, emphasize that leadership effectiveness is largely determined by how followers perceive and respond to the leader. Leaders may set visions and strategies, but without followers' buy-in and active participation, these plans are unlikely to come to fruition. The concept of "followership," as articulated by Robert E. Kelley in his book *The Power of Followership*, highlights that effective followers possess critical thinking, self-management, and the ability to work collaboratively toward a leader's vision. Kelley argues that followers are not merely passive recipients of leadership but active participants whose actions can significantly influence outcomes. This underscores the idea that leaders need followers who are not only competent but also committed, engaged, and invested in the success of their leaders.

The Leader-Member Exchange (LMX) theory, developed by George Graen and Mary Uhl-Bien, posits that the quality of the relationships between leaders and followers impacts various organizational outcomes, including job satisfaction, productivity, and turnover. High-quality LMX relationships are characterized by mutual trust, respect, and obligation, which can lead to enhanced follower performance and discretionary behaviors that benefit the organization. Essentially, leaders are made more effective through the reciprocal and supportive relationships they build with their followers. In addition, the *social identity theory of leadership* suggests that leaders emerge and gain legitimacy through the support of their followers. This theory posits that followers are more likely to endorse leaders who embody the group's values and identity, thereby granting the leaders influence and authority.

13.8 The Business Case for Caring Leadership

Your employees come first. And if you treat your employees right, guess what? Your customers come back, and that makes your shareholders happy.

—Herb Kelleher, cofounder, Southwest Airlines

Leaders who *Care more for their people than others think reasonable foster* a work environment characterized by trust, loyalty, and high morale. Studies have consistently shown that employees who feel valued and cared for by their leaders are more engaged and productive. According to a 2017 Gallup study, companies with highly engaged workforces achieved 115% growth in earnings per share between 2011 and 2015, compared to just 27% among their less engaged peers. Highly engaged workforces also had 41% lower absenteeism and 70% fewer safety incidents. Furthermore, a 2016 report by *Harvard Business Review* Analytic Services concluded that a "highly engaged workforce can increase innovation, productivity, and bottom-line performance while reducing costs related to hiring and retention in highly competitive talent markets." By demonstrating genuine care, leaders can significantly enhance employee retention and performance, driving long-term organizational success.

At Woodard & Curran, a privately owned top-100 engineering design firm based in Portland, Maine, the "People First" value is a cornerstone of its organizational philosophy, emphasizing that the well-being, growth, and satisfaction of employees are paramount. This principle is rooted in the belief that when employees are nurtured and valued, they are empowered to deliver exceptional service and innovative solutions to clients. At Woodard & Curran, *People First* means fostering a supportive and inclusive workplace culture where individuals are encouraged to bring their whole selves to work, collaborate openly, and pursue continuous learning. By prioritizing their workforce, Woodard & Curran not only enhances employee engagement and retention but also drives long-term business success and client satisfaction, demonstrating that taking care of people is the key to thriving in the fiercely competitive landscape of environmental and engineering consulting.

Companies that prioritize employee well-being see tangible benefits, including reduced absenteeism and lower turnover rates. Simon Sinek, author and motivational speaker, observed, "When people are financially invested, they want a return. When people are emotionally invested, they want to contribute." Deloitte studies reveal that mission-driven organizations with a strong sense of purpose and care for their employees report 30% higher levels of innovation and 40% higher employee retention, and they tend to rank first or second in their market segment. This correlation underscores the importance of leaders going above and beyond in their care for employees to cultivate a thriving, innovative workplace.

Treat people like volunteers. The idea is that nobody has to work for you. They all have a choice. It's our assignment to be able to energize them and influence them so that they all want to be around us.
—Bill Amelio, chief executive officer, Lenovo Group Limited

Moreover, caring leadership can enhance a company's reputation and customer loyalty. Businesses known for their ethical and caring practices attract top talent and loyal customers who value those principles. For example, Patagonia's commitment to employee well-being and environmental responsibility has not only driven their business success but also built a strong, loyal customer base. A survey by Cone Communications found that 87% of consumers would purchase a product because a company advocated for an issue they cared about, while 76% would refuse to buy a company's products or services upon learning it supported an issue contrary to their beliefs. Leaders who demonstrate an extraordinary level of care not only benefit their employees but also enhance their company's overall brand and customer loyalty.

13.9 Caring Leadership Must Be Visible

Kindness is the language which the deaf can hear and the blind can see.
                                                    —Mark Twain

Leadership is not a hidden talent; it must be visible in your actions— actions that demonstrate your commitment to something bigger than yourself. That commitment must be evident in your willingness to confront and dismantle the barriers that perpetuate inequality and injustice in the workplace.

This principle is powerfully illustrated in the 2016 American movie *Hidden Figures*, which tells the inspiring story of three Black mathematicians who worked at NASA in the 1960s. During a time of intense racial segregation, these women faced enormous challenges, including being denied access to the same restrooms as their white colleagues. Yet their perseverance and dedication were instrumental in America's space race.

In one memorable scene from the movie, the project leader, Al Harrison (portrayed by Kevin Costner) discovers that one of his top mathematicians, Katherine Johnson (played by Taraji P. Henson), has been running half a mile several times a day to use the restroom designated for black employees. Upon learning this, Harrison takes decisive action. He smashes the *Colored Ladies Room* sign, declaring that at NASA, everyone can use the same restroom. His actions are not just about addressing a logistical issue; they symbolize his commitment to equality and his understanding that true leadership requires visible, impactful actions.

This scene powerfully demonstrates that caring leadership must be visible. Harrison's actions send a clear message to his team that he values all his employees equally and that he is committed to eliminating barriers that hinder their productivity and well-being. By publicly addressing the issue, Harrison not only solves a practical problem but also fosters a more inclusive and supportive work environment. His leadership extends beyond the immediate goal of sending an American to space; it encompasses creating a workplace where every individual feels valued and empowered.

In 2015, Dan Price, cofounder and CEO of Gravity Payments, made global headlines by slashing his $1.1 million salary to $70,000 and redirecting company profits to fund a $70,000 minimum wage for all 120 employees—a move aligned with the principles of caring leadership. While the policy reduced turnover and helped increase revenue from $3.8 million in 2015 to $14 million in 2021, it also faced criticism regarding pay equity and long-term sustainability. Price's personal sacrifices—including taking on debt during COVID-19 to maintain employee salaries—underscored his commitment to the initiative. The case remains a polarizing yet landmark example of radical wage reform that prioritized the happiness and well-being of the entire team.

13.10 Show You Care: Shield, Don't Shame

If you shut the door to all errors, truth will be shut out.
—Rabindranath Tagore

A truly caring leader understands that mistakes are an inevitable part of growth and should never be met with punishment or harsh words. Instead of reacting with frustration, great leaders recognize mistakes as valuable learning opportunities that can strengthen individuals and teams.

Instead of penalizing mistakes, leaders should focus on guiding employees through the resolution process in a way that builds confidence and trust. When mistakes happen, follow these steps to turn challenges into opportunities:

Pause and assess. Instead of reacting emotionally, take a moment to evaluate the situation objectively. Is the mistake due to lack of knowledge, unclear instructions, or process gaps? Understanding the root cause helps you respond constructively.

Lead with curiosity, not judgment. Ask open-ended questions to encourage employees to reflect,

"What do you think went wrong?"
"What could we do differently next time?"
"How can I support you in improving this?"

This approach fosters problem-solving rather than fear of punishment.

Create a fix-it plan together. Instead of pointing fingers, collaborate on a solution. Encourage employees to take ownership by asking, "What steps can we take to correct this?" Offer support while allowing them to lead the resolution process, which builds confidence and accountability.

Turn it into a learning experience. Reinforce that mistakes are not failures but stepping-stones to growth. Share past examples of how similar challenges have led to improvements and innovation. Consider hosting team debriefs where lessons learned are discussed openly to prevent repeated errors.

Shield, don't shame. When mistakes affect clients or stakeholders, own the responsibility as a leader instead of shifting blame to employees. Protect your team from undue criticism and work behind the scenes to address concerns professionally. Strong leaders uplift their teams rather than expose them to blame.

Too often, managers react with anger or punitive measures when things go wrong—sometimes out of ego, sometimes out of fear that failure will reflect poorly on them. This pressure can trickle down from their own leaders, creating a toxic cycle of blame that stifles creativity, discourages risk-taking, and ultimately weakens the organization. This cycle must be broken. True leadership means standing up for your team, ensuring that they feel supported even in difficult situations. A culture of trust and accountability, rather than fear, fosters stronger teams, better results, and long-term success.

13.11 Show You Care: Combat Bad Leadership

Bad leaders do not typically wake up one morning and say, "Golly gee, I've been bad. I need to change my ways." They will stop being bad only if someone else or something else stops them. And if nothing stops them and no one stops them, they will go from bad to worse.

—Barbara Kellerman

Leadership is not just about holding a title or position; it is about taking visible actions that reflect your commitment to a purpose greater than yourself. Nothing undermines this visibility of care more than tolerating or ignoring bad leadership within your organization. Poor leadership is not merely an annoyance; it is a destructive force that sows mistrust, diminishes morale, and spreads unhappiness. A Gallup study found that 50% of employees leave their jobs to escape bad managers, while a McKinsey report revealed that toxic workplace behaviors are the top reason employees resign, outranking even pay and benefits. Additionally, the American Psychological Association (APA) reports that toxic workplaces, often driven by poor leadership, contribute to a 70% increase in employee mental health issues.

These statistics make one thing clear: combating bad leadership within your organization is essential. Addressing it firmly yet respectfully within your power or sphere of influence can transform your workplace into an environment where leaders and followers alike can thrive. Harvard University professor Barbara Kellerman, an esteemed authority on leadership studies, argues persuasively in *Leadership from Bad to Worse* that leadership failure is not isolated to a few "bad apples." Instead, it exists on a spectrum, ranging from incompetence and negligence to outright unethical behavior. Kellerman's extensive research highlights that bad leadership persists not only because of the actions of those in power but also due to systemic complicity and followers' reluctance to challenge the status quo. Addressing these failures is not the sole responsibility of those at the top; it requires shared accountability at every level of an organization. When you actively combat poor leadership, you demonstrate genuine care for your team, shielding them from the harmful effects that undermine individual and collective success.

Unchecked power erodes trust and ethical standards, leading to a cascade of negative outcomes, as Kellerman emphasizes. Embedding practices that promote transparency—such as regular performance reviews, 360-degree feedback, and leadership training focused on ethical decision-making—can counteract this. These mechanisms are not mere formalities; they send a clear message that bad behavior will not be tolerated. Implementing such structures reinforces that care extends beyond words into tangible actions, creating an environment where integrity is nonnegotiable. Moreover, promoting diversity and inclusion is crucial in preventing the stagnation that bad leadership often fosters. Kellerman underscores that leadership operating within a homogeneous environment—where backgrounds, perspectives, and experiences lack diversity—is prone to toxic behaviors and group-think. By assembling diverse leadership teams, organizations empower individuals to voice concerns and hold each other accountable, bolstering ethical decision-making and safeguarding against complacency. Research confirms that when organizations prioritize inclusivity, they cultivate cultures in which accountability is collectively embraced, lowering the risk of unethical leadership.

Another pivotal step in combating bad leadership is dismantling toxic workplace cultures. Such cultures—which reward unchecked ambition, aggression, and rigid hierarchies—enable leaders who prioritize personal gain over their teams' well-being. A 2022 *MIT Sloan Management Review* article titled "Why Every Leader Needs to Worry about Toxic Culture" revealed that toxic workplace environments cost US employers nearly $50 billion a year due to avoidable turnover. The article identified the "Toxic Five" elements most predictive of a toxic culture:

1. **Disrespect,** where employees feel dismissed or under-valued.
2. **Noninclusiveness,** marked by a lack of diversity, equity, and belonging.
3. **Unethical behavior,** involving violations of integrity or company values.
4. **Cutthroat competition,** which undermines collaboration and fosters internal sabotage.
5. **Abusive management,** characterized by bullying, intimidation, or mistreatment by those in power.

Combating these elements requires both top-down leadership reform and grassroots empowerment. Leaders must model humility, transparency, and a commitment to serving their teams, while followers need safe channels to report the Toxic Five without fear of retaliation.

Breaking the cycle of toxic leadership involves redefining organizational standards to prioritize respect, mutual accountability, and constructive dialogue. Furthermore, continuous education, development, and oversight are essential to sustaining high leadership standards. Bad leadership often persists because systems reward stagnation, not merely because leaders lack training. Many leaders refuse to evolve and focus solely on the mechanics of power without cultivating the moral compass needed to wield it effectively. Therefore, sustainable change requires institutional accountability, such as removing protections for toxic leaders. Demonstrating visible care for your organization means addressing bad leadership head-on, fostering accountability, and creating environments where ethical leadership can thrive. By doing so, you ensure that leadership fulfills its promise as a force for trust, growth, and ethical stewardship.

13.12 Show You Care: Select Good Leaders

The greatest leader is not necessarily the one who does the greatest things. He is the one that gets the people to do the greatest things.
—Ronald Reagan

One of the most defining responsibilities of senior leaders is selecting and promoting individuals into management and leadership roles. This single decision shapes the culture of an organization for years to come, influencing the well-being, engagement, and success of employees at every level. A well-chosen leader fosters a thriving, ethical, and high-performing environment, while a poor selection can stifle growth, create toxicity, and push talented individuals out the door.

If you care about your people, you will ensure they work under good leaders. Just as combating bad leadership is essential, so is actively selecting and promoting the right leaders—those who inspire, uplift, and create environments where people thrive. Every time you are in a position to select or advocate for a leader, you are making a statement about what you value. Do you prioritize the well-being of your employees by ensuring they work under strong, compassionate leaders, or do you default to outdated promotion models that reward technical skills over leadership ability? Research from McKinsey reveals that the quality of leadership is the number-one driver of employee engagement and organizational performance. Every leadership selection is, therefore, a direct investment in—or risk to—a company's health.

Despite this immense responsibility, many organizations fail to approach leadership selection with the necessary rigor and intentionality. A Gallup study found that companies fail to hire the right person for management roles 82% of the time, often prioritizing technical skills or tenure over emotional intelligence, humility, and ethical decision-making. Research cited in a *Harvard Business Review* article revealed that a staggering 75% of American employees consider their direct manager to be the most stressful part of their job, and 65% said they would willingly accept a pay cut if it meant having a better boss.

Tomas Chamorro-Premuzic's *Why Do So Many Incompetent Men Become Leaders?* highlights a troubling pattern in leadership selection. Many organizations unknowingly favor confidence over competence and charisma over humility, leading to the frequent promotion of individuals who appear strong and assertive but ultimately lack the qualities necessary to lead effectively. He argues that traditional leadership pipelines reward traits associated with narcissism, overconfidence, and dominance, despite evidence that the best leaders exhibit humility, self-awareness, and a commitment to developing others. This misalignment between who is promoted and who should be promoted has long-term consequences, resulting in low employee morale, high turnover, and poor decision-making at the highest levels.

One of the biggest mistakes organizations make is promoting based on past performance rather than leadership potential. Just because someone excels in their current role does not mean they are equipped to lead others. Many organizations promote top performers into management positions, only to find that they lack the interpersonal skills, vision, and adaptability needed to succeed as leaders. Chamorro-Premuzic's research further reveals that organizations often conflate leadership emergence with leadership effectiveness. Just because someone rises quickly through the ranks does not mean that person is a good leader. Many individuals receive promotions because they are bold, decisive, and self-promoting, rather than having the ability to mentor, inspire, or build trust. This fundamental flaw in leadership selection explains why so many ineffective leaders remain in power, while more competent but less self-promotional individuals are overlooked.

The best leaders are not just high achievers—they enable success for others. They demonstrate empathy, emotional intelligence, ethical decision making, adaptability, and the ability to inspire. When leadership selection is based solely on past performance, organizations risk promoting individuals who lack these critical traits, creating a cycle of ineffective management. If you wouldn't entrust your best employees to a poor leader, why promote one in the first place?

To ensure that the right people step into leadership roles, organizations must institutionalize better selection processes that prioritize leadership potential over technical proficiency alone. As Chamorro-Premuzic warns, "If we want better leaders, we must change the way we define, select, and reward leadership." The future of leadership depends on intentional, courageous choices—because who we promote today will define the workplace for generations to come.

13.13 Show You Care: Turn Employee Feedback into Action

He who knows all the answers has not been asked all the questions.
                                                    —Confucius

Throughout this book, you'll notice frequent mention of the actionable step "Seek and value feedback." However, organizations and leaders often fall into the trap of merely seeking feedback without truly valuing it. Valuing feedback means taking meaningful action based on what employees share—a visible sign that you care. As emphasized in the 2024 *Harvard Business Review* article "Turn Employee Feedback into Action," the core challenge in many organizations is not "survey fatigue" but rather "inaction fatigue." When employees see their input solicited repeatedly but rarely acted upon, they disengage, losing trust in leadership and the feedback process. Conversely, taking visible steps—even small ones—signals care, builds credibility, and fosters a stronger employer-employee relationship. Turning feedback into action is not just a process; it is a hallmark of caring leadership.

The *HBR* article highlights a structured and transparent approach as essential to overcoming inaction fatigue. Organizations must address seven key challenges: (1) Making sense of extensive data, (2) ensuring employees feel heard, (3) identifying root problems, (4) protecting privacy, (5) navigating conflicting views, (6) addressing negative feedback, and (7) following up meaningfully.

For example, Microsoft has successfully tackled these issues by creating centralized systems and specialized listening teams composed of data scientists, organizational psychologists, and analysts. These teams not only streamline feedback collection but also ensure that insights are actionable and address employees' most pressing concerns. By taking visible and measurable actions, leaders demonstrate to employees that their concerns matter, reinforcing trust and commitment.

Clear and consistent communication is equally vital. Leaders who excel in acting on feedback openly share survey results, summarize actionable themes, and outline the steps being taken. For instance, a CEO addressing survey findings in company-wide meetings or town halls can set the tone for transparency and accountability, visibly showing care through their engagement. Such transparency reassures employees that their voices matter and builds trust by demonstrating follow-through.

By addressing feedback thoughtfully and visibly, leaders create a culture of care where employees feel valued and empowered. This approach not only improves satisfaction and retention but also drives innovation, boosts morale, and enhances customer satisfaction. Leadership that turns feedback into action sends a powerful message: "We hear you, and we care." This visible action transforms feedback into a cornerstone of organizational success and caring leadership.

13.14 Caring Leadership: Reimagining Performance Appraisal

Performance appraisal aims at controlling an individual's behavior to the satisfaction of his or her manager.

—Peter Scholtes

Have you ever considered that performance appraisal could be more than what it is today—a system of judgment and rankings, tied to bonuses, rewards, promotions, and even subtle or overt punishment? Caring leadership challenges us to reimagine performance appraisals— not as backward-looking evaluations, but as forward-focused commitments to unlocking potential, fostering excellence, and inspiring continuous growth.

Performance appraisals were introduced into corporate settings in the 1920s and 1930s, influenced by Frederick Taylor's scientific management principles (Taylorism), with a focus on efficiency, productivity, and structured evaluation. As the command-and-control management system became entrenched in organizations over time, so did a performance appraisal system. However, cracks in the system began to appear in the 1970s. In 1982, W. Edwards Deming, the father of Total Quality Management (TQM), published *Out of the Crisis*, in which he identified "evaluation by performance, merit ratings, and annual reviews" as one of the seven deadly diseases of management. He argued that these practices cripple organizations and hinder long-term success. In 1993, Peter Scholtes, a quality management expert and author of *The Leader's Handbook*, published an article titled "Total Quality or Performance Appraisal: Choose One" in the *National Productivity Review* advocating for the complete abolition of performance appraisals.

Yet more than 30 years later, performance appraisals remain deeply entrenched in organizational practices. A 2023 report by the Talent Strategy Group indicates that 90% of companies still use performance ratings, with the majority employing a 5-point rating scale as a standardized evaluation method. A 2015 *Harvard Business Review* article revealed that Deloitte "found that completing the forms, holding the meetings, and creating the ratings consumed close to 2 million hours a year" for its 65,000 employees, averaging approximately 31 hours per employee annually.

Despite the widespread use and staggering costs, the effectiveness of performance appraisal systems remains in question. According to a Gallup survey, only 21% of employees strongly agree that their performance is managed in a way that motivates them to do outstanding work—meaning that the vast majority, 79%, lack confidence in the performance management process. Even more striking, only 2% of chief human resource officers (CHROs) from Fortune 500 companies strongly agree that their performance management system inspires employees to improve. In 2023, the Society for Human Resource Management reported that 95% of managers are dissatisfied with their organization's performance review system. This overwhelming dissatisfaction is a clear sign that most performance management practices are outdated—yet many companies continue relying on the same ineffective tactics, hoping for different results.

A *Vanity Fair* article based on interviews with Microsoft employees revealed that after implementing stack ranking —a performance management system that forces managers to rank employees against one another, typically designating a set percentage as low performers—employee engagement plummeted, and top talent left due to a toxic performance culture. A 2017 Adobe study showed that 47% of Millennials started looking for a different job after receiving their performance review, highlighting the potential negative impact of conventional evaluation methods on employee retention among younger generations, who increasingly value continuous feedback over formal reviews. Earlier studies suggest that Gen X and baby boomers were more accustomed to traditional reviews, though many also found them transactional rather than useful.

These findings suggest that while performance ratings remain deeply embedded in corporate structures, they often weaken trust, suppress collaboration, and create a fear-driven environment where employees focus more on securing a favorable rating than on actual growth and contribution. The question at hand is this: has the time come to abandon performance appraisals entirely, or should they be reimagined under a purpose-driven and caring leadership paradigm? For decades, performance reviews have operated on a carrot-and-stick model, rewarding top performers while subtly or overtly penalizing those who struggle. The intent may have been to drive efficiency and accountability, but the result has often been low morale, disengagement, and a lack of trust between employees and leadership. Annual reviews that look backward rather than forward fail to capture real progress, leaving employees disconnected from their growth potential and managers frustrated by an outdated tool. Quantum Workplace research reveals that a lack of recognition is one of the top three reasons employees leave their jobs. I experienced this firsthand. My motivation and sense of value steadily declined in my first job due to the absence of acknowledgment for my efforts, ultimately leading me to resign. Traditional annual performance evaluations and sporadic recognition are no longer effective in today's workplace. Studies show that increasing the frequency of recognition from quarterly to monthly can boost employee engagement and productivity by 40%, and increase job commitment by 25%. These findings underscore the importance of consistent and timely recognition in building up a committed and motivated workforce.

If performance appraisals are to serve their true purpose, they must shift from a judgment tool to a development framework. Leaders who truly care about their teams recognize that performance evaluations should be designed to create success, not just measure it. This means replacing rigid ranking systems with continuous, meaningful conversations that focus on learning, development, and goal alignment.

Feedback—actionable, constructive, trackable, and influential—is the informational and motivational coin of the digital realm in the post-pandemic distributed workforce.

—Michael Schrage,
MIT Sloan Management Review

Companies like Adobe, Microsoft, and Accenture have already abandoned annual reviews in favor of real-time feedback loops, coaching sessions, and data-driven performance tracking.

Leaders should take the following actions to drive modern performance management:

◇ **First fix systemic issues.** Proactively identify and eliminate barriers in processes, resources, and workplace culture that hinder performance. Instead of blaming individuals, leaders must first optimize systems to create an environment where employees can thrive and succeed.

◇ **Conduct frequent check-ins.** Provide timely, constructive feedback to keep employees engaged and on track, rather than waiting for an annual review.

◇ **Coach, don't judge.** Mentor employees to foster a supportive environment where they feel empowered to learn, grow, and contribute. Actively develop employees' skills and guide their career progression instead of merely assessing past performance.

◇ **Create personalized development plans.** Align employees' contributions with their professional growth and business success to drive meaningful progress.

◇ **Develop a culture of frequent recognition.** Move beyond annual or quarterly acknowledgments by recognizing employee contributions at least monthly. Encourage managers to regularly celebrate small wins, personalize appreciation, and integrate recognition into team meetings, peer feedback, and digital communication channels to foster a motivated and loyal workforce.

This shift is not just an ideological preference; it's a business necessity. Research shows that Millennials and Gen Z, who now dominate the workforce, reject rigid performance rankings and instead seek ongoing feedback, career development, and purpose-driven work. Organizations that fail to adapt their performance management approach risk losing top talent to companies that understand employees thrive in growth-focused, flexible, and values-driven workplaces.

That said, caring leadership does not mean avoiding accountability. High performers still need to be recognized and rewarded—but in a way that acknowledges both their individual contributions and long-term potential. Compensation structures should link performance to growth opportunities, ensuring that employees see a clear connection between their efforts and career advancement. For those struggling, the response should not be punishment, but rather a proactive approach to diagnosing barriers—whether they stem from skill gaps, misalignment with role expectations, or external challenges—and offering meaningful support.

The question is not whether performance appraisals should exist, but rather, are we using them to develop employees or to judge them? The future of performance management must be transparent, growth-oriented, and centered on unlocking human potential. Leaders must ask themselves,

- ◈ Are we empowering employees—or just rating them?
- ◈ Are we measuring what truly matters—or just checking a box?
- ◈ Are we coaches and mentors—or just evaluators?

Performance appraisals should inspire, not intimidate. Organizations that embrace growth-driven performance management build cultures of trust, innovation, and high engagement—where employees and the business thrive. The time for change is now. Caring leaders do not just manage performance; they cultivate it.

13.15 A Caring Leader Is a Multiplier

Great leaders do not create followers. They create more leaders.

—Tom Peters

Our greatest happiness often stems from helping others, a sentiment that philosophers, psychologists, and spiritual leaders have echoed throughout history. This notion extends seamlessly into the realm of leadership, where the focus on creating leaders rather than followers fosters an environment that nurtures and multiplies leadership qualities across an organization. As discussed earlier, Liz Wiseman, in her book *Multipliers: How the Best Leaders Make Everyone Smarter*, categorizes leaders into "multipliers" and "diminishers." *Multipliers* amplify the intelligence and capabilities of their team members, thereby creating more leaders. They encourage innovation, foster collaboration, and challenge their teams to reach their full potential. In contrast, *diminishers* stifle growth and creativity by micromanaging and hoarding decision-making power. Wiseman's research highlights that multipliers enhance team intelligence and productivity while also inspiring and engaging their teams—creating a culture where individuals feel valued and empowered, leading to greater job satisfaction and overall happiness.

Being a multiplier requires a deep commitment to the growth of one's team, involving key behaviors such as encouraging autonomy, fostering a growth mindset, and recognizing and developing talent. These behaviors directly impact the happiness of team members. For instance, when leaders delegate effectively and provide opportunities for professional growth, employees feel more engaged and motivated. This sense of growth and contribution is crucial for long-term happiness. Furthermore, multipliers cultivate a supportive environment where collaboration and innovation are encouraged, resulting in a more dynamic and enjoyable work experience. As Wiseman states, "Multipliers invoke each person's unique intelligence and create an atmosphere of genius—innovation, productive effort, and collective intelligence."

The concept of a leader-as-multiplier is crucial in today's context, where adaptability and resilience are more important than ever. The COVID-19 pandemic disrupted traditional work models, necessitating a shift toward remote and hybrid work environments. In such settings, leaders must inspire and empower their teams without direct oversight. According to Wiseman, multipliers achieve this by fostering a culture of trust, encouraging risk-taking, and valuing diverse perspectives. This approach aligns with contemporary leadership theories that emphasize emotional intelligence and psychological safety. Leaders who act as multipliers not only enhance individual performance but also build cohesive, high-performing teams that can navigate complex and rapidly changing environments.

In today's rapidly evolving world, the significance of teams in driving organizational success cannot be overstated. Research consistently highlights that effective teamwork is a critical determinant of high performance, innovation, and adaptability. In *Nine Lies About Work*, Marcus Buckingham and Ashley Goodall debunk the myth that individual performance is the primary driver of success, emphasizing instead that teams are the fundamental unit of productivity and engagement in any organization. They argue that fostering a sense of belonging and purpose within teams leads to greater commitment and performance, as people are inherently more motivated when they feel connected to a collective mission. Furthermore, the rise of artificial intelligence presents opportunities and challenges for leadership. Multipliers can harness the potential of AI by promoting a culture of continuous learning and innovation. By encouraging team members to stay curious and adaptable, leaders ensure that their organizations remain competitive in a technology-driven world. This approach resonates with insights from other leadership literature, such as *The New Leadership Literacies* by Bob Johansen, which highlights the need for leaders to be futurists, innovators, and integrators in an increasingly digital world. In summary, the principles that multipliers embrace provide a powerful framework for leaders to enhance their effectiveness and create a collaborative, innovative, and resilient organizational culture.

13.16 Forgiveness: The Forgotten Art of Leadership

To err is human; to forgive, divine.

—Alexander Pope

Forgiveness is often thought of as a matter confined to our personal or spiritual lives—relevant to family and friendships, but not to the world of work. Yet in the context of caring leadership, forgiveness becomes a powerful expression of trust, empathy, and respect—qualities that define leaders who truly care about people.

In corporate cultures—where deadlines, deliverables, and results reign supreme—forgiveness may seem too soft, too abstract, or too permissive to have practical value. But neuroscience and leadership research now say otherwise. According to a neuroscientific review published in the May 2025 issue of *Inc.*, forgiving others activates areas of the brain associated with empathy and emotional regulation. It reduces stress hormones, strengthens emotional resilience, and frees cognitive space for creativity and decision-making. In short, forgiveness makes you a better leader—biologically and behaviorally.

But what exactly does forgiveness mean in the business context? It is not excusing poor performance, ignoring accountability, or offering trust where it's been broken. Forgiveness means intentionally releasing resentment toward a teammate while still holding them accountable and upholding performance standards. It does not mean overlooking ethical lapses or condoning poor results—it means letting go of the emotional burden that clouds judgment and erodes trust.

In Ron Carucci's *Harvard Business Review* article "Forgiving a Difficult Colleague," he explores the common frustrations leaders face—from chronic meeting interrupters to moody coworkers and spotlight hoggers. These are not HR violations, but they can wear teams down. In these cases, forgiveness means recognizing that everyone has quirks and limitations—and that our judgment often becomes more corrosive than the behavior we're reacting to.

In fact, many forgiveness situations at work fall into these gray areas: a team member always runs late, another dominates discussions, a third shows flashes of brilliance but lacks interpersonal grace. A leader without the capacity to forgive internalizes resentment, loses objectivity, and often retaliates—directly or subtly. This not only drains emotional energy but also erodes trust within the team. Leaders who practice thoughtful forgiveness, on the other hand, build a climate of psychological safety. They allow others to grow beyond their weaknesses and feel safe enough to own mistakes. Such leadership is not passive—it's transformative.

That said, forgiveness is not without boundaries. It does not apply to ethical breaches, harassment, or racial discrimination—behaviors that destroy psychological safety and demand immediate accountability. Forgiveness is not silence in the face of injustice. Leaders must discern the difference between forgivable flaws and unforgivable violations. As Carucci notes, forgiving someone does not mean you restore trust immediately or condone bad behavior—it means you choose not to carry the emotional burden of retribution. As Dr. Mark Goulston, a psychiatrist and leadership consultant, puts it, "Forgiveness is accepting the apology you're never going to receive."

Critics of workplace forgiveness often worry that it leads to lowered standards or a lack of accountability. But in reality, it allows for excellence without perfectionism. Forgiveness supports the long game: a high-trust, high-performance culture where feedback is welcome, risks are taken, and growth is possible. Studies from Harvard and INSEAD affirm that forgiveness improves team cohesion, boosts innovation, and reduces burnout. A leader who forgives becomes a multiplier—not of errors, but of potential. By acknowledging imperfection and refusing to judge others solely by their faults, leaders become not just supervisors of tasks, but builders of people.

Finally, the importance of forgiveness doesn't stop at the corporate door. In nonprofit leadership, where passion runs deep and resources are often stretched thin, tensions can rise quickly. Here, forgiveness becomes even more vital. It's the difference between collaboration and collapse, between serving a mission and succumbing to burnout. In life and leadership alike, forgiveness is a sacred act of humility and courage—a quiet decision to believe in people more than we judge them, and to lead with grace in pursuit of a greater purpose.

13.17 Small Acts of Care: A Personal Story

No act of kindness, no matter how small, is ever wasted.

—Aesop

From the earliest days of running our engineering consulting firm, I understood that caring for people wasn't just good business—it was the right thing to do. Having worked in large companies where long hours and relentless pressure were the norm, my partner and I had experienced firsthand how such environments could wear down even the most dedicated employees. We wanted to create a different atmosphere, one where people felt valued, supported, and balanced in their work and personal lives. Genuine interest in their well-being had to be at the core of our company culture.

We did everything we could to show that commitment. We offered comprehensive health insurance for all employees at no cost to them and covered more than 50% of the premiums for their dependents. This wasn't an industry standard in our business sector, especially in a very small company, but we believed it was a necessary investment in our people. We also did not choose the cheapest healthcare options simply to benefit our bottom line; instead, we offered a variety of plans—from PPOs to HMOs—so that employees could select the option best suited to their individual circumstances. In addition, our kitchen was always stocked with free snacks and drinks—not just as a perk but as a small way to show that we cared about their comfort. We hosted office Christmas parties where employees' entire families, including children, were invited to join in the festivities and gift-giving, creating a warm and inclusive celebration for all.

One of my most cherished memories as CEO was the year I decided to send personalized thank-you notes to the spouses of our employees. We wanted them to know how much we appreciated their unseen contributions to the success of our employees. To accompany the notes, we sent checks ranging from $200 to $1,000 as tokens of gratitude. I'll never forget the feedback I received; employees told me how much it meant that their families were recognized and valued. That small gesture reinforced a culture of appreciation and helped build a sense of community that went beyond the walls of our office.

I also tried to be attentive to individual situations. One story that stands out is about a bright, young employee who had joined us before completing his PhD. I knew that many talented individuals get stuck at ABD (all-but-dissertation), and I didn't want that to happen to him. He was so focused on work that he kept putting off his dissertation —even though he was only a few weeks away from completing it. It worried me that he wasn't making his dissertation a priority, especially knowing how close he was to finishing and how critical it is for his long-term career and self-fulfillment. I gently prodded him over time and eventually offered him two weeks of paid leave and a plane ticket so he could return to his alma mater and finish what he'd started. He accepted, wrapped up his dissertation, and proudly completed his PhD. Seeing him achieve that milestone was as rewarding for me as it was for him. It reaffirmed that caring for people's growth, even outside of work, made a difference.

We made it a practice to encourage personal and professional development beyond the immediate demands of the job. We paid for writing classes for those who wanted to improve their communication skills. It was not just about writing better reports or preparing compelling presentations for management's benefit; it was about empowering our employees to grow holistically. I also wanted to offer a weekly monetary incentive to those who could self-certify that they had exercised three days a week, but I did not get a chance to implement it.

Looking back, these efforts weren't about grand gestures but about creating an environment where people felt genuinely supported. The way we cared for our employees and their families helped build a team that was loyal, motivated, and willing to go the extra mile—not just because they had to, but because they wanted to. And in that shared sense of commitment, we found our greatest success and happiness.

13.18 The Happiness Advantage of Caring Leadership

I slept and dreamt that life was joy. I awoke and saw that life was service. I acted and behold, service was joy.

—Rabindranath Tagore

Caring for others not only fosters personal happiness but also drives business success through enhanced employee engagement and productivity. Research published in the *Journal of Personality and Social Psychology* indicates that acts of kindness and empathy significantly boost the happiness of both the giver and the receiver, leading to a more positive and collaborative workplace environment. Leaders who show genuine concern for their employees' well-being create a culture of trust and mutual respect, which is essential for job satisfaction and overall happiness. This emotional connection translates to lower turnover rates and higher employee morale, which are critical for sustained business success.

From a business perspective, the economic benefits of a caring leadership approach are substantial. Companies that prioritize employee well-being tend to outperform their competitors in terms of profitability and customer satisfaction. According to a 2024 Gallup report, businesses with high employee engagement levels, fostered by caring leadership, experience 23% higher profitability and 18% higher sales. Additionally, these companies report a 63% reduction in safety incidents and a 78% reduction in absenteeism, illustrating the direct link between a supportive work environment and improved business performance. Organizations like Southwest Airlines and Google have reaped significant financial rewards by embedding care and empathy into their corporate culture, proving that a focus on employee happiness not only creates a better workplace but also drives superior business outcomes.

QUICK TIP

Action: Use AI-driven employee engagement platforms to understand and address individual needs. Implement AI tools for personalized career development and training programs.

Example: Deploying AI-based learning platforms like Coursera or LinkedIn Learning to provide tailored skill development for employees.

Caveat: Balance AI recommendations with human judgment to ensure that career development programs are genuinely beneficial and aligned with individual aspirations.

13.19 Ten Actionable Steps for Applying Principle 7

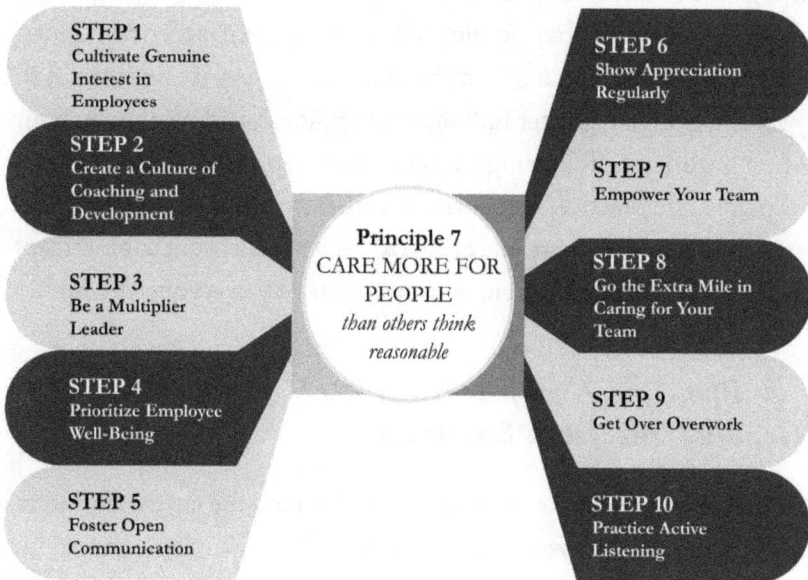

STEP 1
Cultivate Genuine Interest in Employees

STEP 2
Create a Culture of Coaching and Development

STEP 3
Be a Multiplier Leader

STEP 4
Prioritize Employee Well-Being

STEP 5
Foster Open Communication

Principle 7
CARE MORE FOR PEOPLE
than others think reasonable

STEP 6
Show Appreciation Regularly

STEP 7
Empower Your Team

STEP 8
Go the Extra Mile in Caring for Your Team

STEP 9
Get Over Overwork

STEP 10
Practice Active Listening

The heart of leadership: ten actionable steps to applying Principle 7

Balance your thoughts with action. If you spend too much time thinking about a thing, you'll never get it done.

—Bruce Lee

In the preceding pages of this chapter, we have uncovered the many dimensions of caring leadership—from the timeless insights of Tolstoy on human compassion to the modern business case for care, from cultivating mindfulness and genuine concern for employees to combating toxic leadership and transforming performance appraisals into tools of growth and encouragement. We have seen how caring leadership must be visible, how it strengthens trust and engagement, and how even small acts of kindness ripple outward, creating cultures where people feel valued and respected.

But care is not something you merely talk about; it is something you live. It must shine through in your daily interactions, rooted in genuine concern and the inherent goodness that defines great leadership. Caring for others is not only a gift to those around you—it is also a gift to yourself, bringing greater fulfillment, happiness, and purpose to your life and work. The following ten actionable steps will help you put this principle into practice, transforming care from intention into tangible, authentic action. Choose one or two to begin, and let your commitment to caring leadership be seen, felt, and trusted by everyone you lead.

Principle 7, Step 1: Cultivate Genuine Interest in Employees

Action: Spend the time necessary to understand the needs, emotions, and perspectives of your team members. Show genuine concern for and interest in them.

Example: In *To Kill a Mockingbird*, Atticus Finch exemplifies empathy by teaching his children to understand and respect others' perspectives. His advice to his daughter, Scout Finch, in the face of racial injustice in the South, is one of the greatest lessons on empathy: "You never really understand a person until you consider things from his point of view . . . until you climb inside his skin and walk around in it." Starbucks' former CEO Howard Schultz emphasized empathy in the workplace, creating an inclusive and supportive environment, especially during challenging times. During a frightening 2010 mining accident in Chile, President Sebastián Piñera demonstrated empathy by prioritizing the miners' well-being and ensuring constant communication with their families, which fostered trust and unity.

💡 *Principle 7, Step 2: Create a Culture of Coaching and Development*

Action: Establish a culture where continuous coaching and development are prioritized, enabling employees to grow and thrive. High-quality coaching not only builds employees' skills and confidence but also demonstrates a commitment to their long-term success and inclusion. This is particularly valued by Millennial and Gen Z workers who seek purposeful development, and it's essential for nurturing diverse talent within the organization.

Example: HubSpot transitioned from traditional annual performance reviews to a social performance management model. This approach provides employees with continuous, real-time feedback from peers and leaders throughout the organization, encouraging ongoing skill development and fostering a collaborative environment. Additionally, companies like Deloitte have embraced frequent check-ins and coaching sessions, supporting employees' professional growth while creating an inclusive culture that values every individual's contribution.

💡 *Principle 7, Step 3: Be a Multiplier Leader*

Action: Encourage team members to continually seek new knowledge, skills, and experiences by providing resources and opportunities for growth.

Example: In *Dead Poets Society*, Mr. Keating encourages his students to think independently and pursue their passions. LinkedIn's Learning and Development programs offer employees a wide range of courses to enhance their skills and advance their careers. At Pixar, cofounder Ed Catmull emphasizes a culture where employees are encouraged to take risks and learn from their mistakes, nurturing an environment of creativity and innovation. Another example is 3M's "15% rule," which fostered an innovation-friendly culture where employees like Art Fry were encouraged to pursue creative ideas—leading to the development of the Post-it Note from a previously failed adhesive.

💡 Principle 7, Step 4: Prioritize Employee Well-Being

Action: Implement policies and practices that support physical, mental, and emotional well-being of employees.

Example: In *The Lord of the Rings*, Aragorn prioritizes the well-being of his companions, leading them with care and concern. Google's comprehensive wellness programs, including on-site medical services and mental health resources, demonstrate a commitment to employee well-being.

Patagonia provides extensive health benefits and promotes work-life integration, reflecting its dedication to employee well-being and environmental sustainability. Patagonia estimates that it recovers 91% of its annual calculable costs for on-site childcare support through a combination of federal tax credits (50%) and gains in employee retention (30%) and engagement (11%)— a compelling case for investment in such programs. And Patagonia is not alone. JPMorgan Chase Bank, N.A., has reported a 115% return on its internal childcare program, while global consulting firm KPMG found that its corporate clients achieved an average ROI of 125% from implementing family-friendly benefits such as childcare programs.

💡 Principle 7, Step 5: Foster Open Communication

Action: Create channels for transparent and open communication within the organization.

Example: In the movie *12 Angry Men*, Juror 8 fosters open communication, encouraging others to voice their opinions and concerns. Ray Dalio's Bridgewater Associates is known for its culture of radical transparency, where open communication is encouraged and valued. The open communication approach at Pixar encourages employees to share ideas and feedback, fostering innovation and collaboration.

⚡ *Principle 7, Step 6: Show Appreciation Regularly*

Action: Regularly recognize and appreciate the efforts and achievements of team members.

Example: In the Harry Potter series, Headmaster Albus Dumbledore acknowledges the efforts and bravery of his students, boosting their morale. He awards Neville Longbottom 10 points for displaying courage by standing up to his friends, stating, "It takes a great deal of bravery to stand up to our enemies, but just as much to stand up to our friends." At Southwest Airlines, leadership frequently recognizes and celebrates employee achievements, fostering a positive and motivating work environment. Zappos' culture of appreciation includes regular shout-outs and rewards for employees, contributing to high levels of employee satisfaction and engagement.

⚡ *Principle 7, Step 7: Empower Your Team*

Action: Delegate responsibilities and empower team members to make decisions and take ownership of their work.

Example: In *The Avengers*, Nick Fury empowers the superheroes to leverage their unique strengths for the greater good. At Netflix, the culture of freedom and responsibility empowers employees to take initiative and make impactful decisions. The employee empowerment strategy at The Ritz-Carlton, patronized by cofounder Horst Schulze, authorizes every employee to spend up to $2,000 per guest, per incident—without managerial approval—to resolve issues and enhance the guest experience.

💡 Principle 7, Step 8: Go the Extra Mile in Caring for Your Team

Action: Show extraordinary care and support for your team members, going beyond standard expectations to ensure their well-being and success.

Example: In *Les Misérables,* Jean Valjean demonstrates exceptional care and compassion for those around him, often sacrificing his own comfort for their well-being. During the pandemic, Woodard & Curran, led by CEO Doug McKeown, provided all employees with a $1,000 stipend to cover home office setups and other unreimbursed pandemic-related expenses, demonstrating a commitment to employee well-being during a crisis. Another notable example is former PepsiCo CEO Indra Nooyi, who annually handwrote 400 letters to the parents of her senior executives, expressing gratitude for their children's contributions to the company.

💡 Principle 7, Step 9: Get Over Overwork

This step, inspired by the *Harvard Business Review* article "Getting Over Overwork," emphasizes the importance of fostering a workplace culture that supports employee well-being and sustainable productivity by shifting away from overwork and embracing work-life integration. Unlike the traditional concept of work-life balance—which suggests a strict division between work and personal life—work-life integration recognizes that professional and personal responsibilities are inter-connected and should enhance rather than conflict with one another.

Action: Encouraging employees to integrate their work and personal lives in a way that aligns with their individual needs while maintaining productivity is essential for fostering a sustainable and healthy workplace. This approach involves respecting nonworking hours and minimizing unnecessary after-hours communication, ensuring that employees have the time they need to recharge. Instead of emphasizing hours worked, organizations should focus on outcomes, allowing for flexibility in how and when tasks are completed to accommodate different work styles and personal commitments. Employees should be encouraged to prioritize tasks effectively, delegate when necessary, and implement time management strategies that enhance efficiency during regular working hours.

Leaders play a crucial role in setting the standard for work-life integration by demonstrating healthy work habits, such as taking breaks, using vacation time, and refraining from sending emails outside of standard working hours. By modeling these behaviors, leaders reassure employees that they also can manage their work in a way that aligns with their personal needs without fear of negative repercussions. When organizations embrace work-life integration, they create an environment where employees feel empowered to manage their responsibilities holistically, leading to greater well-being, engagement, and long-term success.

Example: In the film *The Pursuit of Happyness*, Chris Gardner's perseverance in balancing his job and caring for his son highlights the importance of work-life integration. At Boston Consulting Group (BCG), the implementation of a Predictable Time Off initiative ensures that consultants have designated time away from work that the entire team respects. This practice not only helps in reducing burnout but also enhances productivity and job satisfaction. Social media platform

Buffer's fully remote work model and flexible schedules exemplify a commitment to work-life integration, resulting in increased employee happiness and engagement. Similarly, HubSpot offers its employees "Results-Only Work Environment" (ROWE) policies, allowing them to work when and where they are most productive, prioritizing outcomes over rigid schedules. Salesforce promotes work-life integration through its Success from Anywhere initiative, enabling employees to blend their professional and personal commitments seamlessly by providing flexible schedules and remote work options.

💡 *Principle 7, Step 10: Practice Active Listening*

Action: Engage in active listening to understand the concerns and ideas of your team members. Open yourself up during conversation, Ask questions to facilitate discovery and understanding.

Example: In *To Kill a Mockingbird*, Atticus Finch demonstrates active listening with his children, fostering mutual respect and understanding. At Southwest Airlines, active listening is part of the company's culture, helping to resolve conflicts and improve employee relations. Google's Project Aristotle found that active listening and conversational turn-taking were critical to the success of high-performing teams, emphasizing the importance of genuinely hearing team members.

13.20 Ten Barriers to Applying Principle 7

Efforts and courage are not enough without purpose and direction.
                                                            -John F. Kennedy

Caring deeply for others is one of the most humanizing and courageous acts of leadership—but it's not always easy, especially when it exceeds cultural or organizational norms. Here are ten common barriers to caring more for people than others think reasonable—and how to overcome them.

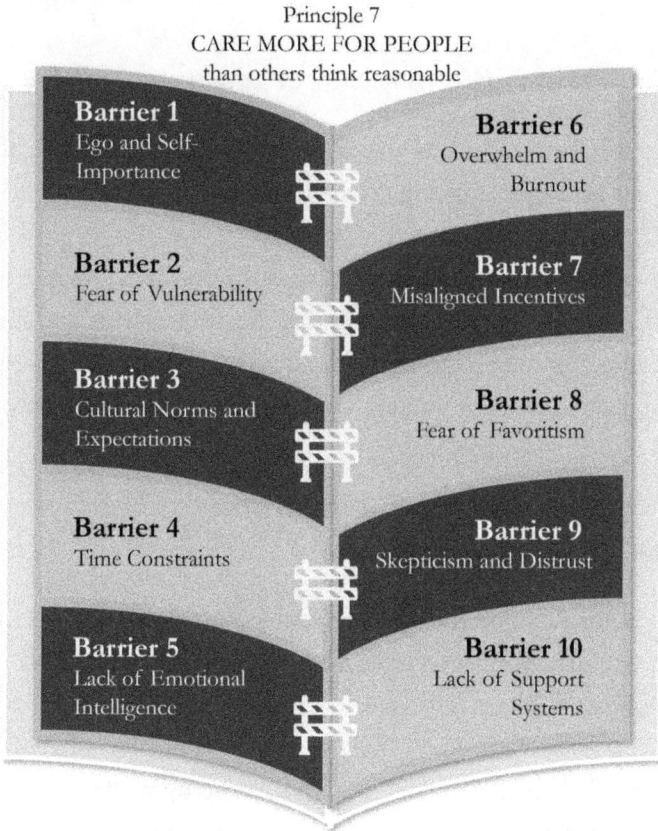

Principle 7
CARE MORE FOR PEOPLE
than others think reasonable

Barrier 1
Ego and Self-Importance

Barrier 2
Fear of Vulnerability

Barrier 3
Cultural Norms and Expectations

Barrier 4
Time Constraints

Barrier 5
Lack of Emotional Intelligence

Barrier 6
Overwhelm and Burnout

Barrier 7
Misaligned Incentives

Barrier 8
Fear of Favoritism

Barrier 9
Skepticism and Distrust

Barrier 10
Lack of Support Systems

The empathy blockers: ten barriers to applying Principle 7

⚠ *Principle 7, Barrier 1: Ego and Self-Importance*

Barrier: A leader's inflated sense of self can prevent them from genuinely caring for others, as they prioritize their own status and achievements.

Solution: Practice humility by seeking regular feedback and focusing on servant leadership. Encourage a culture where everyone's contributions are valued equally. By putting the team's needs first, leaders can foster a more caring and inclusive environment.

⚠ *Principle 7, Barrier 2: Fear of Vulnerability*

Barrier: Leaders might fear that showing too much care will be perceived as a weakness, making them vulnerable.

Solution: Embrace vulnerability as a strength. Leaders like Brené Brown have demonstrated that vulnerability fosters trust and connection. Encourage open communication and share personal experiences to build deeper, more authentic relationships within your team.

⚠ *Principle 7, Barrier 3: Cultural Norms and Expectations*

Barrier: Organizational culture or societal norms might discourage leaders from showing excessive care, deeming it unprofessional or unnecessary.

Solution: Challenge and change cultural norms by leading by example. Highlight successful companies that prioritize empathy and care, like Patagonia or Zappos. Integrate care into the company's core values and reward empathetic behaviors.

⚠ *Principle 7, Barrier 4: Time Constraints*

Barrier: Leaders often feel that they don't have enough time to show care due to their busy schedules.

Solution: Prioritize and schedule time for one-on-one meetings, team-building activities, and regular check-ins. Employ tools for effective time management and delegate tasks to free up time for relationship-building.

⚠ *Principle 7, Barrier 5: Lack of Emotional Intelligence*

Barrier: Some leaders may not naturally possess high emotional intelligence, making it difficult for them to connect with others on a deeper level.

Solution: Invest in EI training for leaders. Encourage self-awareness practices, such as mindfulness and reflection, to help leaders better understand and manage their own emotions and those of others.

⚠ *Principle 7, Barrier 6: Overwhelm and Burnout*

Barrier: Taking on too much at once can lead to overwhelm and burnout, which in turn can trigger self-sabotaging behaviors as a way to cope with stress.

Solution: Prioritize tasks and break them down into manageable steps. Learn to say no and delegate responsibilities when necessary. Make time for rest and relaxation to prevent burnout and maintain balance.

⚠ *Principle 7, Barrier 7: Misaligned Incentives*

Barrier: Incentive structures that focus solely on performance metrics can discourage leaders from investing time in caring for their team.

Solution: Align incentives with caring behaviors by incorporating metrics related to employee well-being and team satisfaction into performance evaluations. Recognize and reward leaders who demonstrate exceptional care for their team members.

⚠️ *Principle 7, Barrier 8: Fear of Favoritism*

Barrier: Leaders may worry that showing care for some individuals will be perceived as favoritism, leading to resentment among other team members.

Solution: Ensure that care and attention are distributed fairly across the team. Develop transparent criteria for recognition and support. Communicate openly about the importance of caring for everyone and maintaining fairness.

⚠️ *Principle 7, Barrier 9: Skepticism and Distrust*

Barrier: Team members might be skeptical of a leader's genuine intentions when they start showing more care, especially if it's a new behavior.

Solution: Build trust gradually by consistently demonstrating genuine care and empathy. Be transparent about your intentions and listen actively to concerns. Over time, your consistent actions will build credibility and trust.

⚠️ *Principle 7, Barrier 10: Lack of Support Systems*

Barrier: Without adequate support systems, leaders may struggle to provide the necessary care for their team.

Solution: Develop robust support systems within the organization, such as employee assistance programs, mentorship opportunities, and wellness initiatives. Ensure that leaders have access to resources that help them support their team effectively.

By addressing these barriers and implementing the suggested solutions, leaders can more effectively embody the principle *Care more for people than others think reasonable.* This approach not only enhances team morale and productivity but also fosters a positive organizational culture that values empathy and human connection.

13.21 Ten Examples of Applying Principle 7

1. Olivia advocates for better mental health resources in the workplace, even if it means reallocating the budget from other areas.
2. Michelle regularly organizes idea-sharing sessions to encourage innovative solutions and actively implements the best ideas, demonstrating her role as a multiplier.
3. Jessica organizes a fundraiser to support a colleague facing medical expenses.
4. James covers a colleague's workload during their personal crisis without expecting anything in return.
5. Sarah regularly checks in on her team's well-being, offering support and resources as needed.
6. Sophie arranges for additional training for struggling employees, giving them a second chance to meet performance standards.
7. A manager provides extra support for an employee going through a tough time, offering flexible hours and understanding.

8. A community volunteer organizes food drives to support local families in need, going above and beyond.
9. A family member without hesitation takes on additional responsibilities to care for an ill relative.
10. A neighbor regularly checks on an elderly resident, ensuring that they have everything they need.

13.22 Closing Reflections

A true leader is one who places the welfare of others above his own.
—Ramayana

Caring for people more than others think reasonable is not just a moral imperative; it is a strategic business decision that leads to tangible benefits. The evidence is clear: organizations that prioritize the well-being of their employees foster environments of trust, loyalty, and high morale. Research from Gallup shows that companies with highly engaged employees experience significantly higher profitability and productivity. Moreover, Deloitte's study underscores that a strong sense of purpose and care leads to higher innovation and employee retention rates.

Leaders who go above and beyond in their care for employees cultivate a thriving, innovative workplace. Companies like Patagonia and Google have demonstrated that a caring leadership approach attracts top talent, reduces turnover, and builds a loyal customer base.

Ultimately, integrating care into the core of business practices enhances reputation, customer loyalty, and overall performance. Leaders who demonstrate extraordinary levels of empathy and concern create better workplaces and drive superior business outcomes. By embedding this ethos into their organizational culture, businesses can achieve sustained success and a competitive advantage—proving that caring for people is as much about business acumen as it is about compassion.

13.23 Daily Practice

1. **Listen and engage:** At the end of each day, ask yourself, *Did I listen more than I spoke?* and *Did I engage with the person while listening with the intent to understand others' perspectives fully?*

2. **Practice compassion:** Understand the needs of the employees and be genuinely concerned about their well-being.

3. **Put people first:** Do not manage by metrics only. Understand the emotional needs of people and help them grow and perform.

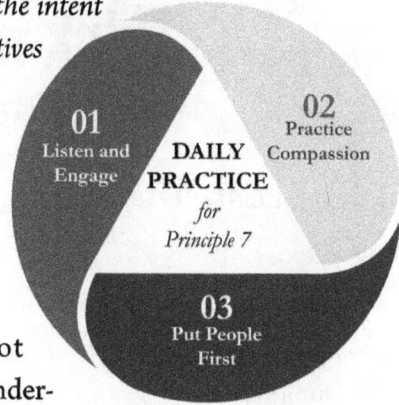

14 Principle 8: Trust More Than Others Think Logical

14.1 Trust, The Magic Glue

Trust is the glue of life. It's the most essential ingredient in effective communication. It's the foundational principle that holds all relationships.

—Stephen M. R. Covey

Trust is indeed the magic glue that binds relationships, societies, and organizations. Its origin, deeply rooted in human history, has been shaped and refined through centuries of philosophical thought and practical application. From Socrates and Confucius to modern thinkers like Stephen M. R. Covey, the consensus is clear: Trust is indispensable. It accelerates business processes, fosters healthy relationships, and underpins effective leadership.

The word "trust" originates from the Old Norse word *traust*, meaning "confidence, protection, support." This term evolved through Old English as *treowth* or *trost*, embodying a sense of loyalty and faithfulness. In Sanskrit, the ancient language of India, the equivalent word for "trust" is *vishwas*. The term *vishwas* derives from the root word *vish*, meaning "to enter" or "to permeate," and *vas*, meaning "to dwell" or "to abide." Thus, *vishwas* encapsulates the idea of a deep-seated belief or confidence that permeates one's being. In Indian philosophy and culture, *vishwas* is more than just a concept; it represents a fundamental aspect of interpersonal relationships, faith, and reliance. This profound sense of trust is integral to the functioning of societal bonds, spiritual practices, and ethical behavior in the Indian context.

In ancient Greek philosophy, trust (*pistis*) was considered a cornerstone of ethical behavior and effective leadership. Socrates, though not leaving behind written works himself, emphasized the importance of trust in his discussions on virtue and knowledge. He believed that trust was fundamental to fostering a sense of community and moral integrity. Socrates is quoted as saying, "The greatest way to live with honor in this world is to be what we pretend to be." The idea "Be what you pretend to be" is what is called a person's "authenticity" and is a fundamental requirement to be respected as trustworthy.

Plato, Socrates's most famous student, developed this notion further in *The Republic*, where he presents the philosopher-king as the ideal leader—one who governs not through force or popularity but through wisdom and virtue. According to Plato, such a leader earns trust by embodying justice and moral clarity, making trust in leadership essential to achieving a just and harmonious society.

Plato's student Aristotle saw trust as the glue of genuine friendship (*philia*), particularly in relationships grounded in shared virtue and mutual respect. For Aristotle, trust was not merely a feeling but a moral practice—integral to *eudaimonia*, or human flourishing. In his view, flourishing required friendships built on reciprocal goodwill and ethical character. Contemporary scholars, such as Martha Nussbaum, emphasize the rigor of this model, noting that "Aristotelian trust is active—it requires continual ethical practice, not passive belief." This interpretation underscores that, for the ancients, trust was both a private virtue and a public necessity—an enduring foundation of ethical leadership and cohesive communities.

Trust is an indispensable virtue—one that forms the bedrock of ethical behavior and social cohesion as emphasized by numerous philosophical traditions. In the modern age, Stephen M. R. Covey's works, particularly *The Speed of Trust*, reiterate that trust is a tangible and measurable asset that accelerates efficiency and enhances organizational performance.

14.2 The Flaw in Machiavellian Logic

Means we use must be as pure as the ends we seek.
—Martin Luther King Jr,

Many argue, citing Machiavelli, that a certain level of cunning and broken promises is necessary to navigate the fiercely competitive organizational landscape, contending that idealistic notions of trust (or too much trust) may be impractical in real-world scenarios. Niccolò Machiavelli was an Italian Renaissance political philosopher and historian, best known for his seminal work *The Prince* (*Il Principe*), written in 1513 as a gift to the new prince of Florence, Lorenzo de' Medici. Although not published until 1532, *The Prince* offers supposedly pragmatic and, at times, controversial advice on political leadership, emphasizing the importance of cunning, strategy, and sometimes ruthless tactics to maintain power and achieve political goals.

Machiavelli's work has sparked extensive debate over the ethics of leadership and the nature of power. His assertion "The promise given was a necessity of the past: the word broken is a necessity of the present" reflects a cynical view of leadership that prioritizes manipulation and expediency over ethical consistency. Those who cite Machiavelli in favor of their position believe that the realities of business often require leaders to make tough decisions that may involve deceit or manipulation to protect their interests and achieve strategic goals. This perspective holds that absolute transparency and unwavering trust can be exploited by competitors, leaving leaders and their organizations vulnerable. Additionally, in high-stakes environments, they argue that flexibility in ethical standards is sometimes needed to adapt to rapidly changing circumstances and ensure survival and success. This viewpoint suggests that a pragmatic approach, which includes the strategic use of deception, can be more effective than rigid adherence to idealistic principles, which may be seen as naïve or unrealistic.

While Machiavelli's advice may have been practical in the tumultuous political landscape of Renaissance Italy, it is fundamentally flawed when applied to modern leadership. Contemporary leadership demands a foundation of trust and integrity, principles that are deeply rooted in Aristotle's philosophy of virtue and crucial for sustainable success in today's interconnected world. Contrary to Machiavelli's view, Aristotle argued that a virtuous leader, who keeps promises and acts consistently with ethical principles, fosters a stable and flourishing community. Breaking promises—as explicitly endorsed by Machiavelli—undermines social stability and erodes the moral fabric of society, leading to widespread distrust and discord.

The virtuous ethic of means and ends was later championed by two of the twentieth century's most revered moral leaders. Gandhi insisted, "They say, 'means are after all means.' I would say, 'means are after all everything.' As the means, so the end." Martin Luther King Jr. echoed this principle, asserting, "Means we use must be as pure as the ends we seek." Both rejected the notion that good ends justify immoral means. For them, integrity of action was nonnegotiable—virtue was not a tool to achieve results; it was the result.

Stephen M. R. Covey, in his works *The Speed of Trust* and *Trust and Inspire*, provides practical insights that counter Machiavelli's advice. Covey argues that trust is a critical asset that accelerates business processes, reduces costs, and enhances performance. Leaders who are trustworthy and consistent in their actions build strong, loyal teams and create environments where innovation and collaboration can thrive. Conversely, a leader who breaks promises and acts deceitfully may achieve short-term gains but will ultimately face long-term consequences such as high turnover, low morale, and reputational damage.

Modern corporate examples further illustrate the pitfalls of Machiavellian tactics. Consider the downfall of companies like Enron and Volkswagen, where deceit and broken promises led to catastrophic failures. Enron's fraudulent activities and Volkswagen's emissions scandal eroded trust with stakeholders, leading to severe financial and reputational damage. These cases underscore that ethical breaches, far from being a necessity, are a liability that modern leaders cannot afford. On the other hand, companies that prioritize integrity, like Patagonia and Salesforce, have built strong, loyal customer bases and are celebrated for their ethical leadership.

Machiavelli's advice, while historically contextual, is not suitable for modern leadership. Aristotle's philosophy of virtue and Covey's practical insights on trust illustrate that integrity and ethical consistency are foundational to effective leadership. Trustworthy leaders build strong organizations that can withstand challenges and thrive in the long term. By discarding Machiavellian tactics and embracing principles of trust and virtue, leaders can inspire their teams, foster loyalty, and achieve sustainable success.

14.3 Why Trust More?

Once again, I affirm that nothing is as fast as the speed of trust. Nothing is as fulfilling as a relationship of trust. Nothing is as inspiring as an offering of trust. Nothing is as profitable as the economics of trust. Nothing has more influence than a reputation of trust.
                                        —Stephen M. R. Covey

Trust is a cornerstone of effective leadership and a critical component in fostering a productive and harmonious organizational environment.

Stephen M. R. Covey, in *The Speed of Trust*, posits, "When trust goes up, speed goes up and cost goes down." This simple yet profound statement highlights the tangible benefits of trust within an organization. High-trust environments facilitate faster decision-making processes, reduce operational costs, and enhance overall efficiency. Trust acts as a lubricant, reducing friction and enabling smoother, more effective interactions and transactions.

Nelson Mandela, the former president of South Africa, demonstrated remarkable trust in the power of reconciliation during the country's transition from apartheid to democracy. Despite decades of racial segregation and violence, Mandela extended trust to his former oppressors, advocating for forgiveness and cooperation rather than retaliation. His willingness to trust in the capacity for change and reconciliation played a crucial role in healing the wounds of apartheid and uniting South Africans across racial divides.

In *Avengers: Endgame*, Tony Stark (Iron Man) and Steve Rogers (Captain America) must rebuild their trust after the events of *Captain America: Civil War*. Their reconciliation, based on mutual respect and a shared mission, is essential for their united effort to defeat Thanos. Their journey demonstrates the importance of repairing trust to achieve common goals.

In *The Lord of the Rings*, the bond between Frodo Baggins and Samwise Gamgee exemplifies the essence of trust. Frodo trusts Sam implicitly to help him carry the burden of the One Ring, and Sam's unwavering loyalty and support enable Frodo to complete his mission. Their mutual trust underscores the importance of faith and reliability in achieving extraordinary goals.

Stephen M. R. Covey's 2022 *Trust and Inspire* delves deeper into the transformational impact of trust in leadership. Covey argues that leaders who trust and inspire their teams unlock greater levels of creativity, commitment, and performance. This approach contrasts sharply with command-and-control leadership styles, which often stifle innovation and reduce employee engagement.

One significant benefit that Covey highlights is the enhancement of organizational agility. In a high-trust environment, teams are more adaptable and responsive to change. Trust fosters open communication and collaboration, enabling quicker decision-making and more effective problem-solving. This agility allows organizations to navigate market shifts and disruptions more efficiently, maintaining a competitive edge.

Another crucial benefit of a trust-based leadership approach is increased employee engagement and retention. Covey points out that employees who feel trusted and valued are more likely to be engaged and committed to their work. This leads to lower turnover rates and higher levels of job satisfaction. By fostering an environment of trust, leaders can cultivate a loyal and motivated workforce, which is essential for long-term success. These are not merely theoretical assertions—a *Harvard Business Review* article provided compelling quantitative research-based data. According to the article, "Compared with people at low-trust companies, people at high-trust companies report: 74% less stress, 106% more energy at work, 50% higher productivity, 13% fewer sick days, 76% more engagement, 29% more satisfaction with their lives, 40% less burnout." Great Place To Work has conducted extensive research on workplace culture since 1992, surveying over 20 million employees annually across hundreds of countries through its proprietary analytics platform. Their findings consistently highlight the significant advantages of cultivating a high-trust workplace culture. Employees in such environments report more positive experiences, show higher levels of commitment, and are less likely to leave the organization. Additionally, these employees experience lower rates of burnout, demonstrate greater effort, and contribute to faster innovation. Companies that successfully foster high-trust cultures not only achieve stronger financial performance but also enjoy higher stock market returns.

Moreover, trust enhances a leader's credibility and authority, which are essential for inspiring people and leading them through challenges. The philosopher Lao Tzu observed, "He who does not trust enough will not be trusted." This wisdom underscores that trust must be mutual. Leaders who demonstrate reliability and integrity earn the respect and loyalty of their team members. In a business context, this trust translates into higher employee engagement and retention. In his book *The Five Dysfunctions of a Team*, Patrick Lencioni emphasizes that trust is the foundation of a cohesive team. Trust enables open and honest communication, which is crucial for problem-solving and innovation. When team members trust each other and their leaders, they are more likely to share ideas, take risks, and collaborate effectively, driving the organization toward its objectives. By cultivating trust, leaders not only enhance their own credibility but also create a thriving, productive, and committed workforce.

In today's interconnected world, success often depends on the ability to collaborate effectively with others. Yet collaboration requires a foundation of trust: in the expertise, integrity, and commitment of team members. By *trusting in teams more than others think logical*, leaders can unleash the collective potential of their organizations and drive meaningful change. Imagine a startup founded on the principle of radical trust, where employees are empowered to take ownership of their work and contribute their unique talents and perspectives. In such a company, leaders prioritize transparency, open communication, and mutual respect, creating a culture where trust permeates every aspect of the organization. As a result, employees feel valued, motivated, and inspired to innovate, leading to breakthroughs that propel the company to success in a competitive market.

Trust empowers individuals to take initiative, innovate, and contribute to collective success. Leaders who trust their teams create an environment where people feel valued and motivated. Franklin D.

Roosevelt's leadership during the Great Depression and World War II involved trusting his advisors and the American people to overcome significant challenges. Roosevelt's New Deal programs and wartime strategies relied on empowering others to take action and implement solutions. His trust in the collective effort of his nation led to transformative changes and victories.

In *Coach Carter*, Samuel L. Jackson plays the role of a high school basketball coach who trusts his players to uphold academic and personal standards. By setting high expectations and showing faith in their potential, Coach Carter empowers his team to excel on and off the court. His trust in his players' abilities fosters discipline, teamwork, and success.

In Disney's *Frozen*, Elsa's journey involves learning to trust herself and others with her magical powers. Initially fearful and isolated, Elsa's eventual embrace of vulnerability and trust in her sister Anna leads to the restoration of their relationship and the kingdom's safety. Her story highlights the transformative power of embracing vulnerability and risk.

Trust is especially critical during times of uncertainty and crisis. Leaders who provide clear communication, support, and stability can help their followers navigate challenges with confidence. Winston Churchill's leadership during World War II was marked by his ability to foster trust during a time of extreme uncertainty. Through his inspiring speeches and steadfast resolve, Churchill provided the British people with the confidence and resilience needed to endure the war. His transparent communication and unwavering leadership built trust and unity.

In today's fast-paced and interconnected world, leaders are often faced with the challenge of balancing risk and reward, uncertainty, and trust. Yet it is precisely in moments of uncertainty that the power of trust becomes most evident. At its core, radical trust is about believing in the potential of others beyond what is considered conventional or safe. It is about extending trust even when doubt lingers and uncertainty looms. In the business world, radical trust can manifest in various forms—from empowering employees to make decisions autonomously to forging strategic partnerships based on mutual respect and shared values. By embracing radical trust, leaders can create an environment where innovation thrives and creativity flourishes.

A legacy built on trust endures, inspiring future generations to uphold the values of integrity, authenticity, and mutual respect. In times of adversity and uncertainty, trust becomes both a shield and a catalyst for resilience. Leaders who *trust more than others think logical* inspire confidence, instill hope, and rally their teams to overcome challenges with courage and determination.

14.4 Think Win-Win: Say No to Command-and-Control

Good reasons must, of force, give place to better.
—William Shakespeare, *Julius Caesar*

In today's rapidly evolving business environment after the pandemic, the traditional command-and-control management style has become an anachronism that stifles innovation and suppresses employee engagement. Despite its prevalence, this approach is increasingly recognized for its significant downsides. Stephen M. R. Covey, in *Trust and Inspire* and *The Speed of Trust*, highlights the profound impact of trust and empowerment on organizational success, making a compelling case for moving beyond command-and-control leadership. His father, Stephen R. Covey—founder of the Covey Leadership Center—emphasizes a critical leadership habit in *The 7 Habits of Highly Effective People*: "Think Win-Win," which promotes mutually beneficial solutions in all interactions. The win-win mindset reinforces that when leaders prioritize the growth and success of their team members alongside their own, it results in higher morale, improved collaboration, and sustained organizational success. Adopting a win-win approach helps leaders move away from rigid control and fosters an atmosphere where trust flourishes.

First, command-and-control management inherently undermines trust within an organization. Managers who rely heavily on oversight and strict directives signals a lack of trust in their employees' abilities and judgment. This lack of trust breeds a culture of fear and compliance rather than creativity and initiative, ultimately reducing overall productivity and job satisfaction. In addition, the command-and-control model, which relies on closely monitoring and micromanaging employees, is ineffective in a remote work environment because it undermines trust and autonomy, essential for maintaining motivation and productivity when direct oversight is impractical. Instead, a trust-based approach is crucial, as it fosters employee engagement, accountability, and innovation, allowing remote teams to thrive independently.

Moreover, the command-and-control style fails to tap into the full potential of employees. Covey's trust-and-inspire approach advocates for leadership that empowers individuals, arguing that people perform best when they are trusted and inspired to take ownership of their work. He states, "When you trust people, you bring out the best in them." This empowerment leads to higher levels of engagement, motivation, and innovation, as employees feel valued and capable of making meaningful contributions. Research data presented earlier in this chapter support this perspective.

The rigidity of command-and-control also hampers agility and adaptability, crucial traits for thriving in today's fast-paced market. High-trust organizations can make decisions faster and respond more effectively to changes and challenges, providing a significant competitive advantage. Command-and-control, with its layers of approval and rigid hierarchies, slows down decision-making and stifles responsiveness.

Additionally, a command-and-control management model often leads to higher turnover rates. Employees today seek workplaces where they can grow, contribute, and feel appreciated. By contrast, environments dominated by micromanagement and stringent control measures see higher levels of dissatisfaction and attrition, as employees look elsewhere for more supportive and empowering work cultures.

Finally, the command-and-control approach is at odds with fostering a collaborative and innovative culture. A win-win approach supports collaboration by emphasizing the shared success of both leaders and their teams. This collaborative environment is essential for innovation, as it allows for the free exchange of ideas and the collective problem-solving necessary to drive growth and improvement. Command-and-control stifles this dynamic, leading to missed opportunities and a stagnant organizational culture.

14.5 Trust and Employee Productivity: Arguments and Counterarguments

Trust men and they will be true to you; treat them greatly, and they will show themselves great.

—Ralph Waldo Emerson

The idea that more trust in employees increases productivity is a widely discussed concept in management and organizational behavior. It is important to recognize and understand both the arguments and counterarguments around trusting more, in order to apply the principle *Trust more than others think logical* more effectively. The following sections examine key arguments that support this principle, as well as important counterarguments that highlight its limitations.

Persuasive Arguments Supporting Trust in Employees

The following key arguments illustrate how cultivating trust in employees can serve as a powerful driver of productivity, engagement, and organizational performance.

1. Increased Autonomy and Empowerment

Argument: Trusting employees leads to greater autonomy and empowerment, which in turn fosters a sense of ownership and responsibility. This can enhance motivation and drive higher productivity.

Evidence: A 1995 study by Spreitzer, published in the *Academy of Management Journal*, found that empowered employees exhibit higher levels of job satisfaction and productivity. Empowerment, which stems from trust, allows employees to make decisions and take initiatives that improve performance.

2. Enhanced Job Satisfaction and Engagement

Argument: Trusting employees contributes to higher job satisfaction and engagement, which are critical drivers of productivity.

Evidence: Gallup reported in 2017 that companies with high levels of employee engagement, which is closely linked to trust, outperform those with lower engagement levels by 115% growth in earnings per share, compared to 27% among their less engaged peers. Trust creates an environment where employees feel valued and respected, leading to greater commitment and productivity.

3. Reduced Stress and Burnout

Argument: When employees feel trusted, they experience lower levels of stress and burnout, leading to better health and sustained productivity.

Evidence: Research by Dirks and Ferrin published in the *Journal of Applied Psychology* in 2001 found that trust in management reduces stress and increases job performance. Trust minimizes the need for micromanagement, allowing employees to work in a more relaxed and efficient manner.

4. Improved Innovation and Creativity

Argument: A trusting environment encourages innovation and creativity, as employees feel safe to experiment and propose new ideas without fear of negative repercussions.

Evidence: Studies by Amabile and colleagues published in 1996 in the *Creativity Research Journal* showed that trust and psychological safety are critical for fostering creativity and innovation. Organizations that trust their employees see higher rates of innovative solutions and improvements in processes.

Counterarguments against Trust Increasing Productivity

While trust offers many potential benefits, leaders must also weigh counterarguments that expose important risks and nuances in applying trust-based approaches to workforce productivity. The following key counterarguments highlight important considerations for applying trust-based approaches effectively.

1. Potential for Abuse of Trust

Counterargument: Trusting employees too much can lead to complacency or even abuse of trust, where employees might take advantage of the freedom given to them, leading to decreased productivity.

Evidence: Claus W. Langfred's study "Too Much of a Good Thing? Negative Effects of High Trust and Individual Autonomy in Self-Managing Teams," published in the *Academy of Management Journal*, demonstrates that in self-managing teams, high levels of trust combined with significant individual autonomy can result in reduced performance due to decreased monitoring among team members.

Solution: Implement balanced accountability mechanisms alongside trust. Regular performance reviews, clear communication of expectations, and setting measurable goals can help ensure that trust is not abused. Trust should be coupled with transparency and mutual accountability to maintain high productivity and prevent potential complacency.

2. Need for Supervision and Guidance

Counterargument: Some employees and certain types of jobs require greater supervision and guidance to maintain productivity. Trust alone might not be sufficient for those who need clear direction and support to perform well.

Evidence: Hackman and Oldham's job characteristics model (JCM) emphasizes five core dimensions—skill variety, task identity, task significance, autonomy, and feedback—that collectively enhance the intrinsic motivation and meaningfulness of work. According to this model, jobs lacking these essential characteristics, especially autonomy and feedback, may lead to reduced motivation and productivity, prompting the need for increased structure or oversight.

Solution: Provide tailored supervision and support based on individual needs. Hackman and Oldham argue that the optimal solution is not greater supervision but rather a deliberate redesign of jobs to incorporate these motivating factors, ultimately fostering higher levels of employee engagement and effectiveness. Use a situational leadership approach, where the level of supervision and guidance is adjusted according to the employee's competence and confidence in their role. This way, employees who need more direction receive it, while those who thrive on trust and autonomy can operate more independently.

3. Variability in Individual Motivation

Counterargument: Not all employees are equally motivated by trust. Individual differences in work ethic and motivation mean that some employees may not respond positively to increased trust.

Evidence: According to Herzberg's motivation-hygiene theory, workplace factors are divided into *motivators* (e.g., achievement, recognition, growth opportunities), which inherently lead to job satisfaction and intrinsic motivation, and *hygiene factors* (e.g., compensation, job security), which, if unmet, result in dissatisfaction but do not directly inspire motivation. Trust can be associated with either motivators, such as responsibility and recognition, or hygiene factors, such as interpersonal relationships, depending on the context. Additionally, Deci and Ryan's self-determination theory highlights that motivational drivers vary among individuals: some employees prioritize intrinsic factors like trust, autonomy, and recognition, while others are more motivated by extrinsic factors, such as compensation or job security.

Solution: Recognize and address diverse motivational drivers. Conduct regular employee surveys and one-on-one meetings to understand individual motivations and tailor strategies accordingly. Combining trust with other motivational factors such as recognition, career development opportunities, and competitive compensation can create a more holistic approach to enhancing productivity across a diverse workforce.

The persuasive arguments and supporting evidence suggest that trust in employees can significantly increase productivity through enhanced autonomy, job satisfaction, reduced stress, and improved innovation. However, counterarguments highlight potential risks such as abuse of trust, the need for supervision, and variability in individual motivation.

Balancing trust with accountability and providing appropriate support and guidance is crucial for optimizing productivity. Organizations should tailor their approach to trust based on the specific needs and characteristics of their workforce to achieve the best outcomes. Ultimately, fostering a culture of trust, combined with clear expectations and support, can lead to sustained improvements in productivity and organizational performance.

14.6 The Trust Equation

To be trusted is a greater compliment than to be loved.
—George McDonald

David Maister, Charles Green, and Robert Galford, in their book *The Trusted Advisor*, propose the trust equation to provide a tangible measure of the trust a consultant can earn from a client. This equation is equally applicable to leaders, offering a concrete way to measure the trust a leader can garner from their employees. It is expressed as

$$T = \frac{C + R + I}{S}$$

$$\underset{\text{Trustworthiness}}{T} = \frac{\underset{\text{Credibility}}{C} + \underset{\text{Reliability}}{R} + \underset{\text{Intimacy}}{I}}{\underset{\text{Self-orientation}}{S}}$$

Trust decoded: A formula for building authentic relationships

Credibility refers to the advisor's credentials, skills, and experience. For example, a financial advisor with extensive knowledge and certification in financial planning demonstrates high credibility. A technical consultant can enhance credibility by demonstrating a track record of success in similar projects, providing case studies, and maintaining professional certifications. Leaders can demonstrate credibility by consistently showcasing expertise and knowledge in their field and maintaining transparency and honesty in all communications.

Reliability is about consistency and dependability. An advisor or a leader who consistently follows through on promises and delivers results as expected is seen as reliable. Individuals can demonstrate reliability by setting clear expectations, meeting deadlines consistently, and communicating proactively if obstacles arise.

Intimacy involves the safety and security that a client or an employee feels when sharing personal information. A trusted advisor or leader builds intimacy by being empathetic and maintaining confidentiality, while showing genuine care.

Self-orientation pertains to the advisor's or leader's focus, whether they prioritize their own interests over those of their clients or employees. Lower self-orientation indicates a greater focus on a client's or employee's needs. An advisor or leader who actively listens and tailors advice to the client's or employee's situation exemplifies low self-orientation.

The trust realms of the components of the trust equation are shown with examples in the table below. By understanding and enhancing the components of the trust equation—credibility, reliability, intimacy, and minimizing self-orientation—leaders can systematically build and sustain trust within their teams, enhancing their overall effectiveness and fostering a supportive organizational culture.

Trust Realms

Component	Realm	Example
Credibility	Words	I can trust what she/he says about.... Her/his explanations are accurate and truthful.
Reliability	Actions	I can trust her/him to deliver products.... She/he consistently meets deadlines.
Intimacy	Emotions	I feel comfortable discussing this.... I can openly share my concerns without judgment.
Self-orientation	Motives	I don't trust that she/he cares about.... She/he seems focused mainly on personal gain.

14.7 Transparency, Trust, and Integrity: Interconnected Pillars of Happy and Great Leadership

Transparency breeds trust, and trust is the foundation of great teamwork.

—Simon Sinek

Trust is not a one-way street; it is a mutual relationship between leaders and their employees. When trust exists, it significantly enhances a leader's sense of fulfillment and happiness. Research consistently shows that CEOs who foster trust within their organizations have employees who report higher levels of happiness and job satisfaction, experiencing reduced stress and increased energy. This improved sense of well-being is not merely a personal benefit—it directly contributes to higher organizational performance. Moreover, trusted leaders are more likely to engage in meaning-making activities, where their work aligns with their core values and purpose. This meaningful work, in turn, leads to greater happiness and a stronger commitment to the organization's mission. For trust to be established and sustained, leaders must trust and inspire their employees to perform their duties effectively while also doing the right things to earn the trust of their employees and stakeholders. This is where transparency plays a crucial role.

Transparency involves the open and honest communication of information, decisions, and processes, fostering an environment where employees and stakeholders feel informed and valued. Trust is built when stakeholders, including employees, customers, and investors, believe that an organization is honest and reliable. Transparency reinforces this belief by providing clarity and openness about the organization's operations and decisions. In the corporate world, transparency can differentiate between a trusted, resilient organization and one that faces skepticism and distrust. For example, during the 2008 financial crisis, many banks faced a trust deficit due to opaque practices.

On the other hand, Costco has built significant customer trust through its transparent pricing strategy. The company caps markups at 14% for brand-name products and 15% for its private-label Kirkland Signature items. This approach has been a key element of Costco's business model since its founding in 1983. Through this transparent pricing approach, Costco has achieved membership renewal rates exceeding 90% in key markets like the United States and Canada. This high retention rate reflects strong customer loyalty and satisfaction.

Another prime example of the interdependence of trust and transparency is seen in the operations of Salesforce. The company has embedded transparency into its corporate values by openly sharing its financial results, product roadmaps, and strategic initiatives with both employees and the public. This transparency has cultivated a high level of trust, enabling Salesforce to foster strong relationships with its stakeholders.

When organizations practice transparency, they demonstrate accountability and honesty, which are crucial for maintaining trust. By consistently aligning actions with transparent communication, companies not only enhance trust but also drive long-term success, loyalty, and engagement among all stakeholders.

Integrity is closely linked to transparency, as it represents adherence to moral and ethical principles. For integrity to be credible, it must be demonstrated through transparent actions and communications. IBM exemplifies this integration by publicly disclosing its AI ethics guidelines, data privacy controls, and third-party audit results—ensuring that stakeholders understand how data are used and protected. Similarly, Microsoft is acknowledged for proactive transparency, particularly in cybersecurity, data privacy, and responsible AI. Its open disclosure of vulnerabilities, as demonstrated during the SolarWinds cyberattack, has enhanced its reputation for trustworthiness. Patagonia sets industry standards by openly sharing its supply chain practices and environmental impact data.

These companies go beyond compliance, using transparency to prove their integrity—whether in AI ethics, cybersecurity, sustainability, or corporate governance. The result is measurable trust: IBM ranks among Ethisphere's Most Ethical Companies (2024), Microsoft achieves high customer confidence in its responsible AI, and Patagonia enjoys exceptional consumer trust and loyalty.

When organizations align actions with values through verifiable transparency, they don't just meet expectations—they build lasting credibility and stakeholder loyalty. This alignment fosters a culture of trust, where employees, customers, and partners feel respected, informed, and valued. Over time, such integrity-driven practices become a competitive advantage, reinforcing the organization's reputation and resilience in times of change or crisis. Transparency, integrity, and trust ultimately form the bedrock of a strong, sustainable foundation upon which long-term success is built.

QUICK TIP

Action: Leverage AI to predict market trends and inform strategic decisions, showing trust in data-driven insights. Use AI collaboration tools to foster trust and transparency within remote teams.

Example: Relying on AI algorithms to make bold investment decisions based on predictive analytics and trend forecasting.

Caveat: Validate AI predictions with human expertise and contextual understanding to avoid overreliance on automated systems, which might not capture all nuances of complex situations.

14.8 Challenge of Trusting More: A Personal Story

You may be deceived if you trust too much, but you will live in torment if you do not trust enough.

—Frank Crane, American minister and columnist

Fortunately, I grew up with belief in the principle that trust can accelerate progress and strengthen relationships, even if it sometimes defies logic. As a result, I'm naturally inclined to trust others, perhaps more than most, and I've experienced both the benefits and the risks of that approach throughout my career and personal life. But my conviction is that the speed of trust can create an environment where people thrive and achieve more than they thought possible.

At one point, I was so inspired by Stephen M. R. Covey's book *The Speed of Trust* that I bought multiple copies and shared them with my business partner and senior colleagues involved in decision-making. I wanted to instill the idea that trusting people's capabilities and giving them the opportunity to succeed—or fail—was essential. I believed that letting go of control, even if it felt risky, was the only way to harness the full potential of our team. I would give presentations to the employees on the concept, explaining the trust equation discussed earlier in this chapter: moving away from self-orientation and keeping one's word to build credibility with clients and colleagues alike.

Practicing this principle was not always easy, especially when managing complex projects where the stakes were high. I reminded myself constantly not to micromanage, even when every instinct told me to do so. There was a time when we undertook a particularly critical project involving multiple moving parts. I had to fight my perfectionist tendencies and trust the team to handle their respective roles. It wasn't without its hiccups—there were times when mistakes were made, and I had to resist the urge to take over. But in the end, the project was delivered successfully, and I could see the pride and ownership in my team's eyes. It taught me that while trusting others has risks, the payoff in team growth and efficiency is immeasurable. I must admit, though, that even today I occasionally find it difficult to resist my urge to take over when I see a drop in quality—and that has delayed my building a team that can take over after I retire. To be honest, I am constantly working on this principle.

Trust is even more crucial in voluntary organizations. I had managed a large and complex community event for years, pouring time and effort into every detail to make it successful. When the time came to pass the responsibility to a group of young volunteers, it was a test of my commitment to trust. I provided enough guidance but stepped back to let them lead. There were moments of anxiety—times when I worried they might overlook something crucial—but they rose to the occasion. Their success reinforced my belief that trusting others, even when it feels illogical or risky, can yield incredible results and empower others to grow in confidence and skill.

As a parent, I found that trusting my children was perhaps one of the hardest and most rewarding tests of this principle. Letting them make their own decisions, knowing they might fail, was challenging for a perfectionist and overcautious parent like me. I would catch myself wanting to step in, to guide them away from potential missteps. Over the years, I failed many times in resisting myself from intervening. But I learned that giving them the space to experience success and failure on their own terms was essential for their growth. There were times they faltered, and it was difficult to watch, but those moments taught them resilience and built their decision-making skills. It also reinforced to me that trust isn't just a professional value—it's a cornerstone of personal relationships and parenting.

Reflecting on these experiences, I've come to understand that *trusting others more than seems logical* requires humility. It means accepting that things might not go perfectly and being okay with that. But it's in that space of trust that people step up, learn, and grow. Whether in the workplace, in voluntary settings, or at home, I've seen firsthand that trusting others can be transformative, not just for them but for me as a leader and as a person.

14.9 Communication: The Lifeblood of Trusting Leadership

The single biggest problem in communication is the illusion that it has taken place.

—George Bernard Shaw

Throughout this journey of leadership, the topic of communication has appeared in almost every chapter, accompanied by actionable steps that reinforce its significance. This is no coincidence; communication is the thread that weaves through every facet of great and fulfilling leadership. Without clear, consistent, and compassionate communication, trusting leadership cannot thrive. Only through honest and meaningful connection does trust take root and grow. We revisit it here before concluding this book to avoid falling prey to the illusion that everything that needs to be said about communication has already been communicated—a trap against which George Bernard Shaw aptly warned.

If trust is the glue that holds relationships together, then communication is the lifeblood that nourishes them. It affects everything: how a vision is shared, how values are lived, how purpose is articulated, and how success is ultimately achieved. Good communication and happiness are deeply intertwined, as effective communication lays the foundation for understanding, trust, and connection—all essential elements of personal and collective well-being and fulfillment. To ignore or underplay the importance of communication is to limit the potential of both individuals and organizations. Communication is, quite simply, the force that turns intention into action and connects people to the purpose behind every pursuit.

Warren Buffett, one of the most successful investors and business leaders of all time, famously argues that communication skills dramatically enhance personal value. Speaking to a group of Columbia University business students, Buffett once said, "Now, you can improve your value by 50 percent just by learning communication skills—public speaking and writing." His emphasis on communication is not merely theoretical; Buffett himself exemplified the importance of mastering this skill. In his office, the only diploma he chooses to display is not one from an Ivy League school but the certificate he received from the Dale Carnegie Institute in 1952 for completing a course on public speaking. This decision speaks volumes: to Buffett, the ability to communicate effectively is more valuable than any traditional academic accolade. This example underscores that communication is not just a skill but an essential leadership tool that affects how a message is received and acted upon.

Understanding the content and its reception is essential to mastering communication. A leader must grasp that what is said and how it is received can be vastly different. The content of the message represents the information being conveyed, but its impact hinges on how the audience perceives, interprets, and internalizes it. As such, leaders should consider not only the clarity and accuracy of their words but also the emotional and contextual nuances that affect how the message is received. To ensure that the intended impact aligns with the content, leaders should use active listening, encourage feedback, and observe nonverbal cues, making adjustments as necessary to bridge any gaps between intention and perception.

A leader's capacity to communicate shapes an organization's future. Effective communication articulates a clear vision, inspires teams to pursue excellence, and clears up misunderstandings that can erode productivity and morale. Transparent communication builds trust—a foundational pillar of any successful relationship or enterprise. When people trust that their leader is honest and open, collaboration flourishes and loyalty deepens. Furthermore, communication demonstrates care powerfully. When leaders engage in active listening, share insights, and maintain open channels for feedback, they show their teams that their voices are valued, creating a culture where employees feel seen and heard.

According to a 2013 study from the Project Management Institute (PMI), poor communication is a major factor in project failure, contributing to the breakdown of nearly one-third of all projects. The study also found that ineffective communication accounts for more than half of the budgetary risks in project execution, with over 50% of failed projects falling short of their business goals due to communication issues. Specifically, PMI's *Pulse of the Profession* communication report highlights that out of every $1 billion invested in projects, $135 million is at risk—and astonishingly, $75 million of that risk is directly tied to poor communication. These findings underscore the critical role of clear, consistent, and effective communication in achieving project success.

These stark numbers reflect the reality that even the best ideas can die without the right channels of expression and understanding. Communication is the catalyst that transforms vision into action and connects people to the shared purpose that drives success. As such, a leader must pay special attention to this vital aspect of leadership and recognize that effective communication requires clarity and simplicity, active listening, emotional intelligence to connect empathetically, awareness of nonverbal cues to reinforce authenticity, and adaptability through feedback to ensure the message is understood as intended.

14.10 Ten Actionable Steps for Applying Principle 8

Trust is like the air we breathe—when it's present, nobody really notices; when it's absent, everybody notices.

—Warren Buffett

In the preceding pages of this chapter, we have explored trust as the essential glue that binds teams, strengthens relationships, and fuels lasting success—from challenging the outdated Machiavellian mindset to understanding the power of transparency, from learning to think win-win rather than command-and-control to examining the link between trust, productivity, and organizational health. We have seen how communication sustains trust, how integrity and transparency reinforce it, and how fragile it can be in the face of missteps and careless leadership.

Trust is not a gift you claim; it is one you earn, day by day, through your actions and behaviors. It cannot be demanded or fabricated—it must be built patiently and protected fiercely. Trust accelerates collaboration, inspires people to do their best work, and kills the inefficiencies that drain organizations of time, energy, and morale. The following ten steps will help you create a high-trust environment where creativity, commitment, and performance thrive. Choose the practices that fit your context and begin embedding trust into every conversation, every decision, and every part of your leadership. Let trust speak for itself through what you do, not just what you say.

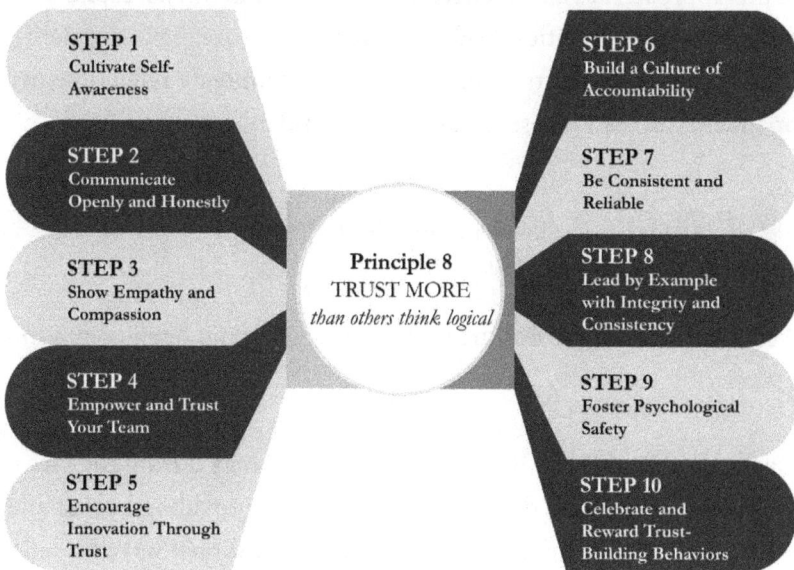

STEP 1	STEP 6
Cultivate Self-Awareness	Build a Culture of Accountability
STEP 2	STEP 7
Communicate Openly and Honestly	Be Consistent and Reliable
STEP 3	STEP 8
Show Empathy and Compassion	Lead by Example with Integrity and Consistency
STEP 4	STEP 9
Empower and Trust Your Team	Foster Psychological Safety
STEP 5	STEP 10
Encourage Innovation Through Trust	Celebrate and Reward Trust-Building Behaviors

Principle 8
TRUST MORE
than others think logical

The trust multiplier: ten actionable steps for applying Principle 8

💡 *Principle 8, Step 1: Cultivate Self-Awareness*

Action: Understand your own biases, strengths, and weaknesses to build authentic relationships.

Example: Abraham Lincoln, renowned for his deep self-reflection and moral deliberation, regularly evaluated his decisions and their ethical consequences. This introspective leadership style—coupled with his willingness to listen to dissenting views—gradually earned him the trust of his cabinet and the nation, even among former rivals. Ray Dalio, founder of Bridgewater Associates, institutionalized a culture of radical transparency and self-awareness, where employees are encouraged to openly critique mistakes and refine their thinking. While Dalio's principles have driven Bridgewater's success as one of the world's largest and most influential hedge funds, the uncompromising nature of this approach has also drawn criticism for its intensity. Despite their different arenas (political leadership versus corporate management), Lincoln and Dalio both demonstrate how deliberate reflection and openness can foster trust, accountability, and long-term success.

💡 *Principle 8, Step 2: Communicate Openly and Honestly*

Action: Foster an environment of transparency and open communication.

Example: Franklin D. Roosevelt's Fireside Chats during the Great Depression reassured the American public by providing honest and clear updates on the nation's challenges and solutions. Satya Nadella, CEO of Microsoft, transformed the company culture by promoting open communication and transparency. Under Nadella's leadership, Microsoft's open communication culture led to increased innovation and market competitiveness.

💡 *Principle 8, Step 3: Show Empathy and Compassion*

Action: Demonstrate genuine care for the well-being of your team members.

Example: Howard Schultz, former CEO of Starbucks, focused on creating a supportive and compassionate work environment. Schultz's empathy-driven leadership led to high employee morale and customer loyalty, significantly contributing to Starbucks' global success. Arne Sorenson, former CEO of Marriott International, was known for his compassionate leadership. During the COVID-19 pandemic, Sorenson delivered an emotional video message to Marriott employees, explaining the tough decisions the company had to make while expressing deep empathy for those affected. He waived his salary for the rest of the year and ensured that Marriott supported its employees to the best of its ability during the crisis.

💡 *Principle 8, Step 4: Empower and Trust Your Team*

Action: Delegate responsibilities and trust your team to deliver.

Example: Mahatma Gandhi trusted his followers to carry out nonviolent protests and civil disobedience movements. Richard Branson of Virgin Group encourages entrepreneurial spirit and trusts his team to take risks. Branson's trust in his employees' abilities has led to numerous successful ventures under the Virgin brand.

Principle 8, Step 5: Encourage Innovation through Trust

Action: Create a safe space for experimentation and innovation.

Example: Thomas Edison trusted his team to experiment and fail in the pursuit of inventing the electric lightbulb. Google's 20% time policy gives employees the freedom to pursue projects they are passionate about during work hours. This policy led to the creation of successful products like Gmail and Google Maps, demonstrating the power of trusting employees' innovative capabilities.

Principle 8, Step 6: Build a Culture of Accountability

Action: Foster a sense of responsibility and accountability within your team.

Example: George Washington's leadership during the American Revolution emphasized accountability and discipline. Netflix promotes a culture of freedom and responsibility, holding employees accountable for their results. In his 2020 book *No Rules Rules: Netflix and the Culture of Reinvention*, Reed Hastings, cofounder of Netflix, described how Netflix's high-trust culture had been pivotal in its rapid innovation and market dominance.

💡 *Principle 8, Step 7: Be Consistent and Reliable*

Action: Maintain consistency in your actions and decisions to build reliability.

Example: Abraham Lincoln's consistent ethical stance during the Civil War earned him enduring trust. Warren Buffett's consistent investment principles have earned him immense trust from shareholders. Buffett's reliability and integrity have made Berkshire Hathaway a model of stable and trustworthy leadership.

💡 *Principle 8, Step 8: Lead by Example with Integrity and Consistency*

Action: To build credibility, demonstrate integrity and consistency in your actions and decisions.

Example: Jim Sinegal, cofounder and former CEO of Costco, was known for his modest compensation relative to industry standards. During his tenure, he maintained an annual base salary of $350,000, significantly lower than the average for Fortune 100 CEOs at the time, which was around $1 million. Johnson & Johnson's handling of the Tylenol crisis exemplifies leading with integrity, prioritizing customer safety over profit.

💡 *Principle 8, Step 9: Foster Psychological Safety*

Action: Create an environment where team members feel safe to express ideas and concerns.

Example: Martin Luther King Jr.'s leadership created a safe space for civil rights activists to voice their struggles. Google's Project Aristotle found psychological safety to be crucial for high-performing teams. Organizational town halls with anonymous questions have become a crucial tool for fostering transparency, trust, and open communication between leadership and employees. These meetings allow employees to voice their concerns, seek clarifications, and share ideas without fear of judgment or retaliation. Employees who feel safe to take risks and voice their opinions are more innovative and effective.

💡 *Principle 8, Step 10: Celebrate and Reward Trust-Building Behaviors*

Action: Recognize and reward behaviors that contribute to building trust.

Example: Winston Churchill's recognition of bravery and loyalty during World War II strengthened trust among his allies. Salesforce recognizes and rewards employees who demonstrate trustworthiness and collaboration. Salesforce's culture of recognition and reward has led to high employee engagement and loyalty.

14.11 Ten Barriers to Applying Principle 8

It always seems impossible until it's done.

—Nelson Mandela

By addressing the barriers listed below with practical solutions, leaders can cultivate an environment where trust thrives, leading to enhanced creativity and commitment—and overall organizational success.

Principle 8
TRUST MORE
than others think logical

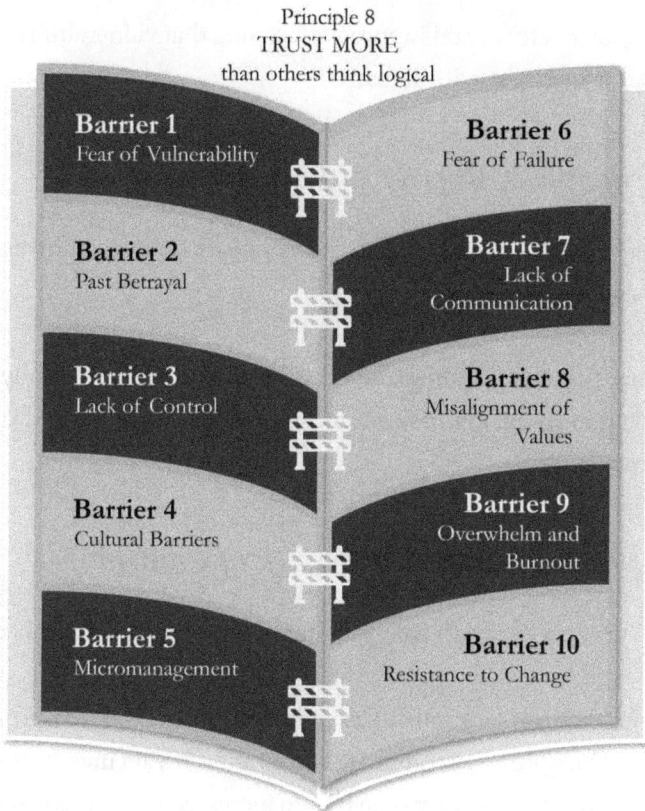

Barrier 1	Barrier 6
Fear of Vulnerability	Fear of Failure
Barrier 2	Barrier 7
Past Betrayal	Lack of Communication
Barrier 3	Barrier 8
Lack of Control	Misalignment of Values
Barrier 4	Barrier 9
Cultural Barriers	Overwhelm and Burnout
Barrier 5	Barrier 10
Micromanagement	Resistance to Change

Trust blockers: ten invisible barriers to applying Principle 8

⚠ *Principle 8, Barrier 1: Fear of Vulnerability*

Barrier: Many leaders fear that trusting others will expose their weaknesses or be perceived as a sign of vulnerability.

Solution: Embrace vulnerability as a strength. Leaders can share their own challenges and mistakes to create a culture of openness and honesty. Brené Brown, a research professor at the University of

Houston, advocates for this approach, arguing that vulnerability fosters connection and trust within teams.

⚠ *Principle 8, Barrier 2: Past Betrayal*

Barrier: Previous experiences of betrayal can make leaders hesitant to trust again.

Solution: Focus on healing and rebuilding trust incrementally. Start by trusting in small, low-risk situations and gradually extend trust as confidence builds.

⚠ *Principle 8, Barrier 3: Lack of Control*

Barrier: Leaders often fear losing control when they place trust in others.

Solution: Shift from a control-based to an empowerment-based leadership style. Delegate responsibilities and empower team members to take ownership of their tasks. This can lead to increased motivation and innovation, as illustrated by Google's approach to employee empowerment.

⚠ *Principle 8, Barrier 4: Cultural Barriers*

Barrier: Some organizational cultures harbor a deep-seated belief that trust must be earned rather than given.

Solution: Foster a culture of trust by leading by example. Demonstrate trustworthiness through consistent and transparent actions. Jeff Weiner, CEO of LinkedIn, emphasizes the importance of embodying the values you wish to see in your organization.

⚠ *Principle 8, Barrier 5: Micromanagement*

Barrier: Leaders who micromanage often struggle to extend trust to their team members.

Solution: Practice delegating tasks and stepping back to allow team members to take the lead. Trust them to find their own solutions and provide support when needed. This approach has been successfully implemented at companies like Netflix, where a culture of freedom and responsibility is promoted.

⚠ *Principle 8, Barrier 6: Fear of Failure*

Barrier: The fear that team members might fail can prevent leaders from extending trust.

Solution: Reframe failure as a learning opportunity. Encourage a growth mindset within the team, where mistakes are seen as chances for development rather than setbacks. Carol Dweck's research on growth mindset supports this approach.

⚠ *Principle 8, Barrier 7: Lack of Communication*

Barrier: Poor communication can lead to misunderstandings and a lack of trust.

Solution: Establish clear and open lines of communication. Regular check-ins, feedback sessions, and transparent sharing of information can help build and maintain trust. Satya Nadella's transformation of Microsoft's culture through open communication is a prime example.

⚠ *Principle 8, Barrier 8: Misalignment of Values*

Barrier: When team members' values do not align with the organization's values, trust can be eroded.

Solution: Ensure alignment of values during the hiring process and reinforce them through continuous engagement and dialogue. Patagonia's commitment to environmental sustainability and its alignment with employee values has built a strong culture of trust.

⚠ *Principle 8, Barrier 9: Overwhelm and Burnout*

Barrier: Taking on too much at once can lead to overwhelm and burnout, triggering self-sabotaging behaviors.

Solution: Prioritize tasks and break them down into manageable steps. Learn to say no and delegate responsibilities when necessary. Make time for rest and relaxation to prevent burnout and maintain balance. This approach helps sustain long-term trust and productivity.

⚠ *Principle 8, Barrier 10: Resistance to Change*

Barrier: Some team members may resist changes that involve greater trust due to comfort with the status quo.

Solution: Gradually introduce changes and involve team members in the process. Explain the benefits of a high-trust environment and seek team members' input to make the transition smoother. John Kotter's change management model highlights the importance of creating a vision and communicating it effectively.

14.12 Ten Examples of Applying Principle 8

1. A CEO empowers employees by giving them decision-making authority, boosting morale and innovation.
2. Alex allows his team to make strategic decisions independently, even if it means accepting potential failures.
3. Michael implements a flat hierarchy, encouraging open communication and decision-making across all levels.
4. Tom gives his remote team complete autonomy over their schedules, trusting them to manage their time effectively.
5. Olivia allows her team to set their own project deadlines, confident in their time management skills.
6. Mia entrusts a new employee with a critical client presentation, demonstrating her belief in their abilities.
7. A team leader delegates critical tasks to team members, trusting their capabilities and fostering a collaborative environment.
8. A community leader delegates the organization of a major event to a group of volunteers, trusting their abilities.
9. A partner supports their significant other's career change, trusting their judgment and potential.
10. A parent trusts their teenager to plan a family vacation, building their confidence and responsibility.

14.13 Closing Reflections

The measure of a man is what he does with power.

—Plato

Trust is a powerful and transformative force in leadership and organizational success. By *trusting more than others think logical*, leaders can unlock unparalleled benefits that drive performance and innovation. Trust reduces transactional costs by eliminating the need for excessive monitoring and control mechanisms, allowing for quicker decision-making and streamlined operations.

Moreover, trust significantly boosts productivity and creativity within teams. When employees feel trusted and valued, they are more likely to take initiative, propose innovative ideas, and collaborate effectively. This is supported by Gallup's findings that high-trust cultures experience 50% higher employee productivity. Google's Project Aristotle further reinforces this, showing that psychological safety, a component of trust, is crucial for high-performing teams, enabling them to be more innovative and effective.

Decreased turnover is another critical advantage of a trust-based leadership approach. Employees who trust their leaders and feel trusted in return are more engaged and committed to their organization, leading to lower turnover rates. This retention of talent not only saves on recruitment and training costs but also ensures continuity and stability within the organization.

In essence, *trusting more than others think logical* fosters an environment where efficiency, innovation, and loyalty thrive. By embracing trust, leaders can create resilient, dynamic, and successful organizations that are well-equipped to navigate the complexities of the modern business landscape. Cultivating trust is not only an ethical imperative but a strategic necessity for sustained organizational success.

14.14 Daily Practice

1. **Put trust in others:** Trust your team members with significant responsibilities and decision-making authority.
2. **Be transparent:** Openly communicate your goals and expectations, be transparent about the decision-making process, and nurture a culture that encourages open, honest communication.
3. **Inspire with a higher purpose:** Communicate a noble purpose for the work and align your values and actions with a purpose that is bigger than yourself.

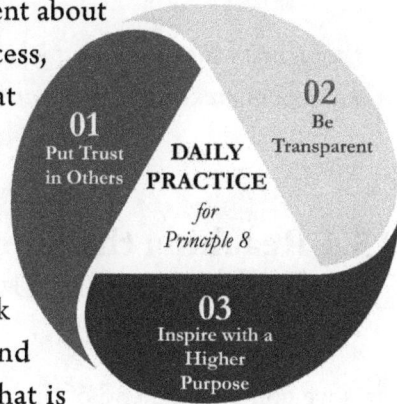

01
Put Trust
in Others

02
Be
Transparent

DAILY PRACTICE
for
Principle 8

03
Inspire with a
Higher
Purpose

15 Epilogue: Personal Commitment

The highest education is that which does not merely give us information but makes our life in harmony with all existence.

—Rabindranath Tagore

15.1 Reaching the Summit: Reflections on Our Path

As we come to the end of this journey, it is essential to reflect on the path we have traveled and the transformative insights we have uncovered. At the beginning of this book, we posed fundamental questions: Why DEEP PACT? Why does happiness matter? As we reach the conclusion of the book, it is time to revisit these questions with fresh perspectives. T. S. Eliot, in his poem "Little Gidding" from *Four Quartets*, poignantly captures the essence of our journey with these lines:

> *We shall not cease from exploration*
> *And the end of all our exploring*
> *Will be to arrive where we started*
> *And know the place for the first time.*

This idea of rediscovery is central to our journey through this book. By reflecting on the same questions after absorbing the insights and principles discussed, we gain a deeper understanding and appreciation for their significance. Through this exploration, we find out that the answers to the above fundamental questions are richer and more profound, having been shaped by our experiences and the wisdom gained along the way.

In a world fraught with complexities and challenges, the need for effective leadership has never been more pressing. Leadership is not confined to titles or positions; it is about influence, vision, and the ability to inspire others toward a common goal. This book aims to redefine leadership by presenting a new definition and eight powerful principles that challenge conventional wisdom and encourage a proactive, inclusive, and dynamic approach.

Leadership is a necessity, not just for organizational success, but for personal well-being and fulfillment. Initially, we might have viewed leadership as a role confined to positions of authority or as a means to achieve external success. However, our exploration has revealed that true leadership transcends titles and positions. It is about influencing others positively, fostering growth, and creating meaningful impact. Leadership, as we now understand, is intrinsically linked to our personal health, happiness, and job satisfaction. It is about finding purpose and making a difference, which in turn enriches our own lives.

The DEEP PACT framework, with its emphasis on lofty ideals and actionable principles, might have seemed idealistic at first glance. However, through our journey, we have seen how each principle— *Decide, act, and lead; Examine your beliefs and actions; Ensure excellence; Protect yourself from self-sabotage; Practice more humility; Act with more integrity; Care more for people; and Trust more*—provides a practical roadmap for personal and professional growth. The power of DEEP PACT lies in its ability to integrate these lofty ideals into everyday actions, leading to lasting change and fulfillment.

After reading this book, our perspectives on these questions may have evolved. We now recognize that leadership is not an abstract concept reserved for a select few, but a tangible practice that each of us can develop and embody. The principles of DEEP PACT are not just lofty ideals but actionable steps that can transform our approach to leadership and life. By continually examining our beliefs and actions, we align ourselves more closely with our values and aspirations, leading to greater coherence and satisfaction in both our personal and professional lives.

15.2 The Journey of Self-Discovery

The journey of self-discovery is powerfully illustrated through an allegorical narrative in Fariduddin Attar's mystical masterpiece *The Conference of the Birds*. The story follows a group of birds, led by the Hoopoe, as they embark on a quest to find their king, the Simorgh. This journey is not just a physical expedition but a profound spiritual quest representing the search for enlightenment and self-realization. Along the way, the birds face numerous trials and tribulations, each symbolizing the inner challenges and distractions that one must overcome to achieve true understanding and self-awareness.

The key points of this allegorical journey highlight the transformative power of self-discovery. Each bird represents a different human flaw or attachment, such as greed, pride, or fear, which must be confronted and transcended. As the birds proceed through the seven valleys—Quest, Love, Knowledge, Detachment, Unity, Bewilderment, and Self-Annihilation—they shed their egos and misconceptions, ultimately realizing that the Simorgh they seek is none other than themselves. This revelation underscores the central theme that the divine—or true self—is within us all; the journey's purpose is to awaken us to this reality.

The power of Attar's allegory lies in its depiction of the inner journey toward self-discovery. The birds' quest teaches that true enlightenment is not found in external pursuits but through introspection and spiritual growth. By overcoming personal obstacles and purifying their hearts, the birds symbolize the potential for transformation and the realization of one's true nature. This timeless message resonates with the idea that self-discovery is a journey of continuous exploration and inner reflection, leading to the profound understanding that we are inherently connected to the divine essence within.

The allegory in *The Conference of the Birds* underscores a vital lesson for leadership: the necessity of personal commitment in the journey of self-discovery and growth. Just as the birds must individually confront and overcome their personal flaws to reach enlightenment, aspiring leaders must commit to an ongoing process of self-reflection and improvement. This journey requires dedication, resilience, and the willingness to face uncomfortable truths about oneself. Personal commitment in leadership means embracing the DEEP PACT principles—continually examining beliefs, fostering integrity, and caring for others—while navigating the daily challenges and distractions that arise in the course of our lives. By committing to this path, leaders not only transform themselves but also inspire and elevate those around them, much like the birds of Attar's tale that, through their collective journey, discover the divine essence within. This personal dedication to growth and self-awareness is what ultimately enables leaders to guide others with authenticity, empathy, and a profound sense of purpose.

Rediscovery, as Eliot and Attar suggest, is a powerful process. It allows us to revisit familiar questions with new insights, deepening our understanding and commitment. As we ponder, "Why DEEP PACT?" once more, we find that our answers are richer and more nuanced. Leadership is essential because it fosters a sense of purpose, drives personal and collective growth, and enhances our overall well-being. DEEP PACT, with its holistic approach, equips us with the tools to navigate the complexities of modern life, ensuring that our pursuit of excellence is both meaningful and sustainable. Through this journey of exploration and rediscovery, we come to know the place—our purpose and potential—as if for the first time.

15.3 DEEP PACT Needs Personal Commitment

In this epilogue, let us take time to reflect on the DEEP PACT principles and the inspirational stories that bring them to life, with the intention of guiding our leadership journey through sincere personal commitments. This final chapter invites you to turn knowledge and understanding into action—to personalize each principle and apply it in ways that reflect your unique context and convictions. Leadership, at its core, is not about acquiring power or prestige; it is about embodying purpose and integrity in the pursuit of something greater than oneself.

Why, one might inquire, aspire to leadership? Beware the siren call of avarice, for the pursuit of power and prestige shrouds in darkness the path to true leadership. Instead, seek solace in endeavors larger than oneself, for therein lies the true essence of leadership. Amid the labyrinthine complexities of life, leadership assumes paramount importance, for its absence exacts a heavy toll on individuals and institutions alike. Consider the staggering cost of poor leadership—a toll measured not only in monetary terms but also in the erosion of commitment and performance. Consider the staggering cost of human lives—workplace stress contributing to over 120,000 deaths annually in the United States alone.

Leadership is the cornerstone of progress and innovation. It shapes the future, drives change, and creates a sense of purpose and direction. This book was written to provide a comprehensive framework for understanding and practicing effective leadership. By exploring eight foundational principles, we have delved into the essence of what it means to lead in today's world. Each principle offers a unique perspective on leadership, urging us to think beyond traditional boundaries and embrace a more visionary approach. In the pages that follow, we revisit each of the eight principles of DEEP PACT—not to summarize them, but to invite deeper reflection. Each subsection offers a final thought and personal commitment challenge, calling on you to live the principle, not just understand it. Whether you are at the start of your journey or far along the path, these closing reflections are designed to help you internalize the values of decisive action, empathy, ethics, and purpose that define whole-person leadership.

Principle 1: Decide, Act, and Lead without Waiting for Approval

The first principle sets the stage for proactive leadership. It emphasizes the importance of initiative and autonomy, encouraging us to step forward and take charge without waiting for external validation.

This principle is exemplified by historical figures like Harriet Tubman, who, despite immense risks, led countless slaves to freedom via the Underground Railroad. Tubman did not wait for permission; she saw a need and acted upon it with courage and determination. Her leadership was rooted in a deep sense of purpose and unwavering commitment to her vision.

In fiction, we see a similar spirit in characters like Katniss Everdeen from *The Hunger Games*. Katniss did not wait for permission to lead the rebellion against a tyrannical regime. She stepped up, inspired others, and became a symbol of hope and resistance. Her journey teaches us that true leadership is about recognizing opportunities for change and taking bold actions to make a difference. While fictional, her journey mirrors real-world leadership lessons: transformative change often begins when individuals act on conviction, not waiting for validation, much like Rosa Parks.

When leaders stop waiting for permission, they break free from self-imposed constraints and societal expectations. This liberation allows them to envision possibilities that others might deem unrealistic. The courage to lead without asking for permission lays the foundation for dreaming bigger and setting visionary goals that can transform organizations and inspire others.

Dreaming big is not about idle fantasies; it is about setting audacious goals that inspire you and those around you to reach for greatness. Think of the pioneers who have changed the world with their dreams. Steve Jobs revolutionized personal computing, music, and mobile technology with Apple, transforming how people interact with technology on a global scale. Jeff Bezos, driven by the dream of creating a seamless online marketplace, built Amazon into a behemoth that redefined e-commerce, logistics, and even cloud computing. Sara Blakely, with no background in fashion or business, turned a simple idea—comfortable shapewear—into Spanx, a billion-dollar brand that disrupted the apparel industry. Malala Yousafzai, despite facing grave danger, dreamed of a world where every girl has access to education, and her advocacy has sparked global movements and policy changes. These individuals prove that dreaming big is not just about ambition—it ignites a sense of purpose and passion that drives progress, fuels resilience, and turns the impossible into reality.

Personal commitment: I will take the initiative to lead without asking for permission and dream boldly. I will identify a vision that excites and challenges me. I will write it down, share it with others, and take actionable steps toward making it a reality. I will remember that the size of my dreams reflects the depth of my ambition and the scope of my impact.

Principle 2: Examine Your Beliefs and Actions More Than Others Think Wise

The second principle is about cultivating a mindset of continuous learning and introspection. True leaders are not rigid in their thinking; they are open to new ideas, willing to challenge their assumptions, and committed to personal growth.

Mahatma Gandhi exemplified this principle through his lifelong dedication to self-reflection and growth. His ability to adapt his beliefs and strategies in response to changing circumstances made him a formidable leader in the fight for India's independence. By examining your beliefs, you gain a deeper understanding of your values and motivations, enabling you to lead with greater clarity and authenticity.

In the realm of fiction, we find inspiration in Atticus Finch from *To Kill a Mockingbird*. Atticus's unwavering commitment to justice and equality, despite societal prejudice, demonstrates the power of examining one's beliefs and standing firm in the face of adversity. His introspective approach and moral clarity make him a timeless example of ethical leadership.

Personal commitment: I will regularly reflect on my beliefs and values. I will seek feedback from others, read widely, and engage in thoughtful discussions. I will be willing to change my perspective in light of new information and experiences. This practice of introspection will enhance my self-awareness and strengthen my leadership.

Principle 3: Ensure Excellence More Than Others Think Imaginable

The third principle challenges you to set the highest standards for yourself and your team. Excellence is not about perfection; it is about striving to be the best you can be and inspiring others to do the same.

Steve Jobs's relentless pursuit of excellence at Apple revolutionized multiple industries. His commitment to creating products that combined functionality with beauty set a new standard for innovation and design. By ensuring excellence, you create a culture of high performance and continuous improvement.

In fiction, we see a similar dedication in characters like Hermione Granger from the Harry Potter series. Hermione's pursuit of knowledge and her meticulous attention to detail often saved her friends from dire situations. Her commitment to excellence in her studies and her willingness to go above and beyond demonstrate the importance of striving for the highest standards in everything we do.

Personal commitment: I will set ambitious goals for myself and my team and communicate them clearly. I will focus on quality in everything I do and encourage others to do the same. I will celebrate achievements and learn from failures, always striving to improve. Excellence will be the hallmark of my leadership.

Principle 4: Protect Yourself from Self-Sabotage More Than Others Think Necessary

The fourth principle involves recognizing and overcoming the behaviors and thought patterns that undermine your success. Self-sabotage can take many forms, from procrastination to negative self-talk.

Thomas Edison's perseverance in the face of countless failures exemplifies the importance of protecting oneself from self-sabotage. His ability to view setbacks as learning opportunities allowed him to ultimately succeed in inventing the lightbulb. By cultivating resilience and a positive mindset, you can navigate challenges more effectively.

In fiction, we find a powerful example in Elizabeth Bennet from *Pride and Prejudice*. Elizabeth's initial prejudices and quick judgments could have sabotaged her happiness. However, her self-reflection and willingness to confront her biases allowed her to grow and ultimately find love and fulfillment. Her story teaches us the importance of overcoming self-imposed limitations and embracing personal growth.

Personal commitment: I will identify and address the ways in which I may be sabotaging my own success. I will develop strategies to overcome these behaviors, such as arrogance, a fixed mindset, micromanagement, and a profit-only mindset. I will seek feedback, conduct introspection, nurture a growth mindset, and trust others.

Principle 5: Practice More Humility Than Others Think Possible

The fifth principle underscores the importance of humility in leadership. Humility allows you to recognize your limitations, seek feedback, and value the contributions of others.

Nelson Mandela's humility and willingness to listen to others were key to his success in leading South Africa out of apartheid. His ability to forgive and his commitment to reconciliation demonstrated profound moral strength. By practicing humility, you build stronger relationships and foster a collaborative environment.

In fiction, we see humility exemplified by Samwise Gamgee from *The Lord of the Rings*. Sam's unwavering loyalty and selflessness were crucial to Frodo's success in destroying the One Ring. Sam's humility, despite his significant contributions, underscores the importance of supporting others and recognizing that leadership is often about serving those around you.

Personal commitment: I will approach leadership with humility. I will acknowledge my strengths and weaknesses and be open to feedback. I will value the contributions of others and create opportunities for them to shine. Humility is a powerful tool for building trust and fostering collaboration.

Principle 6: Act with More Integrity Than Others Think Prudent

The sixth principle emphasizes the importance of ethical leadership. Integrity is about making decisions based on your principles, even when it is difficult or unpopular.

Abraham Lincoln's leadership during the American Civil War was guided by his commitment to justice and equality. His integrity and moral conviction were instrumental in preserving the Union and abolishing slavery. By acting with integrity, leaders inspire trust and create a culture of ethical behavior.

In fiction, we find a compelling example in Albus Dumbledore from the Harry Potter series. Dumbledore's unwavering commitment to fighting against dark forces, even at great personal cost, reflects his deep sense of integrity. His leadership teaches us that acting with integrity, even when it seems irrational, is essential for inspiring trust and creating lasting change.

Personal commitment: I will make integrity the cornerstone of my leadership. I will ensure that my actions align with my values and make ethical decisions even when faced with pressure or temptation. I will be fair and consistent. Integrity is essential for building credibility and trust.

Principle 7: Care More for People Than Others Think Reasonable

The seventh principle highlights the importance of empathy and compassion in leadership. Caring for your team members and creating a supportive environment is crucial for their well-being and performance.

Mother Teresa's selfless service to the poor and sick exemplified her deep care for humanity. Her compassion and dedication to helping others made her a global symbol of kindness and altruism. By caring for people, you foster loyalty, engagement, and a positive organizational culture.

In fiction, we see this principle in action with Jean Valjean from Victor Hugo's *Les Misérables*. Valjean's transformation from a hardened criminal to a compassionate and caring individual reflects his deep commitment to helping others. His leadership, marked by empathy and selflessness, shows the profound impact of caring for people beyond what is considered reasonable.

Personal Commitment: I will prioritize the well-being of my team members. I will actively listen and show empathy and compassion in my interactions. I will create a supportive environment where everyone feels valued and respected. Caring for people is not just wise; it is essential for effective leadership.

Principle 8: Trust More Than Others Think Logical

The eighth and final principle underscores the importance of building trust within your team or organization. Trust is the foundation of effective collaboration and innovation.

Warren Buffett's decentralized management style at Berkshire Hathaway is based on trusting the leaders of subsidiary companies to make independent decisions. This approach has fostered a culture of responsibility and innovation. By extending trust, you empower others and create a high-performance environment.

In fiction, we find a powerful example in Gandalf from *The Lord of the Rings*. Gandalf's trust in the diverse members of the Fellowship of the Ring empowered each to play a crucial role in the quest to destroy the One Ring. His leadership demonstrates the strength that comes from trusting others and recognizing the unique contributions they can make.

Personal commitment: I will extend trust to my team members and encourage them to take initiative. I aim to create a culture of accountability and support, where everyone feels empowered to contribute their best. Trust is the glue that holds our team together and drives our success by inspiring us.

15.4 DEEP PACT's Character Ethic and Rumi's Seven Maxims

There are seven days in the week, seven colors in a rainbow, seven notes on a musical scale, seven seas, and seven continents.

—Unknown

As you make a personal commitment to DEEP PACT and incorporate its principles into your daily routine, remember that it is ultimately a character-building tool. Jensen Huang's assertion that "greatness comes from character" and Stephen Covey's "character ethic" paradigm reinforce the idea that happy and great leadership is rooted in fundamental principles of integrity, resilience, humility, and moral values rather than superficial skills or tactics. To build strong character, leaders must draw inspiration and guidance from multiple sources, ensuring a well-rounded foundation of principles. This diverse approach allows for resilience, as a breach or failure in one source of guidance can be compensated for by the strength of others.

At the beginning of this book, we shared with you a story about a fictional monk and three boys who climbed a mountain to test the monk's abilities and returned with the enlightenment that choice lies within us. Now, let us meet a real monk, a 13th-century Sufi teacher and poet who has become the best-selling poet in America. Mevlana Jalaluddin Rumi, commonly known as Rumi, is renowned for his profound spiritual teachings and poetry. His works transcend time and cultural boundaries, offering timeless wisdom that resonates deeply with contemporary audiences.

One of Rumi's most celebrated contributions to spiritual literature is his seven maxims, which provide a simple yet profound guide for living a life of integrity, compassion, and authenticity. These maxims, elaborated below, resonate deeply with the principles of DEEP PACT and can serve as a complementary and buttressing framework. By integrating these timeless teachings, leaders can reinforce and expand upon the character-building aspects of DEEP PACT, ensuring a robust and resilient approach to leadership that is both dynamic and ethical.

1. **In generosity and helping others, be like a river.** Effective leaders understand the importance of generosity and support within their teams. Like a river that continuously flows and nourishes the land, leaders should consistently offer their time, resources, and encouragement to help their team members grow and succeed. This fosters a culture of care, enhancing overall team performance and satisfaction.

2. **In compassion and grace, be like the sun.** Leaders should embody compassion and grace, treating their team members with warmth and kindness, much like the sun provides

light and warmth to all it touches. By leading with empathy, leaders can build trust and create a positive, inclusive work environment where individuals feel valued and understood. This servant leadership approach not only boosts morale but also drives engagement and loyalty.

3. **In concealing others' faults, be like the night.** Great leaders protect the privacy and dignity of their team members by handling mistakes discreetly and constructively. Instead of public criticism, they offer guidance and support in private, much like the night conceals the imperfections of the day. This respectful approach creates a space of psychological safety and encourages a culture of continuous improvement and mutual respect.

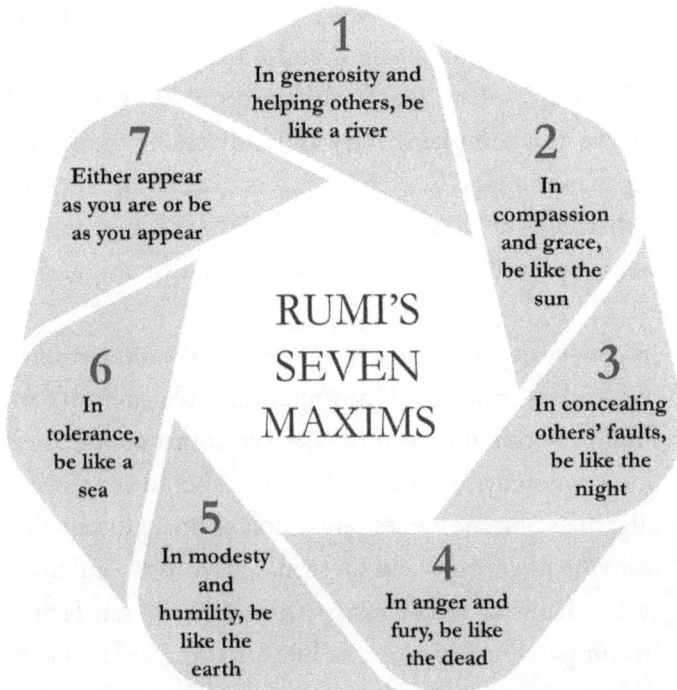

1
In generosity and helping others, be like a river

2
In compassion and grace, be like the sun

3
In concealing others' faults, be like the night

4
In anger and fury, be like the dead

5
In modesty and humility, be like the earth

6
In tolerance, be like a sea

7
Either appear as you are or be as you appear

RUMI'S SEVEN MAXIMS

The geometry of life: Rumi's seven maxims

4. **In anger and fury, be like the dead.** Leaders who practice self-regulation and manage their emotions effectively, especially anger, set a powerful example for their teams. Just as the dead are unmoved by anger, leaders should maintain their composure to make rational decisions and foster a stable and positive environment of psychological safety. This emotionally intelligent approach helps in navigating conflicts and maintaining stability within the organization.

5. **In modesty and humility, be like the Earth.** Leaders should learn from the Earth's humility in nurturing all life without seeking recognition because humility is a cornerstone of strong leadership. Leaders who remain grounded and approachable, like the Earth, inspire respect and loyalty. They recognize that leadership is about serving others and facilitating their success, rather than seeking personal glory. This humble approach fosters a collaborative environment and encourages team members to contribute their best ideas.

6. **In tolerance, be like a sea.** Embracing diversity and practicing tolerance are essential for effective leadership. Leaders who, like the vast sea, accept and value different perspectives and backgrounds create an inclusive culture that fosters innovation and creativity through continuous self-examination. This openness not only enhances team dynamics but also drives the organization toward greater achievements.

7. **Either appear as you are or be as you appear.** Authenticity is crucial for building trust and credibility. Leaders who are genuine and transparent in their actions and decisions, matching their words with their deeds, cultivate an environment of trust and integrity. This authenticity encourages team members to also be their true selves, leading to a more honest and effective workplace.

15.5 Final Reflections: Making the DEEP PACT

In the long run, we shape our lives, and we shape ourselves. The process never ends until we die. And the choices we make are ultimately our responsibility.

—Eleanor Roosevelt

As we conclude this journey, it is time to make a DEEP PACT with yourself. This pact is a commitment to embody and integrate these eight powerful principles into your leadership journey. By doing so, you are not only transforming your own leadership but also inspiring those around you to reach for greatness.

The DEEP PACT is a promise to lead with courage, integrity, and purpose. It is a commitment to dream boldly, examine your beliefs and actions, ensure excellence, protect yourself from self-sabotage, practice humility, act with integrity, care for people, and trust deeply. This pact is not just a set of principles; it is a call to action, a guide to becoming the best leader you can be.

As you move forward, remember the stories of visionary leaders from history and fiction who have embodied these principles. Let their journeys inspire you to take bold actions and make a positive impact in your organization and community. Leadership is not a destination but a continuous journey of growth and learning. It is not merely about efficiency and business results, but about continuous reinvention through outside-the-box thinking. Embrace the DEEP PACT and lead with the confidence, resilience, and compassion needed to create a better future for all.

Make a copy of the eight principles and hang it in front of your desk so that you can read and reflect on them every day. Focus on the daily practices listed at the end of any chapter for one week or one month. This consistent reinforcement will help you internalize these principles and integrate them into your daily routine, fostering a more mindful and effective approach to leadership.

By committing to the DEEP PACT, you are making a profound promise to yourself and to those you lead. This commitment will guide you through challenges, inspire you to achieve great things, and leave a lasting legacy of positive change. Let this pact be the foundation of your leadership journey, inspiring you to become the visionary leader you were meant to be. Let us continue this journey of leadership with a renewed sense of purpose and a commitment to making a positive impact in our organizations and communities. The future of leadership is in our hands, and it begins with the choices we make and the actions we take today.

It does not matter how slowly you go as long as you do not stop.
—Confucius

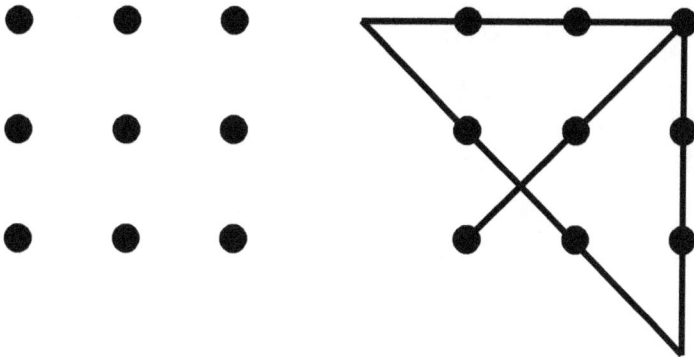

The classic nine-dot problem (left), as presented in Chapter 1, and its solution (right), which requires thinking beyond the perceived boundaries of the grid.

Notes and References

Part 1: Problem and Solution

2   **Tao Te Ching on wisdom and knowing:** Lao Tzu. *Tao Te Ching*. Translated by D. C. Lau. New York: Penguin Classics, 1963.

2   **Marcus Aurelius on obstacles:** Aurelius, Marcus. *Meditations*. Translated by Gregory Hays. New York: Modern Library, 2003.

2   **Viktor Frankl on changing oneself:** Frankl, Viktor E. *Man's Search for Meaning*. Translated by Ilse Lasch. Boston: Beacon Press, 2006.

Chapter 1: Introduction: Why This Book, Why Now

3   **Simon Sinek on purpose in leadership:** Sinek, Simon. *Start with Why: How Great Leaders Inspire Everyone to Take Action*. New York: Portfolio, 2009.

3   **Frederick Winslow Taylor on scientific management:** Taylor, Frederick Winslow. *The Principles of Scientific Management*. New York: Harper & Brothers, 1911.

5   **Mary Parker Follett on collaborative management:** Follett, Mary Parker. *Creative Experience*. New York: Longmans, Green and Co., 1924.

5   **Peter Drucker on Follett as prophet of management:** Drucker, Peter F. *The Essential Drucker: The Best of Sixty Years of Peter Drucker's Essential Writings on Management*. New York: HarperCollins, 2001.

7   **Hersey and Blanchard on situational leadership:** Hersey, Paul, and Kenneth H. Blanchard. *Management of Organizational Behavior: Utilizing Human Resources*. Englewood Cliffs, NJ: Prentice-Hall, 1969.

7   **James MacGregor Burns on transformational leadership:** Burns, James MacGregor. *Leadership*. New York: Harper & Row, 1978.

7   **Robert K. Greenleaf on servant leadership:** Greenleaf, Robert K. *Servant Leadership: A Journey into the Nature of Legitimate Power and Greatness*. New York: Paulist Press, 1977.

7   **Bernard Bass on transactional leadership:** Bass, Bernard M. *Leadership and Performance beyond Expectations*. New York: Free Press, 1985.

8   **Agile Manifesto, Agile leadership:** Beck, Kent, et al. *Manifesto for Agile Software Development*. 2001.

8   **Authentic leadership:** George, Bill. *Authentic Leadership: Rediscovering the Secrets to Creating Lasting Value*. San Francisco: Jossey-Bass, 2003.

8   **Coaching leadership:** Whitmore, Sir John, and Tiffany Gaskell. 2024. *Coaching for Performance: The Principles and Practice of Coaching and Leadership: Fully Revised Edition for 2024.* 6th ed. London: John Murray Business.

8   **2016 HOW Report:** *The HOW Report: A Global, Empirical Analysis of How Governance, Culture and Leadership Impact Performance.* New York: LRN Corporation, 2016.

9   **Stephen M. R. Covey on trust and inspire:** Covey, Stephen M. R. *Trust and Inspire: How Truly Great Leaders Unleash Greatness in Others.* New York: Simon & Schuster, 2022.

10   **Great Resignation:** World Economic Forum. "What Is the 'Great Resignation?' An Expert Explains." November 2021.

10   **Deloitte on leadership change:** Deloitte. *Global Human Capital Trends Report 2023.* New York: Deloitte Insights, 2023.

10   **Harvard leadership development study:** *2024 Global Leadership Development Study: Time to Transform.* Boston: Harvard Business Publishing, 2024.

12   **Gallup on what followers want:** Gallup. *Global Leadership Report: What Followers Want.* Washington, D.C.: Gallup, 2025.

13   **Follett on leadership and power:** Follett, Mary Parker. *Dynamic Administration: The Collected Papers of Mary Parker Follett.* Edited by Henry C. Metcalf and L. Urwick. New York: Harper & Brothers, 1941.

14   **U.S. News & World Report on New Year's resolutions:** "Why Most New Year's Resolutions Fail." *U.S. News & World Report,* January 3, 2024.

14   **Robert Kegan and Lisa Lahey on immunity to change:** Kegan, Robert, and Lisa Laskow Lahey. *Immunity to Change: How to Overcome It and Unlock the Potential in Yourself and Your Organization.* Boston: Harvard Business Press, 2009.

14   **Plato's Allegory of the Cave:** Plato. *The Republic.* Translated by Allan Bloom. New York: Basic Books, 1968.

18   **Forbes article by Vibhas Ratanjee:** Ratanjee, Vibhas. "The Leadership Competency Few Talk About: Unlearning What No Longer Serves You." *Forbes,* April 18, 2025.

18   **Alvin Toffler on future illiterates:** Toffler, Alvin. *Rethinking the Future: Rethinking Business, Principles, Competition, Control & Complexity, Leadership, Markets, and the World.* Edited by Rowan Gibson. London: Nicholas Brealey Publishing, 1997.

18   **Kluge and Gronau on intentional forgetting:** Kluge, Annette, and Norbert Gronau. "Intentional Forgetting in Organizations: The Importance of Eliminating Retrieval Cues for Implementing New Routines." *Frontiers in Psychology* 9 (2018).

19   **Deloitte on burnout:** Deloitte, *Global Human Capital Trends Report 2023.*

19　**HOW Institute report on moral leadership:** *The State of Moral Leadership in Business: 2025.* New York: The HOW Institute for Society, 2025.

20　**Gallup on employee engagement:** *State of the Global Workplace Report 2024.* Washington, DC: Gallup Press, 2024.

21　**Top Employers Institute on Gen Z:** "Gen Z: Redefining the Future of Work." Top Employers Institute, June 2024.

21　**Gartner report on 2025 top priorities:** *Top 5 Priorities for HR Leaders in 2025: Actionable Insights to Navigate Challenges and Drive Business Impact.* Stamford, CT: Gartner, 2023.

22　**Center for Creative Leadership on lack of training:** Gentry, William A. *Developing New Managers? How to Set Your First-Time Leaders Up for Success.* Greensboro, NC: Center for Creative Leadership, 2022.

22　**Failure of managers:** CEB Global. "Why Most New Managers Fail and How to Prevent It." *Forbes,* February 15, 2023.

22　**Impact of leadership on employees:** Development Dimensions International (DDI). "Measuring the Impact of Leadership on Employee Engagement." *DDI Blog,* February 20, 2024.

22　**Bad managers creating unnecessary work and stress:** Society for Human Resource Management. "Survey: 84 Percent of U.S. Workers Blame Bad Managers for Creating Unnecessary Stress." SHRM.org, August 12, 2020.

24　**Anne Frank on happy people:** Anne Frank. *The Diary of a Young Girl.* Edited by Otto H. Frank and Mirjam Pressler, translated by Susan Massoty. Westminster, MD: Bantam Books, 1997.

Chapter 2: What's New and Why It Matters to Your Growth

25　**Mahmud Shabistari on inner potential:** Shabistari, Mahmud. *The Secret Rose Garden.* Translated by Florence Lederer. London: John M. Watkins, 1914.

27　**Gallup on employee engagement:** *State of the Global Workplace Report 2024.* Washington, DC: Gallup Press, 2024.

27　**Harvard Business Review on happiness and productivity:** Achor, Shawn. "The Happiness Dividend." *Harvard Business Review,* June 23, 2011.

27　**Oxford research on happiness:** Bellet, C. S., J.-E. De Neve, and G. Ward. *Does Employee Happiness Have an Impact on Productivity?* Centre for Economic Performance Discussion Paper No. 1655. London School of Economics and Political Science, 2019.

27　**Canada Human Resources on unhappy workers:** Employee Engagement, February 15, 2010.

27 *Harvard Business Review* on happiness and productivity: Peppercorn, Susan. "Why You Should Stop Trying to Be Happy at Work." *Harvard Business Review,* July 26, 2019.

27 *MIT Sloan Management Review* on happiness and meaning: Bailey, Catherine, and Adrian Madden. "What Makes Work Meaningful—Or Meaningless." *MIT Sloan Management Review* 57, no. 4 (Summer 2016).

28 MIT research on employee experience: Dery, Kristine, and Ina M. Sebastian. "Building Business Value with Employee Experience." *MIT Sloan Center for Information Systems Research, Research Briefing* 18, no. 6 (June 15, 2017).

28 12 data-driven habits that set best leaders apart: Vanderbloemen, William. *Be the Unicorn: 12 Data-Driven Habits That Separate the Best Leaders from the Rest.* Nashville: Thomas Nelson, 2023.

29 Stanford Graduate School of Business on emotional intelligence in AI workplaces: "Emotional Intelligence and AI in the Workplace." *Stanford Insights,* September 2024.

29 MIT Sloan on ethical AI practices: MIT Sloan School of Management. "Ethical AI: Leadership Insights." *MIT Sloan Management Review* (Winter 2024).

29 Harvard Business Publishing on global leadership trends: *2024 Global Leadership Development Study: Insights on Leadership and Learning Trends.* Boston: Harvard Business Publishing, 2024.

29 David Epstein on generalists in leadership: Epstein, David. *Range: Why Generalists Triumph in a Specialized World.* New York: Riverhead Books, 2019.

29 Simon Sinek on the importance of "why" in leadership: Sinek, Simon. *Start with Why: How Great Leaders Inspire Everyone to Take Action.* New York: Portfolio, 2009.

30 David A. Kolb's experiential learning theory: Kolb, David A. *Experiential Learning: Experience as the Source of Learning and Development.* Englewood Cliffs, NJ: Prentice Hall, 1984.

33 Gallup on employee departure: *State of the American Manager: Analytics and Advice for Leaders.* Washington, DC: Gallup Press, 2015.

33 Workplace bullying: *2017 WBI U.S. Workplace Bullying Survey.* Bellingham, WA: Workplace Bullying Institute, 2017.

34 Edelman Trust Barometer on trust decline: *2021 Edelman Trust Barometer.* New York: Edelman, 2021.

34 Gallup Poll on managers: *Why Great Managers Are So Rare.* Washington, DC: Gallup Press, 2016.

34 Cost of employee disengagement at work: The Engagement Institute. *Study on Employee Engagement and Its Financial Impact.* Collaboration of the

Conference Board, Sirota-Mercer, Deloitte, ROI Institute, the Culture Works, and Consulting LLP, 2017.

34   **Jeffrey Pfeffer, Stefanos Zenios, and Joel Goh on workplace stress mortality:** Goh, Joel, Jeffrey Pfeffer, and Stefanos A. Zenios. "Workplace Stressors and Health Costs in the U.S." *Management Science* 61, no. 3 (2015): 510–528.

35   **Deloitte on employee purpose and engagement:** *Millennial and Gen Z Workplace Values Report 2024*. New York: Deloitte Insights, 2024.

35   **McKinsey on flexibility:** "American Opportunity Survey: Flexibility Remains Key for Workers." McKinsey & Company, June 23, 2022.

35   **Purdue Global on career growth expectations of Gen Z:** "Generational Differences in the Workplace" [infographic]. Purdue University Global, 2025.

36   **Global Strategy Group on societal issues:** *Business & Politics: Do They Mix?* New York: Global Strategy Group. January 27, 2016.

36   **Economic Policy Institute on CEO pay:** Bivens, J., E. Gould, and J. Kandra. "CEO Pay Declined in 2023: But It Has Soared 1,085% since 1978 Compared with a 24% Rise in Typical Workers' Pay." Economic Policy Institute. September 19, 2024.

36   **Institute for Policy Studies on CEO pay:** Anderson, S., and O. Alperstein. "Executive Excess 2024: The Low-Wage 100—The U.S. Corporations Squeezing Workers to Boost Shareholder Value." Institute for Policy Studies. August 29, 2024.

37   **US Bureau of Labor Statistics on the Great Resignation:** US Bureau of Labor Statistics. "Record High Quit Rates amid the Great Resignation." *Monthly Labor Review*, August 2021.

37   **Microsoft on employee turnover during pandemic:** *"The Next Great Disruption Is Hybrid Work—Are We Ready?:* Redmond, WA: Microsoft, March 22, 2021.

38   **McKinsey on AI economic potential:** *Global AI Economic Impact Report 2023*. New York: McKinsey & Company, 2023.

39   *Harvard Business Review* **on leadership training failures:** Yemiscigil, Ayse, Dana Born, and Horace Ling. "What Makes Leadership Development Programs Succeed." *Harvard Business Review* (February 2023).

44   **Statistics on performance of ethical business:** Corporate Executive Board. *The Business Case for Ethical Culture: 2016 Ethics and Compliance Risk Management Practices Report.* Arlington, VA: CEB, 2016.

44   **Kahneman on cognitive ease:** Kahneman, Daniel. *Thinking, Fast and Slow.* New York: Farrar, Straus and Giroux, 2011.

45   **Adam Grant,** *Think Again:* Grant, Adam. *Think Again: The Power of Knowing What You Don't Know.* New York: Viking, 2021.

45   **Quote on gift of life:** Goodall, Jane. *Reason for Hope: A Spiritual Journey.* New York: Warner Books, 1999.

46   **Stephen M. R. Covey on potential in leadership:** Covey, Stephen M. R. *The Speed of Trust: The One Thing That Changes Everything.* New York: Free Press, 2006.

47   ***Harvard Business Review* on compassionate leadership:** Trzeciak, Stephen, Anthony Mazzarelli, and Emma Seppälä. "Leading with Compassion Has Research-Backed Benefits." *Harvard Business Review* (February 21, 2023).

48   **Stephen Covey on habits and leadership:** Covey, Stephen R. *The 7 Habits of Highly Effective People: Powerful Lessons in Personal Change.* New York: Free Press, 1989.

50   **Lao Tzu quote:** Lao Tzu. *Tao Te Ching.* Translated by Stephen Mitchell. New York: Harper & Row, 1988.

51   **Goal attainment and social support:** Shteynberg, Garriy, and Adam D. Galinsky. "Implicit Coordination: Sharing Goals with Similar Others Intensifies Goal Pursuit." *Journal of Experimental Social Psychology* 47, no. 6 (2011): 1291–1294.

51   **David Kelley on inherent creativity:** Kelley, David, and Tom Kelley. *Creative Confidence: Unleashing the Creative Potential within Us All.* New York: Crown Business, 2013.

52   **Teresa Amabile on creativity in leadership:** Amabile, Teresa M. *Creativity in Context: Update to the Social Psychology of Creativity.* Boulder, CO: Westview Press, 1996.

52   **World Economic Forum on future workforce skills:** *Future of Jobs Report 2023.* Geneva: World Economic Forum, 2023.

52   **Jensen Huang on greatness and character:** Huang, Jensen. "Greatness and Character in Leadership." Speech presented at the Stanford Institute for Economic Policy Research (SIEPR) Economic Summit, Stanford University, Stanford, CA, March 7, 2024.

53   **Heraclitus on character:** Heraclitus. *Fragments.* Translated and edited by T. M. Robinson. Toronto: University of Toronto Press, 1987.

54   **Stephen Covey on character and leadership:** Covey, Stephen R. *The 7 Habits of Highly Effective People: Powerful Lessons in Personal Change.* New York: Free Press, 1989.

54   **The HOW Report on character:** *The HOW Report: Character, Trust, and Behavior as the Key to High Performance and Innovation.* LRN Corporation, 2016.

55   **Theodore Levitt on future leadership:** Levitt, Theodore. *The Marketing Imagination.* New York: Free Press, 1983.

56   **Kanter on vision:** Kanter, Rosabeth Moss. *The Change Masters: Innovation and Entrepreneurship in the American Corporation.* New York: Simon & Schuster, 1983.

56   **Fariduddin Attar on self-discovery and personal transformation:** Attar, Fariduddin. *The Conference of the Birds.* Translated by Afkham Darbandi and Dick Davis. London: Penguin Books, 1984.

Chapter 3: Why Happiness Matters

57   **Aristotle on happiness:** Aristotle. *Nicomachean Ethics.* Translated by Terence Irwin. Indianapolis, IN: Hackett Publishing, 1985.

58   **Martin Seligman on happiness:** Seligman, Martin. *Flourish: A Visionary New Understanding of Happiness and Well-Being.* New York: Free Press, 2011.

58   **Oprah Winfrey on happiness:** Winfrey, Oprah, and Arthur C. Brooks. *Build the Life You Want: The Art and Science of Getting Happier.* New York: Portfolio/Penguin, 2023.

58   **Bertrand Russel on happiness:** Russell, Bertrand. *The Conquest of Happiness.* New York: Liveright Publishing, 1930.

59   **Arthur Brooks on happiness at work:** Ignatius, Adi, and Arthur C. Brooks. "Harvard's Arthur C. Brooks on the Secrets to Happiness at Work." *Harvard Business Review,* September 1, 2023.

60   **Shawn Achor and Michelle Gielan on optimism:** Achor, Shawn, and Michelle Gielan. "What Leading with Optimism Looks Like." *Harvard Business Review,* October 2020.

62   **Shawn Achor on happiness:** Achor, Shawn. *The Happiness Advantage: How a Positive Brain Fuels Success in Work and Life.* New York: Crown Business, 2010.

63   **Charles Dickens's *A Christmas Carol*:** Dickens, Charles. *A Christmas Carol.* London: Chapman & Hall, 1843.

64   **Liz Wiseman on diminishers and multipliers:** Wiseman, Liz. *Multipliers: How the Best Leaders Make Everyone Smarter.* New York: HarperCollins, 2010.

64   **Clayton Christensen on leadership and people development:** Christensen, Clayton. "How Will You Measure Your Life?" *Harvard Business Review,* July–August 2010.

64   ***International Journal of Happiness and Development*:** Díaz-García, Gustavo A., Marta Ortiz-de-Urbina-Criado, and Rafael Ravina-Ripoll. "Happy Leadership, Now More Than Ever." *International Journal of Happiness and Development* 8, no. 3 (2024): 223–243.

66   **World Health Organization on depression:** "Depressive Disorder (Depression)." Fact sheet. World Health Organization, Geneva, March 31, 2023.

66   **Gallup Poll on depression:** "U.S. Depression Rates Reach New Highs." *Gallup News,* May 17, 2023.

66 **Epictetus on Stoic philosophy:** Epictetus. *The Discourses.* Translated by Robin Hard. London: Everyman's Library, 1995.

67 **Harvard Medical School on social connections and longevity:** Harvard Medical School. "The Health Benefits of Strong Relationships." Harvard Health Publishing, April 2023.

67 **Lack of supervisor support:** Hämmig, Oliver. "Health and Well-Being at Work: The Key Role of Supervisor Support." *SSM—Population Health* 3 (2017).

67 **Viktor Frankl on meaning and happiness:** Frankl, Viktor E. *Man's Search for Meaning.* Translated by Ilse Lasch. Boston: Beacon Press, 2006.

68 **Self-determination theory by Edward Deci and Richard Ryan:** Deci, Edward L., and Richard M. Ryan. *Intrinsic Motivation and Self-Determination in Human Behavior.* New York: Springer, 1985.

68 **Michel de Montaigne on goodness:** Montaigne, Michel de. *The Essays of Michel de Montaigne.* Translated by Charles Cotton. Chicago: Encyclopaedia Britannica, 1952.

69 **Confucius on virtue:** Confucius. *The Analects of Confucius.* Translated by Arthur Waley. New York: Knopf, 1938.

69 **Mencius on human nature:** Mencius. *The Book of Mencius.* Translated by D. C. Lau. New York: Penguin Classics, 2004.

69 **Socrates on virtue and knowledge:** Plato. *Meno.* Translated by W. K. C. Guthrie. Indianapolis, IN: Hackett Publishing, 1976.

69 **Sonja Lyubomirsky on happiness and kindness:** Lyubomirsky, Sonja. *The How of Happiness: A Scientific Approach to Getting the Life You Want.* New York: Penguin Press, 2008.

70 **Arianna Huffington on success:** Huffington, Arianna. *Thrive: The Third Metric to Redefining Success and Creating a Life of Well-Being, Wisdom, and Wonder.* New York: Harmony Books, 2014.

70 **Martin Seligman on positive psychology and flourishing:** Seligman, Martin. *Flourish: A Visionary New Understanding of Happiness and Well-Being.* New York: Free Press, 2011.

70 **Anne Frank on goodness:** Frank, Anne. *The Diary of a Young Girl.* Translated by B. M. Mooyaart-Doubleday. New York: Doubleday, 1952.

71 **Marcus Aurelius on virtue:** Aurelius, Marcus. *Meditations.* Translated by Gregory Hays. New York: Modern Library, 2002.

71 **Robert Waldinger's TED Talk on happiness:** Waldinger, Robert. *What Makes a Good Life? Lessons from the Longest Study on Happiness.* Filmed November 2015. TEDxBeaconStreet video, 12:46. Posted January 25, 2016.

72 **Harvard Study on adult development (overview):** Mineo, Liz. "Over Nearly 80 Years, Harvard Study Has Been Showing How to Live a Healthy and Happy Life." *Harvard Gazette,* April 11, 2017.

72 **Diener and Seligman on happiness and social relationships:** Diener, Ed, and Martin E. P. Seligman. "Very Happy People." *Psychological Science* 13, no. 1 (2002): 81–84.

73 **Plato on leadership and choice:** Plato. *The Republic.* Translated by Benjamin Jowett. New York: Vintage Books, 1991.

74 ***Harvard Gazette* on COVID-19 frontline heroes:** "Nurses Lead the Way: Extraordinary Efforts in COVID-19 Response." *Harvard Gazette,* July 15, 2021.

75 **Nelson Mandela on leadership and purpose:** Mandela, Nelson. "Speech at Walter Sisulu's 90th Birthday Celebration." May 18, 2002. Nelson Mandela Foundation.

75 **Steger on purpose and happiness:** Steger, Michael F., Shigehiro Oishi, and Selin Kesebir. "Is a Life without Meaning Satisfying? The Moderating Role of the Search for Meaning in Satisfaction with Life Judgments." *The Journal of Positive Psychology* 6, no. 3 (2011): 173–180.

76 **Abraham Maslow on self-actualization:** Maslow, Abraham. *Motivation and Personality.* New York: Harper & Row, 1954.

76 **Enron scandal and leadership failure:** McLean, Bethany, and Peter Elkind. *The Smartest Guys in the Room: The Amazing Rise and Scandalous Fall of Enron.* New York: Portfolio, 2003.

76 **Uber leadership crisis:** Isaac, Mike. *Super Pumped: The Battle for Uber.* New York: W. W. Norton & Company, 2019.

77 **Anne M. Mulcahy on employee satisfaction:** Mulcahy, Anne M. "Lessons in Leadership from the Xerox Turnaround." *Harvard Business Review,* August 2004.

80 **Robin Sharma's quote:** Sharma, Robin. *The Leader Who Had No Title: A Modern Fable on Real Success in Business and in Life.* New York: Free Press, 2010.

80 **Stephen R. Covey's quote:** Covey, Stephen R. *The 7 Habits of Highly Effective People: Restoring the Character Ethic.* New York: Free Press, 1989.

81 **Marcus Aurelius's quote:** Aurelius, Marcus. *Meditations.* Translated by Gregory Hays. New York: Modern Library, 2002.

82 **Deloitte on burnout:** *Workplace Burnout Survey: Burnout without Borders.* Deloitte, 2021.

82 ***Harvard Business Review* on overwork:** Carmichael, Sarah Green. "The Research Is Clear: Long Hours Backfire for People and for Companies." *Harvard Business Review,* August 19, 2015.

83 **World Health Organization on overwork and mortality risk:** "Long Working Hours Increasing Deaths from Heart Disease and Stroke: WHO, ILO." World Health Organization, May 17, 2021.

83   **Erin Reid on overwork:** Reid, Erin A. "Why Some Men Pretend to Work 80-Hour Weeks." *Harvard Business Review,* June 2015.

83   **Leslie Perlow and Jessica Porter on overwork:** Perlow, Leslie A., and Jessica L. Porter. "Making Time Off Predictable—and Required." *Harvard Business Review* 87, no. 10 (2009): 102–109.

85   **Melody Wilding on sideways delegation:** Wilding, Melody. "How to Delegate to Someone Who Doesn't Report to You." Harvard Business Review, May 22, 2025.

87   **Mihaly Csikszentmihalyi on flow:** Csikszentmihalyi, Mihaly. *Flow: The Psychology of Optimal Experience.* New York: Harper & Row, 1990.

88   ***Harvard Business Review* on joy:** Perlow, Leslie A., Sari Mentser, and Salvatore J. Affinito. "How the Busiest People Find Joy." *Harvard Business Review,* July–August 2025.

88   ***Leadership Quarterly* on mood contagion:** Johnson, Stefanie K. "Do You Feel What I Feel? Mood Contagion and Leadership Outcomes." *The Leadership Quarterly* 20, no. 5. 2009.

88   **Barbara Fredrickson on broaden and built theory:** Fredrickson, Barbara L. "The Broaden-and-Build Theory of Positive Emotions." *Philosophical Transactions of the Royal Society, B: Biological Sciences* 359, no. 1449 (2004).

88   **Leslie Perlow on the subjective value of time:** Perlow, Leslie, and Salvatore J. Affinito. "Time Well Spent: A New Way to Value Time Could Change Your Life." *MIT Sloan Management Review* 66, no. 4 (Summer 2025).

91   **Kuykendall et al on lesisure:** Kuykendall, Lauren, Louis Tay, and Vivian Ng. "Leisure and Subjective Well-Being: A Meta-Analysis." *Psychological Bulletin* 141, no. 2 (2015).

91   **Etkin and Mogliner on variety of activities:** Etkin, Jordan, and Cassie Mogilner. "Does Variety Among Activities Increase Happiness?" *Journal of Consumer Research* 43, no. 2. 2016.

91   **Sonnentag and Fritz on unwinding from work:** Sonnentag, Sabine, and Charlotte Fritz. "The Recovery Experience Questionnaire: Development and Validation of a Measure for Assessing Recuperation and Unwinding from Work." *Journal of Occupational Health Psychology* 12, no. 3. 2007.

Chapter 4: Leadership Failure Is Not an Option

95   **Apollo 13 mission and Gene Kranz:** Lovell, James, and Jeffrey Kluger. *Apollo 13.* New York: Houghton Mifflin, 1994.

97   **Henry Ford on failure:** Ford, Henry. *My Life and Work.* New York: Doubleday, Page & Company, 1922.

97   **American Psychological Association on job stress:** *2023 Work in America Survey: Workplace Health and Well-Being.* Washington, DC: American Psychological Association, 2023.

97   **Jeffrey Pfeffer, Stefanos Zenios, and Joel Goh on workplace stress:** Goh, Joel, Jeffrey Pfeffer, and Stefanos Zenios. "The Relationship between Workplace Stressors and Mortality and Health Costs in the United States." *Management Science* 61, no. 3 (2015): 510–528.

98   **World Health Organization and International Labour Organization on health risks from stress:** Pega, Frank, Natalie C. Momen, Kai N. Streicher, Tim Driscoll, Marilyn Fingerhut, Annette Prüss-Üstün, and Jukka Takala. "Global, Regional, and National Burdens of Ischemic Heart Disease and Stroke Attributable to Exposure to Long Working Hours for 194 Countries, 2000–2016: A Systematic Analysis from the WHO/ILO Joint Estimates of the Work-Related Burden of Disease and Injury." *Environment International* 154 (September 2021).

98   **World Health Organization and International Labour Organization on health risks from overwork:** *Long Working Hours Increasing Deaths from Heart Disease and Stroke: WHO, ILO.* Geneva: World Health Organization, May 17, 2021.

99   **Gallup on employee disengagement costs:** *State of the Global Workplace Report 2021.* Washington, DC: Gallup Press, 2021.

99   **Job report:** US Bureau of Labor Statistics. *Job Openings and Labor Turnover Survey (JOLTS).* August 2021. 100 **Ralph Waldo Emerson on opportunities:** Emerson, Ralph Waldo. *Essays and Lectures.* New York: Library of America, 1983.

100   **Microsoft on the Great Resignation:** *2021 Work Trend Index: The Next Great Disruption Is Hybrid Work—Are We Ready?* Microsoft, 2021.

100   **World Health Organization on mental health:** "Mental Health at Work." Fact sheet. World Health Organization. Geneva. September 2024.

102   **Adam Grant on rethink:** Grant, Adam. *Think Again: The Power of Knowing What You Don't Know.* New York: Viking, 2021.

103   **McKinsey & Company on decentralized decision-making:** "Global Survey of Organizational Structure." *McKinsey Quarterly,* January 2020.

103   **Gallup on employee engagement:** *State of the Global Workplace 2024.* Washington, DC: Gallup Press, 2024.

104   **Work Institute on employee turnover:** *2025 Retention Report: Employee Retention Truths in Today's Workplace.* Franklin, TN: Work Institute, 2025.

104   ***Harvard Business Review* on trust:** Twaronite, Karyn. "A Global Survey on the Ambiguous State of Employee Trust." *Harvard Business Review* 94, no. 7 (July 2016).

104   *Forbes* **on employee trust:** Sturt, David, and Todd Nordstrom. "10 Shocking Workplace Stats You Need To Know." *Forbes*, March 8, 2018.

104   **Society for Human Resource Management on managerial influence on turnover:** "The Real Cost of Poor Leadership." *SHRM Research Highlights*, September 2019.

105   **Zenger Folkman on leadership and profitability:** Zenger, Jack, and Joseph Folkman. *The Extraordinary Leader: Turning Good Managers into Great Leaders.* New York: McGraw-Hill Education, 2009..

105   **Lynn Stout on profit-centric model:** Stout, Lynn. *The Shareholder Value Myth: How Putting Shareholders First Harms Investors, Corporations, and the Public.* San Francisco: Berrett-Koehler, 2012.

105   **Chartered Institute of Personnel and Development on workplace stress absences:** *Health and Well-Being at Work Survey 2020.* London: CIPD, 2020.

105   **Google's wellness program:** Krapivin, Pavel. "How Google's Strategy for Happy Employees Boosts Its Bottom Line." *Forbes*, September 17, 2018.

106   **Deloitte on leadership and innovation:** *Human Capital Trends Report 2020.* New York: Deloitte Insights, 2020.

106   **American Psychological Association on stress-related absenteeism costs:** Cynkar, Amy. "Whole Workplace Health." *Monitor on Psychology* 38, no. 3 (March 2007).

106   **Robert K. Greenleaf on servant leadership:** Greenleaf, Robert K. *Servant Leadership: A Journey into the Nature of Legitimate Power and Greatness.* New York: Paulist Press, 1977.

107   **Servant leadership in nonprofit organizations:** Ngah, Nor Syamaliah, Nor Liza Abdullah, and Norazah Mohd Suki. "Servant Leadership, Volunteer Retention, and Organizational Citizenship Behavior in Nonprofit Organizations: Examining the Mediating Role of Job Satisfaction." *Nonprofit and Voluntary Sector Quarterly* 50, no. 5 (2021): 1031–1053.

108   **Lisa Earle McLeod on noble purpose selling:** McLeod, Lisa Earle. *Selling with Noble Purpose: How to Drive Revenue and Do Work That Makes You Proud.* Hoboken, NJ: John Wiley & Sons, 2012.

108   **Lisa Earle McLeod on noble purpose leadership:** McLeod, Lisa Earle. *Leading with Noble Purpose: How to Create a Tribe of True Believers.* Hoboken, NJ: John Wiley & Sons, 2016.

108   *Harvard Business Review* **on noble purpose leadership:** McLeod, Lisa Earle, and Elizabeth Lotardo. "How to Be a Purpose-Driven Leader without Burning Out." *Harvard Business Review*, July 26, 2023.

110   *MIT Sloan Management Review* **on noble purpose leadership:** Cross, Rob, Amy C. Edmondson, and Wendy Murphy. "A Noble Purpose Alone Won't

Transform Your Company." *MIT Sloan Management Review* 61, no. 3 (Spring 2020).

112   **Friedman on total leadership:** Friedman, Stewart D. *Total Leadership: Be a Better Leader, Have a Richer Life. With new preface.* Boston: Harvard Business Review Press, 2014.

114   **Harvard Business Review on leadership training failures:** Beer, Michael, Magnus Finnström, and Derek Schrader. "Why Leadership Training Fails— And What to Do about It." *Harvard Business Review*, October 2016.

115   **Harvard Business Review on successful leadership training:** Yemiscigil, Ayse, Dana Born, and Horace Ling. "What Makes Leadership Development Programs Succeed?" *Harvard Business Review*, February 2023.

116   **Simon Sinek on generational expectations:** Sinek, Simon. *The Infinite Game.* New York: Portfolio, 2019.

116   **US Department of Labor on US labor supply:** *Trendlines: Changes in the U.S. Labor Supply. August 2024.* Washington, DC: US Department of Labor, August 2024.

119   **Viktor Frankl on purpose and meaning:** Frankl, Viktor E. *Man's Search for Meaning.* Translated by Ilse Lasch. Boston: Beacon Press, 2006.

119   **George Kohlrieser on modern leadership challenges:** Kohlrieser, George. *Hostage at the Table: How Leaders Can Overcome Conflict, Influence Others, and Raise Performance.* San Francisco: Jossey-Bass, 2006.

119   **Stephen M. R. Covey on trust and inspire:** Covey, Stephen M.R. *Trust and Inspire: How Truly Great Leaders Unleash Greatness in Others.* New York: Simon & Schuster, 2022.

120   **McKinsey & Company on digital transformation:** "How COVID-19 Has Pushed Companies over the Technology Tipping Point—And Transformed Business Forever." McKinsey & Company. October 2020.

120   **Catalyst's report on empathy in leadership:** Van Bommel, Tara. "The Power of Empathy in Times of Crisis and Beyond." Catalyst, January 13, 2025.

120   **Edelman Trust Barometer on trust decline:** *2021 Edelman Trust Barometer.* New York: Edelman, 2021.

121   **McKinsey & Company on diversity and profitability:** "Diversity Wins: How Inclusion Matters." *McKinsey Reports*, May 2020.

122   **Charles Handy on organizational purpose:** Handy, Charles. *The Age of Unreason.* Boston: Harvard Business School Press, 1989.

122   **Report by Global Sustainable Investment Alliance:** *Global Sustainable Investment Review, 2020.* London: GSIA, 2021.

122   **Satya Nadella on AI and human augmentation:** Nadella, Satya. *Hit Refresh: The Quest to Rediscover Microsoft's Soul and Imagine a Better Future for Everyone.* New York: Harper Business, 2017.

123   **Harvard Business Publishing blog on AI:** "AI-First Leadership: Embracing the Future of Work." *Harvard Business Publishing* (blog), January 24, 2025.

123   **Ethan Mollick on living and working with AI:** Mollick, Ethan. *Co-Intelligence: Living and Working with AI.* Philadelphia: University of Pennsylvania Press, 2023.

124   **Lao Tzu on the importance of starting small:** Lao Tzu. *Tao Te Ching.* Translated by D. C. Lau. New York: Penguin Classics.

Chapter 5: DEEP PACT: A Whole-Person Approach

126   **Norman Vincent Peale on inspiration:** Peale, Norman Vincent. *The Power of Positive Thinking.* New York: Prentice Hall, 1952.

128   **William Blake on imagination:** Blake, William. *The Marriage of Heaven and Hell.* Oxford: Oxford University Press, 1975.

128   **Lisa McLeod on leading with purpose:** McLeod, Lisa Earle. *Leading with Noble Purpose: How to Create a Tribe of True Believers.* Hoboken, NJ: John Wiley & Sons, 2013.

128   **Oxford University on purpose:** *First of Its Kind Global Study of 450 C-Suite Execs Highlights Shift from Shareholders to Stakeholders.* Saïd Business School, University of Oxford. January 10, 2024.

129   ***The Davos Manifesto* on purpose of a company :** *The Davos Manifesto 2020: Universal Purpose of a Company in the Fourth Industrial Revolution.* World Economic Forum. December 2, 2019.

131   **Simon Sinek on infinite leadership:** Sinek, Simon. *The Infinite Game.* New York: Portfolio/Penguin, 2019.

131   ***Harvard Business Review* on leadership training failures:** Yemiscigil, Ayse, Dana Born, and Horace Ling. "What Makes Leadership Development Programs Succeed." *Harvard Business Review*, February 2023.

132   **Peter Senge on personal mastery:** Senge, Peter M. *The Fifth Discipline: The Art and Practice of the Learning Organization.* New York: Doubleday, 1990.

132   **Robin Sharma on personal mastery:** Sharma, Robin. *The Leader Who Had No Title: A Modern Fable on Real Success in Business and in Life.* New York: Free Press, 2010.

132   **Robin Sharma on personal mastery:** Sharma, Robin. *The 5 AM Club: Own Your Morning. Elevate Your Life.* Toronto: HarperCollins, 2018.

133   **John C. Maxwell on leadership influence:** Maxwell, John C. *The 21 Irrefutable Laws of Leadership: Follow Them and People Will Follow You.* Nashville: Thomas Nelson, 1998.

134 **Arthur Schopenhauer on stages of truth:** Schopenhauer, Arthur. *The World as Will and Representation.* Translated by E. F. J. Payne. New York: Dover Publications, 1966.

135 **Malala Yousafzai on leadership and education:** Yousafzai, Malala, and Christina Lamb. *I Am Malala: The Girl Who Stood Up for Education and Was Shot by the Taliban.* New York: Little, Brown and Company, 2013.

136 **Nelson Mandela on self-reflection:** Mandela, Nelson. *Long Walk to Freedom: The Autobiography of Nelson Mandela.* Boston: Little, Brown and Company, 1994.

137 **Steve Jobs on pursuing excellence:** Isaacson, Walter. *Steve Jobs.* New York: Simon & Schuster, 2011.

138 **Howard Schultz on protecting vision:** Schultz, Howard. *Pour Your Heart into It: How Starbucks Built a Company One Cup at a Time.* New York: Hyperion, 1997.

139 **Mahatma Gandhi on humility and service:** Gandhi, Mahatma. *The Story of My Experiments with Truth.* Translated by Mahadev Desai. Ahmedabad: Navajivan Publishing House, 1927.

140 **James Burke and Johnson & Johnson on integrity:** *Johnson & Johnson and the Tylenol Murders: Crisis Communication Case Study.* New Brunswick, NJ: Johnson & Johnson, 1982.

141 **Jacinda Ardern on empathy in leadership:** Ardern, Jacinda. "New Zealand's Response to COVID-19." *Parliamentary Record,* April 28, 2020.

142 **Warren Buffett on trust-based leadership:** Buffett, Warren. *Berkshire Hathaway Annual Shareholder Letters.* Omaha, NE: Berkshire Hathaway, 1986–2023.

143 **Jonah Berger on social influence:** Berger, Jonah. *Invisible Influence: The Hidden Forces That Shape Behavior.* New York: Simon & Schuster, 2016.

143 **Arthur Schopenhauer on social influence:** Schopenhauer, Arthur. *Parerga and Paralipomena: Short Philosophical Essays,* Volume 1. Translated by E. F. J. Payne. Oxford: Clarendon Press, 1974.

144 **Stephen Covey on habits and leadership:** Covey, Stephen R. *The 7 Habits of Highly Effective People: Powerful Lessons in Personal Change.* New York: Free Press, 1989.

147 **Hellen Keller quote:** Keller, Helen. *Optimism: An Essay.* New York: T. Y. Crowell & Co., 1903.

148 **William Vanderbloemen on leadership habits:** Vanderbloemen, William. *Be the Unicorn: 12 Data-Driven Habits That Separate the Best Leaders from the Rest.* Nashville: Thomas Nelson, 2023.

148 **James Clear on incremental changes in behavior:** Clear, James. *Atomic Habits: An Easy & Proven Way to Build Good Habits & Break Bad Ones.* New York: Avery, 2018.

148 **BJ Fogg on habit formation:** Fogg, BJ. *Tiny Habits: The Small Changes That Change Everything*. Boston: Houghton Mifflin Harcourt, 2020.

153 **Failure of managers:** CEB Global. "Why Most New Managers Fail and How to Prevent It." *Forbes*, February 15, 2023.

154 **MIT Sloan Management Review on failure of managers:** Morela Hernandez, Jasmien Khattab, and Charlotte Hoopes, "Why Good Leaders Fail," *MIT Sloan Management Review* (Summer 2021): 1–4.

159 **Mahatma Gandhi on meeting our capabilities:** Gandhi, Mahatma. *Selected Works of Mahatma Gandhi*, Volume 3. New Delhi: Navajivan Trust, 1968.

159 **Benjamin Franklin's virtue practice:** Franklin, Benjamin. *The Autobiography of Benjamin Franklin*. Edited by Leonard W. Labaree. New Haven, CT: Yale University Press, 1964.

Chapter 6: The AI Playbook of DEEP PACT

162 **Sundar Pichai on AI:** Pichai, Sundar. Interview by CBS News. *60 Minutes*, April 16, 2023.

163 **Homer on Hephaestus:** Homer. *The Iliad*. Translated by Robert Fagles. New York: Penguin Classics, 1998.

163 **Mahabharat on Brahmastra:** Ganguli, Kisari Mohan, trans. *The Mahabharata of Krishna-Dwaipayana Vyasa*. New Delhi: Munshiram Manoharlal Publishers, 2004.

164 **Hephaestus and Talos:** Hesiod. *Theogony*. Translated by Hugh G. Evelyn-White. Cambridge, MA: Harvard University Press, 1914.

164 **Pygmalion myth:** Ovid. *Metamorphoses*. Translated by David Raeburn. London: Penguin Classics, 2004.

164 **Chinese legends:** Liezi. *The Book of Liezi*. Translated by A. C. Graham. New York: Columbia University Press, 1990.

164 **Mark Cuban on AI:** Mark Cuban. Interview by Jason Hirschhorn. Upfront Summit, Los Angeles, CA, February 8, 2017. YouTube.

166 **HBR on AI resistance:** De Freitas, Julian. "Why People Resist Embracing AI." *Harvard Business Review* 103, no. 1 (January–February 2025): 52–56.

167 **New work versus old work:** Autor, David. "Most Work Is New Work, Long-Term Study of US Census Data Shows." *MIT News*, April 1, 2024.

167 **On AI job displacement:** World Economic Forum. *The Future of Jobs Report 2020*. Geneva: World Economic Forum, 2020.

168 **JP Morgan's COIN:** Weiss, Debra Cassens. "JPMorgan Chase Uses Tech to Save 360,000 Hours of Annual Work by Lawyers and Loan Officers," *ABA Journal*, March 2, 2017.

168   **AI success in drug:** Jumper, John, et al. "Highly Accurate Protein Structure Prediction with AlphaFold." *Nature* 596, no. 7873 (2021): 583–589.

169   **Netflix story:** "Role of Artificial Intelligence in Enhancing OTT Content Recommendation Algorithms." *Medium*, December 2024.

169   **Chipotle's use of AI:** Chipotle Mexican Grill. "Chipotle Introduces New AI Hiring Platform to Support Its Accelerated Growth." News release, October 22, 2024.

169   **Recruitment statistics:** "100 Recruitment Statistics and Trends for 2025 and Beyond." WeCP. January 17, 2025.

169   **Salesforce data:** "New Salesforce Research Links Lower Stress Levels and Business Automation." *Salesforce News*, December 2, 2021.

170   **Deloitte study:** "AI in the Workplace: Impact, Trends, and Challenges." Deloitte Insights, 2024.

170   **McKinsey report on AI:** "The Economic Potential of Generative AI: The Next Productivity Frontier." *McKinsey Digital*, June 14, 2023.

170   **Accenture report:** "AI Integration and Business Performance: Driving Growth through Intelligent Automation." Accenture Research, 2024.

170   **Eric Brynjolfsson on AI:** Brynjolfsson, Erik, and Andrew McAfee. "The Business of Artificial Intelligence." *Harvard Business Review*, July 2017.

170   **Gartner survey on flexible work:** "Gartner HR Survey Reveals 64% of Employees Are More Likely to Choose a Job with Flexible Work Options." Gartner, October 7, 2021.

171   ***Harvard Business Review* study on leadership characteristics:** Kabacoff, Robert. "Leadership Characteristic That Is Most Important to Future Success." *Harvard Business Review*, February 7, 2014.

172   **AI-driven leader:** Woods, Geoff. *The AI-Driven Leader: Harnessing the Power of Artificial Intelligence for Strategic Leadership.* n.p.: AI Thought Leadership, 2024.

173   **Ethan Mollick on co-intelligence:** Mollick, Ethan. *Co-Intelligence: Living and Working with AI.* New York: Penguin Random House, 2024.

178   **MELDS approach:** Daugherty, Paul R., and H. James Wilson. *Human + Machine: Reimagining Work in the Age of AI.* Boston: Harvard Business Review Press, 2018.

180   **Fei-Fei Li on AI and human creativity:** Li, Fei-Fei. *The Worlds I See: Curiosity, Exploration, and Discovery at the Dawn of AI.* New York: Flatiron Books, 2023.

183

187   **Boston Consulting Group study:** Dell'Acqua, Fabrizio, Edward McFowland III, Ethan Mollick, Hila Lifshitz-Assaf, Katherine C. Kellogg, Saran Rajendran, Lisa Krayer, François Candelon, and Karim R. Lakhani. "Navigating the Jagged

Technological Frontier: Field Experimental Evidence of the Effects of AI on Knowledge Worker Productivity and Quality." Harvard Business School Working Paper No. 24-013, September 2023.

187 **NIST study on AI bias:** National Institute of Standards and Technology (NIST). *Face Recognition Vendor Test (FRVT)*, Part 3: *Demographic Effects.* US Department of Commerce, December 2019.

187 **Georgia Tech study on AI bias:** Wilson, Benjamin, Judy Hoffman, and Jamie Morgenstern. *Predictive Inequity in Object Detection.* Georgia Institute of Technology, Atlanta, 2019.

188 **UC Berkeley study on AI bias:** Bartlett, Robert, Adair Morse, Richard Stanton, and Nancy Wallace. *Consumer-Lending Discrimination in the FinTech Era.* UC Berkeley, Haas School of Business, February 2019.

188 **University of Washington study:** Wilson, Kyra, and Aylin Caliskan. "Gender, Race, and Intersectional Bias in Resume Screening via Language Model Retrieval." In *Proceedings of the 2024 AAAI/ACM Conference on AI, Ethics, and Society,* Association for Computing Machinery, October 21–23, 2024. San Jose, CA. .

188 **AI hiring platform reducing bias:** Greenhouse Software. "Anonymize Resumes." Greenhouse Support Center, January 22, 2025.

190 **LinkedIn on upskilling:** *Workplace Learning Report.* LinkedIn Learning, 2024.

190 **Microsoft trend index:** *Work Trend Index: Will AI Fix Work?* Microsoft WorkLab, 2023.

Part 2: Personal Mastery

192 **Lao Tzu on inner strength:** Lao Tzu. *Tao Te Ching.* Translated by Stephen Mitchell. New York: Harper & Row, 1988.

192 **Carl Jung on the unconscious mind:** Jung, Carl G. *Collected Works of C. G. Jung,* Volume 7: *Two Essays on Analytical Psychology.* Princeton, NJ: Princeton University Press, 1972.

192 **Peter Senge on personal mastery:** Senge, Peter M. *The Fifth Discipline: The Art and Practice of the Learning Organization.* New York: Doubleday, 1990.

Chapter 7: Principle 1—Decide, Act, and Lead without Waiting for Approval

193

195 **Franz Kafka's "Before the Law" parable:** Kafka, Franz. *The Trial*. Translated by Willa and Edwin Muir. New York: Schocken Books, 1998.

195 **Steve Jobs on bold initiative and innovation:** Isaacson, Walter. *Steve Jobs*. New York: Simon & Schuster, 2011.

196 **Sheryl Sandberg on leading without permission:** Sandberg, Sheryl. *Lean In: Women, Work, and the Will to Lead*. New York: Knopf, 2013.

196 **George Bernard Shaw on creating opportunity:** Shaw, George Bernard. *The Collected Works of George Bernard Shaw*. London: Constable and Company, 1930.

197 **Mark Twain on taking risks:** Twain, Mark. *Following the Equator: A Journey around the World*. New York: Harper & Brothers, 1897.

197 **Vincent van Gogh on overcoming doubt:** Van Gogh, Vincent. *Letters to Theo*. Edited by Irving Stone. Boston: Houghton Mifflin, 1937.

198 **Rosa Parks on civil rights leadership:** Parks, Rosa, and Gregory J. Reed. *Quiet Strength: The Faith, the Hope, and the Heart of a Woman Who Changed a Nation*. Grand Rapids, MI: Zondervan, 1994.

198 **Malala Yousafzai on education for all:** Yousafzai, Malala, and Christina Lamb. *I Am Malala: The Girl Who Stood Up for Education and Was Shot by the Taliban*. New York: Little, Brown and Company, 2013.

198 **Amelia Earhart on breaking barriers:** Earhart, Amelia. *The Fun of It: Random Records of My Own Flying and of Women in Aviation*. New York: Brewer, Warren & Putnam, 1932.

199 **Viktor Frankl on personal transformation:** Frankl, Viktor E. *Man's Search for Meaning*. Boston: Beacon Press, 2006.

206 **Eleanor Roosevelt on the power of dreams:** Roosevelt, Eleanor. *You Learn by Living: Eleven Keys for a More Fulfilling Life*. New York: Harper & Brothers, 1960.

206 **Muhammad Yunus on microfinance and poverty alleviation:** Yunus, Muhammad. *Banker to the Poor: Micro-Lending and the Battle against World Poverty*. New York: PublicAffairs, 1999.

207 **The Yoga Sutras of Patanjali on inspiration:** Patanjali. *The Yoga Sutras of Patanjali*. Translated by Sri Swami Satchidananda. Buckingham, VA: Integral Yoga Publications, 2012.

208 **Gary Pisano on innovation in organizations:** Pisano, Gary P. *Creative Construction: The DNA of Sustained Innovation*. New York: PublicAffairs, 2019.

208 **King's "I Have a Dream" speech:** King, Martin Luther, Jr. *I Have a Dream: Writings and Speeches That Changed the World*. Edited by James M. Washington. San Francisco: HarperSanFrancisco, 1992.

209   **Muhammad Yunus on a world of three zeros.** Yunus, Muhammad, and Karl Weber. *A World of Three Zeros: The New Economics of Zero Poverty, Zero Unemployment, and Zero Net Carbon Emissions.* New York: PublicAffairs, 2017.

210   **Steve Jobs on innovation and visionaries:** Isaacson, Walter. *Steve Jobs.* New York: Simon & Schuster, 2011.

211   **Seize-the-day story in *Dead Poets Society:*** *Dead Poets Society.* Directed by Peter Weir. Touchstone Pictures, 1989.

212   **T. E. Lawrence on daydreaming and action:** Lawrence, T.E. *Seven Pillars of Wisdom: A Triumph.* London: Jonathan Cape, 1935.

212   **Will Smith in *The Pursuit of Happyness:*** *The Pursuit of Happyness.* Directed by Gabriele Muccino. Columbia Pictures, 2006.

214   **William Shakespeare on doubt and inaction:** Shakespeare, William. *Measure for Measure.* London: G. G. Harrap, 1914.

215   **Martin Luther King Jr. on faith and vision:** King, Martin Luther, Jr. *Strength to Love.* Philadelphia: Fortress Press, 1981.

216   **Aristotle on excellence:** Aristotle. *Nicomachean Ethics.* Translated by W. D. Ross. Oxford: Oxford University Press, 2009.

217   **John Quincy Adams on leadership:** Adams, John Quincy. *The Diary of John Quincy Adams, 1794–1845.* Cambridge, MA: Harvard University Press, 1981.

217   **Nelson Mandela on social justice:** Mandela, Nelson. *Long Walk to Freedom: The Autobiography of Nelson Mandela.* Boston: Little, Brown and Company, 1994.

217   **The HP Way:** Packard, David. *The HP Way: How Bill Hewlett and I Built Our Company.* New York: HarperBusiness, 1995.

219   **Ed Catmull on creative leadership:** Catmull, Ed, and Amy Wallace. *Creativity, Inc.: Overcoming the Unseen Forces That Stand in the Way of True Inspiration.* New York: Random House, 2014.

219   **Maya Angelou on legacy:** Angelou, Maya. *Letter to My Daughter.* New York: Random House, 2008.

219   **Victor Hugo on dreams and the future:** Hugo, Victor. *Les Misérables.* New York: Carleton, 1862.

220   **Oprah Winfrey's story:** Kelley, Kitty. *Oprah: A Biography.* New York: Crown Publishers, 2010.

220   **Rabindranath Tagore on aspiration:** Tagore, Rabindranath. *Stray Birds.* New York: Macmillan, 1916.

221   **Steve Jobs quote:** Siltanen, Rob. "The Real Story behind Apple's 'Think Different' Campaign." *Forbes,* December 14, 2011.

223   **Seneca on courage and difficulty:** Seneca. *Letters from a Stoic.* Translated by Robin Campbell. New York: Penguin Classics, 1969.

234   **Rumi on barriers:** Rumi, *The Essential Rumi.*

234   **Carol Dweck on growth mindset:** Dweck, Carol S. *Mindset: The New Psychology of Success.* New York: Random House, 2006.

235   **Albert Bandura on self-efficacy:** Bandura, Albert. *Self-Efficacy: The Exercise of Control.* New York: W. H. Freeman, 1997.

236   **James MacGregor Burns on transformational leadership:** Burns, James MacGregor. *Leadership.* New York: Harper & Row, 1978.

236   **James Kouzes and Barry Posner on leadership challenge:** Kouzes, James M., and Barry Z. Posner. *The Leadership Challenge: How to Make Extraordinary Things Happen in Organizations.* San Francisco: Jossey-Bass, 1987.

237   **Geert Hofstede on cultural dimensions:** Hofstede, Geert. *Culture's Consequences: Comparing Values, Behaviors, Institutions and Organizations across Nations.* Thousand Oaks, CA: SAGE Publications, 2001.

237   **Alice Eagly and Linda Carli on women in leadership:** Eagly, Alice H., and Linda L. Carli. *Through the Labyrinth: The Truth about How Women Become Leaders.* Boston: Harvard Business Review Press, 2007.

239   **John P. Kotter on leading change:** Kotter, John P. *Leading Change.* Boston: Harvard Business Review Press, 1996.

240   **Winston Churchill on perseverance:** Churchill, Winston S. *The End of the Beginning.* New York: Houghton Mifflin Company, 1943.

Chapter 8: Principle 2—Examine Your Beliefs and Actions

242   **Lao Tzu on self-knowledge:** Lao Tzu. *Tao Te Ching.* Translated by Stephen Mitchell. New York: Harper Perennial, 1988.

242   **Socrates on the unexamined life:** *The Collected Dialogues of Plato.* Edited by Edith Hamilton and Huntington Cairns. Princeton, NJ: Princeton University Press, 1961.

244   **Aristotle on self-awareness and wisdom:** Aristotle. *The Nicomachean Ethics.* Translated by David Ross. Oxford: Oxford University Press, 2009.

245   ***Harvard Business Review* on self-aware leadership:** Goleman, Daniel. "What Makes a Leader?" *Harvard Business Review* 76, no. 6 (November–December 1998): 93–102.

245   **Tasha Eurich on self-awareness:** Eurich, Tasha. *Insight: Why We're Not as Self-Aware as We Think, and How Seeing Ourselves Clearly Helps Us Succeed at Work and in Life.* New York: Crown Business, 2017

245   **Adam Grant on overconfidence cycle:** Grant, Adam. *Think Again: The Power of Knowing What You Don't Know.* New York: Viking, 2021.

246   **Kouzes and Posner on leadership challenge:** Kouzes, James M., and Barry Z. Posner. *The Leadership Challenge: How to Make Extraordinary Things Happen in Organizations.* San Francisco: Jossey-Bass, 2012.

247   **Abraham Lincoln on evolving leadership beliefs:** McPherson, James M. *Abraham Lincoln and the Second American Revolution.* New York: Oxford University Press, 1991.

247   **Carl Sandburg on wisdom:** Sandburg, Carl. *The People, Yes.* New York: Harcourt, Brace, and Company, 1936.

248   **Attar on happiness and meaning-making:** Attar, Fariduddin. *The Conference of the Birds.* Translated by Afkham Darbandi and Dick Davis. New York: Penguin Classics, 1984.

249   **Rumi on embracing vulnerability:** Rumi. *The Essential Rumi.* Translated by Coleman Barks. San Francisco: HarperOne, 1995.

250   **Shakespeare on self-examination:** Shakespeare, William. *Julius Caesar.* In *The Complete Works of William Shakespeare,* edited by W. J. Craig. London: Oxford University Press, 1914.

253   **Maya Angelou on bias and blind spots:** Angelou, Maya. *The Heart of a Woman.* New York: Random House, 1981.

253   **Plato's Allegory of the Cave:** Plato. *The Republic.* Translated by Allan Bloom. New York: Basic Books, 1968.

254   **Eleanor Roosevelt on civil rights and justice:** Roosevelt, Eleanor. *The Autobiography of Eleanor Roosevelt.* New York: Harper & Brothers, 1961.

255   **Oscar Wilde on truth:** Wilde, Oscar. *The Importance of Being Earnest.* London: Leonard Smithers and Co., 1899.

255   **Marcus Buckingham and Ashley Goodall on workplace truths:** Buckingham, Marcus, and Ashley Goodall. *Nine Lies About Work: A Freethinking Leader's Guide to the Real World.* Boston: Harvard Business Review Press, 2019.

257   **Xerox turnaround:** "Anne Mulcahy: Turning Xerox Around." *Harvard Business Review,* August 2004.

258   **Marcus Aurelius on self-examination:** Marcus Aurelius. *Meditations.* Translated by George Long. New York: Modern Library, 2002.

258   **Icek Ajzen on the theory of planned behavior:** Ajzen, Icek. "The Theory of Planned Behavior." *Organizational Behavior and Human Decision Processes* 50, no. 2 (1991): 179–211.

259   **William James on belief:** James, William. *The Will to Believe and Other Essays in Popular Philosophy.* New York: Longmans, Green and Co., 1897.

259   **Belief-value-attitude-behavior spectrum:** "Personal Beliefs, Values, Attitudes and Behaviour." Immigration Advisers Authority, New Zealand Government. Accessed April 12, 2025. 261 **Fishbein and Ajzen on belief:** Fishbein, Martin,

and Icek Ajzen. *Belief, Attitude, Intention, and Behavior: An Introduction to Theory and Research.* Reading, MA: Addison-Wesley, 1975.

260   **Schwartz on values:** Schwartz, Shalom H. "Universals in the Content and Structure of Values: Theoretical Advances and Empirical Tests in 20 Countries." *Advances in Experimental Social Psychology* 25 (1992): 1–65.

262   **Health and wellness:** Biddle, Stuart J. H., and Nanette Mutrie. *Psychology of Physical Activity: Determinants, Well-Being and Interventions.* 2nd ed. London: Routledge, 2008.

263   **Workplace integrity:** Treviño, Linda K., Gary R. Weaver, and Scott J. Reynolds. "Behavioral Ethics in Organizations: A Review." *Journal of Management* 32, no. 6 (2006): 951–990.

263   **Social justice:** Sagiv, Lilach, and Shalom H. Schwartz. "Value Priorities and Subjective Well-Being: Direct Relations and Congruity Effects." *European Journal of Social Psychology* 30, no. 2 (2000): 177–198.

264   **Environmental sustainability:** Kollmuss, Anja, and Julian Agyeman. "Mind the Gap: Why Do People Act Environmentally and What Are the Barriers to Pro-Environmental Behavior?" *Environmental Education Research* 8, no. 3 (2002): 239–260.

264   **Educational achievement:** Eccles, Jacquelynne S., and Allan Wigfield. "Motivational Beliefs, Values, and Goals." *Annual Review of Psychology* 53, no. 1 (2002): 109–132.

264   **Community service:** Penner, Louis A., John F. Dovidio, Jane A. Piliavin, and David A. Schroeder. "Prosocial Behavior: Multilevel Perspectives." *Annual Review of Psychology* 56, no. 1 (2005): 365–392.

265   **Literary example:** Lee, Harper. *To Kill a Mockingbird.* New York: J. B. Lippincott & Co., 1960.

266   **Managers' qualifications:** Gallup. *State of the American Manager: Analytics and Advice for Leaders.* Washington, DC: Gallup Press, 2016.

267   **Camus on irrational:** Camus, Albert. *The Myth of Sisyphus and Other Essays.* Translated by Justin O'Brien. New York: Vintage International, 1955.

268   **PMBOK Guide:** *A Guide to the Project Management Body of Knowledge (PMBOK Guide).* 6th ed. Newtown Square, PA: Project Management Institute, 2017.

268   **Agile development and Scrum methods:** Schwaber, Ken, and Jeff Sutherland. *The Scrum Guide.* Scrum.org and Scrum Alliance, 2020. 268 **2020 CHAOS Report:** The Standish Group. *CHAOS Report 2020.* West Yarmouth, MA: Standish Group International, 2020.

269   **Dan Ariely on rationality:** Ariely, Dan. *Predictably Irrational: The Hidden Forces That Shape Our Decisions.* New York: HarperCollins, 2008; Ariely, Dan. *The Upside of Irrationality: The Unexpected Benefits of Defying Logic at Work and at Home.* New York: HarperCollins, 2010.

270   **Oxford on emotions:** White, A., and A. Canwell. "Prioritizing Emotions Is the Key to Success for Business Transformation, Groundbreaking Research Finds." Saïd Business School, University of Oxford, 2002.

270   **Jane Austen on complete truth:** Austen, Jane. *Emma.* London: John Murray, 1816.

271   **Simon Sinek on leadership and responsibility:** Sinek, Simon. *Leaders Eat Last: Why Some Teams Pull Together and Others Don't.* New York: Portfolio, 2014.

272   **George Orwell on myths and beliefs:** Orwell, George. *1984.* New York: Harcourt, Brace, and Company, 1949.

272   **Edward Deming on management myths:** Deming, W. Edwards. *Out of the Crisis.* Cambridge: MIT Press, 1986.

273   **William Shakespeare on thoughts:** Shakespeare, William. *Antony and Cleopatra.* Edited by Barbara A. Mowat and Paul Werstine. New York: Simon & Schuster, 1999.

273   **Google's 20% rule:** Iyer, B., and T. H. Davenport. "Reverse Engineering Google's Innovation Machine." *Harvard Business Review,* April 2008.

274   **Deloitte Consulting Greenhouses:** "Deloitte Greenhouse Experience: Accelerating Breakthroughs." Deloitte.com, 2021.

275   **Buddha's quote:** Buddha. *The Dhammapada: The Sayings of the Buddha.* Translated by Thomas Byrom. Boston: Shambhala, 1993.

275   **Carol Dweck on mindsets:** Dweck, Carol S. *Mindset: The New Psychology of Success.* New York: Random House, 2006.

277   **Albert Einstein on intuition and rationality:** Einstein, Albert. *The World as I See It.* New York: Philosophical Library, 1949.

277   **Rumi on water and boat:** Rumi. *The Masnavi.* Book One. Translated by Jawid Mojaddedi. Oxford: Oxford University Press, 2004.

278   **Dale Carnegie on emotional intelligence:** Carnegie, Dale. *How to Win Friends and Influence People.* New York: Simon & Schuster, 1936.

279   **Daniel Goleman on emotional intelligence:** Goleman, Daniel. *Emotional Intelligence: Why It Can Matter More Than IQ.* New York: Bantam Books, 1995.

280   **Aristotle on self-awareness:** Aristotle. *Nicomachean Ethics.* Translated by W. D. Ross. Oxford: Oxford University Press, 2009.

280   **Thomas Jefferson on self-regulation:** Jefferson, Thomas. *The Works of Thomas Jefferson.* Edited by Paul Leicester Ford. New York: G. P. Putnam's Sons, 1904.

281   **John Quincy Adams on motivation:** Adams, John Quincy. Quoted in John C. Maxwell's *The 21 Irrefutable Laws of Leadership: Follow Them and People Will Follow You.* Nashville: Thomas Nelson, 1998.

281   **Carl Rogers on empathy:** Rogers, Carl. *A Way of Being.* Boston: Houghton Mifflin Harcourt, 1980. (For the quote "Empathy is a special way of coming to know another and ourselves.")

282   **Dale Carnegie on social skills:** Carnegie, *How to Win Friends and Influence People.*

283   **CareerBuilder survey:** "Seventy-One Percent of Employers Say They Value Emotional Intelligence over IQ, according to CareerBuilder Survey." CareerBuilder, August 18, 2011.

284   **Harvard University Division of Continuing Education on emotional intelligence:** Wilcox, Laura. "Emotional Intelligence Is No Soft Skill." Harvard Division of Continuing Education, Professional & Executive Development blog. Published July 6, 2015. Last updated January 8, 2024.

285   **McKinsey on psychological safety:** "Just 26 Percent of Leaders Create Psychological Safety for Their Teams." McKinsey & Company, 2021.

285   *Harvard Business Review* **on psychological safety:** Edmondson, Amy C., and Michaela J. Kerrissey. "What People Get Wrong about Psychological Safety." *Harvard Business Review*, May–June 2025.

286   **Ludwig Wittgenstein on language and reality:** Wittgenstein, Ludwig. *Tractatus Logico-Philosophicus.* Translated by C. K. Ogden. London: Kegan Paul, 1922.

286   **Amy Edmondson on psychological safety:** Edmondson, Amy C. *The Fearless Organization: Creating Psychological Safety in the Workplace for Learning, Innovation, and Growth.* Hoboken, NJ: Wiley, 2018.

286   **Andy Grove on effective communication:** Grove, Andrew S. *High Output Management.* New York: Random House, 1983.

287   **Marshall Goldsmith on leadership communication:** Goldsmith, Marshall. *What Got You Here Won't Get You There: How Successful People Become Even More Successful.* New York: Hyperion, 2007.

287   **Robert Kegan and Lisa Lahey on language and organizational growth:** Kegan, Robert, and Lisa Laskow Lahey. *How the Way We Talk Can Change the Way We Work: Seven Languages for Transformation.* San Francisco: Jossey-Bass, 2001.

289   **Jonah Berger on magic words:** Berger, Jonah. *Magic Words: What to Say to Get Your Way.* New York: Harper Business, 2023.

295   **Stephen Covey on effectiveness:** Covey, Stephen R. *The 8th Habit: From Effectiveness to Greatness.* New York: Free Press, 2004.

296   *MIT Sloan Management Review* **on effectiveness:** Hooijberg, Robert, and Michael Watkins. "The Future Workplace Depends on Efficiency, Effectiveness, and Balance." *MIT Sloan Management Review* 63, no. 4 (2022).

297   **Peter Drucker on reflection and action:** Drucker, Peter F. *The Effective Executive: The Definitive Guide to Getting the Right Things Done.* New York: Harper Business, 2006.

304   **HBR on addition subtraction:** Sutton, Robert I., and Hayagreeva Rao. "Rid Your Organization of Obstacles That Infuriate Everyone." *Harvard Business Review,* January 2024.

308   **Marcus Aurelius on barriers and growth:** Aurelius, Marcus. *Meditations.* Translated by Gregory Hays. New York: Modern Library, 2002.

314   **Bertrand Russell on openness to doubt:** Russell, Bertrand. *The Problems of Philosophy.* New York: Oxford University Press, 1912.

Chapter 9: Principle 3—Ensure Excellence

316   **Martin Luther King Jr. on excellence in work:** King, Martin Luther, Jr. *Strength to Love.* Philadelphia: Fortress Press, 1981.

316   **Aristotle on excellence and virtue:** Aristotle. *The Nicomachean Ethics.* Translated by David Ross. Oxford: Oxford University Press, 2009.

317   **John F. Kennedy on talent and happiness:** Kennedy, John F. *Public Papers of the Presidents of the United States: John F. Kennedy, 1961.* Washington, DC: Government Printing Office, 1962.

318   **Simon Sinek on employee happiness:** Sinek, Simon. *Leaders Eat Last: Why Some Teams Pull Together and Others Don't.* New York: Portfolio, 2014.

318   **Albert Bandura on self-efficacy:** Bandura, Albert. *Self-Efficacy: The Exercise of Control.* New York: W. H. Freeman, 1997.

318   **Mihaly Csikszentmihalyi on flow:** Csikszentmihalyi, Mihaly. *Flow: The Psychology of Optimal Experience.* New York: Harper & Row, 1990.

319   **Ralph Marston on excellence as an attitude:** Marston, Ralph S., Jr. *The Daily Motivator to Go.* Dallas, TX: Image Express, 1997.

320   **Steve Jobs on teams:** Jobs, Steve. Interview by Leslie Stahl. *60 Minutes.* CBS. Aired on May 18, 2003. **match earlier 60 minutes**

321   **Buckingham and Goodall on teams:** Buckingham, Marcus, and Ashley Goodall. *Nine Lies About Work: A Freethinking Leader's Guide to the Real World.* Boston: Harvard Business Review Press, 2019.

321   **Deloitte Report on teams:** Deloitte Insights. *Belonging: From Comfort to Connection to Contribution.* 2020 Global Human Capital Trends. Deloitte Development LLC, 2020.

323   **Patrick Lencioni on team dynamics:** Lencioni, Patrick. *The Five Dysfunctions of a Team: A Leadership Fable.* San Francisco: Jossey-Bass, 2002.

323 **MIT Human Dynamics Lab on teams:** Pentland, Alex Sandy. "The New Science of Building Great Teams." *Harvard Business Review* 90, no. 4 (2012).

325 **Rabindranath Tagore on striving and perfection:** Tagore, Rabindranath. *Gitanjali: Song Offerings.* New York: Macmillan, 1913.

325 ***Dangal* as an example of high standards in pursuit of excellence:** Sharma, Nitesh, dir. *Dangal.* Aamir Khan Productions, 2016.

325 ***Rocky* as a story of determination and excellence:** Avildsen, John G., dir. *Rocky.* United Artists, 1976.

326 **Mark Twain on continuous improvement:** Twain, Mark. *Notebook.* Edited by Albert Bigelow Paine. New York: Harper & Brothers, 1935.

326 **Jeffrey K. Liker on organizational excellence:** Liker, Jeffrey K. *The Toyota Way: 14 Management Principles from the World's Greatest Manufacturer.* New York: McGraw-Hill, 2004.

327 **Vince Lombardi on #1:** Lombardi, Vince. *What It Takes to Be #1: Vince Lombardi on Leadership.* Edited by Vince Lombardi Jr. New York: McGraw-Hill, 2001.

329 **Lou Gerstner on culture at IBM:** Gerstner, Louis V. *Who Says Elephants Can't Dance? Inside IBM's Historic Turnaround.* New York: HarperBusiness, 2002.

330 **Brian Tracy on excellence as a journey:** Tracy, Brian. *Eat That Frog! 21 Great Ways to Stop Procrastinating and Get More Done in Less Time.* San Francisco: Berrett-Koehler, 2001.

330 **University of Chicago study on skill and happiness:** Gruenberg, Barry. "The Happy Worker: An Analysis of Educational and Occupational Differences in Determinants of Job Satisfaction." *American Journal of Sociology* 86, no. 2 (1980): 247–271.

330 **Gallup study on employee engagement and excellence:** "State of the American Workplace." Gallup, 2019.

330 **Eleanor Roosevelt on leadership and inspiration:** Roosevelt, Eleanor. *The Autobiography of Eleanor Roosevelt.* New York: Harper & Brothers, 1961.

331 **Stephen M. R. Covey on trust and inspiration:** Covey, Stephen M. R. *Trust and Inspire: How Truly Great Leaders Unleash Greatness in Others.* New York: Simon & Schuster, 2022.

331 **Daniel H. Pink on motivation:** Pink, Daniel H. *Drive: The Surprising Truth about What Motivates Us.* New York: Riverhead Books, 2009.

332 **Ralph Waldo Emerson on inspiration:** *Ralph Waldo Emerson: Essays and Lectures.* Edited by Joel Porte. New York: Library of America, 1983.

332 **Adam Galinsky on inspiring:** Galinsky, Adam. *Inspire: The Universal Path for Leading Yourself and Others.* New York: Harper Business, 2025.

333 **Darius Mirshahzadeh on invisible manager:** Mirshahzadeh, Darius. *The Core Value Equation: A Framework to Drive Results, Create Limitless Scale and Win the War for Talent.* Austin, TX: Lioncrest Publishing, 2020.

335 **Amy Gallo on conflict resolution:** Gallo, Amy. "How to Master Conflict Resolution." *Harvard Business Review,* October 21, 2024.

335 **Peter Coleman on conflict intelligence:** Coleman, Peter T. "The Conflict-Intelligent Leader." *Harvard Business Review,* July–August 2025.

336 **On role of dignity in conflict resolution:** Hoben, Merrick. "To Navigate Conflict, Prioritize Dignity," *MIT Sloan Management Review,* May 20, 2024.

337 **On challenging a superior:** Laker, Benjamin. "The Delicate Dynamics of Challenging a Superior." *MIT Sloan Management Review,* October 12, 2023.

338 **On being nice:** Su, Amy Jen. *The Leader You Want to Be: Five Essential Principles for Bringing Out Your Best Self—Every Day.* Boston: Harvard Business Review Press, 2019.

339 **Roger Crawford on resilience and adversity:** Crawford, Roger. *How High Can You Bounce? Turn Setbacks into Comebacks.* New York: Berkley, 2002.

341 *California Management Review* **on collaborative intelligence:** Yoffie, D. B. "Competing in the Age of Digital Convergence." *California Management Review* 61, no. 3 (2019): 5–23.

343 **Jim Collins on First Who Then What:** Collins, Jim. *Good to Great: Why Some Companies Make the Leap... and Others Don't.* New York: HarperCollins, 2001.

343 *Harvard Business Review* **on hiring:** FernándezAráoz, Claudio. "Hire for Potential, Not Just Experience." *Harvard Business Review,* The Idea. July 20, 2021. Video, HBR.org.

346 **McKinsey on leadership development failure:** Gurdjian, Pierre, Thomas Halbeisen, and Kevin Lane. "Why Leadership-Development Programs Fail." McKinsey & Company, January 2014.

346 *MIT Sloan Management Review* **on leadership development failure:** Leroy, Hannes, Moran Anisman-Razin, and Jim Detert. "Leadership Development Is Failing Us. Here's How to Fix It." *MIT Sloan Management Review,* December 6, 2023.

350 **Shannon Alder on legacy:** Alder, Shannon L. Quoted on Goodreads. Accessed May 29, 2025. 351 **Leonardo da Vinci on art and science:** Vasari, Giorgio. *Lives of the Most Excellent Painters, Sculptors, and Architects.* Translated by Gaston du C. De Vere. New York: Knopf, 1996.

351 **Steve Jobs on quality:** Jobs, Steve. "Be a Yardstick of Quality." Quoted in *The Steve Jobs Way: iLeadership for a New Generation,* by Jay Elliot. New York: Vanguard Press, 2011.

352 **A. P. J. Abdul Kalam on excellence as a process:** Kalam, A. P. J. Abdul. *Wings of Fire: An Autobiography.* Hyderabad: Universities Press, 1999.

360 **Unknown on excellence as doing one's best:** *Tiny Buddha.* Accessed June 1, 2025.

365 **Mother Teresa on taking initiative:** Mother Teresa. *No Greater Love.* Edited by Becky Benenate and Joseph Durepos. Novato, CA: New World Library, 2001.

Chapter 10: Principle 4—Protect Yourself from Self-Sabotage

367 **Plato on self-conquest:** Plato. *The Republic.* Translated by Benjamin Jowett. New York: Barnes & Noble, 2004.

367 **Aeschylus on self-will:** Aeschylus. *Prometheus Bound.* Translated by David Grene. Chicago: University of Chicago Press, 1942.

368 **Aristotle on akrasia:** Aristotle. *Nicomachean Ethics.* Translated by David Ross. Oxford: Oxford University Press, 2009.

368 **Epictetus on rational control:** Epictetus. *The Enchiridion.* Translated by Elizabeth Carter. New York: Dover Publications, 2004.

368 **Dr. Judy Ho on self-sabotage:** Ho, Judy. *Stop Self-Sabotage: Six Steps to Unlock Your True Motivation, Harness Your Willpower, and Get Out of Your Own Way.* New York: Harper Wave, 2019.

369 **Bhagavad Gita on conquering the mind:** Vyasa. *The Bhagavad Gita.* Translated by Eknath Easwaran. Tomales, CA: Nilgiri Press, 2007.

371 **Ryan Holiday on ego:** Holiday, Ryan. *Ego Is the Enemy.* New York: Portfolio, 2016.

372 **Research on narcissistic leadership by Resick and colleagues:** Resick, Christian J., Michael T. Whitman, Stephen E. Weingarden, and Nathan S. Hiller. "The Bright-Side and the Dark-Side of CEO Personality: Examining Core Self-Evaluations, Narcissism, Transformational Leadership, and Strategic Influence." *Journal of Applied Psychology* 94, no. 6 (2009): 1365–1381.

373 **Frei and Morriss on leadership is not about you:** Frei, Frances, and Anne Morriss. *Unleashed: The Unapologetic Leader's Guide to Empowering Everyone around You.* Boston: Harvard Business Review Press, 2020.

373 **Clive Woodward on teamship:** Woodward, Clive. *Winning!* London: Hodder & Stoughton, 2004.

373 **Lisa Earle McLeod on importance of team:** McLeod, Lisa Earle. *Leading with Noble Purpose: How to Create a Tribe of True Believers.* Hoboken, NJ: Wiley, 2016.

374 **Peter Hawkins on team coaching:** Hawkins, Peter. *Leadership Team Coaching: Developing Collective Transformational Leadership.* London: Kogan Page, 2014.

374 **Collectivistic leadership approaches article:** Yammarino, F. J., E. Salas, A. Serban, K. Shirreffs, and M. L. Shuffler. "Collectivistic Leadership Approaches:

Putting the 'We' in Leadership Science and Practice." *Industrial and Organizational Psychology: Perspectives on Science and Practice* 5, no. 4 (2012): 382–402.

375 **Jim Collins on level-5 leadership:** Collins, Jim. *Good to Great: Why Some Companies Make the Leap . . . and Others Don't.* New York: HarperCollins, 2001.

375 **Rigid mindset of King George III:** Hibbert, Christopher. *George III: A Personal History.* New York: Basic Books, 1999.

376 **Blockbuster and Netflix business decisions:** Keating, Gina. *Netflixed: The Epic Battle for America's Eyeballs.* New York: Portfolio, 2012.

377 **Satya Nadella on growth mindset:** Nadella, Satya. *Hit Refresh: The Quest to Rediscover Microsoft's Soul and Imagine a Better Future for Everyone.* New York: Harper Business, 2017.

377 **Julius Caesar on distrust:** Suetonius. *The Lives of the Caesars.* Translated by Catharine Edwards. Oxford: Oxford University Press, 2000.

378 **Enron leadership scandal:** McLean, Bethany, and Peter Elkind. *The Smartest Guys in the Room: The Amazing Rise and Scandalous Fall of Enron.* New York: Portfolio, 2003.

378 **Nokia's decline in the smartphone market:** Vuori, Timo O., and Quy Nguyen Huy. "Distributed Attention and Shared Emotions in the Innovation Process: How Nokia Lost the Smartphone Battle." *Administrative Science Quarterly* 61, no. 1 (2016): 9–51.

379 **East India Company and profit obsession:** Stern, Philip J. *The Company-State: Corporate Sovereignty and the Early Modern Foundations of the British Empire in India.* Oxford: Oxford University Press, 2011.

379 **Lehman Brothers and the 2008 financial crisis:** McDonald, Lawrence G., and Patrick Robinson. *A Colossal Failure of Common Sense: The Inside Story of the Collapse of Lehman Brothers.* New York: Crown Business, 2009.

380 **Sears under Eddie Lampert:** Mugford, Kristin, and Sarah L. Abbott. *Sears: The Demise of an American Icon.* Boston: Harvard Business School Publishing, April 15, 2019.

380 **Arthur Miller's *Death of a Salesman* and profit obsession:** Miller, Arthur. *Death of a Salesman.* New York: Penguin Books, 1998.

381 **Bertrand Russell on power:** Russell, Bertrand. *Power: A New Social Analysis.* London: George Allen & Unwin, 1938.

381 **Ray Dalio on ego and blind spots:** Dalio, Ray. *Principles: Life and Work.* New York: Simon & Schuster, 2017.

382 **Dacher Keltner on power paradox:** Keltner, Dacher. *The Power Paradox: How We Gain and Lose Influence.* New York: Penguin Press, 2016.

382   ***Harvard Business Review* on power traps:** Diamond, Julie, Lisa Zigarmi, and Lesli Mones, "5 Traps to Avoid as You Gain Power as a Leader." *Harvard Business Review*, June 13, 2024.

383   **Savior trap—John Sculley and Apple:** Sculley, John, and John A. Byrne. *Odyssey: Pepsi to Apple—A Journey of Adventure, Ideas, and the Future.* New York: Harper & Row, 1987.

384   **Complacency trap—Kodak story:** Anthony, Scott D., David S. Duncan, and Pontus M. A. Siren. *Building a Growth Factory.* Boston: Harvard Business Review Press, 2012.

384   **Avoidance trap—PBS documentary on Boeing:** *Boeing's Fatal Flaw.* Directed by Tom Jennings and produced by FRONTLINE in collaboration with the New York Times. PBS. Aired September 14, 2021.

386   **Friend trap—Yahoo story:** Carlson, Nicholas. *Marissa Mayer and the Fight to Save Yahoo!* New York: Twelve, 2015.

387   **Stress trap—Jacques Nasser and Ford:** Vlasic, Bill. *Once upon a Car: The Fall and Resurrection of America's Big Three Automakers—GM, Ford, and Chrysler.* New York: William Morrow, 2011.

388   **Albert Einstein on pure mathematics:** Einstein, Albert. *Essays in Science.* New York: Philosophical Library, 1954.

391   **Darwin on survival:** Darwin, Charles. *On the Origin of Species.* London: John Murray, 1859.

395   **Dr. Hardy on personality types:** Hardy, Benjamin. *Personality Isn't Permanent: Break Free from Self-Limiting Beliefs and Rewrite Your Story.* New York: Portfolio, 2020.

396   **Peter Bregman on personality test:** Bregman, Peter. "Employees Can't Be Summed Up by a Personality Test." *Harvard Business Review*, August 19, 2015.

398   **Amy Cuddy on presence:** Cuddy, Amy. *Presence: Bringing Your Boldest Self to Your Biggest Challenges.* New York: Little, Brown and Company, 2015.

398   **Bill George on presence:** George, Bill. *True North: Discover Your Authentic Leadership.* San Francisco: Jossey-Bass, 2007.

398   **Amy Blankson on digital balance:** Blankson, Amy. *The Future of Happiness: 5 Modern Strategies for Balancing Productivity and Well-Being in the Digital Era.* Dallas, TX: BenBella Books, 2017.

399   **Cal Newport on distraction:** Newport, Cal. *Deep Work: Rules for Focused Success in a Distracted World.* New York: Grand Central Publishing, 2016.

399   **Insightful on distraction:** *Lost Focus: The Cost of Distractions on Productivity in the Modern Workplace.* Insightful 2024 Research Report.

400   **Seneca on distraction:** Seneca. *Letters from a Stoic.* Translated by Robin Campbell. London: Penguin Books, 1969.

400   **University of California, Irvine research on distraction:** Mark, Gloria, Daniela Gudith, and Ulrich Klocke. "The Cost of Interrupted Work: More Speed and Stress." *Proceedings of the SIGCHI Conference on Human Factors in Computing Systems*, April 2008, Association for Computing Machinery, Florence, Italy, 107–110.

400   **Goleman on focus:** Goleman, Daniel. *Focus: The Hidden Driver of Excellence.* New York: Harper, 2013.

401   **RAND Corporation study on sleep:** Hafner, Marco, Martin Stepanek, Jirka Taylor, Wendy M. Troxel, and Christian Van Stolk. *Why Sleep Matters—The Economic Costs of Insufficient Sleep: A Cross-Country Comparative Analysis.* Santa Monica, CA: RAND Corporation, 2016.

401   **Huffington on sleep:** Huffington, Arianna. *The Sleep Revolution: Transforming Your Life, One Night at a Time.* New York: Harmony Books, 2016.

401   ***National Geographic* on sleep:** Regan, Catherine Zuckerman. "The Science of Sleep." *National Geographic*, August 2018.

401   **National Sleep Foundation on sleep:** Hirshkowitz, Max, et al. "National Sleep Foundation's Sleep Time Duration Recommendations: Methodology and Results Summary." *Sleep Health* 1, no. 1 (2015): 40–43.

401   **Recommendation on sleep:** American Academy of Sleep Medicine and Sleep Research Society. "Recommended Amount of Sleep for a Healthy Adult: A Joint Consensus Statement." *Journal of Clinical Sleep Medicine* 11, no. 6 (2015): 591–592.

403   **World Health Organization on physical activity:** World Health Organization. *Global Recommendations on Physical Activity for Health.* Geneva: WHO, 2010.

403   ***The Lancet Quarterly* on exercise and mental health:** Chekroud, Adam M., Andrew T. Gueorguieva, Jimmy Zhe, et al. "Association between Physical Exercise and Mental Health in 1·2 Million Individuals in the USA between 2011 and 2015: A Cross-Sectional Study." *The Lancet Psychiatry* 5, no. 9. 2018.

403   ***Harvard Business Review* on exercise:** Na Li, Yolanda, and Linda Ng. "To Improve Your Work Performance, Get Some Exercise." *Harvard Business Review*, May 2023.

404   **Harvard Health on exercise and depression:** Harvard Health Publishing. Exercise is an all-natural treatment to fight depression. *Harvard Health Letter*, February 2, 2021.

404   ***MIT Sloan Management Review* on breaks:** Parker, Sharon K., and Gwenith G. Fisher. "How Well-Designed Work Makes Us Smarter." *MIT Sloan Management Review*, March 2, 2022.

405   **Setting and implementing goals: Oettingen, Gabriele, and Peter M. Gollwitzer.** "Strategies of Setting and Implementing Goals: Mental Contrasting and Implementation Intentions." In *From Goal Intentions to Implementation*

Intentions: Basic and Applied Approaches, edited by Peter Gollwitzer and John A. Bargh, 114–35. New York: Psychology Press, 1996.

405 **Booster breaks.** *Booster Breaks: Improving Employee Health One Break at a Time.* Houston, TX: Karrick Press, 2010.

405 ***Harvard Business Review* on wellness program.** *Harvard Business Review.* "What's the Hard Return on Employee Wellness Programs?" *Harvard Business Review,* December 2010.

405 **Theodore Roosevelt on belief and success:** Roosevelt, Theodore. *Theodore Roosevelt: An Autobiography.* New York: Macmillan, 1913.

407 **Benjamin Franklin on net worth:** Franklin, Benjamin. *The Autobiography of Benjamin Franklin.* New York: New American Library, 1961.

408 ***Remember the Titans*—leadership example:** Yakin, Boaz, director. *Remember the Titans.* Walt Disney Pictures, 2000.

408 **Howard Schultz's servant leadership at Starbucks:** Schultz, Howard. *Onward: How Starbucks Fought for Its Life without Losing Its Soul.* New York: Rodale Books, 2011.

408 **Thomas Edison's growth mindset:** Edison, Thomas A. *The Diary and Sundry Observations of Thomas Alva Edison.* Edited by Dagobert D. Runes. New York: Philosophical Library, 1948.

409 **Satya Nadella's cultural shift at Microsoft:** Nadella, Satya. *Hit Refresh: The Quest to Rediscover Microsoft's Soul and Imagine a Better Future for Everyone.* New York: Harper Business, 2017.

409 **Project Aristotle on psychological safety at Google:** Rozovsky, Julia. "The Five Keys to a Successful Google Team." re, Google. November 17, 2015. 409 **Ed Catmull on creative risk-taking at Pixar:** Catmull, Ed, and Amy Wallace. *Creativity, Inc.: Overcoming the Unseen Forces That Stand in the Way of True Inspiration.* New York: Random House, 2014.

411 **Arianna Huffington on burnout and work-life integration:** Huffington, Arianna. *Thrive: The Third Metric to Redefining Success and Creating a Life of Well-Being, Wisdom, and Wonder.* New York: Harmony, 2014.

412 **Patagonia's environmental mission:** Chouinard, Yvon. *Let My People Go Surfing: The Education of a Reluctant Businessman.* New York: Penguin Books, 2006.

412 **Paul Polman's mission at Unilever:** Polman, Paul, and Andrew Winston. *Net Positive: How Courageous Companies Thrive by Giving More Than They Take.* Boston: Harvard Business Review Press, 2021.

412 **Costco's winning strategy:** "Costco History: From Price Club to Retail Giant." Discovery Chepe, April 3, 2025.

412   **Toyota production system and kaizen philosophy:** Liker, Jeffrey K. *The Toyota Way: 14 Management Principles from the World's Greatest Manufacturer.* New York: McGraw-Hill, 2004.

Part 3: Interpersonal Mastery

422   **Confucius on order:** Confucius. *The Analects of Confucius.* Translated by Arthur Waley. London: George Allen & Unwin, 1938.

422   **Brené Brown on vulnerability:** Brown, Brené. *Daring Greatly: How the Courage to Be Vulnerable Transforms the Way We Live, Love, Parent, and Lead.* New York: Gotham Books, 2012.

422   **Maya Angelou on connection:** Angelou, Maya. *I Know Why the Caged Bird Sings.* New York: Random House, 1969.

Chapter 11: Principle 5—Practice More Humility

423   **Ralph Waldo Emerson on humility:** Emerson, Ralph Waldo. *Essays: First Series.* Boston: James Munroe and Company, 1841.

423   **Numbers 12:3 on Moses's humility:** *The Bible*, New International Version. Grand Rapids, MI: Zondervan, 1978.

424   **Prometheus in Greek mythology:** Hesiod. *Theogony.* Translated by Hugh G. Evelyn-White. Cambridge, MA: Harvard University Press, 1914.

424   **Nelson Mandela's story:** Mandela, Nelson. *Long Walk to Freedom: The Autobiography of Nelson Mandela.* Boston: Little, Brown, 1994.

424   **Lao Tzu on leadership:** Lao Tzu. *Tao Te Ching.* Translated by Stephen Mitchell. New York: Harper & Row, 1988.

425   **Rick Warren on humility:** Warren, Rick. *The Purpose Driven Life: What on Earth Am I Here For?* Grand Rapids, MI: Zondervan, 2002.

425   **Satya Nadella's leadership at Microsoft:** Nadella, Satya. *Hit Refresh: The Quest to Rediscover Microsoft's Soul and Imagine a Better Future for Everyone.* New York: Harper Business, 2017.

426   **Augustine on humility:** Augustine of Hippo. *Sermons (230–272B) on the Liturgical Seasons.* Translated by Edmund Hill, edited by John E. Rotelle. Hyde Park, NY: New City Press, 1993.

428   ***Harvard Business Review* on judgmentalism:** Carucci, Ron. "Forgiving a Difficult Colleague." *Harvard Business Review*, March 21, 2023.

429   ***Harvard Business Review* on anchoring bias:** Bouygues, Helen Lee. "Don't Let Anchoring Bias Weigh Down Your Judgment." *Harvard Business Review*, August 30, 2022.

429   **LinkedIn Pulse on judgmentalism:** Heady, Carson V. "Judgment Is the Enemy of Empathy: How Humility Builds Stronger, More Connected Teams." LinkedIn Pulse, April 8, 2025.

430   **Stephen Covey on listening:** Covey, Stephen R. *The 7 Habits of Highly Effective People: Powerful Lessons in Personal Change.* New York: Free Press, 1989.

430   ***Harvard Business Review* on listening:** Gallo, Amy. "What Is Active Listening?" *Harvard Business Review,* January 2, 2024.

433   **Walt Disney's *Pocahontas* on connection:** Gabriel, Mike, and Eric Goldberg, directors. *Pocahontas.* Walt Disney Pictures, 1995.

433   **Jim Collins on leadership:** Collins, Jim. *Good to Great: Why Some Companies Make the Leap . . . and Others Don't.* New York: HarperCollins, 2001.

434   **John Maxwell on connection:** Maxwell, John C. *Everyone Communicates, Few Connect: What the Most Effective People Do Differently.* Nashville: Thomas Nelson, 2010.

435   **Patrick Lencioni on team dynamics:** Lencioni, Patrick. *The Five Dysfunctions of a Team: A Leadership Fable.* San Francisco: Jossey-Bass, 2002.

435   **Brené Brown on vulnerability:** Brown, *Daring Greatly.*

435   **Oxford on vulnerability:** Botsman, Rachel, and Mark Smets. "The Power of Doubt and the Rise of Trust." Saïd Business School, University of Oxford, January 19, 2022.

435   **Jacinda Ardern's leadership example:** Ardern, Jacinda. Interview by David Frost. "Empathy and Leadership in Crisis." *New Zealand Herald,* April 24, 2020.

436   **Rumi on speech and influence:** Rumi, *The Essential Rumi.*

436   **Jack Welch on leadership:** Welch, Jack, with Suzy Welch. *Winning.* New York: Harper Business, 2005.

439   **Howard Schultz and Starbucks:** Schultz, Howard. *Onward: How Starbucks Fought for Its Life without Losing Its Soul.* New York: Rodale, 2011.

439   **Amy Cuddy on influence and warmth:** Cuddy, Amy J. C., Matthew Kohut, and John Neffinger. "Connect, Then Lead." *Harvard Business Review* 91, no. 7–8 (July–August 2013): 54–61.

440   **Nelson Mandela on competence and warmth:** Mandela, Nelson. *Long Walk to Freedom: The Autobiography of Nelson Mandela.* Boston: Little, Brown, 1994.

441   **Steve Jobs and Apple's leadership culture:** Isaacson, Walter. *Steve Jobs.* New York: Simon & Schuster, 2011.

444   **Ernest Hemingway on nobility:** Hemingway, Ernest. *The Sun Also Rises.* New York: Scribner, 1926.

446   **John F. Kennedy on leadership accountability:** Sorensen, Ted. *Counselor: A Life at the Edge of History.* New York: HarperCollins, 2008.

447   **Abraham Lincoln's listening tours:** Goodwin, Doris Kearns. *Team of Rivals: The Political Genius of Abraham Lincoln.* New York: Simon & Schuster, 2005.

447   **Nelson Mandela on team recognition:** Mandela, Nelson. *Conversations with Myself.* New York: Farrar, Straus and Giroux, 2010.

448   **Jacinda Ardern on inclusivity and cabinet diversity:** "New Zealand Election: Jacinda Ardern Swears in Diverse Cabinet." *BBC News,* November 6, 2020.

449   **Howard Schultz's leadership at Starbucks:** Schultz, *Onward.*

449   **Jeff Bezos and Amazon's "Day 1" philosophy:** Bezos, Jeff. *Invent and Wander: The Collected Writings of Jeff Bezos, with an Introduction by Walter Isaacson.* Cambridge, MA: Harvard Business Review Press, 2020.

449   **Pope Francis's humility:** Ivereigh, Austen. *The Great Reformer: Francis and the Making of a Radical Pope.* New York: Henry Holt, 2014.

449   **Warren Buffett's modesty:** Schroeder, Alice. *The Snowball: Warren Buffett and the Business of Life.* New York: Bantam, 2008.

450   **Chade-Meng Tan on mindfulness at Google:** Tan, Chade-Meng. *Search inside Yourself: The Unexpected Path to Achieving Success, Happiness (and World Peace).* New York: HarperOne, 2012.

Chapter 12: Principle 6—Act with More Integrity

459   **Shakespeare quote:** Shakespeare, William. *Hamlet.* Edited by Barbara A. Mowat and Paul Werstine. New York: Simon & Schuster, 2003.

459   **Socrates on the unexamined life:** Plato. *The Trial and Death of Socrates.* Translated by G. M. A. Grube. Indianapolis, IN: Hackett Publishing Company, 1975.

461   **Mahatma Gandhi's philosophy of nonviolence:** Gandhi, Mahatma. *The Story of My Experiments with Truth.* Translated by Mahadev Desai. Ahmedabad: Navajivan Publishing House, 1940.

462   **Martin Luther King Jr. on nonviolence:** King, Martin Luther, Jr. "My Pilgrimage to Nonviolence." *Christian Century* 77, no. 33 (July 13, 1960): 439–441.

462   **Oprah Winfrey on integrity:** Winfrey, Oprah. *What I Know for Sure.* New York: Flatiron Books, 2014.

463   **Harper Lee's *To Kill a Mockingbird* on Atticus Finch:** Lee, Harper. *To Kill a Mockingbird.* New York: J. B. Lippincott & Co., 1960.

463   **Warren Buffett on integrity in business:** Schroeder, Alice. *The Snowball: Warren Buffett and the Business of Life.* New York: Bantam, 2008.

464 **Johnson & Johnson's handling of the Tylenol crisis:** Kaplan, Sheila. "The Tylenol Crisis: How Effective Public Relations Saved Johnson & Johnson." *Public Relations Review* 9, no. 2 (1993): 31–46.

464 **Voltaire on common sense:** Voltaire. *A Pocket Philosophical Dictionary.* Translated by John Fletcher. Oxford: Oxford University Press, 2011.

465 **Volkswagen emissions scandal:** Ewing, Jack. *Faster, Higher, Farther: The Inside Story of the Volkswagen Scandal.* New York: W. W. Norton & Company, 2017.

465 **Wells Fargo fake accounts scandal:** Cowley, Stacy, and Emily Glazer. "Wells Fargo Fined $185 Million for Fraudulently Opening Accounts." *New York Times*, September 8, 2016.

465 **Cambridge Analytica and Facebook data scandal:** Cadwalladr, Carole, and Emma Graham-Harrison. "Revealed: 50 Million Facebook Profiles Harvested for Cambridge Analytica in Major Data Breach." *The Guardian*, March 17, 2018.

466 **Edelman Trust Barometer 2024:** *2024 Edelman Trust Barometer: Global Report.* January 2024.

466 **Ethics & Compliance Initiative:** Ethics & Compliance Initiative. *2024 Global Business Ethics Survey (GBES): U.S. Trends.* Arlington, VA. 2024.

466 **The 2024 and 2025 HOW Reports on Moral Values:** *The State of Moral Leadership in Business: 2024.* New York: The HOW Institute for Society, 2024; *The State of Moral Leadership in Business: 2025.* New York: The HOW Institute for Society, 2025.

467 **Michael Jensen on integrity:** Jensen, Michael C. "Integrity: Without It Nothing Works." Harvard Business School Working Paper No. 10-042, November 2009.

467 **Definition of integrity by Charles Marshall:** Marshall, Charles. *Shattering the Glass Slipper: Destroying Fairy-Tale Thinking before It Destroys You.* Brentwood, TN: Provision Group, 2003.

469 **Bible on integrity:** *The Holy Bible*, English Standard Version. Wheaton, IL: Crossway, 2001.

471 **Warren Buffett on good employees:** Loomis, Carol J., ed. *Tap Dancing to Work: Warren Buffett on Practically Everything, 1966–2012.* New York: Portfolio/Penguin, 2012.

472 **Steve Jobs's management style and ethical practices:** Lashinsky, Adam. *Inside Apple: How America's Most Admired—and Secretive—Company Really Works.* New York: Business Plus, 2012.

472 **Wells Fargo fake accounts scandal:** "Wells Fargo Agrees to Pay $3 Billion to Resolve Criminal and Civil Investigations into Sales Practices Involving the Opening of Millions of Accounts without Customer Authorization." US Department of Justice, February 21, 2020.

472   **Martin Shkreli and Turing Pharmaceuticals:** Pollack, Andrew. "Drug Goes from $13.50 a Tablet to $750, Overnight." *New York Times*, September 20, 2015.

473   **Theodore Levitt on business purpose:** Levitt, Theodore. *The Marketing Imagination*. New York: Free Press, 1983.

474   **Simon Sinek on employee engagement:** Sinek, Simon. *Leaders Eat Last: Why Some Teams Pull Together and Others Don't*. New York: Portfolio, 2014.

475   **Richard Branson on prioritizing employees:** Branson, Richard. *The Virgin Way: Everything I Know about Leadership*. New York: Portfolio, 2014.

475   **ICMA report on leadership integrity during COVID-19:** "Local Government Ethics and Integrity: ICMA COVID-19 Report." International City/County Management Association, 2020.

475   **Harvard Law School study on ethics:** Harvard Law School. "The Business Ethics of Elon Musk, Tesla, Twitter, and the Tech Industry." *Harvard Law School Today*, February 7, 2023.

476   **BBC on quitting:** Christian, Alex. "Are Workers Really Quitting over Company Values?" BBC Worklife, February 23, 2022.

479   **Warren Buffett's consistent and ethical approach:** Schroeder, *Snowball*.

489   **Sophocles on truth:** Sophocles. *Oedipus Rex*. Translated by Robert Fagles. New York: Penguin Classics, 1984.

Chapter 13: Principle 7—Care More for People

492   ***Bhagavad Gita* on selflessness:** *The Bhagavad Gita*. Translated by Eknath Easwaran. Tomales, CA: Nilgiri Press, 2007.

494   **Aristotle on virtue and happiness:** Aristotle. *Nicomachean Ethics*. Translated by W. D. Ross. New York: Oxford University Press, 1925.

494   **Siddhartha Gautama on compassion and care:** Buddha. *The Teachings of Buddha*. Tokyo: Bukkyo Dendo Kyokai, 1966.

494   **Immanuel Kant on moral philosophy:** Kant, Immanuel. *Groundwork for the Metaphysics of Morals*. Translated by Mary Gregor. Cambridge: Cambridge University Press, 1998.

494   **Jean-Paul Sartre on existentialist meaning:** Sartre, Jean-Paul. *Being and Nothingness*. Translated by Hazel E. Barnes. New York: Philosophical Library, 1956.

495   **Mother Teresa on compassionate leadership:** Mother Teresa. *Mother Teresa: Come Be My Light: The Private Writings of the "Saint of Calcutta."* Edited by Brian Kolodiejchuk. New York: Doubleday, 2007.

496   **Gallup on engagement and profitability:** "The Relationship between Engagement at Work and Organizational Outcomes." Gallup, 2017.

496 **SSM Health:** "The Science behind Kindness and How It Is Good for Your Health." *SSM Health Matters*, November 2022.

496 ***Journal of Social Psychology* on caring for others:** Buchanan, Kathryn E., and Anat Bardi. "Acts of Kindness and Acts of Novelty Affect Life Satisfaction." *Journal of Social Psychology* 150, no. 3 (2010): 235–237.

496 **Greater Good Science Center on helping others:** Post, S. G. "Altruism, Happiness, and Health: It's Good to Be Good." *International Journal of Behavioral Medicine* 12, no. 2 (2005): 66–77.

496 **Frances Frei on empowerment in leadership:** Frei, Frances, and Anne Morriss. *Unleashed: The Unapologetic Leader's Guide to Empowering Everyone around You.* Boston: Harvard Business Review Press, 2020.

496 **Tolstoy on three questions:** Tolstoy, Leo. "Three Questions." In *What Men Live By, and Other Tales.* Translated by Aylmer Maude, 23–31. New York: Charles Scribner's Sons, 1906.

498 **Condon and colleagues on mindfulness and compassion:** Condon, Paul, Gaëlle Desbordes, Willa B. Miller, and David DeSteno. "Meditation Increases Compassionate Responses to Suffering." *Psychological Science* 24, no. 10 (2013): 2125–2127.

499 **Boellinghaus and colleagues on empathy and mindfulness:** Bölinghaus, Inga, Fiona C. Jones, and John M. G. Williams. "The Role of Mindfulness and Loving-Kindness Meditation in Cultivating Self-Compassion and Other-Focused Concern in Health Care Professionals." *Mindfulness* 5, no. 2 (2014): 129–138.

501 ***Deloitte Insights* on leader's role:** Ott, Tanya. "Why Corporate Well-Being Initiatives Aren't Doing So Well—and What Companies Can Do about It." *Deloitte Insights*, February 15, 2023.

502 ***Harvard Business Review* on wellness program ROI:** Berry, Leonard L., Ann M. Mirabito, and William B. Baun. "What's the Hard Return on Employee Wellness Programs?" *Harvard Business Review*, December 2010.

502 ***New York Times* on wellness program:** Barry, Ellen. "Workplace Wellness Programs Have Little Benefit, Study Finds." *New York Times*, January 15, 2024.

502 ***Harvard Business Review* on wellness program:** Croft, Jazz, Acacia Parks, and Ashley Whillans. "Why Workplace Well-Being Programs Don't Achieve Better Outcomes." *Harvard Business Review*, October 18, 2024.

505 **Andy Grove on constructive confrontation:** Grove, Andrew S. "How to Make Confrontation Work for You." *Selling Power*, February 2, 2010.

505 ***Harvard Business Review* on DEI:** Dobbin, Frank, and Alexandra Kaleb. "Achieve DEI Goals Without DEI Programs." *Harvard Business Review*, July–August 2025.

506 ***McKinsey* on diversity and inclusivity:** McKinsey & Company. *Diversity Matters Even More: The Case for Holistic Impact.* December 2023.

506 ***Boston Consulting Group* on diversity and inclusivity:** Lorenzo, Rocío, Nicole Voigt, Miki Tsusaka, Matt Krentz, and Katie Abouzahr. "How Diverse Leadership Teams Boost Innovation." Boston Consulting Group, January 2018.

507 ***Glassdoor* on diversity and inclusivity:** Glassdoor, "What Job Seekers Really Think About Your Diversity & Inclusion Stats," *Glassdoor Blog*, July 12, 2021.

508 **Marcus Buckingham on leadership effectiveness:** Buckingham, Marcus, and Ashley Goodall. *Nine Lies About Work: A Freethinking Leader's Guide to the Real World*. Boston: Harvard Business Review Press, 2019.

508 **Robert Kelley on followership:** Kelley, Robert E. *The Power of Followership: How to Create Leaders People Want to Follow, and Followers Who Lead Themselves*. New York: Doubleday/Currency, 1992.

508 **Leader-Member Exchange theory:** Graen, George B., and Mary UhlBien. "Relationship-Based Approach to Leadership: Development of LeaderMember Exchange (LMX) Theory of Leadership over 25 Years." *Leadership Quarterly* 6 (1995): 219–247.

509 **Gallup on performance of engaged employees:** *State of the Global Workplace Report 2017*. Washington, DC: Gallup Press, 2017.

509 ***Harvard Business Review* on performance of engaged employees:** Harvard Business Review Analytic Services, *The Impact of Employee Engagement on Performance*. Harvard Business School Publishing, Boston. April, 2016.

510 **Deloitte on mission driven companies:** Deloitte. "Workplace Culture and the Alternative Workforce." *Deloitte Insights*. ca. 2016–2017.

510 **Deloitte on mission driven companies:** Deloitte. "5 Studies on the Benefits of the PurposeDriven Workplace." *IDEO U (blog)*, March 30, 2018.

510 **Cone communications on corporate advocacy and support:** Cone Communications. *Cone Communications CSR Study*. Denver. 2017.

511 **Kevin Costner in *Hidden Figures*:** *Hidden Figures*. Directed by Theodore Melfi; based on the book by Margot Lee Shetterly. 20th Century Fox, 2016. Film.

514 **Barbara Kellerman on bad leaders:** Kellerman, Barbara. *Leadership from Bad to Worse: What Happens When Bad Festers*. Oxford: Oxford University Press, 2024.

516 ***MIT Sloan Management Review* study on toxic culture:** Sull, Donald, Charles Sull, and Ben Zweig. "Why Every Leader Needs to Worry about Toxic Culture." *MIT Sloan Management Review*, January 11, 2022.

518 **McKinsey research on leadership quality:** De Smet, Aaron, Monica Mugayar-Baldocchi, Anouk Reich, and Bryan Hancock. *Some Employees Are Destroying Value. Others Are Building It. Do You Know the Difference?* McKinsey & Company, October 5, 2023.

518   **Gallup study on managerial selection:** Adkins, Amy. *Only One in 10 People Possess the Talent to Manage.* Gallup Workplace, April 13, 2015.

518   *Harvard Business Review* **on leadership quality:** Chamorro-Premuzic, Tomas, and Clarke Murphy. "When Leaders Are Hired for Talent but Fired for Not Fitting In." *Harvard Business Review,* June 14, 2017.

518   **Chamorro-Premuzic's book on leadership selection:** Chamorro-Premuzic, Tomas. *Why Do So Many Incompetent Men Become Leaders? (And How to Fix It).* Boston: Harvard Business Review Press, 2019.

520   *Harvard Business Review* **on feedback:** Burris, Ethan, Benjamin Thomas, Ketaki Sodhi, and Dawn Klinghoffer. "Turn Employee Feedback into Action." *Harvard Business Review,* November–December 2024.

522   **Deming on seven deadly diseases:** Deming, W. Edwards. *Out of the Crisis.* Cambridge, MA: MIT Press, 1982.

522   **Peter Scholtes on performance appraisal:** Scholtes, Peter R. "Total Quality or Performance Appraisal: Choose One." *National Productivity Review* 12, no. 3 (1993): 349–363.

522   **Talent Strategy Group on performance appraisal:** "Global Performance Management Report 2023." Talent Strategy Group, March 20, 2023.

522   *Harvard Business Review* **on Gallup cost of performance review:** Buckingham, Marcus, and Ashley Goodall. "Reinventing Performance Management." *Harvard Business Review* 93, no. 4 (April 2015): 40–50.

522   **Gallup study on performance appraisal:** Wigert, Ben, and Heather Barrett. "2% of CHROs Think Their Performance Management System Works." Gallup, May 7, 2024.

523   **Adobe study on Millennials:** "Work in Progress: The State of Performance Reviews." Adobe Research, 2017.

523   *Vanity Fair* **article on Microsoft:** Eichenwald, Kurt. "Microsoft's Lost Decade." *Vanity Fair,* August 2012.

524   **Quantum research on employee departure:** "The Importance of Employee Recognition: Statistics and Research." Quantum Workplace, July 6, 2023.

523   **Adobe study on Millennials:** "Work in Progress: The State of Performance Reviews." Adobe Research, 2017.

524   **Importance of employee recognition:** Leung, Iris. "Top 20 Employee Recognition Statistics for HR Leaders in 2025." *Achievers,* January 7, 2025.

524   **Michael Schrage on feedback:** Schrage, Michael. "Rethinking Performance Management for Post-pandemic Success." *MIT Sloan Management Review,* August 2020.

527   **Liz Wiseman on multipliers in leadership:** Wiseman, Liz. *Multipliers: How the Best Leaders Make Everyone Smarter.* New York: HarperCollins, 2010.

528   **Bob Johansen on leadership and digital transformation:** Johansen, Bob. *The New Leadership Literacies: Thriving in a Future of Extreme Disruption and Distributed Everything.* Oakland, CA: Berrett-Koehler, 2017.

529 **Inc. on forgiveness:** Stillman, Jessica. "A Neuroscientist Explains All the Good Things That Happen in Your Brain When You Forgive Someone." *Inc.,* May 7, 2025.

530 ***Harvard Business Review* on forgiveness:** Carucci, Ron. "Forgiving a Difficult Colleague." *Harvard Business Review*, March 21, 2023.

531 **Aesop on kindness:** Aesop. *The Complete Fables of Aesop.* Translated by Olivia Temple and Robert Temple. London: Penguin Classics, 1998.

533 **Rabindranath Tagore on joy in service:** Tagore, Rabindranath. *The Essential Tagore.* Edited by Fakrul Alam and Radha Chakravarty. Cambridge, MA: Harvard University Press, 2011.

533 ***Journal of Personality and Social Psychology* on acts of kindness:** Grant, Adam, and Francesca Gino. "A Little Thanks Goes a Long Way: Explaining Why Gratitude Expressions Motivate Prosocial Behavior." *Journal of Personality and Social Psychology* 98, no. 6 (June 2010): 946–955.

534 **Gallup report on employee engagement:** *State of the Global Workplace: 2024 Report.* Washington, DC: Gallup Press, 2024.

535 **Bruce Lee quote:** Lee, Bruce. *Striking Thoughts: Bruce Lee's Wisdom for Daily Living.* Edited by John Little. Boston: Tuttle Publishing, 2000.

537 **Jeff Weiner on LinkedIn's learning culture:** Weiner, Jeff. "Building a Culture of Learning at LinkedIn." LinkedIn (blog), 2019.

538 **Eric Schmidt and Jonathan Rosenberg on Google's work culture:** Schmidt, Eric, and Jonathan Rosenberg. *How Google Works.* New York: Grand Central Publishing, 2014.

538 **Patagonia on childcare:** Marcario, Rose. "Patagonia's CEO Explains How to Make On-Site Child Care Pay for Itself." *Fast Company*, August 15, 2016.

539 **Ray Dalio on radical transparency at Bridgewater:** Dalio, Ray. *Principles: Life and Work.* New York: Simon & Schuster, 2017.

539 **Ed Catmull and Amy Wallace on creativity at Pixar:** Catmull, Ed, and Amy Wallace. *Creativity, Inc.: Overcoming the Unseen Forces That Stand in the Way of True Inspiration.* New York: Random House, 2014.

539 **Albus Dumbledore in J. K. Rowling's *Harry Potter* series:** Rowling, J.K. *Harry Potter and the Sorcerer's Stone.* New York: Scholastic, 1997.

539 **Freiberg on Southwest Airlines:** Freiberg, Kevin, and Jackie Freiberg. *Nuts!: Southwest Airlines' Crazy Recipe for Business and Personal Success.* Austin, TX: Bard Press, 1996.

539 **Tony Hsieh on Zappos' culture of happiness:** Hsieh, Tony. *Delivering Happiness: A Path to Profits, Passion, and Purpose.* New York: Grand Central Publishing, 2010.

539 **Reed Hastings on Netflix's culture of freedom:** Hastings, Reed. *No Rules Rules: Netflix and the Culture of Reinvention.* New York: Penguin Press, 2020.

540 **Horst Schulze on service excellence at Ritz-Carlton:** Schulze, Horst. *Excellence Wins: A No-Nonsense Guide to Becoming the Best in a World of Compromise.* Grand Rapids, MI: Zondervan, 2019.

540 ***Harvard Business Review* on overwork:** Gavett, Gretchen. "Getting Over Overwork." *Harvard Business Review,* November–December 2024.

542 **Buffer's remote work model:** Gascoigne, Joel. "The 4-Day Workweek Boosted Our Productivity and Happiness." Buffer Open, May 19, 2020.

542 **Sakaguchi on Project Aristotle and team dynamics:** Sakaguchi, K. "The Success Factors of High-Performing Teams." Google Research, 2016.

548 **Ramayana on a true leader:** Valmiki. *Ramayana.* Translated by Hari Prasad Shastri. London: Shanti Sadan, 1952.

Chapter 14: Principle 8—Trust More

550 **Covey on trust:** Covey, Stephen M. R. *The Speed of Trust: The One Thing That Changes Everything.* New York: Free Press, 2006.

550 **Origin of "trust"—Old Norse and Sanskrit etymology:** Hoad, T.F., ed. *The Concise Oxford Dictionary of English Etymology.* Oxford: Oxford University Press, 1993; Monier-Williams, Monier. *A Sanskrit-English Dictionary: Etymologically and Philologically Arranged with Special Reference to Cognate Indo-European Languages.* Oxford: Oxford University Press, 1899.

551 **Plato on the philosopher-king:** Plato. *The Republic.* Translated by G. M. A. Grube. Indianapolis, IN: Hackett, 1992.

551 **Aristotle on friendship and trust:** Aristotle. *Nicomachean Ethics.* Translated by W. D. Ross. Oxford: Oxford University Press, 2009.

551 **Nussbaum on Aristotelian trust:** Nussbaum, Martha C. *The Fragility of Goodness: Luck and Ethics in Greek Tragedy and Philosophy.* Cambridge: Cambridge University Press, 1986.

552 **Niccolò Machiavelli's *The Prince*:** Machiavelli, Niccolò. *The Prince.* Translated by Harvey C. Mansfield. Chicago: University of Chicago Press, 1998.

553 **Covey's trust and inspire:** Covey, Stephen M. R. *Trust and Inspire: How Truly Great Leaders Unleash Greatness in Others.* New York: Simon & Schuster, 2022.

554 **Enron and Volkswagen scandals:** McLean, Bethany, and Peter Elkind. *The Smartest Guys in the Room: The Amazing Rise and Scandalous Fall of Enron.* New York: Penguin Books, 2004; Ewing, Jack. *Faster, Higher, Farther: The Volkswagen Scandal.* New York: W. W. Norton & Company, 2017.

554 **Patagonia's ethical leadership:** Chouinard, Yvon. *Let My People Go Surfing: The Education of a Reluctant Businessman.* New York: Penguin Press, 2005.

555 **Nelson Mandela on reconciliation and trust:** Mandela, Nelson. *Long Walk to Freedom: The Autobiography of Nelson Mandela.* Boston: Little, Brown and Company, 1994.

555   **Tony Stark in *Avengers: Endgame*:** Russo, Anthony, and Joe Russo, directors. *Avengers: Endgame*. Marvel Studios, 2019.

555   **J. R. R. Tolkien's *Lord of the Rings*:** Tolkien, J.R.R. *The Fellowship of the Ring*. Boston: Houghton Mifflin, 1954.

556   ***Harvard Business Review* on high-trust culture:** Zak, Paul J. "The Neuroscience of Trust." *Harvard Business Review*, January–February 2017.

556   **Great Place to Work Institute report:** *Trust in the Workplace: The Impact of Leadership on Employee Engagement and Performance*. San Francisco: Great Place to Work, 2019.

557   **Lao Tzu on trust:** Lao Tzu. *Tao Te Ching*. Translated by Stephen Mitchell. New York: HarperCollins, 1988.

557   **Patrick Lencioni on team cohesion:** Lencioni, Patrick. *The Five Dysfunctions of a Team: A Leadership Fable*. San Francisco: Jossey-Bass, 2002.

558   **Franklin D. Roosevelt and trust:** Alter, Jonathan. *The Defining Moment: FDR's Hundred Days and the Triumph of Hope*. New York: Simon & Schuster, 2006.

558   ***Coach Carter* as an example of trust for high standards:** Carter, Thomas, director. *Coach Carter*. Paramount Pictures, 2005.

558   ***Frozen* as an example of learning to trust oneself:** Buck, Chris, and Jennifer Lee, directors. *Frozen*. Walt Disney Animation Studios, 2013.

558   **Churchill on fostering trust:** Churchill, Winston. *The Second World War*. 6 vols. Boston: Houghton Mifflin, 1948–1953.

559   **Shakespeare on prioritizing better reasons:** Shakespeare, William. *The Tragedy of Julius Caesar*. Edited by Barbara A. Mowat and Paul Werstine. New York: Simon & Schuster, 2005.

561   **Emerson on trust:** Emerson, Ralph Waldo. *Essays: First Series and Second Series*. Edited by Joseph Slater. New York: Library of America, 1983.

562   **Spreitzer on psychological empowerment:** Spreitzer, Gretchen M. "Psychological Empowerment in the Workplace: Dimensions, Measurement, and Validation." *Academy of Management Journal* 38, no. 5 (1995): 1442–1465.

562   **Gallup Organization report:** *State of the American Workplace: Employee Engagement Insights for U.S. Business Leaders*. Gallup, 2013. 563 **Dirks and Ferrin study on role of trust:** Dirks, Kurt T., and Daniel L. Ferrin. "The Role of Trust in Organizational Settings." *Journal of Applied Psychology* 86, no. 5 (2001): 1012–1022. 563 **Amabile and colleagues' study on workplace creativity:** Amabile, Teresa M., et al. "Assessing the Work Environment for Creativity." *Creativity Research Journal* 9, no. 3 (1996): 235–255. 564 **Study on trust and task performance:** Langfred, Claus W. "Too Much of a Good Thing? Negative Effects of High Trust and Individual Autonomy in Self-Managing Teams." *Academy of Management Journal* 47, no. 3 (2004): 385–399.

564   **Hackman and Oldham study on motivation:** Hackman, J. Richard, and Greg R. Oldham. "Motivation through the Design of Work: Test of a Theory." *Organizational Behavior and Human Performance* 16, no. 2 (1976): 250–279.

565   **Herzberg study on motivation-hygiene theory:** Herzberg, Frederick. *Work and the Nature of Man.* Cleveland: World Publishing, 1968.

565   **Self-determination theory on motivation:** Ryan, R. M., and E. L. Deci. "Self-Determination Theory and the Facilitation of Intrinsic Motivation, Social Development, and Well-Being." *American Psychologist* 55, no. 1 (2000): 68–78.

566   **George MacDonald on trust:** MacDonald, George. *The Princess and the Goblin.* Edited by Michael Phillips. New York: Dover Publications, 1999.

567   **David Maister's trust equation in *The Trusted Advisor*:** Maister, David H., Charles H. Green, and Robert M. Galford. *The Trusted Advisor.* New York: Free Press, 2001.

568   **Simon Sinek on transparency and trust:** Sinek, Simon. *Leaders Eat Last: Why Some Teams Pull Together and Others Don't.* New York: Portfolio, 2014.

569   **PwC report on trust and CEO happiness:** "The CEO Survey: Building Trust through Transparency and Purpose." PwC, 2016.

570   **Salesforce on transparency and trust:** Benioff, Marc, and Monica Langley. *Trailblazer: The Power of Business as the Greatest Platform for Change.* New York: Currency, 2019.

570   **IBM's commitment to data privacy:** "IBM's Commitment to Data Responsibility." Accessed March 10, 2023.

574   **George Bernard Shaw quote on communication:** Shaw, George Bernard. *Selected Plays with Prefaces.* New York: Dodd, Mead & Company, 1948.

574   **Warren Buffett quote and story:** Buffett, Warren. Interview and remarks referenced in *The Snowball: Warren Buffett and the Business of Life* by Alice Schroeder. New York: Bantam Books, 2008.

576   **Project Management Institute statistics on communication:** *Pulse of the Profession: The High Cost of Low Performance.* Newtown Square, PA: Project Management Institute, 2013.

576   **Warren Buffett on trust:** Miller, Jeremy C. *Warren Buffett's Ground Rules: Words of Wisdom from the Partnership Letters of the World's Greatest Investor.* Hoboken, NJ: Wiley, 2016.

578   **Dalio on self-reflection and radical transparency:** Dalio, Ray. *Principles: Life and Work.* New York: Simon & Schuster, 2017.

579   **Success of Starbucks:** Schultz, Howard. *Onward: How Starbucks Fought for Its Life without Losing Its Soul.* New York: Rodale Books. 2011.

579   **Marriott video:** Sorenson, Arne. "A Message to Marriott International Associates." Video, 5:49. March 19, 2020.

579   **Virgin brand:** Branson, Richard. *The Virgin Way: If It's Not Fun, It's Not Worth Doing It.* New York: Portfolio. 2015.

580   **Netflix's high-trust culture:** Hastings, Reed. *No Rules Rules: Netflix and the Culture of Reinvention.* New York: Penguin Press. 2020.

583   **Brené Brown on vulnerability and trust:** Brown, Brené. *Daring Greatly: How the Courage to Be Vulnerable Transforms the Way We Live, Love, Parent, and Lead.* New York: Gotham Books, 2012.

584   **Jeff Weiner on LinkedIn embodying the values:** Weiner, Jeff. "From Vision to Values: The Importance of Defining Your Core." LinkedIn, October 28, 2012. Accessed June 1, 2025.

585   **Carol Dweck on mindsets:** Dweck, Carol S. *Mindset: The New Psychology of Success.* New York: Random House, 2006.

586   **John Kotter's change management model:** Kotter, John P. *Leading Change.* Boston: Harvard Business Review Press, 1996.

Chapter 15: Epilogue: Personal Commitment

590   **Rabindranath Tagore on education:** Tagore, Rabindranath. *Sadhana: The Realization of Life.* New York: Macmillan, 1913.

590   **T. S. Eliot on rediscovery:** Eliot, T.S. *Four Quartets.* New York: Harcourt, Brace and Company, 1943.

592   **Fariduddin Attar on self-discovery:** Attar, Fariduddin. *The Conference of the Birds.* Translated by Afkham Darbandi and Dick Davis. London: Penguin Books, 1984.

595   **Harriet Tubman and the Underground Railroad:** Larson, Kate Clifford. *Bound for the Promised Land: Harriet Tubman, Portrait of an American Hero.* New York: Ballantine Books, 2004.

595   **Suzanne Collins's *The Hunger Games* and leadership:** Collins, Suzanne. *The Hunger Games.* New York: Scholastic Press, 2008.

597   **Mahatma Gandhi on self-reflection:** Gandhi, Mahatma. *The Story of My Experiments with Truth.* Translated by Mahadev Desai. Boston: Beacon Press, 1993.

597   **Harper Lee's *To Kill a Mockingbird*:** Lee, Harper. *To Kill a Mockingbird.* Philadelphia: J. B. Lippincott & Co., 1960.

598   **Steve Jobs and Apple's innovation:** Isaacson, Walter. *Steve Jobs.* New York: Simon & Schuster, 2011.

598   **Hermione Granger in J. K. Rowling's *Harry Potter* series:** Rowling, J.K. *Harry Potter and the Sorcerer's Stone.* New York: Scholastic, 1997.

599   **Thomas Edison's perseverance and innovation:** Stross, Randall E. *The Wizard of Menlo Park: How Thomas Alva Edison Invented the Modern World.* New York: Crown Publishing, 2007.

599   **Jane Austen's *Pride and Prejudice*:** Austen, Jane. *Pride and Prejudice*. London: T. Egerton, 1813.

599   **Nelson Mandela on humility:** Mandela, Nelson. *Long Walk to Freedom: The Autobiography of Nelson Mandela*. Boston: Little, Brown and Company, 1994.

599   **J. R. R. Tolkien's *The Lord of the Rings*:** Tolkien, J.R.R. *The Fellowship of the Ring*. Boston: Houghton Mifflin, 1954.

600   **Abraham Lincoln on integrity:** White, Ronald C. A. *Lincoln: A Biography*. New York: Random House, 2009.

600   **Albus Dumbledore in J. K. Rowling's *Harry Potter* series:** Rowling, J.K. *Harry Potter and the Half-Blood Prince*. New York: Scholastic, 2005.

601   **Mother Teresa's compassionate service:** Muggeridge, Malcolm. *Something Beautiful for God: Mother Teresa of Calcutta*. New York: Harper & Row, 1971.

601   **Victor Hugo's *Les Misérables* and Jean Valjean's transformation:** Hugo, Victor. *Les Misérables*. Translated by Charles E. Wilbour. New York: Carleton, 1862.

602   **Warren Buffett's decentralized management at Berkshire Hathaway:** Schroeder, Alice. *The Snowball: Warren Buffett and the Business of Life*. New York: Bantam, 2008.

602   **J. R. R. Tolkien's *The Lord of the Rings*:** Tolkien, *Fellowship of the Ring*.

602   **Jensen Huang on character and leadership:** Fortune editors. "CEO of the Year Jensen Huang on NVIDIA, AI, and His Character-First Leadership." *Fortune*, June 28, 2023.

602   **Stephen Covey's character ethic:** Covey, Stephen R. *The 7 Habits of Highly Effective People: Powerful Lessons in Personal Change*. New York: Free Press, 1989.

603   **Rumi's seven maxims:** Rumi. *The Masnavi*. Translated by Jawid Mojaddedi. Oxford: Oxford University Press, 2004–2017.

606   **Eleanor Roosevelt on responsibility and choices:** Roosevelt, Eleanor. *You Learn by Living: Eleven Keys for a More Fulfilling Life*. New York: Harper & Brothers, 1960.

607   **Confucius on perseverance:** Confucius. *The Analects*. Translated by Arthur Waley. New York: Vintage Books, 1989.

Index of Topics

About the Author

Dr. Saquib Najmus, a distinguished leader and visionary, earned his PhD in civil engineering from the University of California, Davis. Renowned for his pioneering contributions to the field of water modeling, he received the prestigious Hugo B. Fischer Award from from the California Water and Environmental Model-ing Forum. This honor recognizes his exceptional leadership and lasting impact in shaping California's water modeling landscape.

Dr. Najmus founded WRIME Inc., an engineering consulting firm that he led as president and CEO. Under his leadership, WRIME rose to become the leading groundwater firm in California, culminating in two successive mergers into larger corporations. Currently, he serves as vice president of Woodard & Curran Inc., a nationwide engineering firm, where he continues to drive innovation and inspire excellence.

Beyond his professional accomplishments, Dr. Najmus has dedicated two decades to community service as the founder and leader of a nonprofit organization established in 2004. Through his dual roles in professional and community settings, he has provided leadership and project management training for over 20 years, inspiring individuals and organizations to achieve their full potential.

Dr. Najmus's thought leadership extends to invited speeches delivered to corporations, professional associations, client organizations, and universities. A trailblazer in both his professional and philanthropic endeavors, he embodies the values of purpose-driven, whole-person leadership, fostering transformative impact across industries and communities.